# Learning Resource Centre

Park Road, Uxbridge, Middlesex, UB8 1NQ

**Renewals: 01895 853344**

Please return this item to the LRC on or before the
last date stamped below:

| | | |
|---|---|---|
| | | |
| | | |
| | | |
| | | |
| | | 3 0\ |

Twenty-eight years on, and it's still
**For Eirene**

# An Introduction to Sociology

Fifth Edition

Ken Browne

polity

First edition first published in 1992 by Polity Press
This fifth edition first published in 2020 by Polity Press

Polity Press
65 Bridge Street
Cambridge CB2 1UR, UK

Polity Press
101 Station Landing
Suite 300
Medford, MA 02155, USA

ISBN-13: 978-1-5095-2800-4 (pb)


A catalogue record for this book is available from the British Library.
Names: Browne, Ken, 1951- author.
Title: An introduction to sociology / Ken Browne.
Description: 5 Edition. | Medford, MA : Polity Press, [2019] | Revised edition of the author's An introduction to sociology, 2011. | Includes bibliographical references and index.
Identifiers: LCCN 2018059991 (print) | LCCN 2019001892 (ebook) | ISBN 9781509528035 (Epub) | ISBN 9781509527991 (hardback) | ISBN 9781509528004 (pbk.)
Subjects: LCSH: Sociology. | Great Britain--Social conditions.
Classification: LCC HM585 (ebook) | LCC HM585 .B884 2019 (print) | DDC 301/.0941--dc23
LC record available at https://lccn.loc.gov/2018059991

Typeset in 9.5 on 13pt Utopia Regular by
Servis Filmsetting Ltd, Stockport, Cheshire
Printed and bound in Italy by Rotolito

For further information on Polity, visit our website:
politybooks.com

# Contents

# Introduction to the Fifth Edition

This book is intended as an introduction to sociology for both the general reader and those studying at GCSE and other courses at a similar level. It is designed to be accessible to students studying for GCSE on one- or two-year courses, who require a clear and concise account of each topic area. It will also be useful for non-specialist GCSE sociology teachers who need a good grounding in the subject before they start teaching it. It is also suitable for use by students on other introductory courses which have a sociological component, such as nursing, social work, and health and social care courses. There is a chapter on health, for those needing it on such courses, available as a free download at www.politybooks.com/introsoc. This book will enable the content of such courses to be covered easily and thoroughly, and allow time for students and teachers or lecturers to discuss, and acquire, the skills of application, interpretation and evaluation. Students studying at home or on other distance-learning courses will find the book a valuable companion to their studies.

Those who are considering taking an AS- or A-level or Access sociology course, or undergraduates with no sociology background taking a degree with a sociological component, will find the book very useful both as preparatory reading and as an easy-to-read foundation text to get them started in sociology.

No previous knowledge of sociology is assumed. All the key issues and areas included in GCSE and other introductory sociology courses are covered. This fifth edition has been completely restructured and rewritten to provide full in-depth coverage of the latest AQA, WJEC/Eduqas and Cambridge IGCSE sociology specifications, and it is structured around these. See www.politybooks.com/introsoc for more detail on how the book maps onto these specifications. The book will enable students to obtain the highest grades in all the sociology GCSE exams available in the UK at the time of writing.

Thoroughly revised and updated, this fifth edition includes a wide range of new material and statistics reflecting more contemporary social changes and social trends, and new cartoons, photographs and graphics have been added. This book is based on a wide range of sociological evidence derived from official statistics, sociological research, media and government reports, and surveys. In many cases, the source of this evidence is cited in the text. However, this is not always the case, to avoid 'cluttering' the chapters with a large number of references which would be undesirable and unnecessary in what is intended to be a basic introductory text. Nonetheless, readers can be assured that the chapters are based on sociological evidence – it is crucial that sociologists base their work on evidence, and not on anecdotes or hearsay.

# Acknowledgements

I'd like to thank my partner Eirene Mitsos once again for her help and ideas, her constructive criticism and her alertness in reading various drafts of a book she has been re-reading now in various versions for nearly thirty years. I'd also like to thank Polity's anonymous readers who provided valuable feedback in preparing this fifth edition. I'd like to thank all the staff at Polity, particularly Jonathan Skerrett for being such a conscientious and supportive editor, and for so generously putting up with an author who somehow always manages to exceed by some margin the contractual word limit. Leigh Mueller has yet again done a great job copy-editing. Thanks to Evie Deavall and her team at Polity, who have made this latest edition the most attractive yet, and to Breffni O'Connor for his marketing skills.

I am grateful to all those who gave permission to reproduce copyright material. The source of such material is acknowledged in the text.

# How to use this book

Most chapters in this book are fairly self-contained, and it is not necessary to read them in any particular order or to read all of them. Select chapters according to the course you are studying. Those doing research projects of various kinds, or anyone studying for GCSE, should read chapter 2. When issues are discussed or raised in more than one chapter, cross-references are made in the text.

Throughout the book, a range of activities and discussion topics is included. These provide valuable exercises to develop your skills and understanding, and should be attempted whenever possible, though they are not essential for understanding each chapter. These activities also include some exam-style questions you might encounter in GCSE examinations.

Important terms are highlighted in colour when they first appear in the book, and in most cases, when they first appear, are shown in **bold type** in the glossary boxes in the page margins. These terms are normally explained in the text the first time they appear, and are listed at the end of the chapter. They are also included in a comprehensive glossary at the end of the book. If you come across a term you're not familiar with or are unsure about, check the glossary or index for further clarification or explanation. The contents pages or the index should be used to find particular themes or references.

The AQA and Eduqas courses require students to know about the key ideas of a number of named sociologists and related 'classic texts'. These are flagged up in the text with the name and date, such as 'Becker (1963)', and are then listed at the end of the book. The main references to these authors and texts are also included in the index.

Chapter summaries outline the key points that should have been learnt after reading each chapter. These should be used as checklists for revision – if you cannot do what is asked, then refer back to the chapter to refresh your memory. The glossary at the end of the book also provides both a valuable reference source and a revision aid, as you can check the meaning of terms.

A last word: do not look on this book as your final and absolute source of authority – see it as your friend rather than your boss. Much of sociology is controversial and the subject of intense and heated debate, and even apparently factual statistics are open to a variety of interpretations. Be prepared to draw on your own experiences of the social world to help reach a sociological understanding of contemporary society, and to provide examples for use in examination answers. Discuss with others what you read in this book, and adopt a questioning and critical approach to your studies. The truth may be out there somewhere, but, like the executioner's face, it is always well hidden, so take nothing for granted and do not accept things at face value. Above all, enjoy sociology.

# The Sociological Approach: Key Ideas and Concepts

## Contents

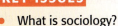

**KEY ISSUES**

- What is sociology?
- What is meant by social structure?
- What are social processes?
- Social issues, social problems and social policy

Newcomers to sociology often have only a vague idea as to what the subject is about, though they frequently have an interest in people. This interest is a good start, because the focus of sociology is on the influences from society which mould the behaviour of people, their experiences and their interpretations of the world around them. To learn sociology is to learn about how human societies are constructed, and where our beliefs and daily routines come from and how our social identities are formed; it is to re-examine in a new light many of the taken-for-granted assumptions which we all hold, and which influence the way we think about ourselves and others. Sociology is above all about developing a critical understanding of society. In developing this, sociology can itself contribute to changes in society – for example, by highlighting and explaining social problems such as inequality, crime and poverty. The study of sociology can provide the essential tools for a better understanding of the world we live in, and therefore the means for improving it.

## WHAT IS SOCIOLOGY?

**Sociology** is the systematic (or planned and organized) study of human groups and social life in modern societies. A **society** is a large group of people who are involved with one another and generally share the same geographical territory or country, and a similar way of life, language and beliefs – e.g. British society.

It is concerned with the study of **social institutions.** These are the various organized social arrangements that are found in all societies. For example, the family is an institution which is concerned with arrangements for marriage – such as at what age people can marry, whom they can marry and how many partners they can have – and the upbringing of children. The education system establishes ways of passing on attitudes, knowledge and skills from one generation to the next. Work and the economic system organize the way the production of goods will be carried out, and religious institutions are concerned with people's relations with the supernatural. These social institutions make up a society's **social structure** – the 'building blocks' of society.

Sociology tries to understand how these various social institutions operate, and how they relate to one another – such as the influence the family might have on how well children perform in the education system. Sociology is also concerned with describing and explaining the patterns of inequality, deprivation and conflict which are a feature of nearly all societies.

### How did sociology develop?

Sociology first developed in response to changes in the world around 200 years ago. These changes included industrialization, as people began to work in factories and cities, rather than in agriculture and villages in the countryside; and science began to challenge religious belief, popular myths and superstition as ways of understanding the world. Many men and women across the world and over the centuries have asked questions about how society works, though not all have received equal credit or attention. The

**Sociology** The systematic (planned and organized) study of human groups and social life in modern societies.

**Society** A large group of people who are involved with one another and generally share the same geographical territory or country, and a similar way of life, language and beliefs.

**Social institutions** The various organized social arrangements that are found in all societies.

**Social structure** The social institutions and social relationships that form the 'building blocks' of society.

following male European figures are those who have been most strongly associated with the development of sociology in Europe.

### Auguste Comte (1798–1857)

The Frenchman Auguste Comte (1798–1857) was one of the first to use the term 'sociology', to describe a new social science consisting of the idea that society could be studied in a scientific way, in much the same way as the natural sciences of biology, physics and chemistry studied the natural world.

### Émile Durkheim (1858–1917)

**Functionalism** A sociological approach which sees society as made up of parts – such as the family, education system and religion – which work together to maintain society as a whole. Society is seen as basically harmonious and stable, because of agreement (consensus) on the everyday rules of social life which people learn as they grow up.

The French sociologist Émile Durkheim (1858–1917) is often seen as one of the founding figures of sociology. He set up the first European department of sociology, and was France's first professor of sociology.

He saw the study of sociology as a way of gaining a scientific understanding of society in order to improve it. He was a key figure in the development of the sociological theory of **functionalism** (discussed in the next chapter), which sees society as being based on consensus (agreement) and generally harmonious. Functionalism has been a longstanding sociological approach (or perspective). Many of Durkheim's ideas appear throughout this book.

### Karl Marx (1818–1883)

The German Karl Marx (1818–83) is another towering figure in the history of sociology, as well as being the founder of the political ideology called

Auguste Comte was one of the first to use the term 'sociology'

Émile Durkheim is one of the founders of sociology. He is closely associated with the theory of functionalism and a scientific approach to studying society

The German sociologist Karl Marx is another major figure in the development of sociology. Marxism (a theoretical approach inspired by his work) is still widely applied in sociology today

The ideas of German sociologist Max Weber are still very influential in contemporary sociology

**Marxism** A sociological theory which sees society divided by conflict between two main opposing social classes: a small richer class that owns the majority of society's **wealth**, and exploits a much larger class of non-owners. **Wealth** Property which can be sold and turned into cash for the benefit of the owner.

**Social class** (or socio-economic class). An open system of stratification consisting of broad groups of people (classes) who share a similar social and economic situation, such as occupation, **income** and ownership of wealth. **Income** The flow of money which people obtain from work, from their investments, or from the state in the form of welfare benefits.

**Verstehen** The idea of understanding human behaviour by putting yourself in the position of those being studied, and trying to see things from their point of view. (Pronounced 'fair-shtay-en'.)

'communism'. **Marxism** – a major sociological and political approach – is named after him, and many of his ideas are still used in sociology today, such as the ideas of a society divided by **social class** and by conflict between the rich and the poor. Marx saw the scientific study of society primarily as a means to understanding it in order to change and improve it for the benefit of those who were poor and oppressed. There is more on this in chapter 2, and throughout this book.

### Max Weber (1864–1920)

The final key figure in the history of sociology has been the German sociologist Max Weber (1864–1920). Weber, like Marx, saw society as being based on conflict between social groups, rather than on harmony and consensus as Durkheim did. Weber's ideas have been very influential in sociological theory and on how to do sociological research, and his ideas still have important influences on contemporary sociology. One of his significant contributions was that he recognized that society could not be studied in a purely objective, scientific way. He developed the *verstehen* (pronounced 'fair-shtay-en') approach to society – the view that, to understand why people behave as they do, it is necessary to put yourself in their position and understand things from their point of view.

There is more on Weber's ideas in chapter 2, and they are considered in various places throughout this book.

## Sociology and common sense

Sociology is concerned with studying many things which most people already know something about. Everyone will have some knowledge and understanding of family life, the education system, work, the media and religion simply by living as a member of society. This leads many people to assume that the topics studied by sociologists and the explanations sociologists produce are really just common sense: what 'everyone knows'.

This is a very mistaken assumption. Sociological research has shown many widely held common-sense ideas and explanations to be false. Ideas such as that there is no real poverty left in modern Britain; that the poor and unemployed are lazy; that everyone has equal chances in life; that the rich are rich because they work harder – these have all been questioned by sociological research. The re-examination of such common-sense views is very much the concern of sociology.

A further problem with common-sense explanations is that different societies have differing common-sense ideas. Common-sense ideas also change over time in one society. In Britain, for example, we no longer burn witches when the crops fail, but seek scientific explanations for such events.

Not all the findings of sociologists undermine common sense, and the work of sociologists has made important contributions to some of our common-sense understandings. For example, the knowledge which most people have about the changing family in Britain, with higher rates of divorce and

What is seen as common sense varies between societies and over time. What is seen as common sense in one society may appear as nonsense in another

lower rates of marriage, is largely due to the work of sociologists. However, sociology differs from common sense in two important ways:

- Sociologists use what C. Wright Mills called a sociological imagination. This means that, while they study the familiar routines of daily life, sociologists look at them in unfamiliar ways or from a different angle. They ask if things really are as common sense says they are. Sociologists re-examine existing assumptions, by studying how things were in the past, how they've changed, how they differ between societies, and how they might change in the future.
- Sociologists look at evidence on issues before making up their minds. The explanations and conclusions of sociologists are based on precise evidence which has been collected through painstaking research using established research procedures.

## Sociology and biological explanations: nurture v. nature

Biological or *naturalistic* explanations are those which assume that various kinds of human behaviour are natural or based on innate (in-born) biological characteristics. If this were the case, then one would expect human behaviour to be the same everywhere, as people's biological make-up doesn't change between societies. In fact, by comparing different societies, sociologists have discovered that there are very wide differences between them in **customs**, **values** and **norms**, beliefs and social behaviour.

For example, there are wide differences between societies in the **roles** of men and women and what is considered appropriate masculine and feminine behaviour.

How masculine and feminine behaviour is created in Britain will be discussed later in this chapter.

Similarly, some people have tried to distinguish between humans on the grounds of race, dividing people into different racial groups according to physical and biological characteristics like skin colour. However, sociologists through their work show that White English people behave rather differently in some circumstances from White Polish or German people, and often they have many different cultural traditions; there are many differences in the culture and behaviour of Pakistani Asian Muslims and Indian Sikhs, even though they may share the same skin colour.

Sociological explanations recognize that these differences between people can only be because people learn to behave in different ways in different societies – through nurture or upbringing – rather than being something they have through nature at birth. Individuals learn how to behave from a wide range of social institutions, such as the family, the media and the education system, right throughout their lives. Sociologists call this process of learning **socialization**.

**Customs** Norms that have existed for a long time.

**Values** General beliefs about what is right or wrong, and the important standards and goals that are worth maintaining and achieving in any society.

**Norms** Social rules which define correct or appropriate behaviour in a society or group.

**Roles** The patterns of behaviour which are expected from people in society.

**Socialization** The process of learning the **culture** of any society.

**Culture** The language, beliefs, values and norms, customs, roles, knowledge and skills which combine to make up the way of life of any society.

## Sociology and journalism

Journalism is the gathering of news and information about the state of society, such as current events, trends and issues. Journalists report these news stories aiming to inform large numbers of people through media such as newspapers, magazines, radio, television and the internet. In some ways, good journalism and sociology have a lot in common, as both seek to collect information about society, try to avoid deliberate bias, present the information in a balanced and fair way, and use the evidence they have collected to justify the conclusions they reach. However, journalism often presents information in sensational ways which are designed more to interest media audiences and sell newspapers or attract viewers than to spread accurate information about the world. In recent years, there has been increasing concern about 'fake news' – deliberately sensationalized, exaggerated or false misinformation or hoaxes spread via the media to mislead and grab attention for financial or political gain. This selective use of evidence, producing sensationalized or one-sided reports, is something sociologists generally try to avoid.

Sociology differs from journalism in the following main ways:

- Sociology is based on evidence collected through systematic, planned research methods and rigorous sampling techniques, and that evidence is generally presented in a balanced objective way. Journalists don't necessarily use such systematic methods of collecting evidence – though they may draw on sociological research – and the presentation of news may be biased (one-sided).

- Sociological research is subject to scrutiny for bias, errors and omissions by other sociologists.
- Sociology has a toolkit of theory, concepts and research methods which influence the way the investigation of society is carried out, and sociological work is primarily aimed at other sociologists and social policy makers. Journalism does not require theory, and is in most cases aimed at large mass audiences, rather than the specialized audiences of sociology.
- Sociological research is not driven by the same time pressures as journalism. Journalists work within very tight time constraints, as news is about very recent events, updated on an almost instantaneous rolling basis. This means journalists are often forced to cut corners in collecting evidence.

## Sociology and psychology

Like sociology, psychology also studies people, and has a range of research techniques (such as experiments and sampling) and theories to support this. However, psychology tends to focus on the behaviour of individuals, why they come to think and behave as they do and how their minds work. This includes things like their learning, perception, intelligence, memory, aggression and the development of their personalities. Sociology focuses more on the social groups, communities, organizations and social institutions, like the family and the education system, forming the social structure of society. Sociologists also focus on the wider social processes like socialization and **social control** that influence individuals.

> **Social control**
> The social process of persuading or forcing individuals to conform to values and norms.

## Sociology and science

Sociology is one of a group of subjects, including economics, psychology and politics, which are known as the social sciences. The idea that sociology might be considered a science poses a number of problems. This is because the term 'science' is usually associated with the study of the natural world, in subjects like physics, chemistry and biology, which make up the natural sciences.

However, the study of society by sociologists presents a range of problems which do not exist in the natural sciences, as the comparison in the box suggests.

### *Is sociology scientific?*

The differences between the natural sciences and sociology mean that sociologists cannot follow exactly the same procedures or produce such precise findings as those in the natural sciences. Despite this, sociology might still

| NATURAL SCIENCE | SOCIOLOGY |
|---|---|
|  |  |

**NATURAL SCIENCE**

- Experiments can be carried out to test and prove ideas and it is possible to identify causes in laboratory conditions.

- As a result of experiments, natural scientists can accurately predict what will happen in the same circumstances in the future. For example, the chemist can predict with certainty, as a result of experiments in laboratory conditions, that some combinations of chemicals will cause explosions.

- In the natural sciences, the presence of the scientist doesn't affect the behaviour of chemicals or objects.

- The natural scientist does not have to persuade objects, chemicals or, usually, animals to cooperate in research.

**SOCIOLOGY**

- Human beings might well object to being experimented upon. Sociology also wants to study society in its normal state, not in the artificial conditions of an experiment.

- Human behaviour cannot be predicted with such certainty: in two similar situations, people may react differently, according to how they interpret what is going on around them, and people can change their minds.

- Sociologists studying people may change the behaviour of those being studied, who may become embarrassed, be more defensive and careful about what they say, or act differently because they have been selected for study. If this happens, then the results obtained will not give a true picture of how people behave normally.

- People may refuse to answer questions or otherwise cooperate, making sociological research difficult or impossible. They can lie or otherwise distort and conceal the truth when they are being researched, making the findings of research suspect.

**Value freedom**
The idea that the beliefs and prejudices of the sociologist should not be allowed to influence the way research is carried out and evidence interpreted.

be regarded as adopting a scientific approach to the study of society as long as it has the following features:

- **Value freedom** – the personal beliefs and prejudices of the sociologist should not be allowed to influence the way they carry out the research or interpret the evidence. Obviously, the personal interests and beliefs of the sociologist will influence the choice of topic he or she studies, but the research itself should not be distorted by these beliefs.

- **Objectivity** – the sociologist should approach topics with an open mind, and be prepared to consider all the evidence in a detached way.
- The use of systematic research methods – sociologists collect evidence about topics using planned and organized methods. These are discussed fully in the next chapter.
- The use of evidence – sociological descriptions of social life, and the explanations and conclusions drawn, are based on carefully collected evidence.
- The capacity for being checked – the findings and conclusions of sociological research are open to inspection, criticism and testing by other researchers. Bad sociology – or 'fake sociology' – using inadequate evidence to reach unjustifiable conclusions, is likely to be torn to shreds by others interested in the topic.

> **Objectivity**
> Approaching topics with an open mind, avoiding bias, and being prepared to submit research evidence to scrutiny by other researchers.

## WHAT IS MEANT BY SOCIAL STRUCTURE?

Social structure refers to the social institutions and network of social relationships, and the links between them, which combine to build up the structure of society. These building blocks include institutions like the family, work and the economy, the education system, the media, the legal system and the political system. Many of these social institutions are considered throughout this book. The pattern of inequality or **social stratification** is also part of the social structure, such as the patterns of inequality and **discrimination** based, for example, around gender, ethnicity, religion, social class, sexuality, disability or age. Social stratification and inequality are discussed in depth in chapter 6.

The social structure often has important influences on people's behaviour, controlling and limiting what they can do. For example, differences in **power**, or social rules (norms and values) learnt during socialization, mean we cannot easily act in just any way we like.

> **Social stratification** The division of society into a hierarchy of unequal social groups.

> **Discrimination** The unfair or unfavourable treatment of people because of the group with which they are identified, e.g. by gender, ethnicity, religion, social class or age.

> **Power** The ability of individuals or groups to exert their will over others and get their own way, even if others sometimes resist this.

### Activity

To what extent is our behaviour moulded by the social structure? Suggest *three* ways that each of the following social structures has contributed to the way you are now, and which prevent you from behaving in just any way you like:
- the family
- the education system
- the legal system
- the workplace (if you have a full- or part-time job)
- the pattern of inequality, e.g. the amount of income you (and your family) have, or racial and sexual discrimination.

# WHAT ARE SOCIAL PROCESSES?

**Social processes** The various influences that control and regulate human culture and behaviour, and help to keep societies running more or less smoothly and with some day-to-day stability.

**Social processes** are the various influences that control and regulate human behaviour, and help to keep societies running more or less smoothly and with some day-to-day stability. Two important social processes which are illustrated in Figure 1.1, and considered throughout this book, are socialization and social control.

## Socialization

### *Socialization – learning values and norms*

***Values*** Values are ideas and beliefs about what is right and wrong, and the important standards which are worth maintaining and achieving in any society. They provide general guidelines for behaviour.

In Britain, values include beliefs about respect for human life, privacy and private property, about the importance of family life and of money

**Figure 1.1** Socialization and social control

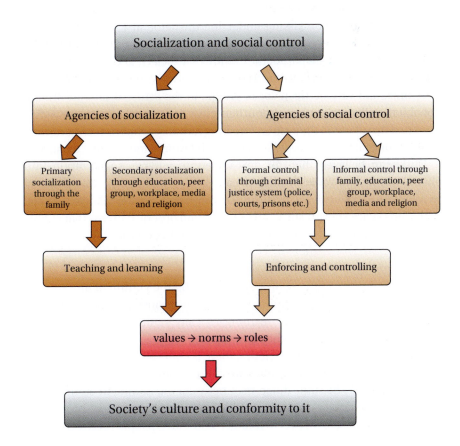

and success. There are often strong pressures on people to conform to a society's values, which are frequently written down as laws. These are official legal rules which are formally enforced by the police, courts and prisons, and involve legal punishment if they are broken. Laws against murder, for example, enforce the value attached to human life in our society.

*Norms*   Norms are social rules which define correct and acceptable behaviour in a society or social group. People are expected to conform to norms. Norms are much more specific than values: they put values (general guidelines) into practice in particular situations. The rule that someone should not generally enter rooms without knocking reflects the value of privacy, and rules about not drinking and driving reflect the value of respect for human life. Norms exist in all areas of social life. In Britain, those who are late for work, jump queues in supermarkets, laugh during funerals, walk through the streets naked, or never say 'hello' to friends are likely to be seen as annoying, rude or odd because they are not following the norms of accepted behaviour. Norms are mainly informally enforced – by the disapproval of other people, embarrassment, or a telling-off from parents.

Customs are norms which have existed for a long time and become a part of society's traditions – kissing under the mistletoe at Christmas, buying Easter eggs, or lighting candles at Diwali are typical customs found in Britain.

Values and norms are part of the culture of a society, and are learned and passed on through socialization. They differ between societies, may change over time, and vary between social groups in the same society. In Britain, cohabitation (living together without being married) is now much more widely accepted than it was in the past, and wearing turbans – which is seen as normal dress among Sikh men – would be seen as a bit weird among white teenagers.

Durkheim believed that, for any society to survive, socialization into shared norms and values, which he called **value consensus**, was essential to maintain **social order**. This means society has to remain relatively stable, with some shared norms and values to maintain orderly patterns that enable people to live together and relate to one another in everyday life.

## Socialization and culture

Socialization is the life-long process of learning the culture of any society. This culture is socially transmitted (passed on through socialization) from one generation to the next. It is learning a society's culture that enables individuals to fit into the society they grow up in.

Both within and between societies, there is **cultural diversity**. This means that different societies have different cultures, and within any particular society there may be some differences between the dominant culture – the main one in a society – and the **subculture** (see glossary box) of particular social groups, e.g. between younger and older people, between richer

**Value consensus** A general agreement around the main norms and values of society.

**Social order** A relatively stable state of society, with some shared norms and values which establish orderly patterns that enable people to live together and relate to one another in everyday life.

**Cultural diversity** Cultural differences between social groups and different societies, based on factors such as history, religious beliefs, ethnic group, social class and age.

**Subculture** A smaller culture shared by a group of people within the main culture of a society, in some ways different from the main culture, but with many aspects in common.

What might happen to you if you didn't know or follow the expected norms of queuing?

**Multicultural society** A society in which there are a range of different cultures (ways of life) which exist alongside the shared overall culture of society.

**Ethnicity** The shared culture, including language, religion, cultural traditions and characteristics, of a social group, which gives its members an identity in some ways different from other groups – e.g. Black, Asian and Minority Ethnic (BAME) groups.

**Globalization** The growing interconnectedness of societies across the world, with the spread of the same culture, consumer goods and economic interests across the globe.

**Consumer (or consumption) goods** Products and services that people buy to satisfy their needs and desires, such as food, clothes, furniture, TVs, tablets, smartphones and leisure activities, like paying to go to cinemas, clubs and concerts.

and poorer people, and between people from Black, Asian and Minority Ethnic (BAME) groups. Cultural diversity is a feature of many contemporary Western societies. Britain is now a **multicultural society** consisting of a range of cultural differences based around **ethnicity**. All these cultures are learnt during the socialization process.

## Culture and globalization

**Globalization** refers to the process whereby societies and cultures across the world become increasingly connected to one another (interconnected). For example, international trade, the internet, global media, international travel and tourism mean people are now much more aware of different cultures, and absorb them into their own national cultures.

Many people in different countries experience the same cultural and **consumer goods** across the world, and they have become part of the ways of life of many different societies. Companies like Apple, Google, Microsoft, McDonald's, Coca-Cola, Starbucks, Nescafé, Sony, Nike, Pizza Hut and Subway now operate in many countries of the world. Television and production companies sell their shows across the globe. The global marketing of films, music, computer games, food, clothes, football and other consumer products has made cultures across the world increasingly similar, with people watching the same TV programmes and films, listening to the same music, following the same sporting events, eating the same foods, wearing the same designer clothes and labels and sharing the same fashions, playing the same computer games, carrying the same smartphones and sharing many other aspects of their beliefs, lifestyles and identities.

This has led to the suggestion there is now a **global culture**, in which cultural products, norms, values and attitudes and ways of life in different countries of the world have become more alike. Socialization into a society's culture has increasingly become socialization into a global culture.

It should be emphasized, however, that much of this global culture is influenced mainly by the countries of the United States and Western Europe. Some cultural influences have gone the other way too, though – Thai, Indian and Chinese foods, and Asian-origin meditation and yoga, are very popular in the UK, and Bollywood movies (from India) are watched in many different countries of the world, though mainly by Indian audiences.

> **Global culture**
> The culture that has developed in different countries of the world have become more alike, sharing increasingly similar consumer goods and ways of life. This has arisen as globalization has undermined national and local cultures.

---

**Activity**

1. Refer to the pictures on this page, and explain in what ways they show global culture. Try to think of two other consumer products (which you might even own yourself) that are also global.
2. Describe two ways in which global culture has affected the culture of people in the UK.
3. Suggest two ways in which your own socialization has involved encounters with cultures from outside the UK, e.g. holidays abroad.

> **Feral children**
> Children who display wild, undomesticated, animal-like behaviour as a result of missing out on some important stages of human learning, as they have been removed from human contact and the normal processes of human socialization.

## *The importance of socialization – feral children*

Evidence of the importance of socialization in binding the individual into society is found in the study of **feral children** ('feral' means wild or undomesticated). Feral children display wild, undomesticated, animal-like behaviour as a result of missing out on some important stages of human learning. This arises if they have been removed from human contact and the normal processes of human socialization at a very early age – for example, if they were raised in isolation or by animals. They remain unaware of human social behaviour and language and therefore fail to develop many aspects of behaviour we would regard as 'human'. Feral children are extremely rare, and many studies of so-called feral children need to be treated with care because:

- some cases are hoaxes, designed to attract publicity;
- some children may have had severe learning or physical impairments rather than lacking human socialization, and were abandoned by their families because of these impairments.

---

**Activity**

Go to https://goo.gl/VJ9b5P and https://goo.gl/YP1UHE.

1  Describe *two* case studies in which children were raised differently from how human children usually are.
2  Identify in each case study two characteristics these children display that children raised in human societies usually don't.
3  Explain carefully the ways feral children might show that human behaviour is learnt rather than naturalistic or based on instinct.
4  Explain two reasons why feral children may have difficulty fitting into society.

---

> **Identity** How individuals see and define themselves, and how other people see and define them.

> **Agencies of socialization** Groups and social institutions that are responsible for, or involved in, the socialization process – e.g. the family, the education system, religion, the media, the workplace and the peer group.

> **Agents of socialization** The actual people who carry out socialization in the agencies of socialization. For example, in the family and education system, parents and teachers may be regarded as agents of socialization.

## Socialization and identity

Socialization plays a crucial part in forming our identities. **Identity** is about how we see and define ourselves – our personalities – and how other people see and define us.

For example, we might define ourselves as gay, black, a Muslim, Welsh, English, a woman, a student or a mother. Many aspects of our individual identities will be formed through the socialization process, with the family, friends, school, the media, the workplace and other **agencies of socialization** and **agents of socialization** helping to form our individual personalities.

While life-long socialization plays a very important part in forming our identities, individuals also have the free will to enable them to carve out their own personal identities and influence how others see them, rather than simply being influenced by them. Individuals are not simply the passive victims of the socialization process.

Figure 1.2 shows a range of factors which influence our identities, and many chapters in this book refer to aspects of this socialization process, and the forming of our identities. Note the arrows go both ways, suggesting that, while individual identities are formed by various agencies of socialization,

In what ways do different forms of media (for example, free newspapers on commuter transport or social media) influence the individual's socialization and sense of identity?

the choices individuals and groups make and how they react to these forces can also have an influence. For example, while the media might influence our lifestyles, attitudes and values, individuals may also react to what they read, see or hear in the media in different ways. A woman from a minority ethnic background may define herself as Black or Asian, but she may also see herself mainly as a woman, a mother, a teacher or a Muslim. Similarly, we have some choices in the consumer goods we buy, the clothes we wear, and the leisure activities we choose to follow. Through these choices, we can influence how others see us, and the image of ourselves we project to them.

## *Agencies and agents of socialization: primary and secondary socialization*

*Primary socialization*  **Primary socialization** refers to socialization during the early years of childhood, and is carried out by the family or close community. It is during primary socialization that children first begin to learn about values and norms and other features making up the culture of their society. They also begin to acquire their sense of individual identity and significant elements of their *social* identities, such as their gender, ethnicity and sexuality. In most cases, these identities formed during childhood will remain throughout people's lives and are much more difficult to change in adulthood than other identities.

> **Primary socialization**
> Socialization during the early years of childhood, carried out by the family or close community.

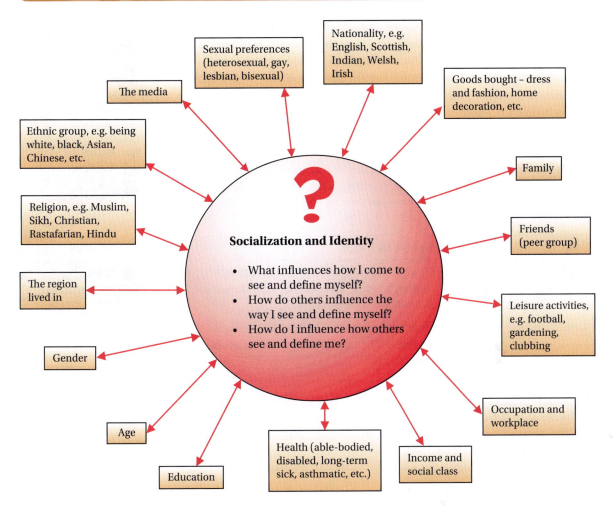

**Figure 1.2** Socialization and identity

Refer to figure 1.2

**Activity**

Refer to figure 1.2

1   Suggest one example in each case of how the various factors may influence the individual's sense of identity.
2   Suggest three ways that individuals can influence how others see them.
3   Describe the three most important factors that you think have influenced how *you* define yourself and how others see you. Explain your answer with examples.
4   Suggest three ways *you* can influence how others see and define you, for example as a particular 'type' of person – cool, odd, sporty, scary, Goth, etc.

*Secondary socialization* **Secondary socialization** refers to socialization which takes place beyond the family and close community. It is carried out through agencies (or by people who are sometimes called 'agents') of secondary socialization such as the education system, the **peer group**, the workplace, the media and religious institutions. For many young people, **social media** – such as Instagram, Snapchat and YouTube – and websites are key influences.

> ### Activity
>
> Below are some important agencies of secondary socialization. In the right-hand column, describe two ways in each case how that agency carries out secondary socialization. The education system has been done for you, but try to do the same for the other agencies.
>
> | Agency | Role in socialization |
> |---|---|
> | Education system | • Teaches knowledge about society, such as history, language and customs, making up key elements of society's culture<br><br>• Teaches values and norms to which young people will be expected to conform as adults. |
> | The peer group | |
> | The workplace | |
> | The media (including social media) | |
> | Religious institutions | |

## Socialization – roles and role conflict

Roles are the patterns of behaviour which are expected from people in different positions in society – they are very much like the roles actors play in a television series, and learning them is an important aspect of the socialization process.

People in society play many different roles in their lifetimes, such as those of a boy or girl, a child and an adult, a student, a parent, a friend, and work roles like factory worker, police officer or teacher. People in these roles are expected by society to behave in particular ways. For example, police officers are expected to show patterns of behaviour – perform roles – that involve things like honesty, obeying the law and generally conforming to social rules. Teachers are expected to show similar patterns of behaviour, and the role of teacher (ideally) involves providing a **role model** – an example to students of proper, socially acceptable, forms of behaviour,

**Secondary socialization** Socialization which takes place beyond the family and close community. It is carried out through agencies of secondary socialization such as the education system, the peer group, the workplace, the media and religious institutions.

**Peer group** A group of people of similar age and **status**, with whom a person often mixes socially.

**Status** The amount of prestige, importance or respect attached to individuals, social groups or positions in any society by other members of a group or society. Status involves people's social standing in the eyes of others.

**Social media** Websites, apps and other online means of communication that are used to create, share and exchange information and connect people together – e.g. Facebook, Instagram, YouTube and Twitter.

**Role model** A pattern of behaviour which others copy and model their own behaviour on.

which hopefully students will copy and model their own behaviour on. Like a teacher and a police officer, a parent too is expected to provide a role model for his or her children's behaviour.

Often, the rules that define roles are not always clear until they are broken, but the police officer who steals, or the teacher who is drunk in the classroom, shows what these rules and expectations of behaviour are.

One person plays many roles at the same time. For example, a woman may play the roles of woman, mother, worker, sister and someone's life partner at the same time. This may lead to **role conflict**, where two or more roles performed at the same time may come into conflict with one another, as in the conflict between the roles of full-time worker and mother which many women experience.

**Role conflict**
The conflict that arises between the successful performances of two or more roles at the same time.

Role conflict for working women

**Activity**

1. List all the roles you play, and briefly outline what others expect of you in each of these roles. For example, how are you expected to behave as a student, and what activities are you expected to carry out which you wouldn't have to if you were not a student?
2. From your list of roles, try to pick out those which conflict with each other, as suggested in the cartoon above.

## Social control

In order for people to know how to behave in society, and therefore to live together in some orderly way, some shared values and norms are necessary. Without some measure of agreement on the basic ground rules, social life would soon fall into confusion and disorder. For example, imagine the chaos on the British roads if drivers stopped following the rules about driving on the left-hand side of the road, or stopping at red traffic lights.

Norms and values are learnt through socialization, and most people show **social conformity** to them. But knowing what the norms are does not necessarily mean people will follow them – some will display **non-conformity** by breaking the dominant social rules. For example, in a school, some students may deliberately set out to break rules, and form a disruptive **anti-school subculture** (sometimes called a counter-school subculture) – a group organized around a set of norms, values, attitudes and behaviour in opposition to the main values, norms and aims of a school.

Social control is the term given to the various methods used to persuade or force individuals to conform to those social values and norms that have been learnt through socialization, and to prevent a failure to conform to social norms. **Deviance** is any behaviour that is in some way socially unacceptable or not approved of – non-conformist behaviour.

**Sanctions** are the rewards and punishments through which social control is achieved, and conformity to norms and values enforced.

These may be either *positive sanctions*, rewards of various kinds, or *negative sanctions*, various types of punishment. The type of sanction will depend on the seriousness of the norm: positive sanctions may range from gifts of sweets from parents to children, to merits and prizes at school, to knighthoods and medals; negative sanctions may range from a feeling of embarrassment, to being ridiculed or gossiped about or regarded as a bit eccentric or a bit odd, to being fined or imprisoned.

> **Activity**
>
> Describe one positive and one negative sanction which affects the way you behave in your daily life.

Together, socialization and social control help to maintain social conformity and social order.

**Social conformity** Acting in a way that follows a society's or group's norms and values.

**Non-conformity** Acting in a way that goes against a society's or group's norms and values.

**Anti-school subculture** A group organized around a set of norms, values, attitudes and behaviour in opposition to the main values, norms and aims of a school. Sometimes called a counter-school subculture.

**Deviance** The failure to conform to social norms and values – rule-breaking behaviour.

**Sanctions** A reward (positive sanction) or punishment (negative sanction) to encourage social conformity.

Social control: people make rules and then enforce them on the carrot-and-stick principle

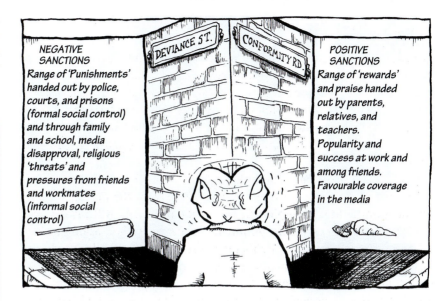

**Agencies of social control** State organizations – e.g. the criminal justice system (police, courts, probation service, prisons, etc.) – or other groups and institutions – e.g. the family, religion, the education system, the peer group and the media – that control people's behaviour to compel conformity to social norms and values.

**Agents of social control** The actual people who carry out social control in the agencies of social control. For example, in the criminal justice system, the agents of social control are people such as police officers, judges and magistrates.

**Formal social control** Control of people's behaviour by agencies of social control and agents of social control that have the specific purpose of ensuring social conformity and the maintenance of social order – e.g. the criminal justice system, police officers and judges.

### Activity

Look at the cartoon above.
1   Explain in your own words the point the cartoon is illustrating.
2   Describe three possible consequences that might face a person who followed a deviant path as an adult.
3   Suggest two reasons why a person might fail to conform to social norms.
4   Explain two reasons why not conforming to social norms might lead to success in society.
5   Much deviance is disapproved of to some extent, but can you think of forms of deviance in any society which might be welcomed by the majority of the public as opening the way for society to change and improve?

### *Agencies and agents of social control: formal and informal social control*

Social control is carried out through a series of **agencies of social control**, by **agents of social control**, many of which are discussed in fuller detail in other parts of this book, but it is useful to summarize them here.

● **Formal social control** is that which is carried out by agencies and agents specifically set up to ensure that people conform to a particular set of norms, especially the law. The criminal justice system – police, courts, the probation service and prisons – force people to obey the law through formal sanctions such as arresting, fining or imprisoning those who break society's laws.

- **Informal social control** is carried out by agencies and agents whose primary purpose is not social control, but they play an important role in it none the less. For example, the family is an important agency of informal social control through primary socialization, and parents act as agents of social control in persuading their children to conform to social norms and values. Children begin to learn the difference between right and wrong, what is good or bad behaviour, norms governing their **gender role**, and acceptance of parental authority. The approval or disapproval of parents can itself be an important element in encouraging children to conform, along with other sanctions such as praise and rewards, threats, teasing or even physical violence.

Table 1.1 shows some examples of how other agencies carry out social control, and seek to limit deviance.

| Table 1.1 Informal social control | |
| --- | --- |
| **Agency** | **How it carries out social control** |
| Education system | Sets standards of 'correct' behaviour, forms of dress and so on which are expected by society. This is achieved by sanctions such as detentions, suspensions, exclusions, merit points and other aspects of the **hidden curriculum** (see later in this chapter and chapter 4 for more discussion of this). Through the actions of teachers and the way the school is organized – for example, through streaming and examinations – pupils are encouraged to accept norms from wider society, such as competitiveness, gender roles, ranking of people with unequal pay and status, and inequalities in power and authority. In this way, the school helps to maintain the way society as a whole is presently organized. |

**Informal social control** Control of people's behaviour by agencies and agents whose primary purpose is not social control, but that act in various ways to ensure social conformity through approval and disapproval of behaviour in everyday life – e.g. social pressure from agencies such as the family and peer groups, and from agents such as parents and neighbours, friends and workmates.

**Gender role** The pattern of behaviour which society expects from a man or woman.

**Hidden curriculum** The learning of values, attitudes and behaviour through the school's organization and teachers' attitudes, but which is not part of the formal timetable – e.g. obedience, punctuality and conformity to school rules.

## Table 1.1 (continued)

| Agency | How it carries out social control |
| --- | --- |
| Peer group | The peer group is very important in providing an individual's sense of identity. The desire for approval and acceptance by peers, and fear of rejection and ridicule, may promote conformity to the wider norms of society, such as acceptance of traditional gender roles. However, conformity to the peer group may also promote deviance. This is particularly likely among young people, where **peer pressure** may encourage them to adopt forms of deviant behaviour, such as playing truant from school, taking illegal drugs or under-age drinking. |
| The workplace | There are frequently strong pressures from fellow workers to conform to work-related norms, and an individual who is labelled as a troublemaker or uncooperative may find herself or himself denied promotion opportunities, allocated unpleasant jobs or even dismissed. Fellow workers may use such negative sanctions as refusing to talk to or mix with workmates, ridiculing them, or playing practical jokes on those who fail to conform to their norms. |
| The media | These are major sources of information and ideas, and can have powerful influences on people's attitudes, opinions and behaviour. The media generally encourage conformist behaviour, by means such as news reports on the serious consequences which follow for those who break society's norms, and their selection of what to report – thereby telling people what they should be thinking about and behaviour they should disapprove of – or advertising promoting conformity to traditional gender roles. |
| Religion | Religion lays down often clear rules about right and wrong behaviour, which may persuade believers to conform. Religious beliefs and teachings often support and reinforce the values and norms of society by giving them a sacred quality. The Ten Commandments in Christianity – 'thou shalt not kill … steal … commit adultery', etc. – reinforce values such as respect for human life, private property and monogamous marriage, and Muslims believe that practices like fasting during the month of Ramadan help them to avoid violence, anger, lust, envy and other antisocial behaviour. Feelings of guilt (a guilty conscience) may result if religious rules are broken by believers – a sort of inner police officer controlling behaviour. |

**Peer pressure**
Pressure from those in a group to which one belongs to encourage conformity to group norms.

### Activity

1 Give examples of three norms in each case, to which you are generally expected to conform, in two of the following: (a) at your school or college; (b) in your peer group; (c) at work.
2 Explain in each case how these norms are enforced, and outline the sanctions applied to encourage you to conform to them.

## An example of a social process: gender role socialization

### *Sex and gender*

- The term **'sex'** (whether someone is male or female) refers to the natural or biological differences between men and women, such as differences in genitals, internal reproductive organs and body hair.
- **Gender** (whether someone is masculine or feminine) is a **social construction**. This means that society and culture construct the idea of gender by creating, encouraging and teaching the two sexes to behave in different ways through socialization.
- A *gender role* is the pattern of behaviour and activity which society expects from individuals of either sex – how a boy/man or girl/woman should behave in society. Gender roles may sometimes be referred to as sex roles.

The difference between the terms *sex* and *gender* is best illustrated by the case of transgender people – those who biologically belong to one sex, but are convinced they belong to, or identify themselves more with, the opposite sex, e.g. a woman 'trapped' in a man's body. When these people try to change their biological sex (transsexuals), through surgery and hormone treatment, they also have to learn to act in a different way and adopt new masculine or feminine gender roles.

### *Gender and biology*

It is sometimes suggested that the different gender roles played by women and men are obvious extensions of the biological differences between the sexes. Therefore, women are thought to be natural mothers, with a maternal and caring instinct and a biological inclination towards domestic tasks. Men, on the other hand, it is suggested, are naturally assertive and dominant members of society, inclined towards the breadwinner role of supporting the family.

If this argument were correct, then socialization would be of little importance, as men and women would naturally adopt their roles, and one would expect the typical roles played by men and women in Britain to be the same in every society – after all, the biological differences between men and women are the same everywhere. However, the comparative study of other societies suggests this is not the case.

***Three Tribes in New Guinea*** Margaret Mead described three tribes in New Guinea (*Sex and Temperament*, 1935) where the roles of men and women were quite different from those found in modern Britain.

**Sex** The biological differences between men and women.

**Gender** The culturally created differences between men and women which are learnt through socialization.

**Social construction** (or social construct) Something that is created by people's actions, beliefs and interpretations in a society or culture, rather than something that exists in biology or nature. It only exists because people have constructed it by choosing to give it a particular meaning, interpretation and label – e.g. the definitions of crime, deviance, health, gender or race.

- Among the *Mundugumor*, both sexes showed what we in Britain would regard as masculine characteristics – both sexes were aggressive, both hated child rearing, and both treated children in an offhand way.
- Among the *Arapesh*, there were few differences between the behaviour of the sexes. Both sexes were gentle and passive, women did the heavy carrying, and the men tried to share the pains of childbirth with their wives by lying with them during it. Both sexes shared equally the tasks of bringing up children (women's traditional role in Britain).
- In the *Tchambuli* tribe, the traditional gender roles found in modern Britain were reversed – it was the men who displayed what we would regard as feminine characteristics, such as doing the shopping and putting on make-up and jewellery to make themselves attractive. Women were the more aggressive, practical ones, who made the sexual advances to men and did all the trading.

These three examples suggest that gender roles are not natural, since they differ between societies even though biology is the same. It is evidence like this which has led sociologists to conclude that masculine and feminine gender identities are primarily constructed through socialization, rather than simply a result of the biological differences between men and women.

> **Activity**
>
> 1 List some of the socially approved ways in which men and women are expected to behave, and how they should *not* behave, in contemporary Britain.
> 2 Suggest ways in which these expectations might be beginning to change.

## *Gender socialization and stereotyping in Britain*

**Stereotype** A generalized, over-simplified view of the features of a social group, allowing for few individual differences among its members. The assumption is made that all members of the group share the same features. An example might be 'all those on welfare benefits are on the fiddle'.

A gender **stereotype** is a generalized view of the typical or ideal characteristics of men and women.

1  *The feminine stereotype* in modern Britain often involves the expectation that girls and women will show the feminine characteristics of being pretty, slim, gentle, caring, sensitive, submissive, non-competitive, dependent and focused on people (people-oriented), for example with concerns for their family and running households, maintaining friendships and keeping customers happy. Girls and women face informal social control through social pressures, from both men and other females, to conform to that stereotype, e.g. ridicule and bullying at school or work for being 'tomboys'.

2   *The masculine stereotype* emphasizes characteristics like physical strength, aggression and assertiveness, independence, competitiveness, ambition and a focus on 'doing things' (task-oriented), such as playing sport, achieving success at work, and DIY in the home. Men and boys are likely to face informal social control through peer pressures to encourage conformity to the masculine stereotype – e.g. being called names like 'wimp'. It is still the case that one of the worst taunts a male child can face is to be called 'a girl' by his peer group.

There is a wide range of social institutions which influence the socialization and social control of males and females into conformity to their gender roles in modern Britain, but here the family, the education system, the peer group and the media will be focused on.

---

### Activity

1   What other groups of people tend to get stereotyped in the world today, apart from men and women?
2   What are the main features of these stereotypes?
3   Do you consider these stereotypes to be flattering or insulting to the groups concerned? Give reasons for your answer.
4   Look at the following list of words, and divide them into three groups: those you might use to describe women, those you might use to describe men, and those you might use to describe both men and women.

| | | | | |
|---|---|---|---|---|
| clever | passive | sulky | thoughtful | bastard |
| powerful | assertive | gentle | caring | attractive |
| bimbo | emotional | spinster | elegant | soft |
| aggressive | pretty | tart | kind | tender |
| cold | sweet | logical | quiet | competitive |
| sly | ruthless | delicate | brave | active |
| muscular | bitchy | weak | clinging | slag |
| domineering | slim | submissive | frigid | gracious |
| hideous | hunk | handsome | raving | plain |
| hysterical | blonde | beautiful | bachelor | stud |
| cute | babe | fit | mover | dickhead |
| loose | dog | trophy bird | easy | slut |

5   Now compare the two lists of words used to describe men and women. Do they present gender stereotypes? You will probably have found there are some words in both lists that have a similar meaning. Why are some words generally restricted to one gender? Discuss why these words are not used to describe both sexes, and how they show stereotyped assumptions about women and men.

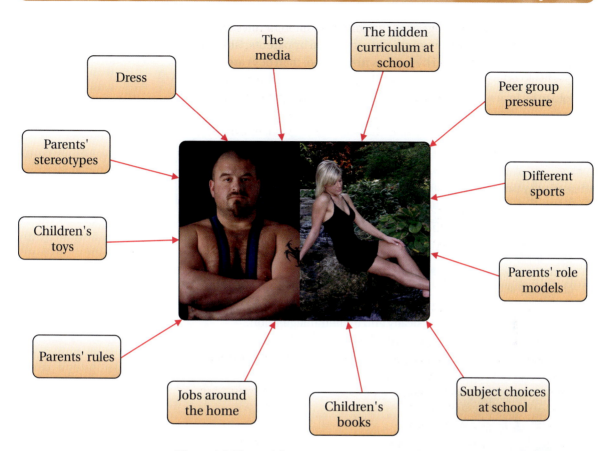

**Figure 1.3** The social construction of gender stereotypes through socialization

## The role of the family

Oakley argues that it is socialization that leads to gender differences, and children begin to learn their gender roles at a very early age. Even before they start school, many children have already learnt much about feminine and masculine roles and identities.

This begins during primary socialization in most families. Parents and relatives tend to hold stereotyped views of the typical or ideal characteristics of boys and girls, and they often try to bring up their children in accordance with this view of what they regard as normal masculine or feminine behaviour. Oakley suggests this is achieved through four processes:

1 **Manipulation** Boys and girls are manipulated or encouraged to adopt behaviour regarded as appropriate to their gender, e.g. by praising a boy for successfully completing some risky or scary activity, but discouraging a girl from even attempting it. From birth, girls and boys are frequently dressed in different styles of clothes and colours – 'blue for a boy, pink

for a girl'. Research has suggested that girls face different rules from boys of the same age, and are more strictly supervised by parents. Girls are more likely to be collected by parents from school than boys are, and are less likely to be allowed to play outside. Girls are also more likely to be told to be in at a certain time, and to have to tell their parents where they are going.

> **Activity**
>
> Go to www.pinkstinks.co.uk. Browse through the website, and identify four reasons why those involved with the website think the association between pink and female socialization is harmful – in short, why they think pink stinks.

2   **Canalization** Boys and girls are channelled towards different toys, games and activities. Boys tend to be given construction kits, footballs, chemistry sets, electronic toys, guns, cars and trucks, and computer games, for example: more active and technical toys, which take them outside the home, both physically and in their imagination.

   On the other hand, girls are generally given toys like dolls, prams, toy vacuum cleaners, cookers, tea sets and drawing books – toys which

More than 1 billion Barbies (and members of her family) have been sold worldwide since 1959. If all the Barbies sold were placed head to toe, they would circle the world more than eleven times. But do such toys make girls overconcerned with their own bodies and image? Games and toys aimed at boys tend to be more active and take them outside the home both physically and in their imaginations. To what extent do you think children's toys and games contribute to socialization into gender stereotypes?

are often played with inside the home, and serve to restrict girls to the domestic situation.

Boys are likely to be encouraged to involve themselves in games such as football or rugby, while girls may be encouraged to do dancing or ballet. A short time in a nursery shows that, by the age of 3, most little girls are already acting out the stereotyped female gender role, while boys play more aggressive and dominant games.

3  **Verbal appellations** Boys and girls are exposed to different nicknames (like 'sweet little angel' or 'scruffy little monster') and are praised or told off in different ways.

4  **Differential activity exposure** Small children mainly learn by watching and imitating the role models – patterns of behaviour on which they model their own behaviour – provided by their parent(s). Boys and girls are exposed to and encouraged to carry out different

### Table 1.2  11-year-olds' participation in household duties

| Duty | Boys % | Girls % | Both % |
|---|---|---|---|
| Washing up | 40 | 63 | 51 |
| Indoor housework (tidying, vacuum cleaning, dusting, bedmaking, etc.) | 19 | 44 | 32 |
| Miscellaneous dirty/outside jobs (gardening, sweeping, cleaning car or windows, making or mending fires, peeling potatoes, shoe cleaning, emptying bin, etc.) | 36 | 8 | 22 |
| Going on errands | 39 | 21 | 30 |

*Source*: Adapted from J. Newson, E. Newson, D. Richardson and J. Scaife, 'Perspectives in Sex Role Stereotyping', in J. Chetwynd and O. Hartnett (eds.), *The Sex Role System: Psychological and Sociological Perspectives* (Routledge & Kegan Paul)

### Activity

1  Study table 1.2 and answer the following questions:
   (a) What household duty is most likely to be performed by both sexes?
   (b) What household duty is least likely to be performed by (a) boys and (b) girls?
   (c) How do you think the divisions in household duties among 11-year-olds could be seen as preparation for adult gender roles? Give examples of particular adult roles.
   (d) Table 1.2 is based on research carried out many years ago. Do you think the same pattern is shown today in your own home?
2  Explain how manipulation by parents may be used to shape gender identity.
3  Explain why gender roles vary from society to society.

activities, e.g. girls staying inside to help their mothers with domestic chores, and boys doing jobs outside the home with their fathers, like cleaning the car.

Children often observe their parents carrying out their respective gender roles every day. If children see their mothers spending more time in the home while their fathers go out to work, their mothers spending more time doing cooking, cleaning and other housework than their fathers, and their mothers, rather than their fathers, taking time off work to look after them when they are sick, or taking them to the doctor, then children may well begin to view these roles as the normal ways for men and women to behave. In general, small children are brought up by women, surrounded by women, and it is women who nearly always care for them, whether as mothers, child-minders or teachers. It is perhaps not surprising, then, that many girls still grow up today seeing childcare as being a major part of their role in life.

Role models are important in socialization, particularly in the early formative years, but also throughout life. How might these role models encourage different behaviours in men and women? Who is important in your life today as role models for behaviour, and to what extent do you try to copy their examples?

## The role of the school

The process of gender socialization begun in the home often carries on through schooling. Much of this socialization goes on through the school's hidden curriculum.

This consists of the hidden teaching of attitudes and behaviour, which are not part of the formal timetable. This is discussed in more detail in chapter 4. Despite equal opportunities policies, the hidden curriculum still often emphasizes the differences between males and females, and encourages different forms of behaviour. Two examples help to illustrate this.

*Teachers' attitudes*  Teachers have also been socialized into gender roles, and there is evidence suggesting that teachers may give different career advice to boys and girls, such as steering girls towards nursing and office work, and boys towards a much wider range of occupations.

Boys demand more of the teacher's time, and disruptive, unruly behaviour from boys is more likely to be tolerated than the same behaviour from girls. Girl troublemakers – who fight in the playground or are disruptive in class, for example – are likely to be punished more severely than boys displaying similar behaviour, since girls are not expected to act in such an 'unfeminine' way.

*Subject choice*  Girls and boys have traditionally been counselled by parents and teachers into taking different subjects. Girls have been more likely to take arts subjects (like English literature, history, sociology, psychology and foreign languages) and study subjects like food technology, business studies, leisure and tourism, and hair and beauty. Boys have been more likely to take sciences, CAD, and design and technology – subjects which are more likely to lead to more skilled and technical occupations after school. This gender division is also found in sport, with rugby and cricket for the boys and hockey and netball for the girls. After age 16, there are quite wide gender differences in subject choice, as chapter 4 on education shows.

### Activity

1  On the basis of your own experiences at both primary and secondary school, make a list of any difficulties or pressures you might have experienced there, because of your sex, in choosing subjects, options and activities that you wanted to do. Take into account factors such as the views of your parents, friends and teachers, and the advice of careers and subject teachers.
2  Suggest explanations for why these difficulties and pressures exist, and discuss your findings and ideas with others in your group.

How do you think the interests and concerns of male and female teenage peer groups differ? How does your peer group influence your behaviour?

## The importance of the peer group

A peer group is a group of people of similar age and status with whom a person mixes socially. Generally, people try to gain acceptance among their peers by conforming to the norms of their peer group. These norms frequently involve stereotyped masculine and feminine roles. For example, among male peer groups, interests and norms often centre on stereotyped activities like football, cars, motor-bikes and computer games. Female interests often centre on stereotyped things such as fashion, diet, celebrities and make-up. The peer group can exert strong pressure to conform to these interests: a boy, for example, who collected soft toys would be quite likely to find himself ridiculed by his peer group; a girl who played rugby might be seen as a bit of a tomboy. Being ridiculed or excluded from group activities can discourage participation in activities which don't conform to gender stereotypes.

*Double standards*  Among teenage boys (and often adult men too), sexual promiscuity and sexual conquest are often encouraged and admired as approved masculine behaviour, and are seen as a means of achieving status in the male peer group. However, males will condemn this same promiscuity among females – promiscuous girls and women are likely to be judged negatively and called insulting terms. This attitude is sometimes reinforced even by the female peer group, where sexual relations are often only approved of in the context of a steady, close relationship. Girls and women who have casual sex – outside some steady relationship – are therefore likely to find themselves condemned by men and women alike. In short, promiscuous men are seen as 'stags' or 'studs'; promiscuous women are seen as 'slags' or 'sluts'. This double standard helps to encourage conformity to separate gender identities for men and women, with the stereotyped man as a sexual athlete, and woman as the passive and faithful wife or girlfriend.

> ### Activity
>
> 1  Describe two influences your peer group has had in forming your gender identity, and, drawing on your own experiences, suggest ways it does this.
> 2  Do you have any evidence that there is a double standard applied to the behaviour of males and females when it comes to sexual activity? Note down your evidence and discuss it with others, and try to establish whether this double standard is a common occurrence.

## The role of the media

The media include radio, television, print and online newspapers and magazines, books, films, advertising, music, computer games and the internet, including social media.

The media create and reinforce gender stereotypes in a number of ways. Comics, for example, present different images of men and women: girls are usually presented as pretty, romantic, helpless, easily upset and emotional, and dependent on boys – strong, independent, unemotional and assertive – for support and guidance, and boys and girls are often presented in traditional stereotyped gender roles such as soldiers (boys) or nurses (girls). A similar pattern is shown on children's television, and much TV advertising shows gender stereotypes. Around 80 per cent of TV advertising voice-overs are male voices – suggesting authority. The media, particularly advertising, often promote the 'beauty myth' – the idea that women should be assessed primarily in terms of their appearance.

> ### Activity
>
> Examine some children's reading-books, comics, or print or online male or female adult magazines, or study TV adverts or shows, websites or social media sites, such as Facebook, Instagram or Twitter, and see whether you can identify any pattern in the different roles and interests allocated to boys and girls or men and women. Provide evidence for your conclusions.

You may have found from the activity above that there are often very different types of story and images aimed at males and females. Romantic fiction is almost exclusively aimed at a female readership. A glance at the magazine shelves of any large newsagents will reveal a range of magazines clearly aimed at women, consisting almost exclusively of magazines on 'true-life' stories, the lifestyles of celebrities, beauty, fashion and haircare, health and

Women's magazines still often portray stereotypical views of women's interests

slimming, alongside traditional fare of cooking, homecare, housekeeping, and weddings, mothers and babies.

This shows very clearly the way the media both encourage and cater for a particular view of a woman's role. Magazines aimed at men often focus on subjects like bodybuilding and fitness, photography, electronic gadgets of all kinds, computers and computer games, DIY, and all manner of transport: cars, motor-bikes, aircraft, trains and boats. The top-shelf soft-porn magazines are aimed exclusively at men.

### Activity

Take two magazines, either print or online, or magazine-like websites you use – one aimed at men, and one aimed at women (https://goo.gl/tKtULP gives a list of men's magazines, and https://goo.gl/Gi9HNS some women's magazines, which you can use to search for their websites).

1  Describe three differences between them, in terms of things like the stories or issues covered and the pictures used.
2  Suggest two ways that these might contribute to differences in the socialization and adult behaviour of males and females.

***Media stereotypes of women***   When women appear in the media, it has traditionally been in a limited number of stereotyped roles, for example:

- *in a narrow range of gender-specific roles*, e.g. nurses, stay-at-home mothers
- *as people prone to emotional and unpredictable behaviour*
- *as WAGS (wives and girlfriends)* – in their relationships to men as wives, girlfriends and lovers
- *as sex objects* – the image of the slim, sexually seductive, scantily clad figure – typically found in the *Sun* newspaper – is used by the advertising industry to sell everything from peanuts to motor-bikes and newspapers
- *as content, capable and caring home-makers and mothers*, living more in the private sphere of the home than in the public world of the workplace and the street. Her constant concern is with the cleanliness of clothes

Gender stereotypes like those shown here are still quite common in the media, and may have harmful consequences for the majority who fail to live up to the stereotype

and floors, the evening meal, getting the kids to school, and being the person who keeps the family together and manages its emotions
- *as ball breakers* – a negative stereotype of sexually active, selfish, independent and ambitious career-minded women who don't depend on men.

*Media stereotypes of men*   The masculine stereotype of the physically well-built, muscular, strong, handsome, brave, independent, unemotional, assertive non-domestic male still often appears in the media. Men are often portrayed:

- *as living in the public sphere outside the home more than women*
- *in a wide range of roles,* often carrying higher status than women's, and which have no particular reference to their gender
- *as strong silent types* – who are in control, act decisively and avoid weakness by not talking about their feelings or showing emotion
- *as jokers* – who use laughter to avoid displaying seriousness or emotion
- *as jocks* – who show aggression to demonstrate power and strength
- *as big shots* – who are economically and socially successful
- *as action heroes* – who are tough, strong and show extreme aggression and often violence
- *as buffoons* – who are totally inept at parenting or housework.

To what extent do you think these shelves of men's magazines reflect gender stereotypes?

> **Activity**
>
> Go to https://goo.gl/xCQuy2 and list and explain briefly the gender stereotypes shown in the video clip. Do you think the clip still gives a fair, if exaggerated, picture of gender stereotypes in advertising? What effects do you think such images might have on the behaviour of men and women, particularly over a long period of time?

*Changing media images of men and women* In recent years, media images of gender have been changing.

**Feminism** A view, and a movement, which believes that women are disadvantaged in society, and aims to achieve gender equality so women have rights, power and status equal to those of men. Anyone who supports this view is known as a *feminist*.

- A new form of popular **feminism** – 'girl power' – emerged in the 1990s, shown in young (pre-teen and teenage) women's magazines and websites. These promoted female assertiveness, self-confidence, independence and ambition.
- Women are being presented more in TV dramas and films as powerful 'tough girls', and 'action heroes', taking on roles that were once the preserve of men.
- Male bodies are being used more as sex objects in advertising, in much the same way that women's bodies have always been used.
- Men's magazines are covering more concerns that were once restricted to women, e.g. diet, health and cosmetics.

*Why have these changes occurred?*

- There is much more flexibility in gender identities, weakening traditional stereotypes. The masculine ideals of toughness, self-reliance and emotional coldness now exist alongside an emphasis on men's emotions, and more men are getting involved with childcare. More women are now becoming important family wage-earners.
- The changing position of women in society and their growing success in education and the job market have created a growing social expectation that women and men should be treated equally. This has made traditional stereotypes seem outdated.
- The presence and influence of women in media management and production have grown.
- Powerful advertisers are tapping into a new profitable men's market for consumer cosmetics.
- Media organizations need to retain advertising revenue and profits by attracting a changing media audience, particularly among women, for whom traditional stereotypes – based on **patriarchy** – have less relevance to their lives.

**Patriarchy** Power, status and authority held by men.

- There is a growing awareness in the advertising industry that gender stereotyping can have harmful consequences, e.g. by having negative effects on how adults and children see themselves and how others see them. This has become a major concern of the Advertising Standards Authority (ASA), the UK's independent regulator of advertising across all media. In 2017, the ASA issued *Depictions, Perceptions & Harm*, a report which urged changes in advertising practice to restrict gender stereotyping. You can read their report here: https://goo.gl/8nvL3k.

Despite these changes, gender stereotypes do still thrive in the mainstream media and advertising, particularly in the red-top print and online newspapers, such as the *Sun* and the *Daily Star*. New media technology has also led to the exploitation of women as sex objects and as victims of sexual violence more extensively than ever, for example through porn websites.

---

**Activity**

Go through the following questions, and write down a couple of points in relation to each one. Then discuss your findings in a group, and try to reach some conclusions about how the socialization of males and females might be changing in contemporary Britain.

1 To what extent is the social process of gender role socialization discussed in the sections above still accurate in contemporary Britain?
2 Does socialization mean that women and men still have different experiences and expectations of life?
3 Does socialization still have the general effect of emphasizing girls' domestic responsibilities of housework and childcare, limiting their self-confidence, and pushing them, eventually, towards marriage and the roles of homemaker and mother (often alongside paid employment) as their primary roles in life?
4 Are boys still more likely to grow up conforming to the stereotype of the non-domestic, practical, unemotional, independent and assertive male, whose role in life is that of 'the provider, the protector, and the impregnator'.
5 Are media stereotypes of men and women changing? If so, how? What examples are there of this?

---

**Activity**

The process of gender socialization shows how the agencies of socialization socially construct culture and identity relating to gender. Suggest some ways that families, schools, peer groups and the media also socially construct and pass on between generations culture and identities relating to social class, ethnicity and age.

# SOCIAL ISSUES, SOCIAL PROBLEMS AND SOCIAL POLICY

## Social issues

> **Social issues** Issues that affect people and the way they live their lives.

**Social issues** are those that affect people and the way they live their lives. They tend to be matters that people worry about, and their causes, effects and solutions are frequently controversial, generating quite heated debate and discussion. They are also matters that may affect in some way many members of society and that are rooted in the wider community, rather than being purely personal issues under the control of any one individual. Such issues might include the causes and consequences of social class, gender and ethnic inequalities; the causes of and solutions to poverty; the welfare state; crime and the fear of crime; the quality of education and healthcare; and **racism**. Many of these and other issues are considered in other parts of this book.

### *Examples of social issues*

> **Racism** Treating people as inferior, and encouraging hostility towards them, on the grounds of racial or ethnic origins – usually based on skin colour or other physical or cultural characteristics.

- **Social class, gender, ethnic and age inequalities** and unequal and unfair treatment can generate hostility and conflict between the haves and the have-nots, between women and men, between different ethnic groups, and between younger and older people. These can contribute to social instability and social conflict. These issues are discussed later in this book (see particularly chapter 6).
- **Poverty** is an issue as the poor find themselves lacking the resources to participate in the activities and obtain the consumer goods and living conditions that others in society take for granted. This can generate resentment and conflict, contributing to an unstable society. This can be made worse as the poor often lack the power to do much to change their position. Poverty is also an issue for government, as there are huge costs in social welfare benefits and tax credits to help the poor, plus potential social disorder if poverty and resentment among the poor about social inequality become too great. (There is a discussion of poverty in chapter 6.)
- **Crime** is a source of fear for many people. Even though crime rates have been falling in recent years, fear of crime remains persistently higher than the real risk of being a victim of crime. Older people have particularly high levels of fear of crime, as they tend to be more home-centred and dependent on the media for information, and the media tend to focus on bad news and make exaggerated reports on crime to sell papers and attract viewers. Similarly, the media often give the impression that most young people are frightening and threatening antisocial, gun- and

A slum neighbourhood in Freetown, the capital city of Sierra Leone. In what ways might such poverty pose threats to the stability of society? In contemporary Britain, such extreme poverty is very rarely found, but how might large numbers of people lacking everyday things others take for granted pose threats to social stability in the UK?

knife-carrying thugs. In fact, most young people are conformist and law-abiding.

- **Racism** is a serious issue for Black, Asian and Minority Ethnic (BAME) groups. Black people and Asians are much more likely to be the victim of a racially motivated **hate crime** than white people, and they often face discrimination in jobs, housing and the law. Racism can also generate wider conflicts, as it can breed resentment, periodically erupting in riots, and cause a fragmented society lacking cohesion.

- **The quality of education** is a social issue as education is a key to **life chances**: the chances of gaining the desirable, and avoiding the undesirable, things in life – for example, gaining a well-paid job, a nice home, consumer goods and good health, and avoiding unemployment, poverty, poor housing and ill health. Poor schools, with a high turnover of teachers, low standards and multiple social problems, mean that young people are being denied opportunities in life.

> **Hate crime** Any crime that is perceived by the victim, or any other person, to be motivated by hostility or prejudice towards someone based on a personal characteristic, such as their ethnicity or race, disability, religion, beliefs or sexual orientation.

> **Life chances** The chances of obtaining those things defined as desirable, and of avoiding those things defined as undesirable, in any society.

> **Social problem** Something that is seen as harmful to society in some way, and that calls for something to be done to sort it out.

## Social problems

Many social issues are also often considered to be **social problems** – things that are in some way harmful to society, and that need something doing to sort them out. The social issues referred to above are also social problems, as they cause difficulties, resentment and instability in society, and harm many people.

## Social policy

**Social policy**
The packages of plans and actions adopted by national and local government or various voluntary agencies to solve social problems or achieve other goals that are seen as important.

Social problems are tackled by the application of **social policy**. Social policy refers to the plans and actions of national and local government and various voluntary agencies designed to solve social problems. Social policy seeks to achieve goals that have an impact on and improve the life chances and welfare of citizens, such as goals concerned with health, housing, employment, social care, education, crime and transport.

There are always different ways of tackling social problems, and the social policy option chosen – if indeed any is chosen – will depend on those with power to make policy, which is nearly always either national or local government. For example, poverty is a social problem, and possible social policy options to tackle it include:

- doing nothing – people might argue that the poor are inadequate and lazy, and have only themselves to blame for their own inadequacy. They therefore don't deserve any help. Not providing help will force them to help themselves.
- forcing people into work, even if jobs are very low-paid.
- redistributing wealth, through higher welfare benefits for the poor, paid for by higher taxes on the rich.
- a guaranteed national minimum income, tax credits and other incentives to help the low-paid.

The option chosen will depend on the views about poverty and its causes held by those with the power to implement social policies.

> **Activity**
>
> Take *one* of the following social problems (or another social issue, of your own choosing, that is also a social problem): teenage pregnancy; obesity; sex discrimination; racism; crime; family breakdown.
> 1  Explain how the issue you have chosen is a social problem.
> 2  Describe two social policies that might be adopted to solve the problem.

## Sociology, social problems and social policy

When tackling social problems, governments are more likely to produce social policies that are effective and work as intended if they base them on proper evidence gained through research. The work of sociologists in areas such as education, health, poverty and crime has contributed to understanding and explaining social issues, and has sometimes had quite important effects on the social policies of governments. Government will often commission research from sociologists in universities to assist policy making.

Sociology can assist social policy making by:

- *identifying social problems*
- *changing assumptions* – for example, sociological research has contributed a great deal to understanding the extent of poverty in contemporary Britain, and has shown that the causes are primarily located in society rather than the individual inadequacies of poor people (these issues are discussed later in this book).
- *providing the evidence* – through surveys, opinion polls, and collecting statistics to either back up or show the inadequacies of particular social policies.
- *identifying the unintended consequences of policies* – for example, have policies designed to reduce crime in one area simply moved it to another?
- *assessing the results* – sociological research can help to establish whether policies have achieved what they set out to do, and whether they need changing or scrapping.

In these ways, sociologists and their research can help to provide the means of improving society.

### Activity

1 Imagine you were creating an ideal society from scratch. Drawing on the ideas of social structure and social processes discussed in this chapter, plan how you would organize your ideal society, with particular reference to the following issues:
   - the care and socialization of children
   - the passing on of society's knowledge and skills from one generation to the next
   - the production of food and other goods necessary for survival
   - how you would allocate food and other goods to members of society
   - the establishment and enforcement of rules of behaviour, and how decisions will be made
   - how you would deal with people who didn't conform to social rules
   - how you would coordinate things and resolve disputes between members of society
   - how you would prevent or deal with any social conflicts.
2 Consider what social issues might arise in your society, and how they might be brought to the attention of everyone.
3 Identify two social problems that might arise, and suggest ways you might resolve them.
4 Suggest ways your ideal society is similar to, or different from, the organization of contemporary Britain. How would you explain these similarities or differences?

## CHAPTER SUMMARY AND REVISION CHECKLIST

After studying this chapter, you should be able to:

- explain what sociology is, how and why it first developed, and the contributions of Comte, Durkheim, Marx and Weber to this development

- explain why sociology is different from common-sense and naturalistic or biological explanations, and how it differs from journalism and psychology

- describe some of the problems sociologists face compared with those working in the natural sciences

- explain why sociology is scientific

- define the meaning of socialization, social order, culture, identity, roles, role conflict, values, norms, social control, deviance, and positive and negative sanctions, and explain their importance in understanding human behaviour in society

- explain what is meant by social structure and social processes, and discuss gender role socialization as a social process

- explain, with examples, what is meant by a social issue, a social problem and social policy, and how sociology can contribute to social policy

## KEY TERMS

Definitions can be found in the glossary at the end of this book, as well as these terms usually being defined in the margin where they first appear in the chapter. You can also find the glossary online by following the link at www.politybooks.com/browne. Put it in your phone for ready reference.

| | | | |
|---|---|---|---|
| agencies of social control | gender | power | social policy |
| agencies of socialization | gender role | primary socialization | social problem |
| agents of social control | global culture | racism | social processes |
| agents of socialization | globalization | role conflict | social stratification |
| anti-school subculture | hate crime | role model | social structure |
| consumer (or consumption) goods | hidden curriculum | roles | socialization |
| cultural diversity | identity | sanctions | society |
| culture | informal social control | secondary socialization | sociology |
| customs | life chances | sex | stereotype |
| deviance | Marxism | social class | subculture |
| discrimination | multicultural society | social conformity | value consensus |
| ethnicity | non-conformity | social construction | value freedom |
| feminism | norms | social control | values |
| feral children | objectivity | social institutions | verstehen |
| formal social control | patriarchy | social issues | |
| functionalism | peer group | social media | |
| | peer pressure | social order | |

There are a variety of free tests and other activities that can be used to assess your learning – mainly aimed at AS- and A-level sociology students, but you might find them useful – as well as an online searchable glossary, at

www.politybooks.com/browne

You can also find new contemporary resources by following Ken Browne on Twitter

@BrowneKen

# Sociological Theories and Research Methods

## Contents

# DIFFERENT VIEWS OF SOCIETY

## Sociological perspectives

A **perspective** is simply a way of looking at something – e.g. from above, or below, or through binoculars. Sociologists have different ways of seeing or approaching the study of society. Each of these different ways of viewing society is called a **sociological perspective**. Newcomers to sociology often find the different perspectives in sociology difficult, as there appears to be no 'right answer'.

**Perspective**
A way of looking at something.

**Sociological perspective** An approach adopted by a sociologist when studying society.

Young woman or old woman? What you see depends on your perspective.

People may view the same scene from different perspectives

A useful insight might be gained from the following situation. Imagine there are five people looking at the same busy shopping street – a pickpocket, a police officer, a roadsweeper, a shopper and a shopkeeper (see cartoon above). The pickpocket sees wallets sticking out of pockets or bags, and an opportunity to steal. The police officer sees potential crime and disorder. The roadsweeper sees litter and garbage left by everyone else. The shopper might see windows full of desirable consumer goods to buy, and the shopkeeper sees only potential customers, and possibly shoplifters. All are viewing the same street, but are looking at different aspects of that street. What they see will depend on their 'perspective' – what they're looking for. They might all be seeing different things, but you can't really say any of their views is more correct than another – though you might think some views provide a more truthful, more rounded and fuller description of the street than others do.

Sociological perspectives are basically similar, in that they are the different viewpoints from which sociologists examine society. Different sociological perspectives simply emphasize and explain different aspects of society.

## Structuralism

**Structuralism** (or structural theory / structural approaches) bases its explanations on the study of the overall social structure and culture of society, rather than by focusing on individuals or small groups. This large-scale, overall study of society is known as a **macro approach**. Structuralist sociologists will look at the various social institutions making up society's structure, and the links between them. For example, they might study the role of the family or the education system in society as a whole, rather than looking at an individual family or family member, or individual school or student. Structuralists believe that the beliefs, identity and behaviour of individuals are largely formed by forces outside them, such as by the agencies of socialization and social control discussed in the previous chapter. People are like puppets, who simply react to the 'strings' pulled by society, as suggested by figure 2.1.

## Social action or interpretivist perspectives

Social action or interpretivist perspectives suggest people actively interpret and give meanings to their experiences in everyday **social interaction**. For example, if a teacher tells a student off, rather than just accepting it at face value and allowing it to change their behaviour, the student may interpret it and act upon it in various ways – for instance, as being unfairly picked on because the teacher is just in a bad mood, doesn't like the student, doesn't think the student is working hard enough, is a racist and has it in for Black, Asian and Minority Ethnic (BAME) students, etc. Those interpretations will affect how the student responds to the telling off – e.g. accepting it, appealing to the rest of the class for support in rebelling, punching the teacher, walking out of school, etc.

To understand and explain society and individual behaviour, sociologists have to understand how, why and what interpretations are made, and how people make sense of the world around them through social interaction. Social action or interpretivist approaches therefore take a small-scale or **micro approach**, studying small-scale social interaction, such as how an individual family operates and the interaction of individual family members, or an intensive case study of one school or classroom.

Unlike the structuralists, social action or interpretivist sociologists emphasize that people have free will and choice, and are not simply puppets moulded by the social structure. They actively create through their social action what schools, families and other social institutions are like, as suggested by figure 2.2.

**Structuralism**
(or structural theory / structural approaches)
A sociological perspective that bases its explanations on the study of the overall social structure and culture of society, rather than by focusing on individuals or small groups.

**Macro approach**
An approach to studying society that focuses on the large-scale structure of society as a whole, rather than on individuals and small groups.

**Social interaction**
The relationship between two or more individuals, and how those individuals act and react to those around them.

**Figure 2.1** Structural perspectives see individuals formed by the wider social forces making up the social structure of society

## Postmodernism

**Figure 2.2** Social action or interpretivist perspectives emphasize the free will and choice of individuals, and their role in creating social structures

### POSTMODERNISM – A NOTE TO STUDENTS

Postmodernism is mainly considered in this book in relation to the media chapter, and so will only be considered briefly here. It is not normally required for GCSE and similar-level introductory courses, but if you are doing the Cambridge IGCSE you will need some awareness of it. More general introductory courses to sociology may wish you to have at least some familiarity with postmodernist ideas. Having said this, if you do mention postmodernism (correctly) in GCSE answers, the examiners are likely to be extremely impressed.

**Postmodernism** suggests that society has entered a new phase that follows (comes after – or 'post') modernism. In modernism, the world can be explained through logic and rational and scientific evidence, such as is found in sociological research based on structural and interpretivist approaches. Postmodernists argue:

- Society is changing so rapidly that it is marked by chaos, risk and uncertainty about the future.
- Social structures have ceased to exist. This has undermined the ability of structuralist and interpretivist approaches to understand society.
- There is a growing emphasis on individual self-interest in postmodern societies.
- People have more choice in their relationships, which are no longer controlled by tradition and norms of what is socially acceptable, and they are free from traditional constraints such as social class, gender or ethnicity. For example, postmodernists argue that it is nonsense to talk of an institution called the family, as people now live in such a wide range of ever-changing personal relationships.
- Society is now composed of a mass of individuals making individual choices about their lifestyles and identities. This means people can now form their own identities – how they see and define themselves and how others see and define them – and they can be whatever they want to be.
- There can be no general perspectives for understanding society. Structuralist and social action approaches, and theories like the functionalist and Marxist approaches discussed below, are redundant, as society has been fragmented by unlimited individual choice, leading to such wide differences in identities and lifestyles that it is impossible to use any general theory or perspective to understand society.

# CONSENSUS AND CONFLICT VIEWS OF SOCIETY

Is society based on harmony and agreement between individuals and groups? Or is society based on conflict and antagonism between them? These two questions reflect different views among sociologists about the way society works. These two approaches are often referred to as consensus and conflict theories (or perspectives).

## Consensus theory

**Consensus theory** is the approach adopted by **functionalism** (see pages 51–2), which has its origins in the work of Émile Durkheim in the nineteenth century, and Talcott Parsons (1902–79) in the twentieth century. Functionalism sees social order and stability in society based on socialization into shared norms and values – a value consensus (as discussed in chapter 1).

Consensus theorists, when studying society, emphasize these shared norms and shared values that exist between people, and see society made up of individuals and social institutions working together in harmony, without much conflict between individuals and groups.

## Conflict theory

**Conflict theory** emphasizes that social order is maintained by coercion and power, with power in the hands of those with the greatest political, economic and social resources. Conflict theory has its origins in the work of Karl Marx (1818–83) and Max Weber (1864–1920), and is found in the work of **feminist** writers.

Rather than viewing society as essentially peaceful, harmonious and based on value consensus, as consensus theorists do, conflict theorists emphasize social differences and conflicts between individuals, groups and classes. They emphasize conflicts created by inequalities in wealth, power and status when describing and explaining society, as individuals and groups struggle against one another, pursuing different interests. Conflict theory is associated with Marxist, Weberian and feminist theories (see pages 53–9). Conflicts exist, for example, between White British people and BAME groups, between men and women, between the rich and the poor, between employers and employees, between different religious groups (e.g. Christians and Muslims), and between different age groups (e.g. younger and older people). Figure 2.3 summarizes some of the contrasts between consensus and conflict theories.

**Consensus theory** A sociological approach that emphasizes the shared norms and shared values that exist between people, and sees society made up of individuals and social institutions working together in harmony, without much conflict between people and groups.

**Functionalism** A sociological perspective which sees society as made up of parts – such as the family, education system and religion – which work together to maintain society as a whole. Society is seen as basically harmonious and stable, because of the agreement on basic values (value consensus) established through socialization.

**Conflict theory** A sociological approach that emphasizes social differences and conflicts, with inequalities in wealth, power and status all creating conflicts between individuals and groups.

**Feminist** Someone who believes that women are disadvantaged in society, and should have rights, power and status equal to those of men.

Conflict theorists emphasize social divisions and conflict in society, shown by the demonstration here in London against public-sector cuts and austerity, with a heavy police presence protecting the 5* luxury-class Ritz Hotel in London.

**Figure 2.3** Some differences between consensus and conflict theories of society

**Consensus theory**

Society based on:
- value consensus
- agreement
- shared interests
- stability and harmony

**Conflict theory**

Society based on:
- values and interests of dominant groups
- disagreement and control by powerful groups
- conflicting interests
- instability, tension and conflict

## The consensus perspective of functionalism

Functionalism is a structural consensus theory (or perspective), and is associated with the work of Durkheim and Parsons. It argues that:

**Functional prerequisites** Basic needs that must be met if societies are to survive.

- Societies have **functional prerequisites** – basic needs that must be met if societies are to survive, e.g. the production of food and housing; socialization so people learn the culture and rules of society, and social control to make sure people conform to those rules.
- Society works a bit like the human body, as Parsons suggests. All body parts (social institutions) work together to maintain the needs (or functional prerequisites) of the human body (society) as a whole.

- Social order – the avoidance of social chaos and disorder – is maintained by encouraging people to cooperate by sharing some common beliefs, norms and values – a value consensus.
- Social institutions (such as the economic system, family, education and the criminal justice system) play a key role in building value consensus, and work together to satisfy functional prerequisites and to establish and maintain social order.
- To understand the workings and importance of one part of society – e.g. the family – it is necessary to discover its function or purpose in maintaining the whole – e.g. the family's role in socializing young children so they are prepared for the education system and the world of work.
- All social phenomena have some function in society, e.g. crime has the function of reminding people about the rules of what is right and wrong, what happens to those who break them, and alerting others to problems in society.

For functionalists, value consensus maintains a peaceful, harmonious society without much conflict between people and groups.

## Evaluation of functionalism

✓ It is a reasonably successful attempt to produce a general theory of the overall workings of society.

✓ It recognizes the importance of social structure in controlling individual behaviour, and how the major social institutions often have links between them.

✓ It provides an explanation for social order and stability, and why most people generally conform to the rules of social life.

✗ It sees individuals as simply passive products of society – it doesn't allow for individual choice and action.

✗ It paints a rosy picture of society, and over-emphasizes the beneficial functions of social institutions – e.g. families and schools don't always produce well-behaved and conformist young people.

✗ It has no sense of inequalities in life chances and power, which mean not everyone necessarily shares the same values.

## Functionalism and the New Right (or neoliberal) approach

The functionalist perspective is often associated with policies adopted by the **New Right**, sometimes also called *neoliberalism*. The New Right first emerged in the United States and the UK in the 1970s and 1980s, and is found today in many policies of Conservative governments. It shares much in common with functionalist theories of society.

**New Right** An approach to social and political policies that stresses individual freedom; self-help and self-reliance; reduction of the power and spending of the state; the free market and free competition between private companies, schools and other organizations; and the importance of traditional institutions and values.

## Features of the New Right

- An emphasis on the importance of socialization into shared values for the maintenance of social stability.
- An emphasis on protecting the important functions of traditional institutions in building shared values, e.g. conventional marriage and family life, and traditional education.
- An emphasis on individual freedom and self-interest, and the need to reduce the power of the state/government to the minimum. Self-interest is given priority over the needs and welfare of others.
- Reduced spending by the state, by making individuals more self-reliant – e.g. cutting welfare benefits and encouraging people into work to make them 'stand on their own two feet'. Lower taxes are seen as a means of increasing incentives for individuals and businesses to succeed.
- A defence of the free market. This means that free competition between individuals, companies, schools and other institutions is encouraged, to give individuals maximum choice between competing products, for instance in healthcare and education.
- Support for private companies to provide basic services such as gas, electricity, water and healthcare. The assumption is that private companies with more competition will lead to lower prices and better-quality services or products.
- The need for strong social control, such as cracking down hard on criminals and deviants, to maintain social order through socialization, reinforcement of a value consensus and the prevention of deviance.
- A condemnation of anything that challenges traditional values, or undermines the important functions of social institutions in maintaining social stability, as suggested in the box below on the work of Charles Murray.

**Means of production** The key resources like land, labour, raw materials, property, factories, businesses and machinery which are necessary for producing society's goods.

**Capitalism** A form of society or economic system in which the means of production are privately owned; goods are produced for sale in the free market (rather than for personal use) to make profits for their owners; and the majority of people only make the money needed to survive by selling their labour to the owners in exchange for wages.

## The conflict perspective of Marxism

Marxism is a structural conflict theory (or perspective), and is associated with the work of Karl Marx (2000).

Marxists suggest that the main reason for social conflict lies in the private ownership of the **means of production** – the key resources like land, property, factories and businesses which are necessary to produce society's goods.

In **capitalism** (or capitalist societies), most of the means of production are privately owned, rather than collectively owned by the state on everyone's behalf. Goods are produced for sale in the free market (rather than for personal use), with the aim of making profits for their owners. Most people can only make the money they need to survive by selling their labour in exchange for wages to the owners, who then reap the profits.

## THE NEW RIGHT ON THE FAMILY, THE WELFARE STATE AND THE UNDERCLASS

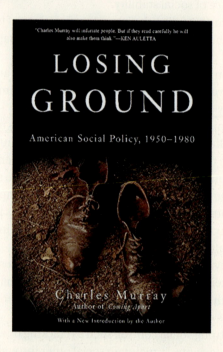

New Right theorist Charles Murray in *Losing Ground* (1984) argues that the welfare state has undermined personal responsibility and self-help. It has devalued the importance of support from families, and the traditional functions families have carried out. He sees the decline of the traditional family, and especially growing numbers of female-headed lone-parent families, as threats to the adequate socialization and disciplining of children, particularly because of the lack of male/father role models. He views the interference of the welfare 'nanny' state and the decline of traditional family life as contributing to the emergence of a **dependency culture** and a culture of laziness. This encourages the creation of a deviant workshy **underclass** which wants to avoid work by living off welfare benefits, and which is associated with high levels of illegitimacy, lone parenthood and family instability. The New Right sees the decline of the conventional nuclear family unit and an over-generous welfare state as undermining traditional values such as honesty, a commitment to traditional marriage and family life, and hard work as important goals in life. This contributes to wider social problems, such as immorality, the lack of a work ethic, alcohol and drug abuse, antisocial behaviour and 'yob culture', crime, fiddling of the benefit system, and failure at school.

**Dependency culture** A set of values and beliefs, and a way of life, centred on dependence on others. Normally used in the context of those who depend on welfare-state benefits. Sometimes called a 'culture of dependency'.

**Underclass** A social group who are right at the bottom of the social class hierarchy, who are in some ways cut off or excluded from the rest of society.

Marx argued that the concentration of ownership of the means of production in the hands of the few laid the basis for social class inequalities in wealth and income, and ongoing conflict. Marx argued there were two basic social classes in capitalist industrial society:

**Bourgeoisie** The class of owners of the means of production.

- The **bourgeoisie** (or capitalists) – a small, wealthy and powerful class of owners of the means of production. This class was also a ruling class, with power in society. It maintained its rule and protected its interests through its control of society's major institutions and the dominant ideas. For example, the laws protected the owning class rather than the workers, and the bourgeoisie's ownership of the media meant it was mostly its ideas that were spread among the population. In this way, the working-class were almost brainwashed into accepting their position as normal and natural.

**Proletariat** The class of workers, who have to work for wages to survive as they do not own the means of production.

- The **proletariat** (or working class) – a large, relatively poor (compared to the bourgeoisie) class of non-owners. Since they owned no means of production, in order to survive the proletariat had no alternative other than selling their labour to the bourgeoisie in exchange for wages.

## Exploitation and class conflict

According to the Marxist view, the bourgeoisie exploited the proletariat, making the highest profits out of them they could by paying them as little as possible, instead of giving them the full payment for their work. Marx predicted the working class would become increasingly poorer compared to the bourgeoisie, and society would become increasingly divided.

The exploitation of the proletariat by the bourgeoisie, Marx believed, laid the basis for ongoing social conflict over growing inequalities in life chances in many areas of life, such as in health, housing, levels of educational achievement and job security.

## Evaluation of Marxism

✓ It is a reasonably successful attempt to produce a general theory of the overall workings of society.

✓ It recognizes the importance of social structure in controlling individual behaviour, and how the major social institutions, such as the family, education and the economy, often have links between them and support the interests of the bourgeoisie.

✓ It provides an explanation for growing social inequalities in life chances and power, lack of stability, and conflicts in contemporary societies.

✘  It sees social conflict arising only between the two basic classes of bourgeoisie and proletariat. It does not consider inequalities and conflicts between, for example, men and women, between ethnic and religious groups, or between age groups.

There is more on Marx's theory of social class in chapter 6.

## The conflict perspective of Weber

Weber's conflict theory combines both a structural and social action approach. He saw, like Marx, that people's behaviour was shaped by the social structure, but he recognized other factors also affected their behaviour, such as the meanings they gave to everyday encounters.

Weber agreed with Marx that ownership and non-ownership of the means of production form the most important basis of social class divisions, but criticized Marx for concentrating only on conflict created by social class inequality. Weber argued that conflicts could be caused by three factors, which could be independent of one another:

- social class – e.g. doctors and professional footballers have rarer skills than a refuse worker or checkout worker, so they get higher pay. Different social classes have unequal life chances.
- **status** – the amount of social standing or prestige a person has in the eyes of others. A **status group** is a group of people who share similar social standing in any society, e.g. having similar occupations or educational background.
- **party** – a group of people who work together to pursue power to influence policies in their interests. This involves power inequalities – some are more able than others to get their own way in society, despite any opposition they face.

Weber recognized that class, status and party may coincide – e.g. people with a high class will often have high status and power as well. But status and party can also cut across class – e.g. black and white workers may have a similar social class, but be divided by the status differences of ethnicity or gender. Similarly, a person with high status, such as a priest, may have a low income more like that of someone from the working class.

### *Evaluation of Weber*

For Weber, the sources of social conflict, social divisions and power differences are much wider-ranging than those of Marx. Weber's distinction between class, status and party has the advantage over functionalist and Marxist theories of being able to explain a wider range of conflicts in

**Status** The amount of prestige, importance or respect attached to individuals, social groups or positions in any society by other members of a group or society. Status involves people's social standing in the eyes of others. Status inequalities only exist as long as other people in a group or society continue to recognize them.

**Status group** A group of people who share a similar social standing (status) and lifestyle in any society.

**Party** Any group which is concerned with holding power, making decisions and influencing policies in the interests of its membership.

contemporary societies, such as those based around not just class, but also, for example, gender, ethnicity or age status groups.

## The conflict perspective of feminism

**Feminism** A view, and a movement, which believes that women are disadvantaged in society, and aims to achieve gender equality so women have rights, power and status equal to those of men. Those supporting this are known as *feminists*.

**Feminism** argues there are inequalities in power and status between men and women, with women dominated by men and subordinate to them in most areas of social life. These inequalities generate differences of interest and conflict between men and women. Feminist theories are therefore conflict theories. There are a number of strands within feminist approaches, but what they all share is that they examine the way society controls and limits the power, opportunities and interests of women. Feminists argue that a lot of mainstream sociology has been traditionally focused on the concerns of men – 'malestream sociology' – and has failed to deal with the concerns and interests of women and the unequal position they have traditionally occupied in society.

- *Marxist feminism* takes a Marxist approach to the study of women and women's interests. It emphasizes the way in which women are doubly exploited – both as workers and as women.
- *Radical feminism* tends to focus more on the problem of patriarchy – the system whereby males dominate in every area of society, such as the family, the workplace and politics. For radical feminists, the main focus is on the problem of men and male-dominated society.
- *Liberal feminism* emphasizes the rights of women as individuals, and believes in removing all forms of discrimination to establish equality of opportunity for women with men. They want to ensure that women have equal opportunities with men within the present system, through steps such as changes to the law to stop sex discrimination, establishing equal pay, removing obstacles to women's full participation in society, and better childcare measures so that all women can play their full part in paid employment.

Marxist feminism and radical feminism fundamentally challenge the way society is presently organized and seek major social change, while liberal feminism basically accepts the system as it is but seeks to ensure women have equal opportunities with men within that system.

### *Patriarchy*

**Patriarchy** Power, status and authority held by men.

Feminists see **patriarchy** – power, status and authority held by men – as the main cause of gender inequality. Walby (1990) argues there are six patriarchal structures, illustrated in figure 2.4, which restrict women to a

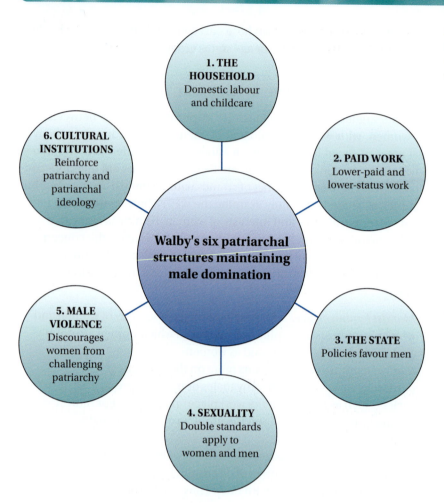

subordinate social position and help to maintain male domination of society:

1  *The household* – in which women have the primary responsibility for **domestic labour** and childcare, limiting their access to and advancement in paid work. Men benefit from women's unpaid labour in the home.

2  *Paid work* – women are disadvantaged in the labour market. They get lower-paid and lower-status work, and are more likely than men to be in part-time and temporary jobs.

3  *The state* – whose policies are mainly in the interests of men, e.g. not tackling the gender pay gap whereby men earn more than equivalent women.

4  *Sexuality* – where different standards are expected from women and men. Women who have casual sex with multiple partners are often

> **Domestic labour**
> Unpaid housework, including cooking, cleaning, childcare and looking after the sick and elderly.

condemned with vicious terms of contempt. Equivalent men are more likely to be grudgingly admired or seen as 'just doing what men do'.

5 *Male violence* – the use or threat of violence discourages women from challenging patriarchal authority. This is most obvious in domestic violence and rape cases.

6 *Cultural institutions* – which reinforce patriarchy and **patriarchal ideology**, e.g. advertising and the media.

> **Patriarchal ideology** A set of ideas that supports and justifies the power of men over women.

## *Evaluation of feminism*

✓ It has produced much evidence demonstrating the extent of lack of opportunities and the barriers facing women.

✓ It has had important effects on social policy, e.g. the passing of anti-discrimination laws such as the Equal Pay Act (1970), the Sex Discrimination Act (1975) and the Equality Act (2010).

✓ It has been influential in bringing women and their concerns more into the centre of sociological work (as will be seen throughout the rest of this book).

✓ It has shown that patriarchal power inequalities and conflicts are found in all public (outside the home) and private (family and personal relationships) spheres of life.

✗ It sometimes assumes all women share the same interests, and downplays inequalities and conflicts between women – e.g. women from different ethnic or religious groups, or from different social classes (see the 'What is intersectionality?' box on page 415 in chapter 6 for more on this).

## INTERACTIONISM OR INTERACTIONIST THEORIES

> **Interactionism** A social-action perspective that is concerned with understanding human behaviour in face-to-face and small group situations, and how individuals, groups and situations come to be defined in particular ways through their everyday encounters with other people.

**Interactionism** is a social-action or interpretivist perspective. It differs from functionalism and Marxism as it doesn't focus on the overall 'macro' structure of society. Instead, it takes a 'micro' approach and focuses on understanding human behaviour in face-to-face situations and in small-scale settings – e.g. a school classroom, or an individual family.

It doesn't see individuals as entirely shaped and moulded by the social structure, but recognizes that people have free will and make choices. Their behaviour is often influenced by the way they interpret situations, and their interpretations are formed through the meanings they give to their everyday encounters ('interactions') with other people.

> **Labelling** Defining a person or group in a certain way and as having particular characteristics – as a particular 'type' of person or group.

It is also concerned with the **labelling** process – how individuals and groups come to be defined ('labelled') as having certain characteristics – and the consequences for individual behaviour once a label is attached. The sociologist's task is to understand the point of view and experience of, say, the disillusioned and hostile student who hates school, as well as of the teachers and others who label him or her as 'deviant'. Sociologists should try to understand how and why teachers classify some students as deviant, and what happens to the behaviour of those students once they have been labelled in that way.

## Evaluation of interactionism

✓ It highlights the importance of understanding the meaning and interpretations that lie behind the way people act.

✓ It emphasizes that people have free will and choice, and how their choices may be influenced by their everyday interactions with others.

✓ It shows how attaching labels can have consequences for the way people behave.

✗ Its focus on micro small-group settings means its findings may not apply to other situations, and so don't necessarily build up into understanding society as a whole.

✗ It doesn't pay sufficient attention to how social structures limit free will and choice – people cannot easily do just anything they want without facing sanctions from family, school, the law, etc.

---

### Activity

Test your understanding – go through each of the following statements, and classify them as one or more (e.g. conflict approach and Marxist) of the following:

- Conflict approach
- Consensus approach
- Feminist
- Functionalist
- Interactionist
- Marxist
- New Right
- Postmodernist
- Social action / interpretivist
- Structuralist
- Weberian

1 The family is one of the main building blocks in creating the shared values which are such an important part of a stable society.

2 There are conflicts between the rich and the poor in our society. This is hardly surprising, given that the richest 10 per cent of the population own over half the country's wealth.

3 To make sure women have equal opportunities with men, there must be more free childcare provided.

4 Society is divided by conflicts between social classes, status groups and parties.

5 Women are exploited both as women and as workers – they get exploited in paid employment, and they get exploited at home, where they do most of the housework and childcare and get nothing for it.

6 The ruling ideas in society are those of the ruling class.

7  Some people may see an amber traffic light as a warning to speed up before it turns red. Others may see it as a sign to slow down before stopping. In order to understand such behaviour, you need to understand the meaning people give to events.

8  Black workers may share the same social class as white workers, but their ethnicity may mean they have more in common with black people in other classes than they do with their white co-workers.

9  A woman needs a man like a fish needs a bicycle.

10 The education system is of major importance in preparing a well-trained and qualified labour force so the economy can develop and grow for everyone's benefit.

11 Society is made up of individuals and social institutions working together, mostly in harmony.

12 People are just social puppets, whose strings are pulled by the social structure.

13 You can't blame society for people's behaviour. They have free will and make their own choices.

14 If you think people are out to get you, even if they're not, then this is likely to affect the way you behave. To understand behaviour, we have to understand people's point of view.

15 It is in everyone's interests to pull together at work for the benefit of society as a whole.

16 Some students are almost bound to fail, because teachers give them the impression that they're thick, and this undermines the self-confidence of the students, who then think it isn't worth bothering.

17 The welfare state has produced an underclass of people who are idle and don't want to work, and are content to scrounge off overgenerous welfare-state benefits rather than get a job to support themselves.

18 A person's identity is purely a matter of her or his personal choice, regardless of social factors like their social class, gender or ethnicity.

## READING STATISTICAL DATA

The evidence that sociologists use in their research comes in a variety of forms, but often consists of statistical data presented in the form of tables, graphs and charts. These often prove difficult for newcomers to sociology to understand. This section is designed to introduce you to the use and interpretation of these forms of data, and give you practice in understanding them. This should make it easier to read the tables and figures appearing in this book, and construct your own, should you wish. Answers to all activities in this section (except the graphs you are asked to draw) are at the end of the book on page 597, but don't look until you've done the activities.

## Statistical tables

When confronted with a statistical table, you should first read carefully the heading of the table – this will tell you what subject the statistics refer to. Tables generally show the relationship between two or more factors, and the key thing to note is what the statistics refer to – whether they are in actual numbers or percentages and what units the numbers are in. For example, the numbers might be in thousands or millions, or they might be in the form of numbers per thousand of the population.

Table 2.1 is adapted from official government statistics on divorce. The data in this table will be used to show the variety of ways in which statistical evidence can be presented.

Table 2.1 shows the relationship between a number of factors (shown in the left-hand column) and how these have changed over time (the dates shown along the top row). Notice that:

- The table refers to the different countries making up the United Kingdom. There are references to England and Wales, Scotland, Northern Ireland and the United Kingdom.
- There are three ways in which the figures are expressed:
    - 'Number of couples divorcing' and divorces 'Granted to husband' and 'Granted to wife' are expressed in *thousands*.
    - 'Persons divorcing' are expressed as '*per thousand* married people' (this is known as the divorce rate).

### Table 2.1  Divorce: 1971–2011

|  | 1971 | 1981 | 1991 | 2001 | 2011 |
|---|---|---|---|---|---|
| Number of couples divorcing (thousands) United Kingdom | 79 | 157 | 172 | 157 | 130 |
| England and Wales | 74 | 146 | 158 | 144 | 118 |
| Scotland | 5 | 10 | 12 | 11 | 10 |
| Northern Ireland | 0.3 | 1 | 2 | 2 | 2 |
| Divorces granted (thousands), England and Wales |  |  |  |  |  |
| Granted to husband | 30 | 42 | 44 | 44 | 40 |
| Granted to wife | 44 | 102 | 114 | 99 | 77 |
| Persons divorcing per thousand married people, England and Wales | 5.9 | 11.9 | 13.5 | 12.9 | 10.1 |
| Percentage of divorces where one or both partners had been previously divorced, England and Wales | 8.8 | 17.1 | 25.4 | 29.4 | 29.3 |

Figures may not always add up due to rounding up or down to the nearest whole number

*Source*: Office for National Statistics

> **Activity**
>
> Study table 2.1 carefully and answer the following questions to check whether you are reading the table correctly:
> 1  How many divorces were granted to husbands in England and Wales in 1991?
> 2  How many couples divorced in Scotland in 2001?
> 3  By how many had the number of divorces in the United Kingdom increased between 1971 and 2011?
> 4  How many divorces were granted to wives in England and Wales in 2001?
> 5  How many persons were divorcing per thousand married people in England and Wales in 1981?
> 6  What percentage of divorces in England and Wales in 2011 involved at least one partner who had been previously divorced?
> 7  What was the total number of divorces in England and Wales in 1991?

- 'Divorces where one or both partners had been previously divorced' are expressed in *percentages* (how many divorces *per hundred*).

## Describing a trend

> **Trend** How the pattern shown in statistics changes over time, such as an increase or decrease.

When interpreting statistical data, you will often be expected to describe a **trend**, or how the pattern shown changes over time. In describing a trend, you should normally say whether it is upward or downward, stating whether the figure has increased or decreased (or increased until a certain time, and then later decreased), and by how much, and give the starting figure and date and the finishing figure and date.

For example, with table 2.1 you might be asked: 'What trend is shown in the number of couples divorcing in the United Kingdom between 1971 and 1991?' Your answer might take the form: 'The number of couples divorcing has shown an upward trend, increasing by 93,000, from 79,000 in 1971 to 172,000 in 1991' (the figure of 93,000 being obtained by subtracting the figure of 79,000 in 1971 from 172,000 in 1991).

> **Activity**
>
> Using table 2.1, practise describing the following trends:
> 1  What trend is shown in the number of persons divorcing per thousand married people in England and Wales between 1971 and 2011?
> 2  What trend does the table show in the number of couples divorcing in England and Wales in the period covered by the table?
> 3  Comparing the number of divorces granted to husbands and wives in England and Wales between 1971 and 2011, identify three trends that are shown.

## Graphs

Statistics are commonly presented in the form of graphs. These show the relationship between two factors and how they change over time. These factors are shown on the vertical (top to bottom) and horizontal (left to right) axes (lines), which are labelled to show what they represent. Trends can be spotted immediately by studying whether the line rises or falls between two dates. It is always important to note what the figures on the axes refer to – numbers, percentages, dates, and so on.

Figure 2.5, using the data given in table 2.1, illustrates how the number of couples divorcing in the United Kingdom has changed over time. Notice how the horizontal axis gives the date and the vertical axis gives the number of divorces (in thousands).

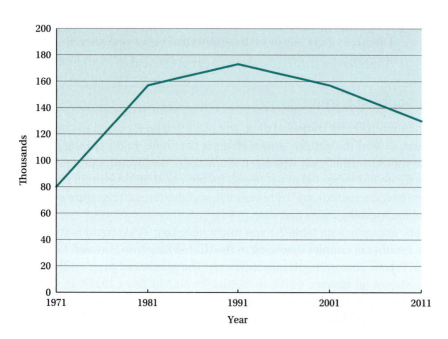

**Figure 2.5** Couples divorcing: United Kingdom, 1971–2011

*Source:* data from table 2.1

---

**Activity**

Using figure 2.5:
1 About how many couples divorced in 1971 in the United Kingdom?
2 About how many couples divorced in 1991?
3 What trend is shown in the graph?
4 Using the data given in table 2.1, practise drawing your own graph to illustrate the changing number of persons divorcing per thousand married people in England and Wales between 1971 and 2011. Make sure you label the axes correctly and put a title on your graph.

## Cumulative graphs

Sometimes graphs may show how a total figure is made up by adding one set of figures to another. This is called a cumulative graph, as the figures 'build up' to the total. This is illustrated in figure 2.6, using the data from table 2.1 on 'divorces granted to husbands and wives in England and Wales'.

In figure 2.6:

– the top line shows the total number of divorces granted
– the bottom line shows the number of husbands granted a divorce
– the coloured space between the two lines represents the number of wives granted a divorce.

By subtracting the number of husbands (the bottom line) from the total (the top line), it is possible to calculate the number of wives granted a divorce. For example, in 1991, there was a total of about 158,000 divorces (point A), with 44,000 granted to husbands (point B). The number of wives granted a divorce was therefore about 114,000 (A minus B).

It is immediately obvious from looking at the graph that:

– far more wives are granted divorces than husbands, as the gap between the top line and the bottom line is much wider than the gap between the bottom line and the horizontal axis.
– the gap between the curves widens over time (although it narrows after about 1991), showing that the number of wives granted a divorce grew at a faster rate, until 1991, than that of husbands granted a divorce.

**Figure 2.6** Number of divorces granted to husbands and wives: England and Wales, 1971–2011

*Source:* data from table 2.1

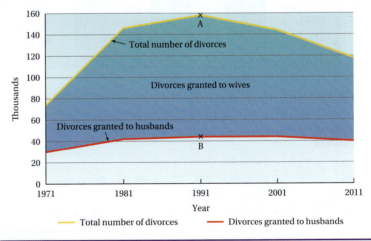

Activity

Referring to figure 2.6:
1  About how many wives were granted a divorce in 1971?
2  Identify three trends that are shown in the graph.

## Bar charts

Bar charts are another very commonly used way of presenting data and showing comparisons and trends in a visually striking way. Bar charts are constructed in much the same way as graphs, but columns are used instead of lines.

Figure 2.7 shows a bar chart comparing the percentage of divorces where one or both partners had been previously divorced in England and Wales between 1971 and 2011.

### *Cumulative bar charts*

Bar charts may, like graphs, be cumulative and show how totals are made up. Compare figure 2.8 with figure 2.6, in which exactly the same information is presented in a different form.

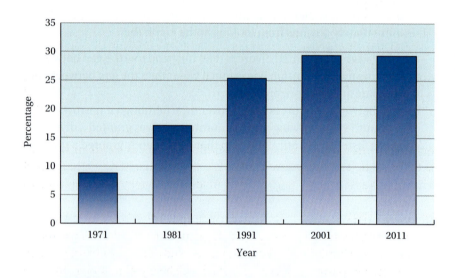

**Figure 2.7** Percentage of divorces where one or both partners had been previously divorced, 1971–2011

*Source:* data from table 2.1

---

**Activity**

Referring to figure 2.7, answer the following questions:
1   In 2001, about what percentage was there of divorces where one or both partners had been previously divorced?
2   Identify the trend that the bar chart shows.

---

## Pie charts

Pie charts present data by dividing a circle into sectors, with the size of each sector being proportional to the size of the item it represents. Pie charts are

**Figure 2.8** Number of divorces granted to husbands and wives: England and Wales, 1971–2011

*Source:* data from table 2.1

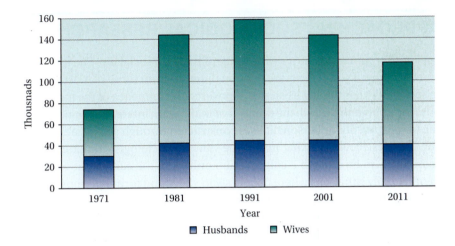

Husbands   Wives

very effective in showing statistics in an easily digestible and striking way. For example, using the data given in table 2.1, the number of divorces granted to husbands and wives in England and Wales in 2011 might be presented as in figure 2.9.

Throughout this book, there are many examples of statistics presented in a variety of forms, often with activities to develop your understanding of them. You should not simply ignore them, but try to read and interpret them. They often contain important information which will help you to understand the text better.

**Figure 2.9** Divorces granted to husbands and wives: England and Wales, 2011

*Source:* data from table 2.1

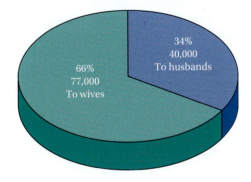

# APPROACHING SOCIOLOGICAL RESEARCH

Sociology is concerned with a wide range of issues in social life. The interests and concerns of sociologists are not that different from those of most people in society: the continuing existence of poverty, the influence of the media on our views about the world, the things that make work interesting or not, how the very centre of our personalities is constructed through socialization into gender roles. However, what makes the views of sociologists different from those likely to be aired in a conversation online, in the canteen at work, or in other daily situations where people swap views and form opinions is that sociologists try to provide evidence to back up what they say. This evidence is collected from a variety of sources and through the use of a number of research methods. In the rest of this chapter, we will examine a range of practical, ethical and theoretical factors that influence research, the types of data (or information) sociologists collect and the range of sources they use, the research process, and the methods sociologists use to collect their own information.

# POSITIVISM AND INTERPRETIVISM

The choice of research methods used in sociology flows from two different approaches to the study of society. These two approaches are known as **positivism** and **interpretivism**.

## Positivism and quantitative data

Positivists believe that sociology can and should use the same or similar methods and approaches to study society that the natural sciences such as physics, chemistry and biology use to investigate the physical or natural world. Positivists believe sociology should be concerned with the study of what Durkheim called **social facts**. These are social phenomena which exist outside individuals but act upon them in ways which mould their behaviour – e.g. social institutions like the family, the criminal justice system (the police, the courts, the law, prisons, etc.) and the education system. These social facts can be – and should be – studied objectively, using methods that enable researchers to remain relatively personally detached from the social facts they are studying. They therefore use similar scientific methods to those used in the natural sciences. These are **quantitative methods** used to produce **quantitative data** – statistical data – on social patterns and trends which can be used to explain society.

**Positivism** An approach that believes society can be studied using similar methods to those used in the natural sciences, such as physics, chemistry and biology.

**Interpretivism** An approach that believes it is only possible to understand society by using methods that provide an understanding of the interpretations and meanings people give to social situations, and of how they see and understand the world around them.

**Social facts** Social phenomena which exist outside individuals but act upon them in ways which mould their behaviour – e.g. social institutions such as the family, the criminal justice system and the education system.

**Quantitative methods** Research methods used to collect quantitative/statistical information.

**Quantitative data** Information that can be expressed in statistical or number form.

Quantitative data are things that can be expressed in number form or can be measured in some way, such as age, qualifications or income. Such data are usually presented in the form of statistical tables, graphs and charts. For example, questionnaires might be used to find out what percentage of criminals suffered abuse when they were children to check whether this is a possible cause of criminality in adults. These quantitative methods include (explored later in this chapter):

- the laboratory experiment (which is very rarely used in sociology)
- social surveys
- structured/pre-coded questionnaires
- formal/structured interviews
- non-participant observation
- official statistics
- content analysis.

> Hint: remember quantitative methods and data by thinking of quantitative as quantity = number / amount / how many.

**Verstehen** The idea of understanding human behaviour by putting yourself in the position of those being studied, and trying to see things from their point of view.

**Qualitative methods** Research methods used to collect information about people's feelings and the meanings and interpretations they give to some issue or event, usually in their own words.

**Qualitative data** Information about people's feelings and the meanings and interpretations they give to some issue or event, expressed in their own words rather than in statistical form

## Interpretivism and qualitative methods

Interpretivists believe that sociology cannot use the quantitative methods that positivists use. Human beings aren't just puppets reacting to social forces, so the study of social facts is inadequate for understanding society. Interpretivists suggest that people have consciousness involving personal beliefs, meanings, values and interpretations, and these influence the way they act. The researcher's job is to gain an in-depth understanding of how people see and understand the world around them by putting him- or herself in the position of those being studied, by trying to develop empathy with them and understand things from their point of view. It's about people telling their own stories, rather than sociologists deciding what's important and telling it for them. This process is what Weber called (in German) **verstehen** (pronounced 'fair-shtay-en') or 'empathetic understanding'.

This involves **qualitative methods** used to produce **qualitative data**. Qualitative data are concerned with people's feelings about some issue or event, and try to get at the way they see things. Such data are normally in the form of the sociologist describing and interpreting people's feelings and lifestyles, often using direct quotations from the people studied. Personal diaries, journals, letters, interview data, video, audio-recordings, photographs and documents such as newspaper reports and emails are all forms of qualitative data. Qualitative research methods are those which aim to produce in-depth information describing the feelings people have, and the meanings and interpretations they give to some issue or event – e.g. in-depth interviews with criminals to try and discover what made them turn to crime.

These qualitative methods include (explored later in this chapter):

- uncontrolled field experiments
- open-ended questionnaires
- unstructured (informal/in-depth/open-ended) interviews
- overt or covert participant and (sometimes) non-participant observation
- personal documents, giving personal accounts – such as diaries, journals and letters
- historical documents
- case studies and life histories.

## KEY ISSUES AND PROBLEMS IN EVALUATING SOCIAL RESEARCH

There are five key issues that should always be considered when carrying out, or evaluating the strengths and weaknesses of, research.

1 **Validity** is concerned with notions of truth: how far the findings of research actually provide a genuine or authentic picture of what is being studied. Data can be reliable without being valid. For example, official crime statistics may be reliable, in so far as researchers repeating the data collection would get the same results over and over again, but they are not valid if they don't give us the full picture on the extent of crime.

2 The **Hawthorne effect** (sometimes referred to as the '*observer effect*') is when the presence of a researcher, or an individual's or group's knowledge that it is the focus of attention, changes the usual behaviour of the individual or group. This can potentially affect the validity of most research methods – e.g. people may not tell the truth in questionnaires or interviews, 'play up' for the researcher in participant observation, or otherwise behave or respond differently from their usual, everyday behaviour.

3 **Reliability** is concerned with replication: whether another researcher repeating research using the same method for the same topic on the same or a similar group would achieve the same results. For example, if different researchers used the same questionnaire on similar samples of

**Validity** Whether statistics or the findings of research provide a true, genuine and authentic picture of what is being studied.

**Hawthorne effect** (or observer effect) When the presence of a researcher, or an individual's or group's knowledge that it has been specially chosen for research, changes the usual behaviour of the individual or group, raising problems for the *validity* of research.

**Reliability** Whether another researcher, if repeating research using the same method for the same topic on the same or a similar group, would achieve the same results.

**Representativeness/ generalizability**
Whether a group being studied contains similar characteristics to those of a wider group, enabling the results of research to be applied more generally to a wider population beyond just the one studied.

the population, then the results should be more or less the same if the techniques are reliable.

4    **Representativeness/generalizability** is concerned with whether the results of research can be applied (generalized) to a wider group beyond those studied. This is only possible if the group studied is representative – that is, it contains a good cross-section of the wider population.

5    The **ethics** of research are concerned with morality and standards of behaviour when sociologists carry out research. These important ethical considerations are considered in the box below.

**Ethics** Ideas about what is morally right and wrong.

---

**THE ETHICS OF RESEARCH**

When doing research, sociologists should always consider the following points:

- They should take into account the sensitivities of those helping with their research. For example, it would not be appropriate to ask about attitudes to abortion in a hospital maternity ward where women may be having babies or have suffered miscarriages.
- Findings should be reported accurately and honestly.
- The physical, social and mental well-being of people who help in research should not be harmed by it – for example, by the disclosure of information given in confidence which might get the person into trouble, or cause them embarrassment.
- The anonymity, privacy and interests of those who participate in your research should be respected. Their personal information should be kept confidential. Sociologists should not identify them by name, or enable them (or an institution) to be easily identified.
- As far as possible, research should be based on the freely given consent of those studied. Researchers should make clear to those participating what they're doing, why they're doing it, any risks taking part might have, and what they will do with their findings. This is known as obtaining **informed consent**.

**Informed consent** The ethical requirement that those taking part in research should, whenever possible, have agreed to do so and have given this consent based on a full understanding of the nature, aims and purposes of the research, any implications or risks taking part might have, and the uses of any findings of the research.

---

# WHERE DO SOCIOLOGISTS GET THEIR INFORMATION FROM?

## Primary and secondary sources

Secondary sources of data are those which already exist. **Secondary data** have already been collected by others. Secondary sources provide sociologists with both quantitative and qualitative data. Figure 2.10 shows a range of secondary sources which might be used by sociologists in carrying out research.

**Secondary data** Information that already exists and which the researcher hasn't collected herself or himself.

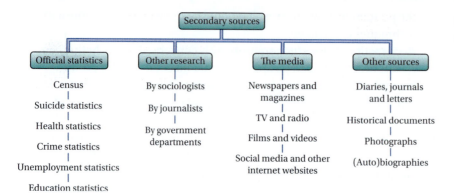

**Figure 2.10** Secondary sources of data

### Activity

Describe *two* ethical problems that may arise in each of the following research situations, and suggest ways of overcoming them.

1. You want to investigate what sort of men get involved with prostitutes. In order to do this, you photograph the number-plates of cars hanging around in a well-known local red-light district. You then track down the names and addresses of the owners, with help from a friend in the police, and call on the men in their homes to interview them about their lives, pretending your survey is about healthy eating.

2. You want to study, using a questionnaire, to what extent students at a local college have been in trouble with the police. The questionnaire involves asking students about all their illegal activities as well as encounters with the police. In collaboration with the college authorities, completion of the questionnaire is made a compulsory requirement of enrolment at the college, although students are not told what the questionnaire is for.

3. You want to study how much time parents spend playing with and talking to their small children. You plan to ask children about this, selected from those at a local infant school, but you can't mention it to their parents in case they distort the results by telling the children what to say.

4. You want to observe teachers as they are teaching in an infant school to see how far they stereotype boys and girls and treat them differently in classes. You decide not to tell the teacher what you're doing, because otherwise you're afraid they'll behave differently. You therefore pretend you're interested in the behaviour of children in the classroom.

Because the existing data required for research may be unreliable or may simply not have been collected, sociologists often have to collect their own data from primary sources. **Primary data** consist of information that is collected by sociologists themselves – it only exists because the sociologist has collected it. Such information is usually obtained by using a range of research methods which will be discussed shortly.

**Primary data**
Information that sociologists have collected themselves.

> **Activity**
>
> 1 Go through the following examples, marking each as primary or secondary *and* quantitative or qualitative data:
>   - exam results of schools in your area published in a local newspaper
>   - newspaper stories from the 1930s
>   - information collected by you showing the proportions of students doing different GCSE subjects
>   - teenage magazines
>   - statistics produced by the local NHS showing inequalities in health
>   - video-recordings of a week's news reports
>   - letters in a newspaper complaining about the risks of accidents arising from cyclists riding on footpaths
>   - the published diaries or journal of a former prime minister.
> 2 Explain, with reasons, in what circumstances you might, or might not, consider each of the above pieces of data to be (a) reliable, and (b) valid, as sources of evidence.

## The advantages and disadvantages of using secondary sources of data

✓ The material is readily available and so is cheap and easy to use. There is no need to spend time and money collecting data. Some data, such as that provided by the census, would be impossible for an individual to collect.

✓ They may be the only sources of information available in an area, such as in historical research.

✗ The information may be unrepresentative, and it may therefore not be possible to apply (or generalize) it to the whole population. For example, before the beginning of compulsory education in Britain in 1880, it was mainly only the well-off who could read and write, and so it was mainly they who left documents behind them.

✗ The information may be inaccurate in some way, and therefore unreliable or lacking in validity. It may be forged or biased, contain errors or be exaggerated. Newspaper reports, for example, are notoriously unreliable as sources of evidence.

This means that when sociologists use any secondary data, they must be very aware of their limitations, question their *representativeness/ generalizability*, *validity* and *reliability*, and therefore approach such data with care.

## The advantages and problems of qualitative secondary sources of data: personal and public documents

Documents provide mainly qualitative data and are preferred by interpretivists.

**Personal documents** are (usually) private documents for a person's own use, which record part of a person's life – e.g. personal diaries (a record of appointments, what you ate, what happened, when, who you saw, etc.) and journals (like a diary – and sometimes called a diary – but usually more detailed and containing thoughts, emotions and an interpretation of events); personal letters, emails, photographs or videos; pupils' school reports or personal medical files.

**Public documents** are those produced for public knowledge and are available to all – e.g. reports from government, councils, charities, voluntary organizations and businesses, and media content, such as newspaper, TV and online photos and reports, novels and autobiographies.

✓ They are already available, so cheap to use.
✓ They may be the only data available for gaining insight, especially for historical research.
✓ They provide valid in-depth qualitative data – give insights into the attitudes, values and meanings of those who produced them. *Personal documents* may be more honest, as they are produced for private use.
✓ *Public documents* are publicly available, so there are no ethical difficulties in using them.
✗ They may not be genuine, or may not mean the same thing now as they did at the time they were produced (for historical documents).
✗ They may not be representative, so findings cannot be generalized.
✗ They may not be reliable or valid – they may be exaggerated, biased and selective, and provide only one particular view. Public documents present only the views of the organization, government, newspaper, etc.
✗ Using *personal documents* without permission poses ethical difficulties around not having informed consent, and may be harmful if anonymity is not protected.
✗ They can take a long time to analyse and interpret, and may contain a lot of irrelevant material in terms of the research aims.

## The use, advantages and limitations of content analysis

**Content analysis** is a way of trying to analyse the content of documents and other qualitative material – such as books, newspapers, magazines, films and advertisements – by quantifying it. An example of this might include a researcher analysing comics for children when seeking evidence of gender role stereotyping. The researcher might select categories such as 'male leader / female follower' or 'female works or plays indoors / male outdoors',

> **Personal documents** Those produced for a person's own use, which are usually private, and record part of a person's life.

> **Public documents** Those produced for public knowledge and available to all.

> **Content analysis** A way of analysing documents and other qualitative material by quantifying them – e.g. counting the number of times a particular item appears in the media.

and so on. They would then go through a number of comics systematically, recording the number of times items in each category appear.

### Advantages of content analysis
✓ It is a relatively cheap means of research.
✓ There is no involvement with people that can sometimes lead to distorted results if people's normal behaviour changes because of the Hawthorne effect (see page 70).
✓ It is a reliable research method, as it produces quantitative statistical data that other researchers can easily check.

### Disadvantages of content analysis
✗ It depends on the categories chosen by the researcher and how he or she interprets what they see. For example, the researcher decides in analysing a children's comic to use the categories of 'male leader / female follower', but these categories and what is happening depend on the researcher's personal judgements.
✗ It is mainly concerned with *describing* what is being studied, and is not very good at *explaining* it.
✗ Items may not fit neatly into one particular category.

---

**Activity**

Refer to the section above on content analysis.
1 Look at a selection of red-top daily or Sunday newspapers (these are the *Sun*, *Daily Mirror*, *Daily Star*, *The Sun on Sunday*, *Sunday Mirror*, *Sunday People*, *Sunday Sport* and the *Daily Star Sunday*, plus, in Scotland, the *Daily Record* and *Sunday Mail*), or their online equivalents, and carry out a content analysis of the photographs of men and women, and how they are portrayed. You will need to decide what you want to discover, work out suitable categories, and then work through the newspapers, or their websites, classifying photos into the categories you've chosen, and counting them up.
2 Draw conclusions from your findings, saying what you think you discovered and outlining any problems you had in categorizing the photographs.

---

## The advantages and problems of quantitative secondary sources of data: official statistics

Sociologists very often use official statistics in their research. These are produced by the Office for National Statistics and other government agencies like the NHS and the Department for Education. Official statistics are available on a vast range of topics, such as on crime, health, education, employment and unemployment, population size and trends, marriage, divorce, cohabitation, and births and deaths.

*Advantages/strengths*

✓ They are useful for planning and evaluating social policies, e.g. those relating to education or the elderly.

✓ They are often the only available source of data in a particular area.

✓ They are cheap and easy-to-access data, some of which would be impossible for an individual to collect – e.g. census data.

✓ Positivists see them as objective and reliable, as they are usually collected following strict statistical rules which are publicly available and can be scrutinized by others for errors.

✓ They cover a long time span; comprehensive in coverage and use either large samples or the whole population (as in the ten-yearly census), so likely to be representative and generalizable. Enable discovery of patterns and trends over time – e.g. how the size and characteristics of the population have changed.

✓ They provide useful background material helping researchers identify links between data – e.g. poverty and exam results – which can help in identifying hypotheses for further research.

✓ They are publicly available, so unlikely to breach ethical guidelines.

*Disadvantages/problems/limitations*

✘ They are collected for administrative/policy purposes rather than for sociological research – so the definitions and classifications adopted may be unsuitable for research.

✘ They are produced by the state, so they may be biased and 'massaged' to avoid political embarrassment to the government – e.g. unemployment statistics often underestimate the real numbers of the unemployed, as they exclude those in part-time work who are really looking for full-time work, and those reluctantly staying on at school or college because they can't find jobs.

✘ They may not provide a valid picture if they are not accurate and complete – e.g. official crime statistics don't include the large number of crimes not discovered by or reported to the police (there is more on crime statistics in chapter 5); health statistics exclude sick people who don't go to the doctor. Interpretivists argue they are not objective, reliable or valid, but simply social constructions: the product of a process of interpretation and decision-making by those with authority – e.g. which statistics to collect or not to collect.

These mean official statistics must be treated very cautiously by sociologists. Such limitations also mean that other (non-official) statistics – not produced by government bodies – such as those produced by private businesses, must be treated with even more caution, as they are not bound by the same strict statistical rules as official statistics.

## Activity

1 To get a flavour of some of the official statistics available, go to www.ons. gov.uk. Take a look at 'People, population and community' or use 'search' for any topic that interests you, using a keyword like 'family', 'divorce', 'crime' or 'education'. Make a note of three statistics on three different areas, noting the source from which the information is derived. How useful do you think such official statistics and websites are for sociologists trying to find out about society?

2 Describe two strengths and two limitations of using official statistics in sociological research.

3 Read the following passage and then answer the questions:

Suicide is, by definition, the death of a person who intended to kill him or herself. The problem for coroners is they can't ask dead people if they meant to kill themselves, so they can only guess at the truth by looking for 'clues' in the circumstances surrounding the death. Atkinson has suggested there are four main factors which coroners take into account when deciding whether a death is a suicide or not.

- Whether there was a suicide note.
- The way the person died, for example by drowning or a drug overdose. Death in a road accident rarely results in a suicide verdict.
- The place the death occurred and the circumstances surrounding it – for example, a drug overdose in a remote wood would be more likely to be seen as a suicide than if it occurred at home in bed. A coroner might also consider circumstances such as whether the person had been drinking before taking the drugs, and whether the drugs had been hoarded or not.
- The life history and mental state of the dead person, such as her or his state of health, and whether the victim was in debt, had just failed exams, lost her or his job, or got divorced, or was depressed or not.

Coroners do not always agree on the way they interpret these clues. For example, Atkinson found one coroner believed a death by drowning was likely to be a suicide if the clothes were left neatly folded on the beach, but another coroner might attach little importance to this.

(a) How is suicide defined in the passage?

(b) Why do you think coroners attach such importance to suicide notes?

(c) Suggest two reasons why the presence or absence of a suicide note might be an unreliable clue to a dead person's intention to die.

(d) Suggest ways relatives and friends might try to persuade a coroner that a death was not a suicide but an accident.

(e) On the basis of the evidence in the passage, suggest reasons why: (i) some deaths classified as suicides may have been accidental; and (ii) some deaths classified as accidents may in fact have been suicides.

(f) With reference to the evidence in the passage, suggest reasons why a sociologist should be very careful about using official statistics on suicide as a record of the real number of suicides in society.

# THE RESEARCH PROCESS

When researching society, sociologists generally approach their research in a systematic and organized way. Figure 2.11 shows the path that research takes in sociology. Much of this will be developed in the following pages.

## Choosing a topic and research method

When deciding which topic and method to choose, sociologists must ask themselves several questions, and address several issues. You can remember these issues with the word PET – Practical, Ethical and Theoretical.

### *Practical issues*

- Is this the best method to use to research the particular topic?
- Does the time and cost of using the chosen method make it a practical option?
- Is the method chosen likely to work in the particular setting or for gaining information from the people who are being researched?
- Is the method suitable for overcoming any resentment, resistance or hostility from those being researched? Will it help to overcome any reluctance by people to talk about very personal, sensitive, embarrassing or emotionally upsetting activities?
- Will the chosen method be successful in identifying samples or individuals to conduct research on?
- Will the researcher have the right personal characteristics, such as age, gender, ethnicity, language, etc., to accomplish research successfully using the proposed method?
- In the case of using secondary data, are these available on this topic?

### *Ethical issues*

- Does the method respect the privacy, interests and confidentiality of those being researched?
- Is investigating the topic or using this method likely to upset or harm in some way those being researched?
- Will the method suggested enable informed consent? For example, can very young children realistically give informed consent?
- Is the method likely to involve deception?

**Figure 2.11** The stages of the research process

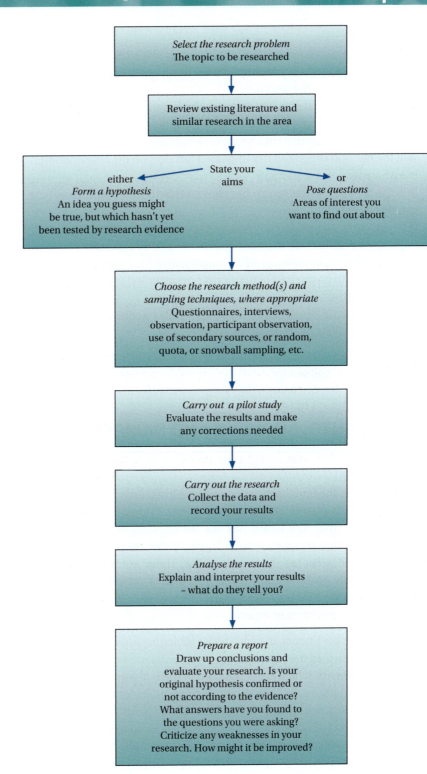

## *Theoretical issues*

- Is the method suggested reliable? Would other researchers who repeated the research using the same or similar methods get the same results? Could others check the results?
- In the case of using secondary data, are those data reliable and valid?
- Is the method the most suitable to produce valid – true, genuine and authentic – information about the people or topic being studied?
- Will the method suggested risk imposing answers on the **respondent**(s) (those answering questions)?
- Will the presence of the researcher cause a Hawthorne effect? How best can this be avoided?
- Is the group of people chosen for investigation representative, and likely to produce results that can be generalized to all other groups?
- Will the suggested method produce quantitative information (more associated with positivists) or qualitative information (more associated with interpretivists)?
- Is the approach adopted linked with structural or action theorists, or with functionalists, Marxists or feminists?

> **Respondent**
> The person answering – responding to – questions in questionnaires and interviews.

These, and other issues influencing the choice of research topic and methods, are summarized in figure 2.12

# EXPERIMENTS, SURVEYS AND SAMPLING

## Experiments

The experiment is the main means of conducting research in the natural sciences. Experiments are used to test a **hypothesis** – an idea that the researcher guesses might be true, but which has not yet been tested against the evidence. They are not used much in sociology by either positivists or interpretivists. This is because, as discussed earlier, there are wide differences between the study of the natural world and that of society (see page 9 in chapter 1).

> **Hypothesis** An idea that a researcher guesses might be true, but which has not yet been tested against the evidence.

There are two main types of experiment:

- **Laboratory experiments**, in which all variables (or possible causes) are under the control of the researcher.
- **Field experiments**, which are conducted in the real world under normal social conditions, but follow similar procedures to the laboratory experiment – e.g. Rosenthal and Jacobson aimed to find out whether teacher labelling affected student progress. They told teachers that a randomly chosen group of school students were bright and could be expected to make good progress, even though they were no different

**Figure 2.12** Influences on choices of research topic and method

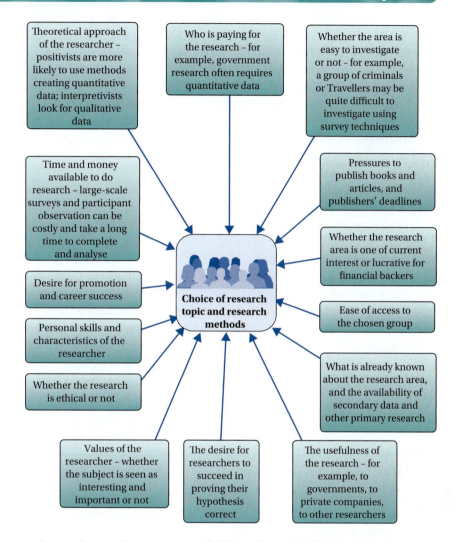

Theoretical approach of the researcher – positivists are more likely to use methods creating quantitative data; interpretivists look for qualitative data

Who is paying for the research – for example, government research often requires quantitative data

Whether the area is easy to investigate or not – for example, a group of criminals or Travellers may be quite difficult to investigate using survey techniques

Time and money available to do research – large-scale surveys and participant observation can be costly and take a long time to complete and analyse

Pressures to publish books and articles, and publishers' deadlines

Desire for promotion and career success

Whether the research area is one of current interest or lucrative for financial backers

**Choice of research topic and research methods**

Ease of access to the chosen group

Personal skills and characteristics of the researcher

Whether the research is ethical or not

What is already known about the research area, and the availability of secondary data and other primary research

Values of the researcher – whether the subject is seen as interesting and important or not

The desire for researchers to succeed in proving their hypothesis correct

The usefulness of the research – for example, to governments, to private companies, to other researchers

from other students in terms of ability. Those labelled 'bright' did, in fact, make more progress than those not so labelled.

## *Advantages/strengths of experiments*

✓ Hypotheses can be tested in controlled conditions.
✓ They are easy to isolate and manipulate variables to identify the causes of events (except in field experiments).
✓ They are reliable – they should achieve the same results if repeated.
✓ They enable comparisons to be made with other experimental research.
✓ Positivists see them as a detached, objective and scientific means of studying society.
✓ Participants may not be aware they are being studied, so the Hawthorne effect is avoided.

## Disadvantages/problems/limitations of experiments

✗ Interpretivists emphasize that experimental conditions are artificial, so may not provide valid explanations of real-world behaviour (field experiments are more valid than laboratory experiments, in their view).

✗ The Hawthorne effect may reduce validity – those taking part may act differently from their usual behaviour because they know they are part of an experiment.

✗ They are often only possible in small-scale settings, which may therefore be unrepresentative of the bigger picture.

✗ It is impractical to observe large-scale social processes in a laboratory or in a small-scale field experiment.

✗ In sociology, it is difficult to isolate a single cause of a social issue, and to isolate variables for testing.

✗ They have ethical problems:

👎 Experiments need to treat one group of people differently from another and compare results. This may have harmful effects on the experimental group – e.g. in Rosenthal and Jacobson's experiment mentioned above, those who suffered because they were not labelled 'bright'.

👎 To avoid the Hawthorne effect, it is often necessary to deceive subjects as to the true nature of the experiment so that they do not act differently from their usual behaviour. This involves deception and therefore lack of informed consent.

## Social surveys

A **survey** involves the sociologist systematically gathering information about some group of people. This is done by questioning them using question-naires and interviews.

### The survey population

One of the first steps in any social survey is the selection of the target group of people to be studied. This target group is called the **survey population**. The choice of survey population will depend on the hypothesis which the sociologist is investigating.

For example, a hypothesis like 'teachers treat high-achieving girls more favourably than lower-achieving girls' might mean the survey population would just include female pupils and their teachers, in a particular school.

If the survey population is small, such as a class of college students, it may be possible to question all the female students in it. Some organiza-tions doing research have enough time and money to investigate everyone, even in a very large survey population. For example, the government has

**Survey** A means of collecting primary data, often from large numbers of people, in a standardized statistical form, by questioning them using interviews and questionnaires.

**Survey population** The section of the population which is of interest in a survey.

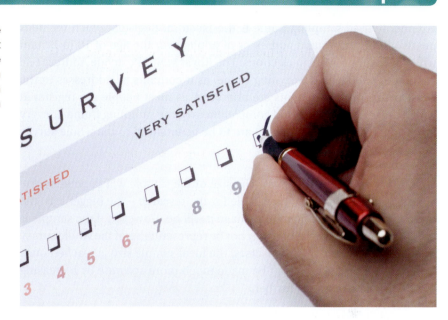

Surveys often use questionnaires to collect information from large numbers of people, with results usually presented in statistical form

the resources to survey the entire population of the United Kingdom in the census every ten years – at a cost of £480 million in 2011. Such costs are way beyond the reach of most sociologists and market research organizations, and, because of cost and time, most surveys are limited to studying a sample of the survey population.

## Sampling

A **sample** is simply a small group drawn from the survey population. Taking a sample is a way of making general statements about the whole survey population based on the responses of only a small percentage of it.

If the results obtained from the sample are to be used to make valid (true) generalizations about the whole survey population, it is important that the sample is *representative*. A **representative sample** is one that contains a good cross-section of the survey population, such as the right proportions of people of different ethnic origins, ages, social classes and sexes. The information obtained from a representative sample should provide roughly the same results as if the whole survey population had been questioned.

Sociologists obtain representative samples by using various sampling methods.

## Methods of obtaining a representative sample

*1 Drawing up a sampling frame* A **sampling frame** is simply a list of names of all those included in the survey population from which the sample will eventually be selected – for example, the names of all schoolchildren in a school taken from registers, or all the doctors in a town. A

**Sample** A small representative group drawn from the survey population for questioning or interviewing.

**Representative sample** A smaller group selected from the survey population for study, containing a good cross-section of the characteristics of the survey population as a whole.

**Sampling frame** A list of names of all those in the survey population, from which a representative sample is selected.

commonly used sampling frame is the Electoral Register, which includes nearly all the names and addresses of adults over the age of 18 in Britain who are eligible to vote in elections. The Royal Mail's Postcode Address File is another widely used sampling frame, as it contains all addresses in the UK. Doctors' lists of patients are also used, as most people are registered with a doctor. The choice and completeness of the sampling frame are very important if the results obtained are to be generalized to the whole survey population.

*2 Deciding on the sample size*   The size of the sample will depend on the amount of time and money available for the research – the bigger it is, the more expensive and difficult to manage it will be. However, if the sample is too small, the results obtained may not be representative of the whole survey population. To balance these factors, the ideal sample size is reached once the results of the survey won't be made much more accurate by increasing the size of the sample any further.

*3 Deciding on a sampling method*   A sampling method is the process by which the sociologist selects, from the sampling frame, representative individuals to question. There are a number of sampling methods used by sociologists to try to gain a representative sample.

- **Simple random sampling**   means that every individual in the survey population has an equal chance of being picked out for questioning.

A random sample is a bit like a lottery draw – every person has an equal chance of being selected but, like the lottery, you've got to be in it to win it, or, in surveys, to be in the sampling frame to have a chance of being selected

For example, all names in the sampling frame are given a number and a computer is used to select enough numbers at random to make up the size of sample required.

The problem with this method is that, purely by chance, the random sample may not be representative of the survey population. For example, there may be too many people of one sex, of one age group, or who live in the same area.

- **Systematic sampling** is a sampling method in which names are selected from the survey population at regular intervals until the size of sample is reached. For example, every tenth name in the sampling frame is selected.

- **Quota sampling** is a method in which interviewers are told to go and select people who fit into certain categories, according to their proportion in the survey population as a whole. For example, an interviewer may be asked to ensure that half of the people they question are women, and half are men.

- **Stratified random sampling** is a way of attempting to avoid the possible errors caused by simple random sampling. In this case, the sampling frame is divided into strata (layers) or sub-groups relevant to the hypothesis being investigated – such as groups of a similar age, sex, ethnic group or social class – and a random sample is then taken from each sub-group. For example, in a survey of school students, we may know from earlier research that 10 per cent of all students are Indian Asian, and so the sociologist must make sure 10 per cent of the sample are also Indian Asian. To do this, the sociologist will separate out the Indian Asian students from the sampling frame of all students, and then take a random sample from this list of Indian Asian students to make up the 10 per cent of the sample of all students. In this way, the final sample is more likely to be representative of all students in the survey population. Stratified random sampling has the advantage of being much more representative than simple random sampling, because all the characteristics of the survey population are more certain to be represented in the sample.

The sampling methods discussed above and shown in the box (below) provide results that can be generalized with great accuracy to the whole survey population. For example, opinion polls on the voting intentions of electors often produce extremely accurate predictions of the outcome of general elections from questioning only about 1,000 voters.

## EXAMPLES OF SIMPLE RANDOM, SYSTEMATIC AND STRATIFIED RANDOM SAMPLING

| | |
|---|---|
| Survey population | 400 students in a school |
| | 50 per cent are male and 50 per cent are female |
| | This information would be known from earlier research, such as school records |
| | In each group, 75 per cent are White British and 25 per cent are from BAME (Black, Asian and Minority Ethnic) groups |
| Sample size required | 10 per cent (40 students) |

### A simple random sample

To obtain a simple random sample:

1   Draw up a sampling frame: a list of the names of 400 students in the survey population.
2   Pick out 40 names at random.

### A systematic sample

To obtain a systematic sample:

Pick out every tenth name from the sampling frame until 40 names are collected.

A possible problem with these random and systematic samples is that, purely by chance, they might consist of too many males or females, or too many White British or BAME students. If this happened, the sample would be unrepresentative of the survey population, and therefore the survey results would give biased, inaccurate and unrepresentative results. Stratifying the sample can avoid this problem.

### A stratified random sample

To obtain a stratified random sample, complete the following stages:

1   Draw up a sampling frame (list of names) of the 400 students in the survey population.
2   Divide this sampling frame into the same proportions as the survey population. We know 50 per cent are male and 50 per cent are female, so in this case divide the sampling frame into two groups, one with 200 males, one with 200 females.
3   We know 25 per cent of males and of females are from BAME groups, and 75 per cent are White British (White B.), so divide *each* of these sampling frames into two further groups.
4   Now take a 10 per cent random sample from each sampling frame. This produces a sample made up like the one here.

This stratified random sample should be representative of the sex and ethnic characteristics of the entire school population, as these features of the survey population are now certain to be included in the 10 per cent sample

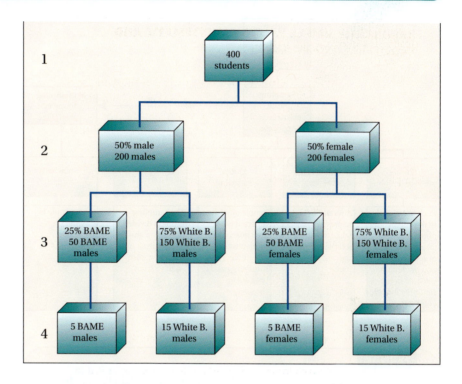

## Snowball sampling

Snowball sampling is used when a sampling frame is difficult to obtain or doesn't exist. The researcher may identify one or two people with the characteristics they're interested in, and ask them to introduce the researcher to other people willing to cooperate in the research, and then ask these people to identify others. In this way the sample gradually builds up, just like a snowball getting bigger as you roll it in the snow. For example, Laurie Taylor in *In the Underworld* used this technique to investigate the lifestyles of criminals. There was no readily available sampling frame, but Taylor happened to know a convicted criminal, who was able to put him in touch with others who were willing to cooperate in his research. These criminals in turn put him in touch with more, and so he was able gradually to build up his sample of criminals.

Such samples may be useful, but they are not random or representative. They rely on volunteers recommending other volunteers to the researcher, and the sample is therefore self-selecting, and this may create bias. For example, such volunteers may have particular views for or against a particular issue, which is why they volunteered.

## Longitudinal studies

Most sociological researchers study a group of people only for a short period of time, producing a snapshot of events. It is therefore difficult to study change

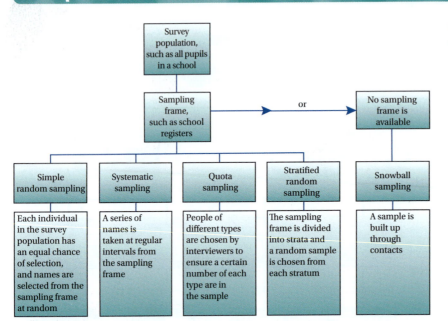

**Figure 2.13** Sampling methods

---

**Activity**

1  In each of the following cases, suggest a hypothesis you might wish to test, how you might obtain your sampling frame, and the sampling method you would choose to select your sample, giving reasons in each case.

- The attitudes of family doctors (GPs) to changes in the NHS.
- The reasons why shoplifters commit the crime.
- The amount of support that parents give to their children's education.
- The reasons why few female school-leavers in a town go on computer courses at a local college.
- A survey of young mothers.
- A survey of pensioners.
- The opinions of adults in your neighbourhood about how they will vote in the next election.
- The attitudes of gay men.

2  Ellova College has 3,000 full-time students, and 6,000 part-time students. Half of the full-time students are women, and three-quarters of the part-time students are men. You want to conduct a survey among students at Ellova College. You haven't the time or the money to question every student, so you need to take a 10 per cent sample. In order to make this as representative as possible, you have decided to use a stratified random sampling method.

(a) Explain how you would select this 10 per cent sample.

(b) Give the actual numbers of the different groups in the survey population which will be included in your sample.

Longitudinal studies show change over a period of time. Why might this provide more useful information than the one-off snapshot provided by most research?

**Longitudinal study** A study based on a sample of people from whom data are collected at regular intervals over a period of years.

over time. A **longitudinal study** is a type of survey that attempts to overcome this problem by selecting a sample – sometimes called a panel or cohort – from whom data are collected at regular intervals over a period of years (each one of these data-collecting surveys is commonly known as a 'sweep'). The census, carried out every ten years since 1801 (with the exception of 1941), is in effect a longitudinal study of the entire population. This enables researchers to trace broad patterns of social change, and to make comparisons between the social conditions of one period and those of another.

*Understanding Society* is a UK household longitudinal study that began in 2011. It interviews all members of a representative sample of 40,000 households drawn from all over the UK. It interviews the same people in the same households each year, to follow changes in people's lives over time, and to investigate the causes and consequences of them. The questions asked cover a wide range of areas such as family life, parenthood, household arrangements, education, employment, finance, health and well-being, and how these change over time. (You can find out more about *Understanding Society* at www.understandingsociety.ac.uk/about.)

### The advantages/strengths of longitudinal studies

✓ It is possible to study change over time, and provide detail on the changes that occur, compared to the one-off snapshot picture provided by most research.

✓ It may be possible to discover the causes of change, as long as the sample remains the same. By comparing earlier studies with later ones, researchers can be sure that the changes measured do not result from changes in the composition of the sample.

✓ They may provide more valid data than other surveys. Studies which ask people about past events rely on human memories, and people may forget, distort or exaggerate things that happened in the past. Longitudinal studies help to avoid this, as there are previous studies to refer back to.

## The limitations/weaknesses of longitudinal studies

✗ The sample selected must be available and willing to participate over a long period. However, it is likely that the original sample size will drop as people die, move home or go abroad, can't be traced, or become unwilling to cooperate. This may reduce the representativeness of the sample.

✗ The *Hawthorne effect* may undermine the validity of findings. Those in the sample are conscious of the fact that they are being studied. This may change their behaviour and responses.

✗ Time and cost – most funding agencies are unwilling to take on a commitment over a long period of time.

---

### Activity

1 If people drop out of the original sample during a longitudinal study, suggest reasons why sociologists should be cautious about using the results to make general statements about society.

2 Suggest *one* reason why longitudinal studies might provide a more valid picture of society, and *one* reason why they might not.

3 Go to the Centre for Longitudinal Studies at www.cls.ioe.ac.uk.
   (a) Identify two aims of the Millennium Cohort Study.
   (b) Find out how large the sample is, and what steps have been taken to make the sample representative.
   (c) Find out how many sweeps have taken place, and when they were carried out.

---

### OPINION POLLS

Opinion polls are social surveys that aim to find out people's attitudes and opinions. They are often used in market research to discover people's opinions towards some product or service, and they are widely used to discover how people intend to vote in elections. Opinion polls don't always give a valid, or true and genuine, picture of what the public really thinks, despite often employing sophisticated research methods. For example, almost all polls ahead of the UK referendum on EU membership in June 2016 predicted that most people would vote to remain in the EU, but in fact more people voted to leave (Brexit). Why are opinion polls sometimes inaccurate?

● They may not contain a representative sample, which may lead to inaccurate results.

● Respondents might give any answer just to get rid of the pollster.

● Interviewer bias (see below) may mean people give inaccurate answers. People in face-to-face interviews may give the answer that they think is socially acceptable rather than what they really believe.

● The format and wording of questions may affect the results. For example, respondents prefer to agree rather than disagree with statements which are put to them.

**Pilot survey** A small-scale practice survey carried out before the final survey to check for any possible problems in the way it is designed.

## The stages of a survey

Before carrying out a large-scale survey, it is important to carry out a **pilot survey** (sometimes called a pilot study).

This is a trial run of the final survey, using fewer people than the final sample. Its purpose is to iron out any problems which the researcher might have overlooked. For example, some questions may be unclear, some of the sample may have died or moved away, or there may be problems with non-response or non-cooperation by respondents.

After the pilot survey is completed, the results are reviewed, any necessary changes are made, and the main survey can then proceed. The stages of a survey are shown in figure 2.14.

**Figure 2.14** The stages of a survey

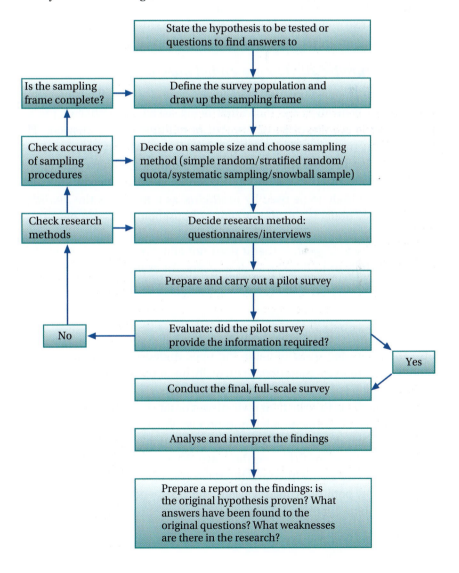

# RESEARCH METHODS USED IN SURVEYS AND OTHER SOCIOLOGICAL RESEARCH

There are two main methods that are used in social surveys to collect data: questionnaires and interviews.

## Questionnaires

Most surveys involve the use of a questionnaire of some kind. A questionnaire is a printed list of questions to be filled in either personally by the respondent (the person answering the questions) or by an interviewer. All respondents answer exactly the same questions.

There are two main types of questionnaire: the structured (closed or precoded) questionnaire and the more unstructured open-ended questionnaire.

### The structured, closed or pre-coded questionnaire

The structured questionnaire (sometimes called a *closed* or *pre-coded questionnaire*) involves the individual being asked a number of pre-set *closed* questions with a limited number of multiple-choice answers. The person filling in the questionnaire will tick off the answer. A typical question might be 'Do you think wages should be paid for housework?' with available answers being 'Yes' / 'No' / 'Don't know'. This type of questionnaire is more likely to be used by *positivists*, as it produces the *quantitative data* they prefer – e.g. 70 per cent of household tasks are performed exclusively by women. The problem with this type of closed questionnaire, as *interpretivists* suggest, is that it does not allow respondents to explain their views fully or to develop their answers. An example of a structured/closed questionnaire (to be self-completed by the respondent) is shown in figure 2.15.

### The open-ended questionnaire

Like the pre-coded questionnaire, the open-ended questionnaire (sometimes called an *open questionnaire*) usually has a number of pre-set questions, but there is no pre-set choice of answers. They are *open* questions that allow respondents to write their own answer or dictate it to an interviewer.

An example of an open-ended question is: 'What is your opinion of the role parents should play in their children's education?' Such open questions give respondents scope to express their own views. Such a questionnaire may form the basis for an unstructured interview (see below).

In a survey, both pre-coded (closed) and open-ended (open) questions may be combined in the same questionnaire.

**Figure 2.15** Example of a structured/closed questionnaire to be completed by the respondent in couple households with children. Note the wording at the top of the questionnaire. This addresses the ethical issues of confidentiality and informed consent

## HOUSEWORK IN THE HOME

This is an anonymous and voluntary survey. By completing the questionnaire, you are giving consent. Your answers will be kept in strictest confidence and will only be used as part of a national survey into households and families. You may withdraw your participation at any time, and you may skip any questions you do not want to answer. Please tick (✓) the box that most applies to you.

**Your age**: 18–30 ☐  31–40 ☐  41–50 ☐  51–60 ☐  61–70 ☐ Over 70 ☐

**Your sex**: Male ☐  Female ☐

**Do you live**: With a female partner ☐  With a male partner ☐

**Do you have children under 15 living at home?** Yes ☐  No ☐

**Do you have pets?** Yes ☐  No ☐

**Are you employed?** Full-time ☐  Part-time ☐  Unemployed ☐ Not seeking work ☐  Retired ☐

**Who is mainly responsible for the following household jobs?** (Please put a tick ✓ in the column that normally applies in your household).

| Household job | Mainly me | Mainly my partner | Shared equally |
|---|---|---|---|
| Taking out the garbage | | | |
| Cooking evening meal | | | |
| DIY repairs | | | |
| Gardening | | | |
| Non-food shopping | | | |
| Food shopping | | | |
| Cooking a meal (special occasions) | | | |
| Decorating | | | |
| Tidying the house | | | |
| Helping children with homework | | | |
| Washing clothes | | | |
| Getting children's school gear ready | | | |
| General cleaning and dusting | | | |
| Cleaning the kitchen, bathroom and toilet | | | |
| Arranging childcare | | | |
| Organization/payment of household bills / money | | | |
| Sorting out home and car insurance, car tax, MoTs, etc. | | | |
| Teaching children discipline | | | |
| Changing the sheets and towels | | | |
| Looking after / caring for pets | | | |
| Sorting recycling / putting recycling out | | | |
| Attending school parents' evenings | | | |
| Buying family presents/cards | | | |

## DESIGNING A QUESTIONNAIRE

To design a successful questionnaire, you should follow these rules:

- It should be clearly laid out and well printed, and instructions for completing it should be easily understood by the respondent. The questionnaire should be easy to follow and complete.
- Questions should only be asked which the respondents are likely to be able to answer accurately. For example, people can only give opinions on things they know about and can remember correctly.
- The number of questions should be kept to the minimum required to produce the information. Respondents may be unwilling to spend a long time answering questions, or might stop answering the questions seriously.
- Questions should be simple and direct, and able to be answered briefly.
- Questions should be phrased in simple, everyday language so they are easily understood by the respondent. Technical words and jargon should be avoided as the respondents may not understand the question. For example, a question about 'marital status' should be avoided – it is better to ask if someone is married, cohabiting, single or divorced.
- Questions should be unambiguous, and their meaning quite clear. For example, a question like 'Do you watch television often?' is a bad question because people might interpret 'often' in different ways – it is better to specify actual time periods such as 1–2 hours a day, 3–4 hours a day, and so on.
- **Leading questions**, which encourage people to give particular answers, should be avoided – otherwise the respondent might feel he or she is expected to give a particular response. This might then produce invalid (or untruthful) answers. An example would be a question beginning '*Do you agree* that … ?'
- Pre-coded questionnaires should provide enough alternative answers to apply to all the respondents. There should be an opportunity for the respondents to give a 'Don't know' answer.

> **Leading questions** Questions which are worded in such a way as to encourage people (lead them) into giving a particular answer.

Questionnaires should be phrased in straightforward, everyday language

**Activity**

1  The following questions, which are intended to be filled in by the respondent, all have *at least* one thing wrong with them. In each case, describe what is wrong with the question and re-write the question in a more correct or more appropriate way.

  (a)  Do you watch television:  1–2 hours a night?
  2–4 hours a night?
  4–6 hours a night?

  (b)  Don't you agree sex outside a steady relationship is wrong?  YES/NO

  (c)  Don't you think you should vote Labour if there were a general election tomorrow?  YES /NO/ DON'T KNOW

  (d)  Which recommendation of the Government Road Safety Committee regarding the change in the upper speed limit on class A roads and motorways do you support?

  (e)  Are you happy with your washing machine?  YES / NO / DON'T KNOW

  (f)  Do you have joint conjugal roles in your household?  YES / NO / DON'T KNOW

  (g)  Which social class do you belong to?

  (h)  Do you bonk with your partner a lot?  YES/NO

  (i)  Are you a good driver?  YES / NO / DON'T KNOW

  (j)  Do you read newspapers:  A LOT?
  QUITE A LOT?
  OFTEN?
  SOMETIMES?
  A BIT?
  NOT MUCH?
  NEVER?

2  Do you think any of the questions above in their present form would be either unlikely to be answered or answered dishonestly? How would this affect the *validity* of the research? Give reasons for your answer.

## The postal/mail, internet-based or self-completion questionnaire

This kind of questionnaire (which may contain both closed and open questions) is either left with the respondent and picked up later, or sent through the post with a pre-paid addressed envelope for the reply, or posted on an internet site or emailed for people to reply to. The respondents fill in the form themselves (self-completion). Many surveys, including opinion polls

**Activity**

A useful site for devising computer-based surveys, which can be used either online or offline, is www.surveymonkey.com. If you want to try your hand at a computer-based survey, have a go at devising a questionnaire using Survey Monkey, preferably relating to a topic of some sociological interest. Practise using your friends as a sample. Outline any conclusions you might reasonably reach and discuss with others any difficulties or problems you experience.

and government surveys like the Crime Survey for England and Wales (see chapter 5), are now using computerized and web-based self-completion questionnaires, sometimes recorded onto computer for those who are illiterate, and this can help in getting answers to embarrassing questions – such as those on a person's criminal or sexual activity – that might otherwise remain unanswered if asked by a researcher in person.

A key problem with postal and other self-completion questionnaires is that of a low **response rate** – the number of people who reply compared to the total number of questionnaires distributed. People often don't bother to reply, and the percentage returning them may sometimes be less than 20 per cent of the sample, and this may mean the results obtained are not valid, but inaccurate, biased and unrepresentative. For example, those who choose to reply may be more interested in the topic being investigated, or be more educated, than those who don't reply, or they may have some axe to grind.

To try to overcome the problem of non-response, postal questionnaires often have covering letters from well-known individuals or organizations. Postal and online questionnaires often offer free gifts, competition prizes and other rewards. A reply-paid envelope is essential if the questionnaire is not to be dropped into the nearest paper recycling bin.

> **Response rate** The number of people who respond to questionnaires compared to the total number of questionnaires distributed.

### THE IMPOSITION PROBLEM

The **imposition problem** is the risk that, when asking questions in self-completion questionnaires or interviews (interviews are discussed in the next section), researchers might be imposing their own views and framework on the people being questioned, rather than getting at what they really think. For example, the question the respondent really wants to answer is never asked, or the limited choice of answers offered in a questionnaire means the answer the respondent wants to give simply isn't there. This imposes limits on what kind of information can be given or collected. This poses problems of *validity* as the researcher is giving priority to their own concerns rather than those of the respondent.

> **Imposition problem** The risk that, when asking questions in interviews or self-completion questionnaires, the researcher might be imposing their own views or framework on the people being researched, rather than getting at what they really think.

### The advantages/strengths of postal/mail, internet-based and other self-completion questionnaires

✓ They are fairly cheap compared to paying interviewers.
✓ Large numbers of people over a wide geographical area can be questioned, providing more representative samples.
✓ Results are obtained quickly.
✓ They are generally reliable, getting similar replies if repeated.
✓ People have more time to reply than when an interviewer is present, so more accurate answers may be obtained.
✓ Questions on personal, sensitive, controversial or embarrassing subjects are more likely to be answered than if they are asked by an interviewer.
✓ The problem of interviewer bias (see below) is avoided.
✓ Answers are easy to compare and put into statistical (quantitative) form – for example, '87 per cent of women questioned said they had to do all the housework.' *Positivists* prefer them for this reason.

### The limitations/weaknesses of postal/mail, internet-based and other self-completion questionnaires

✗ Non-response, leading to unrepresentative, invalid, biased results.
✗ Extra questions cannot be asked or added, to get the respondents to expand or explain themselves more fully. The quality and depth of information is therefore limited.
✗ With pre-coded questionnaires, the limited range of questions and answers may mean the researcher isn't getting at what the respondent really thinks, so results may not be valid – the *imposition problem*.
✗ The wording may be confusing to the respondent, and the questions therefore misunderstood. There is no interviewer present to explain the question if necessary.
✗ You can't be sure the right person completed it, undermining the validity and representativeness of the sample.
✗ People with literacy problems may have difficulty completing them, undermining the representativeness of the sample.

## Interviews

There are two main types of interview: the structured or formal interview and the unstructured or informal interview.

### The structured or formal interview

The structured interview is based on a structured/pre-coded questionnaire. The interviewer asks the questions and does not probe beyond the basic answers received. It is a formal question-and-answer session. This type of interview is preferred by *positivists*, as it produces more *quantitative* data.

## The unstructured, informal or in-depth interview

The unstructured, informal or in-depth interview is based on an open-ended questionnaire, or simply a list of topics the interviewer wishes to discuss. The interviewer will ask the respondent open-ended questions which may trigger discussions or further questions. The interviewer will try to put the respondent at ease in a relaxed, informal situation and encourage him or her to express his or her feelings and opinions. This means the interviewer can obtain much greater depth of information than is possible in a structured interview or in a postal or other self-completion questionnaire. It is a bit like a TV chat show. This method is much preferred by *interpretivists*, as it produces more in-depth *qualitative* information.

*Group interviews and focus groups*   Group interviews and focus groups are both forms of in-depth interview, and produce the *qualitative* information much preferred by *interpretivists*.

● A **group interview** is an interview in which the researcher interviews several people at the same time, often about a range of topics. The interviewer's role is to question, and to control the direction the interview takes as she or he is seeking to obtain particular information; usually, responses will be to the interviewer, though people may well develop their answers through discussion with others in the group.

● A **focus group** is a form of group interview in which the group focuses on a particular topic to be explored in depth, and people are encouraged to talk to one another as well as the interviewer. This is so people's views

**Group interview**
Where the researcher interviews several people at the same time, with the researcher controlling the direction of the interview, with responses directed to him or her.

**Focus group** A form of group interview in which the group focuses on a particular topic to explore in depth, and people are encouraged to talk to one another as well as the interviewer.

How do you think interviewing people in a group might affect the validity of the information obtained, compared to interviewing someone on their own?

on the issue under discussion are drawn out and well explored. The researcher's role is to feed in ideas or questions and get people discussing an issue and to draw out their feelings, experiences, ideas and opinions. The researcher also has to make sure the group remains focused on the topic under discussion.

## The problem of interviewer bias

Interviews involve face-to-face social interaction between people, and the success of interviews often relies on the personality and personal skills of the interviewer. There is always the possibility that the respondent might adapt his or her answer according to the class, ethnicity, age, sex, speech, accent, tone of voice, style of dress, or behaviour of the interviewer. The interviewer may give the impression of wanting to hear a certain answer. The respondent may try to impress the interviewer by giving answers she or he thinks the interviewer wants to hear and would approve of, rather than giving her or his real opinions. This isn't really surprising, as nearly everyone likes to obtain the approval of the person they're talking to. The way in which the presence or behaviour of the interviewer, or their social

What possible sources of interviewer bias might there be in this interview? What steps might you take to overcome them?

and personal characteristics, may influence in some way the answers given by the respondent is referred to as **interviewer bias** (sometimes called the **interviewer effect**).

Interviewer bias is a serious problem, as it could mean that respondents do not give answers that they really believe, and therefore the results of an interview may not be valid (not give a true, genuine or authentic picture of what is being studied) or reliable (other interviewers may not get the same results). To overcome interviewer bias, interviewers are trained to avoid giving any impression of approval or disapproval based on their own opinions and feelings about the answers they receive. They should give the impression of polite and friendly indifference to the answers received. Another way of overcoming interviewer bias is to avoid face-to-face interviews altogether, and use telephone interviews instead.

> **Interviewer bias/ interviewer effect**
> The answers given in an interview being influenced or distorted in some way by the presence or behaviour of the interviewer.

### Activity

Consider the following situations, and in each case:
1. Suggest possible ways in which interviewer bias might occur.
2. Suggest what might be done to help remove the bias.
   (a) A white person being questioned by a black interviewer about his or her racial attitudes.
   (b) An adult interviewing pupils in a school.
   (c) An adult interviewer asking teenagers about their attitudes to illegal drug use.
   (d) A well-dressed, middle-class sociologist asking adults on welfare benefits questions about their lifestyle.
   (e) A female interviewer asking a married or cohabiting couple about how household tasks are divided between them.
   (f) An older woman asking questions of a young mother about the way children should be brought up.
   (g) An interviewer who is a committed Christian asking questions about religious belief.

Interviewers may not always get the cooperation they hope for ... especially if they choose the wrong moment

## The advantages/strengths of interviews

✓ The problem of non-response found with self-completion question-naires is much rarer. Skilled interviewers can persuade people to answer questions.

✓ There is more flexibility than with self-completion questionnaires – questions may be explained and, except with interviews using pre-coded questionnaires, extra questions can be asked and more detail obtained.

✓ Unstructured interviews allow the respondent to be more open and honest, and therefore more valid information about the respondents' attitudes, values and opinions can be obtained. This is why *interpretivists* prefer them.

✓ With unstructured interviews, the interviewer can adjust questions and change direction as the interview is taking place if new ideas and insights emerge. By contrast, structured interviews have already decided the important questions.

✓ Group interviews and focus groups can help to trigger discussions and thereby gain more detailed and in-depth *qualitative* information.

## The limitations/weaknesses of interviews

✗ They are more time-consuming and costly than self-completion questionnaires – interviews are often slow and interviewers have to be paid.

✗ Because interviews tend to be slow and expensive, often only a small number can take place – this means the sample size may be small, and therefore risks being unrepresentative of the survey population.

✗ There is no way of knowing whether what people say in an interview is what they really believe or how they behave in real life – the problem of *validity*.

✗ The success of interviews depends heavily on the skill and personality of the interviewer, especially in unstructured interviews. It can be difficult to repeat or replicate such interviews. *Positivists* are concerned about this problem of *reliability*.

✗ There is a risk of interviewer bias, leading to results that are neither reliable nor valid.

✗ Group interviews or focus groups may act as a form of peer pressure and individuals may conceal their true feelings in case others disapprove. They may be reluctant to reveal personal issues in such a group setting. They may also exaggerate or distort their views to impress others.

### Activity

1  Make up a short five-question structured questionnaire (with a choice of answers) to find out about attitudes to some social topic you're interested in.

2  Test this out on three people, using a structured interview, and record your findings.

3  Now, using the same questions as prompts, do unstructured interviews with two people. Be prepared to probe further and ask extra questions and enter discussions. Record your findings.

4  Compare the data collected by each type of interview, and the time it took to complete the interviews. Is there any difference between the information collected by these two types of interview, and the time taken to carry them out? Explain why you think this might be the case.

5  Identify and explain *two* reasons why an interpretivist sociologist might choose to use an unstructured interview rather than a structured interview in sociological research.

6  Identify *two* ways in which unstructured interviews might be unreliable as a method of research.

7  Suggest *two* examples in each case below in which group interviews or focus groups might:
   (a)  provide a greater depth of qualitative information than interviews with a single individual;
   (b)  provide less valid information than interviews with a single individual.

## Observation

Apart from surveys, sociologists also collect data by observation. There are two main kinds of observation: non-participant observation (or direct observation) and participant observation.

### *Non-participant observation*

The researcher observes a group or situation without taking part in any way, and records his or her observations. For example, a researcher may observe school students by sitting at the back of a classroom to see whether boys and girls are treated differently by teachers. By counting up the number and type of different interactions between students and teacher, the quantitative data positivists prefer can be produced.

#### *Advantages*

✓  The sociologist can study people in their natural or normal setting with less chance of their behaviour being influenced and changed by the presence of the researcher (but not always, as the cartoon suggests).

✓  As the observer is not involved with the group being observed, he or she can be more detached, and, as positivists would suggest, produce more objective quantitative information.

### Limitations

✘ As interpretivists suggest, observation without involvement in the group means it is often not possible to understand what is really happening, or to find out more by questioning people about the behaviour the researcher is observing. It describes *what* is happening, but provides no *qualitative* information telling you why or what it means.

✘ The data produced may well reflect simply the assumptions and interpretations of the researcher, raising serious issues over their reliability and validity.

✘ The presence of the researcher may cause the Hawthorne effect, as the cartoon suggests. This may make the findings invalid.

Because of these difficulties, sociologists more often join in with a group to observe it. This is known as participant observation.

## Participant observation

Participant observation is a very commonly used observation technique. In this method, the researcher actually joins in the group or community she or he is studying. The researcher tries to become an accepted part of the group and to learn about the group as a member of it. For example, the sociologist may spend time as a mental patient in a hospital, join a gang, live as a homeless person, spend time in prison, or teach in a school. This technique is used by *interpretivists* who seek to understand a group from its members' point of view – what Weber called *verstehen* – and to obtain in-depth *qualitative* information about how it sees the world.

> **Overt role** The role of a researcher in participant observation who reveals to the group being studied his or her true identity and purpose.

***Overt and covert roles*** Joining a group raises many questions about the researcher's role. The researcher may adopt an **overt role**, where the

How do the cartoons show the Hawthorne effect (or observer effect), and how might this affect the validity of some kinds of sociological research?

Is this a romantic encounter or are the couple fighting? Are they having a séance or has there been a power cut or haven't they paid their electricity bill? Observation alone is not always adequate for finding out what is really going on

researcher declares his or her true identity to the group and the fact he or she is doing research. Alternatively, the researcher may adopt a **covert role** (concealing her or his role as a researcher) or a cover story (partially declaring his or her role as a researcher, but concealing elements of it).

> **Covert role** A hidden role, where the researcher in participant observation conceals from the group being studied his or her true identify as a researcher, to gain access to the group and avoid disrupting its normal behaviour.

### ADOPTING A COVERT ROLE
✓ It avoids the risk of people's behaviour changing if they know they are being studied (the *Hawthorne effect*).
✗ It raises ethical concerns over observing and reporting on people's activities in secret, without first trying to obtain their informed consent.

### ADOPTING AN OVERT ROLE
✓ People may share with a trusted researcher things that they hide from other members of the group.
✓ The researcher may be able to ask questions or interview people without arousing suspicion.
✓ Ethically, it is right that people should be aware they are being studied.
✗ It carries the risk that the behaviour of those being studied may be affected – the *Hawthorne effect* – raising questions over the validity of the research.

### The advantages/strengths of participant observation
✓ The sociologist gains that first-hand knowledge of a group seen through the eyes of its members that interpretivists prefer. This provides much more detail, depth and rich *qualitative* information than other methods like questionnaires and interviews.

## Activity

1 What does the cartoon above suggest might be some of the difficulties involved in a participant observation study of a gang?
2 Many participant observation studies have been concerned with the study of groups not fully accepted into society, such as street gangs, religious cults or drug users. Suggest ways you might get in touch with and be accepted by such a group to study it, and outline any difficulties you might have with staying in the group.
3 Suggest two advantages and two disadvantages of adopting a covert role in participant observation.
4 What ethical problems are there with adopting a covert role? Can adopting a covert role ever be justified?
5 Explain the ways, with examples, in which being a successful participant observer might depend on the personality and personal characteristics of the researcher, such as their age, sex or ethnic group.

✓ It takes place over a long period and can therefore give a much fuller and more valid account of a group's behaviour than the snapshot provided by most questionnaires and interviews.

✓ It enables new ideas to emerge during the research itself. The sociologist may discover things she or he would not even have thought of asking about, producing more valid results.

✓ It may be the only practical method of research. For example, a criminal gang is hardly likely to answer questionnaires or do interviews for fear of the consequences. By adopting a covert role – keeping her or his identity secret – the researcher may be able to investigate such groups. Even if the group knows who the researcher is (an overt role), the researcher may, after a time, win the trust of the group.

✓ People can be studied in their normal social situation, rather than in the somewhat artificial context of an interview or questionnaire.

### The limitations/weaknesses of participant observation

✗ It is very time-consuming and expensive compared to other methods, as it involves the sociologist participating in a group for long periods.

✗ Because only a small group is studied, it is difficult to make generalizations.

✗ It depends a great deal on the personality and personal characteristics of the investigator and his or her ability to fit in with the group.

✗ There is a danger of the researcher becoming so involved with the group and developing such loyalty to it that he or she may find it difficult to stand back and report his or her observations in a neutral way. Positivists argue the research would not then be valid.

✗ As positivists suggest, there is no real way of checking the findings of a participant observation study. There is no real evidence apart from the observations of the researcher, and what one researcher might regard as important may be missed or seen as unimportant by another.

✗ There may be a problem of gaining the group's confidence (getting into the group) and maintaining it (staying in), especially if criminal and other deviant activities are involved. What does the researcher do if a group involves itself in criminal activities such as theft, drug-dealing or acts of violence? Failure to take part may result in loss of the group's confidence and trust, and effectively cause the research to end before it is completed.

✗ The presence of the researcher in an overt role may change the group's behaviour simply because they know they are being studied – the Hawthorne (or observer) effect.

✗ With a covert role, the researcher has to be very careful when asking questions or taking notes, in case her or his real identity is revealed or people become suspicious. This may limit the information obtained.

✗ There are serious ethical difficulties involved in a researcher adopting a covert role and not obtaining informed consent.

## THE MIXED METHODS APPROACH (OR METHODOLOGICAL PLURALISM) AND TRIANGULATION

The methods chosen in a piece of research will be influenced by:

- the practical, ethical and theoretical (PET) issues mentioned on pages 78 and 80
- the questions or hypothesis being investigated

- whether *quantitative* or *qualitative* information is required
- the scale of the research
- the time and money available to complete it.

Figure 2.16 illustrates the relationship between some of these factors.

In an actual piece of research, many sociologists, whether they are positivists or interpretivists, will use a range of methods to collect the data they require. The **mixed methods** approach (or methodological pluralism) is the use of a variety of methods to collect both quantitative and qualitative data in a single piece of research. For example, the researcher might use participant observation combined with unstructured interviews to study a group, providing qualitative data, and then collect quantitative data using structured questionnaires to find out details about occupation, income or educational qualifications.

**Mixed methods**
The use of both quantitative and qualitative methods within a single study (also referred to as methodological pluralism).

**Figure 2.16** Methods of data collection

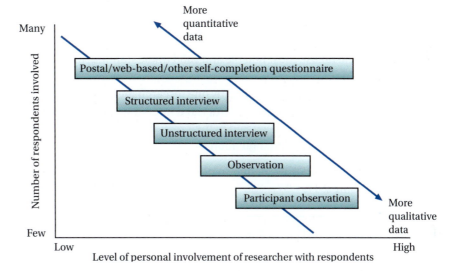

**Activity**

1 According to figure 2.16, which method of data collection involves the largest number of respondents?
2 Which method has the highest level of personal involvement of the researcher with the respondents?
3 Which method, apart from observational methods, provides the most qualitative data?
4 Which method do you think provides the most *valid* information? Give reasons for your answer.
5 Which method do you think is the most *reliable* method of collecting information? Give reasons for your answer.

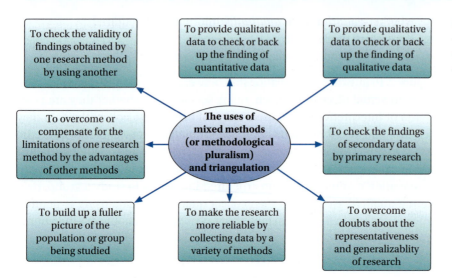

To check the validity of findings obtained by one research method by using another

To provide qualitative data to check or back up the finding of quantitative data

To provide qualitative data to check or back up the finding of qualitative data

To overcome or compensate for the limitations of one research method by the advantages of other methods

The uses of mixed methods (or methodological pluralism) and triangulation

To check the findings of secondary data by primary research

To build up a fuller picture of the population or group being studied

To make the research more reliable by collecting data by a variety of methods

To overcome doubts about the representativeness and generalizablity of research

**Figure 2.17** The uses of mixed methods (or methodological pluralism) and triangulation

Mixed methods are used for two main aims:

- To provide the fullest, most reliable and valid understanding possible of the topic being studied.
- To cross-check information gained by one research method by using another – e.g. using qualitative unstructured interviews to check whether people really meant what they said in their responses to questionnaires in a survey. This is called **triangulation**.

The use of mixed methods (or methodological pluralism) and triangulation are shown in figure 2.17.

**Triangulation**
The use of a variety of methods, and different types of data, to cross-check that the results obtained by another method are valid and reliable.

## Mixed methods and case studies

The mixed methods approach is commonly used in a **case study**. This is a research approach that focuses on the intensive study of a single case, such as a place, person, group, institution or event, rather than a population or sample. This enables a very detailed, in-depth study, and can provide useful insights for further research.

An example of mixed methods used in a case study is *Reading the Riots* (available here: goo.gl/Ks8u8T). This set out to gain insights into the factors behind England's summer of disorder in early August 2011. It used in-depth unstructured qualitative interviews, content analysis to study riot-related tweets, and survey-like structured questionnaires to collect quantitative data about factors such as age, ethnicity, education, employment and criminal history.

**Case study**
Research that focuses on the intensive study of a single case of a place, person, group, institution or event.

## Activity

Test your understanding of research methods.

Imagine you have two months to carry out a small-scale research project on one of the following issues (or one of your own choosing), using both primary and secondary sources:

- the role of grandparents in childcare
- the opinions of adults in your neighbourhood about crime
- how household tasks are divided between couples in the home
- gender stereotyping in a school or college
- the attitudes of people towards gay marriage
- the lifestyle of teenagers.

Select one of the issues above, and:

(a) Suggest a hypothesis you might wish to test, or questions you want to find answers to.

(b) Identify at least one secondary source of information you might use, and explain what information you would expect to obtain from it.

(c) Explain how you might select the group of people to be studied, and how you would try to make sure any sample was representative.

(d) Explain carefully what research method you would use to collect your primary data, why it would be particularly suited to the hypothesis you would be investigating, and why it would be more suitable than other methods you could use.

(e) Identify three problems or difficulties you might face in carrying out your research, and in each case suggest how you might overcome them.

(f) Identify two ethical issues you might encounter, and how you would try to avoid or overcome them.

## CHAPTER SUMMARY AND REVISION CHECKLIST

After studying this chapter, you should be able to:

- explain briefly what is meant by a sociological perspective, including structuralism, social action or interpretivist perspectives, macro and micro approaches, and consensus and conflict approaches to the study of society

- outline the features of the consensus perspective of functionalism and the New Right; the conflict perspectives of Marxism, Weber and feminism, and the interactionist perspective

- be able to read and interpret statistical data presented in a variety of forms

- outline and explain the main approaches to research adopted by positivism and interpretivism

- outline the difference between quantitative and qualitative methods and data

- explain what is meant by the issues of validity, the Hawthorne (or observer) effect, reliability, representativeness/generalizability, and ethics in social research

- explain, with examples, the difference between primary and secondary sources of data, and their advantages and disadvantages

- describe the use, advantages and disadvantages of content analysis

- outline the advantages and limitations of using official and non-official statistics in research

- describe the main stages of the research process

- describe a range of practical, ethical and theoretical (PET) issues influencing the choice of research topic and method

- outline the main features of experiments, their strengths and limitations, and why sociologists use them only rarely

- describe the main features of social surveys, and the various sampling techniques sociologists use to obtain representative samples to study.

- outline the features, strengths and weaknesses of longitudinal studies

- outline the main stages of a survey, including the importance of pilot surveys

- describe the nature and use of questionnaires, interviews (including group interviews and focus groups), and non-participant and participant observation in sociological research, whether positivists or interpretivists are more likely to use them, and explain their various strengths and limitations

- explain what is meant by the 'imposition problem' in questionnaires and interviews

- explain what is meant by 'interviewer bias' (the interviewer effect)

- outline the mixed methods approach and why it's used (including triangulation)

- plan a small-scale piece of research of your own, using the various sources, sampling techniques and research methods covered in this chapter.

## KEY TERMS

Definitions can be found in the glossary at the end of this book, as well as these terms usually being defined in the margin where they first appear in the chapter. You can also find the glossary online by following the link at www.politybooks.com/browne. Put it in your phone for ready reference.

| | | | |
|---|---|---|---|
| bourgeoisie | hypothesis | patriarchy | respondent |
| capitalism | imposition problem | personal documents | response rate |
| case study | informed consent | perspective | sample |
| conflict theory | interactionism | pilot survey | sampling frame |
| consensus theory | interpretivism | positivism | secondary data |
| content analysis | interviewer bias | postmodernism | social facts |
| covert role | labelling | primary data | social interaction |
| dependency culture | leading questions | proletariat | sociological perspective |
| domestic labour | longitudinal study | public documents | status |
| ethics | macro approach | qualitative data | status group |
| feminism | means of production | qualitative methods | structuralism |
| feminist | micro approach | quantitative data | survey |
| focus group | mixed methods | quantitative methods | survey population |
| functional prerequisites | New Right | reliability | triangulation |
| functionalism | overt role | representative sample | underclass |
| group interview | party | representativeness/ | validity |
| Hawthorne effect | patriarchal ideology | generalizability | *verstehen* |

There are a variety of free tests and other activities that can be used to assess your learning – mainly aimed at AS- and A-level sociology students, but you might find them useful – as well as an online searchable glossary, at

## www.politybooks.com/browne
You can also find new contemporary resources by following Ken Browne on Twitter

@BrowneKen

# CHAPTER

# 3 Families

## Contents

**KEY ISSUES**

- What is the family?
- Different forms of family, marriage and household structure
- Alternatives to the family
- Consensus and conflict theories of the role of the family in society
- Family and household diversity
- Social change and family types, structures and relationships
- Social change and relationships inside the family
- A summary of changes in families
- Critical views of the family: the darker side of family life

The family unit is one of the most important social institutions, which is found in some form in nearly all known societies. It is a basic unit of social organization, and plays a key role in socializing children into the culture of their society, and forming their identities – how they see themselves and how others see them.

Most people are raised in families, and so we might think we know all about them. We may make assumptions that people will fall in love with someone of the opposite sex and get married, start having children, and form their own family. We may have the impression that the 'best' kind of family consists of parents and a couple of children, with Dad out working and Mum always available for looking after the kids, but with both partners sharing a lot of jobs around the home. We may believe the family is the only place where children can be properly brought up, and that it is a source of unconditional affection – a place to retreat to whenever things get too much or go wrong in the outside world.

On the other hand, you may believe that this vision of the family is in decline, pointing to high rates of divorce and increasing numbers of lone-parent families. You might point to rising levels of child abuse and violence against women in families, with vandalism, crime and drug abuse arising from inadequate socialization of children. You would not be alone in holding such a belief – the media, politicians, the police, social workers, teachers and religious leaders have all at some time or other tried to blame the family and lack of parental control for a wide range of problems in society.

There is, whatever way you look at it, a controversy over the family. This chapter will review many of the key issues that are arising in contemporary families.

## WHAT IS A FAMILY?

Defining a family is not necessarily straightforward. For example, some people will clearly distinguish between what they see as their family – parents, brothers and sisters, grandparents, uncles and aunts and cousins, etc. – and their friends. For others, friends may blur into or be treated as family, or even become a kind of substitute 'family of choice'. Some may regard close neighbours or pets as part of their family. For the sake of clarity, this chapter takes a key defining feature of a family or a family relationship to be that it is made up of people who are related by **kinship** ties: relations of blood, marriage / civil partnership or adoption.

For couples, cohabitation (living together without the legal bonds of a marriage or civil partnership) ought also to be included as a family relationship, as it is now becoming a very common alternative to marriage or a civil partnership.

For the purposes of this chapter, we will include in the family all of the following:

- any group of people who are related by kinship ties
- any married / civil partnership or cohabiting couple (of the same or opposite sex), with or without children (**dependent** or non-dependent), who live at the same address
- a lone parent, with at least one child (dependent or non-dependent) who lives at the same address.

**Kinship** Relations of blood, marriage / civil partnership or adoption.

**Dependent** Someone who is maintained by another person, e.g. a dependent child is supported by his or her parent(s).

### What is a household?

It is important to make the distinction between families and households. A **household** is either one person living alone or any group of people who live at the same address and share living arrangements. Most families will live in a household, but not all households are families. For example, students sharing a house together make up a household, though they are not a family. In the UK in 2017, around two-thirds of households consisted of families, but around one in three households consisted of either people living alone or two or more unrelated adults.

**Household** One person living alone or a group of people (not necessarily related) who live at the same address and who share cooking facilities and a living room, sitting room or dining area.

## DIFFERENT FORMS OF FAMILY, MARRIAGE AND HOUSEHOLD STRUCTURE

Even though the family is found in nearly every society, it can take many different forms. Family life in other societies can be organized in quite different ways from family life in modern Britain, and in Britain it has changed a lot over time. Sociologists use a number of different terms to describe the wide varieties of the family, marriage and household.

## Monogamy

In modern Britain and the rest of Europe, the USA and most Christian cultures, monogamy is the only legal form of marriage / civil partnership. Monogamy is a form of marriage / civil partnership in which a person can have only one legal partner at a time. Monogamy has not traditionally been the most common form of marriage in the world, though it is rapidly becoming so as societies modernize and Western ideas of marriage spread around the world through globalization. In a society where monogamy is the only form of legal marriage, a person who marries while still legally married to someone else who is still alive is guilty of the crime of bigamy – a serious offence punishable by imprisonment.

### *Serial monogamy*

In modern Britain, most of Western Europe and the USA, there are high rates of divorce and remarriage. Some people keep marrying and divorcing (or cohabiting with, then leaving), a series of different partners, but each relationship is monogamous. The term 'serial monogamy' is sometimes used to describe this pattern. This form of marriage / civil partnership or cohabitation has been described as 'one at a time, one after the other and they don't last long'.

**Monogamy** A form of marriage / civil partnership in which a person can only be legally married/civil-partnered to one partner at a time.

**Bigamy** In societies where monogamy is the only legal form of marriage / civil partnership, the offence of marrying/ civil-partnering another person while still legally married/civil-partnered to someone else who is still living.

**Serial monogamy** A form of relationship in which a person keeps marrying / civil-partnering / cohabiting with and divorcing or separating from a series of different partners, but only forms a relationship with one person at a time.

# Arranged marriages

**Arranged marriage**
A marriage which is arranged by the parents of the marriage partners, with a view to compatibility of family background and status. More a union between two families than two people, and romantic love between the marriage partners is not necessarily present.

**Arranged marriages** are those in which the marriages of children are organized by their parents or other family members, who try to match their children with partners of a similar background and status. Such arranged marriages are more a union between two families than between two people, and romantic love is not necessarily present between the marriage partners. They are typically found among Muslims, Sikhs and Hindus (though not all Muslims, Sikhs and Hindus form arranged marriages). Arranged marriage is still common (though declining) in the South Asian community in Britain, where the custom is often more strictly enforced than in the Indian sub-continent. This is because the older generations of parents and grandparents here often still stick to the customs which existed when they left India for Britain many years ago.

It is important not to confuse an arranged marriage with a **forced marriage**. While arranged marriages involve the family in selecting marriage partners, the couple are normally free to accept or reject the arrangement. They are therefore consensual, involving the consent of both parties to the marriage. In contrast, a forced marriage is one that takes place without the consent of both parties. This involves, for example, emotional and psychological pressure (e.g. the accusation of bringing shame on their family), threats and physical or sexual violence to force marriage on someone against their will.

The Antisocial Behaviour, Crime and Policing Act of 2014 made it a criminal offence to force someone to marry, and aimed to protect both adults and children at risk of being forced into marriage.

**Forced marriage**
One in which someone is compelled, often by violence or the threat of violence, to marry without their consent.

> **Activity**
>
> What are the advantages and disadvantages of arranged marriages? How do you think arranged marriages might be changing in Britain, and what pressures do you think there might be on the survival of the custom in Britain?

# Civil partnership

A civil partnership is a legal relationship, first available throughout the UK in 2005, which originally could be registered only by two people of the same sex. It gave gay and lesbian couples equal treatment to married couples in a wide range of legal matters. In 2019, civil partnership became available to all couples, not just same-sex couples.

From 2014, changes in the law opened up marriage, too, as an option for same-sex couples on the same basis as opposite-sex couples (except in Northern Ireland). Civil partnerships declined as the majority of same-sex

couples opted for marriage instead, and only a minority of same-sex couples – mainly men – still prefer this option to marriage.

Same-sex families are becoming more common, though they are still quite rare – in 2017, they made up only about 1 per cent of all couple families. Most same-sex couples with children tend to be lesbian couples. However, there is an increase in the number of gay male couples adopting children or having children through surrogate mothers.

## Polygamy

While marrying a second partner without divorcing the first is a crime in Britain, in many societies it is perfectly acceptable to have more than one marriage partner at the same time. **Polygamy** is a general term referring to marriage between a member of one sex and two or more members of the opposite sex at the same time. There are two different types of polygamy: polygyny and polyandry.

### *Polygyny*

**Polygyny** is the marriage of one man to two or more women at the same time. It is widely practised in some Muslim-majority countries in Africa and Asia, as Islam grants a man the right to take up to four wives, as long as he can provide for and treat them all equally. It is also practised (illegally) among some Mormons in the state of Utah in the USA.

The possession of several wives is often seen as a sign of wealth and success, and generally only those men who can afford to support several

**Polygamy** A form of marriage in which a member of one sex can be married to two or more members of the opposite sex at the same time.

**Polygyny** A form of marriage in which a man may have two or more wives at the same time.

wives practise polygyny. Because of this, even where polygyny is allowed, only a small number of men actually practise it. In any case, the numbers of men and women in most societies are usually fairly evenly balanced, and there are not enough women for all men to have more than one wife.

## *Polyandry*

**Polyandry** is the marriage of one woman to two or more men at the same time. This is rare, and is illegal in virtually every country of the world. It is

> **Polyandry** A form of marriage in which a woman may have two or more husbands at the same time.

found in only about 1 per cent of all societies, often in small, isolated, tribal or minority subcultures. Polyandry appears to arise where living standards are so low that a man can only afford to support a wife and child by sharing the responsibility with other men; where there is an imbalance in the population and a shortage of women; and a desire to limit population size by controlling the number of births. It is found among the Toda of southern India, the Marquesan Islanders, and has been reported as occurring in parts of Tibet, Bhutan and other Himalayan countries.

## The nuclear family

In a **nuclear family**, there are just one or two parents and their children, living together in one household. It is sometimes called the two-generation family, because it contains only the two generations of parent(s) and children. In Britain in 2017, around 57 per cent of people lived in this type of family. The **privatized (or isolated) nuclear family** refers to the way the nuclear family has become separated and isolated from its extended kin, and has become a more private, self-contained, self-reliant, home-centred unit. Life for the modern privatized nuclear family is largely centred on the home – free time is spent doing jobs around the house, and leisure is mainly home- and family-centred. DIY, gardening, watching television or going out as a family to pleasure parks like Alton Towers are typical family activities. The contemporary nuclear family has thus become a very private institution, isolated from wider kin and often from neighbours and local community life as well.

> **Nuclear family** A family with two generations, of parents and children, living together in one household.

> **Privatized (or isolated) nuclear family** A self-contained, self-reliant and home-centred nuclear family unit that is largely separated and isolated from its extended kin, neighbours and local community life.

In 2017, 57 per cent of people in Britain lived in nuclear families. In what other types of family or household do you think the remaining 43 per cent of people live today?

## The extended family

The **extended family** is a grouping consisting of all kin. There are three main types of extended family: the classic extended, the modified extended, and the 'beanpole' family.

### *The classic extended family*

The **classic extended family** is made up of several nuclear families or family members joined by kinship relations. The term is mainly used to describe a situation in which many related nuclear families or family members live in the same house, street or area, and the members of these related nuclear families see one another regularly. It may be horizontally extended, where it contains just two generations, with aunts, uncles, cousins, etc., or vertically extended, where it contains more than two generations, such as grandparents and grandchildren as well as parents and their own children.

While the most common type of family found in modern Britain is the nuclear family or the modified extended family (see below), there is evidence that the classic extended family still survives today in modern Britain in three types of community:

- TRADITIONAL WORKING-CLASS COMMUNITIES These are long-established communities dominated by one industry, such as fishing or mining, in the traditional working-class industrial centres of the north of England, and in inner-city working-class areas. Such extended family life declined in the 1990s, as traditional industries closed down and people were forced to move away in search of new employment. In such communities, children usually remain in the same area when they leave home. People stay in the same community for several generations, and this creates a close-knit community life. Members of the extended family live close together and meet frequently, and there is a constant exchange of services between extended family members – such as shopping and babysitting between female kin, and shared work and leisure activities between male relatives.
- THE SOUTH ASIAN COMMUNITY As discussed below, the classic extended family is still very common among those who came to Britain in the 1960s and 1970s from India, Pakistan and Bangladesh.
- SMALL COMMUNITIES OF TRAVELLERS (Gypsies/Roma).

### *The modified extended family*

The **modified extended family** is one in which related nuclear families, although they may be living far apart geographically, nevertheless maintain regular contact and mutual support through visiting, phone calls, Skype,

---

**Extended family**
A family grouping including all those linked by kinship ties.

**Classic extended family** A family in which several related nuclear families or family members live in the same house, street or area. It may be horizontally extended – where it contains aunts, uncles, cousins, etc. – or vertically extended – where it contains more than two generations.

**Modified extended family** A family type in which related nuclear families, although living apart geographically, nevertheless maintain regular contact and mutual support through visiting, phone calls, Skype, letters, email and social media: continuing close relations made possible by modern communications. This is probably the most common type of family arrangement in Britain today.

letters, email, photo sharing and social media: continuing close relations made possible by modern communications. This is probably the most common type of family arrangement in Britain today.

## The 'beanpole family'

As discussed later in this chapter, Britain now has an **ageing population**, with people living longer and a growing proportion of older people compared to younger people. At the same time, couples are having fewer children and nuclear families are getting smaller. This means that there is an increase in the number of extended four- and five-generation families, with more children growing up in extended families alongside several of their grandparents and even great-grandparents. This new shape of the extended family is sometimes called the **beanpole family**, shown in figure 3.1. This is because the family tree is long (multi-generational) and less 'bushy' (fewer brothers and sisters in one generation leads to fewer aunts and uncles and cousins in the next). This trend towards a new emerging beanpole form of the extended family can only be expected to increase with the growing numbers of the elderly, and fewer children being born.

## The symmetrical family

The **symmetrical family** is one in which the male and female roles of cohabiting couples (e.g. full-time work, cooking, cleaning, DIY, childcare, etc.) have become more alike (symmetrical) and equal. There are more shared tasks within relationships, rather than a clear division between the jobs of male and female partners. Both partners are likely to be wage earners

**Ageing population** A population in which the average age is getting higher, with a growing proportion of elderly people, and a declining proportion of younger people.

**Beanpole family** A multi-generation extended family, which is long (multi-generational) and thin, with few people in each generation. This is because fewer children are being born in each generation, but people are living longer.

**Symmetrical family** A family in which the roles of partners who live together in couple relationships have become more alike (symmetrical) and equal.

The 'Beanpole' family

*Great-grandparents*

↓

*Grandparents*

↓

*Parents*

↓

*Children*

↓

*Grandchildren*

↓

*Great-grandchildren*

**Figure 3.1** The beanpole family

**Activity**

1  Carry out a brief survey among your friends or workmates and find out how many live in nuclear families, how many live in classic extended or modified extended families, and how many have beanpole families. You will have to think of suitable ways of measuring the features of these families, such as how near relatives live, how often they see one another, what other relatives live in the household apart from parents and children, and so on.
2  Ask them what it is like living in these different types of family. On the basis of your findings, and using also your own experience of family life, make a list of the advantages and disadvantages of living in each type of family.

**Dual-earner family** A family in which both partners earn money from paid employment.

**Dual-career family** A family in which both partners have their own careers, with the hope and expectation of future promotions.

**Reconstituted (blended or step-) family** A family in which one or both partners have children from a previous relationship, combining to form a new family.

(a **dual-earner** (or **dual-career**) **family**). It remains a popular impression that most families in modern Britain are symmetrical, but evidence which will be discussed later in this chapter suggests this is not the case, and that many families remain patriarchal and benefit men the most.

## The reconstituted (blended or step-) family

The **reconstituted family** (also called a stepfamily or a blended family) is a family in which one or both partners have children from previous relationships, but they have combined to form a new family. This 'reconstitutes' the family with various combinations of stepmother, stepfather and stepchildren. Such families are increasingly common in Western societies, as a result of higher divorce rates, remarriages and serial monogamy. In England and Wales, around one in every three marriages in 2016 was not a first-time marriage, but a remarriage for one or both partners, and around one in ten of all couple families with dependent children today are stepfamilies, with parents having children from one or more previous relationships.

## The lone-parent family

The lone-parent or single-parent family is increasingly common in Western societies. In 2017, around 13 per cent of people in the UK lived in this type of family. Around a quarter of all families with dependent children were lone-parent families. Nearly nine out of ten of these lone parents were women. This is because women are more likely to take on the main caring responsibilities for any children when relationships break down.

Although lone-parent families can also arise from the death of a partner, they are today largely a result of divorce and separation, or because women lack or don't want a traditional couple relationship. Those in lone-parent families are nearly twice as likely to be in poverty as those in couple-parent families.

## One-person households

Just over one in four households today contains only one person (compared to about one in twenty in 1901). Around half of these households are made up of older adults in their sixties and above (over pensionable age). In 1971, a larger proportion than this (two-thirds) was made up of adults over pensionable age. This means there is a growth in the number of younger people living alone.

---

**Activity**

Refer to the previous section. Fill in the blanks in the following passage, using *some* of the following terms: nuclear family; extended family; classic extended family; modified extended family; beanpole family; lone-parent family; reconstituted family; symmetrical family; civil partnership; bigamy; patriarchal; forced marriage; monogamy; serial monogamy; arranged marriages; polygamy; polyandry; gay families.

Each term should only be used once, and each dash below represents one word.

The ___ ___ means just one or two parent(s) and children, living together in one household. This is sometimes called the two-generation family, because it contains only the two generations of parents and children. The ___ ___ is a grouping consisting of all kin. The ___ ___ ___ consists of several related nuclear families or family members who live in the same household, street or area and who see one another regularly.

The ___ ___ ___ is one in which related nuclear families, although they may be living far apart, maintain close relations made possible by modern communications, such as car travel, Skype or social media. This is probably the most common type of family arrangement in Britain today.

The ___ ___ is a form of the extended family in a pattern which is long and thin (many generations, but few people in each generation), reflecting the fact that people are living longer but are having fewer children.

The ___ ___ ___ is today largely a result of the rise in the divorce rate, although it may also arise from the death of a partner, the breakdown of cohabiting relationships, or a simple lack of desire to form a couple relationship. Nine out of ten of these families are headed by women.

The ___ ___ is one in which one or both partners have had children in a previous relationship, and they bring these children with them to a new couple relationship.

It remains a popular impression that the most usual kind of family in contemporary Britain is the ___ ___ in which both partners are likely to be wage earners, and to share the housework and childcare. However, some argue that men still dominate in the family and make most of the decisions, and it therefore remains ___.

___ is the only legal form of marriage allowed in Britain. In modern Britain, there are high rates of divorce, remarriage and separation of cohabiting couples, and some people keep marrying, divorcing or cohabiting with a series of different partners. The term ___ ___ is sometimes used to describe these patterns, and has been described as 'one at a time, one after the other and they don't last long'.

___ ___ are those where parents organize the marriages of their children to try to ensure a good match with partners of a similar background and status. This custom is coming under pressure in Britain as younger people in these groups demand greater freedom to choose their own marriage partner in the same way as in wider society.

While marrying a second partner without divorcing the first is a crime in Britain, in many societies it is perfectly acceptable to have more than one marriage partner at the same time. ___ is a general term used to describe this form of marriage.

# ALTERNATIVES TO THE FAMILY

Most societies in the world have some established arrangements for the production, rearing and socialization of children, and the nuclear family is probably the most common arrangement for this. However, it would be wrong to assume that the conventional nuclear family is a universal institution. This is particularly the case today, when new forms of relationship are developing, and when the idea of a lifetime relationship is increasingly disappearing as people have a series of partners during their lifetimes, abandon traditional styles of family living, or simply choose to live alone in one-person households.

The following examples illustrate some alternative arrangements which suggest the family is not always the main way of bringing up children – nor does it necessarily have to be the family that does this.

## Foster care and children's homes

It is worth remembering that a considerable number of 'looked-after' children – around 75,000 in England in 2018 – are brought up in care, looked after by foster parents or in residential children's homes. This does demonstrate that the link between natural parents and the rearing of children can be, and sometimes is, broken.

## Communes

Communes are self-contained and self-supporting communities. They developed in Western Europe, the UK and the USA in the 1960s, among groups of people wanting to develop alternative lifestyles to conventional society because of the political or religious beliefs they held.

Communes often try to develop an alternative style of living and a kind of alternative household, with the emphasis on collective living rather than individual family units. A number of adults and children all aim to live and work together, with children being seen as the responsibility of the group as a whole rather than of biological parents. Many communes tended to be very short-lived, and only a few remain in Britain today.

## The kibbutz

The Israeli kibbutz is a form of commune, and is one of the most famous and successful attempts to establish an alternative to the family. Here, the emphasis is on collective child rearing, with the community as a whole taking over the tasks of the family. In the early kibbutzim (plural of 'kibbutz'), children were kept apart from their natural parents for much of the time and brought up in the Children's House by *metapelets* – a kind of 'professional parent' combining the roles of nurse, housemother and educator. Children were seen as the 'children of the kibbutz' – they were the responsibility of the community as a whole, which met all of their needs.

In recent years, the more traditional family unit has re-emerged in the kibbutzim, with biological parents and children sharing the same accommodation, but the kibbutz remains one of the most important attempts to find an alternative to conventional family structures.

In Israeli kibbutzim, children from various couples are raised together as the shared responsibility of the whole community

### The Nayar

Among the Nayar of south-west India before the nineteenth century, there was no nuclear family. A woman could have sexual relations with any man she wished (up to a maximum of twelve) and the biological father of children was therefore uncertain. The mother's brother, rather than the biological father, was responsible for looking after the mother and her children. Unlike in Britain – where in most cases the biological parents marry, live together and are responsible for rearing their children – among the Nayar, there was no direct link between having sexual relations, childbearing, child rearing and cohabitation.

### Shared households and 'families of choice'

As discussed later (see page 147), households shared with peers are becoming much more common, particularly among young people, given the high costs of buying or renting their own homes. Such shared households, in which people choose to live and form relationships with a group of people with whom they may have closer relations than with their families of birth, might be regarded as a 'family of choice' and an alternative to the conventional idea of what a family is. However, there is not much evidence as yet of such arrangements providing a secure alternative means of bringing up children, though the potential is there for them to do so.

## CONSENSUS AND CONFLICT THEORIES OF THE ROLE OF THE FAMILY IN SOCIETY

Consensus and conflict theories or perspectives were considered in chapter 2 (see pages 50–9). This section will apply these competing theories to the role of the family in society.

### The consensus approach of functionalism

The consensus perspective of functionalism sees the family as a vital organ maintaining the health of the 'body' of society. Functionalists argue the family plays a key role in meeting society's functional prerequisites – basic needs that must be met if societies are to survive.

Murdock argued there are four main functions of the family, which he argued were so necessary that some form of the nuclear family was found in every society to carry them out. These functions are:

- *sexual* – providing a socially approved context for the expression of sexuality, and thereby binding couples together in stable relationships.
- *reproduction* – providing a stable and safe unit for the reproduction and rearing of children.
- *socialization and education* – providing primary socialization, whereby children learn socially acceptable behaviour and the culture of their society. This helps to build the shared ideas and beliefs (value consensus) that functionalists regard as important to maintaining a stable and harmonious society.
- *economic* – providing food and shelter for family members.

Parsons (1959) focused on the family in the United States. Unlike Murdock, he argued that the nuclear family is not the only form of arrangement possible for carrying out the functions Murdock identified. Parsons suggested there was a process of **structural differentiation**. This means that, as societies develop, families lose some of their functions as more specialized institutions emerge to take over or share them, as suggested in table 3.1. This is commonly referred to as the 'loss of functions debate'.

> **Structural differentiation** The process of more specialized institutions emerging to take over functions that were once performed by a single institution. For example, some once-traditional functions of the family have been transferred to the education system and the welfare state.

### Table 3.1 The loss of functions debate

| Traditional functions of the family | How they have changed |
|---|---|
| *Reproduction.* Having children was traditionally seen as the main reason for marriage, as a means of passing on family property and providing a healthy future workforce. | In Britain in 2017, nearly half (48 per cent) of children were born outside marriage / civil partnership. These changes are explained later in this chapter. |
| The family and kinship network traditionally played a major role in *maintaining and caring for dependent children* – housing, clothing and feeding those children who were still unable to look after themselves. | The modern nuclear family is less dependent on relatives for help and assistance in maintaining and caring for children. Welfare benefits, such as social security and child tax credits, and social services all help parents to maintain their children. |
| The family provided most of the *help and care for the young, the old, the sick and the poor* during periods of illness, unemployment and other crises. | This has become shared with the state through the NHS and the social services. Homes for the elderly, hospitals, welfare clinics, GPs, state pensions, unemployment benefits and income support reduce the dependence on kin for money and support. |
| The *primary socialization and social control of children.* The family is where society's new recruits first learn the basic values and norms of the culture of the society they will grow up in. For example, it is in the family that children first learn the difference between what is seen as right and wrong, good and bad behaviour, and the acceptance of parental and other adult authority. | The family still retains the major responsibility for the socialization of very young children, but the increase in the number of children's centres, child-minders, pre-schools and playgroups, and free nursery education has meant this is no longer restricted to the family. The state educational system now helps the family with the socialization of school-age children, and the media also play an important role. |

## Table 3.1 (continued)

| Traditional functions of the family | How they have changed |
|---|---|
| • The family used to be one of the only sources of *education* for young people in Britain. Before compulsory schooling was provided by the state in Britain from 1880, many children from working-class families were very poorly educated by today's standards, and illiteracy rates were extremely high. | • The education of children has been mainly taken over by the state, and is now primarily the responsibility of professional teachers rather than parents. However, the family continues to play an important socializing and supporting role in preparing a child for school, and encouraging and supporting her or him during school years. The family still has a major effect on a child's level of educational achievement. |

### Activity

1 Go carefully through table 3.1 above on the traditional functions or responsibilities of the family and how they have changed. Make a list summarizing these changes under two main headings: (a) the tasks traditionally performed by the family; and (b) who performs these functions today: family, or government and state, or shared between them.
2 Identify two ways in which the family provides for the well-being of its members.
3 Do you think the changes that have occurred in the family's functions have made it more or less important in society today? Back up your viewpoint with evidence.
4 Imagine all families were banned by law tomorrow. What tasks currently carried out in your own family would someone else have to perform? Who would do these tasks, do you think?
5 Consider all the ways you can think of in which the family a child is born into might affect the chances she or he gets in life, such as in health, education and job opportunities. Be sure you explain the connection between family background and the life chances you identify.

Parsons argued that, despite structural differentiation and the loss or sharing of some functions, the family retains two basic functions that are found in all families in every society:

- *The primary socialization of children* – the passing on of society's culture. Parsons argues that society would cease to exist if the new generation were not socialized into accepting society's basic norms and values by the family. Parsons argues that families are factories producing human personalities.
- *The stabilization of human personalities* In industrial societies, there are many possible causes of stress and anxiety, such as the need for

work and money, and the pressure to achieve success and support the family. Parsons suggests the family acts like a 'warm bath', relieving stress and providing emotional warmth and security to help stabilize people's personalities. This is achieved by the **sexual (or gendered) division of labour** in the family, with men and women performing different roles:

— The *expressive role* (see glossary box) is performed by women, who fulfil themselves by providing warmth, security and emotional support to their children and male partner.

— The *instrumental role* (see glossary box) is performed by men, who fulfil themselves by acting as the family breadwinner, earning money to support the family. The male partner's instrumental role leads to stress and anxiety. However, the wife's expressive role relieves this tension by providing love and understanding.

The sexual division of labour into expressive and instrumental roles therefore contributes to the stabilization of human personalities, and a generally more harmonious society.

## The New Right (or neoliberal) approach to the family

The New Right (or neoliberal) view of society was outlined on pages 52–3 and 54 in chapter 2. Its views of the role, importance and functions of the traditional family unit in society are very similar to the functionalist approach.

The New Right emphasizes, like the functionalists, the importance of:

- the traditional opposite-sex married-couple family and the kinship network in securing social stability
- the traditional gendered division of labour: it sees expressive roles for women and instrumental roles for men as the best means of bringing up children to become conformist, responsible adults
- a return to traditional family values.

The New Right sees traditional family life as under threat from social changes such as the rising divorce rate, more stepfamilies, more lone parenthood, cohabitation as an alternative to the commitment of marriage, births outside marriage, gay marriage or civil partnership, and welfare-state policies that support relationships outside the conventional nuclear family.

It argues these changes and the decline of traditional family life undermine social stability and contribute to wider social problems, such as:

- uncontrollable children, a rising lack of respect and antisocial behaviour among the young.

**Sexual (or gendered) division of labour** The division of tasks into 'men's jobs' and 'women's jobs'.

**Expressive role** The nurturing, caring and emotional role, often seen by functionalists as the natural role for women in the family, linked to women's biology.

**Instrumental role** The provider/breadwinner role, often seen by functionalists as the natural role for men in the family.

- lack of discipline in school, school exclusion and educational underachievement
- alcohol and drug abuse, and crime
- the emergence among poor families of a dependency culture and a work-shy underclass fiddling the benefit system (see pages 54, 484–5 and 486–7). This dependency culture is passed on to children through socialization, and living off welfare benefits becomes to them an acceptable and normal way of life.

The New Right argues that these arise from inadequate socialization and supervision of children, and the lack of successful male role models providing discipline for young people in fatherless families. It therefore argues for a return to traditional family values. Governments should adopt social policies to reverse the decline of the traditional family unit, such as the reduction of welfare-state benefits to non-conventional family units, like lone parents. This is to make alternative means of living or bringing up children less attractive options, and to support and strengthen conventional nuclear family units.

## Criticisms of the functionalist / New Right perspective

- *It is based on a very traditional (largely American) middle-class family.* It does not consider the wide diversity of family and household types in which people live. These are considered on pages 137–48 below.
- *It paints very rosy pictures of family life*, presenting it as a harmonious and integrated institution, but ignores the harmful effects caused by a **dysfunctional family**. This is a family which doesn't work as it should – for example, where children are not properly socialized, where there is constant conflict, and where there is a 'darker side' to family life, such as violence against women, and child neglect and abuse (see pages 191–8 below).
- *It's out of date.* Parsons's view of the instrumental and expressive roles of men and women is very old-fashioned. In most families today, both partners are likely to be income-earning breadwinners and both are likely to be playing expressive and instrumental roles at various times, especially if men are taking on greater responsibilities for childcare, as we are sometimes led to believe.
- *It ignores the exploitation of women, which feminists consider* (see below). Women suffer from the sexual division of labour in the family. For example, their responsibility for housework and childcare undermines their position in paid employment, through restricted working hours because of the need to prepare children's meals, take them to and from school, and look after them when they are ill.

**Dysfunctional family** A family which doesn't work as it should, causing physical and psychological harm affecting the safety and development of children and other family members, particularly women.

## The conflict approach of Marxism

Marxist conflict theory emphasizes the way the family reproduces social inequality from one generation to the next. The family is concerned not with building value consensus as the functionalists suggest, but with settling down the social conflict that is bound to appear in unequal societies. It teaches its members to submit to the values and beliefs of the wealthy and powerful, and not to be critical of the society around them.

### *Reproducing labour power*

Marxists see the family's main role in society as reproducing **labour power** – people's capacity to work. The family supplies the capitalist class of employers with a readily available and passive labour force for its factories and offices. The family achieves this in five ways, by:

1  *providing a place where children can be born and raised* with a sense of security and safety, and ensuring that a new workforce is produced.
2  *producing and maintaining labour free of cost to the capitalists* through the domestic labour (housework and childcare) of (usually) women, who are not paid for their work in rearing children and looking after male partners.
3  *socializing children into the **dominant ideology*** – the ideas and beliefs of the most powerful and wealthy groups in society – and preparing them for the necessity of working for a living, and the routines of work, such as the need for punctuality and obedience. Through day-to-day relationships in the family where parents have power and control over their children, and men generally over women, people come to accept, often without questioning them, the power inequalities they will face as adults in capitalist society. The family therefore lays the groundwork for a submissive and obedient workforce.
4  *the pressure put on parents to provide material comforts and good life chances for their children*. This helps to keep people in unsatisfying, boring and unrewarding jobs. It is harder for workers to go on strike for higher pay if there is a family to support, because it might mean cuts in the living standards of themselves and their children. This discourages workers from taking action that might disrupt the system.
5  *providing a private sphere and 'safety valve'*. Zaretsky (1976) suggests the family appears to be a private sphere or 'sanctuary' in which adults can enjoy a personal life and be valued as individuals, have some measure of control over their lives, and enjoy the feel-good emotional factors of friendship, love and support. The family therefore provides an outlet or 'safety valve' to release people from the tedium, frustration and lack of

**Labour power**
People's capacity to work. According to Marxism, labour power is sold to the owners of the means of production in exchange for wages.

**Dominant ideology** The ideas and beliefs of the most powerful and wealthy groups in society, which influence the ideas and beliefs of the rest of society.

**Alienation**
The feeling of a lack of power and control over their lives that many people experience. Marxists link this to oppression and exploitation in capitalist societies, and the unfulfilling work that people have to perform.

power and control at work, and over their daily lives, that many experience (what Marx referred to as **alienation**). This enables members of the workforce to go to work each day with their ability to work (their labour power) renewed. This helps to stabilize capitalism by undermining opposition to it.

Zaretsky argues that the idea that the family is a private place separate from the economy and the world of work is an illusion. He believes the family acts as a cushion against the effects of capitalism, but at the same time it props up the system. It does this in two ways:

- *By producing future generations of workers* (as described above), mainly through the unpaid, and stressful, domestic labour of women.
- *By being an important unit of consumption* Families buy and consume large quantities of goods and services produced by the capitalist system (houses, food, toys, household goods, cars, holidays, etc.), often in stressful competition with other families, to improve their own and their children's life chances (compared to their neighbours). This bolsters the profits of those who produce these products.

## Criticisms of the Marxist perspective

- It suggests a very romanticized view of the family, without family conflicts and rows, or dysfunctional families.
- As feminists have pointed out (see below), it is very much a male Marxist perspective on the family, as much of the work that might make the family a haven and refuge is done by, and at the expense of, women.
- It's out-of-date, and tends to be based on a conventional instrumental/expressive model of the family, in which the man is the primary breadwinner, and the woman is primarily concerned with the home. It doesn't really take into account that most women nowadays are in paid employment, and are increasingly more successful than men in both education and the labour market.
- The idea that families exist basically to reproduce labour power and pass on the dominant ideology ignores the many other things that go on in families. For example, not all parents will simply pass on the dominant ideas to their children, nor expect them simply to prepare for the world of work. There is an emphasis on love, affection and personal growth and fulfilment in many contemporary families.
- Day-to-day relationships in the family are less likely today to create an unquestioning and obedient workforce. Children have much more status and power in the family than they used to, and families have become more child-centred (see pages 185–8). Children are empowered by knowledge and experience gained through exposure

to a much wider range of socializing experiences outside the family, such as education and the media – particularly social media and the internet – and are not simply fodder for employers, as some Marxists might suggest.

## The conflict approach of feminism

Feminist writers see the family as a unit based on patriarchy, reproducing and supporting a society in which men have most of the power, status and authority.

Delphy and Leonard (1992), writing from a feminist perspective, believe that the family has a central role in maintaining patriarchy. They see the family as an 'economy in miniature', in which women are exploited through unpaid domestic labour, which is for the benefit of men: women cook men's meals, look after men's children, and clean men's homes. This is just like the wider economy, in which workers work for the benefit of the profits of capitalists. Women in the family are generally in a more subordinate position, with their male partners having more power and control over family resources. Relations in the family are therefore patriarchal and they reflect, maintain and reproduce patriarchy in wider society.

Feminists make the following criticisms of the family, which suggest women have much to lose from its present organization.

- *The dual burden and the triple shift* Women still have most of the responsibility for housework and childcare, even when they are in full-time paid employment (this is discussed on pages 179–84 below). They have a **dual burden** of paid work and unpaid housework – two jobs to the man's one – and work a '**triple shift**': time spent in paid work, time spent on domestic labour, and time spent on '**emotional work**'. Delphy and Leonard describe emotional work as concerned with maintaining the bonds of affection, moral support, friendship and love which make family members feel good, with a sense of belonging and feeling they are cared for. The dual burden and the triple shift mean that in many cases, quite literally, a woman's work is never done.
- *Housework is, in fact, unpaid labour.* Legal and General's 2015 'Value of a Parent' research found that the value of the work that Mums do for unpaid childcare and household tasks alone is £29,535 a year – that's £567 a week.
- *It is still mainly women who give up paid work (or suffer from lost/restricted job opportunities) to look after children, the old, the sick and male partners.* Women still take most of the responsibility for childcare and

**Dual burden**
The two jobs of paid employment and unpaid domestic labour taken on, nearly always, by women.

**Triple shift**
The three periods of working time spent, nearly always by women, on paid employment, unpaid domestic labour and emotional work.

**Emotional work**
Tasks concerned with maintaining the bonds of affection, moral support, friendship and love.

Many female partners in couple families now often have the dual burden of two jobs of paid work and unpaid domestic labour (including childcare), and work a triple shift of paid employment, domestic labour and emotional work, compared to their male partner's one.

child rearing, and are most likely to get the blame from society if these tasks are not performed properly.

- *Women's position in the family remains a primary source of discrimination and disadvantage in the labour market.* Employers are often unwilling to employ or promote married women – particularly in jobs with high levels of pay and responsibility, for example – in case they get pregnant and take maternity leave. Marriage poses no such problem for men.
- *The family is a major source of gender role socialization* (see pages 27–30), which teaches girls to believe that they are in a secondary position to boys and men in many areas of social life.
- *It is still mainly women who make sacrifices* to buy the children clothes, and to make sure other family members are properly fed.
- *Women are less likely than men to make the most important decisions* in the family (see pages 183–4).
- *Women are far more likely than men to be the victims of serious domestic violence* (see pages 195–6).

### Activity

1 Describe two ways in which men might gain from family life at the expense of women.
2 Explain why functionalists argue that nuclear families are important, and identify two criticisms of this.

## Criticisms of feminist approaches

- Women's roles are not the same in all families. Many families now consist of dual-earner couples, with both partners in paid employment, with consequently more sharing of housework, childcare and decision-making in recognition of this.
- These perspectives assume that women are passive victims in the family, and do not have any choices. Women's inequality in the family may be the result of some women's personal choices and preferences, and some men and women may have different career aspirations, life goals and priorities (though feminists might argue that this is because they have been socialized into it).
- More women are working and have independent incomes, and this means they may have more power in the family than some feminist writers imply.
- Around two-thirds of divorces are initiated by women, which shows that some women can, and do, escape from relationships which are unsatisfactory, exploitative or oppressive.

## Table 3.2 Consensus and conflict perspectives on the family

| Functionalism / New Right (consensus approach) | Marxism (conflict approach) | Feminism (conflict approach) |
|---|---|---|
| The family meets the basic needs of society and all its members. It socializes children into a culture based on value consensus, leading to social harmony and stability. | The family meets the needs of capitalism by socializing children into the dominant ideology, leading to a submissive and obedient workforce for capitalism. | The family meets the needs of patriarchy by socializing children into traditional gender roles, with men as 'breadwinners' and women having responsibility for housework and childcare. |
| The family provides security for the conception, birth and nurture of new members of society. | The family is responsible for the reproduction of labour power for capitalism. | The family is responsible for the reproduction of patriarchal inequality between women and men. |
| The family is a supportive and generally harmonious and happy social institution. | The family is an oppressive institution that stunts the development of human personalities and individuality. | The family is an oppressive institution that dominates, controls and exploits women for the benefit of men. There is a 'dark side' to family life that includes violence and abuse against women and children. |
| The sexual (or gendered) division of labour in the family (instrumental and expressive roles) stabilizes adult personalities. This helps to maintain a stable society. | The male's role as wage earner maintains the family, pays for the reproduction of labour power, and acts as a strong control on workers' behaviour in the workplace. The family is a unit of consumption, and provides a temporary refuge from alienation. These help to maintain the stability of an unequal, exploitative capitalist society. | The sexual division of labour in the family exploits women, through their dual burden and triple shift. Women's responsibility for unpaid domestic labour and childcare undermine their position in paid employment and increase dependency on men. It therefore maintains an unequal patriarchal society. |

Table 3.2 shows a summary contrasting consensus and conflict approaches to the family.

# FAMILY AND HOUSEHOLD DIVERSITY

## Oakley and the conventional family

**Conventional family** A nuclear family composed of a legally married couple living with their children.

Writing from a feminist perspective, Oakley (1982) explored the idea of what she called the 'conventional family'. She defined conventional families as 'nuclear families composed of legally married couples, voluntarily choosing the parenthood of one or more children' (this was before civil partnerships). She suggested that this was an 'official stereotype', but even then – nearly forty years ago – she concluded that this stereotype of the conventional family was becoming 'increasingly archaic [very old-fashioned and out-of-date] and that ... certain groups in the community may be moving towards a more open appraisal of other ways of living – both in and without families'.

Nevertheless, even in the second decade of the twenty-first century and after dramatic changes in family life, the popular impression that many people have of the family in Britain is still that of the conventional family. This takes the form of what has been described as the '**cereal packet family**'.

**Cereal packet family** The stereotype of the best and most desirable family found in the media and advertising. It is generally seen as involving first-time married opposite-sex parents and their own natural children, living together, with the father as the primary breadwinner and the mother as primarily concerned with the home and children.

## The 'cereal packet' family

This is the stereotype often promoted in advertising and other parts of the media, with 'family-size' breakfast cereals, toothpaste and a wide range of other consumer goods. This popular happy family image – reflected in functionalist and New Right ideas of the family – often gives the impression that most people live in a typical family with the following features.

- It is a privatized, nuclear family unit consisting of two opposite-sex parents living with one or two of their own natural dependent children.
- These parents are married to one another, and ideally neither of them has been married before.
- The husband is the main breadwinner and responsible for family discipline, with the wife staying at home and primarily concerned with housework and childcare, or perhaps doing some part-time paid employment to supplement the family income.

This image also often includes ideas that this family is based on romantic love, as well as love of children (particularly maternal love), and that it is a safe and harmonious refuge from an uncaring outside world.

**Family diversity**
The wide range of different family types and family lifestyles.

This stereotype of the typical family is very mistaken, because there is a wide range of different family types and family lifestyles, of all shapes and sizes, in contemporary Britain. This is known as **family diversity**.

## Why is the cereal-packet stereotype misleading?

The growing diversity of relationships in which people in Britain live shows that traditional family life is being eroded as people constantly develop new forms of relationship and choose to live in different ways. The meaning of 'family' and 'family life' is therefore changing for a substantial number of parents and children.

*Households and families*  Figure 3.2 shows the different types of household in the UK in 2017, and what percentages of people were living in them. In 2017:

- only 29 per cent of households contained a couple with dependent or non-dependent children, and only 47 per cent of people lived in such a household
- 28 per cent of households consisted of one person living alone
- at least 70 per cent of households had no dependent children in them
- 11 per cent of people lived in lone-parent families, and 10 per cent of households were lone-parent families
- conventional families (opposite-sex married couples with children) made up just 35 per cent of all families.

This alone shows that the cereal-packet image of the nuclear family does not represent the arrangement in which most people in the UK live.

*Families with dependent children*  Figure 3.3 examines families with dependent children. In 2017:

- 22 per cent of such families were lone-parent families, with nearly nine out of ten of them headed by women
- only 61 per cent of families with dependent children were headed by a married couple (the rest were either lone parents, or civil-partnered or cohabiting couples).

This doesn't mean that even most of these married-couple families conformed to the conventional cereal-packet stereotype:

- A number were reconstituted families, in which one or both partners were previously married. About 11 per cent of couple families with dependent children are now stepfamilies.

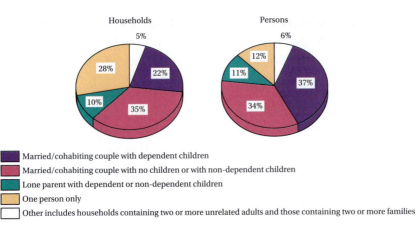

**Figure 3.2** Households and people, by type of household, United Kingdom, 2017

*Source:* data from Labour Force Survey Household datasets, Office for National Statistics

Households
5%
28%
10%
35%
22%

Persons
6%
12%
11%
34%
37%

■ Married/cohabiting couple with dependent children
■ Married/cohabiting couple with no children or with non-dependent children
■ Lone parent with dependent or non-dependent children
■ One person only
□ Other includes households containing two or more unrelated adults and those containing two or more families

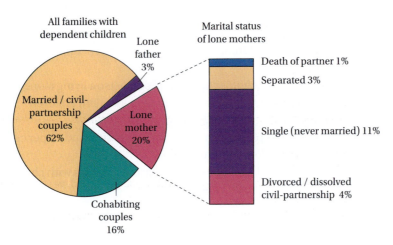

**Figure 3.3** Families with dependent children, by family type and, for lone mothers, by marital status, United Kingdom, 2017

*Source:* data from Labour Force Survey Household datasets, Office for National Statistics

All families with dependent children

Lone father 3%

Married / civil-partnership couples 62%

Lone mother 20%

Cohabiting couples 16%

Marital status of lone mothers

Death of partner 1%

Separated 3%

Single (never married) 11%

Divorced / dissolved civil-partnership 4%

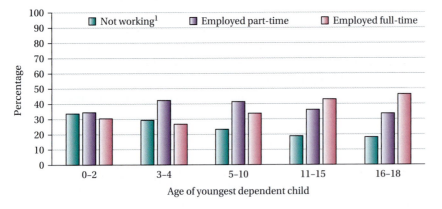

**Figure 3.4** Working patterns (in paid employment) of women with dependent children living with them, United Kingdom, 2019

[1] 'Not working' includes: unemployed; not seeking work; and looking after family home.

*Source:* adapted from *Working and Workless Households in the UK: January to March 2019*, Office for National Statistics

■ Not working[1]  ■ Employed part-time  ■ Employed full-time

Percentage

Age of youngest dependent child
0–2  3–4  5–10  11–15  16–18

- Most of these families were dual-earner families, in which both parents were working. In 2019, around 85 per cent of couples with dependent children were both either in or looking for paid employment. As figure 3.4 shows, large numbers of mothers with dependent children work in paid employment, with the proportion working full-time increasing as children get older.

The cereal-packet happy-family stereotype of a working father married to a home-based mother caring for two small children now makes up probably around 5 per cent of all households.

### Activity

Refer to figure 3.2.
1 What percentage of households in 2017 consisted of one person only?
2 What percentage of people in 2017 were living in households consisting of a married or cohabiting couple with no children or with non-dependent children?

Refer to figure 3.3.
3 In 2017, what percentage of all families with dependent children were lone-parent families?
4 What percentage of families with dependent children were headed by a lone mother who was separated?
5 What was the main cause of lone motherhood?

Refer to figure 3.4.
6 About what percentage of mothers whose youngest child was aged 0–2 years were not working in paid employment in 2019?
7 Identify two trends which occur as the youngest dependent child gets older.
8 What does figure 3.4 suggest might be the main restriction on mothers with young children working in paid employment? Suggest ways this restriction might be overcome.
9 How do you think having young dependent children might affect the working lives of fathers? Give reasons for your answer.
10 Describe two reasons why many people seem to believe that the cereal-packet family is the most common type of family.

## Five types of family diversity

Rapoport and Rapoport (1982) were pioneering family researchers, who drew on secondary sources (existing studies of families) to describe five different aspects of family diversity: organizational; cultural; social class; life course; and cohort. These are applied and updated below.

The cereal-packet stereotype of the conventional family is very misleading, and conceals the wide diversity, or range, of family types and household arrangements in contemporary Britain

## 1 Organizational diversity

Organizational diversity refers to organizational differences within and between families. For example, there are differences between families in the way they organize the **domestic division of labour** – how they divide up tasks within the home – and whether or not they are dual-earner families where both partners work in paid employment. There are also differences in family structure, such as lone-parent families, reconstituted families, and nuclear and extended families.

Six examples of organizational diversity in family structure in contemporary Britain were considered earlier (see pages 120–3).

(a)  The privatized nuclear family
(b)  The modified extended family
(c)  The classic extended family
(d)  The beanpole family
(e)  The lone-parent family
(f)  The reconstituted family

> **Domestic division of labour**
> The division of roles, responsibilities and work tasks within a family or household.

## 2 Cultural diversity

Cultural diversity refers to the way ethnicity or religion affects family structures and lifestyles arising from different cultural beliefs and values. The way religion may affect families is shown in Catholicism, where opposition to divorce and remarriage, and disapproval of contraception, may lead to Catholics separating rather than divorcing in broken marriages, and therefore cohabiting with a new partner rather than remarrying. Disapproval of contraception may lead to larger families.

The effect of ethnicity on family diversity is shown in the following two examples.

- *British South Asian families* (originating from Pakistan, Bangladesh and India) tend to have more extended and close-knit family relationships than White British families. Such families are commonly patriarchal in structure, with seniority going to the eldest male, and males in general. British Pakistani and Bangladeshi women have the highest rates of marriage in the UK, and a very high proportion of British South Asians with a partner are in a formal marriage. In many ways, the traditional British cereal-packet family stereotype of a working male married to a home-based female who has the main responsibility for domestic labour – looking after the home and family – is more likely to be found among British Pakistanis and Bangladeshis than any other ethnic group. This is, however, changing among younger people, especially young women, as they become more ambitious for themselves in the labour market, and resistant to cultural traditions. Divorce rates are low in such families because of strong social disapproval and a wide support network of kin for families under stress. Arranged marriages are still common in such communities.

- *British Black African and Black Caribbean (African-Caribbean) families* often take the form of a **matrifocal family**, in which the mother heads the family and is in many cases the main breadwinner.

**Matrifocal family**
Where mothers head families and fathers play a less prominent role in the home and in bringing up children.

Lone parenthood is higher among African-Caribbean British mothers than any other ethnic group in the UK. According to the Runneymede Trust (http://bit.ly/2ILi8cU), African-Caribbean fathers are twice as likely as White fathers to live apart from their children. This does not mean African-Caribbean fathers are not concerned with their children, and, according to the Fatherhood Institute (http://bit.ly/2y9mAhw), African-Caribbean fathers often continue to play an important role in childcare and spend a good deal of time with their children, maintaining strong relationships with them. There are also lower levels of marriage and higher levels of cohabitation, though just over half of mothers who are Black Caribbean are married when the child is born, compared with about 70 per cent of mothers who are White.

These patterns partly reflect a cultural tradition based in slavery, and now high rates of black male unemployment and lower rates of pay, leading to many men's reduced ability to support families. African-Caribbean families often have a female network of friends and kin to support women with children.

## 3 Social-class diversity

Social-class diversity refers to the influence of social stratification – social class – on family structure, organization and lifestyles. A family's position in the social-class system – the differences in income and wealth between upper-class, middle-class and working-class families – leads to differences in lifestyle between families, for example in the consumer goods they can buy, the types of homes they live in, their ability to afford help with domestic labour, and financial support they can offer to other family members.

The Rapoports also found that middle-class families have a little more equality between partners in the domestic division of labour (see pages 179–83) than working-class families, and there were differences in the way they reared their children – for example, middle-class families placed greater emphasis on reasoning and discussing with their children, whereas the working class emphasized obedience to parents.

Classic extended families are still sometimes found in traditional working-class communities, but modified extended families are now more common in the working class. In Swansea, for example, Nicola Charles found that classic extended families were practically extinct, even in the working class, but modified extended families were common, with working-class people more likely to live near their families. They were also likely to remain in the same home for much longer periods than middle-class people. The privatized nuclear family tends to be the most common form of middle-class family.

## 4 Life-course (or life-cycle) diversity

**Life-course** diversity refers to the way families may change as they go through their life cycle of significant events that occur during their lives. These include, for example, events such as partners having children; children growing older and eventually leaving home; partners separating and forming new relationships; people retiring, growing older and having grandchildren.

All these factors mean the family will be constantly changing. For instance, levels of family income will change as children move from dependence to independence, levels of domestic labour and childcare will differ, and levels of participation in paid employment will alter, particularly for women, depending on the absence or presence of children and their age. This means there will always be a diversity of family and household types at different stages of the family life cycle. Figure 3.5 shows an example of a possible family life course.

> **Life course**
> The various significant events individuals experience during the course of their lives – e.g. marriage or cohabitation, becoming a parent, divorce and retirement.

## 5 Cohort diversity

Cohort diversity (a **cohort** is a group of people with a shared characteristic) refers to groups of families who come from different historical periods, and therefore pass through the family life course at different times.

> **Cohort** A group of people with a shared characteristic.

**Figure 3.5** The life course of a family

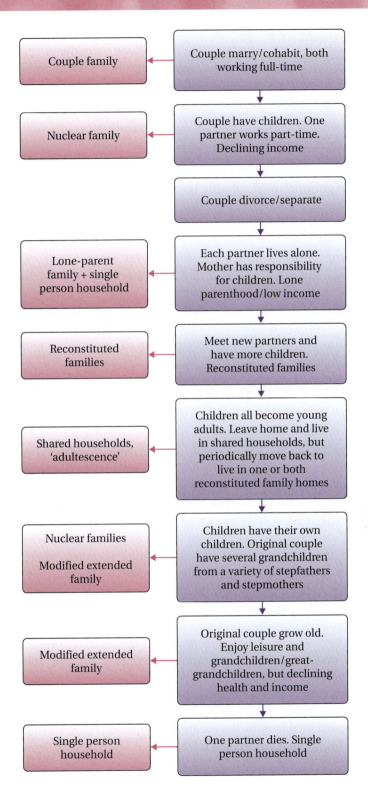

Younger families may be accustomed to, and accepting of, issues such as abortion, sex outside marriage, cohabitation, divorce, lone parenthood and gay and lesbian families. Older families may remember times when many or all of these carried a severe social **stigma** – extreme disapproval in the eyes of others – or were even illegal.

> **Stigma** A label or mark of shame or disgrace showing strong disapproval of behaviour that is seen as wrong, abnormal or immoral – e.g. the shame (stigma) attached to having a criminal record.

## Other dimensions of family diversity

There are two further dimensions of family diversity to consider – regional diversity, and the growing trend towards boomerang families and other family-like households.

### Regional diversity

Regional diversity refers to the way family life differs in different geographical locations around the country. There are distinctive patterns of family life in different areas of Britain. For example, there is a high proportion of elderly couples living in coastal areas; older industrial areas and very traditional rural communities tend to have more extended families; and the inner cities have a higher proportion of families in poverty, lone-parent families and ethnic-minority families.

### Boomerang families, adult-kids, the 'clipped wing' generation, kippers, shared households and 'families of choice'

Young people are now less likely to follow the traditional route of living at home, leaving school, going into a job or higher education, and then settling down into an adult role of living alone or in a married or cohabiting couple relationship in their own homes. Increasingly, they are adopting a wider range of living arrangements before or instead of forming couple relationships later in life. Postmodernists (see page 49) see this as part of the growing individual choice and diversity found in contemporary societies, where identity is now freely chosen according to individual taste and lifestyle preferences, without the constraints arising from tradition and norms of what is socially acceptable.

*Adult-kids, the 'clipped wing' generation and kippers*  In 2017, one in three young men, and one in five young women (aged 20 to 34) were still living with their parents – around 25 per cent more than in 1996. Some of these 'adult-kids' live with their parents because they can't afford to rent or buy their own homes. This has been called the 'clipped wing' generation, as it has been unable to fly the family nest. But others are staying through choice. This group is sometimes referred to as 'kippers' – 'kids in parents' pockets' – as it's cheaper, easier and often more comfortable to live at home. Even by their early thirties (aged 31–4), around one in ten men and about one in twenty-six women are still living with their parents. This transitional period between youth and independent adulthood has been described as 'kidulthood' ('kid' + 'adulthood') or 'adultescence' ('adult' + 'adolescence').

*The boomerang generation and boomerang families*    The increase in adult children who have left home but then return (sometimes repeatedly) has given rise to the boomerang generation and the boomerang family. Just as a boomerang is designed to be thrown, but returns to the thrower, so there is a growing generation of young adults returning to live with their parents (the boomerang generation), and parents facing returning children after they thought they'd left home for good (boomerang families). This often leads to higher unexpected costs (household bills) for parents, who find they are once again having to support children they thought had become independent and financially self-supporting. It can also re-create once-forgotten family rows – e.g. over adult children who come home at all hours, expect their laundry to be done, leave a mess and argue about housework.

*Shared households and 'families of choice'*    For those who have finally left their family home, shared households are becoming much more common, particularly among young people. There may often be a greater loyalty among young people to their friends than to their family. Such shared households, where people choose to live and form relationships with a group of people with whom they have closer relations than with their families of birth, have therefore sometimes been called 'families of choice'. Such households may involve shared domestic life (cooking, eating and socializing together), and shared leisure, sporting activities and holidays.

These households and families are on the increase because of the high costs of buying or renting houses, the growing numbers of young people entering higher education, and the desire of young people to explore alternative living arrangements rather than simply settling down into a conventional couple household.

## Conclusion on family diversity

This section has suggested that it is very misleading to assume that the cereal-packet image of the conventional family represents the reality of family life in Britain. Only a small minority of families are of this type. It is much more realistic to recognize that families and households are constantly changing. There is a wide diversity, or variety, of family types and

---

**Boomerang generation**
A generation of young adults who return – or keep leaving and returning – to live with their parent(s).

**Boomerang family** A family in which adult children who had left home return to live with their parent(s).

household relationships in contemporary Britain. Trends suggest there will be growing numbers of extended, dual-earner, reconstituted, cohabiting, gay and lesbian, and lone-parent families, and more single-person households.

Figure 3.6 summarizes the various forms of family and household types you might consider as making up the patterns of family diversity in contemporary Britain, some of which will be explored later in the chapter.

# SOCIAL CHANGE AND FAMILY TYPES, STRUCTURES AND RELATIONSHIPS

Many of the forms of family diversity considered above have arisen from a series of social changes which have led to shifts in family structure and organization. Social changes have also affected relationships between family members. These changes will now be examined.

## Demographic change and families

**Demography** is the term used for the study of the characteristics of human populations, such as their size and structure and how these change over time. There have been a number of demographic changes in the population of Britain which have had several effects on family structures.

> **Demography**
> The study of the characteristics of human populations, such as their size and structure and how these change over time.

### Activity

1  Using an imaginary family, your own, or one that you know, describe three ways in which family life might change during its life course. Think about issues like how housework (domestic labour) and childcare, conjugal roles (the roles played by partners in couples living together), caring for family members and paid employment might all change during the life cycle of your chosen family.
2  Suggest *two* ways an increase in divorce might contribute to family diversity in contemporary Britain.
3  Suggest two ways that the lifestyles of upper-class and lower-working-class families might differ.
4  Suggest reasons why the cereal-packet family is most likely to be found in the British Pakistani and Bangladeshi communities.
5  Go to https://goo.gl/Z9p5ob and/or https://goo.gl/a1XJUN. Explain how people from Kihnu island and/or the Mosuo tribe in China show different cultural and family arrangements from families in contemporary Britain.
6  How far is it realistic to talk of a typical family in contemporary Britain? Suggest some arguments, and evidence both for and against.
7  Describe and explain two reasons why adult children may remain in the family instead of leaving home.

**Figure 3.6** Family and household diversity

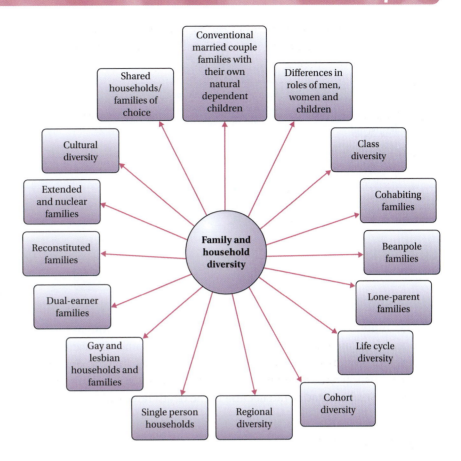

**Death rate** The number of deaths per 1,000 of the population per year.

**Infant mortality rate** The number of deaths of babies in the first year of life per 1,000 live births per year.

**Life expectancy** An estimate of how long people can be expected to live from a particular age. It is commonly estimated from birth, but it can be given from any age.

## *The decline in the death rate and the infant mortality rate, and greater life expectancy*

In 1902, the **death rate** was 18 per 1,000 of the population, and this had declined to around 9 per 1,000 in 2017. The **infant mortality rate** has also fallen, from around 130 per 1,000 live births in 1902 to just under 4 per 1,000 in 2017. Average **life expectancy** has consequently risen. Today, men can expect to live from birth, on average, to around the age of 79, and women to around 83, though of course many will live beyond or less than these average ages. These changes are explained by the following factors:

*Improved hygiene, sanitation and medicine* Public hygiene and sanitation have improved enormously since the early nineteenth century, with the construction of public sewer systems and the provision of clean running water. These changes, together with improved public awareness of hygiene and the causes of infection, have contributed to the elimination in Britain of the great epidemic killer diseases of the past, such as

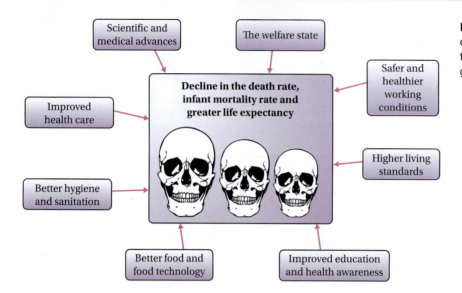

**Figure 3.7** Reasons for the decline in the death rate and the infant mortality rate, and greater life expectancy

cholera, diphtheria and typhoid, which were spread through infected water and food. Advances in medicine and science, such as vaccines and the development of penicillin, antibiotics and other life-saving drugs, and advances in surgery and medical technology, such as transplant surgery, have further contributed to the decline in the death rate, and increased life expectancy.

*Higher living standards and better nutrition*   Higher wages, better food, more amenities and appliances in the home, and greatly improved housing conditions have all assisted in improving the health and life expectancy of the population. Because of improved transportation and food technology, a wider range of more nutritious food is available, with improved storage techniques (such as freezing) making possible the import of a range of foodstuffs, providing more affordable fresh fruit and vegetables all the year round.

*Improved public health and welfare*   There has been a steep rise in state intervention in public welfare, particularly since the establishment of the welfare state in 1945. The NHS, since its foundation in 1948, has provided free and comprehensive healthcare in Britain, and there is much better ante-natal and post-natal care for mothers and babies. More women have children in hospitals today; there are health visitors to check on young babies, and vaccination programmes for babies meaning that many more now survive serious illnesses that would once have killed them. These factors help to explain the decrease in the infant mortality rate. The wide range of welfare benefits available helps to maintain standards of health in times of hardship, and older people in particular are better cared for today, with pensions and a range of services such as home helps, social workers and old people's homes.

*Better health education*   Coupled with these changes has been a growing awareness of nutrition and its importance to health. Improved educational standards generally, and particularly in health education, have led to a much-better-informed public, who demand better hygiene and public health, and welfare legislation and social reforms to improve health. Governments provide national guidance on the promotion of good health and the prevention and treatment of ill health, such as emphasizing the benefits of exercise, giving up smoking, limiting alcohol consumption and eating a balanced diet. NHS Choices (www.nhs.uk/pages/home.aspx) provides online advice on health matters, enabling people to take more control of their own health. National health screening programmes – such as for bowel, cervical and breast cancer, and diabetes – and national vaccination programmes for things like measles, mumps, meningitis, flu and pneumonia have all contributed to the improvement of health.

*Improved working conditions*   Working conditions for most workers improved dramatically in the twentieth century. Technology has taken over some of the more arduous, health-damaging tasks, and factory machinery is often safer than it was 100 years ago. Higher standards of health and safety at work, shorter working hours and more leisure time have all made work physically less demanding, and therefore have reduced risks to health.

## The ageing population

The decline in the death rate and increased life expectancy have been combined with a decline in the **birth rate** and fewer children being born (considered below). This means that the UK, like most Western industrialized countries, today has an ageing population.

**Birth rate** The number of live births per 1,000 of the population per year.

The age structure of the population is therefore changing: the average age of the population is getting higher, with the numbers of those of pension age increasing, while those of working age are shrinking, leading to a greater proportion of older people and a smaller proportion of young people. For example, in 1901, only about 4 per cent were over age 65. By 2018, the proportion over 65 had risen to about 18 per cent, and by 2050, it is expected that one in every four people in the UK will be over the age of 65. Figure 3.8 shows this ageing population between 1901 and what it is projected to be in 2050. The pyramid shape in 1901 shows that there was quite a rapid decline in the proportion of people in each older age group the higher up the pyramid you go, as fewer and fewer people survived to older ages. By 2001 there is more of a bulge in the middle age groups, and by 2050 the older age

Britain has an ageing population. What advantages and disadvantages might there be for families with older, retired relatives?

groups make up a much larger proportion of the population, with almost all age groups taking up similar proportions – the pyramid looks more like a rectangle. A quick glance at the proportion of over 70s in 1901 compared to 2050 shows this clearly.

**Activity**

Look at figure 3.8 and answer the following questions:

1  Approximately what percentage of females were over the age of 80 in 1901?
2  Approximately what percentage of males were aged over 80 in 1901?
3  By approximately how much did the percentage of females in the 70–9 age group increase between 1901 and 2001?
4  About what percentage of females are expected to be over the age of 80 by 2050?
5  Comparing 1901 with 2050, by how much is the percentage of (a) men and (b) women over the age of 60 estimated to increase by 2050?
6  Explain briefly how figure 3.8 shows that the UK has an ageing population.

**Figure 3.8** The ageing population: United Kingdom, 1901–2050

*Source:* Office for National Statistics

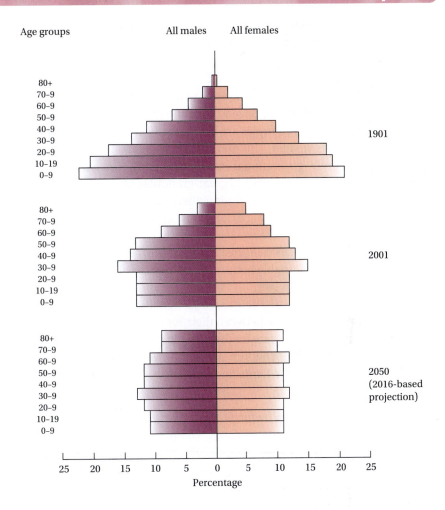

***The consequences of an ageing population***   There is in many cases a long gap between people retiring from work and becoming dependent on others. Men and women will reach state pension age at 66 by 2020, and the state pension age for both men and women looks set to rise in the future, possibly to age 67 by 2028, but it may still change. Many people in their sixties and seventies remain very healthy, active, self-supporting and involved in the lives of their families and communities. However, the growing proportion of elderly people, together with the relatively smaller proportion of young people, leads to a number of potential effects on family and household structures, and on individuals:

● **More one-person households**, as partners die. Many of these will be among older women, who live longer than men.

- **More classic extended families**, as older relatives move in with their younger families. There may be emotional strain and overcrowding if an elderly, and possibly infirm, relative moves in with his or her child's family. This might cause conflict between couples, or between children and grandparents, as well as increasing costs to the family.
- **More beanpole families** (see page 122). At the same time as more people are reaching old age, couples are having fewer children and nuclear families are getting smaller. This means that there is an increase in the number of multi-generational extended families, with children growing up with grandparents and great-grandparents. With fewer children being born in each generation, there are fewer aunts, uncles and cousins in the next, leading to long and thin beanpole family structures.
- **More boomerang families** (see page 147) as young people may have difficulty in finding affordable homes of their own, as older people occupy their homes for longer.
- **The emergence of the sandwich generation**. This is a generation of people (typically aged anywhere between their 30s and 60s) who are sandwiched between having to care for their ageing parents and at the same time supporting their own children. There may well be increased stress and ill health, and financial hardship for these people responsible for the care of two generations.

> **Sandwich generation** A generation of people (typically aged anywhere between their 30s and 60s) who are sandwiched between having to care for their ageing parents and, at the same time, supporting their own children.

This financial hardship can be made worse if one partner has to give up paid work to care for elderly dependants. The practical burdens of caring for the elderly tend to fall mainly on their fully adult children, and particularly women, even though they already carry most of the burden of housework and childcare in their own homes, as discussed later in this chapter. Increasingly, with longer life expectancy, many of these adult children in the sandwich generation are themselves elderly and facing more infirmity; for example, 65-year-olds caring for their 90-year-old parents.

- Elderly relatives can help with childcare and babysitting, and maybe financially (especially in the middle class). With many families in contemporary Britain having both parents in paid employment, grandparents now often play an important role in providing unpaid childcare, such as babysitting services and taking small children to school and collecting them afterwards.
- The growing isolation and loneliness of older people, as friends and partners die and health deteriorates. This may lead to:
  - growing dependence on their neighbours for informal support, or children to visit and support them. This can create problems for moving for work or promotion.

○ a growing risk of **social exclusion** among older people, where they are marginalized (pushed to the edge or margins of society) and are unable to take part in (or excluded from) the everyday life enjoyed by the majority of people in society.

---

**Social exclusion**
The situation where people are marginalized or excluded from full participation in mainstream society, as they lack the resources and opportunities most people take for granted.

---

### THE EMERGENCE OF ACCORDION FAMILIES

One of the consequences of the combination of 'kidulthood', boomerang families, the sandwich generation and the ageing population is the emergence of the 'accordion family'. These are multigenerational families, where fully adult children either don't leave and continue to live with their parents, or keep leaving and returning, and grandparents leave their own homes and come to live either permanently or temporarily with their adult children, who may themselves be quite elderly. Like an accordion, such families keep on getting bigger or smaller as people constantly move into or out of the family home.

---

**Activity**

1 If you have, or were to have, an elderly parent, grandparent or great-grandparent living with you, describe two advantages and two problems that this might create for family life.

2 Go to www.ageuk.org.uk/latest-press (Age UK) and look at 'Later life facts and stats'. This collection of statistics, which is regularly updated, is the best source of publicly available, general information on people in later life in the UK. Identify three issues of concern to older-person households, and what this organization suggests might be done to resolve them.

3 Suggest three possible consequences, for society as a whole, of a growing proportion of older people in society.

---

## *The decline in the birth rate, fertility rate and average family size*

Since the mid twentieth century, the birth rate has been declining in the UK, from about 16 per 1,000 in 1950 to just over 11 per 1,000 in 2017. Both the **fertility rate** and the **total fertility rate** have also been declining. There was an average number of 2.78 children per woman in 1961, but this had reduced to 1.74 by 2017. This has meant that average family and household size have been dropping, from around 6 children per family in the 1870s to an average of around 1.9 children per family in 2017. The average household size in Britain has also almost halved in the last 100 years, from around 4.6 people to around 2.4 people per household in 2017. The trend towards smaller families, and more people living alone, explains this reduction in average household size.

---

**Fertility rate** The number of live births per 1,000 women of childbearing age (15–44) per year.

---

**Total fertility rate** The average number of live children born to women of childbearing age.

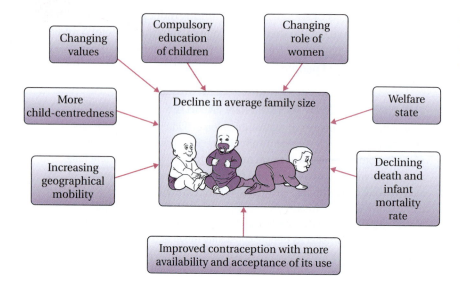

**Figure 3.9** Reasons for the decline in the birth rate, fertility rate and average family size

### *Reasons for the decline in the birth rate and smaller families*

#### CONTRACEPTION

More effective, safer and cheaper methods of birth control have been developed over the last century, and society's attitudes to the use of contraception have changed from disapproval to acceptance. The availability of safe and legal abortion since 1967 has also helped in terminating unwanted pregnancies. Family planning is therefore easier, and women now have more control over their fertility. These changes are partly because of growing **secularization** – the declining influence of the church and religion on people's behaviour and morality.

#### THE COMPULSORY EDUCATION OF CHILDREN

Since children were barred from employment in the nineteenth century, and education became compulsory in 1880, they have ceased to be an economic asset making a contribution to family income through working at an early age. Children are expensive, and have therefore become an economic liability and a drain on the resources of parents, because they have to be supported for a long period in compulsory education, and often in post-16 education and training, including university and college years. Parents today often have to support their children well into their 20s. Parents have therefore begun to limit the size of their families to secure for themselves and their children a higher standard of living. The move to a more child-centred society (discussed later in this chapter) has assisted in this restriction of family size, as smaller families mean parents can spend more money and time on and with each child.

> **Secularization**
> The process whereby religious thinking, practice and institutions decline and lose influence in society.

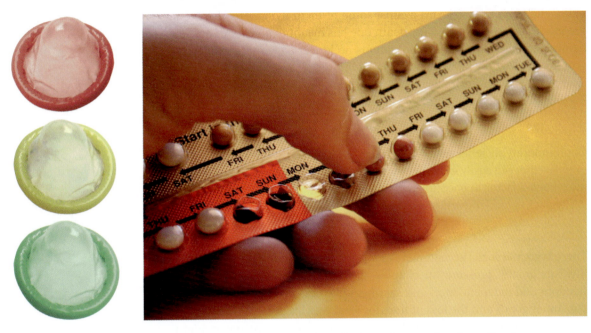

More effective methods of birth control, combined with changing attitudes to the use of contraception, have contributed to the decline in the birth rate and smaller families

### THE CHANGING POSITION OF WOMEN

The changing position of women, particularly since the 1960s, has gradually involved more equal status with men and greater employment opportunities. Women today have more options, other than or in addition to motherhood. Many wish to, and do, pursue their own careers. This means many women want to settle in their careers, pay back student loans, save for a house deposit and so on before having children, and are therefore having fewer children and having them later in life than previously.

While most women do eventually have children, there is a growing proportion who are choosing not to do so. For example, around 18 per cent of women born in 1972 (aged 45 in 2017) were childless in 2017, compared to about 10 per cent of their mothers' generation at a similar age. This trend towards childlessness can be expected to continue with women's growing position in paid employment. This may mean there will be more couple-only families or one-person households in the future.

### THE DECLINING INFANT MORTALITY RATE

Until the 1940s, the absence of a welfare state meant that many parents relied on their children to care for them in old age. It was still often uncertain whether children would outlive their parents. Parents therefore often had many children as a safeguard against some of them dying. The decline in the infant mortality rate and the death rate has meant that fewer people die before adulthood and old age, so parents no longer have more children as security against only a few surviving. In addition, the range of agencies which exist to help the elderly today means that people are less reliant on care from their children when they reach old age.

### A GEOGRAPHICALLY MOBILE LABOUR FORCE

Contemporary societies generally require a workforce that is **geographically mobile** – that can easily move to other areas for work or promotion. This may have been a factor in encouraging smaller families, because they can more easily pack up and move elsewhere.

> **Geographically mobile** Able and willing to move home from one area to live in another area, region or country.

### CHANGING VALUES

There is greater social acceptability today of a childfree lifestyle. Parenthood involves greater pressure on couples, a life-long commitment, a loss of freedom and independence, and sacrifices like cuts in money to spend on consumer goods and the loss of time for work and leisure. Not having children is becoming a positive life choice for many couples. As postmodernists suggest (see page 49), in a society where people seek to develop their identities through their consumer spending and leisure choices, couples are becoming more reluctant to have children.

Most women in the UK work in paid employment today, and many will combine this with childcare responsibilities. Many wish to pursue careers and will therefore either limit the number of children they have, often putting off having them until their careers are established, or choose to have none at all

# Migration and family and household structures

**Migration** refers to the movement of people from one country or area to another. It is used here to refer mainly to **immigration** – people who move to the UK from another country and who make it their place of residence for at least a year.

In the 1950s and 1960s, there was large-scale immigration into the UK from the Caribbean, India and Pakistan (since divided into Pakistan and Bangladesh) to meet a shortage of labour in unskilled and poorly paid occupations. There was also immigration by Kenyan and Uganda Asians who were fleeing persecution. This influx of people began to transform the UK into a more ethnically and culturally diverse country, with different cultures and ways of life coming into contact with one another.

Immigration has been higher than **emigration** since the early 1990s. This means **net migration** (the *difference* between immigration and emigration) has been increasing, as there are more people entering the country than leaving. From the 2000s onwards, there has been an increase of immigration from the European Union countries, particularly young people seeking work from Eastern European countries such as Poland and Romania. There has also been immigration by asylum-seekers, fleeing persecution, torture and potential death in their countries of origin, and refugees, fleeing famines, war and conflict.

Migration has created more cultural and organizational diversity (see pages 142–3) in families and households in the following ways:

- *More classic extended families among migrants*, both vertically extended (including grandparents) or horizontally extended (e.g. including brothers and their wives in many Sikh families). This led to larger households, mainly arising from the large-scale immigration from India and Pakistan (South Asia) in the 1960s.
- *More 'cereal packet'-type families* (in South Asian communities) with a traditional domestic division of labour, as mothers in Asian families, particularly Muslim families, are less likely to work outside the family than mothers from other ethnic groups (including White British mothers).
- *More arranged marriages* (see page 117).
- *More lone-parent families* arising from African-Caribbean migration – over 50 per cent of African-Caribbean families are matrifocal mother-led lone-parent families (Runnymede Trust online Fact Sheet, and see page 143).
- *More one-person households* among African-Caribbean males, and among young recent migrants who live alone while they establish their lives in the UK.
- *More cultural diversity*, with families from different cultural backgrounds.

**Migration** The movement of people between one country or area and another, who remain for at least a year.

**Immigration** The flow of people entering another country, and making it their new country of residence for at least a year.

**Emigration** The flow of people leaving their usual country of residence and entering another country, which then becomes their new country of residence for at least a year.

**Net migration** The *difference* between immigration and emigration, and therefore whether the population of a country has gone up or down when both immigration and emigration are taken into account.

- *More 'hybrid families'* Hybrid families are made up of couples coming from two different ethnic or cultural backgrounds. They merge the two cultures to create new family values and relationships. This is most commonly found between White British and African-Caribbean ethnic groups.
- *Larger one-family households*, often among migrants from Eastern Europe and multi-generational South Asian households. There is wide variation in the size of immigrant households, but on average their household size is greater than the White British equivalent, and they are more likely to live in overcrowded conditions. East European migrants tend to be younger people, and there are more women of childbearing age. Fertility rates are higher and they tend to have larger families.
- *More shared households* Either those containing two or more unrelated adults or multi-family households, as recent migrants may need to share houses as they settle in the UK, due to the costs of renting or buying their own homes.
- *More families separated by national borders* Recent immigration rules mean UK citizens cannot bring in their non-British, foreign-born partners and children without meeting a minimum income requirement. This can leave some UK citizens separated from their partners and children who live in other countries. This is most likely to affect those who are low-paid.

Figure 3.10 summarizes how migration has affected families and households.

**Hybrid families**
Those where the couple come from two different cultural or ethnic backgrounds, creating new family relationships and values arising from the merging of the two cultures.

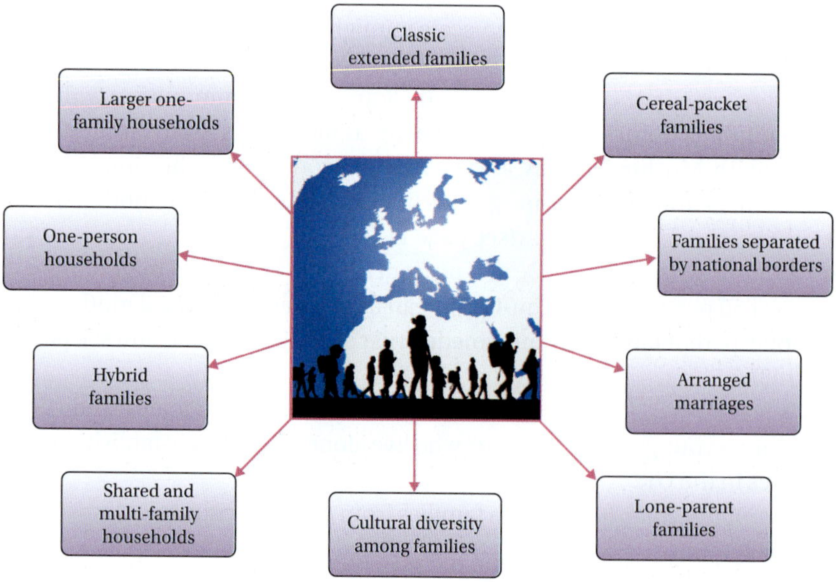

**Figure 3.10** How migration has affected families and households

## The emergence of the privatized (or isolated) nuclear family and the modified extended family as the most common family structures

Over about the last 100 years, classic extended families have become much less common. In contemporary Britain, the privatized (or isolated) nuclear family (see page 120) is the most common form of family structure in which people live. This is a more private institution, isolated from wider kin and often from neighbours and local community life as well.

The following explanations have been offered for the decline of extended family life and the process of privatization.

- *Contemporary societies require a labour force that can be geographically mobile*, with people able and willing to move to other areas of the country to find work, improve their education or gain promotion. This often involves leaving relatives behind, thus weakening and breaking up traditional classic extended family life. The small size of the modern isolated nuclear family and its lack of permanent roots in an area (such as wider kin) mean that it is geographically mobile, which some sociologists argue makes it ideally suited for life in contemporary society.

- *Contemporary Britain is a more **meritocratic society*** – the jobs people get are mainly achieved on the basis of talent, skill and educational qualifications, rather than of whom they know. Extended kin therefore have less to offer family members – such as job opportunities – reducing reliance on kin.

- *Educational success and promotion often involve upward **social mobility***. This leads to differences in income, status, lifestyle, and attitudes and values between kin. Kin have less in common, and this contributes to the weakening of extended family ties.

- *The development of higher standards of living, and the provision of welfare services by the state* for security against ill health, unemployment and poverty, have meant people have become less dependent on kin for help in times of distress.

- *The changing role of the family in society and its loss of functions* to more specialized institutions through the process of what the functionalist

**Meritocratic society** A society in which social and occupational positions (jobs) and pay are allocated on the basis purely of people's individual experience, talents, abilities, qualifications and skills – their individual merits.

**Social mobility** The movement of groups or individuals up or down the social hierarchy.

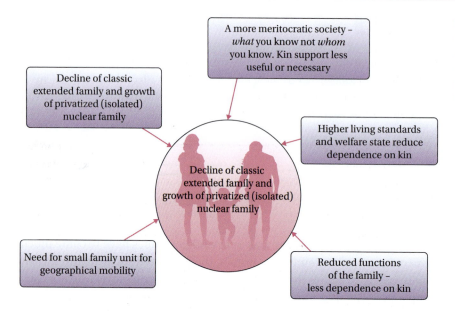

**Figure 3.11** Reasons for the decline of the classic extended family and the emergence of the privatized (isolated) nuclear family as the main family structure

Parsons called 'structural differentiation' (see pages 128–9), has reduced reliance on the extended family.

Figure 3.11 summarizes these changes.

## *The modified extended family and the continued existence of the classic extended family*

While privatized nuclear families have become the most common form of the family in the UK, geographical separation does not necessarily mean all links with kin are severed. As seen on pages 121–2, the closeness and mutual support between kin, typical of classic extended family life, are retained by telephone/Skype, email and social media, or through visiting. The typical family today in Britain is probably not simply the isolated nuclear family, but this modified form of the extended family.

It also doesn't mean that the classic extended family has completely disappeared, as it is still found in traditional working-class communities, the South Asian community and among the small group of Travellers (Gypsies/Roma).

**Activity**

1  Describe *two* characteristics of the privatized nuclear family.
2  Give *two* reasons for the decline of the classic extended family.
3  Explain what is meant by the modified extended family.
4  Suggest *two* advantages and *two* disadvantages of living in a beanpole family.

## Changes in the pattern of divorce

One of the most startling changes in the family in Britain since 1945 has been the general and dramatic increase in the number of marriages ending in divorce, as shown in figure 3.12. Figure 3.13 shows the changes in the **divorce rate** (the number divorcing per 1,000 married people per year) between 1955 and 2015.

The number of divorces of opposite-sex couples in England and Wales rose from 16,000 in 1945 to 101,669 in 2017, with the number of divorces more than doubling during the 1970s. A similar pattern is shown in the divorce rate. The number of divorces is now declining, with 2017 having the lowest number of divorces since 1971, with the divorce rate the lowest since 1973. This decline is not because fewer relationships are breaking up. Fewer people are marrying and so there is a declining number of married couples to get divorced. Britain is in the top third of countries with the highest divorce rates compared to those in the European Union, and estimates have suggested more than 40 per cent of new marriages are likely to end in divorce. The average length of marriages ending in divorce was twelve years in 2017.

### DIVORCE, 'EMPTY-SHELL MARRIAGES' AND 'BROKEN HOMES'

Divorce is the legal termination of a marriage, but this is not the only way that marriages and homes can be 'broken'. Homes and marriages may be broken in an **empty-shell marriage**, where the marital relationship has broken down, but the couple continue living together and no divorce or separation has taken place. Separation – through either choice or necessity (as in working abroad or imprisonment) – may also cause a 'broken home', as may the death of a partner. So homes may be 'broken' for reasons other than divorce, and divorce itself is often only the end result of a marriage which broke down long before.

## *Who gets divorced?*

While divorce affects all groups in the population, there are some groups amongst whom divorce rates and risks of divorce are higher than the average:

- *Couples marrying in their teens and early twenties* are about twice as likely to divorce as couples overall.
- *Men aged 45–9 and women in their late 30s and mid-40s* had the highest divorce rate among opposite-sex couples in 2017.
- *Women mainly start divorce proceedings:* 62 per cent of divorces in 2017 were initiated by women.
- *There is a high incidence of divorce in the first five to seven years of marriage and after about ten to fourteen years* (when the children are older or have left home).

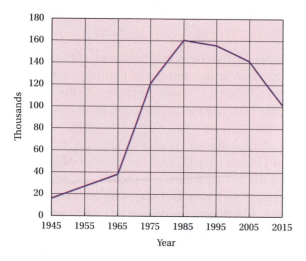

**Figure 3.12** Number of divorces (opposite-sex couples): England and Wales, 1945–2015

*Source: Vital Statistics: Population and Health Reference Tables*, Office for National Statistics, 2017

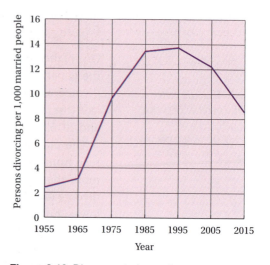

**Figure 3.13** Divorce rate (opposite-sex couples): England and Wales, 1955–2015

### Activity

Study figures 3.12 and 3.13 and answer the following questions:

1  Approximately how many divorces were there in 1965?
2  How many divorces were there in 1975?
3  In what year was there the highest number of divorces?
4  About how many more divorces were there in 2015 than in 1945?
5  What was the divorce rate in 1955?
6  Between which years was there the largest increase in the divorce rate?
7  Explain the difference between the number of divorces and the divorce rate.
8  Between the early 1970s and mid-1980s there was a very large increase in the number of divorces and the divorce rate. Suggest possible explanations for this.

- *The working class* (particularly semi-skilled and unskilled workers) has a higher rate of divorce than the middle class.
- *Childless couples and partners from different social class or religious backgrounds* face a higher risk of divorce.

### Activity

Go through the groups above, and suggest explanations for why each of them is more at risk of divorce than most of the rest of the population. Can you think of other groups who might have a higher risk of divorce than most people?

Around four in every ten marriages today are likely to end in divorce, with teenage marriages having about twice the risk of probable divorce compared to couples overall

## Explanations for the rising divorce rate

Rising divorce rates must be assessed against changing legal, financial and social circumstances, so as to avoid misleading conclusions about the declining importance of marriage and the family. The increase may simply reflect easier and cheaper divorce procedures enabling the legal termination of already unhappy empty-shell marriages, rather than a real increase in marriage breakdowns. There are two broad groups of reasons for the increase in the divorce rate: changes in the law which have gradually made divorce easier and cheaper to get, and changes in society which have made divorce a more practical and socially acceptable way of terminating a broken marriage. Figure 3.14 summarizes these changes.

***Changes in the law as a reason for the rising divorce rate*** Until the twentieth century, divorce could only be obtained by the rich because of its high cost, and men had more rights in divorce than women until 1923. As a result, there were very few divorces.

Changes in the law during the twentieth century made divorce easier, faster and cheaper to get, and gave men and women equal rights in divorce. This partly accounts for the steep rise in the divorce rate over the last fifty years, particularly in the 1970s and 1980s. These changes in the law are listed in the box on the next page. However, changes in the law reflect changing social attitudes and norms, and there are a number of wider social explanations that must also be considered.

**SOME RECENT CHANGES IN THE DIVORCE LAWS**

**The Divorce Law Reform Act of 1969 (came into effect in 1971)**

Before the 1969 Act, a person wanting a divorce had to prove before a court that his or her spouse had committed a 'matrimonial offence', such as adultery, cruelty or desertion. This frequently led to major public scandals, as all the details of unhappy marriages were aired in a public law court. This may have deterred many people whose marriage had broken down from seeking a divorce. Also, marriages may have broken down – become empty-shell marriages – without any matrimonial offence being committed.

The 1969 Act changed all this, and made 'irretrievable breakdown' of a marriage the only grounds for divorce – it is now no longer necessary to prove one partner guilty of a matrimonial offence. This change in the law led to a massive increase in the number of divorces after 1971.

**The Matrimonial and Family Proceedings Act of 1984**

This Act allowed couples to petition for divorce after only one year of marriage, whereas, previously, couples could normally divorce only after three years of marriage. This led to a record increase in the number of divorces in 1984 and 1985.

**The current legal position**

In England and Wales (it differs in Scotland and Northern Ireland), a couple can get a divorce if they have been married at least a year and their relationship has permanently broken down. This can be demonstrated on the grounds of adultery (extra-marital sex); unreasonable behaviour (e.g. violence and abuse); desertion; living apart for more than two years (if both partners agree to the divorce); living apart for at least five years (even if one partner disagrees with the divorce). In 2018, the UK government was considering changes to the divorce laws to allow couples to apply for a 'no-fault' divorce where neither party is blamed for the marriage breakdown.

### Changes in society as a reason for the rising divorce rate

#### THE CHANGING ROLE OF WOMEN

This is a very important explanation for the rising divorce rate. Women are much more likely than men to take the first steps in ending their marriages. In 2017, 62 per cent of divorces were initiated by women.

● *Feminists suggest this is because more women than men are unhappy with the state of their marriages.* This may well be because women's expectations of life and marriage have risen during the course of the last century. Women are less willing to accept the traditional patriarchal nature of marriages, and the inequalities they face. They are rejecting the

**Figure 3.14** Causes of the rising divorce rate

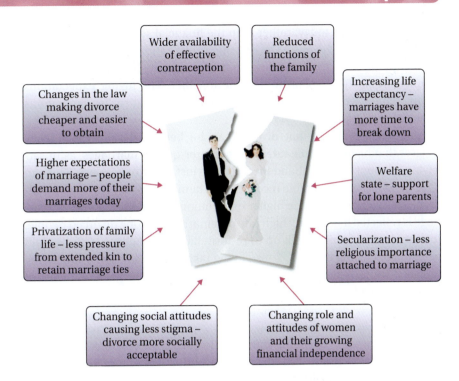

Wider availability of effective contraception

Reduced functions of the family

Increasing life expectancy – marriages have more time to break down

Changes in the law making divorce cheaper and easier to obtain

Higher expectations of marriage – people demand more of their marriages today

Welfare state – support for lone parents

Privatization of family life – less pressure from extended kin to retain marriage ties

Secularization – less religious importance attached to marriage

Changing social attitudes causing less stigma – divorce more socially acceptable

Changing role and attitudes of women and their growing financial independence

traditional homemaker/mother role, and the dual burden and the triple shift (see pages 134–5) which they encounter in many marriages.

- *Marxists take a similar view to the feminist one, with divorce a logical way of escaping an exploitative relationship.* They emphasize the conflicts within marriage that inevitably arise when women experience inequalities.

The employment of married women has increased, and in 2019 around 75 per cent of women were active in the labour market. This has increased their financial independence, and reduced the extent of dependence on their husbands. There is also a range of welfare-state benefits to help divorced women, particularly those with children. Marriage has therefore become less of a financial necessity for women, and this makes it easier for them to escape from unhappy marriages.

### RISING EXPECTATIONS OF MARRIAGE

As feminists and Marxists suggest, the divorce rate may have risen because couples (especially women) expect and demand more in their relationships today than their parents or grandparents might have settled for. Love, companionship, understanding, sexual compatibility and personal fulfilment, so often portrayed in the media, are more likely to be the main ingredients of a successful marriage today, rather than the financial security which seemed more important in the past. The growing privatization and isolation of the nuclear family from extended kin and the community have also meant that couples are likely to spend more time together. The higher expectations mean couples are more likely to end a relationship that earlier generations might have tolerated.

Functionalists argue that divorce can be beneficial for society. They suggest that higher divorce rates reflect better-quality marriages, as unsatisfying relationships are abandoned, leaving just the stronger ones. This can have the effect of more stable reconstituted family units for bringing up children. This suggestion of the higher expectations and better quality of marriage is reflected in the fairly high rate of remarriage among divorced people. In other words, families split up to re-form happier families – a bit like 'old banger' cars failing their MOT test, being taken to the scrapyard and being replaced with a better-quality car, thereby improving the general quality of cars on the road.

### GROWING SECULARIZATION

Secularization – the declining influence in society of religious beliefs and institutions – has resulted in marriage becoming less of a sacred, spiritual union and more a personal and practical commitment which can be abandoned if it fails. Evidence for this lies in the fact that less than a quarter of marriages in England and Wales now involve a religious ceremony. The church now takes a much less rigid view of divorce, and many people today probably do not attach much religious significance to their marriages.

### CHANGING SOCIAL ATTITUDES

Divorce has become more socially acceptable, and there is less social disapproval and condemnation (stigmatizing) of divorcees. As a result, people are less afraid of the consequences of divorce, and are more likely to seek a legal end to an unhappy marriage, rather than simply separating or carrying on in an empty-shell marriage.

### THE GREATER AVAILABILITY OF – AND MORE EFFECTIVE – CONTRACEPTION

The greater availability of – and more effective – contraception has made it safer to have sex outside the marital relationship, and with more than one person during marriage. This weakens traditional constraints on fidelity to a marriage partner, and potentially exposes relationships to greater instability.

### THE GROWTH OF THE PRIVATIZED NUCLEAR FAMILY

The growing privatization and isolation of the nuclear family from extended kin and the community in contemporary society has meant it is no longer so easy for marriage partners to seek advice from or temporary refuge with relatives. This isolation can increase the demands on and expectations of each partner in a marriage. There is also less social control from extended kin pressuring couples to retain marriage ties. In this sense, there is both more pressure on marriage relationships arising from the points above, and fewer constraints preventing people abandoning marriage, and increasingly the decision whether to divorce or not lies with the married couple alone.

### THE REDUCED FUNCTIONS OF THE FAMILY

As seen earlier in this chapter, over time a number of family functions have been transferred to other social institutions. This has perhaps meant that marriage has become less of a practical necessity, and there are fewer bonds linking marriage partners. Love and companionship and personal compatibility are the important dimensions of contemporary marriages, and if some or all of these disappear, there may be nothing much left to hold marriages together.

### INCREASING LIFE EXPECTANCY

People live to a greater age today than they did in the early years of the last century, and this means the potential number of years a couple may be together, before one of them dies, increases as life expectancy lengthens. This gives more time for marriages to go wrong and for divorces to occur.

"I'VE GOT ANOTHER FORTY YEARS TO LIVE!"

**Activity**

1  Write a short essay (10–15 minutes) answering the following question: 'How far do sociologists agree with the view that changes in society rather than changes in the law are mainly responsible for changes in the divorce rate?'

2  Study media advertisements or television soaps for a few days. What kind of overall impressions are given of married life today? Refer to particular advertisements or soaps as evidence for your findings. Do you agree or disagree with the view that these create higher expectations of marriage today? Explain the reasons for your answer.

3  'Of men and women marrying today, around 87 per cent of opposite-sex couples, and over 90 percent of same-sex couples, lived with their partners beforehand, and cohabitation before marriage was seen as one of the major social changes of the late twentieth / early twenty-first centuries. However, many cohabiting couples eventually marry.'

   Describe three social pressures that continue to push people towards conforming to the norm of marriage.

## The consequences of divorce

The ending of marriages (or any relationship) is often a very painful process, and the high proportion of marriages today ending in divorce has a number of consequences, for individuals, families and society.

*Consequences for children*   Couples divorcing in 2014 had between them around 118,000 children aged 16 and under, and it is often such dependent children who live with their parents who face the greatest personal distress when their parents divorce. They often face the following problems:

- conflicts of loyalty over which parent they should live with (though in practice most courts award custody to the mother).
- the difficulty of moving between two different households, as they visit the parent they don't live with.
- possible loss of contact with some grandparents and uncles, aunts and cousins and the emotional support they may have had from them.
- having to cope with and adapt to living in new reconstituted (blended) families, in the event of one or both of their parents forming a new couple relationship. They may have to adapt to different expectations of behaviour from their new stepparent, and get along with various combinations of stepmothers and stepfathers, and stepbrothers and stepsisters.
- the risk of losing contact with their fathers altogether. After divorce or separation, estimates suggest between 10 and 35 per cent of fathers who don't live with their children lose contact with them, and many separated fathers say they do not have a close relationship with their children.

Children often suffer great personal distress when their parents divorce, difficulties moving between different households, and conflicts in loyalty to both parents. In most cases, the courts award custody of children after divorce to mothers rather than fathers. Why do you think this is?

- the distress of seeing on-going conflicts between divorced and separating parents, over issues such as childcare support and parenting styles, and possible court battles relating to which parent has custody of children. Research suggests some children may react to such conflicts by playing truant from school, committing crime and turning to alcohol and drug abuse.

*Consequences for adults*   Divorce not only involves the legal ending of a marriage, it also involves dividing up property and savings, and there are often serious legal disputes fought through the courts between divorcing partners over the division of money and property, and also over who has custody of the children and visiting rights. Divorce nearly always means a decline in income, as setting up and running two new households costs a lot more than one. Lone-parent families with dependent children, particularly, may face financial hardship. Lone parents face higher risks of poverty, and more difficulties juggling childcare and employment commitments than couple families. Grandparents may consequently be called upon more to help with childcare.

*Consequences for family and household structures*    Rising divorce has meant a growing range of different household and family structures. There is an increase in:

- lone-parent families
- reconstituted (blended) families
- one-person households
- more cohabiting couples and births outside marriage
- remarriages.

These issues are discussed below.

## Remarriage and the growth of reconstituted (blended or step-) families

While marriage / civil partnership is still the usual form of partnership between couples, marriages / civil partnerships in which it is the first time for both partners are declining substantially. The number of these has more than halved since 1970. About 45 per cent of marriages now involve a remarriage for one or both partners. More divorced men remarry than divorced women, reflecting women's greater dissatisfaction or disillusionment with marriage. This is perhaps not surprising, given the way women often have to balance the competing demands of paid employment, domestic labour and childcare, and emotional management of the family.

These trends have meant that there are more reconstituted families (stepfamilies or blended families) with stepparents, stepchildren, and step-brothers and stepsisters arising from previous relationships of one or both partners. Official estimates suggest there are over half a million stepfamilies with dependent children in the UK – about 11 per cent of all couple families with dependent children. Stepfathers are more common than stepmothers. In 2011 (the latest available statistic), more than 85 per cent of stepfamilies with dependent children consisted of a couple with at least one child from a previous relationship of the woman, compared to 11 per cent for men, and 4 per cent where children came from previous relationships of both partners. This reflects the fact that most children remain with the biological mother after a break-up, and it is nearly always women who gain legal custody of children.

## The growth of the lone-parent family

One of the biggest changes in the family has been the growth of the lone-parent family (also known as the single-parent or one-parent family). The percentage of lone-parent families has tripled since 1971, and Britain has one of the highest proportions of lone-parent families in Europe. Just over one in five (22 per cent) of all families with dependent children were lone-parent families in 2017 – nine out of ten of them headed by women. Over one in five dependent children now live in such families, compared to just 7 per cent in 1972.

### *Why are there more lone-parent families?*

The rapid growth in the number of lone-parent families can be explained by a number of factors, some of which have already been discussed earlier in explaining the rising divorce rate (see pages 165–9). These include:

- *The greater economic independence of women*, making support by a partner less of an economic necessity today compared to the past.
- *Improved contraception, changing male attitudes and fewer 'shotgun weddings'*. With the wider availability and approval of safe and effective contraception, and easier access to safe and legal abortion, men may feel less responsibility to marry women who have unintentionally become pregnant, and women may feel under less pressure to marry the future father. There are, therefore, fewer 'shotgun weddings' (where reluctant couples are forced into marriage by the father of the pregnant women wielding an imaginary shotgun to ensure that the man marries his daughter).
- *Reproductive technology is available to women*, enabling them to bear children without a male partner, through surrogate motherhood and fertility treatments such as IVF (in-vitro fertilization).
- *Changing social attitudes and secularization*. There is less social stigma (or social disapproval and condemnation) attached to lone parenthood today. Women are therefore less afraid of the social consequences of becoming lone parents.

The New Right (see pages 52–3, 54 and 130–1) has seen the growth in lone parenthood as one of the major signs of the decline of conventional family life and marriage. Lone-parent families – and particularly lone never-married mothers – have been portrayed by some of the media and conservative politicians as promiscuous parasites, blamed for everything from rising juvenile crime through to housing shortages, increasing drug abuse, educational failure of children and the general breakdown of society. The problems created by lone parenthood, particularly for boys, are usually explained by the lack of a male role model in the home, and consequently inadequate socialization.

Lone parenthood has therefore been presented as a major social problem, and the media have periodically, by their exaggerated and sensationalized reporting, stirred up waves of public concern about lone parents, and presented them as threats to society and the stability of family life. Such a wave of unjustified public concern stirred up by exaggerated and sensationalized reporting in the media is known as a **moral panic**.

A number of policies have been introduced in an effort to cut the welfare costs to the state of lone parents, such as encouraging absent fathers to take financial responsibility for their children, and encouraging lone parents to support themselves through paid employment. In 2017, about 70 per cent of lone parents were in employment.

### Nailing the myths of the New Right

Single never-married lone mothers only account for about 57 per cent of all lone parents with dependent children. Many of these mothers formerly cohabited with the father, as in many couple families now: such lone parenthood is now little different from that arising from married/civil-partnered couples who divorce/dissolve civil partnerships, or who separate in married/civil-partnered or cohabiting relationships. Lone motherhood now mostly arises from divorce/dissolution of civil partnerships and separation, and occasionally the death of a partner, as figure 3.15 shows.

The problems allegedly created by absent fathers have been questioned on the grounds that it is not the presence or absence of a father that is important, but whether fathers actually involve themselves in the children's upbringing. There are probably many fathers in two-parent families as well who fail to involve themselves in the care and discipline of their children, and problems like juvenile delinquency are likely to arise in any household where children are inadequately supervised and disciplined.

> **Moral panic**
> A wave of public concern about some exaggerated or imaginary threat to society, stirred up by overblown and sensationalized reporting in the media.

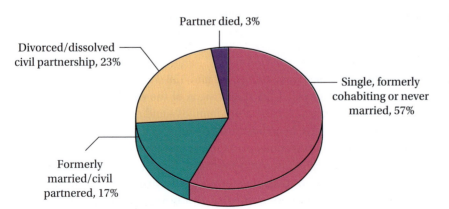

Partner died, 3%

Divorced/dissolved civil partnership, 23%

Single, formerly cohabiting or never married, 57%

Formerly married/civil partnered, 17%

**Figure 3.15** Lone-mother families with dependent children, by marital status: UK, 2015

*Source:* Labour Force Survey, Office for National Statistics

This problem, often blamed on lone parenthood, is more likely to be caused by poverty rather than lone parenthood, as lone-parent households are about four times more likely to be in poverty than couple households with dependent children, and they are more likely to live in overcrowded or poor-quality housing. This probably explains other factors linked in the popular imagination to lone parenthood, such as lower educational achievement.

A misleading myth is that of lone teenage mothers getting pregnant to jump the queue for social housing (from councils and housing associations). There is very little evidence for this. Gingerbread (www.gingerbread.org.uk) pointed out, in 2017, that less than 2 per cent of lone parents are teenagers (aged 16–19 years), and the average age of a lone parent is around 38.

### Activity

1  Suggest reasons why, in the event of divorce, women are more likely than men to be given custody of the children.
2  Suggest explanations why most lone-parent families are headed by women.
3  To what extent do you agree or disagree with the following statements, and why?
   - 'A lone mother can bring up her child as well as a married or cohabiting couple.'
   - 'People who want children ought to get married.'
   - 'To grow up happily, children need a home with both their mother and father.'
4  Suggest and explain two advantages and two disadvantages of lone parenthood, compared to two-parent families?
5  Visit the following website, www.gingerbread.org.uk, and identify five issues that seem to be of particular concern to lone parents. Describe each issue briefly, and outline any solutions that are suggested.

## Changing patterns of marriage and cohabitation

The decline of marriage and the growth of living together before or outside marriage were two of the major social changes at the turn of the twenty-first century. **Marriage rates** (the number of marriages per 1,000 unmarried people aged 16 and over per year) are declining in the UK.

In 2016, there were 242,774 marriages between opposite-sex couples (97 per cent of all marriages) in England and Wales. This was the lowest marriage rate since records began, with first-time marriages for both parties nearly halved since 1945. In the same period, marriage rates fell from 72 to 22 for men, and 55 to 20 for women. The number of marriages in 2016 was only about 60 per cent of those in 1945, despite a steep rise in population.

**Marriage rate**
The number of marriages per 1,000 unmarried people aged 16 and over per year.

People are also marrying at an older age: the average bride in 1945 was aged about 23, but about 35 in 2016 (aged 37 for gay couples), while the average groom was about 25 in 1945 and about 37 in 2016 (aged 41 for gay couples). This is largely because people are putting off marriage until education is completed and careers established.

One of the main reasons behind the declining marriage rate is the rising number of couples who are choosing to cohabit rather than to marry.

Around 17 per cent of people living in couple families were cohabiting in 2017, including people who were separated but not divorced. By 2017, over eight in ten people marrying had lived with their partner beforehand. Around 15 per cent of dependent children are now being brought up by unmarried, cohabiting couples. Cohabitation is now the norm rather than the exception, though many cohabiting relationships eventually end up in marriage.

The reasons for the decline of marriage and growing cohabitation have been considered earlier, including:

- *the changing role of women*, whose growing economic independence has given them more freedom to choose their relationships
- *the growing divorce rate*, and the message it is sending out to potential marriage partners
- *growing secularization*
- *changing social attitudes and reduced social stigma*: before the 1960s and 1970s, it was regarded as socially unacceptable for unmarried women

Cohabitation and giving birth to children outside marriage are both rising rapidly, and younger people are more likely to do both, though many cohabiting couples do eventually get married

(not men) to be sexually active. Young people are more likely to cohabit than older people. This reveals more easy-going attitudes to cohabitation among the young, showing the reduced social stigma attached to cohabitation.

- *the greater availability of – and more effective – contraception*
- *higher expectations of marriage.*

## More births outside marriage

Nearly half of all births (48 per cent in 2017) are now outside marriage or civil partnership – about five times more than the proportion in 1971. Despite the record numbers of children being born outside marriage / civil partnership, in 2017 about two-thirds of those babies had parents who lived together. This reflects the increase in the number of couples cohabiting rather than entering into marriage or civil partnership.

This suggests that children are still being born into a stable couple relationship, even if the partners are not legally married / civil-partnered.

The explanations for the increase in births outside marriage / civil partnership are very similar to those for the increase in the divorce rate, the decline in the marriage rate and the increase in cohabitation, which were discussed above.

> ### Activity
>
> Read the sections above, and explain carefully four reasons why there are more births outside marriage or civil partnership today.

## Living alone: the growth in singlehood and one-person households

There is a general increase in the number of one-person households. About three in every ten households in 2017 contained only one person, compared to one in twenty in 1901. An increasing proportion of these households are among younger people living alone. Only around half of one-person households are now over state pension age (age 65, rising to 66 by 2020), compared to two-thirds in 1971.

Men are more likely to live alone than women: of those living alone aged 16–64 in 2017, 59 per cent were men. There are nearly twice as many men as women living alone in the 25–44 age group, but there are twice as many women as men aged 65 and over.

## *Explanations for these trends*

- The general decline in marriage
- The higher proportions of men than women who never marry, or who marry at older ages than women and marry women younger than themselves
- The rise in couple breakdowns and separations, leading to more men living alone while women may live with any children from the relationship
- The fact that people are delaying marriage / civil partnership or cohabitation until they are older
- The greater life expectancy (longer lives) of women, leading to an increase in the number of women over 65 living alone.

**FAMILIES AND HOUSEHOLDS SINCE 1945**
**A SUMMARY OF TRENDS**

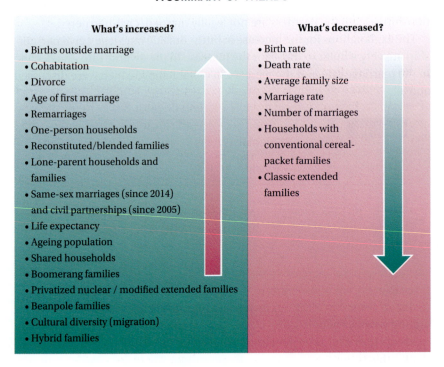

**What's increased?**

- Births outside marriage
- Cohabitation
- Divorce
- Age of first marriage
- Remarriages
- One-person households
- Reconstituted/blended families
- Lone-parent households and families
- Same-sex marriages (since 2014) and civil partnerships (since 2005)
- Life expectancy
- Ageing population
- Shared households
- Boomerang families
- Privatized nuclear / modified extended families
- Beanpole families
- Cultural diversity (migration)
- Hybrid families

**What's decreased?**

- Birth rate
- Death rate
- Average family size
- Marriage rate
- Number of marriages
- Households with conventional cereal-packet families
- Classic extended families

# SOCIAL CHANGE AND RELATIONSHIPS INSIDE THE FAMILY

The previous sections considered how social change has led to changes in family structure and organization. The following sections consider how social change has led to relationships *inside* families changing. This is particularly concerned with the roles of partners, children and other relatives within families.

## Is there a new 'symmetrical family' emerging?

The term 'symmetrical family' was first used by the functionalists Young and Willmott (1973) following a large-scale survey of family life in Greater London. They claimed to have discovered the emergence of a more symmetrical (the same on both sides) privatized nuclear family – less patriarchal or male-dominated, and much more a balanced partnership of equals. Both partners were making similar contributions to the running of the household, sharing household chores, childcare, and family decisions, and couples shared leisure time both inside and outside the home.

This contrasted with previous classic extended family forms in which there was a big gulf between male and female roles in the domestic division of labour. These reflected the classic instrumental/expressive roles that Parsons and other functionalists regard as the natural roles of men and women in the family (see page 130). Then, men made all the family's major decisions, and they had very little involvement in domestic chores or childcare. Wives typically spent leisure time with female kin inside the home, and husbands with male kin and workmates outside the home (often in the pub).

This emergence of a more symmetrical family from the 1960s onwards is generally described as a change in **conjugal roles** (the roles played by partners in couples who live together) from **segregated conjugal roles** to more equally balanced **joint (or integrated) conjugal roles**.

- Segregated conjugal roles are those where partners who live together have very different household and other tasks in their relationship, with a clear division and separation between the male and female roles.
- Joint (or integrated) conjugal roles are those where there are few divisions in household and other tasks and the roles performed by partners in couples who live together.

Some of these differences are identified on the next page.

Young and Willmott's research came under fire at the time, particularly from feminists, who argued Young and Willmott's research actually showed little evidence of symmetry. Nonetheless, since the 1970s the idea

**Conjugal roles**
The roles played by partners in couples who live together.

**Segregated conjugal roles** Where there is a clear division and separation in household and other tasks and the roles performed between the partners in couples who live together.

**Joint (or integrated) conjugal roles** Where there are few divisions in household and other tasks and the roles performed by partners in couples who live together.

| Segregated conjugal roles | Joint (or integrated) conjugal roles |
|---|---|
| • Partners in couples who live together have clearly separated roles. | • Partners in couples who live together have interchangeable and flexible roles. |
| • One partner (usually a man) takes responsibility for bringing in money, major decisions and doing the heavier and more technical jobs around the home, such as fixing household equipment and doing repairs. The other partner (usually a woman) takes responsibility for housework, shopping, cooking, childcare, etc. He or she is unlikely to have full-time paid employment. | • Both partners are likely to be either in paid employment or looking for a job. Household chores and childcare are shared, with males taking on traditional female jobs such as housework, cooking, shopping, etc., and female partners taking on traditional male jobs, such as household repairs, looking after the car, etc. |
| • Partners are likely to have separate friends and different leisure activities. | • Partners share common friends, leisure activities and decision-making. |

has continued that families are becoming more symmetrical. For example, there has been an on-going debate about the emergence of a so-called 'New Man'. This New Man is allegedly more caring, sharing, gentle, emotional and sensitive in his attitudes to women, children and his own emotional needs, sharing decision-making with his partner and willing to do his fair share of housework and childcare.

The emergence of the symmetrical family, the New Man and more joint or integrated conjugal roles is thought to have occurred for a number of reasons.

- *The rise of feminism, and the improved status and rights of women* have forced men to accept women more as equals and not simply as home-makers and mothers.
- *The increase in the number of working women, and more* **dual-career** or **dual-earner families**, where both partners have careers and are working in paid employment, have increased women's independence and authority in the family.
- *Women are now outperforming men in education and are therefore more often earning the same as, or more than, their male partners.* The importance of female partners' earnings in maintaining the family's standard of living, and women's growing equality in the workplace, may have encouraged men to help more with domestic labour – a recognition that the women cannot be expected to do two jobs at once.
- *Improved living standards in the home*, such as streaming TV, Wi-Fi and broadband internet, and tablets, have encouraged both partners to spend more time at home and share home-centred leisure activities.
- *The commercialization of housework* refers to the way in which new technology has enabled a whole host of consumer goods and services to help with reducing the burden of housework, compared to previous

**Dual-career families** Those in which both partners have their own careers, with the hope and expectation of future promotions.

**Dual-earner families** Those in which both partners earn money from paid employment.

generations – e.g. fridges, freezers, microwaves, washing machines and dryers, vacuum cleaners, takeaway foods and supermarket ready-meals, online shopping and home delivery services, and pet-care and cleaning services. This has made housework less skilled and time-consuming, perhaps encouraging men to do a bit more, and enabling women to do a bit less. This option, though, is likely to be available only to the most well-off, as all these products and services have to be paid for.

- *The decline of the close-knit extended family and a more geographically mobile population* in contemporary society have meant there is less pressure from kin on newly married or cohabiting couples to retain traditional roles – it is therefore easier to adopt new roles in a relationship.

- *Weaker gender identities and changing norms* mean that men and women now have more choice in how they see themselves and their roles, and they are less tied to traditional gender roles and gender divisions in the home. This reflects the argument postmodernists make – that there is more choice and diversity in contemporary life, and people have greater freedom from traditional norms and identities.

The view that there is more equality in modern family relationships has been widely criticized, particularly by feminists, and there is not really much evidence that the family is now typically 'symmetrical'. While there is some evidence of more role integration in leisure activities and some decision-making, housework and childcare remain predominantly women's work. Men are perhaps more involved in childcare than they used to be – and this rises among higher-class higher-income households.

The Office for National Statistics suggested in the late 1990s that rising numbers of men were choosing to become 'house-husbands', or stay-at-home dads who raise children rather than work, leaving their partner to become the family breadwinner. This reversal of traditional roles reflects the growing earning power of women at work, and provides some evidence of changing attitudes among some men towards childcare and housework. However, this trend appears to be mainly happening only in those relatively few families where the woman earns more than the man and it is financially practical to swap roles. Evidence from a number of surveys shows that, in most cases, traditional segregated roles still remain.

## Criticisms of the view that modern family relationships are really partnerships of equals: the myths of joint conjugal roles and the 'symmetrical family'

### Inequalities in the domestic division of labour

- As figure 3.16 shows, women still perform the majority of tasks in the domestic division of labour. The only area where men put in more unpaid work hours than women is in the provision of transport, but

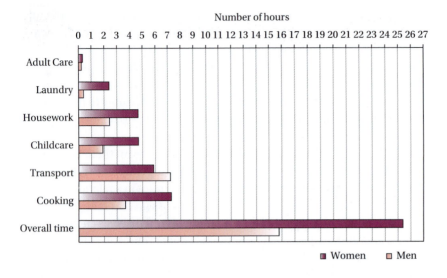

Number of hours

**Figure 3.16** Average hours of unpaid work done per week in each category by men and women, UK, 2015

*Source:* UK Harmonised European Time Use Survey (HETUS), 2015, and Office for National Statistics

this includes driving themselves and non-family members around, as well as travelling to work. Women spend on average between two and three times more hours than men each week on household tasks such as housework, childcare and cooking, and six times longer on the laundry. It is perhaps unsurprising that housework is the second-largest cause of domestic rows, after money.

- Despite fathers spending seven times more time interacting with their children than their own fathers did in the 1970s, it was very little time then, so seven times more still isn't very much. The more routine jobs such as bathing and feeding and taking children to the doctor are still done mainly by women.

- Mothers were still providing around 74 per cent of total childcare time in 2015. In terms of its contribution to the national economy, the annual value of childcare provided by women in 2015 was between 67 per cent and 72 per cent, depending on the age of the youngest child, compared to a 33 per cent to 28 per cent share for men.

- It is women who are most likely to have to make sacrifices to buy the children clothes, and to make sure other family members are properly fed. It is still mostly women who get the blame if the house is untidy or children are dirty or badly dressed.

- Despite some improvements, men's involvement in household work has increased less since the 1970s than women's involvement in paid employment.

- Women also provided, in 2015, 60 per cent of adult care (caring for elderly or disabled adults) in the family – a significant commitment in the sandwich generation (see page 154).

Have conjugal roles really become more equal?

- The inequality of women in the domestic division of labour is found across the world in both developed and developing countries. In 2014, on average across sixty-six countries (representing two-thirds of the world's population), women spent 3.3 times as long as men on household tasks.
- Women still take the major responsibility for managing the emotional side of family life. This refers to things like talking to, listening to, understanding and supporting children, and also their partners. In addition, it involves liaising between family members when there are rows, and acting as the family mediator.

*Inequalities in power and authority*    Power and authority are not equally distributed in couple families. The evidence suggests:

- Women are less likely than men to have the final say on the most important decisions in the family, such as whether to move house or take out loans. Such decisions are mostly taken by men alone.
- While some decisions are taken jointly, very few are taken by women alone, and those decisions that are taken by women alone are often only in relatively unimportant areas such as home decoration and furnishing, children's clothes, food and other domestic spending.
- There is more consultation on money matters, though more men than women make the financial decisions for the family.
- Younger couples, particularly those without children and where both partners are working full-time, are more likely to have financial independence from each other, such as their own bank accounts and credit cards. This is less common when women work part-time or aren't in paid

employment. Given that more men than women are in paid employ-ment, and of those women who are in employment, around 41 per cent in 2019 worked part-time – compared to just 13 per cent of men – this does not point to much sharing or financial independence in many fami-lies. In many households, men still hold the purse strings.

- Men are still often the major or sole earners, and this puts men in a stronger bargaining position than women, and often puts their female partners in a position of economic dependence.
- Surveys suggest many working mothers are limited in the jobs they can do and the hours they can work because they are still expected to take the main responsibility for housework and childcare, and to be at home for the children leaving for and returning from school. It is often women who have to leave work early to pick up children, and it is mothers who are most likely to take time off work to look after children who can't attend school or nursery because they are sick. Women consequently have less pay, less security of employment, and poorer promotion pros-pects than men. This reinforces men's economic superiority and greater authority in the family.
- It is mainly women who give up paid work (or suffer from lost/restricted job opportunities) to look after children, the elderly or the sick. This reduces their financial authority in the home.
- There is evidence of widespread male violence in relationships. Such violence is all too often not taken seriously by the police or courts, being dismissed as a 'domestic dispute'. This might be interpreted as a view that such violence is almost seen as a normal part of a relationship. Violence in the family is discussed later in this chapter.

The points discussed in this section mean many female partners now often have a *dual burden* of paid employment and domestic labour, and work a *triple shift* of paid work, domestic labour and childcare, and emotional work – to their male partner's one job.

While there does seem to be some evidence of changes to the gender roles in the family, in a majority of couple relationships, the traditional roles of women and men remain. The family remains, generally, a patriarchal institu-tion, where men hold the most power and money, and make most decisions, but contribute far less than women to the domestic division of labour.

## Activity

1 Describe what is meant by a 'symmetrical family'.
2 Identify and explain one advantage and one disadvantage of using postal or internet structured questionnaires to investigate the domestic division of labour.

3 Identify and describe one example of how far patriarchy can affect the power relationships between couples in families.
4 Write an essay answering the following question: 'How far do sociologists agree that feminism has changed the relationships between couples in contemporary society?'
5 Identify what you regard as the most suitable research method for discovering the contribution each partner makes to the domestic division of labour, and explain why you think this might be the best method.
6 Identify and explain one ethical issue that may arise in researching relationships between couples, and suggest how you might overcome it.
7 Describe two family issues that are most likely to interfere with or make difficult men's and women's roles in paid employment.
8 Drawing on all the work you have done on the issue, to what extent do you agree or disagree with the view that it is largely a myth that the contemporary family is a partnership of equals? List in two columns all the evidence for and against, and draw a conclusion.

Families have become more child-centred over the past fifty years

## The changing position of children in the family

During the last fifty years or so, families have become more child-centred, with family activities and outings often focused on the needs and interests of the children. The amount of time parents spend with their children has more than doubled since the 1960s – for fathers (as seen above), it has increased seven times – and parents (particularly mothers) are more involved with their children and are taking more of an interest in their activities. Relationships between parents and children are less authoritarian – parents are more likely

Children today are often at the centre of family life, with the lives of parents dominated by the demands and needs of their children

to discuss decisions with children, treating them more as equals, though this is more common in middle-class than working-class families. Often, the children's welfare is seen as the major family priority, frequently involving the parents in considerable financial sacrifice and cost.

## The causes of child-centredness

- Families have got smaller over the last century: more individual care and attention can be devoted to each child.
- The typical working week has got shorter: parents have more time to spend with their children.
- Increasing affluence, with higher wages and a higher standard of living, has benefitted children: more money can be spent on them and their activities.
- The welfare state provides a wide range of benefits designed to help parents care for their children, but also a range of measures to give children a good start in life through early-years education. There are now increased demands on parents to look after their children properly. Social workers, for example, have a wide range of powers to intervene in families on behalf of children who are at risk, and have the ultimate power to remove children from families if parents fail to look after them properly. The United Nations Convention on the Rights of the Child (1989) and the Children Acts of 1989 and 2004 established children's legal rights, and there is now a Minister for Children and Families and a Children's Commissioner (see www.childrenscommissioner.gov.uk) to champion the views of children and protect and promote their interests.
- Paediatrics, or the science of childhood, has developed rapidly over the last 100 years or so, with a wide range of research, popular books, websites and TV programmes, suggesting how parents should bring

**Figure 3.17** Reasons why families have become more child-centred

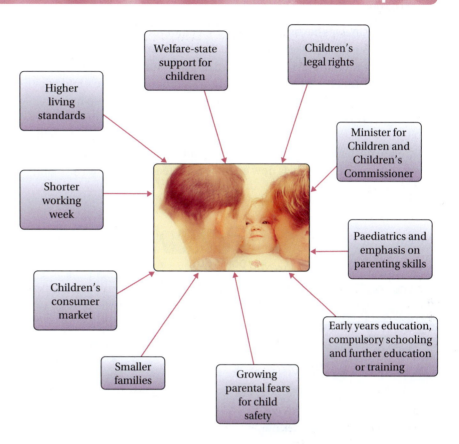

- Higher living standards
- Welfare-state support for children
- Children's legal rights
- Minister for Children and Children's Commissioner
- Shorter working week
- Paediatrics and emphasis on parenting skills
- Children's consumer market
- Early years education, compulsory schooling and further education or training
- Smaller families
- Growing parental fears for child safety

up their children to encourage their full development. The nurturing, protection and education of children are now seen as a vital and central part of family life, with parenting skills and early-years education now recognized as an important aspect of children's educational and social development.

- Compulsory education, and further education or training to the age of 18, have meant young people are financially dependent on their parents for longer periods of time. Tuition fees for higher education and the abolition of student grants have in recent years extended this period of dependency of young people on their parents. In this respect, childhood, including the dependency on adults it involves, has itself become extended.
- Children's lives have become more complex, with more educational, medical and leisure services for them. This frequently involves parents in ferrying children to schools, cinemas, friends, clinics and so on.
- Growing traffic dangers and parental fears (largely unjustified) of assaults upon their children have meant that children now travel more with parents rather than being left to roam about on their own as much as they used to.

- Large businesses have encouraged a specific childhood consumer market. Businesses like Mothercare, Nike, publishers, confectionery and clothing manufacturers, and the music industry aim at the childhood consumer market, encouraging children to consume – and parents to spend – to satisfy their children's demands. Even top fashion designers like Stella McCartney and Gucci are now designing children's clothes. 'Pester power', the principle behind advertisers targeting children to pester their parents into buying them sweets, smartphones, clothes, toys and so on, is now an important feature of the advertising business.

### Activity

Drawing on your own experience, how far do you think advertisers target young people to encourage them to consume things? How does advertising influence you and the things you buy, and how far does it encourage you to badger your parents into buying them for you?

## The role of grandparents in families

Grandparents have always played an important role in family life, particularly in the classic extended families of the past, but shorter life expectancy meant this was often for a more limited period than it is today.

Many working mothers rely on grandparents for childcare

## Why grandparents are more significant in family life today

- *The ageing population and increased life expectancy* – grandparents are healthier and around for much longer.
- *Smaller families mean fewer wider kin and siblings* (aunts and uncles) and, combined with the ageing population, more beanpole families, so grandparents take on a greater significance.
- *More women working in paid employment*, which has meant that grandparents have taken on childcare duties in respect of their grandchildren.
- *The growing wealth of some pensioner families.* In 2017, pensioner households held a larger share of total UK wealth than working households, and, on average, were £20 a week better off than typical working households. This means grandparents can be an important source of financial support to their adult children, and particularly their grandchildren.

## What grandparents contribute to family life

- *Providing childcare.* Time spent on childcare by the over-60s had risen by more than 20 per cent between 2000 and 2016. It is overwhelmingly mothers who change their work patterns when children are born, and childcare by grandparents plays a crucial role in enabling mothers' participation in paid employment. Many women would not be in paid employment today were it not for grandparents' childcare, particularly for pre-school children. Grandparents also help working parents with school-age children by picking them up from school, and by caring for them during school holidays or when schools are otherwise closed.
- *Acting as substitute parents.* In some cases, grandparents may choose to take over full responsibility for bringing up grandchildren when the parents are unable to do so themselves.

- *Socializing grandchildren* – for example, by passing on to their grand-children cultural knowledge, as well as family history and community traditions, and children can learn about what their parents were like when they were themselves children.
- *By providing help and advice.* Grandparents can provide advice when their children's relationships experience difficulties. Grandmothers, particularly, can provide a useful source of help and advice based on their own experience when their daughters have their first children, or when their children are growing up.
- *By 'financial caretaking' – financial support.* Research in 2017 by OneFamily found that grandparents are twice as likely to offer financial support to their grandchildren as the children's parents. Grandparents were using their savings to help their own children, and their grandchildren, to buy homes, pay off debts like student loans, and to help with the ongoing cost of education or training, paying for holidays or helping with monthly bills. Three-quarters (73 per cent) of grandparents who provide their families with financial support give the money with no strings attached.

This means that, for many families throughout the UK, grandparents have become the backbone of family life. However, with the rising state pension age, older people may be working longer, making it more difficult for them to provide support to their children's families.

> **Activity**
>
> Identify and explain one advantage of using unstructured interviews to investigate the contribution of grandparents to family life.

## A SUMMARY OF CHANGES IN FAMILIES

To conclude the changes in family structures and relationships that have been covered in this chapter, figure 3.18 provides a brief summary.

> **Activity**
>
> Refer to figure 3.18, and, in each case, write a short paragraph describing what change has occurred, and give two short explanations of why that change occurred. (**Note:** three boxes have a question mark (?). This means that there is some discussion about the extent to which this change has really occurred, so think about this when you're describing the change.)

**Figure 3.18** Changes in the family

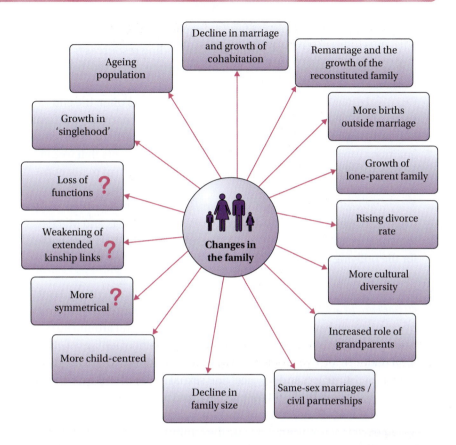

## CRITICAL VIEWS OF THE FAMILY: THE DARKER SIDE OF FAMILY LIFE

While the family is often a warm and supportive unit for its members, it can also be a harmful, hostile and dangerous place for individuals as the following examples suggest.

● *Isolation and conflict* – the privatization of family life can lead to emotional stress in the family. Family members are thrown together, isolated from and lacking the support of extended kin, neighbours and the wider community. Tempers become easily frayed, emotional temperatures and stress levels rise, and – as in an overloaded electrical circuit – fuses blow, and family conflict is the result. This may lead to violence, divorce, psychological damage to children, perhaps even mental illness and crime.

● *Dysfunctional families* show traits such as constant conflict, bullying and abusive relationships; drug and alcohol abuse; criminal behaviour; very poor parenting and out-of-control children; and family life marked by power struggles, violence and fear. Such families can also be a cost to wider society, demanding resources from the police and ambulance workers, and interventions and visits by social workers.

- *The breakdown of marriages* which leads to divorce is often the end result of initial unrealistic expectations glamorizing marriage and family life, and long-running and bitter disputes between partners. The intense emotions involved in family life often mean that incidents that would appear trivial in other situations take on the proportion of major confrontations inside the family.

- *The inequalities that women face in family life* – the dual burden and the triple shift, for example – have been blamed by feminists and Marxists for women's wider inequality in paid employment, and, as seen below, for the bullying and violence by men many women often face in families.

- *Violence in the family* is coming increasingly to public attention. Around 40 per cent of adult murders took place in the family in 2017 – committed by partners, ex-partners or other family members – and around 80 per cent of the victims were women. Around 60 per cent of killings of children under 16 are by parents or other family members. There are rising reports of the neglect and physical and sexual abuse of children, the rape of women by their husbands or partners, and wife- and baby-battering. Because of the private nature of the family, accurate evidence on the extent of violence and abuse inside the family is difficult to obtain, and fear or shame means that it is almost certain that most of such incidents are covered up.

All of these contribute to what is generally referred to as the 'darker side of family life'.

---

## The abuse of children

The abuse of children is increasingly brought to everyone's attention through the media, though much child abuse is likely to remain undiscovered and hidden behind the closed doors of family life. Children may be too young, too scared or too ashamed to tell anyone about what is happening to them.

There are several different types of abuse of children, as figure 3.19 shows.

- *Sexual abuse* – adults using their power to force or persuade a child to take part in sexual activities, whether or not the child is aware of what is happening.

- *Physical abuse* – non-sexual violence.
- *Emotional abuse* – persistent or severe emotional ill-treatment or rejection of children, which has severe effects on their emotional development and behaviour.
- *Neglect* – the failure to protect children from exposure to danger, including cold and starvation, and failing to care for them properly, so that their health or development is affected. Growing levels of poverty are fuelling higher levels of child neglect.

Government figures show that, in 2018, 581,000 children (up to age 18) in England – around 1 in 20 (5 per cent) of all children – were referred to children's services over concern for their well-being and safety; 53,790 children and young people were the subject of a Child Protection Plan because they were at continuing risk of harm from various forms of abuse. These figures are just for England, and only for abuse which was brought to the attention of social services departments. It is very likely that much abuse goes on without being discovered. Some indication of this is shown by statistics from ChildLine, the free confidential counselling service for children, established in 1986. In 2017–18, its website (www.childline.org.uk) received over 3.1 million visits, and of children referred for further help, around 15 per cent were for physical, sexual or emotional abuse, and neglect. Four out of five calls to the NSPCC helpline (www.nspcc.org.uk) related to these same types of abuse and neglect in 2016–17.

For many children, families are not a safe or happy place to be.

**Figure 3.19** Children and young people who were the subject of a Child Protection Plan (total: 53,790), by category of abuse: England, year ending 31 March 2018

*Source:* Department for Education (DfE)

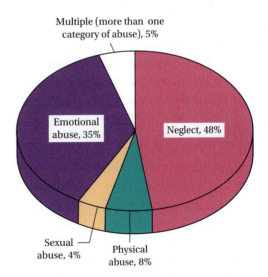

Multiple (more than one category of abuse), 5%

Emotional abuse, 35%

Neglect, 48%

Sexual abuse, 4%

Physical abuse, 8%

## Domestic abuse

There is widespread evidence of domestic abuse of various kinds. Domestic abuse involves any repeated patterns of abusive behaviour to maintain power and control in a relationship. The definition of domestic abuse, used by Women's Aid (see www.womensaid.org.uk), and very similar to the government and police definition, is:

> Any incident or pattern of incidents of controlling, coercive, threatening, degrading and violent behaviour, including sexual violence, in the majority of cases by a partner or ex-partner, but also by a family member or carer.

Domestic abuse is very common, and in the vast majority of cases the victims are women and it is carried out by men.

- The Crime Survey for England and Wales (CSEW) estimated there were 2 million adults aged 16 to 59 years who experienced domestic abuse of some kind in the year ending March 2018. Of these, 65 per cent were women, and 35 per cent men.
- *Police-recorded crime* (PRC) – a different measure from the CSEW – recorded 1.2 million domestic abuse-related incidents and crimes in England and Wales in the same period. Of these, half were criminal offences. This made up one in ten of all offences recorded by the police. In three-quarters of domestic abuse-related offences (according to the PRC measure) the victim was female (75 per cent).

Domestic abuse, often carried out over long periods of time, can have long-term effects on its victims, with harmful mental, emotional, physical, social and financial consequences. It also has wider social consequences – for example, the costs of police, health and other service responses, and time off having to be taken by survivors from paid employment and caring responsibilities.

Each year, on average, about 150 people are killed by a current or former partner or family member, and about 80 per cent of them are women. Most of the assaults and physically most violent incidents are committed by men against their female partners. Why do you think domestic violence is overwhelmingly committed by men against their female partners?

Spotlight Initiative

**Violence against**
# WOMEN

**30%**
of women over the age of 15 have experienced physical or sexual violence by a partner in their lifetime

SpotlightEndViolence

## *Domestic violence*

Domestic violence is only one aspect of domestic abuse, but has more immediate and serious consequences in terms of the physical harm to victims. It is estimated that 1 in 4 women, and 1 in 6 men, will suffer some form of domestic violence at some point in their relationships. Most of the assaults and physically most violent incidents – 89 per cent – are committed by men against their female partners. Each year about 150 people are killed by a current or former partner, and 80 per cent of them are women – an average of about 2 women every week.

- Domestic violence made up one-third (33%) of all 'violence against the person' crimes recorded by the police in 2017–18. In three-quarters (75%) of these domestic violence offences, the victims were women. Over half (53%) of all violence-against-the-person offences experienced by women is domestic, compared to 21% where the victim was male.
- In domestic-related sexual violence (mainly rape and sexual assaults) in 2017–18, 96% of the victims were women.
- Of domestic homicides (murder and manslaughter) between April 2014 and March 2017, 73% of victims were women, and four in five of them were killed by a male partner or ex-partner. Around 80% of all femicides – the murder of women because they are women – are domestic femicides, according to the Women's Aid Femicide Census (see goo.gl/idomiM).

This cartoon from 1896 shows domestic violence was the norm then, but are things really much better today?

'Can I have a black eye, too, Ma?' asks the little girl. 'Wait till you're old enough to get married, pet,' says her mother.

Research suggests female victims of domestic violence will suffer an average of 35–7 assaults for an average period of seven years before informing any agency. Despite the high level of violence against women in family relationships, many women do not leave their violent partners. This is often because of fear, shame and embarrassment, financial insecurity, lack of alternative housing, and concerns about disruption to their children's lives.

Men are also the victims of domestic abuse and violence, and a quarter of domestic violence has male victims (though this doesn't mean it is all committed by women). It is likely that male under-reporting of domestic abuse and violence is greater than that of women, because of masculine expectations and embarrassment at being abused by female partners.

Statistics such as those above reflect the extent and seriousness of the problem of violence in the home, particularly against women, much of which goes unreported and undiscovered. For many women, and some men, home is neither a secure nor a safe place to be.

## SIBLING ABUSE

While most people think of domestic abuse as occurring between adult partners, it can also occur between brothers and sisters, and may take similar forms to that between adults, or that of adults who abuse children. According to the NSPCC, a quarter of 18- to 24-year-olds, and more than 30 per cent of 11- to 17-year-olds, have been a victim of abuse by a sibling.

Sibling abuse may involve emotional, physical and sexually aggressive behaviour, such as name calling, ridiculing, put-downs, hitting, slapping and punching, and unwelcome sexual touching (or worse). While most of us will probably have hit, or been hit by, our brothers or sisters as part of normal sibling rivalry, if it gets out of hand it can have very damaging consequences on the development of young people, and may even establish a pattern of abuse which resurfaces in their own adult relationships.

### *Rape inside the family*

Rape is when someone is forced to have sex against her or his will, often accompanied by the actual or threatened use of violence. Estimates suggest more than one in four women has been raped, with over half of rapes being committed by men on their female partners, yet government estimates suggest that as many as 95 per cent of rapes are never reported to the police at all. About two-thirds of rapes, according to the Crime Survey for England and Wales, take place in the home of the victim or offender. Nearly half of rapes in couple relationships are accompanied by the actual or threatened use of violence, and one in five women suffer physical injury. Such sexual violence in the family, then, would appear to be disturbingly common, but it was only as recently as 1991 that rape within marriage was confirmed as a criminal offence by the Court of Appeal. Nonetheless, only about 7–8 per cent of all reported rapes lead to a rapist being convicted, and rapes in marriage or cohabiting relationships are the most difficult cases in which to prove in court that there was no consent.

## Explanations for domestic abuse and violence

- *Feminists* explain domestic abuse and violence as a means for men to exercise patriarchal power, to control and intimidate women, and to keep them in a state of submission. They argue domestic abuse is rooted in social inequality between women and men. It is about men showing women who's in charge. It may well be that female violence against men takes place to prevent this happening, as resistance to it, or for the same reason as men – so they alternatively assert control in relationships.
- *Marxists* emphasize wider factors as well, such as poverty, overcrowded homes and low incomes generating stress and disputes, erupting in violence. This doesn't explain, though, why domestic abuse and violence occur even in the richest families in society.

Feminists and Marxists agree that domestic abuse can only be tackled at its roots by improving women's power and independence in society – for example by making housing, childcare and employment policies, and the criminal justice system, more responsive to their needs.

---

### Activity

1 Describe two reasons why domestic abuse statistics are likely to understate the extent of this social problem.
2 Identify and describe one reason why domestic violence by women against men is less likely to be reported to the police than domestic violence by men against women.
3 Identify and describe one research method that sociologists might use to investigate domestic abuse and violence, and explain why you think this might be a suitable method.
4 Identify and describe two practical difficulties sociologists might face in trying to investigate the causes of domestic violence.
5 Go to www.womensaid.org.uk (the Women's Aid site), and find out the extent of domestic abuse and the policy measures being taken to combat it.

---

### Activity

Having completed this chapter, give three arguments for, and three against, the view that the family is of less importance in society today than it used to be.

## CHAPTER SUMMARY AND REVISION CHECKLIST

After studying this chapter, you should be able to:

- describe some social issues and social problems linked to families

- explain what is meant by a family, and how it differs from a household

- describe the different forms of marriage, families and households

- describe some alternatives to the family

- describe and criticize consensus and conflict theories of the role of the family in society, and explain the differences between functionalist, New Right, Marxist and feminist approaches to the family

- outline Parsons's functionalist view, Zaretsky's Marxist view and Delphy and Leonard's feminist view of the family

- explain the extent to which the family has lost its functions in society

- outline Oakley's view of the 'conventional family'

- explain what is meant by the cereal-packet image of the family, and why it is a misleading stereotype of the family in modern Britain

- describe Rapoport and Rapoport's five types of family diversity, giving examples of each

- describe how region, ethnicity and social class may affect family diversity

- explain what is meant by the beanpole family and why it has developed

- explain what is meant by the 'boomerang generation' and 'boomerang families' and why they arise

- explain why demographic changes – such as the decline in the birth rate, fertility rate, death rate and infant mortality rate, and increasing life expectancy and the ageing population – have occurred, and how these changes have affected families, including decreasing family size, family and household structures, and the emergence of the 'sandwich generation' and the rise of 'accordion families'

- explain how migration has affected families and households

- explain why the privatized nuclear family, or modified extended family, became the most common forms of families, and provide evidence for the continued existence of the classic extended family

- explain the links between the privatized nuclear family and features of contemporary society

- explain the reasons for the rising divorce rate, identify the groups most at risk of divorce, and describe some consequences of divorce for children, adults and family structures

- explain why remarriage and reconstituted families have become more common

- explain why there has been a large increase in the number of lone-parent families

- explain why there has been a decline in the numbers of people getting married, and increased cohabitation

- explain why there are now more births outside marriage

- explain why there is now more singlehood and an increase in one-person households

- outline Young and Willmott's view of the 'symmetrical family' and the reasons suggested for more symmetry in couple relationships, and the emergence of a 'new man'

- critically examine the view that roles in couple relationships have become more equal, with an apparent change in the domestic division of labour from segregated to integrated conjugal roles, and a growing partnership of equals

- explain why families have become more child-centred, including the roles of each parent
- describe and explain the role of grandparents in families
- describe and explain, with examples, what is meant by the darker side of family life

- briefly outline feminist and Marxist explanations for domestic abuse and violence
- identify some arguments and evidence for and against the view that the family may be of declining social importance

## KEY TERMS

Definitions can be found in the glossary at the end of this book, as well as these terms usually being defined in the margin where they first appear in the chapter. You can also find the glossary online by following the link at www.politybooks.com/browne. Put it in your phone for ready reference.

accordion family
ageing population
alienation
arranged marriage
beanpole family
bigamy
birth rate
boomerang family
boomerang generation
cereal-packet family
classic extended
 family
cohort
communes
conjugal roles
conventional family
death rate
demography
dependent
divorce rate

domestic division of
 labour
dominant ideology
dual burden
dual-career families
dual-earner families
dysfunctional family
emigration
emotional work
empty-shell marriage
expressive role
extended family
family diversity
fertility rate
forced marriage
geographically mobile
household
hybrid families
immigration
infant mortality rate

instrumental role
joint (or integrated)
 conjugal roles
kibbutz
kinship
labour power
life course
life expectancy
marriage rate
matrifocal family
meritocratic society
migration
modified extended
 family
monogamy
moral panic
net migration
nuclear family
polyandry
polygamy

polygyny
privatized (or isolated)
 nuclear family
reconstituted (blended or
 step-) family
sandwich generation
secularization
segregated conjugal
 roles
serial monogamy
sexual (or gendered)
 division of labour
social exclusion
social mobility
social policy
stigma
structural differentiation
symmetrical family
total fertility rate
triple shift

There are a variety of free tests and other activities that can be used to assess your learning – mainly aimed at AS- and A-level sociology students, but you might find them useful – as well as an online searchable glossary, at

www.politybooks.com/browne

You can also find new contemporary resources by following Ken Browne on Twitter

@BrowneKen

CHAPTER

# 4 Education

## Contents

**KEY ISSUES**

- Education as a social issue
- The role of education in society
- Education in Britain before the 1970s
- Comprehensive schools and selection
- Education from 1988 onwards: the free market in education
- School diversity
- Factors influencing educational achievement
- Inequality in education
- Is equality of educational opportunity possible to achieve?

The sociology of education covers a vast area, and it is impossible in this book to cover all aspects. This chapter therefore takes as its main focus the school system, rather than further and higher education, and concentrates on three main aspects of this: what the purposes of education are; the main features and changes which have occurred in the school system since around the 1970s; and the continuing inequalities in education, including the factors that influence whether students succeed or fail in education.

## EDUCATION AS A SOCIAL ISSUE

Public spending on education amounted to around £88 billion a year in the UK in 2018 – about 11 per cent of total national and local government spending. It is perhaps not surprising then that politicians spend a lot of time discussing what the education system is for.

Examples of these social issues include the questions below.

- What are the aims and purposes of education? For example, should schools be concerned with serving the needs of the economy, and providing the skills that employers want? Or should education be particularly concerned with giving the most disadvantaged a helping hand up to improve their life chances? Or stimulating the interests and creativity of children?
- Should children be selected for particular schools by ability?

- Should children be tested to measure their achievements, and how and when?
- Are educational standards sufficiently high, and how can they be improved?
- Should parents be given the opportunity to choose any school they like for their children, and should the government provide schools for every kind of interest group, such as every religious faith?
- Who should run schools? Should they be run by local authorities (local councils)? Or should they be run by private businesses, or groups of parents? Or should they run themselves as free-standing, state-funded, independent institutions?

The on-going uncertainty among politicians about whether the education system is doing what it should is shown by the pace of change, and every year since at least 1988 there has been some new reform of the education system, and every new government or new education minister seems to have different ideas about what the education system should do and how it should be working.

Education is an important social issue in contemporary society because parents want the best for their children, yet there are huge inequalities in educational opportunities and in attainment between the richest and poorest social groups. Not all children of the same ability have the same chance of succeeding in education. Yet education is still, for most people, the key and only means to a healthy, comfortable and secure adult life, and a poor-quality education can have damaging and lasting consequences throughout a person's life.

## THE ROLE OF EDUCATION IN SOCIETY

Education is a major social institution, and schools in Britain command a captive audience of virtually all children between the ages of 5 and 16, though everyone has to stay in some form of full-time education or training until they are 18. During this period of compulsory schooling, children spend about half of the time they are awake at school during term time – about 15,000 hours of their lives.

Why is such importance attached to the provision of education in contemporary society? What does education contribute to society? Why are schools necessary in industrial societies, and why is education to the age of 16 compulsory?

The answer to these questions lies in the *functions* that education performs in society.

Full-time education is compulsory in the UK from ages 5 to 16 (and education or training to age 18), though many children start younger in reception classes at primary and infant schools, at pre-schools, nurseries and playgroups. About 11 per cent of everything national and local government spends goes on education. Why do you think such importance is attached to education?

### Activity

1 List all the reasons you go/went to school. What benefits (if any) do you think going to school has brought you?
2 How do you think your life would differ if you didn't have / hadn't had to go to school?
3 What problems might there be for individuals and society if compulsory education were to be abolished tomorrow?

## The consensus approach to education: the functionalist perspective

The functionalist approach (or perspective) on education follows the same principles as all functionalist approaches to the study of society. It is concerned with the links between education and other social institutions, such as the family and the workplace, and the functions or role of education for society as a whole. Education is seen by functionalists as playing a key role in preparing young people for adulthood, **citizenship** and working life. Émile Durkheim, Talcott Parsons and other functionalists identified four basic functions of education.

### 1 Passing on society's culture and building social cohesion

Durkheim (1973 [1925]) saw education as a key agency of secondary socialization, continuing the process of primary socialization which begins in the family.

Durkheim saw education as playing a key function in the transmission (or handing on) of society's culture and shared norms and values from one generation to the next. Education was important in building a value consensus and **social cohesion**. This would give new generations a sense of belonging and commitment to wider society, and enable the development of **social solidarity** which underpinned a stable society.

For example, in Britain the school curriculum teaches young people about history, geography, science, English language and literature, and so on. Citizenship and PSHE (Personal, Social, Health and Economic) education helps pupils develop the knowledge, skills and characteristics they need to keep themselves healthy and safe, and prepare for adult life and work as citizens in modern Britain.

Pupils learn about the rights and responsibilities, and duties and freedoms, of people living in a democratic society, and develop knowledge, skills and understanding about laws and justice, and respect for different national, religious and ethnic identities. Citizenship is now part of the National Curriculum in England for 11- to 16-year-olds (Key Stages 3 and 4), with the aim of encouraging and equipping young people to play a full, active and responsible role in public life and in running the society to which they belong. Citizenship in England also involves some understanding of what it means to be British, with awareness of the history, beliefs, values and other features making up the British way of life. Through their formal education, pupils then begin to identify with British culture and see themselves as British citizens.

In Wales, citizenship is included as part of PSE (Personal and Social Education), with the teaching of Welsh to foster a sense of Welsh national

**Citizenship**
The legal, social and political rights and responsibilities of individuals (citizens) living in a society.

**Social cohesion**
The bonds or 'glue' that bring people together and integrate them into a united society.

**Social solidarity**
The integration of people into society through shared values, a common culture, shared understandings, and social ties that bind them together.

What are the things that make up Britishness (or substitute any other national identity you have)? Is it traditional British foods? Symbols like flags and Big Ben? Our language? Our values and beliefs? What do you think makes you British, and how does/did your schooling contribute to this?

### Activity

In the activity below, if you see yourself as having some other national identity, such as being Welsh, Scottish, Irish and so on, answer these questions, where appropriate, by replacing 'British' with your own national identity.

1 Suggest three ceremonies, three symbols and three values which you think might show a *British* identity, and which make the British in some ways different from people of other nations.

2 Drawing on your citizenship education, discuss what rights and responsibilities you have as a British citizen.

3 To what extent do you think the education system helps – or doesn't help – to build social cohesion? Give examples to illustrate your answer.

**Hidden curriculum** The learning of values, attitudes and behaviour through the school's organization and teachers' attitudes, rather than as part of the formal timetable – e.g. obedience, punctuality and conformity to school rules.

**Particularistic values** Standards and rules that give priority to personal relationships.

**Universalistic values** Standards and rules that apply equally to everyone, regardless of who they are.

**Ascribed status** Status which is given to an individual at birth and usually can't be changed. Examples of such status include a person's age, ethnic group, sex, or place or family of birth. Members of the royal family in Britain have ascribed status.

**Achieved status** Status that individuals have achieved through their own efforts, such as in education, through skills and talents, or via promotion at work and career success.

**Equality of opportunity** The opportunity to compete on the same terms as everyone else.

identity. In Scotland, similar aims are met through the Social Studies curriculum area, and in Northern Ireland by Personal Development & Mutual Understanding (PD&MU) and Learning for Life and Work (LLW).

Through the **hidden curriculum** (see page 214 below), pupils learn things like respect for others, obeying adult authority, and conformity to rules. These all contribute to building social cohesion.

## 2 Providing a bridge between the particularistic values and ascribed status of the family and the universalistic values and achieved status of contemporary advanced societies

Parsons (1964) argues that, in the family, people's status is ascribed (given at birth) and children are judged in terms of **particularistic values** – standards and rules that give priority to personal relationships. For example, in the family, children are judged as special individuals and by standards that apply only to them. In wider society, status is achieved – people have to earn it. They are judged in terms of **universalistic values** – standards and rules that are applied equally to everyone, regardless of who they are. For example, a teacher marking student essays might reasonably be expected to give marks to everyone according to the same rules (universalistic values), not give different marks depending on whether they liked the student or not (particularistic values). Similarly, students might be expected to achieve a place at university because of their exam grades (universalistic), not because they knew someone who worked there (particularistic).

Parsons argues that, in contemporary societies, universalistic values are meritocratic – people achieve their status on the basis of merit (talents, skills and qualifications): *what* they know rather than *who* they know.

Parsons believes schools provide a bridge between the particularistic standards and **ascribed status** of the family, and the universalistic standards and **achieved status** of wider society.

Durkheim argued that schools were a society in miniature, where children learn to cooperate with those who are neither their family nor their friends. They are judged by their individual achievements, where everyone has **equality of opportunity** – the opportunity to compete on the same terms as everyone else. As children move from primary school to the end of secondary schooling, they are gradually encouraged to take on more responsibilities, to become more independent and to stand on their own two feet, as they will have to when they leave school. This small-scale version of society as a whole then prepares young people for life in the wider adult society.

## 3 Preparation for working life – providing a trained and qualified labour force for the economy

Durkheim and other functionalists see education as crucial in providing a properly trained, qualified and flexible labour force. In a complex industrial society with a specialized **division of labour** (where the world of work is divided into lots of different jobs requiring different kinds of skills), the education system plays an important role in developing the knowledge and skills in the workforce that are needed to enable the economy to prosper.

A literate and numerate workforce is more or less essential in an industrial society, and the skills of use and application of number, communication and information technology are much in demand by employers. There is also the need for specific skills related to particular jobs, such as computing, engineering and science.

As well as encouraging people to accept traditional ideas which will lead to order and stability in society, schools and colleges also prepare students for a rapidly changing industrial society (see the box on vocational education). Since the 1970s, for example, there has been a massive expansion of ICT (Information and Communication Technology) in schools and colleges, in an attempt to prepare young people for a world after school in which ICT plays a central role.

> **Division of labour** The division of work or occupations into a large number of specialized tasks, each of which is carried out by one worker or group of workers.

Schools have played a key role in making young people computer-literate in a society in which information and communication technology is increasingly dominant in all spheres of life

## VOCATIONAL EDUCATION

The emphasis on making education meet the needs of industry, and preparing young people for work, is known as vocational education. A key feature of this has been improving the quality of the basic skills of the workforce, with a particular focus on the 14–18 age group. Measures to achieve this have included:

- *Work experience programmes* for pupils in school years 10 and 11 to ease the transition from school to work, and help/encourage them to get jobs successfully and carry them out well, with a better understanding of work and the economy. Such programmes are no longer compulsory in schools though some schools still provide them.
- *More educational courses, and government training schemes* for those leaving school, which are more closely related to the world of work, and concerned more with learning work-related skills. For example, work-based City and Guilds, BTECs, Diplomas, NVQs (National Vocational Qualifications) and apprenticeships, combining practical training in a job with study.
- *An expansion of post-16 education and training.*

### Criticisms of vocational education

- Work experience is sometimes seen by school students as boring and repetitive, involving little development of their skills and little to do with their future ambitions. Some complain of having been given too little work to do, or having to undertake menial or repetitive tasks. There is sometimes limited support or poor supervision/management from their employer, and students are sometimes reluctant to ask busy workers for support as they have their own jobs to do.
- Post-school training schemes are often similarly criticized for providing little development of skills, for being used as a source of cheap labour by employers, and for not leading to 'proper' jobs at the end of the training.
- Vocational education and qualifications are often seen as having lower status than more traditional academic subjects and courses. Vocational qualifications are, in general, less likely to lead to university entry, and are more likely to lead to lower-status, lower-paid jobs as adults.

Do you think work experience programmes at school are useful? Do you think vocational courses are more or less valuable to students compared to doing more academic courses such as traditional GCSEs and AS- and A-levels?

---

**Activity**

1  Should schools be concerned mainly with meeting the needs of business and industry, and fitting people into the job market? Or should they be concerned with the development of individuals, allowing them to pursue and develop their interests? Suggest two advantages and two disadvantages of each view.
2  Think about any school work experience programmes you have been involved in. Were/are they very useful to you? Give reasons for your answer.
3  Drawing on your own experiences at school, what features of your education do you think prepared you / will prepare you most for adult and working life after school? Think of the particular subjects studied and activities undertaken. To what extent do you think these were successful?
4  What other things do you think should be taught at school to enable people to play a full and responsible part in adult and working life?
5  Do you think GCSEs, AS- and A-levels have the same status as vocational qualifications in schools? Explain your answer.

---

## 4  Selecting and allocating people for roles in a meritocratic society, and justifying social inequality

Parsons believed that schools functioned as an important mechanism for the selection of individuals for their future occupations in society.

The things learnt at school will generally affect the kind of job and training opportunities open to people after school. Schools and colleges act like a sieve, grading young people through streaming and testing according to their individual merits, abilities and educational qualifications. This sieving and grading process is used by employers and other educational institutions to select suitable people for work and further courses. Functionalists argue this ensures that the best and most-qualified people end up in the jobs requiring the greatest skills and responsibilities.

This important result of education has been reflected in the attempts to establish **equality of educational opportunity**, so that all children can have the same educational opportunities in life, regardless of their social-class background, ability to pay school fees, ethnic origin, gender or disability. However, despite these attempts, inequality in educational opportunity remains, as will be considered later.

Education will therefore influence the individual's eventual social-class position as an adult and their life chances. These are the chances of obtaining those things defined as desirable – such as secure, well-paid jobs, good housing and health – and of avoiding those things defined as undesirable in a society, such as poverty and unemployment. In a few cases, education can be a means of upward **social mobility** into the middle class for children from a working-class family. Figure 4.1 illustrates this link between education and the class structure.

> **Equality of educational opportunity** The idea that every child, regardless of his or her social-class background, ability to pay school fees, ethnic origin, gender or disability, should have an equal chance of doing as well in education as his or her ability will allow.

> **Social mobility** The movement of groups or individuals up or down the social hierarchy.

**Figure 4.1** Education and the class structure

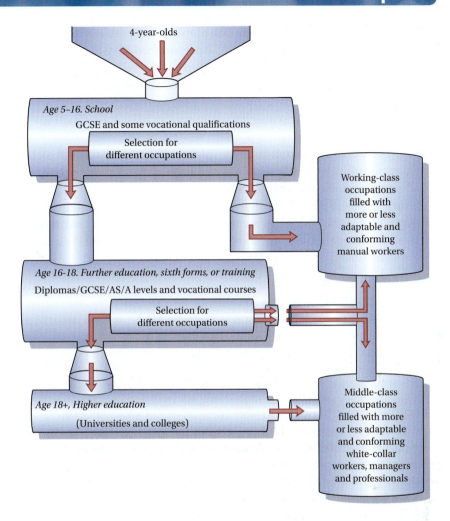

4-year-olds

Age 5–16. School
GCSE and some vocational qualifications

Selection for different occupations

Working-class occupations filled with more or less adaptable and conforming manual workers

Age 16-18. Further education, sixth forms, or training
Diplomas/GCSE/AS/A levels and vocational courses

Selection for different occupations

Age 18+, Higher education
(Universities and colleges)

Middle-class occupations filled with more or less adaptable and conforming white-collar workers, managers and professionals

**Meritocracy** (or meritocratic society) A society in which social and occupational positions (jobs) and pay are allocated purely on the basis of people's merits, such as their individual experience, talents, abilities, qualifications and skills – their individual merits. In Britain today, this nearly always means educational qualifications.

Functionalists see modern industrial societies as generally meritocratic – a **meritocracy** in which most social positions are achieved by merit, such as experience, talent, skill and exam qualifications, and in which everyone has equality of educational opportunity. Everyone who has the ability and talent and puts in the effort has an equal chance of coming out ahead. Functionalists therefore regard this selection process as fair, and social inequality in society is justified as it is those who are most able and qualified who reach the top positions in society. Those lower down lack ability or have failed to work hard at school, so have only themselves to blame.

## Criticisms of the functionalist perspective

- Marxists argue that the values passed on by the education system are not shared by everyone, but are imposed by those with power in society – the wealthy dominant class – to protect their own interests.

- Schooling isn't simply concerned with preparation of the workforce to enable the economy to run smoothly. It prepares working-class children for working-class jobs, and teaches them to be passive making them easier to exploit at work (see Bowles and Gintis's correspondence principle below).
- Feminists argue that schooling passes on patriarchal values, disadvantaging girls and women.
- Society is not based on universalistic values – inherited wealth and social characteristics like social class background, gender and ethnicity still affect access to the highest positions.
- Education is not meritocratic, and there is no equality of educational opportunity – social class, gender and ethnicity are still major barriers to success in education and the development of talents, even for those with the same ability.

---

**SOCIAL CONTROL AND THE HIDDEN CURRICULUM**

Functionalists, Marxists and feminists all recognize schools act as important agencies of social control. Functionalists argue this is a good thing as it encourages children to learn and conform to the values and norms expected by a society based on value consensus, preparing them for adult life. The *conflict view* of Marxists and feminists suggests this social control is repressive – as the values and norms are not based on consensus, but imposed by the dominant groups in society – and prepares children to be docile and submissive adults.

This social control is mainly carried out through what is known as the hidden curriculum. This consists of the learning of values, attitudes and behaviour – such as obedience, punctuality and conformity to school rules – through the school's organization, school rules and teachers' attitudes. This includes things like school assemblies, merit points and prizes, detentions and suspensions, and learning to accept the authority hierarchy of the school. This teaching is 'hidden' because there are no obvious, organized courses in 'obedience and conformity', as there are in the formal curriculum of timetabled subjects, lessons and exams, such as in mathematics or English.

This hidden curriculum is often reflected in the **school ethos** – the character and atmosphere of a school – e.g. what the school rules are; whether there's a school uniform or dress-code policy, an emphasis on academic success or sporting achievements, a focus on religious/spiritual development; whether pupils feel valued and respected; whether parents are encouraged to get involved; whether there's an emphasis on equal opportunities for all, or concern with SEND (**S**pecial **E**ducational **N**eeds and **D**isabilities) pupils, etc.

The hidden curriculum is present throughout schooling, and those who conform to it are likely to be rewarded, while those who don't are likely to be branded as non-conformists by the school and may find themselves getting into trouble. The Marxist view of this hidden curriculum, and what is being taught, is explored further below.

**School ethos**
The character and atmosphere of a school.

---

**Activity**

1 Describe one feature of the hidden curriculum found in your school, or the one you once attended, and explain how this reinforces the wider values of society outside school.
2 Describe two features of the hidden curriculum in your school, or the one you once attended, which might be regarded as discriminating against students from minority ethnic groups or either boys or girls.
3 Are/were there any features of the hidden curriculum in your school which you think might encourage students to take more power and control in schools, such as democratic decision-making, free choice of dress or school councils? Explain your answer.

---

## A conflict approach to education: the Marxist perspective

Marxists regard education, and particularly schooling, as a form of repressive social control. Schooling:

**Ruling-class ideology** The ideas and beliefs of the dominant class which controls society.

- *passes on* **ruling-class ideology** – the ideas and beliefs of the dominant class which controls society.
- *attempts to justify the capitalist system*, and make sure future workers are passive conformists who don't rock the boat or question the power and interests of the dominant class (see Bowles and Gintis, below)
- *tries to persuade future workers to accept their social position* and current patterns of inequality in power, wealth and income.
- *reproduces and legitimizes (explains and justifies) the existing class structure* – For most young people, it is not a means of upward social mobility, but simply confirms pupils' class of origin (the one they were born into) as their class of destination (the one they end up in as adults). Those who fail in education are blamed for their own lack of ability and effort, rather than considering the material and cultural barriers they face in schooling.

### *Bowles and Gintis: schooling, the correspondence principle and the 'long shadow of work'*

Marxists Bowles and Gintis (2011 [1976]), in a study based on 237 members of the senior year of a New York high school, argue that the major role of education in capitalist societies is the reproduction of a hard-working, submissive and disciplined workforce, which is too divided to challenge management at work. Bowles and Gintis argue that such a workforce is reproduced in two main ways.

1 *Through the hidden curriculum of schooling and the correspondence, or very close similarity, between the social relationships at school and at work*

## Table 4.1 The Marxist correspondence principle and the hidden curriculum

| What pupils are socialized to accept through the hidden curriculum | What it corresponds with at the workplace –'the long shadow of work' |
|---|---|
| ❖ Privileges and responsibilities given to older pupils | ➔ Respect for elders, and superiors/managers at work |
| ❖ Pupils' lack of power and control about the subjects taught, how the school is run or the school-day organized | ➔ Workers' lack of power and control at work |
| ❖ The authority hierarchy of the school involving pupils fitting into a complex organization of heads, deputies, heads of department, year heads, etc. | ➔ Learning about their place in the hierarchies of power and control in society and accepting it – for example, in the authority hierarchy at work |
| ❖ Males and females often having different dress rules, being expected to conform to different standards of behaviour, and being counselled into different subjects, further education courses, and careers | ➔ Males and females doing different jobs with unequal pay and opportunities |
| ❖ Respecting authority of teachers regardless of what they say or do | ➔ Respect for bosses at work |
| ❖ Punctuality / being on time: time belongs to the school, not the pupil | ➔ Good time-keeping at work: the employer pays for the worker's time, so it belongs to the company, not the worker |
| ❖ Grading by ability (streaming and setting) and exam success/failure | ➔ Accepting that different jobs, such as managerial, skilled and unskilled manual occupations, and the differences in power, status and pay between them, are natural and justified, as those higher up have worked harder, are more intelligent and better qualified |
| ❖ Rewarding (by high grades) and exam success qualities of dependability, punctuality and acceptance of authority; lower grades to those who show creativity, assertiveness and independence | ➔ Workers are expected to be dependable, be punctual and accept bosses' authority. |
| ❖ Motivating pupils by marks, grades and qualifications | ➔ Working for pay in unfulfilling and powerless jobs. |
| ❖ Concentrating on schoolwork, whether or not it's boring and whether or not you want to do it | ➔ Workers having to accept boring, menial and repetitive jobs |
| ❖ Value being placed on hard work and getting on | ➔ Everyone being able to make it to the top if she or he tries hard enough |
| ❖ The school curriculum being broken up into separate subjects which are clearly separated from one another. | ➔ Work is divided into many separate jobs (the division of labour) which keeps the workforce from having knowledge of the whole process |
| ❖ Competitive sports / competing for grades, merit badges, prizes, exam results, etc. | ➔ Workers competing for jobs |

<table>
<tr><td>

**Correspondence principle** (or theory) The way the hidden curriculum in schools corresponds closely to, or mirrors, many features which are expected in the workplace.

</td></tr>
</table>

The correspondence theory – or **correspondence principle** – is the idea that the hidden curriculum in schools corresponds closely to, or mirrors, many features of the workplace. The norms and values pupils are socialized to accept at school correspond to the norms and values which will make it easy for future capitalist employers to exploit them at work. Schooling then operates in what Bowles and Gintis called the 'long shadow of work'. This is illustrated in table 4.1.

2  *Through the role of the education system in legitimizing or justifying inequality and the class structure.* Bowles and Gintis argue that the educational system:

- helps to maintain, justify and explain (legitimize) the system of social inequality and the class structure in capitalist society
- helps people to accept their own position in it
- therefore helps to reduce discontent and opposition to inequality.

Bowles and Gintis reject the functionalist view that social class inequalities in capitalist society arise from fair competition in education, in which everyone stands an equal chance. In contrast, they argue that social-class background (and also ethnicity and gender) are the main factors related to success or failure in education and the job market. People from upper- and upper-middle-class backgrounds (and who are white and male) tend to obtain higher qualifications and better jobs than working-class children of similar ability.

***The myths of equality of educational opportunity and meritocracy***  Bowles and Gintis see both equality of opportunity and meritocracy as myths that socialize working-class children into accepting that failure in education arises from lack of ability or hard work, when in most cases it arises because those who succeed have advantages arising from their social class and family background (this is discussed more later in this chapter – see pages 246–64).

Education is therefore seen as acting as a kind of confidence trick, which hides the fact that it maintains and reproduces the existing pattern of social class inequalities between generations. In most cases, the education system is not a means of upward social mobility, but seems to be sending children from working-class homes into working-class jobs as adults, and children from middle-class homes into middle-class jobs. The education system, from this point of view, is involved in reproducing and justifying the inequalities that already exist in society, and simply confirming individuals' class of origin (the one they were born into) as their class of destination (the one they end up in as adults).

## Criticisms of the Marxist perspective

- Pupils are not passive conformists and consumers of education. They often rebel against the school, and frequently have little regard for teachers' authority, school rules and discipline (as Willis's research below shows).

- Marxists place too much emphasis on the role of education, and ignore wider influences on young people, such as the family and the media.

- Marxists place too much emphasis on the hidden curriculum, and ignore some influences of the formal curriculum. This does not always seem designed to promote the ideal employee for capitalism, and to develop uncritical, passive and unquestioning conformist behaviour. The humanities and subjects like sociology produce critical thinkers, while work-related courses remain of relatively low status.

- Employers often complain that the education system does not produce the well-qualified and conformist workers with suitable skills and attitudes that Marxist writers suggest it does.

***The work of Willis***   Willis (1977) adopted a Marxist approach, but also draws on the interactionist perspective. He disagreed with Bowles and Gintis that education was successful as an agency of socialization preparing a willing and obedient workforce for capitalism. A quick glance at almost any secondary school provides evidence that students do not always obey teachers, and that they can be disruptive and challenge the school.

Willis used observation and participant observation, group discussions, informal interviews and diaries to study a group of twelve working-class male pupils in a school on a working-class housing estate in Wolverhampton in the 1970s. He referred to this group as 'the lads', and aimed to understand the experience of schooling from their point of view.

Willis found the lads saw through the system and realized they couldn't all be socially mobile; they saw that there was no such thing as equal opportunity for them, as, no matter how hard they tried, they would be less successful than middle-class students. The lads consequently developed a **counter-school (or anti-school) subculture** opposed both to the main aims of the school, and to the 'pen-pushing' of the 'ear 'oles' – conformist pupils who generally complied with school values.

The lads did not see school as relevant to them, and attached little value to its aims, such as gaining qualifications. Their priorities were to reject school and free themselves from its control – for example by avoiding or disrupting lessons, to have a laugh, to get their hands on money, to impress their mates, to keep up with older drinkers in the pub, to impress the girls, and to leave school and get into the world of work as soon as possible and show they could 'graft' in male manual jobs as well as the next man.

Willis found a similarity between the counter-school culture and the workplace culture of male lower-working-class jobs, such as **sexism**, a lack

**Counter-school (or anti-school) subculture** A group within a school organized around a set of norms, values, attitudes and behaviour in opposition to the main values, norms and aims of a school.

**Sexism** Prejudice or discrimination against people (especially women) because of their sex.

of respect for authority, and an emphasis on 'having a laugh' to escape the boring and oppressive nature of both school and work.

Willis's research suggests that schools are not directly preparing the sort of obedient and docile labour force required by capitalism that Bowles and Gintis suggest. Young, working-class males are not forced or persuaded by the school to leave and look for manual jobs, but actively reject school through the counter-school culture and willingly enter male semi-skilled and unskilled work the minute they leave school.

## A conflict approach to education: the feminist perspective

There are a range of inequalities facing girls in schools on top of any other inequalities relating to their social class or ethnic backgrounds. For example, there are differences in subject options which affect future career choices; there is some evidence that, even though girls are beating boys in educational achievements, they could do better still if boys didn't dominate and disrupt lessons, take up more teacher time than girls, and sideline girls in the classroom.

Francis (2005) and other feminists see education – particularly through the hidden curriculum – as perpetuating patriarchy, and the ongoing inequalities between women and men in wider society. Francis emphasizes the patriarchal nature of schools is revealed through:

- their role in the secondary socialization of boys and girls into different gender roles, which first begins during primary socialization in the family
- their reinforcement of patriarchal control by males over females, particularly in mixed classrooms
- their teaching of patriarchal norms and values – for example women's role as carers and limiting access to certain subjects and career options, such as science and engineering, ensuring that males remain more powerful in society.

**Marginalization**
The process whereby some groups or individuals are pushed by poverty, ill health, lack of education, racism, sexism and so on to the margins of society, and are unable to take part in the life enjoyed by the majority of people.

Fitting in at school and with your peers often involves adopting gender-appropriate behaviour linked to gender stereotypes. Ridicule, bullying and **marginalization** – being pushed onto the margins of school and classroom life – threaten those who don't conform.

Francis suggests schooling creates and reinforces gender identities and the patriarchal power of boys over girls through:

- *Gendered verbal behaviour* – Boys dominating talk in mixed-sex classrooms, interrupting girls, belittling girls' contributions, making put-down remarks, making sexist jokes and using terms of sexual abuse for girls, creating an atmosphere that degrades girls.

- *Gendered physical behaviour* – Boys and girls sitting in different groups; boys dominating physical space in the classroom and being more boisterous generally, and getting into confrontations with teachers. This means they take up much more of the teacher's time, and – literally – crowd out the girls, who become almost 'invisible' in the classroom.
- *Gendered pursuits* – Girls' classroom talk and activity focus on their appearance and femininity (e.g. hair, make-up and diet) to please boys. By contrast, boys boast of their (alleged) sexual conquests.
- *Gendered classroom behaviour and power* – Girls helping boys and deferring to them in classroom interaction. Girls may find themselves silenced, ridiculed or physically or sexually abused by boys if they challenge their dominance.
- *Teachers' different expectations of boys and girls* – 'Boys will be boys', but girls are expected to be quiet, conformist, obedient and conscientious. Girls who don't conform are more likely to be penalized by teachers, as girls are expected to be good, while boys aren't.

### Activity

1 Suggest a research method to find out whether and how boys and girls behave differently in class or are treated differently by male and female teachers. Explain why you chose that method, and identify two strengths and two weaknesses of it.
2 Describe three ways in which schools may socialize children into gender roles.

### A SUMMARY OF CONSENSUS AND CONFLICT APPROACHES TO EDUCATION

| | | |
|---|---|---|
| Education teaches shared norms and values, and socializes children into a value consensus | Education socializes children into acceptance of the dominant ideology | Education socializes children into a patriarchal ideology of unequal male and female gender roles |
| Education carries out social control to prevent threats to social cohesion and social solidarity | Education carries out social control to prevent resistance to a society based on inequality and class conflict | Education carries out social control to prevent opposition to a patriarchal society |
| Education allocates roles on a meritocratic basis in societies with equality of opportunity for all | Education is not meritocratic, and there is no equality of opportunity | Education provides different and better opportunities for boys, compared to girls |
| Education provides a means for upward social mobility for those who have the ability and work hard | Education confirms class of origin as class of destination | Education leads to girls and boys having unequal gender roles in a patriarchal society |

| Functionalist consensus perspective | Marxist conflict perspective | Feminist conflict perspective |
|---|---|---|
| Education provides the knowledge and skills needed for a disciplined, qualified labour force, with the best qualified getting the best jobs | Education puts working-class children into working-class jobs, and middle-class children are more likely to succeed and get middle-class jobs | Education reinforces patriarchy by encouraging girls to choose different subjects leading to lower-paid jobs and unpaid work in the home |
| Education justifies inequality, as it is based on a meritocracy | Education only pretends it's meritocratic. It teaches children that educational failure is their own fault, so persuading them to accept inequality | Education justifies patriarchy through the hidden curriculum of gendered behaviour in classrooms |
| The hidden curriculum prepares children for the rules of adult life and belonging to society | The hidden curriculum corresponds to features of the workplace, and encourages children to accept authority and inequality without questioning them | The hidden curriculum prepares girls for a working life in which they will face patriarchal discrimination and inequality. |

## EDUCATION IN BRITAIN BEFORE THE 1970S

Until the 1960s, all children went first to primary schools (as they do now) but then were selected, at age 11, by whether they passed or failed a special intelligence quotient (IQ) test (the 11+ / Eleven-plus examination), to go to one of three types of secondary school – grammar, technical and secondary modern schools. These three types of secondary school became known as the **tripartite system**.

The 15–20 per cent of children with the best 11+ exam results went to grammar schools, with most children going to secondary modern schools. There were hardly any technical schools established. Figure 4.2 illustrates the tripartite system, and the social classes young people were being prepared for as adults.

During the 1960s, the tripartite system came increasingly under attack:

- The 11+ exam was seen as an unfair and inaccurate selection test, which damaged the self-esteem and educational opportunities of children who failed to win a place at a grammar school.
- Secondary modern schools were seen as inferior, second-rate schools, compared to higher-status grammar schools which offered better life chances to their pupils.
- Research suggested that the talent, ability and potential of many children in the secondary modern schools were being wasted, and could be better developed in a **comprehensive school** (see below).

**Tripartite system** The system of secondary education established in 1944 in which pupils were selected for one of three types of secondary school according to their performance in the 11+ exam.

**Comprehensive school** One which accepts children of all abilities, without any selection by examination.

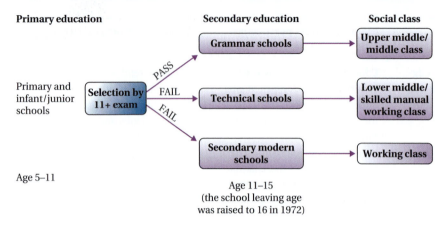

Figure 4.2 The tripartite system

As a result, the tripartite system was abolished in most of the country, and by the 1970s most children attended comprehensive schools, as they do today.

## COMPREHENSIVE SCHOOLS AND SELECTION

Comprehensive education abolished both selection by the 11+ exam and the three types of secondary school. Children in most areas now, regardless of their ability, generally transfer to the same type of school at the age of 11, with no selection by examination. Around nine out of ten young people in the UK now attend some form of comprehensive school, with only 163 state grammar schools remaining in England in 2018, attended by around 5 per cent of all pupils in state-funded secondary schools.

---

### SELECTION REMAINS AN ISSUE TODAY

The issue of selection by ability for secondary education, and whether this is necessary to give young people the most suitable form of secondary education, are still hotly disputed matters. Many state-funded schools are allowed to select up to 10 per cent of their pupils by ability in a particular specialist subject they offer, though many do not use this, but there has been a return to streaming and a move away from mixed-ability teaching. In 2016, the government announced its intention to allow state schools to start selection by ability, and to allow more grammar schools, which are allowed to select by ability. This was fiercely opposed by many parents and educators, and plans were later dropped. School and college league tables and the judging of schools and colleges on their results (see later in this chapter) constantly raise the issue of whether students should be selected by ability, so some schools get the best, most able students in an area – though this, of course, disadvantages other schools.

True comprehensive schools have no selection by ability at all, and children of all abilities are admitted to the same types of school and taught in mixed-ability classes. However, some selection by ability does continue in the education system and – through **streaming** and **setting** – in many comprehensive schools as well.

---

## The case against selection: the advantages of comprehensive schools

### *Opportunities remain open*

In comprehensive schools, the possibility of educational success and obtaining qualifications remains open throughout a child's school career, since moving between streams and classes within one school is easier and more likely to happen than moving between different types of school in a selective system.

### *Late developers benefit*

Late developers, whose intelligence and ability improve after the age of 11, can be catered for better in the comprehensive system, rather than having their opportunities limited at an early age.

Middle-class parents are generally better placed to coach a less bright child – who might therefore have once got a grammar school place at age 11 – than parents from a less well-off background with a late-developing bright child, who might have failed to get a grammar school place. Comprehensives cater for both, and disadvantage neither.

### *More get better qualifications*

Fewer students leave school without any qualifications in the comprehensive system, and more obtain higher standards than under selective systems, such as where grammar schools continue to exist or where there are other forms of selection by ability.

### *More social mixing and fewer social divisions*

As all children attend the same type of school, there is more social mixing between students from homes of different social-class and ethnic backgrounds, and this helps to overcome divisions between different social groups and build social cohesion. Selection by ability in education often benefits the middle class, which dominates selective schools and the top streams in streamed comprehensive schools. The reasons for this are discussed later in this chapter.

**Streaming**
Putting school students into the same group for all subjects according to their ability.

**Setting** Putting school students into different groups – sets – for a particular subject, according to their ability in that subject.

## Reduced risk of the self-fulfilling prophecy

Children are less likely to be branded as failures at an early age – lowering their self-esteem (how they feel about themselves and their ability) – and thus avoiding the damaging effects of the **self-fulfilling prophecy**. This is the process whereby the prediction that children won't do well, as a result of testing and selection by ability, actually comes true, due to the low expectations of teachers, and the consequent poor image students have of their own ability. This is discussed further later in the chapter.

> **Self-fulfilling prophecy** The process in which people act in response to a prediction of their behaviour, thereby making the prediction come true. Often applied to the effects of streaming in schools.

## Benefits of mixed-ability teaching

Where all pupils of the same age, regardless of their ability, are taught in the same type of school and in the same classroom (mixed-ability teaching), the more intelligent pupils can have a stimulating influence on the less able, and the problems created by the self-fulfilling prophecy are easier to avoid. Research has shown that mixed-ability teaching has no negative effect on the 'high flyers', improves the performance of the less able, and makes no difference to a school's overall examination performance.

## More choice and opportunity

The large size of many comprehensive schools, designed to contain all pupils in an area, means there are more teachers teaching a wider range of subjects to meet the needs of pupils of all abilities, with a great variety of equipment and facilities. This benefits all pupils and gives them greater choices and opportunities to develop their talents, to reach their full potential and to gain some educational qualifications.

Selection by ability can have harmful effects on the self-esteem of students, and create a self-fulfilling prophecy

## Table 4.2 The effects of streaming on children's recorded ability between the ages of 8 and 11 years

| Measured ability at 8 years of age – test scores | Average change in test scores between 8 and 11 years | |
|---|---|---|
| | Children in an *upper* stream | Children in a *lower* stream |
| 41–5 | +5.67 | −0.95 |
| 46–8 | +3.70 | −0.62 |
| 49–51 | +4.44 | −1.60 |
| 52–4 | +0.71 | −1.46 |
| 55–7 | +2.23 | −1.94 |
| 58–60 | +0.86 | −6.34 |

+ indicates improvements in score, − indicates deterioration in score.

*Source*: adapted from J. W. B. Douglas, *The Home and the School* (Panther / Grafton Books)

### Activity

Study table 4.2 and answer the following questions.
1 What average change occurred in the test scores of children in a lower stream whose test score at 8 years of age was 55–7?
2 What average change occurred in the test scores of children in an upper stream whose test score at 8 years of age was 46–8?
3 Which ability group in which stream showed (i) the greatest deterioration in test scores, and (ii) the greatest improvement in test scores?
4 What does table 4.2 suggest about the effects of streaming on children's educational performance? List all the factors you can think of which might explain this, drawing on your own experiences at school.
5 With reference to table 4.2 and the arguments above over selection, and drawing on examples from your own experiences at school, describe one argument for and one against selection by ability in education.
6 Do you think streaming and setting or mixed-ability teaching is better for pupils' progress? Give some evidence to back up your view from your own experiences at school.
7 Describe one way in which the self-fulfilling prophecy could affect a pupil's progress in education.

## The case for selection: criticisms of comprehensive education

The lack of selection by ability is not without its critics.

## 'High flyers' are held back

Because comprehensive schools contain pupils of all abilities, brighter children are held back by the slower pace of learning of the less able. Critics argue this wouldn't happen with selection, as 'high flyers' are taught in the same school or streams within a school.

## Overlooked talents and discipline problems

The large size of some comprehensives, containing all students in an area, may make it impossible for staff to know all pupils personally, and this may create discipline problems, and the talents of individuals may not be noticed and developed.

## Stretching the most able

Selection by ability through streaming or setting (rather than mixed-ability teaching) in the same school means brighter students can be 'stretched', rather than being held back by slower learners who take up the teacher's time, and who may be disruptive because they are unable to cope with the work.

# EDUCATION FROM 1988 ONWARDS: THE FREE MARKET IN EDUCATION

While the comprehensive system has succeeded in improving overall educational standards, the system came under increasing criticism in the 1980s and 1990s for:

- not meeting the needs of employers and industry closely enough
- not reaching high enough standards
- failing to benefit the most disadvantaged, poorest groups in society.

As a result, attempts have been made to tie all parts of the education system more closely to the needs of industry and business, and to raise educational standards – particularly of the most disadvantaged groups.

## The key aims of educational change

The move to comprehensive schooling, and more recent changes in the education system, have been driven by four main aims:

1   to raise educational standards, partly by providing more parental choice in schooling, and by creating competition between schools and colleges;

2   to create a more diverse school system, promoting different types of school to give parents more choice in the type of school their children go to;

3   economic efficiency: developing the talents of young people to improve the skills of the labour force so Britain maintains a successful position in the world economy, and making the education system meet the needs of industry and employers through more emphasis on vocational education;

4   to create equality of educational opportunity in a meritocratic society, and to establish a fairer society by opening up opportunities for secondary and further/higher education to the working class and other disadvantaged groups.

## The marketization of education

The 1988 Education Reform Act was the most important piece of educational legislation since the 1944 Education Act. It reduced local control of the education system, for example by teachers and local authorities (councils). At the same time, it increased control by the central government over some aspects of schools – such as the national curriculum, testing and the inspection of schools – but it also handed over more control to school governors, head teachers and the consumers of education – parents and students – in the running of schools. These changes were based on the ideas of schools having control over their own activities and competing with each other for students, with parents having the right to choose whichever school they thought best for their children (as long as there were enough school places).

This process has become known as the **marketization** of education, and has been largely driven by New Right (see pages 52–3) ideas that free competition between schools and giving parents a free choice of schools as consumers of education are the best ways to provide an efficient and business-like education system.

The main features of marketization of education can be summarized as:

> **Marketization** In education, the process whereby schools and colleges become more independent, compete with one another for students, and become subject to the free-market forces of supply and demand, based on competition and parental choice.

- *independence* – allowing schools and colleges to control their own affairs and to be run like private businesses
- *competition* – making schools and colleges compete with one another for customers (students)
- *choice* – giving customers (parents and students) a choice of schools, enabling them to choose whatever education they think best suits their needs.

Since 1988, parents and students have had a wider choice of which schools or colleges to attend, instead of being obliged to go to their nearest one.

The free market in education has made schooling a bit like supermarket shopping, where parents can 'read the labels' and pick and choose the type and quality of school they want. However, the more better-off and educated middle-class parents and young people have gained the most benefits from the marketization of education. Why do you think this is?

It was thought that, by increasing parental choice and competition for students, schools and colleges would become more efficient and accountable to parents and students. Giving parents a choice as consumers of education in a free market – rejecting some schools or colleges in favour of others, in the same way that people choose between competing supermarkets or products – was expected to drive up education standards. Poorly performing schools or colleges would risk losing money as student numbers fell, and might face closure, while those that performed well would grow and improve even more.

Table 4.3 illustrates some of the main features and policies linked to the marketization of education since 1988, and a number of these are explained and discussed in the pages that follow.

## Raising standards: competition, diversity and choice in schooling

### *The national curriculum, target-setting and national testing*

To improve standards across the country, and ensure all students had access to the same high-quality curriculum, the 1988 Education Reform Act set up the national curriculum, a range of subjects and set programmes of study that must be followed by all state schools (except for academies and free schools) in England (there are different requirements in Scotland, Wales and Northern Ireland). There are attainment targets (goals which all teachers are expected to enable students to reach).

## Table 4.3 The marketization of education

| Policy | Aims |
|---|---|
| *Target setting*<br><br>*National testing* (SATs, GCSEs, GCEs and other exams) with publication of results<br><br>*National league tables* of school performance, including exam results<br><br>*Office for Standards in Education, Children's Services and Skills (Ofsted)* – inspecting and publishing reports on the strengths and weaknesses of schools | • to identify the best schools, and shame the worst into improving their standards or face closure<br><br>• to give parents and students the information to choose the best schools<br><br>• to encourage schools to compete for students and money |
| *More independence for schools* (with less control by local councils) | • to give schools the control to make changes to compete and attract students by improving quality and standards |
| *Formula funding* (money allocated per student) | • to enable popular schools that attract students to get the most money so they can expand and improve. Those that don't attract students will risk being closed |
| *Parental choice*<br><br>*Open enrolment*<br><br>*A diversity of school types*, like academies and faith schools | • to enable parents to choose the schools they consider best for their children, rather than just having to go to the local one |

### National 'league tables'

Schools are now required to publish 'Progress 8' performance tables of testing and exam results to show how much schools have added to students' achievements during their schooling. These include a range of information on student progress, and have become known as 'league tables' because – like league tables in football – they are designed to give parents and students an idea of how well schools and colleges are doing so they can choose the best. By encouraging competition for students between schools and colleges, these league tables aim to raise overall standards.

### Local management of schools (LMS)

Local management of schools (LMS) gives schools (rather than local authorities – county and city councils in most areas) much greater control of their budgets, and of a wide range of other aspects of the school. This is designed to make schools more responsive to local needs and the wishes of parents – to encourage schools to run on market principles, where they compete with one another for students, and therefore funds.

National testing through SATs, exams and formal teacher assessment have been used to improve, check and measure the quality and standards of education

## Formula funding

Schools and colleges are funded by a formula which is largely based on the number of students they attract. It was thought this would drive up standards by rewarding successful schools and colleges that attracted students (and hence money), giving less successful schools and colleges the incentive to improve.

## Open enrolment and parental preference

Parents are now allowed to express a preference for the school of their choice, and a school cannot refuse a pupil a place if it has vacancies. This was again designed to encourage competition between schools. Unpopular schools run the risk of losing pupils, and therefore money, and the government has taken steps to close what it sees as 'failing' schools where exam and test results, and standards of behaviour, are poor. In most cases, parents don't really have much choice of school, as places are usually filled up by those living in the school's 'priority area' (the area from which children are admitted first).

## More information for parents

To help parents to choose the best schools and encourage schools to improve their standards and performance, schools now have to provide, by law, a wide range of information for parents, including school ethos, admission arrangements, the standards achieved, Ofsted reports, and examination and national curriculum test results.

## The Office for Standards in Education, Children's Services and Skills (Ofsted)

The Office for Standards in Education, Children's Services and Skills (Ofsted) * was established to conduct inspections of all state schools and sixth-form and further education colleges in England, to ensure schools and colleges were doing a good job. It publishes its inspection reports and requires action to be taken on any weaknesses identified.

---

**Activity**

1. Describe and explain two ways in which the educational reforms from the late 1980s to the present have introduced market forces into the education system.
2. Suggest one advantage and one disadvantage of competition between schools.
3. Do you think the changes in education considered above will succeed in raising standards? Go through each of the changes since the 1980s, and explain why they might or might not improve standards.
4. Do you think schools alone can be held responsible for exam results and truancy rates? What other factors might influence how good a school's exam results are, and whether pupils play truant or not?

---

## Criticisms of the free market in education and other changes

While the changes in education may have given individual schools more control of their affairs, and made them more responsive to parents, the development of the free market in education and the growing independence of schools have been very controversial, and criticized in a number of ways. The main criticisms are outlined below.

### The middle class has gained the most

Middle-class parents have been able to make the greatest use of parental choice and open enrolment, and it is they who are better placed to make the most effective use of the education system to their children's advantage. The educational system remains socially selective, and the higher the social class of the parents, the better are the schools to which they send their children. The reasons why the middle class are able to take more advantage of the education system than the working class are considered later in this chapter, but

---

* Ofsted only operates in England. Similar functions are carried out in Wales by *Estyn* (Her Majesty's Inspectorate for Education and Training in Wales), in Scotland by *Education Scotland*, and in Northern Ireland by *ETI* (the Education and Training Inspectorate).

include the fact that their own higher levels of income and education means they are better placed than many working-class parents to:

- shop around and find the best schools
- know more about how to assess school Ofsted inspection reports and what constitutes a good school
- afford more easily to move into the priority areas of the best schools
- afford higher transport costs, giving their children a wider choice of schools
- make more effective use of appeals procedures should they be refused a place at their chosen school.

This means that those who have already benefitted from education the most will gain more, while those who are more disadvantaged may become further disadvantaged.

### Activity

To understand the difficulties involved in choosing a school, and why the more educated middle class are most successful at it, examine the advice given on the following government website on how to choose a school. Draw up a list of what steps parents are expected to take, and how difficult you think this might be.

www.gov.uk/schools-admissions

## Student needs at risk and social divisions increased

Ball, Bowe and Gerwitz (1994) carried out a study of fifteen schools in neighbouring areas that were different in terms of the social class and ethnicity of people who lived there. Their research shows that parental choice and the publication of school league tables have led to increasing pressures on schools to reintroduce streaming and setting by ability, with some schools giving greater attention to the more able students. Brighter students, or those, for example, on the 4/3 (formerly C/D) grade borderline at GCSE, are likely to get more resources spent on them. This disadvantages weaker students who are less likely to deliver the prestige results, such as grades 9–4 (formerly A*–C) at GCSE, necessary to gain or maintain for parents the image of a good school or college. Weaker students, who are more likely to come from working-class backgrounds (for reasons discussed later in this chapter), may find their needs are neglected because the risk of them getting poorer results might undermine the league-table position of the school or college. As a result, social divisions between the middle class and the working class are widened.

## The unfairness of league tables

League tables of test and exam results don't really reveal how well a school or college is doing. This is because, as later parts of this chapter show, the social-class and ethnic backgrounds and gender of students can affect how well they perform in education. For example, schools and colleges in more deprived working-class areas may produce results that are not as good as those in middle-class areas, yet their GCSE students may have actually made much more progress since starting at the school in Year 7 than middle-class students.

Schools with challenging students, who come from vulnerable or disadvantaged backgrounds, such as from families living in poverty, or who have a high proportion of SEND students (those with **S**pecial **E**ducational **N**eeds and **D**isabilities) are the most likely to be unfairly represented in the performance (league) tables. Such schools are more likely to be found in deprived working-class communities, and they are the least likely to be attractive to potential parents, even though they might be doing excellent work in helping their students. Performance tables, then, may conceal underperforming schools in advantaged middle-class areas, where students, although they might do reasonably well, should be doing a lot better given the advantages they have arising from their home backgrounds. Schools and colleges in more deprived working-class areas might be performing better in improving students' progress given the disadvantages they face, even if their results aren't as good as the schools in middle-class areas.

## Difficulties in improving schools and colleges

Competition between schools and colleges for students (and therefore for money), the emphasis on exam results, and the need to present a good image to parents in the free market may make it harder for poorer schools and colleges to improve, as students go elsewhere. Such schools and colleges may therefore lack the resources to improve their performance – the opposite of what was intended by reforms.

## 'Dumbing down'

The need for schools and colleges to retain students – and the money they bring with them – means that, if students have too much work to do or find the work difficult, they may go to another course or educational institution where things seem easier and less demanding. Retaining (keeping) students may mean not pushing students too hard for fear of losing them.

## Problems with the national curriculum and testing

The national curriculum in England (and possibly Welsh, Scottish and Northern Ireland equivalents) has been criticized for not giving teachers enough opportunity to respond to the needs of their pupils, as teachers are told what they have to teach and when they have to teach it. Testing (the SATs) has been criticized for putting too much pressure on young children, and possibly giving them a sense of failure early in their schooling. More generally, teaching may become too focused on the content of the tests as a way to get the good test results needed for a high position in the league tables, at the expense of the wider school curriculum.

---

**Activity**

1  Identify and explain *two* educational policies that have attempted to improve standards in education in about the last thirty years.
2  Identify and explain *two* reasons why league tables of test and exam results may not give a fair impression of how effective a school or college is.
3  Identify and explain *two* reasons why middle-class parents might be more effective in achieving better schooling for their children than those from working-class backgrounds.
4  Suggest *two* reasons why selection by ability in education may have harmful effects on some children.

---

# SCHOOL DIVERSITY

Education policy in recent years, and the process of promoting greater parental choice in schooling, have meant that there is now a greater diversity (or range of different types) of state-funded schools than ever before.

This section will outline some of the types of state-funded school, and also private, fee-paying (independent) schools, and some of the debates surrounding them. The schools mentioned below often do not exist in a pure form, but may involve elements of different types. For example, an academy may also be a faith school and a grammar school.

## Grammar schools

Grammar schools are the only state-funded schools that are allowed to select their pupils by ability. This selection is carried out by the 11+ exam. There are now only about 163 grammar schools left in England.

## Community or maintained schools

These are state-funded schools that are largely maintained by the local authority (local council) and are not influenced by business or religious groups. In 2018, around 73 per cent of primary schools and 28 per cent of secondary were local authority-maintained schools in England.

## Academies and free schools

These are independently run schools, found only in England, that are funded by central government and manage their own affairs, rather than being funded and controlled by local authorities (local councils). Although they involve no fees and are part of the state system of education, they operate like independent schools in the state system.

Academies were originally set up in 2000 in England as new schools to replace those which were seen to be giving poor education to their students, particularly in the most deprived areas. It was thought that more independence, more control by headteachers, and links with sponsors such as private businesses could give schools more power and new expertise (like that in business) to improve educational standards. In 2010, the focus of academies changed from improving education in deprived areas to giving more independence to all schools by encouraging them to opt out of council control to become independent academies. Academies are the fastest-growing type of school.

In 2018, around 27 per cent of primary schools, and 72 per cent of secondary, were academies or free schools. Academies are often part of a chain of linked schools called MATs – multi-academy trusts.

Free schools are similar to academies, and can be established by charities, universities, independent schools, community and faith groups, teachers, or parents who are concerned about poor educational standards in other schools. They tend to be smaller schools than academies and other state schools, with smaller budgets, fewer facilities and smaller buildings. In early 2018, there were around 391 free schools open in England (with around 290 more approved to open), containing about 1 per cent of the total number of pupils in state-funded schools in England.

Academies and free schools have been very controversial because:

- they don't have to follow the national curriculum, so not all pupils will necessarily be getting a similar standard of education.
- their success record in disadvantaged areas before 2010 was not very good, and some did not improve education standards compared to the schools they replaced.
- they show little difference in pupil performance compared to community/maintained schools run by local authorities.
- they control their own admissions policies, and those that have improved standards have often done so by being more selective in the students they encourage to apply. They may try to select students who are the best behaved and likely to do well – students more likely to be from middle-class homes and those without SEND. They are more likely to exclude 'difficult' pupils than other schools. Some academies are

therefore denying educational help to those students who most need it, and other schools in the area have an unfair proportion of lower-ability, more disruptive and/or SEND students who have been rejected by the academies.

- they weaken a state system of schooling planned to improve education for all across the country, breaking it up into independent, competing schools, with the most favoured schools now likely to be those in the most advantaged middle-class areas.
- free schools, which are potentially smaller schools with smaller budgets in more modest buildings, may lack the range of facilities, subject choices and experiences children in most other schools have, disadvantaging rather than helping those in the poorest areas.
- interested and motivated groups of parents setting up free schools may hold extremist beliefs of one form or another, creating a curriculum and a school ethos (or character) that denies children exposure to the wide range of opinions, experiences and cultural lifestyles available in most community schools.
- lots of extra money has gone into academies and free schools. This money has been removed from the local authority-run community/maintained school system. Free schools receive around 60 per cent more funding per pupil than local authority primary and secondary schools, and money intended to improve underperforming schools has been unfairly redistributed to academies.

The points above suggest the development of academies and free schools is widening existing inequalities in education (discussed later in this chapter), with the most advantaged in society having even more access to the best schools than they do already, and the most disadvantaged losing out even more.

## Faith schools

Faith schools are schools with a religious character. In England in 2018, 37 per cent of state-funded primary schools, and a fifth of secondary, were faith schools, and around a quarter of all pupils attended them. Faith schools make up around 40 per cent of independent schools (fee-paying private schools). They have existed a very long time in the UK. Well before state education began in 1870, there were a range of Church of England, Catholic, Methodist, Jewish and Quaker schools. Although faith schools have been overwhelmingly Christian (96 per cent of them are Church of England and Roman Catholic), in recent years there has been a drive to meet the faith needs of minority ethnic groups, with Muslim and Sikh schools, for example. In England in 2018, there were forty-nine Jewish, twenty-nine Muslim, twelve Sikh and six Hindu schools.

Faith schools are those with a religious character. Although faith schools have been overwhelmingly Christian, in recent years there has been a drive to create more to meet the faith needs of minority ethnic groups, including Muslim and Sikh schools

## Strengths of faith schools

- They enable parents to choose an education for their children in accordance with their religious beliefs.
- They often have a character and ethos (attitudes and beliefs) which many parents, even if they are not religious, think will be good for their children's moral and social development.
- Many faith schools have above-average exam results.

## Problems of faith schools

- *They discriminate on religious and ethnic grounds.* If the school has too many applications, they are allowed to give priority to children on the basis of religious belief and factors like attendance at the church/mosque/synagogue, baptism, knowledge of holy texts, or religious lifestyle aspects, such as eating Halal meat at home.
- *They could damage a multicultural society and social cohesion.* Faith schools segregate/divide children from different religions. As children are being divided and educated on the basis of what separates them from other children, they won't grow up with the same

understanding of a variety of faiths as they might in a non-faith school. This could breed intolerance, divide communities and cause religious hatred.

## DESCHOOLING AND HOME SCHOOLING

'Deschooling' is a term used in two different ways.

1 Sociologists such as Illich use it to refer to the idea that institutional education through schools is concerned with promoting conformity and repressing children, and that it stifles creativity and independent critical thinking. This view suggests society should be deschooled – schools should be abolished and alternative forms of education developed.

2 The term is also used to describe the process whereby parents decide to take their children out of formal schools – to deschool them.

While education is compulsory in the UK until age 16, school is not, and some parents decide to educate their children at home – home schooling. There are often a variety of reasons for this. For example, parents may feel that the local schools aren't good enough and they can do a better job themselves, or that their children have been bullied, have special needs, found it hard to fit in, suffer anxiety, or haven't made progress at school.

Some see home schooling as disadvantageous for children, as they miss out on the social aspects of schooling, such as making new friends and mixing with others, and the resources, specialist teachers and range of subjects available in schools.

You can read more about home schooling at www.education-otherwise.org.

- *They encourage parents to lie about their faith* or pretend to be religious for a while, just to get into their chosen school and avoid what they regard as the worst schools.
- *They are often not representative of the local population.*
- *They may discriminate in their employment or promotion of staff on religious grounds.*
- *Religious institutions and religious leaders are choosing parents*, not parents choosing schools. This gives them too much power in a society where the majority of the population never attend any religious ceremonies or claim to hold religious beliefs.

## Special schools

Special schools cater for SEND students, with a range of learning difficulties from mild to severe, which may sometimes be combined with physical disabilities. They have specialized facilities (like soft play areas, low-level benches, wheelchair access and sensory rooms), specially trained teachers and higher levels of staffing than mainstream schools, and very small groups or one-to-one teaching to cater for the often-complex learning difficulties of pupils.

More and more children with special needs are now being taught in mainstream schools. This has the advantage of enabling students with SEND to grow up alongside other children without SEND, rather than them becoming marked out as different from an early age. However, some students require the specialized education, specially trained and experienced teachers, one-to-one support and resources that only special schools can provide. There is also a potential risk of bullying and ridiculing in mainstream schools that is rarely found in special schools. One way around this has been for children to spend time in both types of school – for example, attending mainstream schools only for some subjects and activities.

### Activity

1 Describe one argument for and one against the view that children with special educational needs and disabilities (SEND) are best taught in mainstream schools.
2 Describe two reasons why parents might choose to educate their children at home rather than at school.
3 Surveys suggest that a majority of the population is opposed to the state funding any faith schools. Many are particularly concerned about the growth of separate faith schools for minority ethnic groups as a threat to social cohesion. Describe two arguments for, and two against, faith schools. (If you're in a group, you could divide into two groups, for and against, and debate the issue).

## Private education: the independent schools

Private schools (also known as 'independent schools') charge fees for children to attend, instead of being funded by the government. Pupils don't have to follow the national curriculum.

There are many poor-quality schools in the private sector of education, but most research and discussion has been about what are known as the 'public schools'. Despite their name, these are not in fact 'public' at all, but very expensive private schools. The public schools are a small group of independent schools belonging to what is called the 'Headmasters' and Headmistresses' Conference' (HMC). Pupils at these schools are largely the children of wealthier upper-middle- and upper-class parents who have decided to opt out of free, state-run schooling and can afford to pay for a private education.

The public schools are long established, many dating back hundreds of years, and charge fees running into thousands of pounds a year. For secondary-age students in 2018, annual fees for day students averaged around £15,000, and for boarders (living in) £33,000. The two most famous boys' public schools are probably Eton and Harrow (boarding fees around £41,000 a year, plus extras, in 2018–19), and many of the 'top people' in this country have attended these or other public schools.

Eton College, one of Britain's most famous public schools, with fees of £40,668 a year plus extras in 2018–19, counts among its former students twenty British prime ministers, numerous princes, kings, archbishops, judges, generals, admirals and other members of Britain's elite

## *The advantages of independent schools*

Compared to state schools, they offer:

- smaller class sizes and better facilities, giving children a better chance of educational success
- a wider range of extra-curricular activities
- better-paid teachers and more teaching and learning resources
- above-average examination results
- much better chances for pupils to get into top universities
- more power to deal with disruptive pupils
- more parental choice, giving parents greater opportunities to protect and improve their children's life chances.

> **Activity**
>
> Go to the websites of either Eton College (www.etoncollege.com), or Harrow School (www.harrowschool.org.uk), and explore how the educational facilities and lifestyle of these schools differ from your school. Do you think those attending such schools have unfair advantages in education compared to the typical student?

## *The case against independent schools*

- *They undermine the principle of equality of educational opportunity.* Most people do not have the money to purchase a private education for their children. It is unfair that the children of the well-off should be given more advantages in education than the poor.
- *They are selective schools* – they only admit pupils who pass an entrance exam and/or whose parents can afford the school fees.
- *They are subsidized by all taxpayers*, the vast majority of whom can't afford for their children to attend them. They have traditionally had the same tax subsidies and benefits as charities. As well as these tax subsidies through charitable status, the taxpayer also pays the cost of training the teachers in these schools, since they attend state-run universities and colleges.
- *The quality of teaching in independent schools is often no better than in state-run schools.* However, their pupils may obtain better results because classes tend to be smaller than in comprehensives, allowing more individual attention, and the schools often have better resources and facilities.
- *They tend to recruit pupils from similar backgrounds*, so pupils often do not mix with people from different social-class and ethnic groups. This reproduces social inequality and class divisions, and undermines social cohesion.

- *They undermine meritocracy in education and society.* Research has shown that even when children who go to private schools, especially the public schools, get worse examination results than children who go to state comprehensive schools, they still get better jobs in the end. This suggests that the fact of attending a public school is itself enough to secure them good jobs, even if their qualifications are not quite as good as those of pupils from comprehensives.
- *They provide a means for the already privileged to obtain the* **elite** *jobs in society* – that small number of jobs in the country which involve holding a great deal of power and privilege.

> **Elite** A small group holding great power and privilege in society.

*Elite education and elite jobs*   Although only about 7 per cent of the population have attended independent schools (and public schools are only a proportion of these schools), many of the top positions in politics, the civil service, medicine, the law, the media, the Church of England, the armed forces, industry, banking and commerce are held by ex-public-school pupils.

In many cases, even well-qualified candidates from state schools will stand a poor chance of getting such jobs if competing with public-school pupils. A typical route into the elite jobs is through a public school and Oxford and Cambridge universities (where around 38–44 per cent of students came from independent schools in 2017). This establishes the 'old boys' network', illustrated in figure 4.3, through which those in positions of power recruit others who come from the same social-class background and who have been to the same public schools and universities as themselves. This shows one aspect of the clear relationship that exists between wealth and power in modern Britain, and how being able to afford a public-school education can lead to a position of power and influence in society.

A public-school education therefore means well-off parents can almost guarantee their children will have well-paid future careers bringing them similar levels of power and status in society to their parents. This undermines the principle of equality of educational opportunity, and any idea that Britain might be a meritocracy. This is because social-class background and the ability to pay school fees, rather than simply academic ability, become the key to success in education. Not all children of the same ability have the same chance of having parents able to afford this route to educational success.

**Activity**

Should private education be abolished? List the arguments for and against. If you are in a group, debate this issue.

**Figure 4.3** The old boys' network

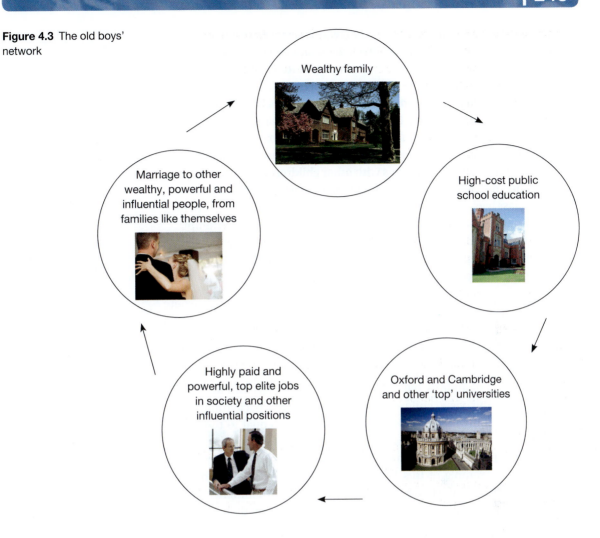

## FACTORS INFLUENCING EDUCATIONAL ACHIEVEMENT

### 1 Government policies and spending

There are various ways in which the government can influence how well young people perform in their education, particularly those who come from the most disadvantaged backgrounds. These include:

- *How much money governments spend on education:* whether it is enough to enable schools to employ experienced and well-qualified teachers and teaching assistants, and to educate pupils in well-resourced and well-equipped classrooms. In 2019, many schools were facing funding shortages, and were finding it harder to recruit and keep teachers, who were put off by larger class sizes, fewer teaching assistants and a shortage of basic classroom resources. Schools were often short of teachers in some subjects, such as maths, science and languages.

- *Support for **compensatory education*** – extra educational help for those facing the greatest obstacles to success. In order for all young people to have an equal chance in the education system, those coming from deprived backgrounds need extra support and resources to enable them to compete on equal terms with other children, and help them overcome the disadvantages in education arising from their deprived social-class backgrounds. This idea of extra help is known as compensatory education, and involves **positive discrimination** as an attempt to overcome working-class **underachievement** – the failure of pupils to fulfil their full potential and do as well in education as they should, given their ability.

Positive discrimination means schools in disadvantaged areas, where home and social-class background are seen as potential obstacles to success in education, are singled out for extra-favourable treatment, such as more, and better-paid, teachers and more money to spend on buildings and equipment, to help the most disadvantaged to succeed in education.

Positive discrimination is based on the idea of equality of educational opportunity. In this view, children from disadvantaged backgrounds and poor homes can only get an opportunity in education equal to those who come from non-disadvantaged backgrounds if they get unequal and more generous treatment to compensate (hence the term '*compensatory education*'). A recent example of this is the pupil premium. This is additional funding for state-funded schools in England, to raise the attainment of disadvantaged pupils of all abilities and to close the gaps between them and their more advantaged peers.

- *Equal opportunities policies and legislation*, which make it illegal for schools to discriminate on the basis of gender or ethnicity.
- *Policies on marketization, competition between schools and parental choice,* which, as seen above (see pages 231–2), have proven to have benefitted the middle class more. These policies have made accessing educational opportunities more difficult for many disadvantaged working-class and some minority ethnic students.
- *School performance (league) tables* have, as seen above (see pages 232–3) encouraged schools to focus on higher-achieving students, who are more likely to be from middle-class homes. League tables can hinder the progress of lower-achievers from disadvantaged working-class homes, who find their needs are neglected as they are less likely to deliver the good results needed for a high league-table position.

**Compensatory education** Extra educational support for those coming from disadvantaged groups to help them overcome the obstacles they face in the education system and the wider society.

**Positive discrimination** Giving disadvantaged groups more favourable treatment than others to make up for the disadvantages they face.

**Underachievement** The failure of people to achieve as much as they are capable of, and to fulfil their full potential – they do not do as well in education (or other areas) as their talents and abilities suggest they should.

## 2 External factors – those outside the school

These are influences from outside the school which affect how well individuals do at school, and after leaving school. These are largely factors over which schools and teachers have little control. These include:

- *material factors:* social and economic conditions in pupils' homes and communities, e.g. poverty and low wages, unemployment, poor housing, poor diet and ill health, availability of educational resources – such as computers – and other facilities for studying at home, and the effects of racism in society. These are the kind of factors that Marxists emphasize.
- *cultural factors:* these are concerned with aspects of the cultural life of some social groups. They include issues such as parental attitudes and values – their level of interest, support, expectations and encouragement for their children's education; parents' level of education; language use in the home; and role models among peers and the wider community. Some groups are seen as culturally deficient or deprived in various ways in relation to the demands of schooling. This is known as **cultural deprivation** and may act as a barrier to success in education.

The blame for underachievement in education is placed on young people's socialization in the family and community, and on the cultural values with which they are raised. These are the kind of factors that functionalists are most likely to emphasize.

**Cultural deprivation** The idea that some young people fail in education because of supposed cultural deficiencies in their home and family background, such as inadequate socialization, failings in pre-school learning, inadequate language skills and inappropriate attitudes and values.

## 3 Internal factors – those inside the school

These are the various influences and processes inside schools which affect pupil progress and achievement. These include factors such as:

- the resources available
- streaming and setting
- teacher attitudes and expectations
- labelling and the self-fulfilling prophecy
- school subcultures
- marketization and selection
- racism and the ethnocentric curriculum
- the language used in school.

The effects of streaming, setting, teacher expectations, labelling and the self-fulfilling prophecy are generally associated with the interactionist perspective (see pages 59–60).

These external and internal factors are explained and discussed in the following sections with regard to how they affect achievement according to social class, ethnicity and gender.

# INEQUALITY IN EDUCATION

The development of the education system in Britain aimed to secure equality of educational opportunity for all children, regardless of their social class, ethnic background or gender. However, despite these efforts, sociological evidence has made it clear that not all children of the same ability achieve the same success in education, and inequalities in educational opportunity remain.

The evidence suggests that social-class origins (the social class of a child's parents or guardians), ethnicity and gender appear to be more important than innate (inborn) ability in influencing people's level of educational achievement or success, even when they are of the same ability. The following sections describe and explain these patterns of inequality in education. It is important to remember that the overall statistics disguise wide variations between individuals – some children may be very successful in the education system, even if they come from a group that generally has higher levels of underachievement. Equally, some children may perform badly in education even if they come from a group that generally has higher levels of achievement.

## Social class and educational achievement

### The facts

Social class is the key factor that affects whether a child does well or badly at school. There are major differences between the levels of achievement of the working class and the middle class and, in general, the higher the social class of the parents, the more successful a child will be in education. Social-class inequality in education begins even before children start in primary school, and the gap between the classes becomes wider as children move through the education system, with the higher levels of the system dominated by middle-class students.

Recent evidence suggests that lower-working-class children, compared to middle-class children of the same ability:

- are already well behind in their educational development *even before they get to school.*
- do less well in national curriculum tests (often referred to as SATs).

Inequality in education begins even before children start primary school, with those from disadvantaged backgrounds up to a year behind more privileged youngsters educationally by the age of 3

- are less likely to get places in the best state schools.
- are more likely to be placed in lower streams or sets.
- generally get poorer exam results – e.g. fewer GCSEs and at lower grades.
- are more likely to leave school at the minimum leaving age of 16 (but they have to stay in some form of education or training until they are 18), many of them with few or no qualifications of any kind. Only about half of young people from unskilled manual families stay on in post-16 full-time education (as opposed to training), compared to about nine in every ten from managerial and professional families.
- are more likely to undertake vocational or training courses at the end of compulsory schooling (age 16), rather than the more academic AS- and A-level courses which are more likely to be taken by middle-class students and which are more likely to lead to university education.
- are less likely to go into higher education.

## Explaining working-class underachievement

***External factors 1: material explanations*** These are some of the social and economic factors from outside the school – in a child's home and community background – that can affect their chances in education.

### POVERTY AND HOME CIRCUMSTANCES
- Poor housing conditions, such as damp homes, overcrowding and insufficient space and quiet, can make study at home difficult.
- Inadequate and unhealthy diets and higher levels of sickness in poorer homes may mean more absence from school and falling behind with lessons.

**A. H. Halsey, A. F. Heath and J. M. Ridge (1980)** *Origins and Destinations: Family, Class and Education in Modern Britain*

Early research in the 1970s by Halsey, Heath and Ridge revealed stark class inequalities in education. They studied a sample in England and Wales of over 8,000 males born between 1913 and 1952. Their sample was divided into three social classes, based on father's occupation:

1 *Service class* – consisting of professionals, administrators and managers
2 *Intermediate class* – consisting of clerical and sales workers, the self-employed and lower-grade technicians and foremen
3 *Working class* – consisting of manual workers in industry and agriculture.

The authors found that a boy from a service-class background, compared to one from the working class, had:

- four times more chance of being at school at age 16
- eight times more chance of being at school at age 17
- ten times more chance of being at school at age 18
- eleven times more chance of attending a university.

Halsey, Heath and Ridge's research was criticized at the time for excluding girls, and basing their definition of class only on the father's occupation. If girls had been included, it is likely that the inequalities in educational life chances would have been even greater, as at that time girls tended to underachieve more than boys.

---

- Low income or unemployment may mean that educational books and toys are not bought, and computers and internet connections are not available in the home. This may affect a child's educational progress before or during her or his time at school. There may also be a lack of money for out-of-school trips, sports equipment and other hidden costs of free state education (see box below). In 2017, the Sutton Trust found that almost one in three 11- to 16-year-old state-school students in England and Wales had private tuition at some point in their life, but poor pupils receive much less of this support than their better-off peers.

- Young people from poorer families are more likely to have part-time jobs, such as paper rounds, babysitting or shop work. This becomes more pronounced after the age of 16, when students may be combining part- or full-time work with school or college work or training. This may create a conflict between the competing demands of study, training and paid work.

- It may be financially difficult for parents on a low income to support students in education after school-leaving age, no matter how bright their prospects might be. In higher education, the potential debts arising from student loans to cover tuition fees and living costs while studying are likely to be a source of anxiety to those from poorer backgrounds, deterring them from going to university.

## THE HIDDEN COSTS OF 'FREE' STATE SCHOOLING

For many families, the idea of a free education is very far from reality, and school-related costs make up a large portion of family budgets. The hidden costs of sending a child to a state school amounted to an estimated £800–£1,600 a year in 2013–14, for basic school-related expenses such as school uniform, PE kit, school trips, class materials, stationery, swimming lessons, school lunches, travel, photographs, charity contributions and other school activities. Even when these costs are voluntary, some schools still pressure parents to pay up, even if they have difficulty in affording them. Children whose families can't afford such expenses may miss out on valuable educational experiences available to other children.

*Sources: The Aviva Family Finances Report, July 2013*, and E. Holloway, S. Mahony, S. Royston and D. Mueller (2014) *At What Cost? Exposing the Impact of Poverty on School Life*. London: Through Young Eyes – the Children's Commission on Poverty, The Children's Society

The effects of these material factors tend to be cumulative, meaning that social deprivation gradually builds up, as one aspect of deprivation can lead to others. For example, poverty may mean overcrowding at home *and* ill health *and* having to find part-time work, building up like a snowball and making all the problems worse, as shown in the cartoon below.

### Activity

Explain in your own words, with examples, how the cartoon shows that the effects of social deprivation on educational achievement are cumulative.

## THE CATCHMENT AREA AND ROLE MODELS

Catchment areas (or priority areas) are the areas from which primary and secondary schools draw their pupils. In deprived areas, there may be a range of social problems such as high unemployment, poverty, juvenile delinquency, crime and drug abuse, and there are often poor role models for young people to imitate. The accumulated effects of the environment on children's behaviour mean schools in such areas are more likely to have discipline problems, and hence a higher turnover of teachers. This may mean that children from the most disadvantaged backgrounds have the most difficult and under-performing schools. In contrast, schools in middle-class neighbourhoods will probably have stronger and more conformist role models for young people, fewer discipline problems, and therefore a better learning environment. Additionally, schools in middle-class areas will have more active and wealthy parent–teacher associations able to provide extra resources for the school.

These material factors are summarized in figure 4.4.

***External factors 2: cultural explanations and cultural deprivation*** These are concerned with deficiencies in the cultural features of the home and family background of pupils (cultural deprivation) which may act as a barrier to success in education.

## PARENTS' ATTITUDES TO EDUCATION

The amount of parental encouragement, expectation, interest and involvement in their children's education, rather than the ability and efforts of the child, have important effects on a child's educational success today.

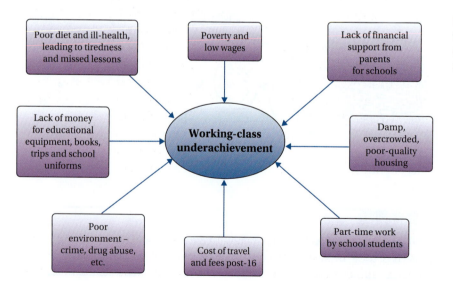

**Figure 4.4** External material factors explaining class differences in educational achievement

Evidence suggests middle-class parents, compared to working-class parents, on the whole:

- *take more interest in their children's progress at school*, shown by them visiting the school more frequently to discuss how their children are getting on
- *become more interested and encouraging as their children grow older*, when exam options are selected and career choices loom
- *are more likely to want their children to stay at school beyond the minimum leaving age* and to expect and encourage them to do so
- *socialize their children into values and attitudes which encourage ambition and educational success*. These include an emphasis on the need for individual effort for educational and future career success, and on the value of **deferred gratification**. This means putting off immediate pleasures for future gains (e.g. staying in and doing homework, putting off getting money in a job to stay longer in education and earn more later) and planning for the future. In contrast, lower-working-class homes are more likely to emphasize **immediate gratification** – taking opportunities and enjoying yourself now rather than waiting for the promise of higher rewards in the future, e.g. obtaining a skill / getting a job and money now, rather than spending more time obtaining educational qualifications.

**Deferred gratification** Putting off immediate rewards and pleasures in order to achieve higher rewards in the future.

**Immediate gratification** Taking opportunities and enjoying yourself now, rather than waiting for higher rewards in the future.

Middle-class parents can also more easily afford to continue to support their children in education after the age of 16. The interest shown by middle-class parents may be due to the importance of educational qualifications in obtaining their own middle-class occupations. By contrast, working-class parents may see education as of less importance because they may have found their own education had little relevance to their working-class jobs. This may lead to poor motivation of some working-class children in school, and therefore lower levels of achievement, regardless of ability.

Parental attitudes can also affect the child's learning by the lower value placed on books or educational toys in some lower-working-class homes. A survey in 2017 found that more than 750,000 schoolchildren in the UK do not have a single book of their own, and such children are more likely to be from lower-working-class homes. Children without books are 15 times less likely to be good readers than their book-owning peers, and this will affect their progress in education (see also the section on 'Cultural capital' below).

### Parents' level of education

Because they are generally themselves better educated, middle-class parents tend to understand the school system better than working-class parents. Lower-working-class parents may feel less confident in dealing with teachers at parents' evenings, and in dealing with subject options and exam choices. In general, middle-class parents:

- know and understand more about schools, Ofsted reports and school league tables, the examination system and careers, and so are more able to advise and counsel their children on getting into the best schools and onto the most appropriate subjects and courses
- can hold their own more in disagreements with teachers (who are also middle-class) about the treatment and education of their child
- know what games and books to buy to stimulate their children's educational development both before and during schooling (and have the money to buy them)
- are better equipped to help their children with homework and school work generally.

As a consequence, even before they get to school, middle-class children may have learned more as a result of their socialization in the family. These advantages of a middle-class home may be reinforced throughout a child's career at school. By contrast, these same reasons for middle-class success

In what ways might parents influence success or failure in their children's education?

may also explain why many of the poorest working-class children are well behind their middle-class peers even before they start school.

### LANGUAGE USE: THE RESTRICTED AND ELABORATED CODES

Success at school depends very heavily on language – for reading, writing, speaking and understanding. Bernstein argues that there is a relationship between language use and social class, and that the type of language used by the middle class is a better instrument for success at school than the type of language used by the working class. His view is that the language used by the lower working class has a **restricted code,** while the language used by the middle class has an **elaborated code**.

> **Restricted code**
> A form of language use which takes for granted shared understandings between people. The informal, simple, everyday language, sometimes ungrammatical and with limited explanations and vocabulary, which is used between friends or family members.

> **Elaborated code**
> A form of language use involving careful explanation and detail. The sort of formal language used by strangers and individuals in some formal context, such as a job interview, writing a business letter, or in a school lesson or textbook, and which uses a much wider vocabulary than the restricted code.

- *The restricted code* of language is used by both middle-class and working-class people, but is more characteristic of working-class people. It is the sort of language which is used between friends, workmates or family members – informal, simple, everyday language (such as slang), with little explanation, sometimes ungrammatical and limited in vocabulary. This form of language is quite adequate for everyday use with friends because they know what the speaker is referring to – the context is understood by both speakers and so detailed explanation is not required. Bernstein argues that lower-working-class people are mainly limited to this form of language use.

- *The elaborated code* of language is used mainly by middle-class people. It is the language of strangers and individuals in some formal context, where explanation and detail are required – such as an interview for a job, writing a business letter, an essay or an examination answer, or in a school lesson or textbook. It has a much wider vocabulary than the restricted code.

Bernstein argues that the language used in schools is the elaborated code of the middle class, and that it is the middle-class child's ability to use the elaborated code that gives her or him an advantage at school over working-class children. For example, in middle-class homes, parents are more likely to use the elaborated code as they explain, argue and discuss with their children about the things they should do – e.g. 'You should do what I said because otherwise you'll be too tired at school tomorrow.' In contrast, in working-class homes, parents are more likely to use the restricted code to tell/order their children what to do, rather than explaining and discussing with them why they should do it – e.g. 'I'm your mum, so do as you're told.'

The elaborated code of the middle class is more suited to the demands of school work, since understanding textbooks (like this one) and writing essays and answers to examination questions require the detail and explanation which are found mainly in the formal language of the elaborated code. Middle-class children who are used to using the elaborated code at home will therefore find school work much easier and learn more in school than those working-class children whose language is limited only to the restricted code. In addition, the teacher may mistake the working-class child's restricted use of language for lack of ability, and therefore expect less from the child. The self-fulfilling prophecy (discussed further later in this chapter) may then come into effect.

## CULTURAL CAPITAL

The various cultural features mentioned above have been combined in the term '**cultural capital**'. This refers to cultural assets such as parents' educational level and knowledge; language use; books, quality newspapers and other educational resources; visits to museums; manners and forms of behaviour; attitudes and values; and the taste and lifestyle which exist in family homes. Middle-class parents have more cultural capital than is usually found in lower-working-class homes (where there may be cultural deprivation), and this gives middle-class and upper-class students who possess it an in-built advantage in a middle-class-controlled education system.

**Cultural capital**
The educational level of parents, their knowledge, attitudes and values, language use and other educational resources that exist in the home that enable parents to support their children in education, and the children themselves to make good progress at school.

Cultural capital in action

### THE CULTURE CLASH

Schools are mainly middle-class institutions, and they stress the value of many features of the middle-class way of life, such as the importance of hard work and study; making sacrifices now for future rewards; the right form of dress, behaviour, manners and language use; good books, high-quality TV programmes, and so on. This means that middle-class children may find that school greets them almost as an extension of their home life, and they may start school already familiar with and tuned in to the atmosphere of the school – such as the subjects that will be explored there, seeking good marks, doing homework, good behaviour, a cooperative attitude to teachers, and other features of middle-class culture. Consequently, they may appear to the teacher as fairly intelligent and sophisticated.

For the working-class child, the atmosphere and values of the school may be quite unfamiliar and different from those of his or her home. This is likely to result in a **culture clash** between her or his home and social class background and the middle-class culture of the school. This culture clash may mean working-class children have to overcome cultural barriers and work much harder to achieve the same results as middle-class children, and this may partly explain working-class underachievement.

**Culture clash**
A clash or conflict between the cultural values of different individuals, groups and institutions – e.g. between the cultural values of the home and those of the school.

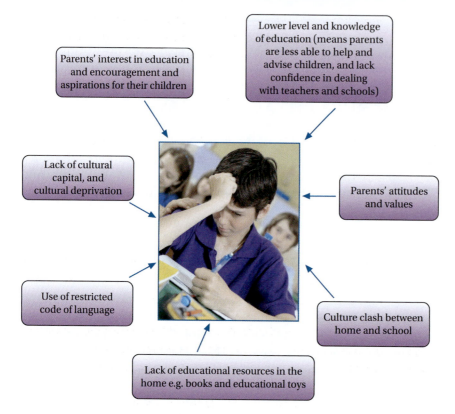

Parents' interest in education and encouragement and aspirations for their children

Lower level and knowledge of education (means parents are less able to help and advise children, and lack confidence in dealing with teachers and schools)

Lack of cultural capital, and cultural deprivation

Parents' attitudes and values

Use of restricted code of language

Culture clash between home and school

Lack of educational resources in the home e.g. books and educational toys

**Figure 4.5** External cultural factors explaining class differences in educational achievement

Cultural explanations have been criticized because:

- *They blame the victims* – Schooling should be about overcoming issues of cultural deprivation in the home and family background. It is schools that are at fault, not the parents.
- *They overlook practical difficulties* – Many working-class parents are very concerned and ambitious for their children's success in education, but working-class parents are more likely to work longer hours, doing shiftwork, overtime or irregular hours, and are less likely than the middle class to get paid for time off work. This may mean it is more difficult, for example, for working-class parents to visit schools, rather than that they don't care about their children's progress.
- *They overlook parents' lack of educational knowledge and self-confidence* – Working-class parents are often less educated than teachers, and this undermines their confidence and assertiveness in dealing with schools and helping their children. This lack of cultural capital, not lack of interest or encouragement, is what prevents working-class people from turning parental interest into practical support for their children's schooling.

- *They ignore the role played by schools themselves* – Schools may discriminate against working-class pupils and have low expectations of them, causing them to fail by the self-fulfilling prophecy (discussed below). If there's a culture clash between home and school, it's not the family's fault, but because the school is failing to meet the needs of working-class children.

*Internal factors – those inside the school*   The material and cultural explanations discussed so far are mainly concerned with factors outside the school that influence children's education. However, there is also a range of factors in the school itself that can affect how well children perform in education.

### TEACHER ATTITUDES, STEREOTYPES AND THE 'HALO EFFECT'

Evidence suggests that teachers' judgements of pupils' ability are influenced by factors other than ability alone. For example, teachers seem to take into account things like standards of behaviour, dress, speech and the types of home children come from, including the social-class background of pupils. Teachers are middle-class, and children from middle-class homes who share the same standards, values and elaborated code as them are often likely to be seen by teachers as brighter and more cooperative than those from working-class homes.

> **Halo effect**
> When pupils become stereotyped, either favourably or unfavourably, on the basis of earlier impressions.

The stereotype held by the teacher (good/bad, thick/bright, 'normal'/deviant student and so on) can produce a **halo effect**. This means that a teacher who has formed a good impression of a student in one way – for example, seeing them as cooperative, polite and helpful – may see that student more favourably in other unrelated ways, too – for instance, as being bright and hard-working (even if they're not) – and therefore encourage and support them. The opposite halo effect may also occur, when a poor impression in one area – for example, for being stroppy, difficult and disruptive – may affect other unrelated impressions, too, with the student also being seen as lazy or not very bright (even if this isn't true).

### STREAMING AND SETTING

Streaming and setting are systems used in schools to separate pupils into different groups according to their predicted ability. Even if children are really of equal ability, teachers are more likely to think working-class children are less intelligent because of the assumptions they hold about their home backgrounds. This may explain why working-class children tend to be found more in the lower streams of streamed comprehensive schools. Streaming and setting therefore seem to divide pupils along social-class lines, and reflect the class divisions in society, with many children from

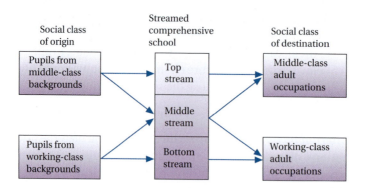

**Figure 4.6** Social class divisions and streaming

lower-working-class homes placed in lower streams or sets. This is illustrated in figure 4.6.

Streaming has been shown to be unfair and harmful to the self-esteem and educational performance of bottom-stream pupils, as teachers expect less from children in lower streams and give them less encouragement than those in higher streams.

This was confirmed by Ball (1981) in *Beachside Comprehensive*. Ball used participant observation in a comprehensive school over a three-year period to study the experience of schooling. Ball found many students were allocated to ability groups on the basis of their social-class background rather than their academic potential.

Ball found that top-stream or top-set students were 'warmed up' by teachers' encouragement and high expectations and were pushed to achieve highly in their courses. On the other hand, lower-stream/set students were 'cooled out' and received less encouragement and lower expectations from teachers. As a consequence, lower-stream or lower-set pupils achieved much less at school.

### LABELLING AND THE SELF-FULFILLING PROPHECY

Ball argues that the way schools put pupils into lower streams or sets involves negative **labelling**, such as defining them as low ability or 'wasters', etc., and pupils so labelled come to accept that they have low ability and underachieve.

Much research by interactionists has suggested that predicting whether a child will be a success or failure through testing, teachers' judgements and streaming or setting, and labelling him or her as bright or slow, can actually make that child a success or failure. Such predictions and labelling can affect an individual's view of himself or herself – their self-esteem – and the individual may act in accordance with the prediction made and the label attached. This process of predicting that something will happen, and of pupils acting in the way teachers expect them to act, in accordance with the

> **Labelling**
> Defining a person or group in a certain way and as having particular characteristics – as a particular 'type' of person or group.

In what ways might the attitudes and behaviour of teachers affect a student's progress?

label they have been given, is known as the self-fulfilling prophecy. Figure 4.7 illustrates this process.

Once placed in bottom streams, pupils may become victims of the self-fulfilling prophecy – those pupils labelled as 'bottom-stream material' may take on the characteristics expected of them by teachers. Because more working-class children tend to be put into bottom streams and sets by teachers, and middle-class children continue to dominate the higher streams and sets, schools may actually create working-class underachievement in education, adding to the material and cultural difficulties working-class children already face in school.

### Activity

1  In a school which puts pupils into ability groups (streams or sets), the best and most-qualified teachers are often kept for the most able classes. Why do you think this is the case? How might it affect the progress of those facing the greatest difficulties in the lower streams and sets?
2  Describe and explain *two* reasons why pupils from lower-working-class homes are more likely to be placed in lower streams and sets than those from middle-class homes.
3  Suggest one research method you might use to investigate how putting students into ability groups might affect their self-esteem. Explain carefully why you chose that research method rather than another, and identify any problems you might come across in using it.

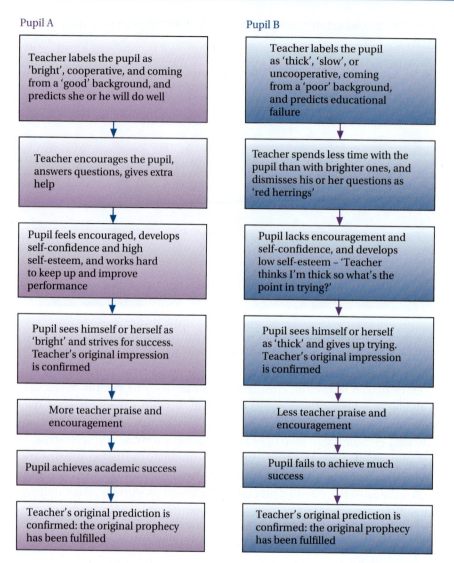

**Figure 4.7** The self-fulfilling prophecy: two examples

**Pupil A**

Teacher labels the pupil as 'bright', cooperative, and coming from a 'good' background, and predicts she or he will do well

↓

Teacher encourages the pupil, answers questions, gives extra help

↓

Pupil feels encouraged, develops self-confidence and high self-esteem, and works hard to keep up and improve performance

↓

Pupil sees himself or herself as 'bright' and strives for success. Teacher's original impression is confirmed

↓

More teacher praise and encouragement

↓

Pupil achieves academic success

↓

Teacher's original prediction is confirmed: the original prophecy has been fulfilled

**Pupil B**

Teacher labels the pupil as 'thick', 'slow', or uncooperative, coming from a 'poor' background, and predicts educational failure

↓

Teacher spends less time with the pupil than with brighter ones, and dismisses his or her questions as 'red herrings'

↓

Pupil lacks encouragement and self-confidence, and develops low self-esteem – 'Teacher thinks I'm thick so what's the point in trying?'

↓

Pupil sees himself or herself as 'thick' and gives up trying. Teacher's original impression is confirmed

↓

Less teacher praise and encouragement

↓

Pupil fails to achieve much success

↓

Teacher's original prediction is confirmed: the original prophecy has been fulfilled

### ANTI-SCHOOL SUBCULTURES

Most schools generally emphasize values such as hard work, good behaviour and exam success. One of the effects of streaming and labelling is to label those in the bottom streams and sets as failures, thereby depriving them of status.

In response to this lack of status, bottom-stream pupils often rebel against the school and develop an **anti-school (or counter-school) sub-culture** of their own. This takes different forms, but consists of an alternative set of values, attitudes and behaviour, in opposition to the aims of the school. Anti-school subcultures provide a means for bottom-stream pupils to achieve a feeling of self-worth through some success and status in their

**Anti-school (or counter-school) subculture** A group within a school organized around a set of norms, values, attitudes and behaviour in opposition to the main values, norms and aims of a school.

peer group. This is the type of subculture that was identified by Willis earlier (see pages 218–19).

Among such pupils, peer-group status is achieved by generally disrupting the smooth running of the school by, for example:

- truancy
- winding up teachers and challenging their authority
- not doing homework
- messing about and disrupting lessons
- breaking the school rules.

Such behaviour becomes a way of getting back at the system and resisting a schooling which has labelled them as 'failures' and denied them status.

Because of all the factors discussed above causing the underachievement of working-class pupils in schools, bottom-stream pupils are very often working-class, and such pupils will often be found in anti-school subcultures. Such pupils often leave school at the earliest possible opportunity, sometimes before taking any GCSEs or other formal qualifications.

Some forms anti-school (or counter-school) subcultures might take

## Activity

1 Describe and explain, with examples and giving at least two reasons, why some pupils form anti-school subcultures.
2 Write a short essay (10–15 minutes) answering the following question: 'How far do sociologists agree that working-class pupils tend to underachieve in education mainly because of socialization in the home?'

## ITEM A
## DO SCHOOLS MAKE A DIFFERENCE?

Rutter et al., in their book *Fifteen Thousand Hours: Secondary Schools and their Effects on Children*, reported research they had carried out in twelve schools. This study attempted to show, in the face of much previous research suggesting the opposite, that good schools can make a difference to the life chances of all pupils. Rutter et al. suggest that it is features of the school's organization which make this difference. These features are summarized below.

- Teachers are well prepared for lessons.
- Teachers have high expectations of pupils' academic performance, and set and mark classwork and homework regularly.
- Teachers set examples of behaviour – for example, they are on time and they use only officially approved forms of discipline.
- Teachers place more emphasis on praise and reward than on blame and punishment.
- Teachers treat pupils as responsible people – for example, by giving them positions of responsibility looking after school books and property.
- Teachers show an interest in the pupils and encourage them to do well.
- There is an atmosphere or ethos in the school which reflects the above points, with all teachers sharing a commitment to the aims and values of the school.
- There is a mixture of abilities in the school, as the presence of high-ability pupils benefits the academic performance and behaviour of pupils of all abilities.

## ITEM B
## THE BRUTAL TRUTH

… but what do we mean by a good school? Examination results are the only criteria we accept, and politicians imply these have something to do with quality of teaching, sound leadership, strong discipline, clarity of aims and so on. And these can all make a difference. The brutal truth, however, is that the surest way to turn a bad school into a good one is to change the pupils who attend it…. Parents, particularly middle-class parents, look at exam results and choose [schools] accordingly. Some don't bother with the results: they see well-scrubbed, nicely dressed and well-behaved pupils, and say that's the one for their child. They are right: home background, as you'd expect when you think how much more time children spend at home than at school, is another guide to attainment … A school can change the head, sack teachers, crack down on truancy and bad behaviour … these things may make the school happier, more peaceful, more businesslike. They may even improve exam results. They will make no long-term difference at all unless the intake changes … Rebranding the school may make a difference … a bright new wrapper always helps, for schools as well as chocolate bars, … but as long as schools have differing pupil intakes, some will be deemed 'good' and some 'bad'.

*Source*: adapted from Peter Wilby, 'Parents' admissions trauma is down to gross inequality outside school gates', *Guardian*, 5 March 2009

**The 'double test' for working-class children**  Taken together, the factors in the home, social-class background and the school help to explain why working-class students tend to do less well at school than middle-class students with the same ability. Schools test all pupils when doing subjects like mathematics, English or science. However, for the working-class student, there is a double test. At the same time as coping with the academic difficulties of school work which all students face, working-class youngsters must also cope with a wide range of other material and cultural disadvantages and difficulties.

These problems, on top of the demands of academic work, explain working-class underachievement in schools. These disadvantages start in the primary school and become more and more emphasized as children grow older, as they fall farther and farther behind and become more disillusioned with school. In this context, it is perhaps not surprising that a large majority of those who leave school at the minimum leaving age of 16 every year, many with few or no qualifications, and who afterwards become **NEET**s (**N**ot in **E**ducation, **E**mployment or **T**raining) come from lower-working-class backgrounds.

**NEET** A young person (aged 16–24) who is **N**ot in **E**ducation, **E**mployment or **T**raining.

## Activity

1 Describe *two* material factors in pupils' home and family backgrounds that may affect how successful they are in education. Be sure to explain how the factors you identify affect their education.
2 Describe *two* cultural factors that may affect pupils' educational achievements.
3 Explain in your own words what is meant by 'cultural capital', and identify three features (e.g., a lot of books) you might expect to find in the family and home life of those with high cultural capital.
4 Explain, with examples, what is meant by a 'culture clash' between the home and the school.
5 Identify *two* ways in which a school's catchment area might influence the education of pupils from the area.
6 Describe and explain *three* factors inside schools which may explain the underachievement of pupils from disadvantaged backgrounds.
7 Explain what is meant by 'labelling' and how it might influence the educational achievements of pupils.
8 Put the following explanations for working-class underachievement in what you think is their order of importance, and then explain why you consider your first choice as more important than all the others: home circumstances; parents' attitudes to education; parents' level of education; the catchment area; language use; possession of cultural capital; the culture clash; teachers' attitudes, streaming and setting, labelling and the self-fulfilling prophecy; the anti-school subculture.
9 In the light of your list, suggest ways that schools and teachers might improve the performance of pupils who face social-class disadvantages in education.
10 Do you think schools can make up for problems that begin outside school, such as in the home and the neighbourhood? Give reasons for your answer.
11 Suggest three policies governments might adopt to overcome the obstacles to success in education facing the most disadvantaged.

## Ethnicity and educational achievement

### *The facts*

Many children from BAME (Black, Asian and Minority Ethnic) backgrounds tend to do as well as – and often better than – many White British children, particularly lower-working-class White British boys and girls. Overall, gaps in educational achievement by ethnic group have narrowed considerably over the last twenty years. Since the early 2000s, most ethnic groups have, on average, seen a greater improvement in attainment at age 16 compared with the poorest White British pupils, and the major concern in 2018 was with the educational underachievement of the poorest White British pupils, who were eligible for free school meals.

- *The highest-achieving groups* are Chinese and Indian Asian pupils. They are more likely than White British students overall to get better GCSE and A-level results, to stay in education post-16, and to enter university.
- *The lowest-achieving groups* are the poorest White British boys and girls who are eligible for free school meals, and Black Caribbean, Mixed White and Black Caribbean, Pakistani, and the small number of Gypsy/Roma and Traveller-of-Irish-Heritage pupils. Most pupils from such backgrounds do less well than they should, given their ability. Underachievement by these groups is shown by the following types of evidence:
  - → below-average reading skills
  - → lower levels of attainment across national curriculum key stages, and in GCSE results
  - → over-representation (that is, there are more than there should be given their numbers in the population as a whole) – particularly Black Caribbean young people – in special schools for those with learning difficulties, and in special units for children with emotional, behavioural and social difficulties
  - → higher rates of permanent exclusion from school. This is particularly the case for Black Caribbean pupils, who are three times more likely to be permanently excluded from schools than White British students of the same sex, and to be temporarily excluded for longer periods for the same offences
  - → over-representation in lower streams (where schools are streamed by ability). Evidence suggests they are put in lower streams even when they get better results than pupils placed in higher streams
  - → more likely than other groups to leave school without any qualifications
  - → less likely to stay on in education after the end of compulsory schooling, and, when they do, they are more likely to follow vocational courses rather than the higher-status academic courses, like AS- and A-levels
  - → fewer going on to higher education at universities
  - → more likely to be NEET
  - → are less qualified in the population as a whole.

## Explaining ethnic differences in achievement

A range of factors work together to produce the lower levels of achievement of some ethnic groups. The previous section on working-class underachievement explained the lack of progress of the poorest groups of White British students, and the following sections identify some additional explanations for differences between ethnic groups. Figure 4.8 summarizes these.

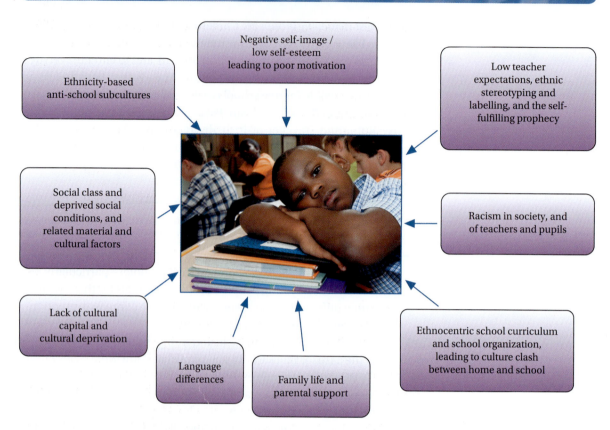

**Figure 4.8** Ethnicity and educational achievement

## *External factors (outside the school)*

### SOCIAL CLASS AND MATERIAL FACTORS

Young people from some minority ethnic backgrounds often face a series of disadvantages in social conditions, such as poor-quality housing, overcrowding and higher rates of unemployment in their homes, which contribute to difficulties in coping with school work. BAME groups are twice as likely overall to live in poverty as White British. In 2017–18, 18 per cent of White British people lived in the poorest fifth of the population, compared to 40 per cent of Black people, and 33 per cent of Asians. All the external material and cultural factors explaining working-class underachievement considered earlier therefore apply even more so to the poorest working-class BAME groups.

### LANGUAGE

Around 21 per cent of pupils in state-funded primary schools, and 17 per cent in secondary (with much higher proportions in some areas), did not have English as their first language or the main language used in their homes, according to official statistics published by the Department for Education in 2018. English is no longer the first language for the majority of pupils in more than 1 in 9 schools. Pupils for whom English is an additional language often have lower levels of attainment on starting school than pupils whose first language is English. Language differences may cause difficulties in doing some schoolwork and communicating with the teacher. However, evidence suggests that such language difficulties are rapidly overcome as children grow older.

### FAMILY LIFE AND PARENTAL SUPPORT

Parental involvement in their children's education has been shown to be a key factor in pupils' attainment. While many ethnic minority parents have high aspirations for their children and see education as a route to upward social mobility, pupils from some BAME groups enjoy higher levels of cultural capital and greater parental support than others, and this in part reflects social-class differences between them.

British Asian family life often has close-knit extended families, which have high aspirations for their children and very supportive attitudes to education, although Pakistani and Bangladeshi parents may be less confident about helping their children with homework, largely because they lack the cultural capital and educational expertise to do so.

British Black Caribbean communities have a higher level of lone parenthood than other ethnic groups, and this may pose financial and practical problems for poorer lone parents in supporting their children's education, no matter how much concern they may have about their children's progress.

Evidence suggests that lower-working-class White British families in the most disadvantaged areas have a fairly indifferent or negative attitude towards learning and towards school, and low aspirations for their children. These family cultures may contribute to differences in attainment between ethnic groups.

### RACISM IN SOCIETY

Racism in society may mean BAME groups face higher risks of the material disadvantages affecting achievement in school. Racism may also create a low self-esteem among young people, which can lead to poor motivation and influence their behaviour in school.

### Internal factors (inside the school)

### LANGUAGE DIFFERENCES

As suggested above, these may cause some difficulties in doing schoolwork and communicating with teachers. This only applies to a small minority of pupils, but it may be unconsciously penalized in the classroom, because most teachers are white and middle class, and they may mistake language difficulties for lack of ability. This may lead to negative labelling by teachers, resulting in lower expectations and the self-fulfilling prophecy, and may be an obstacle to pupil motivation and progress at school.

### RACISM: TEACHER EXPECTATIONS, STEREOTYPING, LABELLING, THE SELF-FULFILLING PROPHECY AND CONFLICT IN THE CLASSROOM

All schools are now legally obliged to have an anti-racist policy, and teachers are trained in equality legislation. Racism is not as widespread in teaching as in some professions, such as the police and legal professions, and teachers have often been, and are, among the first to tackle racism, but there is still racism among teachers and pupils, as there is in the rest of society.

Racism among pupils may result in race-related name-calling, abuse, bullying and harassment, lowering minority ethnic pupils' self-esteem.

Research in primary and secondary schools has found an unusually high degree of conflict between white teachers and Black Caribbean pupils. Teachers often hold stereotypes, with more positive expectations of Asians, particularly Asian girls (as relatively quiet, well-behaved and highly motivated), than of Black Caribbeans, of whom they often have low expectations, and whom they expect to be troublemakers. This may mean teachers negatively label Black Caribbeans and take swift action against them. Black Caribbean students, unlike whites and Asians, are often punished not for any particular offence but because they have the 'wrong attitude'.

Some ethnic groups, especially Black Caribbean boys and poor White British boys and girls, are more likely to be regarded as probable failures and placed in lower streams and sets, and so are effectively written-off as unlikely to succeed.

Such stereotyping and labelling may lead to the self-fulfilling prophecy of failure.

### ANTI-SCHOOL SUBCULTURES

Black Caribbean male pupils, in particular, are more likely to fight racism and form anti-school subcultures to achieve peer-group status denied by the school. There is some evidence they go to school with negative attitudes, reinforcing their labelling by teachers as troublemakers. This might explain why Black Caribbean pupils have an exclusion rate three times higher than the school population as a whole, since most exclusions are for persistent disruptive behaviour and verbal and physical assaults on pupils and staff.

### THE ETHNOCENTRIC SCHOOL CURRICULUM

**Ethnocentrism** means seeing other cultures through the eyes of one's own culture – in this case, White British culture – rather than recognizing and taking into account the cultures of different ethnic communities. Schools

**Ethnocentrism**
A view of the world in which other cultures are seen through the eyes of one's own culture, with a devaluing of the others. For example, school subjects may concentrate on White British society and culture, rather than recognizing and taking into account the cultures of different ethnic communities.

> **Ethnocentric curriculum** The curriculum of a school which gives priority to the culture of a particular ethnic group, whilst disregarding or downplaying other cultures.

tend to have an **ethnocentric curriculum** – for example, teaching history from a White British perspective, and ignoring the UK's complex racial history, and the brutalities and crimes of the British empire, and teaching only European languages instead of those of UK BAME groups.

### ETHNOCENTRISM IN SCHOOL ORGANIZATION

The white middle-class culture of the school means other cultures may be devalued or marginalized in school organization and school rules, e.g. by uniform or dress requirements that don't respect the cultural/religious rules of minority groups, such as banning the wearing of the hijab; school holidays reflecting only Christian festivals; and school meals that don't cater for minority-group diets.

### THE CULTURE CLASH

Because of racism in both the school and the wider society, BAME children in Britain may grow up with a negative self-image – a lack of self-respect and confidence because they feel they are in some ways rejected and their culture is devalued. The ethnocentric school curriculum, school organization and school rules may create a culture clash between home and school,

---

### Activity

1  What evidence can you think of, if any, from your own experiences at school, which suggests that the cultures of minority ethnic groups are either ignored or treated in a degrading way? Think about the subjects you studied, the textbooks you used, and the kinds of activity you undertook.
2  Many schools today are trying to include the cultures of BAME groups in school subjects and activities. What evidence is there of this happening in your experience? Give examples.

Refer to figure 4.8 (on page 266) and the sections above.

3  Write a brief description of each box in figure 4.8, and explain how each one contributes to the underachievement of some BAME groups.
4  Explain how the factors identified in figure 4.8 might combine to create low self-esteem in some BAME students, and how this might affect their progress in the education system.
5  Write a short essay (10–15 minutes) answering the following question: 'How far do sociologists agree with the view that cultural factors are the main reasons for the underachievement of some minority ethnic groups?'
6  Imagine you wanted to investigate parents' attitudes to schooling among different ethnic groups.
   (a)  Describe one way you might select a representative sample to investigate.
   (b)  Identify a research method you might use to collect information. Explain carefully why you chose that research method, and why you think it would be better than other methods you could have used.

contributing further to this low self-esteem. This may lead to low motivation in school and explain the poor educational performance of underachieving minority ethnic groups.

A lot of work has been done in schools in recent years to promote equality and understanding between different ethnic groups, to tackle racism and discrimination, and to reduce ethnocentric biases in teaching, textbooks and school organization, so this explanation for educational underachievement may be of declining significance.

## Gender and educational achievement

While the educational achievements of both males and females have improved in recent years, there are still big differences between them. Until the 1980s, the major concern was with the underachievement of girls. This was because, while girls used to perform better than boys in the earlier stages of their education, they tended to fall behind at GCSE, were less likely than boys to get the three A-levels required for university entry, and were less likely to go into higher education. However, in the early 1990s, girls began to outperform boys, particularly working-class boys, in all areas and at all levels of the education system. The main problem today is with the underachievement of boys, though many argue girls are still underachieving even though they are doing better than boys.

### *The facts*

- Girls do better than boys at every stage in national curriculum tests (the SATs) in English, and science, and outperform boys in language and literacy.

Girls now outperform boys in all areas and at all levels of the education system, and the main problem today is with the underachievement of boys

| GCSE subjects | Grades | Females (%) | Males (%) |
|---|---|---|---|
| All subjects | A*–C (9–4 equivalent) | 73 | 61 |
| English, English Literature and Maths (2017) | 9–4 | 74 | 63 |
| English | A*–C | 71 | 53 |
| | 9–4 | 70 | 55 |

- Girls are more likely to be entered for, and achieve, the EBacc standard, and are more successful than boys in most GCSE subjects, outperforming boys in every major subject, as shown below for the UK in 2018:
- A higher proportion of females stay on in post-16 sixth-form and further education, and post-18 higher education.
- Female school leavers are now more likely than males to get three or more A-level passes, and achieve higher average point scores than males.
- More females than males apply for and get accepted for full-time university degree courses. Young women are now around 35 per cent more likely to go to university than men. They are less likely to drop out, and are more likely than men to get a top 1st-class or upper 2nd-class degree.
- In 2017–18, 57 per cent of all students in higher education were female.

## Table 4.4   Some female and male differences in educational achievement, 2018

| | Female | | Male | |
|---|---|---|---|---|
| Percentage of 16-year-olds achieving at least a GCSE grade A*–C/9–4 (England) | 71 | | 61 | |
| All subjects | Entries (UK) | Pass rate[a] (%) | Entries (UK) | Pass rate[a] (%) |
| GCSE | 2,744,492 | 71 | 2,725,584 | 62 |
| AS-level | 177,317 | 91 | 168,809 | 88 |
| A-level | 446,381 | 98 | 363,395 | 97 |
| Accepted to university degree courses (UK applicants, 2017) | 48% | | 37% | |

[a] Passes are grades A*–C/9–4 for GCSE, and grades A*–E at AS- and A-level. Pass rates are rounded up or down to the nearest whole number.

Sources: Joint Council for Qualifications; UCAS; Department for Education

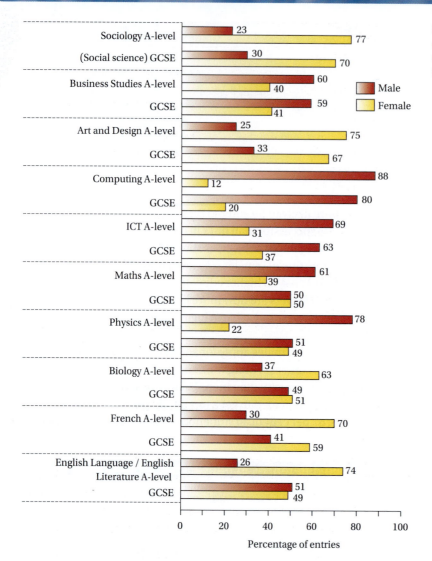

**Figure 4.9** Percentage of entries by subject and sex, GCSE and A-level: United Kingdom, 2018

*Chart data:*

- Sociology A-level — Male 23, Female 77
- (Social science) GCSE — Male 30, Female 70
- Business Studies A-level — Male 60, Female 40
- GCSE — Male 59, Female 41
- Art and Design A-level — Male 25, Female 75
- GCSE — Male 33, Female 67
- Computing A-level — Male 88, Female 12
- GCSE — Male 80, Female 20
- ICT A-level — Male 69, Female 31
- GCSE — Male 63, Female 37
- Maths A-level — Male 61, Female 39
- GCSE — Male 50, Female 50
- Physics A-level — Male 78, Female 22
- GCSE — Male 51, Female 49
- Biology A-level — Male 37, Female 63
- GCSE — Male 49, Female 51
- French A-level — Male 30, Female 70
- GCSE — Male 41, Female 59
- English Language / English Literature A-level — Male 26, Female 74
- GCSE — Male 51, Female 49

Percentage of entries (x-axis: 0, 20, 40, 60, 80, 100)

Male / Female

## Problems still remaining for females

Despite the general pattern of girls outperforming boys, problems do still remain for girls. The focus on girls outperforming boys, and the attention given to the underachievement of boys, can draw attention away from the fact that large numbers of girls, particularly lower-working-class girls, are also low attainers and are underachieving.

- Females and males still tend to do different subjects, which influences future career choices. Broadly, arts subjects are more likely to be chosen by girls, and science and technology subjects by boys. This is found at GCSE, but becomes even more pronounced at A-level and above. Girls

## Activity

Refer to table 4.4.

1 In which qualification was there the largest gap between the pass rates of males and females?
2 In which qualification was there the largest gap between male and female entries?
3 In which qualification did females achieve the best pass rate?
4 In which qualification did males and females achieve the most similar pass rates?

Refer to figure 4.9.

1 In which GCSE subjects were there more female than male entries in 2018?
2 In which three GCSE subjects was the gap between the percentage of male and female entries the greatest?
3 In which A-level subjects were there more male than female entries in 2018?
4 In which three A-level subjects was the gap between the percentage of male and female entries the greatest?
5 Which subject showed the greatest gap between the percentage of male and female entries at both GCSE and A-level?
6 Suggest two explanations for the difference in subjects males and females choose to study at GCSE and A-level.

are therefore less likely to participate after 16 in subjects leading to careers in science, engineering and technology.

- Girls achieve fewer high-grade A-levels than boys with the same GCSE results.
- There is little evidence that the generally better results of girls at 16 and above lead to improved post-school opportunities in terms of training and employment. Women are still less likely than men with similar qualifications to achieve similar levels of success in paid employment, and men still hold the majority of the positions of power in society.

What follows are some explanations for the huge improvement in the performance of girls since the 1980s, the underachievement of boys, and the subject choices that continue to separate males and females. While the key issue here is the underachievement of boys, remember that girls do better despite the obstacles they still face because of their gender.

## Why do females now do better than males?

### External factors (outside the school)

#### THE WOMEN'S MOVEMENT AND FEMINISM

The women's movement and feminism have achieved considerable success in improving the rights and raising the expectations and self-esteem of women. They have challenged the traditional stereotype of women's roles as homemakers and mothers, and raised awareness of patriarchy, gender role stereotyping and sex discrimination, both inside and outside of the education system.

### GROWING AMBITION, MORE POSITIVE ROLE MODELS AND MORE EMPLOYMENT OPPORTUNITIES

There has been a decline in recent years in the number of what were traditionally regarded as 'men's jobs', particularly in semi-skilled and unskilled manual work, while there are growing employment opportunities for women.

As a consequence, girls have become more ambitious, and they are less likely to see having a home and family as their main role in life. Many girls growing up today have mothers working in paid employment, who provide role models for them. Many girls now recognize that the future involves paid employment, often combined with family responsibilities. Sue Sharpe found in *Just like a Girl* in 1976 that girls' priorities were 'love, marriage, husbands, children, jobs, and careers, more or less in that order'. When she repeated her research in 1994, she found these priorities had changed to 'job, career and being able to support themselves'. These factors have raised girls' ambitions and expectations, and provided more incentives for girls to gain qualifications.

### *Internal factors (inside the school)*

#### EQUAL OPPORTUNITIES

The work of sociologists in highlighting the educational underperformance of girls in the past led to a greater emphasis in schools on equal opportunities. This was to enable girls to fulfil their potential more easily. These policies included, among others, monitoring teaching and teaching materials for gender bias to help schools promote 'girl-friendliness', not only in male-dominated subjects but across the whole range of the experience of girls in schools. Campaigns such as WISE (Women into Science and Engineering – www.wisecampaign. org.uk) have aimed to inspire girls and to attract them into studying and following careers in male-dominated STEM subjects (science, technology, engineering and mathematics). Teachers are now much more sensitive about avoiding gender stereotyping in the classroom, and this may have overcome many of the former academic problems which girls faced in schools.

#### GIRLS WORK HARDER

There is mounting evidence that girls work harder, are more conscientious and are better motivated than boys:

- They put more effort into their work.
- They spend more time on doing their homework properly.
- They take more care with the way their work is presented.

Girls read more than boys and talk about their schoolwork, and are more likely to have peer-group support to encourage their learning

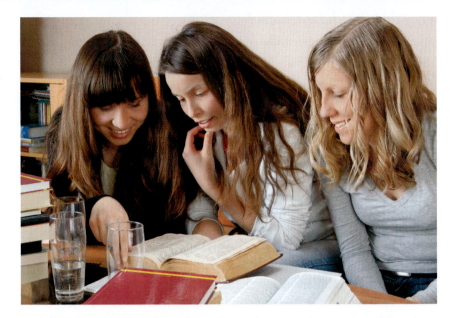

- They concentrate more in class and over a longer period of time (research suggests the typical 14-year-old girl can concentrate for about three or four times as long as her fellow male students).
- They are generally better organized – for example, they are more likely to bring the right equipment to school and meet deadlines for handing in work.
- They are more likely than boys to belong to pro-school subcultures in which they have peer-group support for learning.

### GIRLS MATURE EARLIER THAN BOYS

By the age of 16, girls are estimated to be more mature than boys by up to two years. Put simply, this means girls are more likely to view exams in a far more responsible way, and recognize their seriousness and the importance of the academic and career choices that lie ahead of them.

### TEACHERS HAVE HIGHER EXPECTATIONS OF GIRLS LEADING TO A SELF-FULFILLING PROPHECY OF SUCCESS

Girls are generally more cooperative and better behaved at school, and they generally care more than boys about the opinions of their teachers. This means teachers consequently have higher expectations of them, and girls benefit from a positive self-fulfilling prophecy.

### GIRLS READ MORE

Girls generally read more and talk about their schoolwork. This develops the language and reasoning skills which give them an advantage in education.

## Why do boys underachieve?

Many of the reasons given above for the improved achievements of girls can be reversed to suggest why boys may be underachieving. However, there are some possible additional explanations. These are summarized in figure 4.10.

### External factors (outside the school)

THE DECLINE IN MALE EMPLOYMENT AND THE CRISIS OF MASCULINITY

- The decline in traditional unskilled and semi-skilled male jobs, and the growth of temporary, part-time and insecure work, may be a factor in explaining why some boys (particularly lower-working-class boys) are underperforming in education. They may lack motivation and ambition because they may feel that, whatever they do, they have limited prospects, and getting qualifications won't get them anywhere anyway, so what's the point in working hard and trying to achieve?

- Poor job prospects have been combined with more dual-earner households – with women working and sometimes earning more than men. This has undermined men's traditionally secure identity as the main breadwinner in the family. This has been described as a 'crisis of masculinity', as males feel insecure about their traditional masculine role and position. The future seems bleak and to lack a clear purpose

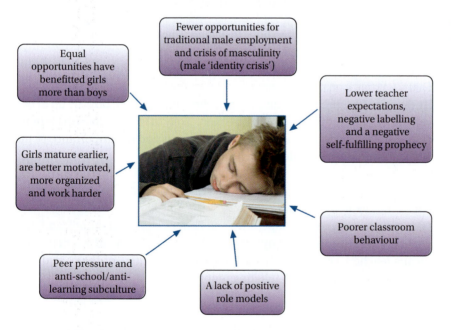

**Figure 4.10** The underachievement of boys

Equal opportunities have benefitted girls more than boys

Fewer opportunities for traditional male employment and crisis of masculinity (male 'identity crisis')

Lower teacher expectations, negative labelling and a negative self-fulfilling prophecy

Girls mature earlier, are better motivated, more organized and work harder

Poorer classroom behaviour

Peer pressure and anti-school/anti-learning subculture

A lack of positive role models

for many lower-working-class boys, and this curbs their ambition. This insecurity is reflected in schools, where some boys see schooling as leading them nowhere, so education just seems like a pointless waste of time.

### Internal factors (inside the school)

#### POORER BEHAVIOUR

Boys are generally more disruptive in classrooms than girls. They may lose more classroom time learning things because they are sent out of the room or sent home. In 2016–17, boys were around three times more likely to receive a permanent or a fixed-period exclusion than girls. Most of these are for persistent disruptive behaviour and verbal and physical assaults on pupils and staff, and usually come at the end of a series of incidents.

#### A LACK OF POSITIVE ROLE MODELS

Teaching is often seen as a mainly female profession, and there is a lack of male role models, especially in primary schools. Learning has therefore come to be seen as a feminine and 'girly' activity, contributing to a negative attitude among boys to schools and schooling.

#### PEER PRESSURE AND ANTI-SCHOOL SUBCULTURES

The 'crisis of masculinity' mentioned above leads boys to attempt to construct a positive self-image through laddish behaviour, aggressive macho posturing and anti-school activity, in attempts to draw attention to themselves. Boys appear to gain 'street cred' and peer-group status by not working, and some develop almost an anti-education, anti-learning, laddish subculture. Some boys achieve peer-group 'macho' status by resisting teachers and schools, through laddish behaviour like messing about in class and not getting on with their work. This may explain why they are less conscientious, and lack the persistence and application required for exam success, contributing to their underachievement.

#### LOWER TEACHER EXPECTATIONS

There is some evidence that staff are not as strict with boys as with girls. They are more likely to extend deadlines for work from them; have lower expectations of boys; are more tolerant of disruptive, unruly behaviour from boys in the classroom; and accept more poorly presented work from them. This can lead to the attachment of negative labels and a negative self-fulfilling prophecy, and this will mean boys perform less well than they otherwise might.

## GIRLS MAY STILL BE UNDERACHIEVING … BECAUSE OF BOYS

Francis's feminist research referred to earlier in this chapter (you should refer now to pages 219–20) showed that school classrooms, in mixed-sex schools, are patriarchal and dominated by boys. Educational research has repeatedly shown that the school's overt and hidden curriculum, interaction with boys, and demands placed on teachers to focus more attention and spend more time on boys, have negative effects on girls' self-esteem and experiences. In the face of the dominance of boys in the classroom, it is perhaps surprising that girls generally tend to do much better at school than boys.

Even though girls are beating boys in educational achievements, they could do better still if boys didn't dominate and disrupt classrooms, take up more teacher time than girls, and undermine and sideline girls in the classroom. Feminists point out that concerns about boys' underachievement mean that girls' experiences of schooling are largely neglected or ignored. The focus on boys means girls remain marginalized, and girls may still be underachieving, even if they are not doing so in relation to the boys.

It is the various distractions and disruptions caused by boys that help to explain why girls in single-sex schools display higher levels of self-esteem and independence, and get even better results – including in typically male-dominated subjects such as maths and science – than their peers in mixed-sex schools.

### Activity

1 Go through the reasons suggested above for why girls outperform boys in education. List the explanations in what you think is their order of importance, and give your reasons for putting them in that order.
2 Drawing on your own experiences at school, try to think of any other explanations for the underachievement of boys not already included above.
3 Discuss the steps that might be taken in schools to improve the performance of boys.
   (a) Identify and explain two reasons why unstructured interviews might be the best research method to investigate how girls feel about their experiences in school in relation to boys, and how this affects their education.
   (b) Identify and explain two reasons why using unstructured interviews in part (a) might not provide valid (or true) information.

*Why do males and females still tend to choose different subjects?* There is still a difference between the subjects that males and females take at GCSE and above, as figure 4.9 on page 272 shows. Females are still more likely to take arts, humanities and social science subjects, such as English literature, history, foreign languages, psychology and sociology, and males are more likely to take scientific and technological subjects, particularly at A-level and above (even though girls generally get better results when they do take them). This is despite the national curriculum, which makes maths, English and science compulsory for all students. However, even within the national curriculum, there are gender differences in option choices. For example, girls are more likely to take drama/performing/expressive arts, home economics / food preparation and nutrition, while boys are more likely to opt for engineering, computing and technology-related subjects. These differences might be explained as follows.

### GENDER SOCIALIZATION

Gender socialization (discussed in chapter 1, see pages 25–38) means that, for example, from an early age boys and girls are encouraged to play with different toys and do different activities at home, and they very often grow up seeing their parents playing different roles around the house. This socialization may encourage boys to develop more interest in technical and scientific subjects, and discourage girls from taking them.

### SUBJECT AND CAREER ADVICE

In giving subject and career advice, teachers may be reflecting their own socialization and expectations, and reinforcing the different experiences of boys and girls by counselling them into different subject options, according to their own gender stereotypes of suitable subjects.

### SUBJECT IMAGES, GENDER IDENTITY AND PEER PRESSURE

The gender perceptions of different subjects are important influences on subject choice, with the arts and humanities seen by students as feminine, and science and technology as masculine. Boys and girls choose subjects which they regard as keeping in line with the appropriate gender identities – femininity or masculinity – or risk ridicule or name-calling by peers.

### SCIENCE AND THE SCIENCE CLASSROOM ARE STILL SEEN AS MAINLY MASCULINE

Boys tend to dominate science classrooms – grabbing apparatus first, answering questions aimed at girls, ridiculing girls' questions and answers, and so on, which all undermine girls' confidence and intimidate them from taking up these subjects. Gender stereotyping is still found in science, with the invisibility of females particularly obvious in maths and science textbooks, where examples are often more relevant to the experience of males than of females. This reinforces the view that these are 'male' subjects.

## Activity

Read the following comments from year 11 boys talking about doing English and science, and then answer the questions beneath:

'I hate it! I don't want to read books.'

'Science is straightforward. You don't have to think about it. There are definite answers. There are no shades to it.'

'In science, everything is set out as a formula, and you have the facts. All you have to do is apply them to the situation.'

'When you read a book, it's like delving into people's lives. It's being nosy.'

'English is about understanding, interpreting … you have to think more. There's no definite answer … the answer depends on your view of things.'

'I don't like having discussions – I feel wrong … I think that people will jump down my throat.'

'That's why girls do English, because they don't mind getting something wrong. They're more open about issues, they're more understanding … they find it easier to comprehend other people's views and feelings.'

'You feel safe in science.'

*Source*: adapted from Eirene Mitsos, 'Boys and English: classroom voices', *English and Media Magazine*, 33, Autumn 1995

1   What are the main points being made about the differences between English and science, and explain whether or not you agree with them, and why.
2   Suggest three reasons why males and females tend to do different subjects.
3   Why do think that, even when girls take traditional boys' subjects such as technology, physics and computing, they still get higher grades than boys?
4   Around three-quarters of students taking GCSE social science and A-level sociology exams are girls. How would you explain this?
5   Suggest any links there might be between subject choices at school and gender role socialization in society as a whole (see pages 25–38 for some discussion of gender role socialization).
6   Applying one of the research methods you studied in chapter 2, carry out a small survey among male and female students to discover what influenced them in making subject and exam choices. Explain why you thought the method you chose was the most suitable, and identify any problems that arose during your research, and how you tried to overcome them.

## IS EQUALITY OF EDUCATIONAL OPPORTUNITY POSSIBLE TO ACHIEVE?

Despite attempts to secure equality of educational opportunity, children of equal ability but from different social classes, from different ethnic backgrounds, and of different sexes are still not achieving the same success in education. The reasons for this are a combination of external material and cultural factors outside the school, and internal factors inside the school. It takes BOTH to explain underachievement.

Social class is the overriding key factor explaining underachievement, and gender and ethnicity sit alongside this. For example, middle-class boys still outperform working-class girls, and middle-class Indian Asian boys will generally outperform working-class White British girls.

Compensatory education has not overcome the disadvantages faced by many pupils.

We live in an unequal society, with wide inequalities in wealth, income and related life chances, where different groups and classes do not start the educational race on equal terms. Until such fundamental inequalities and widespread deprivation are tackled, the combined effects of socialization, home and social-class background, teachers' attitudes, the white, middle-class language and culture of the school, and the continued existence of a privileged private sector of education will mean the realization of the ideal of equality of educational opportunity will remain an impossible dream.

It has been suggested that reforming schools is about as worthwhile an exercise as rearranging the furniture on the *Titanic* – the luxury liner that sank on its first voyage. This is because, in terms of improving life chances, schools often do not make much difference to social class, gender or ethnic inequalities in society as a whole, so reforming schools is basically a pointless exercise. Do you agree?

**Activity**

Write a short essay (10–15 minutes) answering the following question: To what extent is social inequality a major obstacle to educational achievement?

## CHAPTER SUMMARY AND REVISION CHECKLIST

After studying this chapter, you should be able to:

- explain why education is a social and political issue

- describe and explain the role of education in society, including the consensus perspective of functionalism and the conflict approaches of Marxism and feminism

- outline the work of Durkheim, Parsons, Bowles and Gintis, Willis, and Francis in relation to perspectives on education

- describe how education seeks to build social cohesion and citizenship

- describe what is meant by vocational education, and suggest some criticisms of it

- explain what is meant by the 'hidden curriculum', how it carries out social control, and how it reflects the values of society outside school, including the workplace

- outline briefly the education system before the 1970s

- outline the main arguments for and against comprehensive schools and selection in education

- explain what is meant by streaming, setting and mixed-ability teaching, and the problems associated with each of them

- explain what is meant by a meritocracy and equality of educational opportunity

- describe, explain and criticize the various changes in education from 1988 onwards, including attempts to improve standards, league tables, the marketization of education, parental choice and the growing diversity of schools

- outline the work of Ball, Bowe and Gerwitz in relation to parental choice and league tables

- identify the strengths and weaknesses of different types of schools, e.g. comprehensive schools, academies, free schools, faith schools and private schools

- suggest some arguments for and against educating children outside schools at home

- suggest some advantages and disadvantages of children with special educational needs being educated in either special or mainstream schools

- identify a range of ways in which government policies, external factors (outside schools) and internal factors (inside schools) influence educational achievement

- explain what is meant by positive discrimination and compensatory education

- explain what is meant by educational underachievement

- describe and explain a range of external and internal, and material and cultural, factors for the differences in achievement in relation to social class, ethnicity and gender

- outline the work of Halsey, Heath and Ridge in relation to social class and educational achievement

- explain what is meant by labelling and the self-fulfilling prophecy, and the problems associated with streaming and labelling in education, including Ball's findings in relation to social class and streaming

- describe and explain the obstacles to the achievement of equality of educational opportunity

## KEY TERMS

Definitions can be found in the glossary at the end of this book, as well as these terms usually being defined in the margin where they first appear in the chapter. You can also find the glossary online by following the link at www.politybooks.com/browne. Put it in your phone for ready reference.

achieved status

anti-school (or counter-school) subculture

ascribed status

citizenship

compensatory education

comprehensive school

correspondence principle (or theory)

counter-school (or anti-school) subculture

cultural capital

cultural deprivation

culture clash

deferred gratification

deschooling

division of labour

elaborated code

elite

equality of educational opportunity

equality of opportunity

ethnocentric curriculum

ethnocentrism

halo effect

hidden curriculum

immediate gratification

labelling

marginalization

marketization

meritocracy

NEET

particularistic values

positive discrimination

restricted code

ruling-class ideology

school ethos

self-fulfilling prophecy

setting

sexism

social cohesion

social mobility

social solidarity

streaming

tripartite system

underachievement

universalistic values

There are a variety of free tests and other activities that can be used to assess your learning – mainly aimed at AS- and A-level sociology students, but you might find them useful – as well as an online searchable glossary, at

## www.politybooks.com/browne

You can also find new contemporary resources by following Ken Browne on Twitter

## @BrowneKen

## Contents

## KEY ISSUES

- Social control, deviance and crime
- The social construction of crime and deviance
- Public debates over crime and deviance
- Crime, deviance and the media
- Biological and psychological theories of crime and deviance
- Sociological theories (or perspectives) on crime and deviance
- The pattern of crime
- White-collar and corporate crime
- Why are some minority ethnic groups over-represented in the crime statistics?
- Official crime statistics
- What's wrong with official crime statistics?
- Is the crime rate increasing or decreasing?
- The victims of crime
- Crime control, prevention and punishment
- Deviance, crime and social change

**Deviance** The failure to conform to social norms and values – rule-breaking behaviour.

**Crime** Behaviour which is against the law – law-breaking.

**Law** An official legal rule, formally enforced by the police, courts and prison, involving legal punishments if it is broken.

**Criminal justice system** (CJS) All the different agencies and organizations that are involved in law, order and the control and punishment of crime and other offending, such as motoring offences. It includes the police, Crown Prosecution Service (CPS), courts, prisons and the probation service.

## SOCIAL CONTROL, DEVIANCE AND CRIME

As discussed in chapter 1, norms and values are learnt through socialization, and these provide the social rules that enable people to know how to behave in society and to live together in some orderly way. Knowing what norms and values are, though, does not necessarily mean that people will conform to them. Because of this, formal and informal agencies and agents of social control seek to persuade or force individuals to conform to the social values and norms which have been learnt through socialization, and to prevent **deviance** (a failure to conform to social norms – rule-breaking) and **crime** (behaviour which is against the **law** – law-breaking).

These agencies of social control include formal agencies specifically set up to carry out social control, such as the police, courts, the probation service and prisons making up the **criminal justice system** (CJS), and informal agencies like the family, the peer group, education, the media, religion and the workplace. These all seek to maintain social order and stability, and encourage conformity by a range of positive and negative sanctions (rewards and punishments). These issues were discussed more fully in chapter 1, and you may wish to refresh your memory by referring to pages 20–3. The following section provides a brief summary, but check your understanding by completing the activity below.

**Formal rules**
Written rules and laws, which can bring about formal negative sanctions (punishments) if broken.

- *Formal social control* is concerned with the enforcement of **formal rules** – written rules and laws – which, if broken, may result in negative sanctions of various kinds. It is usually associated with control of individual behaviour by the state, through formal agencies of social control, such as the law and the criminal justice system (CJS). It might also include the enforcement of official, formal rules found in schools (e.g. dress rules), workplaces (e.g. wearing hard hats on building sites) and in sports (e.g. the rules of football), to which people are expected to conform or face penalties.

**Informal rules**
Unwritten rules or social norms which aim to control behaviour and ensure conformity in particular situations in everyday life.

- *Informal social control* is concerned with the enforcement of **informal rules** – unwritten rules or social norms which aim to ensure conformity in particular situations. These control behaviour in everyday life to maintain social order and stability. Informal social control is carried out by informal agencies of social control such as the family, the education system, the peer group, the workplace, the media and religion. These try to enforce social conformity and prevent deviance by putting pressure on individuals through rewards and punishments of various kinds, to show approval or disapproval of their behaviour in everyday life – for example, social pressure from parents or neighbours, or peer-group pressure, like that from school friends and workmates, to conform to group norms.

---

### Activity

1 Describe, with examples, two ways in which individuals are encouraged to conform to formal rules. Be sure to give examples of two particular ways and two particular formal rules.
2 Identify three informal agencies or agents of social control that encourage individuals to conform to informal rules, and give an example in each case of how they do this.
3 Describe two positive and two negative sanctions that people may face to encourage them to conform to (a) formal and (b) informal social rules.

**THE DIFFERENCE BETWEEN CRIME AND DEVIANCE**

Deviance is any non-conformist behaviour which is disapproved of by society or a social group, whether it is illegal or not. It is norm-breaking or rule-breaking behaviour, and can range from being eccentric to criminal activity. 'Crime' is the term used to describe behaviour which is against the law – law-breaking. As shown below, while a lot of crime is also seen as deviant, this isn't always the case, and there are many acts people regard as deviant which are not criminal (see below).

**Juvenile delinquency** is crime committed by those between the ages of 10 and 17, though the term 'delinquency' is often used to describe any antisocial or deviant behaviour by young people, even if it isn't criminal.

**Juvenile delinquency** is crime committed by those between the ages of 10 and 17, though the term 'delinquency' is often used to describe any antisocial behaviour by young people, even if it isn't criminal.

# THE SOCIAL CONSTRUCTION OF CRIME AND DEVIANCE

Crime and deviance are socially constructed. This means that something only counts as a criminal or deviant act because it has been given that particular meaning by people. For example, an act only becomes a crime because governments have chosen to pass a law which makes the act illegal. An act only becomes deviant when people interpret or label that act as rule-breaking, antisocial or non-conformist behaviour.

## The difficulty of defining deviance

Crime is easy to define, as the law states what a criminal act is. However, while deviance appears to be easy to define as any non-conformist rule-breaking behaviour, it is, in fact, quite difficult to pin down what members of any society or group actually regard as deviant. Deviance covers a very wide range of behaviour, and what is regarded as deviant will depend on the norms of a group or society. These norms differ between societies and between groups within the same society, and they change over time. The following examples illustrate how definitions of deviance can vary according to a range of circumstances.

### Non-deviant crime?

Most people commit deviant and even illegal acts at some stage in their lives, and there are many illegal acts which most people don't regard as particularly deviant. For example, parking offences, under-age drinking, pinching office stationery or making unauthorized personal calls on the office phone are all illegal but extremely common, and many people would not regard them as particularly deviant. Some offences, such as under-age drinking or use of illegal drugs are sometimes seen as expected behaviour by peers, and

What is deviant? In Ancient Greece, homosexual relationships were not prohibited, though they were governed by social codes. Only since 1967, however, has homosexuality been made legal in the UK after centuries of condemnation and persecution. As another example, in the seventeenth century, elaborate wigs were an accepted part of high-society fashion. Nowadays, wearing such a wig would be seen as deviant, though the practice still persists in the traditional robes of lawyers and judges

those who don't commit the offence may even be seen as deviant by those around them.

### The time

Deviance can only be defined in relation to particular norms or social rules, and these change over time. For example, cigarette smoking used to be a very popular and socially acceptable activity, but is increasingly becoming branded as deviant. Since July 2007, it has been illegal in the UK (and also in a number of other European countries) to smoke indoors in workplaces

Attitudes to smoking have changed

and buildings open to the public, and smokers are now unwelcome in many places. Attitudes to homosexuality have also changed dramatically. Homosexuality was illegal in the UK before 1967, but since then has become legal and widely accepted; it is now possible to have an officially approved gay marriage or a civil partnership. Fashion is an obvious example of changing norms – people today would generally be regarded as deviant were they to wear the fashions of seventeenth-century England, or even those of a few years ago (but not if they come into fashion again).

## The society or culture

Deviance is culturally relative – what is regarded as deviance in one society or group is not necessarily so in another. For example, consumption of alcohol is often seen as deviant and illegal in many Islamic countries, but is seen as normal in Britain.

## The social group

What may be acceptable in a particular group may be regarded as deviant in the wider society. Norms can vary between social groups in the same society. For example, taking illegal drugs is generally regarded as fairly acceptable behaviour among large numbers of young people (according to Home Office statistics, one in five of 16- to 24-year-olds had claimed to have used them in the year 2017–18), although it is regarded as deviant by most adults, and it is illegal.

## The place or context

The place where an act occurs may influence whether it is regarded as deviant or not. For example, it is seen as deviant if people have sex in the street, but

What counts as deviance varies between social groups and places, and sometimes acts are so common it is difficult to see them as deviant at all. For example, smoking cannabis is often regarded as deviant in Britain, and it is a criminal offence. Yet in 2017–18, around one in six 16- to 24-year-olds were using it, and one in fourteen of 16- to 59-year-olds. This is about half the proportion who smoke cigarettes. In the Netherlands, cannabis use is accepted, and there are officially approved premises (coffeeshops) for its sale and consumption. The photo on the right shows one of Amsterdam's oldest coffeeshops

not if it takes place between a consenting couple in a bedroom. Fighting in the street is seen as deviant, but not if it takes place in a boxing ring. The sale of prescription drugs in a local chemist is not regarded as deviant, but selling them at a club would be. Killing someone may be interpreted as heroic, manslaughter, self-defence, murder, a 'crime of passion', justifiable homicide or euthanasia (mercy killing). So it is not the act itself that is deviant but the place or context in which it occurs.

### Activity

Apart from the examples given above:

1   Identify and explain two examples of acts which are against the law but not usually regarded as deviant by most people.
2   Give three examples of deviant acts which are not against the law.
3   Identify and explain two examples of acts which are generally accepted by the majority of people in Britain, but which might be regarded as deviant in some social groups there – for example, among minority ethnic or religious groups.
4   Explain the circumstances in which the following acts might *not* be regarded as deviant or illegal:
    ● killing ten people
    ● driving through red traffic lights
    ● deliberately breaking someone's arm
    ● breaking into someone's house and removing her or his possessions
    ● taking children away from their parents by force.

## Why are some deviant acts defined as criminal while others are not?

Cannabis use in some countries of the Middle East and Africa is a common practice, with few laws enforced to control its use, and yet alcohol consumption is banned by laws which are vigorously enforced. In Britain, the opposite is more or less the case, despite the massive social cost caused by alcoholism in terms of family breakdown, days off work, acts of violence and costs to the NHS, and little evidence that cannabis has any addictive properties. Why are there such differences in the way some acts are defined as criminal while other, similar acts are not? There are two broad competing views on this.

### The consensus approach

The consensus approach, adopted by functionalists, suggests that social rules are made and enforced for the benefit of everyone. The law and the definition of crime represent a consensus – a widespread agreement among most people – that some deviant acts are so serious that they require formal social control and legal punishments to prevent them occurring. This may seem fairly clear in cases such as murder, rape and armed robbery, but it is not so clear on other issues, like those of alcohol and soft drug abuse. From the consensus view, this would be explained by the varying norms found in different societies, which mean alcohol and drugs are viewed differently.

### The conflict approach: inequalities in power

The conflict approach, adopted by Marxists, feminists and interactionists, suggests that the law reflects the interests of the richest and most powerful groups in society. These groups have managed to impose their ideas and way of thinking on the rest of the population through the agencies of social control. Those in positions of influence in society – such as newspaper editors, politicians, owners of industry, powerful pressure groups, judges and the police – are much better placed to make their definition of a crime stick than the ordinary person in the street. They also have the power to define some acts as criminal through media campaigns, by passing laws in Parliament, or by treating some offences more seriously than others.

In this way the powerful are able to maintain their own position of power and influence by defining those activities which are against their interests as deviant or criminal. The issue of alcohol raised above could well be explained by the power of the wealthy large brewers and distillers. Breaches of health and safety regulations by employers are often treated as oversights rather than crimes. Offences such as tax evasion by the well-off are often neither pursued as vigorously, prosecuted, nor punished as severely as a working-class offence such as benefit fraud, which is much more likely to result in prosecution and a prison sentence.

Activity

1   Which view explaining why some deviant acts are defined as criminal while others are not do you find most convincing? Give reasons for your answer.
2   Do you think the law is biased in deciding both which acts are defined as criminal, and which ones get pursued by the police and the courts? Give reasons for your view.

# PUBLIC DEBATES OVER CRIME AND DEVIANCE

Crime and deviance have long been major themes of public debate. In popular culture, fictional and non-fictional crime stories are major sources of spectacle and mass entertainment, and media news is full of stories of crime and deviance.

## Crime as a social issue – its impact on society

Social issues tend to be matters that people worry about, and crime worries many people, and the general public views crime as a major social problem. Crime can cause misery and anxiety to individuals and cast a blight over entire neighbourhoods, and undermine community life and social cohesion. Victims of crime may experience stress and insecurity, physical injury, personal loss, a sense of having their homes violated after burglaries, and a lasting fear of being victimized again, leading to a heightened sense of personal insecurity and a fear of leaving their homes. For some crimes, such as domestic violence, child abuse and racial harassment, there may be a prolonged pattern of repeat victimization having lifetime consequences for those victimized.

## Fear of crime

Even though national crime rates for most offences have been falling in recent years, the 2015–16 Crime Survey for England and Wales (CSEW) showed that 60 per cent of people thought crime was going up. People's fear of crime is much higher than is justified by the actual risk of being a victim of crime. For example, in 2018, 10 per cent of people had a very high level of worry about being burgled, when their risk of being burgled was only about 2 per cent, and homes were around four times less likely to be burgled than they were twenty years earlier. Crime – and particularly serious and violent crime – is not a common experience for most people, with eight in ten adults surveyed by the CSEW in 2018 not being a victim of any of the crimes asked about in the survey.

## Violent crime

The media tend to generate public debates and fuel popular fears with their focus on bad news and exaggerated reporting of crime to sell papers and attract viewers. This can create quite unnecessary levels of anxiety, with sensationalized reports of exceptional crimes of violence and suggestions of crime 'spiralling out of control'. For example, the extent of violent crime is widely exaggerated by the media, with reports of robbery with violence (mugging) and knife and gun crime given very high prominence. Yet over half (55 per cent) of all violent crime involves no injury whatsoever, a further 21 per cent involves minor injury, and less than 2 per cent of adults are likely to be a victim of a violent crime. Knife crime has been rising since 2015, and rose by 12 per cent in 2017–18, and knife crime – including possession of a knife – is a growing problem, especially among young people. Around one young person is stabbed to death every fortnight. But it is important to put knife crime in context. It makes up a tiny proportion of all offences recorded by the police – less than 1 per cent, and the occurrence of gun crime in 2017 was still around a third lower than it was ten years earlier.

## Youth crime and antisocial behaviour

Many people see youth crime and antisocial behaviour as a social problem, and they are often the source of much public debate. Clearly, in some communities, youth crime and antisocial behaviour can have harmful consequences. They can threaten community life and undermine social cohesion, and they are often a source of anxiety among adults, who fear violence, and having their homes burgled or their cars vandalized.

This anxiety is in part fed by the media, which often give the false impression that most young people are frightening and threatening binge-drinking, drug-crazed, antisocial and violent young tearaways, turning town centres and local neighbourhoods into graffiti-saturated, vandalized war zones, ravaged by gun- and knife-carrying gangs of young thugs.

### Youth crime

Young people commit a significant amount of crime. Young offenders (aged 18–25) are the age group most likely to come into contact with the police, and they make up around 27 per cent of all offenders. But it is important to put this into context: only around 7 per cent of 18- to 25-year-olds, and half a per cent of 10- to 17-year-olds, were found guilty of any offence in England and Wales in 2017, and the number of 10- to 17-year-olds who received a **police caution** (a formal warning given to anyone aged 10 or over for minor crimes, such as writing graffiti on a bus shelter) or sentence fell by 81 per cent between 2007 and 2017.

**Police caution**
A formal warning given by the police to anyone aged 10 or over for minor crimes, such as graffiti.

Do you think the media give a false impression of most young people, such as in stories about knife and gun crime, and antisocial behaviour?

Crimes suspected to have been committed by children under 10 (who can't be arrested or charged with a crime) are tiny – estimated at around one-twentieth of 1 percent of all recorded crime in 2015.

This means, despite public impressions, the vast majority of young people are not criminals, nor do they have any contact with the CJS.

## Antisocial behaviour

Antisocial behaviour, shown in the box below, is seen as a common problem often linked to, and blamed on, young people. However, much of it is probably as much the responsibility of adults as young people, and, as the box shows, at least 70 per cent of people don't regard antisocial behaviour as a big problem in their area.

---

**ANTISOCIAL BEHAVIOUR**

Percentage of people aged 16 and over saying there is a very/fairly big problem in their area, year ending March 2018

| | |
|---|---|
| Rubbish or litter lying around | 30 |
| People using or dealing drugs | 23 |
| People being drunk or rowdy in public places | 16 |
| Teenagers hanging around on the streets | 16 |
| Vandalism, graffiti and other deliberate damage to property | 15 |
| Noisy neighbours or loud parties | 10 |
| Abandoned or burnt-out cars | 3 |

*Source: Crime in England and Wales, Year Ending March 2018 – Annual Trend and Demographic Tables,* Office for National Statistics

---

**Activity**

1  Drawing on the evidence above, to what extent do you agree or disagree with the impression sometimes given in the media that youth crime and antisocial behaviour are serious social problems?

2  Suppose you wanted to investigate the extent of crime and antisocial behaviour among young people. Suggest a research method which you think would produce the most valid (or truthful) results, and explain carefully why you think this method might be better than other methods you might have chosen.

## The prison system – an expensive way to make 'bad' people worse

Prison – or Young Offender Institutions, Secure Training Centres or Secure Children's Homes for those aged between 10 and 18 – is the most serious sanction available to the CJS. Public debates and opinion polls generally suggest that many people favour a 'lock 'em up' approach towards offenders, regard most sentencing as too lenient, and believe that prisoners are released too early on parole before completing their sentences. The public view is that prison is a key way of deterring people from offending by increasing the penalties for crime, and politicians are always 'talking tough' on crime and calling for ever more people to be imprisoned. And this is what has happened:

- More people are being sentenced to prison – as shown in figure 5.1, the prison population in England and Wales has more than doubled in the last fifty years. England and Wales have the highest imprisonment rate (per 100,000 people) in western Europe.
- The courts are handing down longer sentences, fewer prisoners are getting parole, and so people are spending longer in prison.

Despite public impressions, prisons are not cushy holiday camps:

- Many prisons are overcrowded (e.g. two prisoners sharing a cell designed for one), and have been every year since 1994. Overcrowding affects whether training and educational activities, staff and other resources are available to reduce the risk of reoffending. Overcrowding also increases stress and tension among prisoners and staff, and harms the mental health of prisoners.
- Safety in prisons has been deteriorating rapidly, with more prisoner suicides, self-harm incidents and assaults than ever before. Self-inflicted death is around eleven times more likely to occur among prisoners than in the general population, and on average one prisoner committed suicide around every four days in the 12 months to December 2018.

**Figure 5.1** Prison population, England and Wales, 1967–2019

*Sources*: *Prison Statistics, England and Wales 2001*, Home Office, 2003; G. Allen and C. Watson, *UK Prison Population Statistics*, Briefing paper number SN/SG/04334, House of Commons Library, 2017; *Prison Population Figures*, Ministry of Justice, April 2019

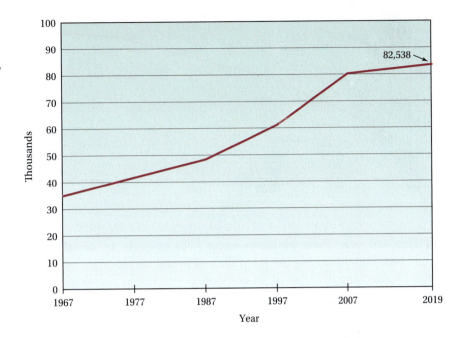

## Does imprisonment reduce crime?

Prison doesn't actually seem to work very well as a way of stopping reoffending, nor are high levels of imprisonment making much impact on reducing crime:

- As figure 5.2 shows, the increase in imprisonment has not resulted in a decrease in the crime rate. In the same period that the numbers in prison more than doubled, the numbers of crimes recorded by the police increased by nearly five times.
- Prison has a poor record for reducing reoffending – nearly half of adults, and 65 per cent of juveniles and young adults, are reconvicted within one year of release. And this is just for those who had their further offending discovered.

If anything, prisons seem to make 'bad' (or already troubled) people worse, rather than reforming them. This is because many prisoners have had very troubled personal histories before entering prison – e.g. chaotic childhoods, during which many have experienced abuse, witnessed violence in the home, and been taken into care. Many lack any educational qualifications, have been unemployed, had problems with accommodation and many have histories of mental illness or learning difficulties. Over half of people entering prison have the literacy skills expected of an 11-year-old – over three times higher than the proportion found in the general adult population.

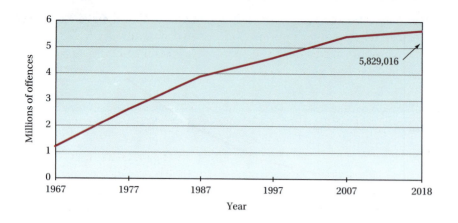

**Figure 5.2** Police-recorded crime, England and Wales, 1967–2018

*Source: Crime in England and Wales*, Office for National Statistics; *Historical Crime Data*, Home Office, 2012, 2016.

Prison can make these problems worse – for example, by destabilizing family ties, and disrupting the possibility of future employment opportunities by attaching the label of 'ex-convict'. Interactionist sociologists (see pages 59–60 in chapter 2 for a reminder of this theoretical approach, and later in this chapter) suggest prisons have their own subcultures, which provide training grounds for criminals, and confirm the 'criminal' label. This makes it difficult for released prisoners to re-enter conforming mainstream society successfully, and increases the likelihood of reoffending as alternative opportunities to live a normal life in society are blocked.

### Activity

The main purposes of prison include:
1 *Rehabilitation* – to make prisoners better people to discourage them from reoffending.
2 *Deterrence* – to discourage or deter others from offending.
3 *Restorative justice* – to force criminals to make amends to victims by repairing or restoring the damage they've done.
4 *Incapacitation* – to protect society from those who are a danger to the public.
5 *Retribution* – to punish criminals simply because they deserve it.

(a) In the light of what you've studied so far, put these five aims in the order you think would be most effective in reducing the extent of crime in society, and explain why you have put them in that order. You might do this as a class exercise, forming groups around your top priority, and then defending it over other people's top priority.

(b) Imagine you were going to try to uncover what people really think about prison sentences (e.g., are they too short / too long / too soft) and the purpose of prisons. You aim to obtain really in-depth information, to uncover their feelings about these things. Suggest a hypothesis you might explore, and the research method you would choose to collect such in-depth information. Give your reasons for choosing that method.

This means prisons can act as 'universities of crime', which create crime rather than rehabilitating (reforming) criminals. It costs about £37,000 a year to keep a prisoner locked up, and in many ways prisons amount to expensive ways of making 'bad' people worse.

# CRIME, DEVIANCE AND THE MEDIA

Surveys such as the CSEW show that the majority of people base their knowledge of crime and the criminal justice system (CJS) on the media – including crime fiction – rather than on their own direct experience. The media – TV, newspapers, magazines, etc., the internet and social media – tend to be very selective in their coverage of crime and deviance. They exploit the possibilities for a 'good story' by dramatizing, exaggerating and sensationalizing some acts, whether criminal or not, out of all proportion to their actual extent in society. This process can create unnecessary fears among people by suggesting that crime is a normal and common feature of everyday life. A Home Office report confirmed this view, arguing that TV programmes which stage reconstructions of unsolved crimes, such as the BBC's *Crimewatch* (axed in October 2017, but living on as *Crimewatch Roadshow* on BBC1 daytime), exaggerate the level of dangerous crime and unnecessarily frighten viewers. This is why, although numbers of most crimes have been steady or falling over the last few years, a majority of the population wrongly think they're rising.

Media news and fiction give a misleading impression of crime in the following ways:

- by hugely exaggerating sex, drug and (particularly) serious violence-related crimes – which are quite rare – such as gun- and knife-crime, sexual assault by a stranger, murder or armed robbery
- by under-reporting the risks of the most common offence of property crime
- by portraying property crime as far more serious and violent than most recorded offences, which are fairly routine, trivial and non-dramatic, and typically involve little or no loss or damage, and no violence or threat to victims
- by over-exaggerating police effectiveness in clearing-up (solving) crimes
- by exaggerating the risks of becoming a victim of crime.

## The media, labelling and deviancy amplification

**News values** The values and assumptions held by journalists, which guide them in choosing what to report and what to leave out, and how what they choose to report should be presented.

What the media choose to report is guided by journalists' **news values** – the values and assumptions which guide them in choosing what to report, and how it should be presented to appeal to their audiences.

The media's news values and their pursuit of what they regard as good stories mean they often distort, exaggerate and sensationalize the activities of some groups. The media have the power to label and stereotype certain groups and activities (such as young people and their behaviours) as deviant, and present them as **folk devils** – individuals or groups causing some imagined or exaggerated threat to society and social values. Even if much of what is reported is untrue, this may be enough to whip up a **moral panic** – growing public anxiety, concern and outrage about the alleged deviance.

This can raise demands for action by the agencies of social control to stop it. Often these agencies, such as schools, social services, the police and magistrates, will respond to the exaggerated threat presented in the media by taking harsher measures against the supposed troublemakers. Such action, particularly by the police, can often make what was a minor issue much worse – for example, by causing more arrests.

It's possible that such action, combined with media coverage, might even create deviance where there was none before, as people get swept away by the excitement of events. The presence and attention of reporters and TV crews might encourage people to act up for the cameras and misbehave when they might not otherwise have done so. The way the media may actually create or make worse (amplify) the very problems they condemn is known as **deviancy amplification**. Figure 5.3 illustrates the way the media can amplify deviance and generate a moral panic.

Young people involved in crime, antisocial behaviour or in youth subcultures are often found among those around whom moral panics develop. For example, fairly trivial acts of antisocial behaviour or vandalism are seen as typical of all young people, who then become stereotyped as a potential threat and as troublemakers. They may then become **scapegoats** – blamed for things which aren't their fault – for all problems in a community. Figure 5.4 shows a range of moral panics which have arisen in Britain since the 1950s.

**Folk devils**
Individuals or groups posing an imagined or exaggerated threat to society and social values.

**Moral panic** A wave of public concern about some exaggerated or imaginary threat to society, stirred up by overblown and sensationalized reporting in the media.

**Deviancy amplification** The process by which the media, through exaggeration and distortion, actually create more crime and deviance.

**Scapegoats**
Individuals or groups blamed for something which is not their fault.

---

**Activity**

1 Describe two reasons why young people are often stereotyped in the media as criminal and antisocial.
2 Describe two reasons in each case, with examples of particular crimes, why exaggerated media reporting of crime might cause unnecessary fears among: (a) older people; (b) women.
3 Describe two consequences for individuals that might follow from being a victim of crime. Illustrate your answer with examples of particular crimes.
4 Identify and explain two ways in which high levels of crime in a neighbourhood might affect communities beyond the actual victims of crime.

Refer to figures 5.3 and 5.4.

5 Try to fill in each of the stages of any current moral panic in society.

6 Suggest ways in which the presence of the media at events might make deviant activity worse – for example, playing up to the cameras.

7 Explain how Muslims might be seen as a source of moral panics in contemporary Britain.

**Figure 5.3** Deviancy amplification, moral panics and the media

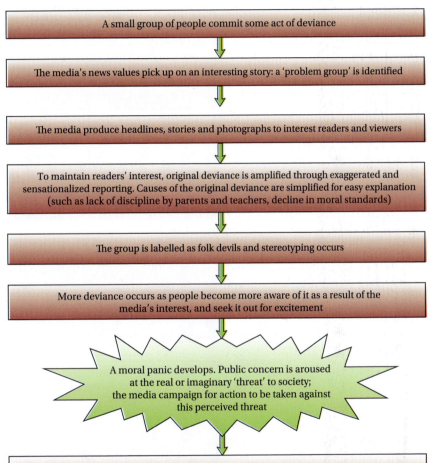

A small group of people commit some act of deviance

The media's news values pick up on an interesting story: a 'problem group' is identified

The media produce headlines, stories and photographs to interest readers and viewers

To maintain readers' interest, original deviance is amplified through exaggerated and sensationalized reporting. Causes of the original deviance are simplified for easy explanation (such as lack of discipline by parents and teachers, decline in moral standards)

The group is labelled as folk devils and stereotyping occurs

More deviance occurs as people become more aware of it as a result of the media's interest, and seek it out for excitement

A moral panic develops. Public concern is aroused at the real or imaginary 'threat' to society; the media campaign for action to be taken against this perceived threat

More social control – politicians, police and magistrates respond to public demands as shown in the media, and law-and-order campaigns are begun to stamp down hard on the deviants. The police take harsher action, with more policing and arrests; judges and magistrates impose heavier penalties, such as fines, community sentences or imprisonment; and governments may pass new laws criminalizing deviant behaviour

**1950s**
Teddy boys and Beatniks

**1960s**
Mods and Rockers
Drug abusers
Student militants
Trade union militants
Hippies

**1970s**
Mugging
Political violence (the IRA)
Trade union militants
Social security 'fraudsters'
Youth culture (punks and skinheads)
Football hooligans

**1980s**
Drug abuse (glue-sniffing; heroin; crack)
Black youth (inner city riots)
Football hooligans
Hippies/travellers
Acid house parties (later called raves)

**1990s**
Satanic ritual abuse of children
Joy-riding
Ecstasy
Handguns and combat knives
Paedophiles
Football hooligans

**2000s**
Asylum seekers
Gun and knife culture
Internet paedophiles
Muslim terrorists
Welfare benefit 'fraudsters'
Knife crime & young people

**Figure 5.4** Folk devils and moral panics: Great Britain, 1950s–2010s

### Activity

Refer to the cartoon opposite, which suggests that social workers are often used as scapegoats, getting blamed for things that are not their fault. Describe two other groups in contemporary society who are often used as scapegoats, and explain why you think they are used in this way.

Every time there is a case of serious child abuse, the media, particularly the red-top newspapers like the *Daily Mail*, *Daily Mirror*, *Sun* and *Daily Express*, attack the social workers responsible for child welfare, whipping up public hostility as suggested in the cartoon. Such newspapers often use social workers as scapegoats, seeming to blame them more for not preventing child cruelty and abuse than the parents and stepparents who nearly always carry out the actual abuse. This is a bit like blaming the police, rather than criminals, for crime, or blaming doctors for disease and ill health

'A paedophile? No, they've cornered a social worker!'

## BIOLOGICAL AND PSYCHOLOGICAL THEORIES OF CRIME AND DEVIANCE

Biological and psychological theories suggest that deviant/criminal behaviour is caused by something in people's biological or psychological make-up, which prevents them from conforming to conventional norms and legal rules. Crime is put down to there being something wrong with criminals and deviants that makes them different from normal people: individuals are to blame, not society.

Sociologists generally reject these explanations, as it is impossible to be born a criminal or a deviant. This is because crime and deviance are socially constructed and do not exist in nature. They involve legal and social rules created by people, and what counts as deviant or criminal will depend on how society defines these rules, and these change between societies and over time, and there is no act that in itself is ever *always* regarded as criminal or deviant. To suggest that criminals are different from normal people also fails to recognize that most people will commit acts of deviance and crime, albeit trivial offences, at some time in their lives, and many criminals are never detected. The sections that follow examine the major sociological perspectives or theories of crime and deviance. These are summarized in figure 5.5.

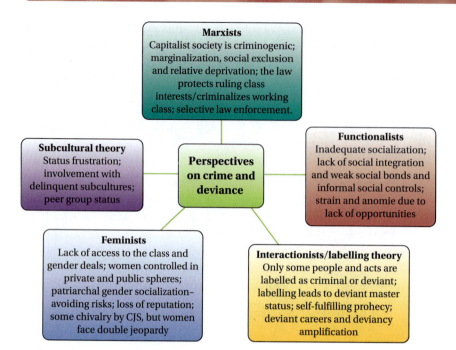

**Figure 5.5** A summary of theories (or perspectives) on crime and deviance

# SOCIOLOGICAL THEORIES (OR PERSPECTIVES) ON CRIME AND DEVIANCE

Deviance and crime cover very wide and different forms of behaviour. Definitions of deviance and crime vary widely between societies, and change over time. There have been a huge number of attempts to explain the causes of deviance, and particularly crime, and why some people commit crime while the majority appear not to. No single explanation can possibly provide an adequate account of all forms of deviance – premeditated murder, armed robbery, making a fraudulent home or car insurance claim, antisocial behaviour, and just being rude and obnoxious are such widely differing acts that no single explanation can cover them all.

## Functionalist theories of crime and deviance

Functionalism (see pages 51–2 in chapter 2) sees crime and deviance arising from the culture and structure of society. Social order and cohesion are based on a value consensus, and the agencies of socialization and social control seek to protect this by controlling the threat posed by crime and deviance.

Despite this, Durkheim saw some (but not too much) deviance and crime as necessary and beneficial in any society. They could perform functions that contribute to the well-being of society and help to make it stronger. Crime and deviance can:

- *strengthen society's values* – values can 'atrophy' (waste away) unless people are reminded of the boundaries between right and wrong behaviour. Offenders who break society's laws and who are punished for it remind everyone else what the boundaries are between acceptable and unacceptable behaviour. This strengthens the values on which the laws are based – e.g. those who break a school's dress rules and are then sent home to change, or are excluded, remind everyone else what the rules are. Widespread media reports of horrific crimes, such as child abuse, can cause public outrage, remind people about how children should be treated, and bring people together in an attempt to stop such crimes.
- *enable social change* – some deviance is necessary to allow problem areas to be identified and for new ideas to develop, e.g. a school's dress rules may be outdated, and a few people breaking the rules might help school authorities realize it is time the rules were changed.
- *act as a 'safety valve'* – to ease stresses and frustrations in society – e.g. school students going on strike for a day to express their frustration at school rules might be seen as a form of release, and preferable to burning the school to the ground.
- *act as a warning device that society is not working properly* – e.g. high rates of divorce, high rates of crime, or masses of students breaking the school rules or playing truant suggest that there are underlying problems that need solving.

The result of this is that some deviance and crime can bring together the conforming members of society against the non-conforming 'outsiders', and strengthen social order – a stable society united by shared values (value consensus). They can also enable social change.

## The functionalist view of the causes of crime

**Inadequate socialization**   Poor socialization, poor parenting and lack of control by families and communities may mean some young people are brought up without proper guidelines on what is right and wrong. This may lead to people choosing deviance and crime over conformity, becoming antisocial, or being indifferent to whether the law is broken or not in their peer group and community. This might help to explain some forms of deviance, like antisocial behaviour or juvenile delinquency among young people, but crime and deviance are so widespread through all social groups in society that it is difficult to put it all down to poor parenting and inadequate socialization.

**Lack of social integration and social control**   Functionalists suggest that most people are fairly weak, and would be tempted to commit crime if they had the chance. What stops them from doing so is their social bonds with other people. These are illustrated in figure 5.6. They include:

- *attachment to those around them*, like family, workmates, neighbours, schoolmates and other friends, and those in their local community
- *beliefs and values shared with others*, such as ideas about right and wrong, respect for fair use of authority, and for the rights of others
- *commitment to conventional activities*, such as working hard at school, getting a job, raising a family and building for the future
- *involvement with a range of social undertakings*, such as sport and school activities.

These social bonds provide a network of support and integrate people into society, tie them to conformity, encourage them to exercise self-control, and limit their desire to commit crime. This is reinforced by informal social control, such as through the family, schools, workplaces, and peer groups.

Functionalists suggests people turn to crime when social bonds and informal social controls encouraging conformity are broken or weakened.

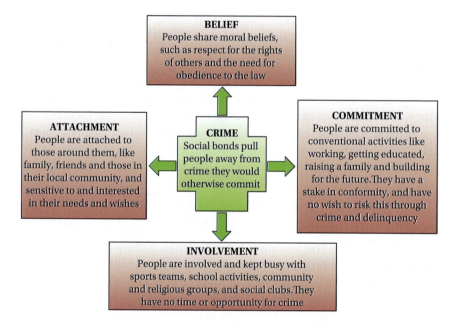

**Figure 5.6** The social bonds that discourage people from committing crime

**Activity**

Identify all the social bonds that you think prevent you from committing crime, or how those bonds were weakened if you have committed crime, been involved in antisocial behaviour or other forms of deviance.

***Merton's strain theory – anomie, strain, and lack of opportunities*** Merton (1968 [1949]) suggests, like all functionalists, that society is stable because all members of society hold similar values – a value consensus. These values include goals which people are encouraged to achieve, such as making money, career success, and buying consumer goods and their own home. Merton argues:

- *Norms or social rules define the socially approved ways of achieving society's goals, such as through hard work and educational qualifications.* Most people are what Merton calls *conformists* – they try to achieve society's goals in approved ways – e.g. by studying hard for educational qualifications leading to well-paid jobs, or by developing talents in sport, entertainment, etc.
- *Some individuals face a strain or tension between achieving the same goals they share with everyone else, and their lack of opportunity to do so by conventional means.* For example, in an unequal society, many disadvantaged groups, such as the poor and the lower working class, have little chance of achieving society's goals by acceptable means; they lack opportunities because they face disadvantages in education, or are unemployed or stuck in dead-end low-paid jobs with no promotion prospects.
- *This strain leads to* **anomie** *– a feeling of confusion and uncertainty over the usefulness of social norms.* These no longer help some people to fulfil their aspirations, given the conditions and lack of opportunities they face, and a situation of 'anything goes' to reach society's goals develops.
- *When the approved ways of achieving society's goals don't work for some people, they break the rules.* They turn to crime and deviance as alternative means of achieving goals and fulfilling their unsatisfied aspirations – e.g. to fraud or theft as an alternative way of gaining wealth, consumer products, etc.

**Anomie** A state of confusion and uncertainty over social norms.

Merton identifies four different types of rule-breaking: innovation, ritualism, retreatism and rebellion. The cartoon in the box on the next page illustrates and explains these four types of deviance.

***Subcultural explanations*** A subculture is a smaller culture shared by a group of people within the main culture of a society, in some ways different from the dominant culture, but with many aspects in common. Figure 5.7 illustrates, with examples, this idea of a subculture.

**INNOVATORS**
Try to achieve society's success goals by illegal or deviant means, such as theft or fraud.

**RETREATISTS**
Abandon both the goals and the approved means of achieving them, and become drop-outs, turning to drink, drugs or some other deviant behaviour.

**REBELS**
Reject society's goals and the accepted means of achieving them, and replace them with their own view of an alternative society with different goals and means of achieving them – e.g. terrorist groups or revolutionaries.

**RITUALISTS**
Continue to work within the system because they have been socialized into conformity, but have little chance of being successful. They are deviant because they give up trying to achieve the conventional goals – e.g. low-status office workers stuck in dead-end jobs who simply go through the motions, with little interest in or enthusiasm for their work, and no career ambition.

Merton's rule-breakers

---

**Activity**

Look at the cartoons of Merton's rule-breakers.

1 Explain in what way each of Merton's rule-breakers is deviant, and how each would have to change to become conformist.

2 Classify each of the following acts/groups as conformist, innovator, ritualist, retreatist or rebel, according to Merton's ideas:
- a successful banker
- a drug-dealer
- a monk living in a monastery
- a shoplifter
- someone cheating in exams
- a teacher who has lost interest in the job, but carries on teaching
- a heroin addict
- a terrorist
- a tramp
- a lazy student who only pretends to do any work
- an indifferent Jobcentre clerk.

3 Suggest one example of your own for each type of rule-breaking (or deviance), and explain how your examples show each type.

Subcultural theories of crime and deviance share the functionalist view that society is based on a value consensus. They focus on:

- how whole groups, rather than just individuals (as in Merton's work), respond to the strain facing them in achieving social goals
- explaining a wider range of criminal and delinquent acts (Merton's strain theory, for example, only explains crime involving material goals such as money; it doesn't explain crime like sexual offences, violence, graffiti or vandalism, or other crimes that bring no obvious material or financial benefit)
- male working-class juvenile delinquents, who constitute the largest group labelled as criminals and deviants.

### STATUS FRUSTRATION AND THE DEVIANT SUBCULTURE

A.K. Cohen (1971 [1955]) studied juvenile delinquency in working-class boys in the USA, drawing on official statistics, existing studies, and other secondary sources. He argues that most lower-working-class youth initially believe in the success goals of mainstream culture, such as obtaining wealth and educational success. However, their experiences of living in deprived areas with many social problems, being labelled as failures at school, with poor chances of getting educational qualifications, and the worst chances in the job market, mean they have little opportunity to attain success by approved

**Figure 5.7** Culture and subcultures

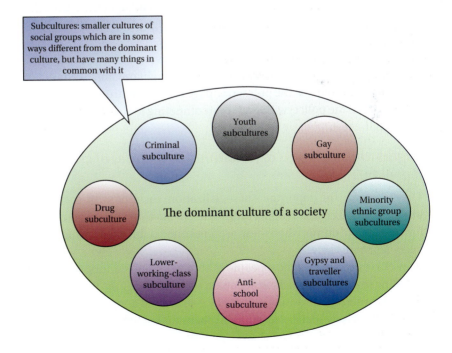

Subcultures: smaller cultures of social groups which are in some ways different from the dominant culture, but have many things in common with it

Youth subcultures

Criminal subculture

Gay subculture

Minority ethnic group subcultures

Drug subculture

The dominant culture of a society

Lower-working-class subculture

Anti-school subculture

Gypsy and traveller subcultures

means. They therefore develop **status frustration**. This simply means they lack status in society, and feel frustration at being unable to achieve such status by accepted means.

Their response to this sense of status frustration is to develop a set of alternative, deviant values which provides them with a means of gaining status among their peers. Delinquency also gives them a way of getting their revenge on the system which has condemned them to failure. Young males form or join deviant subcultures – gangs or other deviant groups – in which delinquent behaviour is expected and rewarded.

Delinquent acts are based on a deliberate reversal of accepted norms. At school, playing truant, messing about in class and destroying school property may replace the values of studying and exam success. Stealing becomes a means of getting money, replacing career success, and vandalism and joy-riding replace respect for property.

Cohen's subcultural approach helps to explain non-utilitarian crime and deviance (behaviour that doesn't produce any financial reward), such as joyriding, vandalism and doing graffiti.

### THE LOWER-WORKING-CLASS SUBCULTURE

Some functionalists suggest that the values of lower-working-class male subculture which young people are socialized into can often lead to crime among young people. This subculture encourages men to demonstrate their toughness, their masculinity and their 'smartness', and to pursue excitement and thrills. These features of working-class life can lead to clashes with the law. For example, the concern with 'toughness' might lead to offences like assault.

These values may become exaggerated in the lives of young males who want to achieve status in their peer group. A 'good night out' might consist of a few drinks, a fight outside the pub, a rampage round the streets with mates, and a run-in with the police, with everyone competing to show they are more macho than the rest.

## Strengths and criticisms of functionalist theories of crime and deviance

✓ They recognize the importance of socialization, social control, social integration and access to opportunities in encouraging people to conform and avoid crime; when these are weakened or blocked, crime becomes more likely.

✗ They don't explain why most people in similar circumstances, such as failing in education, lacking adequate socialization, informal social controls or social integration, or who face strain and anomie in achieving social goals by socially acceptable means do *not* turn to crime and deviance.

> **Status frustration** refers to a sense of frustration arising in individuals or groups because they are denied status in society.

✘ They rely on the pattern of crime shown in official crime statistics, suggesting that most criminals are working class, male and young. However, a lot of crime is never reported, and a lot of offenders are never caught. This makes it difficult to know who the real offenders are, so subcultural explanations are inadequate as they are based on an unrepresentative sample of offenders.

✘ They don't explain the wide variety of forms of deviance and crime.

✘ They only explain, and exaggerate, working-class crime, and underestimate middle-class **white-collar crime** and **corporate crime** (see pages 335–9). They don't explain crime by well-educated and successful middle-class people – such as rich bankers or doctors and dentists committing fraud – who are outwardly respectable, successful, well-off and are socially integrated with tight social bonds.

✘ They take for granted that there is some initial value consensus around society's goals and the means of achieving them, from which people deviate in some way. Marxists and labelling theorists (see below) suggest there is no value consensus. Society's values are those of its dominant and most powerful groups, who have the power to impose their values, goals and means of achieving them on the rest of society. Crime and deviance may just be an expression of resentment against those values they don't share.

**White-collar crime** Offences committed by individuals who abuse their positions in middle-class jobs for personal gain, at the expense of the organization or clients of the organization.

**Corporate crime** Offences committed by large companies, or by individuals on behalf of large companies, which directly profit the company rather than individuals.

**Edgework** Voluntary risk-taking behaviour of any kind that explores and challenges the edges or boundaries of what is normally allowed or accepted.

---

**EDGEWORK AND THE SEDUCTION OF CRIME**

Sociological theories of crime and deviance look for some social causes of what is defined as crime and deviant behaviour. But some suggest that people may commit crimes for no obvious social cause (such as material gain) but simply because they are attractive as forms of **edgework**. Edgework is any voluntary risk-taking behaviour that explores and challenges the edges or boundaries of what is normally allowed or accepted.

Some may commit crime for the sheer thrill of it, to brighten up otherwise routine lives by the excitement and buzz arising from the risk-taking involved in offending. Committing crime may therefore be seductive – a source of pleasure derived from the kicks involved in living 'on the edge', with acts like shoplifting, vandalism, doing drugs, fighting and other fairly petty offences being adventures that are worth any worry about the risk of being caught. The 'thrills and spills' of edgework as a motivation for crime or deviance may appeal to all people at various times. Such an explanation would help to make sense of offences committed not only by young working-class males, but by girls, and middle-class people who don't need to turn to crime for money or status.

---

## Marxist theories of crime and deviance

Marxist conflict theories (see pages 53 and 55–6 in chapter 2) see crime and deviance as arising from the culture and structure of society in the following ways.

The excitement derived from edgework – the kicks derived from living 'on the edge' through risk-taking – may explain why already well-off people turn to crime even though they don't need the money

## Capitalist society is criminogenic

'Criminogenic' means crime is an in-built feature and product of massively unequal capitalist societies that emphasize making profits, self-interest, greed and personal gain. The media encourage people to buy more and more consumer goods, which many can't afford. Crime is a response to the competitiveness, inequality and constant pressure to purchase consumer goods which are major features of life in capitalist societies.

## Marginalization, social exclusion and relative deprivation

**Marginalization** is the process whereby some people are pushed to the margins or edges of society – marginalized – by poverty, ill health, lack of education, disability, racism and so on, and face **social exclusion**. This is where people are excluded from full participation in education, work, community life and access to services and other aspects of life seen as part of being a full member of mainstream society. Those who lack the necessary resources are excluded from the opportunity to participate fully in society, and are denied the opportunities to live the normal life most people take for granted.

**Relative deprivation** is a related idea. This refers to people having a sense of deprivation because they lack things, in relation to the group with which they identify and compare themselves. For example, a young working-class man may want to enjoy the same designer gear, gadgets and lifestyle as those he sees among many of his age group. However, he may lack the educational qualifications, parental support or job making this possible, so he may feel relatively deprived as a result.

**Marginalization**
The process whereby some groups or individuals are pushed by poverty, ill health, lack of education, racism, sexism and so on to the margins of society, and are unable to take part in the life enjoyed by the majority of people.

**Social exclusion**
The situation where people are marginalized or excluded from full participation in mainstream society, as they lack the resources and opportunities most people take for granted.

**Relative deprivation** A sense of lacking things (deprivation) compared to the group with which people identify and compare themselves.

Those who find themselves marginalized, excluded from normal everyday life, and who have a sense of relative deprivation, are vulnerable to committing crime. Crimes such as theft offer a potential route to resolving these problems, and an opportunity to acquire the consumer goods and material possessions that others enjoy, and which media-promoted lifestyles and advertising encourage them to acquire. Antisocial behaviour, vandalism and violence may also be a means of expressing discontent and resentment at their social exclusion.

### The law is designed to protect the interests of the ruling class

Laws are not based on a value consensus, as functionalists suggest, but on the values and interests of the most wealthy and powerful people in society – the ruling class. The law considers serious crime to be offences such as property crime and violence committed by members of the working class, rather than the major harm caused by white-collar and corporate crime (see pages 335–9). The law is rarely used against crimes committed by corporations – such as environmental damage caused by oil spills or the production of dangerous and faulty products – or by governments – such as human rights violations and illegal wars. The agencies of social control protect ruling-class interests and power, and classify as criminals those who oppose them.

### Selective law enforcement

The impression given in official statistics that crime is mainly committed by the working class is largely due to **selective law enforcement**.

**Selective law enforcement** When the police and courts use their discretion to decide whether someone has broken the law, whether to arrest them, to charge them, and whether or how to punish them.

There's one law for the rich and another for the poor, with crime control focused on the working class. It is working-class crimes like theft, burglary and violence that are those most likely to result in arrest and prosecution. For example, benefit fraud (estimated at £2.3 billion in 2018–19) committed by the working class is much more likely to be prosecuted than tax evasion and avoidance by the rich (estimated, at least £7 billion). Those in higher social classes are less likely to be arrested and prosecuted for offences, and, if they are, generally get treated more leniently.

The biggest crimes of all are those committed by the ruling class – 'the crimes of the powerful' – in the form of white-collar and corporate crimes, such as fraud, tax evasion, corporate manslaughter and breaches of health and safety regulations. Such crimes are rarely prosecuted, even if they are discovered. Selective law enforcement gives the false impression most crime is committed by disturbed working-class individuals, and this diverts the working class's attention away from the exploitation they experience and the crimes of the capitalist class. Individuals, not the system of inequality, are blamed for crime.

## Strengths and criticisms of Marxist theories of crime and deviance

✓ They highlight the importance of inequalities in power and wealth, and the conflicts these create, as causes of crime.

✓ They draw attention to white-collar and corporate crimes, and crimes committed by governments.

✓ They show how the law is selectively enforced against working-class people.

✗ They over-emphasize property crime – they say little about offences like rape, domestic violence, child abuse and murder.

✗ They ignore the fact that most working-class people, even the poorest, do not commit crime.

✗ It is difficult to interpret all laws as reflecting the interests of the rich and powerful – e.g. traffic and consumer protection laws, and those against household and vehicle theft and personal violence of all kinds protect everyone, not just the rich.

✗ They don't take into account that most victims of working-class criminals are themselves working class – they're not Robin Hood figures robbing the rich to feed the poor.

---

## Feminist theories of crime and deviance

Feminist theories (see pages 57–9) have criticized much sociological theory and research on crime and deviance because:

- it was **malestream** – it was carried out by men, focused on what interested men – male crime – and female offending and victimization were largely forgotten or ignored
- there was little attempt to explain female offending or other forms of female deviance.

Feminist theories therefore focus on:

- female offending and the experiences of women in the criminal justice system (CJS)
- the gender gap in offending: why women commit less crime and are less involved in other deviance than men.

> **Malestream**
> Sociology that concentrates on men, is mostly carried out by men, and then assumes that the findings can be applied to women as well.

### The class deal and the gender deal

Carlen (1988) undertook research to try to find out why women turned to crime. She carried out in-depth, unstructured interviews with a group of thirty-nine 15- to 46-year-old working-class women who had been convicted of a range of crimes. Twenty were in prison or youth custody at the time of the interviews.

Carlen found that women are encouraged to conform by two types of rewards or 'deals':

- The **class deal** refers to the material rewards – money – that women gain from working in paid employment. These provide women with a route to conformity – a means of purchasing consumer goods, having a reasonable standard of living, and enabling them to follow a fairly conformist lifestyle.
- The **gender deal** refers to the material and emotional rewards and status that women gain from fulfilling their traditional roles in the family and home, with material and emotional support from a male breadwinner.

However, some women lack the rewards gained from these deals:

- *the class deal may be blocked* by poverty, educational underachievement and lack of qualifications, and lack of access to paid work
- *the gender deal may be blocked* by lack of a family through being brought up in care, or by violent and abusive partners.

Carlen suggests such women may then make a rational decision to commit crime as the only alternative way to escape poverty and achieve a decent standard of living. Such a choice has few costs, as they have little to lose (like loss of a job, family or status) and at least crime, such as shoplifting or fraud, offers potential benefits like money, food and consumer goods which are not otherwise available.

Carlen's research has been criticized as it was based on a small sample, so it may not be representative of all women. However, it does suggest – similar to functionalist approaches – that when social control and social integration break down, and conventional opportunities are blocked, criminal behaviour is more likely.

### Socialization, social control and separate spheres

*Socialization* In general, patriarchal gender role socialization (see pages 24–38) encourages women to adopt feminine characteristics such as being less tough and aggressive, and more averse to taking risks than men. This contributes to making many women avoid the risk-taking involved in crime. There is also tighter control of daughters than sons by parents, which limits young girls' opportunities to get involved in juvenile crime.

*Social control and separate spheres* Heidensohn (1985) suggests that women commit less crime than men because, in patriarchal (male-dominated) societies, they face greater pressures to conform through stricter social control, and they have fewer opportunities to commit crime. Heidensohn argues:

- *In the private sphere of the home*, women face patriarchal control (control by men) through being allocated domestic responsibilities for housework and childcare, and where men, in most cases, are responsible for financial and other major decision-making. Women who challenge this face risks of becoming victims of domestic violence.
- *In the public sphere* – outside the home – women are also controlled by men. In a patriarchal society, the public sphere is dominated by men, and it is also where most crime takes place. For example, women are faced with patriarchal controls arising from fear of physical or sexual violence if they go out alone at night, and at work they are often subject to sexual harassment and supervision by male bosses.
- These tighter patriarchal social controls in the private and public spheres reduce the time and opportunity for women to commit crime, even if they wanted to.
- Women face a greater risk of stigma or shame if they get involved in crime and deviance. This is because gender role socialization encourages them to be feminine, respectable and conformist. They then face greater risks of social disapproval and of losing their respectable reputation than men if they get caught committing crime.

Heidensohn proposes that all these put greater pressure to conform on women than on men, because of their greater risks of losing more than they might gain by law-breaking, and also by reducing their opportunities to do so.

## The chivalry thesis

The **chivalry thesis** suggests that the male-dominated criminal justice system (CJS), such as the police and the courts, takes a more benevolent, protective and patriarchal view of female offending. This means that women offenders are seen as 'less guilty', as they are more vulnerable and in need of protection, and they are therefore treated more leniently than men. This partly explains why there are far fewer women offenders recorded in official crime statistics.

> **Chivalry thesis**
> The suggestion that the male-dominated criminal justice system, such as the police and the courts, takes a more benevolent, protective and patriarchal view of female offending, and treats women more leniently than men.

### Evidence for the chivalry thesis

- Female first offenders are about half as likely to be given a sentence of immediate imprisonment as their male equivalents.
- Women are less likely to be remanded in custody when awaiting trial.
- Women are more likely to receive suspended or community sentences, rather than imprisonment.

- Women receive, on average, shorter prison sentences.
- Female offenders are more likely to benefit from more informal approaches to their offences by the police, particularly for minor offences.

### Evidence against the chivalry thesis

Feminists have challenged the chivalry thesis on the following grounds:

- Women's less severe treatment by the CJS is mainly due to the fact that they commit fewer **indictable offences** (more serious offences) than men.
- Women have more 'mitigating factors' which reduce the length of prison sentences, such as showing remorse, having caring responsibilities and a lack of previous relevant convictions; men generally have more 'aggravating factors', leading to their longer sentences.
- Women offenders face 'double jeopardy'. Women offenders who come before the courts often find they are on trial both for the crime they commit and for the extent to which they conform to, or deviate from, stereotypes of femininity. Women who do not conform to socially acceptable patterns of feminine behaviour risk harsher punishment than men. This 'double jeopardy' is shown in rape cases, where women victims often have to prove their respectability and conformity before their evidence is even taken seriously by juries and judges. Carlen suggests that women's sentences reflect this double jeopardy, as judges, magistrates and juries are partly influenced by their assessment of women's characters and performance in relation to their traditional wife/partner and mother roles, rather than simply by the severity of the offence.
- Women who commit serious offences, particularly for violent crime, face more severe punishment than men as this violates socially acceptable patterns of feminine behaviour. This is most obvious in the most serious offences where women violate norms relating to gender roles, motherhood and childcare – such as serious violence, child neglect and abuse, child cruelty or child murder, where they suffer markedly more severe consequences than men who commit similar offences.

In general, then, in a patriarchal society, women might commit less crime, and fewer serious offences, than men, but appear to suffer more serious consequences when they do. Women are expected to be 'good' – feminine and conformist – and punished when they're not, while men are expected to be a bit tough and aggressive and periodically go off the rails, and so are punished less severely when they do so.

**Indictable offences**
More serious criminal offences that are tried at crown court before a judge and jury. Lesser offences are tried at a magistrates' court.

**Activity**

Read carefully the previous section on feminist theories of crime, and why women commit less crime than men.

1  Describe and explain two reasons why women commit less crime and face lesser punishments than men.

2  Carlen used unstructured interviews to explore the circumstances that made women in poverty turn to crime.

    (a)  Identify and explain one strength and one weakness of using this method.

    (b)  Suggest an alternative research method that could be used to investigate why women turn to crime, and give two reasons for choosing it.

3  Suggest two reasons why socialization and social control in the family might make men more likely to commit crime than women.

## Strengths and criticisms of feminist theories of crime and deviance

✔  They draw attention to female conformity and non-conformity, whereas other theories often only concentrated on the pattern of male working-class offending found in official statistics.

✔  They show a range of reasons why women are less likely to commit crime than men.

✔  They challenge the idea that the CJS is more lenient in its treatment of women offenders (the chivalry thesis) and highlight the way women face 'double jeopardy' and are judged for both the crime they commit and whether they conform to stereotypes of femininity.

✗  They don't explain why most women in similar circumstances, such as poverty, do not turn to crime.

## Interactionist theories of crime and deviance: labelling theory

Interactionist theories (see pages 59–60) of crime and deviance, commonly referred to as labelling theory, are concerned with two main features:

● the process whereby some people committing some actions come to be defined or labelled as deviant, while others do not.

● the consequences which follow once a deviant label has been applied, and how this may create more deviance or crime.

Becker (1963), is the key theorist in labelling theory. He argues:

● *There is no act that is in itself deviant* – crime and deviance are social constructions. An act which harms an individual or society only becomes criminal when others react and define or label it as such.

- *Most people commit crimes and other deviant acts at some time in their lives,* but not everyone becomes defined as a deviant or a criminal.
- *Whether the label 'deviant' or 'criminal' is applied depends on:*
  - *who commits the act*
  - *when and where it is committed*
  - *who observes the act and how they react to it*
  - *the negotiations (discussions) – or interactions – that take place between all those involved.* For example, a bunch of young people approached by the police for alleged antisocial behaviour might be able to talk themselves out of being labelled as deviant by being polite and respectful and promising to behave themselves in future. If they're rude and abusive, they might get labelled as young delinquents and arrested.
- *Not everyone who is deviant or criminal gets labelled as such.* The agencies of social control – such as law-makers, the criminal justice system and the media – have the power to define what counts as crime and deviance, to impose their definitions on society, and to make the labels stick. Such labels are generally applied by those with power in society (the upper and middle class) to the powerless (the working class).
- *Agencies of social control, such as the police, have and use considerable discretion and selective law enforcement in deciding how to deal with illegal or deviant behaviour, and they are more likely to label some groups of people as deviant or criminal than others.* Becker suggests that how the police respond to deviant behaviour is influenced by the stereotypes they have of what they regard as typical troublemakers or criminals. These stereotypes are often based on the pattern of crime shown in statistics. Young working-class males and black people, for example, may be treated less favourably than other groups. They are more likely to be stopped and searched by the police, for instance.
- *Official crime statistics are social constructions,* showing only an unrepresentative group of offenders who have been caught and publicly labelled as criminal.

For Becker, the consequences of being caught and publicly labelled are particularly important, as these can have major repercussions for the individual.

### The deviant master status

**Master status**
The dominant status of an individual – such as that of an 'ex-con' or thief – which overrides all other characteristics of that person.

Once someone is caught and labelled as a criminal or deviant, the label attached may become the dominant label or **master status** which overrides all other characteristics of that person – she or he becomes an 'outsider' (outside the boundaries of acceptable behaviour). She or he is no longer seen as someone's partner, mother/father, friend or business associate, but a 'juvenile delinquent', an 'ex-con' or a 'hooligan'. People may assume that the individuals concerned have all the negative characteristics normally associated with the label. This will affect how others see them and respond to them, so people are treated differently according to the label, as the following examples suggest.

Once a person is labelled as 'mad' (mentally ill), as a football hooligan, as a thief or as a failure at school, the label may have quite serious consequences for his or her life. Each label carries with it a range of prejudices and images:

- the football hooligan, for example, is often seen as irresponsible, violent, a drunkard, a racist and a serious threat to society;
- a person with a conviction for theft may be seen as fundamentally untrustworthy and never to be left alone with valuables, and if things go missing this may automatically reinforce suspicions that they have been stolen by the labelled thief;
- the bottom-stream pupil in school may be seen as a waster, and thoroughly untrustworthy and unreliable.

Once labelled, a person's behaviour might be interpreted differently from that of a person not labelled as deviant. For example:

- Teachers may treat some questions from bottom-stream 'delinquents' as red herrings, but regard the same questions from top-stream conformists as intelligent and worthy of discussion.
- Much the same could apply when different pupils offer excuses for not doing homework, missing games, and so on.
- Someone with a history of mental illness may have signs of eccentricity interpreted as evidence of his or her mental illness, but the same behaviour might pass unnoticed in a person not labelled as mentally ill.

## Deviant careers

As people find it hard to shake off a label, labelling may lead to a **deviant career** and people may start acting the way they have been labelled.

For example, a man caught in an isolated act of stealing may be prosecuted, imprisoned and labelled as a 'criminal' and later as an 'ex-con'; friends desert him, employers refuse to offer him jobs, and alternative opportunities of conforming are closed off to him. The man may then begin to see himself primarily as a criminal, and adopts a deviant self-identity. Since everyone treats him as a criminal anyway, he may then turn to crime as a way of life and follow a deviant career of crime.

In this way, labelling theory suggests that labelling people as criminal or deviant can encourage them to become more so. The attachment of a label becomes a self-fulfilling prophecy and generates more deviance – the same *deviancy amplification* discussed earlier on pages 299–301 in relation to the media and crime. For example, adult prisons and young offenders' institutions play a key role in making the labels of 'criminal' and, later, 'ex-con'

> **Deviant career**
> Where people who have been labelled as deviant find conventional opportunities blocked to them, come to accept a deviant self-identity and so are pushed towards deviant subcultures and into committing further deviant acts.

**Figure 5.8** The development of a deviant career

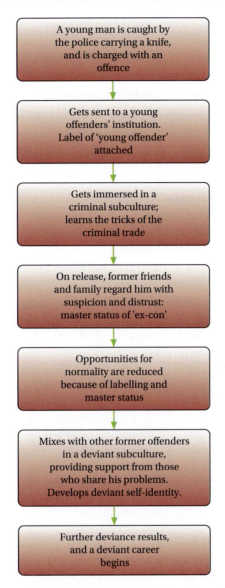

A young man is caught by the police carrying a knife, and is charged with an offence

Gets sent to a young offenders' institution. Label of 'young offender' attached

Gets immersed in a criminal subculture; learns the tricks of the criminal trade

On release, former friends and family regard him with suspicion and distrust: master status of 'ex-con'

Opportunities for normality are reduced because of labelling and master status

Mixes with other former offenders in a deviant subculture, providing support from those who share his problems. Develops deviant self-identity.

Further deviance results, and a deviant career begins

stick. They immerse offenders in a criminal subculture, increase the opportunities to learn about crime, and make it extremely hard for them to go back to living a normal life when they are released. More crime may therefore result as alternative opportunities are limited. An example of a deviant career is shown in figure 5.8.

## Strengths and criticisms of labelling theory

✔ It challenges the idea that deviants are different from 'normal' people.
✔ It shows the importance of the reactions of others in defining and creating deviance.

✔ It reveals the importance of stereotyping in understanding why only some behaviour is labelled as deviant.

✔ It reveals the way official crime statistics are social constructions and a product of selective law enforcement.

✔ It reveals the importance of those with power in defining acts and people as deviant.

✔ It shows how labelling can lead to a self-fulfilling prophecy, deviancy amplification and to deviant careers.

✘ It assumes an act isn't deviant until it is labelled as such, yet many know perfectly well that what they are doing is deviant.

✘ Some people may choose to be criminal regardless of labelling.

✘ It doesn't explain the causes of deviant behaviour before the labelling process, or the different kinds of acts that people commit – for example, taking illegal drugs is a quite different act from murder.

✘ It doesn't explain where the stereotypes of those with power come from in the first place.

✘ It doesn't allow for the possibility that labelling doesn't always lead to a self-fulfilling prophecy and more deviance – e.g. a person caught shoplifting may be so horrified and shamed by the stigma attached through being caught and labelled that they never do it again.

## Activity

In each of the cases listed below:

1 Identify a possible label which may be attached to the person concerned as a result of her or his deviant behaviour.

2 Outline how a deviant career might develop by describing the possible consequences of the labelling for the person's future life and relationships.

3 Suggest ways in which a person might avoid being labelled even after she or he has committed the deviant act.
- A young woman caught shoplifting
- A school teacher who is caught smoking cannabis
- A person who is temporarily admitted to a mental hospital as a result of severe anxiety or depression
- A 17-year-old man who gets arrested during a fight at a football match
- A school student caught cheating in exams

4 Suggest two arguments for, and two against, the view that the agencies of social control, such as the police and the courts, are more likely to label working-class deviance as criminal than the same behaviour by the middle class.

5 Describe how labelling a person as a criminal may cause them to commit more crime.

6 Describe and explain one advantage and one disadvantage of using participant observation to investigate the effects of labelling on a group of juvenile delinquents.

# THE PATTERN OF CRIME

Information on the pattern of crime is obtained from official crime statistics (these are discussed later on pages 344–55). These show the following trends in crime:

- From the 1930s to the early 1950s, there was a gradual rise.
- From the 1950s to the early 1980s, there was a steeper rise.
- From the 1980s to the mid-1990s, there was a rapid increase.
- From the mid-1990s to 2018, there was a substantial fall in most forms of crime – though some offences have been increasing in recent years, such as knife crime, homicides, vehicle-related thefts, burglary, and computer-based 'cybercrimes' (such as computer hacking, identity theft – theft of personal details to commit crime – and online fraud).

Figure 5.9 shows a breakdown of the main types of offence recorded by the police (PRC – police-recorded crime) in 2018, and those revealed by the Crime Survey for England and Wales (CSEW) victim survey (a survey of

**Figure 5.9** The pattern of crime in official statistics: police-recorded crime and Crime Survey for England and Wales; England and Wales, year ending December 2018

*Source:* adapted from *Crime in England and Wales*, Office for National Statistics

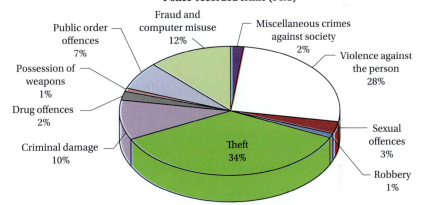

**Police-recorded crime (PRC)**

**Crime Survey for England and Wales (CSEW)**

people who have been victims of crime, whether or not they reported them to the police).

It is notable that, despite wide media coverage of dramatic incidents such as attacks on the elderly, or gun and knife crime, violence made up only just over one in four of PRC offences, and one in ten of CSEW offences, in 2018. Most crimes of violence against the person do not result in any serious physical injury, and 41 per cent of all violent crime reported to the police, and over half (54 per cent) of CSEW violent crimes, in 2018 did not result in *any* physical injury to the victim. Only a small proportion of such cases call for professional medical attention, and in only a few of such cases is the victim admitted to hospital. In fact, most crime is fairly small-scale property and vehicle-related crime, and, as figure 5.9 shows, fraud, theft, computer misuse and criminal damage (vandalism) make up between 56 per cent (PRC) and 86 per cent (CSEW) of all crimes. This offers no great comfort to the victims of these offences, but it is reassuring that the risks of being a victim of crime are falling, and only one in five adults is likely to be the victim of any CSEW crime, including computer-based cybercrimes and fraud.

Criminal statistics are notoriously unreliable, so the pattern of crime shown in them must be treated with considerable caution. The problem of the crime statistics will be discussed later, but for the moment our concern will be with explaining the pattern shown in the official statistics.

## The pattern of offending

The pattern of crime revealed by official statistics shows that most crime is committed:

- in urban areas (large towns and cities)
- against property (around 60–70 per cent of all crime)
- by young people
- by working-class males.

There is also – according to official statistics – an **over-representation** (too large a number given their proportion of the total population) of some BAME (Black, Asian and Minority Ethnic) groups, particularly Black and Asian people.

**Over-representation**
When too many from a particular group are represented, compared to that group's proportion of the total population.

# EXPLANATIONS FOR THE PATTERN OF CRIME SHOWN IN OFFICIAL STATISTICS

The following sections will look at various explanations for the pattern of crime shown in official crime statistics. These are summarized in figure 5.10. These will apply some of the theories discussed above, and can be used as examples to show how the theories work in the real world of crime and deviance.

**Figure 5.10** Some explanations for the pattern of crime shown in official crime statistics

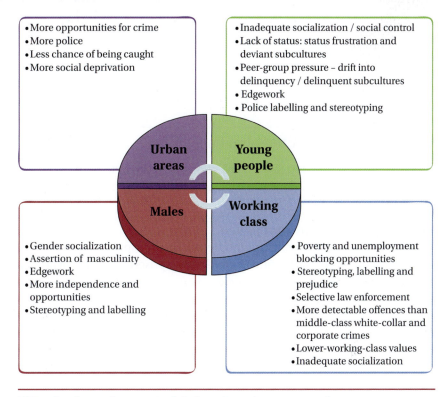

- More opportunities for crime
- More police
- Less chance of being caught
- More social deprivation

- Inadequate socialization / social control
- Lack of status: status frustration and deviant subcultures
- Peer-group pressure – drift into delinquency / delinquent subcultures
- Edgework
- Police labelling and stereotyping

**Urban areas**

**Young people**

**Males**

**Working class**

- Gender socialization
- Assertion of masculinity
- Edgework
- More independence and opportunities
- Stereotyping and labelling

- Poverty and unemployment blocking opportunities
- Stereotyping, labelling and prejudice
- Selective law enforcement
- More detectable offences than middle-class white-collar and corporate crimes
- Lower-working-class values
- Inadequate socialization

## Why is the crime rate higher in urban areas?

### More opportunity for crime

Large urban areas provide greater opportunities for crime: there are more and larger shops, warehouses and business premises, cars, houses and other typical targets of crime.

### Policing

There is a greater police presence in urban areas, so more crime is likely to be detected. Different policing methods also mean the police are more likely to take formal action (arrest and prosecution) in urban areas. In rural areas, they are less likely to arrest offenders for minor offences, preferring merely to issue more informal warnings, or in the case of young people perhaps visiting the offender's parents or her or his school.

### Less chance of being caught

In the large cities, life is more impersonal and people do not know each other so well. Strangers are more likely to go unrecognized, and are therefore more able to get away with offences. Potential criminals are less likely to steal within a small rural community where everyone knows almost everybody else and suspicious strangers in the community are likely to be noticed.

## Social deprivation

Social deprivation and social problems, such as poor housing, unemployment and poverty, are at their worst in the inner cities. These have been linked to crime, as people try to resolve their desperate situations through illegal means.

---

## Why are most convicted criminals young?

Official statistics show roughly a third of all those convicted are under 25. Around 8 per cent of the population of England and Wales are 18- to 24-year-olds, but they make up:

- 17 per cent of the prison population
- a quarter of people serving community orders or suspended sentences
- the most likely group to reoffend after leaving prison – 75 per cent are reconvicted within two years.

### Inadequate socialization and social control

Functionalist theories (see pages 305–6) suggest there may be a breakdown in the socialization of some young people at home, and a lack of social controls to stop them getting involved in crime.

### Status frustration, deviant subcultures and peer-group pressure

Status frustration, discussed earlier under subcultural theories and peer pressure (see pages 309–10), may encourage lower-working-class young people to commit crime through their involvement in deviant subcultures or gangs.

There is also a wider sense in which all young people (not just those from the working class) suffer a form of status frustration. Young people are caught in the transition between child and adult status: they are no longer expected to behave as children, but are denied the full rights and responsibilities of adults. They therefore often feel deprived of status in society and this weakens young people's sense of identity – of who they are. This means that young people often lack a sense of identity and direction and end up in a state of drift. The peer group can provide some support for an identity and status independent of school or family, and therefore takes on a greater importance among young people than at any other age.

Many young people also lack the responsibilities involved in having children, in paying rent or mortgage repayments, and often in keeping down a job. This lack of responsibilities, combined with the search for excitement through *edgework* (see page 311 and below) and peer-group status, means young people may drift into minor acts of delinquency and clashes with the law. Peer-group pressure and support may also give young people the confidence and encouragement to join in with group acts of delinquency which they would not engage in on their own.

This wider idea of status frustration helps to explain why many young people give up crime as they grow older. Adulthood, marriage or cohabitation, parenthood, their own home and employment give them a more clearly defined, independent status in society, and the peer group becomes less important for achieving status.

While many young people will break the law at some time, the kinds of offence they commit are usually less serious and peer-group-related. Research conducted at the Centre of Criminology at Edinburgh University found that about half the offences committed by 11- to 15-year-olds involved rowdiness and fighting in the street, with the rest consisting mainly of shoplifting (usually sweets) and vandalism (usually graffiti). The reasons most often given for their law-breaking are: to impress others, and boredom.

### Activity

How does this picture help to explain why young people are in a state of drift? Using the explanations in this section, suggest how the peer group might help to overcome the types of problem identified in the picture, and how this might be linked to delinquency.

## Edgework

For young people facing status frustration, boredom, and lacking wider responsibilities, committing crime may be seen as a form of edgework (see page 311). It may be a source of pleasure derived from the kicks involved in living 'on the edge', with petty offences being adventures providing excitement and adrenalin flows that are more important than any worry about the risk of being caught.

## Police labelling and stereotyping

Young people tend to commit more visible types of antisocial behaviour and crime than older people, such as vandalism, violent offences like brawls in the street after drinking sessions, street crime and shoplifting, or hanging about in groups in the street making a nuisance of themselves. The police are more likely to stereotype young people as troublemakers and the source of problems. This stereotype means the police are likely to spend time observing and checking youths, telling them off, moving them on, and stopping and questioning or searching them. As a result, more get caught, get labelled as offenders, and appear in the statistics. As labelling theories suggest (see pages 318–21), this may lead to a self-fulfilling prophecy, with a deviant career and further deviance.

## Why are most convicted criminals male?

In England and Wales, men account for around three-quarters of all persons convicted of any offence, and 95 per cent of prisoners. Men are more likely to be repeat offenders, and in general they commit more serious offences. Only about 5 per cent of the prison population are women.

How does this cartoon show police stereotyping of young people?

> **Activity**
>
> 1 What evidence, if any, do you have from your own experience that the police stereotype young people, and unfairly make them out to be troublemakers?
> 2 Suggest reasons why the police might hold such stereotypes.
> 3 Imagine you were going to try to find out the attitudes to the police of a sample of young people aged 10–17.
>    (a) Identify the research method you would use.
>    (b) Explain two reasons why you would choose this method.
>    (c) Explain two weaknesses that you may find using this method.
> 4 Drawing on the theories of crime discussed earlier, and the material in this section, describe two arguments for, and two against, the view that the main reason why young people may commit crime is the formation of subcultures.

## Why do men commit more crime than women?

- *Gender socialization and the assertion of masculinity.* Functionalists might suggest that gender role socialization into a masculine gender identity encourages men to demonstrate macho behaviour such as toughness, aggression and risk-taking. This is more likely to lead to more serious and detectable criminal behaviour, and men are more likely than women to carry out crimes of violence and other serious offences. This expression of masculinity and risk-taking might also explain why some men turn to crime as a form of edgework.
- *Labelling and police stereotyping.* Labelling theory suggests the police are more likely to see men as fitting their stereotypes of potential offenders, to label their behaviour as criminal, and to press charges against them.
- *Men have more independence and opportunities to commit crime* – they are less restricted by the demands of housework and childcare.
- *Men dominate the public sphere* (outside the home) where most crime is committed.

## Why do females appear to commit fewer crimes than males?

Many of the reasons for this were discussed under feminist theories of crime, and you should refer to pages 314–18. Among the reasons why women appear less in official crime statistics (summarized in figure 5.11), besides their offences being under-reported and under-recorded by the police, are:

- *Fewer opportunities to commit crime*, due to:
  - tighter social control and supervision of teenage girls by parents, reducing the chances of their getting into trouble.
  - patriarchal control in the private sphere of the home – the constraints imposed by responsibility for housework and childcare.

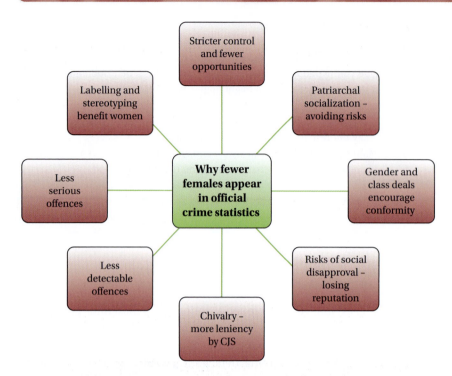

**Figure 5.11** Why fewer females appear in official crime statistics

-   patriarchal control in the public sphere – domination by men at work, in the streets at night, etc.
-   *Patriarchal socialization.* From early childhood, girls are socialized to be passive, caring and gentle, making women more averse to the risk-taking involved in crime.
-   *The gender deal and the class deal* – encourage conformity for most women.
-   *Greater risks of social disapproval and of losing their reputation* than men when they commit crime, so they are more likely to avoid it.
-   *Women commit less detectable offences,* such as prostitution, petty theft such as shoplifting, or drug offences, so are less likely to get caught.
-   *Women offenders commit less serious offences than men,* resulting in lighter sentences and less imprisonment.
-   *The chivalry thesis* – stereotyping by the male-dominated CJS means the police and courts take a more benevolent, protective and patriarchal view of female offending. Women are therefore treated more leniently than men, particularly for minor offences.
-   *Labelling and stereotyping* – women may benefit from the police stereo-type that they are less likely than men to be criminals, and so are less likely to be targeted by the police, have their behaviour watched and get caught. This avoids risks of the self-fulfilling prophecy and deviant careers.

## Growing female criminality

The main offences women commit still tend to be much less serious than those committed by men, and men still commit a lot more crime than women. However, that pattern is slowly changing in the UK and other European countries, and there is a growing increase in the proportion of crime committed by females, most noticeably by young women. In 1957, for example, men were responsible for eleven times as many offences as women, but by 2017 that ratio had narrowed to about three times as many. There were increases in minor assaults, robberies, public-order offences and criminal damage among girls aged 10–17. There was a decrease in the male crime rate between 2002 and 2014, but the female crime rate increased, and although this started decreasing after 2010, it was at a much slower rate than that of men in the same period.

There are several explanations for this:

- *Changing gender roles.* Women in contemporary Britain have more independence than in the past, and they are becoming more successful than men in both education and the labour market. Growing equality

Women generally commit a lot less crime than men, and only about 5 per cent of the prison population is female, but the female crime rate, compared to men's, is slowly rising. How might you explain this?

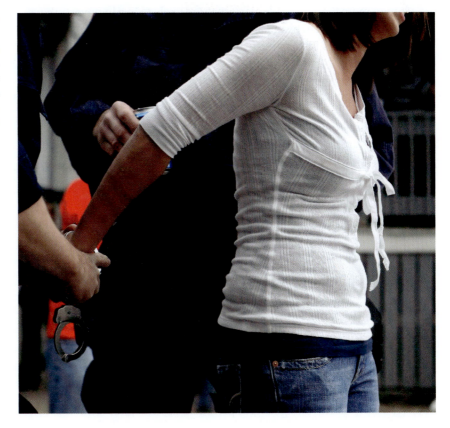

for women may be leading to more opportunities for women to commit crime.

- *Weakening parental and patriarchal control.* Some of the traditional forms of control on women – like the parental supervision mentioned above, the demands of the homemaker/mother role, and patriarchal control at work – are weakening, particularly among younger women, giving them more opportunity for crime.
- *'Ladette' culture.* There's a lot more of a masculinized 'ladette' culture, in which young women are adopting behaviour traditionally associated with young men, as they assert their identity through binge drinking, gang culture, risk-taking and peer-related violence.
- *Changing police stereotypes and labelling, and the decline in the chivalry effect.* There is some evidence that the police and the CJS are now reacting in a more serious way to female offending. They are acting more formally in arresting, prosecuting and labelling and criminalizing girls' bad behaviour. This would increase the statistics for female offenders, as more of their offences are being reported to, and recorded by, the police.
- *Increasing economic inequality.* Britain has become more unequal in wealth and income, and increases in poverty since 2010 have affected women more than men. Women are more likely to live in poverty, have low-paid jobs and to be in part-time work or unemployed. This could explain women's increasing involvement in crime.

---

### Activity

Read carefully the previous section on why most convicted criminals are male.
1. Try to think of any other reasons that you can. Make a list in order of importance of the reasons why men are more likely than women to be criminals, and explain why you have put them in that order.
2. How do you think police attitudes to women and crime could affect the number of female offenders recorded in official crime statistics? Explain your answer carefully, with examples of particular crimes.
3. Describe one reason why women commit less crime than men and explain why some sociologists believe that this may be changing.
4. Women are more likely to be victims of some crimes than men. Suggest, with reasons, examples of some of these crimes.

---

## Why are most convicted criminals working class?

### *Merton's strain theory and blocked opportunities*

Merton's strain theory (see pages 307–8) suggests that, in an unequal society, many disadvantaged groups, such as the poor and the lower working class, have little chance of achieving society's goals by conventional, approved means. They lack opportunities because they face disadvantages in education, or are unemployed or stuck in dead-end jobs with no promotion prospects. This increases the risks of deprived working-class people turning to crime – innovation – as an alternative means of achieving these goals.

## Marxist theories

Marxist theories (see pages 311–14) suggest crime is a response to the competitiveness, inequality and constant desire to purchase consumer goods which are major features of life in capitalist societies. Those who find themselves marginalized by poverty, excluded from normal everyday life, and who have a sense of relative deprivation, are vulnerable to committing crime. In a society where there are wide inequalities in wealth and income, some level of crime is to be expected from those who live a more deprived life than others. Such hardship also provides an obvious explanation for the most common offences of property crime.

Marxists also suggest the law is designed to protect the interests of the ruling class. The impression given in official statistics that crime is mainly committed by the working class is largely due to *selective law enforcement*. It is working-class crimes like theft, burglary and violence that are those most likely to result in arrest and prosecution.

## More visible or public offences

The offences typically associated with the working class tend to be more public, detectable property offences – the 'crimes of the streets'. These offences, such as robbery, theft and burglary, usually have clearly identifiable victims who will report offences to the police, when they will then be recorded in official crime statistics (as opposed to middle- and upper-class 'white-collar crime' – see pages 335–9).

## Labelling, police stereotyping and bias in the CJS

Becker's labelling theory (see pages 318–22) suggests working-class young people fit more closely the police stereotype of the 'typical criminal', and there is therefore a greater police presence in working-class areas than in middle-class ones. This means there is a greater likelihood of offenders being seen and arrested by the police when committing an offence than in middle-class areas. Crime rates will therefore be higher in working-class areas simply because there are more police to notice or respond quickly to criminal acts.

Some groups of people are more likely than others to be labelled as deviant or criminal by the police. Young working-class males may be treated less favourably than other groups. For example, they are more likely to be stopped and searched by the police. The activities of working-class youth are more likely to be defined by the police as criminal than the same behaviour in the middle class. For example, a group of university students getting drunk and wrecking a restaurant might result in their having to pay for the damage, and might be dismissed by the police as a foolish escapade that got out of control – a temporary lapse in otherwise conformist behaviour – but the same behaviour by working-class football supporters would be more likely to be seen as hooliganism, with resulting prosecutions for violence and criminal damage.

The stereotypes and prejudices of middle-class judges and magistrates may mean that, when working-class people appear in court, they are more likely to be seen as typical criminals and found guilty.

## Informal social control

Working-class offenders are also more likely than the middle class to be prosecuted if they are caught. This is perhaps because they are less likely to benefit from informal processes of social control. For petty offences, middle-class young people are more likely to be dealt with by parents and teachers than by the law, with the police perhaps visiting the parents to give them a warning.

## Lower-working-class values

Some have suggested that the values of the lower-working-class subculture (see page 310) often carry with them risks of brushes with the law. This subculture encourages men to demonstrate their toughness, their masculinity and their 'smartness', and to pursue excitement and thrills. These features of working-class life can lead to clashes with the law. For example, the concern with 'toughness' might lead to violent offences such as assault. Young working-class people are also more likely to be part of a delinquent subculture which may stress deviant or criminal behaviour to bring peer-group status.

## Inadequate socialization

Functionalist theories (see pages 305–6) would suggest that poor socialization, poor parenting, and lack of control by some working-class families and communities may mean some working-class people have an inadequate grasp of the boundaries between conformist and deviant behaviour. This may lead to a sense of indifference to whether or not their own actions, or those of others in their peer group or community, are antisocial or illegal. This is often reflected in working-class prisoners, many of whom have had very troubled personal histories before entering prison – e.g. chaotic childhoods, during which many have experienced abuse, witnessed violence in the home, and been taken into care.

*Working-class crime is exaggerated, and middle-class crime underestimated, in official statistics*

Offences committed by members of other social classes may be undetected and unrecorded, or dealt with outside the criminal law. The suggestion that most criminals are working-class may therefore be exaggerated. As labelling theory suggests, powerful people can get away with their crimes, while the powerless can't. This is shown by white-collar and corporate crime, which is discussed below.

---

### Activity

Most judges and magistrates come from white, upper-middle-class or middle-class backgrounds.

1  Suggest ways this might influence judges and magistrates to give more favourable and sympathetic treatment to some groups, and less favourable and unsympathetic treatment to others. Give examples of particular groups.
2  Imagine you are to appear in court on a shoplifting charge. You desperately want to get off lightly. Identify and explain two ways you might try to give a good impression to the judge or magistrate.
3  What might this activity suggest about the real pattern of crime in society?

---

## WHITE-COLLAR AND CORPORATE CRIME

The study of white-collar and corporate crime provides an example of the view of Marxists and labelling theorists that the powerful are often able to conceal their crimes and avoid prosecution. It also shows that official crime statistics may not show the true extent of crime in society.

- *White-collar crimes* (sometimes called 'occupational crimes') are offences committed by individuals who abuse their positions in middle-class jobs for personal gain, at the expense of the organization they work for, or clients of that organization. These include offences such as bribery and corruption in government and business, fiddling expenses, professional misconduct, fraud and embezzlement. Examples include doctors, pharmacists and dentists who defraud the NHS by falsifying prescriptions and patient records to claim millions of pounds more than that to which they are entitled – including one GP who made £700,000 over five years writing fake prescriptions.
- *Corporate crimes* are offences committed by large companies, or by employees on behalf of large companies, which directly profit the company, rather than individuals. These include offences like crimes against consumers, such as the misrepresentation of products

(pretending they're something they're not) and the sale of unfit or dangerous foods – e.g. passing off horsemeat as beef; breaches of health and safety regulations; environmental pollution; and price fixing.

## Examples of corporate crimes

● *Manufacturing offences and dangerous products*: the rigging of test results on the pregnancy morning-sickness drug Thalidomide in the 1960s led to birth defects in thousands of babies. See also the box below on the Ford Pinto.

**PROFITS VERSUS SAFETY**

The Ford Pinto car, advertised in the 1970s as the car that gave you a warm feeling, was found to have a fault that meant the car tended to erupt in flames in rear-end collisions. The car – which became known as 'the barbecue that seats four' – continued in production for eight years before the safety faults were corrected, in which period between 500 and 900 people were thought to have died in burn deaths after accidents. The failure to rectify the fault followed the notorious 'Ford Pinto memo' which showed it was cheaper to pay out to victims ($50 million) than to rectify the safety problems ($121 million).

*Dangerous plant and environmental pollution*: in 1984, the Union Carbide chemical plant leaked poisonous gas in Bhopal in India. This affected half a million people, and by 2018 an estimated 25,000 had died, with a further 120,000 suffering severe symptoms such as cancer, blindness and birth defects in children. The pollution continues today. (See www.bhopal.org for more information.) The Volkswagen emissions scandal of 2015 (see https://goo.gl/BXRA7N) involved the company illegally fitting 11 million cars worldwide with a defeat device – or software – aimed at cheating emissions tests. This breached environmental regulations, and meant the company was responsible for pollution up to 40 times the legal limits.

- *Breaches of health and safety*: in 1987, the *Herald of Free Enterprise* cross-Channel ferry capsized in a calm sea just outside Zeebrugge harbour; 193 people died, as rules governing the closing of the bow doors of the ship had not been complied with. In 2017, Grenfell Tower in London burnt down (see https://goo.gl/FPudHq), killing 71 people, with the fire spreading rapidly because of substandard cladding and insulation on the outside of the building.
- *Computer hacking*: in the early 1990s, British Airways illegally hacked into computers to obtain confidential information about its rival Virgin Atlantic (see https://goo.gl/VZ6Vko).
- *Financial offences*: in the USA in 2001, energy and services company ENRON concealed large debts of around $50 billion, eventually causing the company to collapse, many people to lose large amounts from their investments, and thousands of employees to lose their jobs. Beginning in 2012, global companies like Amazon and Starbucks came under attack in the UK for failing to pay their fair share of taxes, through using various legal foreign locations where taxes were lower than in the UK. Pensions, mortgage endowment policies and payment protection policies (PPP) have all been the subject of proceedings, fines and compensation in the UK over misselling – that is, being sold with misleading information about their benefits.
- *Unfair trade practices – cheating the consumer*: in 2011, UK supermarkets and dairy companies were fined £50 million for fixing the price of milk and cheese so that prices (and profits) were kept artificially high, costing consumers £270m more than they would have paid without price fixing.

Although white-collar and corporate crimes often have no individual victim, as in a household burglary or a violent street attack, the examples above do point to the widespread harm that these offences can cause to the public, such as through dangerous and faulty goods, foods and medicines. The lasting and long-term effects of environmental pollution can impact on thousands of people for generations to come. All too often, the people who suffer the most harm from white-collar and corporate crimes are the poor, who are most likely to buy the cheapest and unsafe products, to be employed in more dangerous workplaces with poor enforcement of health and safety regulations, and to be at risk of being defrauded by middle-class professionals.

## The under-representation of white-collar and corporate crime

White-collar and corporate crimes are substantially under-represented in official statistics – there appear to be fewer than there really are. This means

Seventy-one people lost their lives when Grenfell Tower burned in June 2017. The fire spread so quickly because of substandard cladding and insulation on the outside of the building, and poor design of the building hindered escape

that the impression that the middle class commit fewer offences and that most crime is committed by the working class may therefore be quite misleading.

There are several reasons why white-collar and corporate crimes are under-represented in the official statistics.

- *They are hidden from view:* they are relatively invisible, as they take place in the workplace and offenders simply appear to be doing their normal jobs.
- *They are hard to detect and investigate:* the offences are frequently complex and involve some form of technical or insider knowledge, with investigation requiring a lot of skill and expert knowledge which local police forces often lack.
- *They may benefit both the parties involved.* For example, in offences such as bribery and corruption both parties stand to gain something. Both face trouble if discovered, and so they seek to conceal the offence.
- *They are often without personal or individual victims.* Often the victim is impersonal, like a company, the NHS or the public at large, rather than an individual, so there is no individual victim to report an offence.

- *There is often a lack of awareness that a crime has been committed and so it is not reported.* For example, stealing very small amounts of money from a large number of customers' accounts leads to small losses to individuals which the victims may not notice; victims may lack the expertise to know whether they are being misled, defrauded or sold counterfeit goods or dangerous consumer products or foods that may harm them.

- *Victims may blame themselves, so don't report offences.* For example, they may blame themselves for being gullible for letting themselves be conned, or allowing themselves to become victims of internet scams.

- *Institutional protection means they are often covered up, not reported as criminal acts, and not prosecuted, even if detected.* Violations of health and safety legislation by companies often lead only to a reprimand or fine, and crimes such as professional misconduct, medical negligence and fraud are rarely reported and prosecuted, to protect the interests or reputation of the profession or institution and avoid the loss of public confidence which the surrounding scandal might cause. A private security firm is more likely to lead any such investigation, rather than it being reported to the police, with suspected offenders dealt with by being sacked or forced to retire, rather than by being prosecuted.

- *Even if reported and prosecuted, offenders have a better chance than working-class criminals of being found not guilty, as they benefit from not fitting the stereotype of the 'typical criminal'.* Offenders are often of the same background as judges and magistrates, and may appear more plausible, honest and respectable to juries, and so may be less likely to be found guilty, or, if found guilty, more likely to have their offences seen as temporary lapses in otherwise good behaviour, and to receive more lenient sentences than working-class offenders.

All this means, combined with selective law enforcement, these 'crimes of the powerful' often go undetected and unpunished, and never appear in official crime statistics.

---

In general, the higher up you are in the social class hierarchy:
- the less likely are your crimes to be detected
- the less likely are your crimes, if detected, to result in your arrest
- if arrested, the less likely you are to be prosecuted
- if prosecuted, the less likely you are to be found guilty
- if found guilty, the less likely you are to be given a prison sentence.

# WHY ARE SOME MINORITY ETHNIC GROUPS OVER-REPRESENTED IN THE CRIME STATISTICS?

## The evidence on ethnicity and crime

At first glance, official statistics appear to suggest that some BAME groups are more likely to commit crime than the White population. BAME groups, particularly the Black and Asian population, are over-represented in the criminal population – there are more than there should be given their proportions in the population as a whole. Table 5.1 shows they have a much higher involvement than White people at various stages of the CJS. (You can examine some of the latest statistics at https://goo.gl/xx9er3).

Table 5.1 Percentage of individuals at different stages of the criminal justice system (CJS) process by ethnic group, compared to the general population, England and Wales

| | White % | Black % | Asian % | Mixed % | Chinese or Other/ unknown % | TOTAL |
|---|---|---|---|---|---|---|
| Population aged 10 or over 2011 census | 87 | 3 | 6 | 2 | 2 | 49,443,451 |
| Stop and searches 2017–18 | 55 | 20 | 10 | 4 | 13 | 282,248 |
| Arrests 2017–18 | 72 | 9 | 7 | 4 | 8 | 727,871 |
| Cautions 2016 | 86 | 7 | 5 | – | 2 | 97,710 |
| Court proceedings* 2016 | 79 | 11 | 6 | 3 | 1 | 235,811 |
| Convictions* 2017 | 80 | 10 | 6 | 3 | 1 | 177,348 |
| Sentenced to immediate custody* 2017 | 79 | 10 | 7 | 3 | 1 | 57,744 |
| Prison population (aged 15+) June 2018 | 73 | 13 | 8 | 4 | 2 | 82,773 |

Figures are rounded to nearest whole percentage

* Indictable offences only (more serious offences tried before a judge and jury)

Source: Statistics on Race and the Criminal Justice System 2016, Ministry of Justice, 2017; Offender Management Statistics, Ministry of Justice; Stop and Search Statistics – Police Powers and Procedures, Year Ending 31 March 2018, Home Office

## Sociological explanations for the over-representation of BAME groups in crime statistics

### Age, social class and location

Compared to the White British population, BAME groups are more likely to be working-class, and tend to have higher proportions of young people and those suffering poverty, social deprivation, higher rates of unemployment, and lower pay, and to be living in deprived urban communities. The higher official crime rates therefore might be because of the age and social-class factors discussed earlier as causing crime. BAME groups are no more likely to have criminal tendencies than White British people, but a higher proportion of BAME groups are affected by the same circumstances that push White British working-class people into committing crime.

## Labelling and stereotyping, and racism in the criminal justice system

Many sociologists have argued that the official crime statistics are misleading. Labelling theorists and Marxists argue the statistics are a socially constructed fabrication – a result of racial prejudice and discrimination against BAME groups, especially black people and Asians, by the public and particularly by the police and other criminal justice agencies.

- *Racist canteen culture*: there is some evidence of a racist 'canteen culture' among the police – how they chat about things in the police canteen – which can include suspicion, macho values and racism, and this encourages racist stereotypes and a mistrust of those from non-white backgrounds.
- *Police stereotypes*: how the police go about their work – what they look out for – is guided by their ideas about who the typical troublemakers and criminals are. Black and Asian people (especially youths) fit this police stereotype, and they are therefore more likely to be labelled as untrustworthy, troublemakers and potential criminals, and subjected to heavier policing, than white people.
- *Public stereotypes*: the public view of typical offenders is often fuelled by racist media reporting and stereotypes. It is the public who report most crimes, rather than them being uncovered by the police, and they may consequently be scapegoating BAME groups by reporting more of their offences than white ones.
- *Selective law enforcement*: Marxists argue racism and racist stereotypes in police culture and practice mean the behaviour of black and Asian people is more likely to be labelled as criminal, and the law selectively enforced to target them, accounting for their higher arrest rates compared to whites. Many judges and magistrates hold similar stereotypes, and the evidence suggests that they crack down harder on black and Asian people than on white people, giving them heavier fines and sentences than white offenders committing similar offences.

Evidence on discrimination in the CJS shows that, compared to white people, black and Asian people are:

- between 2 times (Asians) and up to 40 times (blacks) more likely to be stopped and searched by the police
- more likely to be arrested for similar offences
- more likely to be cautioned by the police
- more likely to be charged where white offenders are cautioned for similar offences
- more likely to be remanded in custody than released on bail

People from BAME groups are between two and up to forty times more likely than white people to be stopped and searched by the police

- more likely to be given prison sentences or sent to a young offenders' institution (for juveniles under 18) rather than given a community sentence (compulsory unpaid work in the community)
- more likely to be given longer prison or youth-custody sentences
- more likely to be in prison. In 2018, around 28 per cent of male prisoners, and 18 per cent of females, were from BAME groups, even though they make up only about 13 per cent of the general population.

*Institutional racism*   The Macpherson Report of 1999 into the murder of 18-year-old Stephen Lawrence by five white youths suggests that the view of labelling, stereotyping and racism as an explanation for the links between ethnicity and crime shown in official statistics is a persuasive one. Macpherson's investigation into the police handling of the murder was highly critical of the Metropolitan Police. It pointed to a series of mistakes, professional incompetence and a 'lack of urgency' and mishandling of the police investigation, including their assumption that Stephen Lawrence was involved in a street brawl rather than being the victim of an unprovoked racist attack. It pointed to the existence of **institutional racism** in the police force. The Macpherson Report recommended a series of improvements, which included race-awareness training, more BAME police officers and stronger disciplinary action to get rid of racist police officers. The persistence of this racism in the Metropolitan Police led the Metropolitan Black Police Association, in 2008, to warn people from BAME groups not to join the force, because of 'a hostile atmosphere where racism is allowed to spread'.

Some evidence of institutional racism is also reflected in table 5.2, which shows that minority ethnic groups are under-represented, or not represented at all, in some of the most powerful positions in the CJS.

## OFFICIAL CRIME STATISTICS

Official crime statistics are compiled from several main sources:

1 *Police-recorded crime (PRC).* These are offences either detected by or reported to, and recorded by, the police.
2 *Victim surveys.* These include, for example, the annual Crime Survey for England and Wales (CSEW). They survey the victims of crime and include crimes not reported to, or recorded by, the police. They therefore give a more accurate picture than police-recorded crime.
3 *Self-report studies (or surveys).* These consist of anonymous questionnaires in which people are asked to own up to committing crimes, whether or not they have been discovered. These include the Home Office's *Offending, Crime and Justice Survey*, which ran from 2003 to 2006.
4 *Court and prison records, and records on police cautions.* These reveal the characteristics of offenders who have been caught.

**Self-report studies** and **victim surveys** are discussed later in this chapter (see pages 347–9).

### The use of crime statistics

Crime statistics are used for a variety of purposes:

- for comparison with previous years to discover trends in crime
- to look at the police detection rate (the number of crimes cleared up by the police, with an offender identified and action taken against them – sometimes called the 'clear-up rate') to measure police efficiency
- to show where the police should concentrate resources to reduce crime
- to provide the public (often via the media) with information on crime patterns.

**Institutional racism** 'The collective failure of an organization to provide an appropriate and professional service to people because of their culture, colour or ethnic origin. It can be seen or detected in processes, attitudes and behaviour which amount to discrimination through unwitting prejudice, ignorance, thoughtless and racist stereotyping which disadvantages minority ethnic people' (Macpherson Report, 1999).

**Self-report studies** (or surveys) Studies or surveys where people are asked to own up to committing crimes, whether or not they have been discovered.

**Victim surveys** Surveys that question people on whether or not they have been a victim of a crime, whether or not they reported it to the police. This tries to discover how much crime goes unreported by victims and unrecorded by the police.

## Table 5.2 Ethnic minorities and the criminal justice system (CJS), 2016–17

| Position | Ethnic minority % |
|---|---|
| Whole population aged 10 and over (Census 2011) | 13 |
| Supreme Court & Court of Appeal judges | 0 |
| Crown Prosecution Service | 19 |
| Probation Service | 13 |
| High Court judges | 5 |
| Circuit judges | 4 |
| Recorders | 8 |
| Magistrates | 11 |
| District judges | 8 |
| Barristers | 12 |
| Solicitors | 14 |
| Prison officers | 7 |
| Police Community Support Officers | 12 |
| Police officers | 6 |

(Numbers are rounded to the nearest whole number)

*Source: Statistics on Race and the Criminal Justice System 2016*, Ministry of Justice, 2017; *Judicial Statistics 2017*, Courts and Tribunals Judiciary, Ministry of Justice, 2017; *Practising Barrister Statistics*, Bar Standards Board, 2018; Solicitors Regulation Authority

### Activity

Refer to table 5.2.

1  To what extent does table 5.2 suggest that minority ethnic groups are unequally represented in the CJS? Give evidence for and against from the table to back up your view.

2  Outline and explain two reasons why BAME groups might be poorly represented, or not represented at all, in some parts of the CJS.

3  Suggest two difficulties people from BAME groups might face in joining or staying in the police force.

4  Suggest how the information in table 5.2 might be used to suggest that institutional racism exists not just in the police force but in the CJS as a whole.

5  Explain carefully, with examples, how the evidence in table 5.2 and the sections above might be used to explain the unequal treatment of black and Asian people by the law, and the high proportion of black and Asian people among those in prison.

6  Discuss how far sociologists would agree that crime statistics exaggerate crime levels among particular ethnic groups.

## *The use of crime statistics by sociologists*

Sociologists also draw heavily on official crime statistics to provide a basis for their theories to explain crime, including what is and what is not shown in the statistics.

- *Functionalists* broadly accept official statistics as accurate and representative of most crime. They are useful for showing patterns and trends in crime which they can then try to explain.
- *Marxists* suggest statistics provide a biased view of crime, as they under-represent the crimes of the powerful – white-collar and corporate crime – and give the misleading impression that the majority of criminals are working-class.
- *Feminists* suggest statistics under-represent the extent of female crime, and of unreported or under-reported crimes by men against women, such as domestic violence and rape.
- *Interactionists* (labelling theory) see the statistics as social constructions, which are in part created by the activities of the police themselves and the offenders they choose to pursue and the offences they choose to record. Mainly they are useful only to reveal the stereotypes, labelling and assumptions of the public (fed by the media), and, for example, the racism of the criminal justice system. The pattern shown in statistics further fuels these stereotypes, which generates a self-fulfilling prophecy, as they provide a guide for the police on the 'typical offender' as they go about their work.

## WHAT'S WRONG WITH OFFICIAL CRIME STATISTICS?

The previous sections outlined some explanations of the pattern of crime as revealed in official crime statistics. However, most sociologists are very critical of these statistics, arguing that they are unreliable and inadequate as sources of evidence about the nature and extent of crime and the social characteristics of criminals. Many crimes go undiscovered, unreported or unrecorded. In the year ending September 2018, according to the Home Office, of those that were reported to the police and recorded by them, less than one in ten (9.4 per cent) resulted in someone being charged. In almost half of offences (47 per cent), there was no suspect identified. Estimates suggest less than 3 per cent of all crime in England and Wales ends with a conviction.

This means those appearing in official statistics are an unrepresentative sample of officially classified criminals who happen to have been caught, and we don't really have very reliable evidence about who is committing the majority of offences. This leaves open the possibility that the high proportion of young, urban, working-class males in official statistics may give a misleading impression of the criminal population as a whole. Self-report and victim surveys are the two main sources of evidence showing the inadequacy of official crime statistics.

## Self-report and victim surveys

Sociologists know that the number of crimes is far higher than the official statistics suggest, because of the use of self-report studies and victim surveys.

- *Self-report studies* (or surveys) are anonymous questionnaires in which people are asked to own up to committing crimes, whether they have been discovered or not (the box on page 349 shows an example of a self-report survey questionnaire).
- *Victim surveys* involve people reporting on being the victim of a crime, whether or not they reported it to the police. An example is the CSEW, carried out every year by the Office for National Statistics. This tries to discover how much crime goes unreported by victims and unrecorded by the police. (You can read more about the CSEW at https://goo.gl/k4yqHD; its strengths and weaknesses compared to crime recorded by the police can be found at https://goo.gl/CNxKb3)

Why might victims keep quiet about crime? Imagine each of the people in this picture is a victim of crime (for example, the child perhaps is suffering physical or sexual abuse, or the father could be a victim of blackmail or violent threats to his family), and consider why they might not report the crimes

These surveys mean it is possible to estimate how much crime there really is in society. However, they are only estimates, and even self-report and victim surveys do not give a full picture of the real levels of crime in society. For example, not everyone will admit to being a victim or an offender, and around 25–30 per cent of people approached refuse to cooperate with the CSEW victimization survey. As with all surveys, there is the issue of the extent to which the findings are representative, and can be generalized to the whole population. Some other strengths and weaknesses of these surveys are shown in table 5.3 below.

> **Dark figure of crime** Crimes that are undiscovered, unreported and unrecorded by the police.

## Table 5.3 Strengths and weaknesses of self-report and victim surveys

### Self-report studies

| Strengths/advantages | Weaknesses/disadvantages |
| --- | --- |
| • They provide information uncovering some of the **dark figure of crime**: undiscovered, unreported and unrecorded crime.<br><br>• They may provide information on offenders not caught by the police.<br><br>• They help with finding out about victimless crimes such as fraud, bribery and corruption, or illegal drug use. | • Offenders may exaggerate, understate or lie about the number of crimes they've committed.<br><br>• Offenders may not admit to some offences, particularly more serious ones. This means such surveys tend to over-emphasize more minor or trivial offences, like petty theft, or vandalism/criminal damage.<br><br>• Those who are persistent, prolific and serious offenders are the least likely to participate in such surveys. |

### Victim surveys

| Strengths/advantages | Weaknesses/disadvantages |
| --- | --- |
| • They provide information uncovering some of the dark figure of crimes not reported to or recorded by the police.<br><br>• They provide insights into the victims of crime, such as their perceptions of the police, and attitudes to crime and antisocial behaviour. | • People may forget they were victimized, particularly the more trivial incidents, or forget whether they were victimized in the period covered by the survey (for example, the CSEW covers the last twelve months). This may make results inaccurate.<br><br>• They may not realize they have been the victims of a crime – particularly white-collar and corporate crimes, where they may not realize that they have been duped, conned, scammed or, for example, sold dangerous products.<br><br>• Victims may feel embarrassment or guilt at admitting to being a victim, such as in the case of sexual offences or domestic violence.<br><br>• They often don't include all crimes.<br><br>• Crimes without victims, like drug offences or white-collar crimes like bribery and corruption and fraud, where both parties have something to lose, are not likely to be recorded. |

**EXAMPLE OF A QUESTIONNAIRE FOR A SELF-REPORT STUDY**

1. I have stolen or driven a vehicle without permission, even if the owner got it back.
2. I have stolen or tried to steal parts off the outside, or things from inside, of a vehicle.
3. I have deliberately damaged things that didn't belong to me, for example by scratching, burning, smashing or breaking them, including things like vehicles, trains, rubbish bins, skips, windows, bus shelters, etc.
4. I have gone into someone's home, or buildings like a factory, office, shop, hospital or school without permission, because I wanted to steal or damage something.
5. I have used force, violence or threats against someone in order to steal from them, or from a shop, petrol station, bank or any other business.
6. I have, without using force, violence or threats, stolen things, like something someone was carrying or wearing, for example by taking something from their hand, pocket or bag, or stolen things from a shop, the school or college I attend or used to attend, or where I work, or used to work.
7. I have deliberately used force or violence on someone, whether they were injured or not, for example, by scratching, hitting, kicking or throwing things.
8. I have sold illegal drugs, such as heroin, cocaine, crack, ecstasy and cannabis, to people, including friends.
9. I have had in my possession, or taken, illegal drugs, such as marijuana/cannabis, heroin, crack, cocaine, speed, ecstasy or magic mushrooms.
10. I have travelled on a train or bus without a ticket or deliberately paid the wrong fare.
11. I have taken a weapon, like a knife, out with me in case I needed it in a fight.
12. I have bought something cheap or accepted as a present something I knew was stolen.
13. I have struggled or fought with a police officer to get away from them or to stop them trying to arrest someone.
14. I have written things or sprayed paint on a building, fence, train or somewhere else where I shouldn't have.
15. I have been noisy or rude or acted in such a way in a public place or in or near my home so that someone complained or got me into trouble.
16. I have threatened or been rude to someone because of their skin colour, race or religion.

*Source:* adapted from the *2003 Crime and Justice Survey* and the *2005 Offending, Crime and Justice Survey*, Home Office, 2005, 2006; A. Campbell, *Girl Delinquents* (Blackwell, 1981)

## Activity

1. Work through the self-report study questions in the box above. List any offences you and/or your friends have committed, whether or not you've been caught, no matter how trivial or whether they're on the list or not. Ask your family and people you know, as well as strangers. What conclusions might you draw from your findings about the levels of undiscovered crime in society?
2. List three crimes which a victim might choose not to report to the police, and explain why in each case.
3. Have you or any of your friends ever been a victim (or suspected you might have been a victim) of a crime that you didn't report to the police? Explain the reasons why you didn't report it. What does this tell you about the real extent of crime in society?

## The dark figure of undiscovered, unreported and unrecorded crime

Official crime statistics may lack:

- *Reliability* – there may be differences between individual police officers and police forces in the way they classify offences and the way they count them. This means that a police force in one area may not be collecting statistics in an identical way to that in another.
- *Validity* – they are not a true or complete picture of the real amount and pattern of crime. Official crime statistics only show crimes that are known to the police and are recorded by them, or reported in victim surveys like the CSEW. There is what is called the 'dark figure of crime' – offences that are not discovered (possibly even by victims, as in many computer-based frauds and other cybercrimes), or that are not reported to the police, or recorded by them. The CSEW estimates that, overall, nearly twice as many offences are committed (for those the survey covers) as the number recorded by the police, and 62 per cent of CSEW crimes overall are not reported to the police, as figure 5.12 shows.

Like an iceberg, where most of the ice is hidden beneath the surface, so it is with crime, with a hidden 'dark figure' of undiscovered, unreported or unrecorded crime

## Why don't victims of a crime report it to the police?

- *It was too trivial* – for example, where the incident involved no loss or damage, or the loss was too small, such as losing a small amount of money or garden tools.
- *It was inconvenient to report.*
- *The police could not do anything about it*, by either recovering their property or catching the offenders – for example, cases of shoplifting or being pickpocketed.
- *The victim may fear embarrassment or humiliation at the hands of the police or in court* – for example, many crimes of domestic violence and sexual violence, such as sexual assaults and rapes, go unreported because the victims:
  - are embarrassed
  - think the police won't believe them or take them seriously
  - are made to feel it is their own fault they were beaten or raped
  - don't want to get their attacker – who is often known to them – into trouble.
- Recent rises in the number of reported rapes and crimes of domestic violence are often explained by changing police practice, and their growing willingness to treat such offences in a more serious way and to be more sympathetic to the victim. However, victims may still feel there is little

**Figure 5.12** Percentage of CSEW incidents reported to the police: 2017–18

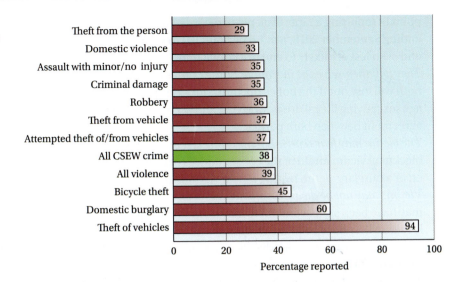

Percentage reported

## Activity

Refer to figure 5.12.

1   Which offence was (a) most likely, (b) least likely, to be reported to the police? Suggest reasons for this in each case.

2   What percentage of the following offences were reported to the police in 2017–18?

3   (a)  thefts from the person
    (b)  bicycle thefts
    (c)  thefts of vehicles
    (d)  domestic violence
    (e)  thefts from vehicles

4   With reference to figure 5.12, suggest reasons, with examples, why some offences are reported to the police much more than others.

5   According to the statistics in figure 5.12, a high proportion of crimes of criminal damage (typically vandalism), assaults, thefts from vehicles, thefts from the person and domestic violence, were not reported to the police. Suggest one reason for this for each offence.

6   Explain how the information given in figure 5.12 might be used to show that police-recorded crime statistics give a misleading impression of the extent of crime in society. Is there any evidence for the opposite view for particular types of crime? Be sure to give statistical evidence from figure 5.12.

7   Suggest examples of offences and/or the circumstances for victims not reporting crimes to the police in each of the following cases:
    (a)  they sympathize with the offender
    (b)  they wish to protect the institution in which the offence occurs.

8   Explain two reasons why the evidence in figure 5.12 might be used to challenge the view that most criminals are young, male and working-class?

point in reporting a rape: of all rapes recorded by the police in the year ending September 2018, just 1.9 per cent led to someone being charged, and even less are likely to end in a conviction.

- *They will themselves be in trouble.* Some crimes benefit both parties, and both will lose out if the police find out – for example, consensual under-age sex, buying illegal drugs, or giving and accepting bribes involve an agreement between both parties.
- *The victim may fear reprisals if the crime is reported* – for example the blackmail victim afraid of the consequences of reporting the blackmailer, or a burglary victim fearing repeat victimization.
- *Victims may not be aware an offence has been committed.* 'Lost' property may have been stolen, and there may be many people who never actually realize they have been the victims of a hoax or a conman. This is commonly the case with the newly emerging internet-based cybercrimes and scams of all kinds.
- *The victim thought it was their own fault* – for example, for falling for a 'get rich quick' internet scam, or for forgetting to lock the shed door.
- Dislike or fear of, or previous bad experiences with, the police and courts.

## Why don't the police record some crimes?

The police may decide not to record an offence that has been reported to or observed by them. According to a 2014 report by Her Majesty's Inspectorate of Constabulary and Fire & Rescue Service (HMICFRS), an estimated one in five offences (19 per cent) that should have been recorded as crimes were not. The greatest levels of under-recording were seen for violence against the person and sexual offences. An estimated one in three violent offences and one in four sexual offences that should have been recorded as crimes were not. This may be because:

- They lack adequate training and knowledge about their own rules for recording crime, or fail to apply them.
- They may regard the matter as too trivial to waste their time on, such as antisocial behaviour or the theft of a very small sum of money.
- It has already been satisfactorily resolved, or because the victim does not wish to proceed with the complaint.
- They may regard the person complaining as too unreliable to take his or her account of the incident seriously, as in the case of complaints made by a tramp, a drug addict or someone who is drunk.
- They may think that a report of an incident is mistaken, or that there is simply insufficient evidence to show that a crime has been committed.

- They may interpret the law in such a way that what is reported is not regarded as an offence.
- They may regard an incident as nothing to do with them, even though an offence has been committed. This has traditionally been true in cases of domestic violence, such as rape and other violence within marriage or cohabiting relationships.

---

### Activity

The police often have a great deal of work to do, and every arrest they make involves considerable paperwork. The police also have discretion over whether to arrest and charge someone for some offences. For example, when people are pubbing and clubbing in town centres, there may be lots of trouble, but the police can choose to move people along rather than arrest them.

1 Suggest two examples of offences which the police might turn a blind eye to. Give reasons for your answer.
2 Suggest two crimes the police would be forced to record and investigate. Give reasons for your answer.

---

## IS THE CRIME RATE INCREASING OR DECREASING?

Much of what was said in the previous section suggests that official crime statistics provide no real guide to the type or extent of crime, and that they must therefore be used with great care. Such care must also be applied to statistics which show increases or decreases in the amounts of some recorded crime.

Much public and media concern is always expressed at any increase in recorded crime, but such increases need not necessarily mean there are more crimes being committed, or that people are at greater risk of being victims of crime. The increases could be explained by a wide range of factors, which suggest more offences are being discovered, reported to and recorded by the police, but not necessarily that more offences are actually being committed. These factors include:

- *The media.* As seen earlier (see pages 299–303), the media may exaggerate and distort the fear of crime and make problems seem worse than they are. This sensitizes people and groups to particular offences or groups of people, which may make people more likely to report such crimes, but this does not necessarily mean that more crimes are being committed.
- *Changing, and stricter enforcement, of police counting rules.* A recent focus on the quality of crime recording by the police is thought to have

led to a greater proportion of reported crimes being recorded by the police, but this does not necessarily mean there is more crime being committed. Changing counting rules have meant, for example, that, since April 2002, a person vandalizing six cars in a street has been counted as committing six separate offences, whereas before this would have counted as one.

- *More sophisticated police training, communication and equipment,* such as the use of computers, CCTV and other surveillance technology, forensic science and DNA testing, and higher policing levels all lead to increasing detection rates. Neighbourhood Watch schemes may also lead to more crimes being reported and detected.
- *Changing police attitudes, policies and priorities* – these can influence the areas, groups or offences targeted by the police. For example, a crack-down on sexual offences, cybercrime, child abuse, knife crime, drug-dealing or drink-driving may give the impression of an increase in crimes of that type, when it is simply that the police are making extra efforts and allocating more officers to tackle such crimes, and therefore catching more offenders.
- *Changes in the law* make more things illegal, such as rape in marriage, forced marriage, hate crime (see pages 450–1), sexual harassment, stalking and sexting (texting sexually explicit messages or photos).
- *Easier communications,* such as mobile phones, email and police community websites, make reporting of crime easier.

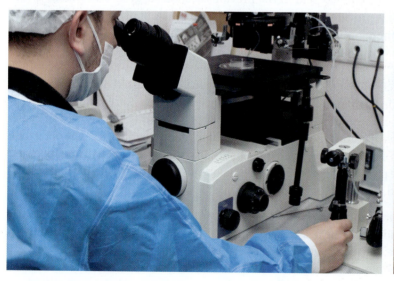 

Forensic science and other sophisticated scientific techniques, together with schemes like Neighbourhood Watch, increase the reporting, recording and detection of crime – but this doesn't necessarily mean there are more crimes being committed

- *Changing social norms and public attitudes* – for example, changing attitudes to rape among the police and the public may have resulted in more rapes being reported, even though no more have been committed. The same might apply to crimes like domestic violence, child abuse and knife crime, which are also statistically on the increase.

- *People have more to lose today* and more have household contents insurance cover. Insurance claims for theft need a police crime number, so more crime is reported. For example, nearly all thefts of cars and burglaries with loss are reported today so people can claim the insurance money.

- *People may be bringing to the attention of the police less serious incidents, which they might not have reported in the past.* For example, they may have become less tolerant of vandalism and antisocial behaviour, particularly by nuisance youth, and expect the police to take action and stop it.

People are now becoming more intolerant of some incidents, such as antisocial behaviour and vandalism, and reporting them to the police for action, though this doesn't necessarily mean there are more incidents than in the past

It is an irony of the official crime statistics that attempts to defeat crime by increased levels of policing, more police pay and resources, and a determination to crack down on offences can actually increase the levels of recorded crime. The more you search for crime, the more you find; and the official crime rate rises.

1 Describe one ethical problem with using a self-report study to investigate the amount of crime in society.
2 Identify and explain one advantage and one disadvantage of using a victim survey to discover the amount of unreported crime in society.
3 Sometimes the police seem to take some offences more seriously than at other times, and this results in increasing numbers of arrests and prosecutions for these offences. Identify and explain, with examples, two reasons why the police might occasionally increase their levels of activity against some offences.
4 Identify and explain two reasons why official crime statistics may not show the true extent of crime in society.
5 Explain what is meant by the 'dark figure of crime'.
6 Describe and explain two reasons why a victim of crime may not report a crime to the police.
7 Explain what sociologists mean when they say crime statistics are socially constructed.
8 Describe one way in which media reporting of crime might increase the amount of crime recorded by the police.

# THE VICTIMS OF CRIME

Since the 1980s, there has been a rapid growth in victim surveys and studies of the impact of crime on victims and their needs and rights. All sections of the criminal justice system (CJS), such as the police and courts, are increasingly paying attention to the interests of victims and the impact of crime on local communities. For example, the police are making greater efforts to engage with the community and keep victims informed about progress in catching offenders, and victims of sexual assault are getting more specialist help and more sympathetic and specially trained police to deal with them. Victim Support schemes (see www.victimsupport.org.uk) are now an integral part of the CJS.

It has been increasingly recognized that if the victims of crime do not have confidence in the CJS to support them and catch and punish offenders, then more crime will remain unreported, victims will be unwilling to give evidence to the police or as witnesses in court, and offenders will go unpunished.

## Who are the victims of crime?

Overall, in 2017–18, 14 per cent of people aged 16 and over in England and Wales said they were victims of crime at least once in the last 12 months, but some social groups are more likely to be the victims of crime than others.

## Social class

The 'hard pressed' – the poor – are, overall, the most likely victims of crime: the unemployed, the long-term sick, low-income families, those living in rented accommodation and in areas with high levels of deprivation. Those living in the 20 per cent of poorest areas face much higher risks of being victims of all crimes covered by the CSEW. The poorest fifth of people in Britain, compared to the richest fifth, face around twice the risk of being victims of burglary and vehicle-related thefts, as well as higher risks of vandalism, and overall household crime.

> Those who have the fewest and least valuable material possessions are those most likely to have them stolen or vandalized, while those who have the most, and most valuable, material possessions are the least likely to have them stolen or vandalized. Those who steal from the poor and vandalize their property are mainly other poor people.

## Age

The likelihood of being a victim of crime decreases with age. The lifestyles of the young, as well as giving them greater opportunity to commit crime, also expose them to greater risk of being victims of crime. Adults aged 16–24:

- face the highest risk of being victims of personal crimes (that is, crimes against the individual – for example assault and theft) than other age groups
- are around nine times more likely to be victims than those aged 75 and over
- men are most likely to be the victims of violent crime, most of it committed by other young men. Older people (age 65+) are the least likely to be victims of violent crime.

## Gender

- Males, particularly young men (aged 16–24), are most at risk of non-sexual violence outside the home.
- Women are far more likely than men to be the victims of sexual violence outside the home, such as sexual assault and rape.
- Women are the most common victims of both physical and sexual violence inside the home – domestic violence. This is one of the least likely offences to be reported to the police, to be recorded in official statistics, or to result in offenders being convicted. Most of the assaults and physically most violent incidents resulting in injury – 89 per cent – are committed by men against their female partners. Many female victims of domestic violence suffer repeat victimization and those men who experience domestic violence suffer less serious attacks and do so less frequently than women. Every week two women die due to domestic violence.

## *Ethnicity*

BAME groups are more likely to be the victims of crime than the White population, with those from the Mixed and Asian ethnic groups at the highest risk in 2017–18. Compared to the White British population, BAME groups:

- face higher risks of being victims of personal crimes
- face twice the risk of being murdered, rising to four times higher for Black people
- are up to fourteen times more likely to be victims of racially motivated hate crimes, such as racist violence, abuse and harassment, most of which are not reported to the police.

---

### Activity

Suggest and describe one reason in each case why each of the following groups are more likely to become victims of the crimes mentioned:
- young men and violence
- people in poverty and burglary
- women and domestic violence
- BAME groups and hate crimes.

---

## The effects of victimization

Becoming a victim of crime, or living in areas where there are high crime levels, can have the following effects, apart from actual, or fear of, physical harm or financial and material loss or damage:

- *psychological effects* – such as anger, depression, panic attacks, disrupted sleep and unwillingness to leave the house
- *greater fear of crime*
- *restrictions over movement* – for example, women victims fearing to go out at night or avoiding certain areas for fear of gender-based violence
- *fear of repeat (further) victimization*
- *wider effects beyond the victims* – for example, whole neighbourhoods or groups of people can be put in fear as a result of hate crimes against BAME groups or gays.

---

## CRIME CONTROL, PREVENTION AND PUNISHMENT

Over the years, both sociologists and governments have suggested a range of different approaches and policies which they suggest would help to prevent or reduce crime.

## Sociological theories and the control of crime

### *Functionalist approaches*

- Making parents take more responsibility for the socialization and super-vision of their children, with penalties for parents who fail to do so.
- Stricter control of young people's behaviour at home and at school.
- Building stronger communities and community cohesion; encouraging communities to pull together to make them safer, with stronger informal social control over potential offenders.
- Establishing community controls over crime, through schemes such as Neighbourhood Watch (www.ourwatch.org.uk), rather than just relying on the police and the CJS.
- Encouraging people to take more responsibility for protecting them-selves from crime – for example, by installing stronger security in their homes – like better locks and a burglar alarm – or avoiding some areas at night, to reduce their risks of becoming victims of crime.
- Reducing opportunities for crime through installing CCTV and other surveillance methods, which increase the risks for potential offenders.
- Zero-tolerance policing – tackling *all* crime, including low-level offences like vandalism, petty theft and criminal (and even non-criminal) antisocial behaviour, to prevent small offences leading to more serious crime.

### *Marxist approaches*

- Tackling social inequality – being tough on the wider social causes of crime. A more equal distribution of wealth and income, more financial help for poorer families, and the elimination of poverty, deprivation, marginalization and social exclusion would reduce the underlying circumstances and risk factors that give rise to working-class crime.
- Better educational and training opportunities, to reduce the temptation to turn to crime.
- Help for parents in raising their children, and early-years childcare support – early intervention to help get children at greatest risk of offending off to a better start in life.
- Stricter measures to reduce white-collar and corporate crime.
- Making the CJS more representative of the population, and reducing selective law enforcement through more democratic and community control of policing. The CJS needs to be made fairer and more responsive to the needs, concerns and priorities of local communities.
- Putting in the resources to divert potential young offenders away from crime, by investing in community projects in sport, arts and apprenticeships.

## *Feminist approaches*

- Tackling female crime means tackling the social inequality and hardship which affect working-class women the most.
- Challenging patriarchy, which lies behind both much female victimization and women's offending. They emphasize policies like opening more rape crisis centres and women's refuges so women can escape male violence.
- Making the patriarchal and male-dominated CJS take a more serious and active approach to male physical and sexual violence against women. This would encourage more women to report crimes against them, expose the extent of male crimes against women, and encourage more action against them.

## *Interactionist/labelling approaches*

Reducing crime means avoiding attaching criminal labels to offenders. Labelling only makes crime worse by reducing opportunities for offenders to return to normal conforming lives and drives them into deviant careers. For example, drug abuse is the single largest cause of crime, lying behind many property crimes. Decriminalizing drug offences – stopping treating them as criminal offences – and treating drug abuse as a health rather than criminal problem could cure addiction, avoid labelling and the development of a deviant career, and reduce crime.

> **Activity**
>
> Study the sociological theories on the control of crime. Identify **one** approach which you think might be the most effective in reducing crime, and explain why you think this approach might be better than the others.

## Government policies and the control of crime

Governments have, over the years, taken a range of measures to tackle crime, but with mixed success. These have predominantly focused on various forms of punishment and control of offenders. Table 5.4 includes a range of measures that have been adopted to try to tackle crime. You can find out more about most of these by searching on www.gov.uk.

## Table 5.4 Policies to tackle crime

| Policy | Description/comment |
| --- | --- |
| Electronic tagging | Electronic tag is fitted to the ankle of offenders to monitor and control their movements. |
| Community sentences | Instead of prison, offenders are given a community sentence, like Community Payback, where they do unpaid work in the community, such as cleaning off graffiti, painting community centres or clearing wasteland. |
| Restorative justice | Offenders and victims meet face-to-face, with the aim of making offenders recognize the harm they have caused, and attempt to restore or repair the harm and damage they caused to their victims. |
| Curfew schemes | To ban young people from specific areas or from being outside their homes during certain hours to keep young tearaways off the streets. |
| Community Protection Notices (CPNs) or Criminal Behaviour Orders (CBOs) | Punishments for antisocial behaviour. Can involve curfews, orders to stop seeing certain people, going to support groups to improve behaviour, fixing damage to someone's property. Those breaking them risk heavy fines and imprisonment. |
| More police on the streets, and more efficient policing | Recruiting more police officers, cutting paperwork so officers have more time patrolling, monitoring police performance, and taking action where results are poor. |
| More targeted policing | Focusing on the areas where crime rates and disorder are highest, to prevent crime in particular locations by making crime more risky and a less attractive choice. |
| Zero-tolerance policing | Tackling *all* crime, including low-level crimes like vandalism, petty theft and criminal (and even non-criminal) antisocial behaviour, where police tolerance and inaction can create an 'anything goes' culture in some communities, leading to more crime. |
| More community involvement in policing | More community policing and schemes such as Neighbourhood Watch, to promote public confidence in the police, and encourage people to report crime and to volunteer evidence that might help to secure convictions. |
| Fast-track justice for young offenders | So punishment follows quickly on the crime. |
| Crime diversion projects | Divert young offenders from crime, through projects like sport, arts and car-maintenance projects. |
| Rehabilitation of offenders to stop them reoffending | Rehabilitate criminals, through education and skills training, and help with finding jobs when they leave prison. In 2016–17, around 48 per cent of all released adult prisoners, 65 per cent of juveniles, and 64 per cent of adults serving sentences of less than 12 months reoffended and were convicted within one year. Others may have reoffended but not been caught. For many prisoners, the present prison regime is not working. |
| Better use of technology and surveillance techniques | Monitoring through round-the-clock surveillance technologies, ANPR (Automatic Number Plate Recognition), more closed-circuit television cameras, video-equipped drones, more DNA testing, photos on credit cards, more alarms and better locks on homes and cars, etc., to deter and catch criminals. |
| Tougher prison sentences | Longer sentences and harsher conditions for offenders, particularly persistent (repeat) offenders. |

**THE ROLE OF PUNISHMENT IN CRIME CONTROL AND PREVENTION**

There are six main reasons for punishing and imprisoning criminals:

1  rehabilitation – trying to change criminals into better people to discourage reoffending
2  deterrence – to discourage (deter) others from offending
3  restorative justice – to force criminals to make amends to victims
4  protection – to protect society from those who are dangerous
5  to reinforce social values and bonds – by showing the boundaries between right and wrong
6  retribution – revenge: to punish criminals simply because they deserve to suffer as much as their victims.

### Activity

1  Look at the range of policies in table 5.4 that have been used by governments to tackle crime. Try to link them to one or more of the six reasons for punishment shown in the box above.
2  Identify and explain **two** policies in table 5.4 which you think are most likely to be effective in tackling crime, giving reasons why you chose those two.
3  Discuss your answer with others in your group, and see whether there is any agreement on the most effective measures to take.
4  Go to the restorative justice website (www.why-me.org) and suggest two ways in which restorative justice might help the victims of crime, and two reasons why it might encourage offenders not to reoffend.
5  'Imprisonment may actually threaten, rather than assist, in re-establishing social order. Rather than rehabilitating offenders, prisons act as "universities of crime", and are simply very expensive ways of making "bad" people worse.' To what extent do you agree with this view?

# DEVIANCE, CRIME AND SOCIAL CHANGE

This chapter has shown that the definition and explanation of deviance and crime are no simple matters. This is hardly surprising given the very wide range of behaviour that the term 'deviance' covers.

We must recognize that deviance, and even crime, are not by any means always harmful to society. Much crime remains fairly trivial, and the wide range of non-conformist behaviour, its quirks and oddities, add a richness of colour and variety to what might otherwise be a drab existence.

Without deviance, even without crime, there would be no possibility of innovation and change. The rebels and the reformers, the heretics and the inventors, and campaigners for peace and justice have all been labelled as deviants or criminals at one time or another. For example, Jesus Christ was seen as a rebel in his time, and crucified for it. Nelson Mandela was imprisoned in South Africa for thirty years for alleged terrorist offences in fighting a white racist society; his role in changing South African society led him later to become President of South Africa and an internationally respected world leader and celebrity. Che Guevara fought in the 1950s against a corrupt and repressive regime in Cuba, later to become Minister of Industry and National Bank President in a new socialist Cuba, as well as the global icon, shown in the picture, which persists to this day. Martin McGuinness was a former commander of the Derry Brigade of the IRA (Irish Republican Army), and was imprisoned in the 1970s for his role in fighting against discrimination and violent attacks against Catholics, and British rule and the presence of British troops in Ireland. His early battles, once defined as deviant and criminal, so changed Northern Ireland that he later became a British MP, a member of the Northern Ireland Assembly and the Deputy First Minister of Northern Ireland. The suffragettes, who fought for votes for women between 1897 and 1918, were once seen as major public enemies who were force-fed, beaten and imprisoned by the British state. In 2018, 100 years later, the British Government allocated £5 million to fund centenary celebrations of the suffragettes. This included a statue of suffragette leader Millicent Fawcett – the first statue of a woman in London's Parliament Square, standing alongside statues of Sir Winston Churchill and Nelson Mandela.

It is often the non-conformists and law-breakers who have contributed to changes which many would regard as of benefit to all. Deviance should be treated with an open mind, for what is regarded as deviant today is often the accepted behaviour of tomorrow.

Nelson Mandela, Che Guevara and Millicent Fawcett: all were seen as deviant at one time, challenging the status quo by sometimes illegal means, but were later honoured and seen by many to have brought about positive change by their once-deviant actions

**KEY ISSUES**

- The significance of social inequality
- Social inequality as a social issue
- What is social stratification?
- Systems of stratification
- Social class stratification and inequality
- Gender stratification and inequality
- Ethnic stratification and inequality
- Age stratification and inequality
- Stratification, inequality and disability
- Religion and sexuality as dimensions of inequality
- Stratification and inequalities in power and authority
- Poverty

# THE SIGNIFICANCE OF SOCIAL INEQUALITY

**Social inequality** refers to the unequal access people have to resources such as wealth, income, power and status, and to the unequal distribution of opportunities linked to these, such as in education, health, housing and employment.

Most people would agree that few societies are really equal. The study of social inequality is of central concern to sociologists because modern societies display such a wide range of inequalities. These include inequalities between rich and poor, between social classes, between men and women, between ethnic groups, and between age groups. Inequalities exist in a wide range of areas of social life, such as in job security, leisure opportunities, health, housing, income and the power to influence events in society. In Britain, income inequality – the gap between the rich and the poor – has grown rapidly since 1979, as shown in figure 6.1, and the gap between the two groups is now one of the largest in comparison with the countries of the European Union.

An understanding of social inequality provides a necessary starting point for the newcomer to sociology because it influences so deeply much of what happens in society.

> **Social inequality**
> The unequal access people have to resources such as wealth, income, power and status, and the unequal distribution of opportunities linked to these, such as in education, health, housing and employment.

imprisoned in South Africa for thirty years for alleged terrorist offences in fighting a white racist society; his role in changing South African society led him later to become President of South Africa and an internationally respected world leader and celebrity. Che Guevara fought in the 1950s against a corrupt and repressive regime in Cuba, later to become Minister of Industry and National Bank President in a new socialist Cuba, as well as the global icon, shown in the picture, which persists to this day. Martin McGuinness was a former commander of the Derry Brigade of the IRA (Irish Republican Army), and was imprisoned in the 1970s for his role in fighting against discrimination and violent attacks against Catholics, and British rule and the presence of British troops in Ireland. His early battles, once defined as deviant and criminal, so changed Northern Ireland that he later became a British MP, a member of the Northern Ireland Assembly and the Deputy First Minister of Northern Ireland. The suffragettes, who fought for votes for women between 1897 and 1918, were once seen as major public enemies who were force-fed, beaten and imprisoned by the British state. In 2018, 100 years later, the British Government allocated £5 million to fund centenary celebrations of the suffragettes. This included a statue of suffragette leader Millicent Fawcett – the first statue of a woman in London's Parliament Square, standing alongside statues of Sir Winston Churchill and Nelson Mandela.

It is often the non-conformists and law-breakers who have contributed to changes which many would regard as of benefit to all. Deviance should be treated with an open mind, for what is regarded as deviant today is often the accepted behaviour of tomorrow.

Nelson Mandela, Che Guevara and Millicent Fawcett: all were seen as deviant at one time, challenging the status quo by sometimes illegal means, but were later honoured and seen by many to have brought about positive change by their once-deviant actions

## CHAPTER SUMMARY AND REVISION CHECKLIST

After studying this chapter, you should be able to:

- define social control and explain how it is carried out formally and informally through agencies, and by agents, of social control
- explain the difference between crime and deviance
- explain how crime and deviance are social constructions
- explain why crime is a social issue and a source of public debate, including its impact on society and on victims, the fear of crime, violent crime, youth crime and antisocial behaviour, and the prison system
- discuss the role of the media in relation to crime, including the exaggeration of crime, labelling, folk devils, moral panics and deviancy amplification
- explain why some crime and deviance may not always be harmful to society
- provide a range of explanations for crime, delinquency and deviance, including the functionalist, Marxist, feminist and interactionist theories of crime, and outline some of their strengths and weaknesses
- describe and explain the ideas of labelling and deviant careers
- outline the work of Merton, Cohen, Carlen, Heidensohn and Becker
- describe and explain the pattern and trends in crime shown in official crime statistics, including the patterns in relation to urban areas, age, gender, social class and ethnicity
- explain what is meant by white-collar and corporate crime, and why they often go undetected, unrecorded and unpunished
- provide a range of reasons why official crime statistics provide no accurate record of the full extent of crime in society, including the dark figure of crime
- describe some strengths and weaknesses of self-report studies and victim surveys
- explain why changes in the official crime rate might not necessarily mean that there have been increases or decreases in the real amount of crime
- outline which social groups face the highest risks of becoming victims of crimes, and some effects of crime on victims
- outline how different sociological theories approach the control and prevention of crime, and outline some government policies that have been adopted to tackle crime.

## KEY TERMS

Definitions can be found in the glossary at the end of this book, as well as these terms usually being defined in the margin where they first appear in the chapter. You can also find the glossary online by following the link at www.politybooks.com/browne. Put it in your phone for ready reference.

| | | | |
|---|---|---|---|
| anomie | edgework | marginalization | self-report studies (or |
| chivalry thesis | folk devils | master status | surveys) |
| class deal | formal rules | moral panic | social exclusion |
| corporate crime | gender deal | news values | status frustration |
| crime | indictable offences | over-representation | subculture |
| criminal justice system | informal rules | police caution | victim surveys |
| dark figure of crime | institutional racism | relative deprivation | white-collar crime |
| deviance | juvenile delinquency | scapegoats | |
| deviancy amplification | law | selective law | |
| deviant career | malestream | enforcement | |

There are a variety of free tests and other activities that can be used to assess your learning – mainly aimed at AS- and A-level sociology students, but you might find them useful – as well as an online searchable glossary, at

### www.politybooks.com/browne
### You can also find new contemporary resources by following Ken Browne on Twitter

@BrowneKen

# Social Stratification and Social Inequality

## Contents

**KEY ISSUES**

- The significance of social inequality
- Social inequality as a social issue
- What is social stratification?
- Systems of stratification
- Social class stratification and inequality
- Gender stratification and inequality
- Ethnic stratification and inequality
- Age stratification and inequality
- Stratification, inequality and disability
- Religion and sexuality as dimensions of inequality
- Stratification and inequalities in power and authority
- Poverty

# THE SIGNIFICANCE OF SOCIAL INEQUALITY

**Social inequality** refers to the unequal access people have to resources such as wealth, income, power and status, and to the unequal distribution of opportunities linked to these, such as in education, health, housing and employment.

Most people would agree that few societies are really equal. The study of social inequality is of central concern to sociologists because modern societies display such a wide range of inequalities. These include inequalities between rich and poor, between social classes, between men and women, between ethnic groups, and between age groups. Inequalities exist in a wide range of areas of social life, such as in job security, leisure opportunities, health, housing, income and the power to influence events in society. In Britain, income inequality – the gap between the rich and the poor – has grown rapidly since 1979, as shown in figure 6.1, and the gap between the two groups is now one of the largest in comparison with the countries of the European Union.

An understanding of social inequality provides a necessary starting point for the newcomer to sociology because it influences so deeply much of what happens in society.

> **Social inequality**
> The unequal access people have to resources such as wealth, income, power and status, and the unequal distribution of opportunities linked to these, such as in education, health, housing and employment.

**Figure 6.1** How inequality has grown in Britain, 1979–2017/18

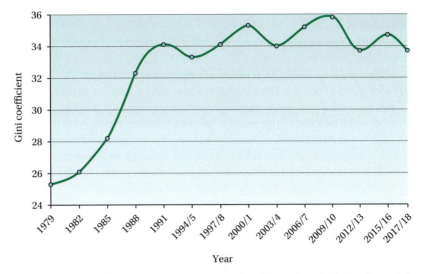

Figure 6.1 shows how inequality has risen in Britain between 1979 and 2017–18. It is based on an index of inequality called the Gini coefficient. This shows income inequality on a scale of 0 (perfect equality - when everyone has the same income) to 100 (perfect inequality – when all income goes to only one person). The higher the figure, the more unequal a country is. In Britain in 1979, the Gini coefficient was 25.3, and in 2017–18, it was 34. There was a particularly large increase between 1979 and 1991, and inequality in 2017–18 was 34 per cent higher than it was in 1979.

*Source*: adapted from *Living Standards, Inequality and Poverty Spreadsheet*. Institute for Fiscal Studies, 2019, and *Households Below Average Income*, Department for Work and Pensions, 2019

## SOCIAL INEQUALITY AS A SOCIAL ISSUE

Social inequality is an important social issue. For example, in societies where there are the widest inequalities, particularly inequalities in income, compared to more equal societies:

- there is less social cohesion – community life is weaker and there is less trust between people
- people are more likely to be depressed and suffer from mental illness
- there is more obesity
- people are imprisoned more, and get harsher prison sentences, if they commit crime.

While these disadvantages affect the poorest people the most, they also affect the rich. For example, the richest people in more equal societies have higher literacy levels than those who are similarly rich in more unequal societies, who also live shorter lives and are more likely to have their children die in their first twelve months of life. Inequality, then, seems to have harmful consequences for all, and not just for those who are poor.

### Activity

Refer to figure 6.1 on page 369.

1  Between which years was there the sharpest increase in inequality in Britain?
2  In what year was inequality at its highest compared to 1979?
3  Much of the evidence in the paragraphs above comes from the Equality Trust, and more detail and explanation on the differences between less equal and more equal societies can be found at www.equalitytrust.org.uk.

   Go to this website and explore (use Search) how inequality influences two of the following issues, and see if you can find explanations for how inequality causes the issues identified: physical health; mental health; drug abuse; education; imprisonment; obesity; social mobility; trust and community life; violence; teenage births; and child well-being.
4  Make a list of what you consider to be the most important inequalities in society today. Explain in all cases why you think they are important in people's lives and how they affect the chances people get in life.

Much of this book, and particularly this chapter, is concerned with describing and explaining a range of these inequalities.

## WHAT IS SOCIAL STRATIFICATION?

Inequality affects not simply individuals, but whole groups of people, and such patterns of inequality between social groups are called **social stratification**.

The word 'stratification' comes from *strata* or layers, as in the way different types of rock are piled on top of one another to form rock strata.

Social stratification refers to the division of society into a pattern of layers or strata made up of a hierarchy of unequal social groups. These stand in relations of advantage and disadvantage to one another in terms of features such as income, wealth, **occupational status** (see glossary box), religion, race, age or sex, depending on the stratification system. Those at the top of the stratification hierarchy will generally have more power in society and better life chances – such as educational success, good-quality housing, better health, longer holidays, and more secure and better-paid jobs – than those at the bottom.

> **Social stratification** The division of society into a hierarchy of unequal social groups.

> **Occupational status** The ranking of occupations based on the amount of status or social standing (admiration and respect) in society attached to a job, usually based on factors such as its power, income and the training and educational qualifications required. Sometimes referred to as socioeconomic status.

A stratification hierarchy

## SYSTEMS OF STRATIFICATION

Sociologists have identified four major types of stratification system, which have important differences between them: slavery, the caste system, feudal estates and social class.

### Slavery

**Slavery** is a form of stratification in which a group of people are held against their will, regarded as the property of others, controlled by their owners, forced to work, and bought or sold like any other possession.

Typical examples included Ancient Rome, Europe for over 400 years from the mid fifteenth century, and what is now the United States of America from the seventeenth to nineteenth centuries, with the enslavement of millions of Africans through the transatlantic slave trade.

Although slavery is now banned in all countries by a series of international laws and treaties, and was abolished in the British Empire and the USA in the nineteenth century, slavery conditions are still found for millions of people today, including children, through human trafficking (illegal international trading in people) for forced labour or sex work in developed countries, and slave-like working conditions in less-developed countries. You can read more about contemporary slavery at www.iabolish.org, www.freetheslaves.net and www.antislavery.org.

**Slavery** A stratification system in which some people are regarded as the property of others.

## The caste system

The **caste system** is the most rigid system of stratification and is associated with India.

- The levels of the social hierarchy are called castes.
- This hierarchy is fixed and clearly defined.
- The social position of individuals is ascribed at birth in accordance with Hindu religious beliefs and customs. Hindus believe in reincarnation – that people are born again after death. Hinduism suggests that people's behaviour in their previous life will decide the caste they are born into after rebirth. Since people believe the social position they are born into (their caste) is god-given, they generally accept their ascribed caste position.
- A caste society is a **closed society**, with no **social mobility** (movement up or down) possible from one caste to another. Each caste is completely closed off from others by religious rules and restrictions, which ensure that very little social contact occurs between members of different castes. The purity of each caste is maintained by **endogamy**. This means that marriage is only permitted to a person of the same caste. Besides the choice of marriage partner, caste membership also determines social status and occupation.

In the Indian caste system, the Hindu religion divides the population into five major castes, shown in figure 6.2

**Caste system**
A stratification system based on Hindu religious beliefs, in which an individual's position is fixed at birth and cannot be changed.

**Closed society** A stratification system in which no social mobility is possible.

**Social mobility**
The movement of groups or individuals up or down the social hierarchy.

**Endogamy** is where marriage must be to a partner of the same kinship or social group.

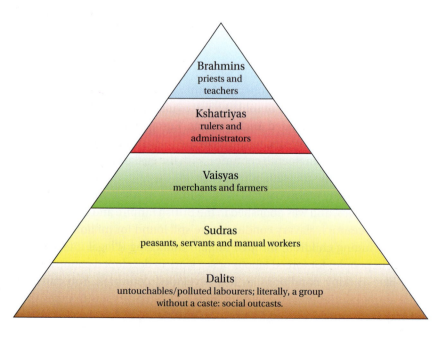

**Figure 6.2** The Hindu caste system

Brahmins
priests and teachers

Kshatriyas
rulers and administrators

Vaisyas
merchants and farmers

Sudras
peasants, servants and manual workers

Dalits
untouchables/polluted labourers; literally, a group without a caste: social outcasts.

Despite attempts by the Indian government to remove the inequalities of the caste system, the system still continues, as many people still accept the Hindu religious beliefs on which it is based.

It has been suggested that the apartheid regime in South Africa, which was only abolished in the 1990s, showed some similarities with the caste system. Here people were stratified according to ascribed racial characteristics (white, coloured, and Bantu or black populations), with legal restrictions on mixing/marriage between different races, and with an almost 'religious' ideology of white supremacy.

## Feudal estates

**Feudalism**
A closed system of stratification based on land ownership and legal inequalities.

**Feudalism** was typically found in medieval Europe.

- The levels of the social hierarchy were called estates, and based on ownership of land.
- There was no legal equality between estates, and people in higher estates had more legal rights and privileges than those in lower ones.
- The lower estates had obligations and duties to those higher up the hierarchy, which were backed up by laws. For example, there was an obligation for serfs to work one day a week on the master's land.
- Membership of any estate was determined largely by birth, with social position, power and status all ascribed at birth.
- Feudalism was, like the caste system, a closed society, with social mobility from one estate to another extremely limited. However, some upward mobility to a higher estate was possible, for example through gifts of land as a reward for outstanding military service.
- In general, estates were preserved by endogamy, and inter-marriage was only rarely allowed between individuals of different estates.

The feudal system of stratification looked something like the diagram in figure 6.3.

## Social class

**Social class** (or *socio-economic class*)
An open system of stratification consisting of broad groups of people (classes) who share a similar social and economic situation, such as occupation, income and ownership of wealth.

**Social class**, sometimes referred to as *socio-economic class*, is the form of stratification found in industrial societies, such as contemporary Britain.

Social classes can be defined as broad groups of people who share a similar economic situation, such as occupation, income and ownership of wealth. Often, these criteria are closely related to each other and to other aspects of individuals' lives, such as their level of education, their status and lifestyle (for example, housing, car ownership and leisure activities), and how much power and influence they have in society.

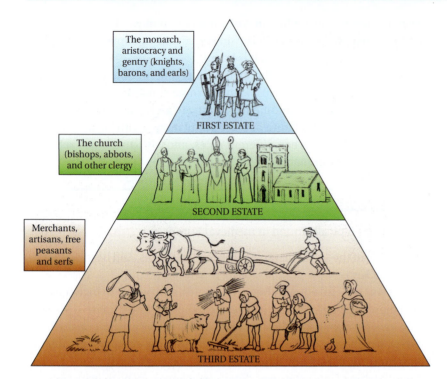

The monarch, aristocracy and gentry (knights, barons, and earls)

FIRST ESTATE

The church (bishops, abbots, and other clergy

SECOND ESTATE

Merchants, artisans, free peasants and serfs

THIRD ESTATE

**Figure 6.3** The feudal hierarchy

The main differences between the social-class system and slavery, the caste and feudal systems are:

- Social class is based not on ownership of people as property, religion or law, but mainly on economic criteria such as occupation, wealth and income.
- The levels of the social hierarchy (social classes) are not clearly separated from one another: the divisions between social classes are frequently quite vague – it is hard to say, for example, where the working class ends and the middle class begins.
- Social-class differences are not backed up by legal differences. All members of society, in theory, have equal legal rights, and those in higher social classes do not have legal authority over those in lower classes.
- There are no legal or religious restrictions on inter-marriage between people of different social classes. In theory, people can marry whom they like; in practice, people tend to marry someone in their own social class.
- Social-class societies are **open societies**. There are no legal or religious restrictions on the movement of individuals from one social class to another, and social mobility is possible.
- The social-class system is generally meritocratic, in which social positions are generally achieved by merit – such as educational

**Open society** A stratification system in which social mobility is possible.

'Look, don't identify me by the size and shape of my body, my social class, my job, my gender, my ethnicity, my sexuality, my nationality, my age, my religion, my education, my friends, my lifestyle, how much money I earn, the clothes I wear, the books I read, where I go shopping, the way I decorate my house, the television programmes and films I watch, my leisure and sports activities, the car I drive, the music I listen to, the drinks I like, the food I eat, the clubs I go to, where I go on holiday, the way I speak or my accent, the things I say, the things I do, or what I believe in. I'm just me. OK?

### Activity

1  If you were trying to decide a person's social class, what features would you take into account? Refer to the cartoon above, and list the issues that are mentioned there and any others you can think of.
2  Now put your list into order of importance, with the most important features first. Explain why you have put them in that order.

qualifications, talent and skill – rather than ascribed from birth. However, the social class of the family into which a child is born can have an important effect on his or her life chances. Entry into the upper class is still mainly through inherited wealth, and therefore social positions here remain largely ascribed rather than achieved.

## SOCIAL-CLASS STRATIFICATION AND INEQUALITY

In the last activity, you listed the most important features that you would take into account in deciding a person's social class. The features you think important, though, may not be the same as those chosen by others. A similar dispute exists among sociologists. While most sociologists would agree that social classes consist of groups of people who share a similar economic situation, there are different views regarding exactly which aspect of that economic situation is the most important in defining a person's social class. The following discussion deals with four of the most common definitions and explanations of social-class inequality that are used by sociologists: the consensus view of the functionalists, the conflict views of Marx and Weber, and the definition of class by a person's occupation.

## The consensus view of stratification and social class: the functionalist theory of stratification

Writing from a functionalist perspective, Davis and Moore (1967 [1945]) argued that social stratification was a 'universal necessity' for every known human society, and it was generally a good thing offering society benefits. They believe that social-class inequalities are necessary for society to survive and operate efficiently because:

- All social roles (occupations) must be filled by those best able to perform them.
- Some jobs are more important than others in maintaining society.
- These jobs will require specialized skills needing more talent or training.
- Not everyone has the talents and/or ability, or is prepared to undergo the necessary training, to do these jobs.
- Those who do have the ability and talent must be encouraged to make the necessary sacrifices (e.g. low pay during education and training) to train for these important positions with the promise of future high rewards in terms of income, wealth, status and power.
- There must therefore be a system of unequal rewards to make sure the most able and ambitious people compete for, and are matched to, the most important social positions that require the highest levels of skill and/or the greatest responsibility to direct and organize others.

### *Strengths and limitations of Davis and Moore's functionalist theory*

✓ It provides a general explanation for why so many societies are stratified.

✗ It assumes society is purely meritocratic, with the most talented rising to the most important positions. But inequality of opportunity in unequal societies prevents disadvantaged individuals from developing their talents and skill (as seen in the education chapter). The system of stratification itself prevents the pool of talent being larger.

✗ It is questionable whether many of those at the top got there by talent – it could be because of luck, inheritance or the influence of social and family background.

✗ It is hard to identify which occupations are more important in maintaining society. There are many poorly rewarded occupations which can still be seen as vital to maintaining society. For example, are highly paid entertainers or footballers more important in maintaining society than nurses, teachers or bus or ambulance drivers?

✗ Not everyone in some of the vital jobs is motivated to do them by higher rewards. No-one goes into teaching and nursing for the money, for example – they do it for reasons of job satisfaction and concern for the welfare of others.

✗ It makes people at the bottom feel less important to society, thus giving them less motivation to participate in society or seek to improve themselves.

✗ Inequality can be a cause of hostility and conflict between people, as those at the bottom resent the wealth, power and superior life chances of those at the top.

✗ Inequality can have a bad effect on society. For example, the more unequal a society is, the more it suffers from social ills such as increased crime, ill health and social disharmony.

---

### Activity

1  Identify and describe one example of the way not everyone has the same chance of developing their talents and skills in society.
2  Write a short essay (10–15 minutes) answering the following question: 'How far do you agree with the view that inequality is necessary to ensure that society works properly for the benefit of everyone?'

---

## Conflict views of stratification and social class (1): the Marxist theory of social class

**Means of production** The key resources like land, labour, raw materials, property, factories, businesses and machinery which are necessary for producing society's goods.

Much sociological discussion about social class has been influenced by the writings of Karl Marx. Marx saw social stratification as a system which allows a privileged few to exploit the many. For Marx, an individual's social class was defined by whether or not she or he owned the **means of production** – the key resources like land, labour, raw materials, property, factories, businesses and machinery which are necessary to produce society's goods. The main explanation for social-class inequalities lies in the private ownership of the means of production in the hands of a small upper class. This brought to their owners an unearned income in the form of profit, and laid the basis for inequalities in wealth and income.

## Bourgeoisie and proletariat

Marx argued there were two basic social classes in capitalist industrial society:

- the bourgeoisie or capitalists – the small but wealthy and powerful class of owners of the means of production.
- the proletariat or working class – the much larger, poorer class of non-owners, who sell their labour to the owners for wages in order to live.

## The petty bourgeoisie

There was a third class of small, often self-employed, business owners between the bourgeoisie and proletariat. Marx called this class the **petty bourgeoisie** (or small bourgeoisie). He thought that eventually this class would disappear as it would be squeezed out between the other two classes. Members of this class would either eventually succeed and grow rich, and join the bourgeoisie, or they would be bankrupted by competition, and join the proletariat. This is like a small shopkeeper growing into a large supermarket chain, which then drives all the other small shopkeepers out of business, who then have to go and look for work in (possibly) the supermarket that drove them out of business in the first place.

> **Petty bourgeoisie**
> A social class of small-business owners, squeezed between the bourgeoisie and proletariat.

## Exploitation

The proletariat, since they owned no means of production, had no alternative means of obtaining a livelihood but working for the bourgeoisie. The bourgeoisie exploited the proletariat, making profits out of them by keeping wages low and paying them as little as possible, instead of giving them the full payment for their work. The relationship between these two classes is exploitative because the workers produce more than is needed for employers to pay their wages. For example, in a burger chain in contemporary

According to Marx, society is split into two groups or classes: those who own the means of production (e.g. a developer with money to buy land to convert into expensive new commercial buildings) and those who work for wages (e.g. builders and construction workers). The builders are paid a fixed wage by the developer on whom they rely for their income, but the developer stands to make large profits out of the labour of employees.

society, it is the workers who make, cook, package and serve the burgers, but only half the burgers they sell are necessary to cover production costs and pay their wages. The rest of the burgers provide profit for the owners of the burger chain. This means the workers who produce the burgers do not get the full value of their work, and they are therefore being exploited.

## The ruling class

According to Marx, political power – who rules – in society is rooted in owner-ship and control of the means of production. The class of owners was therefore also a ruling class. For example, because they owned the means of production, the bourgeoisie could decide where factories should be located and whether they should be opened or closed down, and they could control the workforce through hiring and firing. Marx believed the state, through institutions like the law, the police and the criminal justice system, was fundamentally con-cerned not with protecting everyone, but with protecting the interests of the ruling class. Democratically elected governments could not afford to ignore the power of the bourgeoisie, otherwise they might face rising unemployment and other social problems if the bourgeoisie decided not to invest its money.

## The ruling ideas

The ruling ideas in society – the dominant ideology, which Marx called **ruling-class ideology** – were those of the owning class, and the major institu-tions in society reflected these ideas.

> **Ruling-class ideology** The ideas and beliefs of the dominant class which controls society.

For example:

- the laws protected the owning class rather than the workers – laws are made and strictly enforced to make it difficult for workers to go on strike, but the state is reluctant to pass or enforce laws against such things as pollution, for workers' rights and their health and safety, and against low pay, or other things that might harm the interests of big business
- religion acted as the 'opium of the people', persuading the proletariat to accept their position as just and natural (rather than rebelling against it), by promising future rewards in heaven for putting up with their present suffering
- the education system teaches the myth of meritocracy – it's a fair system and anyone with ability can make it to the top
- the bourgeoisie's ownership of the media meant only their ideas were put forward in the media (e.g. in newspapers, on TV), and kept out ideas harmful to their interests.

In these ways, the working-class were almost brainwashed into accept-ing their position, and persuaded to have a positive image of capitalism as normal and fair. They failed to recognize they were being exploited and therefore did not rebel against the bourgeoisie, because they thought their

A Marxist view of false consciousness and class consciousness

position was 'natural' and they could see no alternative to it. Marx called this lack of awareness of their own interests among the proletariat **false class consciousness** (or simply, 'false consciousness').

## *Exploitation, class conflict and revolution*

Marx argued capitalist society was by its very nature unstable, as at its heart lay a basic conflict of interest between the workers whose labour is exploited and the capitalists who exploit that labour. Marx predicted that growing **economic inequality** – an ever-larger wealth gap – between the working class (or proletariat) and the capitalist class (the bourgeoisie) would mean the differences between the classes would become larger and more extreme. Society would become polarized (divided) into two major social classes: a small, wealthy and powerful bourgeoisie and a large, relatively much poorer, exploited proletariat.

Growing inequality and growing awareness by the working class of their exploitation would eventually lead, Marx believed, to major class conflict – **class struggle** – between the proletariat and the bourgeoisie. He saw this class struggle as the driving force for social change. The proletariat would struggle against the bourgeoisie through strikes, demonstrations and other forms of protest. The proletariat would then develop **class consciousness** – an awareness of their common working-class interests and their exploitation – until eventually they would make a socialist revolution and overthrow the bourgeoisie.

## *Communism*

After the revolution, the proletariat would nationalize the means of production (which were formerly the private property of the bourgeoisie) by putting

**False class consciousness** A failure by members of a social class to recognize their real interests.

**Economic inequality** The differences in all those material things that affect the lives of individuals, such as their wealth, their income and the hours they work.

**Class struggle** Conflict and struggle between the two major social classes in capitalist society – the bourgeoisie (capitalist class) and the proletariat (the working class).

**Class consciousness** An awareness in members of a social class of their real interests.

**Figure 6.4** A summary of the Marxist view of social class

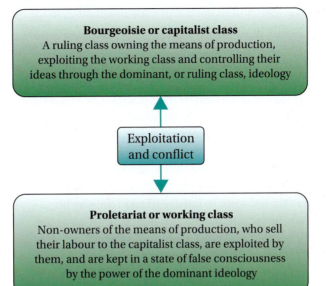

**Bourgeoisie or capitalist class**
A ruling class owning the means of production, exploiting the working class and controlling their ideas through the dominant, or ruling class, ideology

Exploitation and conflict

**Proletariat or working class**
Non-owners of the means of production, who sell their labour to the capitalist class, are exploited by them, and are kept in a state of false consciousness by the power of the dominant ideology

them in the hands of the state. The means of production would therefore be collectively owned and run in the interests of everyone, not just of the bourgeoisie. Capitalism would be destroyed and a new type of society would be created, which would be without exploitation, without classes, and without class conflict. This equal, classless society Marx called **Communism**.

**Communism**
An equal society, without social classes or conflict, in which the means of production are the shared property of all.

## The strengths and limitations of Marx's theory of class

✓ It explains the source of many conflicts and upheavals that periodically surface, many of which are rooted in social-class inequalities.

✓ There is still evidence of opposing class interests and class conflict, such as strikes and industrial sabotage in the workplace; there are growing numbers of exploited part-time, under-employed and temporary workers; and British Social Attitudes has reported that around 75 per cent of the population of modern Britain still believe that society is pyramid-shaped, with a wide divide between a large disadvantaged group at the bottom and a small privileged elite at the top, with conflict between them.

✓ The means of production remain mostly privately owned in the hands of a small minority of the population. In contemporary societies across the globe, there are still great social inequalities of wealth, income, power and life chances, and widespread poverty. In Britain in 2017/18, for example, the richest fifth (20 per cent) of the population owned about 64 per cent of the wealth, compared to nothing for the poorest fifth; and about 22 per cent of the population (14 million people) and over four million children were living in poverty, according to the government's own official statistics.

✓ There remains much evidence of major social-class inequalities in life chances, such as in health, housing, levels of educational achievement and job security.

✓ The owners of the means of production still have much more power and influence than the majority. For example, the major positions in the state, industry and banking are held by the privileged rich who have attended public schools (see pages 240–3), and they own the media, which pump out ideas favouring their interests.

✗ The revolution Marx predicted has not happened in Britain or any of the Western industrialized societies. While many of the class inequalities and conflicts which Marx identified remain, the Communist solutions he proposed do not seem to have worked in the way he foresaw. In those countries where revolutions did occur (such as the former USSR, of which Russia was part), Communism did not succeed in creating an equal society, and there emerged a new ruling class of people who were better-off than the majority. From 1989 onwards, a major wave of popular revolts shook Eastern Europe and the USSR, and swept away the former Communist regimes. There is now no Communist country left in Europe, and only five in the entire world (including China), in many of which large sections of the population are in poverty.

✗ While great inequalities in wealth and income continue to exist, the working class has not got poorer as Marx predicted. Living standards, such as in housing, health and education, are much improved since Marx's day. The welfare state has given the working-class a safety net guaranteeing them a minimum income and health protection, and compulsory state education provides more chances – though still limited – of upward social mobility.

✗ Marx suggested only the two opposing classes of bourgeoisie and proletariat would emerge. This approach does not easily explain the wide inequalities that exist between those people who do not own the means of production. The past century has seen the emergence of a new middle class of professionals, managers and office workers between the bourgeoisie and proletariat. While these groups do not own the means of production, they benefit from exercising authority on behalf of the bourgeoisie and have higher status, better income, and better life chances than the working class. They generally have no interest in overthrowing the bourgeoisie.

✗ Functionalists suggest the Marxist view over-emphasizes social class as a source of inequality and conflict. They point out that society is basically stable, and there is relative consensus on many issues.

✗ It pays little attention to other sources of inequality and conflict, such as ethnicity, age and – as feminists emphasize – gender.

---

**Activity**

1 Explain two ways in which the bourgeoisie are able to rule society in their own interests and maintain their wealth and power.
2 Write a short essay (10–15 minutes) answering the following question: 'How far do you agree that the Marxist view of social class is old-fashioned and out-of-date, and can no longer be applied in today's society?'
3 Imagine you were going to carry out a survey, using a large representative sample, into people's attitudes to social class, inequality and conflict. Identify and explain:
   (a) one way you might obtain your sample
   (b) the research method you would use to collect your information, and why you think this would be the best method.

---

## Conflict views of stratification and social class (2): Weber's theory of stratification

Those following Weber's ideas are known as Weberians. Max Weber (1947), who lived between 1864 and 1920, suggested that stratification is somewhat more complicated than Marx indicated. Weber criticized Marx for concentrating only on economically based class inequality and conflict. He argued that society was stratified in three ways, which could each be a source of conflict:

- *by social class* – into socio-economic groups sharing a similar **market situation** (see below)
- *by status* – into groups sharing a similar social standing or status (esteem in the eyes of others), e.g. gender and ethnicity
- *by party* – into groups that have or try to influence political power and decision-making.

### The Weberian view of social class

Weber agreed with Marx that ownership or non-ownership of the means of production was important in creating social class differences and conflicts between classes. However, Weber suggested that social class should be based on a broader basis than Marx's definition. Weber defined social classes as groups of people who share a similar market situation, giving them similar life chances. 'Market situation' simply refers to the incomes that people are able to get when they sell their abilities and skills in the job market, and differences between these socio-economic groups create inequality and conflict. Some may have a better market situation than others because:

- they have rare skills, talents or qualifications that are in demand – such as doctors, lawyers or Premier League footballers.

**Market situation**
The rewards that people are able to obtain when they compete to sell their skills in the labour market, depending on the scarcity of their skills, the demand for them, and the power they have to obtain high rewards.

**Party** Any group which is concerned with holding power, making decisions and influencing policies in the interests of its membership.

- society values some skills and talents more highly than others and rewards them accordingly, as might be the case with footballers, film and music stars and other celebrities, or with some business executives or company owners.
- some groups have more power to control the rewards they get. For example, some professions have the power to limit who can practise in their fields of work, such as doctors and lawyers, and this can increase their incomes by keeping their skills scarce and valued.

Weber rejected Marx's idea of the polarization of classes into two extremes (the bourgeoisie and proletariat). Weber predicted the groups between the bourgeoisie and proletariat – the middle classes – would expand and grow. He argued there were important differences in the market situations of those who did not own or control the means of production, and that there were many social classes with different market situations, rather than just the two Marx identified.

## Social class and status groups

An individual's social class and status are often closely linked, and a member of a high social class will usually have high status in society as well. This is because the amount of social respect individuals get is often influenced by the same factors as their social class – their wealth, their income and their occupation. But social class and status do not always coincide. For example, religious leaders, such as vicars, priests, rabbis and imams, often earn relatively little money, but are usually given high status by the general public.

While an individual can only belong to one social class, he or she may have several statuses. Links between status and class are shown by the following examples:

- a person with a low-status, working-class job such as a refuse collector may achieve high status as a local magistrate
- black and white male workers may have a similar class by doing the same job, but be divided by the status difference of ethnicity
- women and men may be in the same social class, but women may be given fewer promotion chances simply because employers regard them as of lower status than men
- women may be in different social classes, but still united across classes by their shared status of gender.

Weber therefore thought that, to fully understand social inequality and social conflict, it was also necessary to look at status differences between people as well as their economic position. Status characteristics such as gender, religion, age and ethnicity can all create conflicts between people, regardless of their wealth and income. For example, there are conflicts between

**Status group** A group of people who share a similar social standing (status) and lifestyle in any society.

**status groups** – groups who share some similar status characteristics – such as between men and women; religious groups, such as Protestant and Catholic in Northern Ireland; young people and older people; and between black and white people.

For Weber, therefore, society was divided by conflict between many competing social classes and status groups, rather than just the two social classes Marx considered.

## Parties

Weber rejected the Marxist view that political power was held only by a ruling class owning the means of production.

Weber argued power could be more widely spread among a range of classes, status groups and parties. A party is any group which is specifically concerned with exercising power, making decisions and influencing policies in the interests of their membership. Parties might be linked to a social class (for example, the Conservative Party generally represents the interests of the upper and middle classes, and the Labour Party the working class) or to a status group (e.g. women's/feminist movements represent the interests of women). Or, like the Green Party (www.greenparty.org.uk), they may not be linked to either class or status.

**Pressure group** Any organization that tries to put pressure on those with power in society to implement policies which favour the interests of its membership.

Parties are not identical with only the political parties such as the Labour or Conservative parties, but can include any groups concerned with influencing decision-making. For example, Age UK is a **pressure group** – a form of party – that aims to put pressure on those with power in society to implement policies which protect the interests of older people. There are also **social movements** in which large groups of people, regardless of their class or status, unite around the desire to promote, or block, a broad set of social changes in society, such as around issues like the environment, animal welfare or world peace – e.g. 38 Degrees (https://home.38degrees.org.uk) or Greenpeace (www.greenpeace.org.uk).

Weber then, did not see the relationship between class, status and parties as simple and clear-cut, and party membership could cut across and unite or divide classes and status groups.

**Social movement** A broad movement of people who are united around the desire to promote, or block, a broad set of social changes in society. Unlike political parties or pressure groups, they are often only informally organized through a network of small, independent, locally based groups.

## The strengths and limitations of Weber's view of stratification

✓ It provides a more realistic picture of the stratification system than Marx's, as it recognizes the importance of differences between those who are not owners of the means of production.

✓ It provides the basis for many systems used by governments to classify populations by socio-economic group.

✓ It recognizes that power, inequality and conflict are not only based on economic issues (social class) but can also be based on status groups and parties.

✓ Unlike Marxism and functionalism, Weber's theory can be used to explain stratification and conflicts between status groups, such as those based on gender, ethnicity and age.

✗ Weber's idea of market situation does not easily explain the position of those who inherit their wealth and do not sell any skills in the labour market, as they live on unearned incomes rather than those earned through employment.

✗ It underestimates the power of the ruling class with which Marx was concerned. In most cases, those with the most power in society are those belonging to the highest social classes and status groups, and the most successful parties tend to be those which least threaten the interests of the ruling class.

## Defining class by occupation

Occupation or socio-economic group is the most common indicator of social class used by governments, by advertising agencies when doing market research, and by sociologists when doing surveys. This is because occupation is:

- an easy piece of information to obtain from people
- generally a good guide to people's skills, qualifications, their income, their lifestyle, their health and other life chances, and other important aspects of their lives
- a major factor influencing people's power and status in society, and most people judge the social standing of themselves and others by the jobs they do.

There is a wide range of occupational scales in use, but two of the best-known and most widely used ways of grading occupations into socio-economic classes are the National Statistics Socio-Economic Classification (NS-SEC), shown in table 6.1, and the Institute of Practitioners in Advertising (IPA) Scale (table 6.2). The NS-SEC is used for all official statistics and surveys, and the IPA Scale is widely used in market research and many surveys, including opinion polls. Tables 6.1 and 6.2 include references to what percentage of the population over 16 belong to each of these classes, and what these classes roughly refer to in the everyday language used by sociologists: the middle-class and working-class categories found in this book.

- *Middle-class occupations* are generally non-manual, with people working primarily in offices, doing mainly mental rather than physical work. The term **white-collar workers** is sometimes used to refer to lower-middle-class clerical and sales occupations.
- *Working-class occupations* are mainly manual (literally, people using their hands), with the jobs requiring primarily physical effort and skill.

**White-collar workers** Non-manual clerical workers, sales personnel and other office workers whose work is non-professional and non-managerial.

## Table 6.1 The National Statistics Socio-Economic Classification (NS-SEC)

This occupational scale is based upon occupational status and security of income, prospects of economic advancement (promotion), and the amount of authority and control at work.

| Social Class | Percentage of population (aged 16–74) (2011 census) | Commonly called | Examples of occupations |
|---|---|---|---|
| **Class 1** <br> Higher managerial and professional occupations | 10 | Upper middle class; class 1 | Large employer; higher manager; company director; senior officers in police, fire and prison services and military; newspaper editor; football manager; doctor; solicitor; engineer; teacher; airline pilot |
| **Class 2** <br> Lower managerial and professional occupations | 21 | Middle class; class 2 | Journalist; nurse/midwife; actor; musician; junior police officer (constable); lower manager |
| **Class 3** <br> Intermediate occupations | 13 | Lower middle class; class 3 (non-manual) | Secretary; air stewardess; driving instructor; footballer; telephone operator |
| **Class 4** <br> Small employers and own-account (self-employed) workers | 9 | Self-employed | Small employer/manager; self-employed publican; plumber |
| **Class 5** <br> Lower supervisory and technical occupations | 7 | Upper working class; skilled manual workers; class 3 (manual) | Lower supervisor; electrician; mechanic; train driver; bus inspector |
| **Class 6** <br> Semi-routine occupations | 14 | Working class; semi-skilled manual workers | Traffic warden; caretaker; gardener; supermarket shelf-stacker; assembly-line worker; shop assistant |
| **Class 7** <br> Routine occupations | 11 | Lower working class; unskilled manual workers; class 5 | Cleaner; waiter/waitress; bar staff; road worker |
| **Class 8** <br> Never worked and long-term unemployed | 6 | The poor, and sometimes the underclass | Long-term unemployed; long-term sick; never worked |
| Full-time students | 9 | | In the NS-SEC classification, all full-time students are recorded in the 'full-time students' category whether or not they are looking for work. |

## Table 6.2 The Institute of Practitioners in Advertising (IPA) Scale

Advertisers are mainly interested in selling things to people, so their scale ranks occupations primarily on the basis of income. They obviously want to know how much money people have so they can target their advertising at the right people. This scale is very widely used in surveys of all kinds.

| Social class | Percentage of population (2016) | Commonly called | Examples of occupations |
|---|---|---|---|
| **Class A**<br><br>Higher managerial, administrative or professional occupations | 4 | Upper middle class | Judges; solicitors; senior civil servants; surgeons; senior managers (in large companies); accountants; architects |
| **Class B**<br><br>Intermediate managerial, administrative or professional occupations | 23 | Middle class | Airline pilots; MPs; teachers; social workers; middle managers; police inspectors |
| **Class C1**<br><br>Supervisory or clerical and junior managerial, administrative or professional occupations | 28 | Lower middle class | Clerical workers; computer operators; receptionists; sales assistants; secretaries; nurses; technicians |
| **Class C2**<br><br>Skilled manual workers | 20 | Upper working class | Carpenters; bricklayers; electricians; chefs/cooks; plumbers |
| **Class D**<br><br>Semi-skilled and unskilled manual workers | 15 | Lower working class | Postal workers; bar workers; office cleaners; road sweepers; machine minders; farm labourers |
| **Class E**<br><br>Those on the lowest levels of income | 10 | The poor | State pensioners (on state pensions); casual and lowest-grade workers; unemployed on state benefits only, and others on income support and the lowest levels of income |

## Activity

Owner of small family bakery

Dentist

Road sweeper

Housewife/homemaker

Shop assistant

Sociology lecturer

Postal worker

Car mechanic

Bus driver

Fire fighter

Member of Parliament (MP)

Nurse

1. List all the ways you can think of in which people's occupations might affect other aspects of their lives, such as family life, status, housing, health, leisure activities, beliefs and values, future planning and so on. Make sure you explain precisely how the effects you mention are linked to a person's job.
2. Look at the twelve occupations shown in the pictures, and refer also to the occupational scales above. Rank the pictures 1–12 in four lists in order of: (a) pay, (b) status in society, (c) power, (d) class, numbering them 1–12, beginning with 1 as the highest. Give reasons for your rankings.
3. Do you think the gender or ethnicity of those doing any of these jobs might influence the pay, status or power that is given to the jobs? Explain your answer, with examples of particular jobs.

## Problems with using occupation to measure class

While occupation is very commonly used to define social class, the use of occupation and occupational scales presents a number of problems for the sociologist:

- The use of occupation excludes the wealthy upper class, who own property and have a great deal of power but often don't have an occupation. Occupational scales therefore do not reveal major differences in wealth and income within and between social classes.
- Groups outside paid employment are excluded, such as homemakers (housewives and househusbands) and the never-employed unemployed. Housework is not recognized as an occupation.
- Social class is based primarily on the occupation of the highest-earning member of the household, but the use of a single head of household may ignore dual-earner families, where both partners are working in paid employment. Such families have much better life chances than single-income households in the same class. Their combined incomes might even give them the lifestyle of a higher social class.
- The classes on occupational scales tend to be very broad, and disguise major differences within each class. For example, a grouping like 'professionals' may include both poorly paid junior NHS doctors and rich Harley Street private specialists. There are major differences in income and life chances between such people, yet they are placed in the same class.

## Changes in the class structure

### The changing occupational structure

At the beginning of the twentieth century, the majority of people in Britain were working in manual working-class occupations, with less than a quarter being considered upper or middle class. However, in the last 100 years, changes in the economy have occurred which have altered the occupational structure. The non-manual middle class is now larger than the manual working class, although many so-called middle-class jobs are low-level and routine, and not much different from manual jobs in pay and terms and conditions of employment. These changes include:

- *A growth in the tertiary sector of the economy.* This is concerned with the provision of services, such as administration, sales, finance and insurance, transport, distribution, and the running of government services (like the welfare state and education). This has created more middle-class jobs, particularly routine, low-level, non-manual jobs.

- *A decline in semi-skilled and unskilled manual work*, as technology takes over these tasks, and creates more skilled jobs.
- *A steady increase in the percentage of the workforce engaged in non-manual occupations*, especially occupations such as routine clerical work and customer service work, as in call centres.
- *An increase in professional occupations*, like teaching and social work.
- *The emergence of the precariat* – a new highly insecure section of the workforce (see the box on page 395).
- *The emergence of what some people regard as an underclass* of long-term unemployed, and other groups who are excluded by their poverty from full participation in society. The controversial idea of the **underclass** is discussed later in this chapter (see pages 486–9).

**Underclass** A social group who are right at the bottom of the social class hierarchy, who are in some ways cut off or excluded from the rest of society.

These developments have led to a change in the shape of the social structure, with unskilled and semi-skilled manual occupational groups getting smaller, and skilled manual and lower-middle-class occupational groups getting larger. As shown in figure 6.5, the social structure has changed from the pyramid shape that existed about a century ago to the shape of a diamond.

## The class structure of Britain

Often, when talking of social class, sociologists will refer to terms quite loosely. Tables 6.1 and 6.2 illustrate which groups of occupations are generally being referred to when particular social classes in contemporary Britain are mentioned. Note that the main division between working-class and middle-class is generally accepted as being that between manual and non-manual occupations.

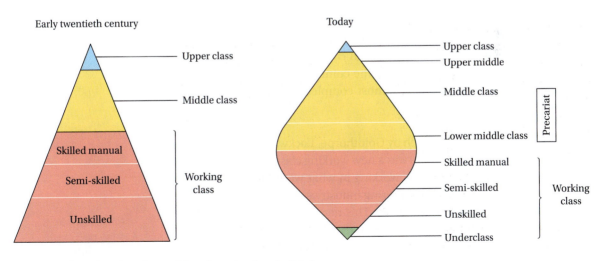

**Figure 6.5** The changing shape of the class structure in Britain

**Activity**

1  What social class do you think you belong to? Give reasons for your answer.
2  Think of all the differences you can between social classes in modern Britain. How would you explain the class differences you have identified?
3  Conduct a survey among people you know, to explore how they see social class.
   (a) Identify a suitable research method (interviews, self-completion structured questionnaires, etc.) and explain two reasons for your choice of this method.
   Find out:
   (b) which social classes they think exist in contemporary Britain.
   (c) which social class they would personally put themselves (or their parents) in.
   (d) their reasons for choosing that class.
   (e) if you're in a group, bring all your results together, and discuss any differences in how people view social class, and any difficulties you found in carrying out the research.

## The changing and declining working class: the traditional and new working classes

*The traditional working class*  The main section of the working class in Britain up to the mid twentieth century was what was commonly called the traditional working class. This was found mainly in the north of England, south Wales and Scotland, in traditional (long-established) basic industries, such as coal mining, docking, iron and steel, and shipbuilding. People worked in the same industry generation after generation and often lived in social (council) or other rented housing near one another and near the place of work. There was, as a result, a close-knit community living and working together, with high levels of involvement in community life, class solidarity and mutual support. These industries, the communities around them and the traditional working class have almost completely disappeared in contemporary Britain.

*The new working class*  Research by Goldthorpe, Lockwood and colleagues in Luton in the 1960s found there was a new working class emerging, initially in the south of England. This was working in what were then newer, more technologically advanced, manufacturing industries, such as the production of cars, electrical goods and chemicals. This new working class had greatly improved pay and living standards compared to the traditional working class, even exceeding those of some of the middle class. These highly paid manual workers, or **affluent workers** as they were commonly described, could afford

**Affluent workers**
Highly paid manual workers.

The traditional working class has almost completely disappeared in contemporary Britain

to buy their own homes and lived a privatized, home-centred family lifestyle, with little involvement with neighbours or the wider community. They lived in what were formerly regarded as middle-class areas, and were able to buy the consumer goods which previously only the middle class could afford.

This gave rise to the idea of **embourgeoisement** – that the upper working class was becoming more like, or merging with, the lower middle class and adopting similar norms and values.

Goldthorpe and Lockwood found affluent workers displayed three characteristics:

**Embourgeoisement**
The idea that the differences between the middle class and working class are disappearing, with well-paid manual workers merging into the middle class.

- *privatization*: living private, home-centred lifestyles – e.g. staying at home watching TV and socializing with their family and friends.
- *instrumentalism*: work was simply a means of – or instrument for – getting money to enjoy life outside work, not a place for making friends, or fulfilling themselves through satisfying work.
- *individualism*: there was a focus on individual self-interest and their family's needs, rather than the sense of solidarity and loyalty to others found in the traditional working class.

Goldthorpe and Lockwood concluded that embourgeoisement was not occurring, as affluent workers still held on to their working-class identity and many of its attitudes. However, their privatized lifestyle, instrumentalism and individualism made them different from the traditional working class, so Goldthorpe and Lockwood maintained there was a new working class, but it was not being absorbed into the middle class.

Devine (1992), in the late 1980s, went back to Luton to re-examine the embourgeoisement thesis, and the work of Goldthorpe, Lockwood et al. She interviewed a sample of male manual workers employed at the Vauxhall car plant in Luton, and their wives. Devine did not find evidence to support the idea of 'privatized instrumentalism'. The lifestyle of her sample was not as community-oriented as that of the traditional working class, but neither had it become as home-centred and privatized as Goldthorpe and Lockwood had predicted. The affluent workers retained many of the values found in the traditional working class, such as resentment at the privileges of inherited wealth, and a sense of injustice at the existence of extreme class inequalities.

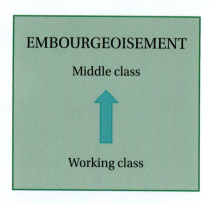

**EMBOURGEOISEMENT**

Middle class

Working class

**Figure 6.6**
Embourgeoisement

Devine concluded that, rather than holding beliefs about politics and society based on instrumentalism and individualism (as the earlier study suggested), the 1980s working class shared both a sense of shared identity with other workers, and a dissatisfaction with the unfair distribution of financial rewards in Britain. There was still evidence of a sense of loyalty to workmates and solidarity among those interviewed, rather than purely self-interested individualism.

The lower-middle-class often have a bit more job security, the opportunity for more flexible working hours (flexitime), and generally work in more pleasant conditions than affluent workers. But in contemporary Britain, in terms of factors like pay, home ownership, consumer goods and lifestyle, there is probably little separating the new working class from the lower middle class.

However, the new working class is today in decline, as manufacturing industries in Britain are closing down as production is moved to other countries where production costs are cheaper. As a result, working-class manual jobs of all kinds are today disappearing, and the working class is shrinking in size.

## The changing and growing middle class

At the same time as working-class jobs have been declining, there has been a growth in middle-class occupations, with a majority of people now engaged in non-manual work of all kinds, and particularly low-level routine non-manual work providing services to people – such as administration, sales, insurance, financial advice, and customer services like call centres – rather than making products.

The new working class was found in more technologically advanced manufacturing industries, such as the production of cars, chemicals, electrical and other consumer goods. The decline of manufacturing industries in contemporary Britain has meant this section of the working class, along with the manual working class in general, has been shrinking, with the middle class growing.

## THE PRECARIAT AND THE 'GIG ECONOMY'

In recent years, the labour market has changed towards more people working on a self-employed basis in highly insecure work, as opposed to permanent jobs. This is typically associated with services like Deliveroo (https://deliveroo.co.uk), Uber (https://goo.gl/qLKBJN) and TaskRabbit (www.taskrabbit.co.uk). This is popularly referred to as the 'gig economy': rather than having a secure wage and income, workers only earn money for each 'gig' (or individual job/task) they perform. This has led to the emergence of a new class grouping – including both manual and non-manual work – sometimes called the *precariat* (formed by merging the words 'precarious' – meaning insecure and unpredictable – with Marx's 'proletariat'). This is a growing group of workers, mainly young people, who face extreme insecurity in their daily lives, creating frustration and stress. The precariat are marked out by:

- self-employment
- low pay
- low-skilled work
- very poor working conditions
- lack of benefits, such as paid holidays, sick pay and pensions
- highly insecure work – temporary, part-time and short-term contracts, or on zero-hours contracts (whereby workers are 'on call', with no guarantee of work, and paid only if and when needed), and high risks of unemployment
- work often below their qualifications
- unpaid work in order to get work, such as waiting around for jobs, filling in forms and retraining / learning new skills
- very poor future prospects.

***The proletarianization of clerical work*** Traditionally, those doing lower-middle-class occupations, such as clerical and administrative work, had higher levels of education, higher pay, shorter working hours, and better working conditions and career opportunities than manual workers, and were seen as having a middle-class status and lifestyle. The **proletarianization** thesis suggests that these advantages, compared to the manual working class, have declined to such an extent that such groups are now virtually indistinguishable from the working class. For example, the pay of clerical workers has declined dramatically, and today is generally little better (and often worse) than that of manual workers; promotion opportunities have been reduced, as higher managerial jobs are often filled directly by university graduates rather than by people who have worked their way up; and the computerization of office work has reduced the skills of clerical work – this is called **deskilling** – and much clerical work has become more like routine and repetitious factory work.

The proletarianization of the lower middle class, combined with some embourgeoisement of the upper working class, has meant that, in terms of educational level, housing, lifestyle and living standards, there are few differences between lower-middle-class and skilled manual or upper-working-class occupations. There is now a 'bulge' in the middle of the social-class hierarchy, as shown in figure 6.5 on page 391, with skilled manual workers and the lower middle class sharing similar status, rewards and lifestyles.

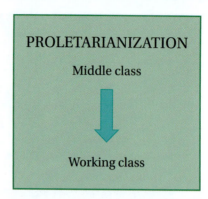

**PROLETARIANIZATION**

Middle class

Working class

**Figure 6.7**
Proletarianization

> **Proletarianization**
> The opposite of embourgeoisement. The process of decline in the pay and conditions of sections of the middle class, so they become more like the working class.

> **Deskilling** The removal of skills from work by the application of new machinery which simplifies tasks.

## Social mobility

Social mobility refers to the movement of people up or down the social-class hierarchy, either during the course of the individual's lifetime or compared to the social class into which she or he was born. Modern societies are said to be open societies because social mobility is possible, and people can move up or down the social-class hierarchy.

### Why study social mobility?

The study of social mobility is useful as it makes it possible to discover:

- The extent to which an individual's life chances are affected by the circumstances into which he or she is born.
- The extent to which society is open and allows people to move freely from class to class, and therefore whether society is based mainly on

ascribed status (given at birth) or on achieved status (achieved during the course of people's lives). This includes questions like:

- ○ Is society fair and meritocratic?
- ○ Is people's social position achieved solely on the basis of their talents, abilities, skills and qualifications?
- ○ Does everyone with talent and motivation, who works hard and plays by the rules, have an equal opportunity to succeed and fulfil their potential?
- ○ Are the life chances of a child and their chances of success largely a result of the social class into which they are born, and other factors like their gender or ethnic origin?

## Measuring social mobility

Sociologists measure social mobility either by income, or by social class defined by occupation, using occupational scales like those mentioned earlier in this chapter. This means that there are problems with the measuring tools used in social mobility studies, as different studies may use different occupational scales, and those using occupational groups tend to produce slightly different results from those using income. This means it can be difficult to compare different studies.

There are two main types of social mobility that sociologists examine to see how open society is:

- **Intergenerational social mobility** compares an adult's present occupational or income group with that of the family she or he was born into. This shows social mobility between two generations. For example, a refuse collector's daughter who becomes a doctor has experienced upward social mobility compared with the class into which she was born.
- **Intragenerational social mobility** compares an adult's present occupation or income with her or his first occupation or income, therefore showing how much mobility she or he has achieved in his or her lifetime. An example would be the person who began her or his working life as a small shopkeeper, but who eventually built up a massive supermarket empire.

## How much social mobility is there in Britain?

Social mobility in modern Britain is relatively limited, and most people stay in the broad social class they were born into. The main findings suggest:

### Intergenerational social mobility

- A considerable number of children from working-class backgrounds now achieve upward mobility to the middle class. This is largely because

**Intergenerational social mobility** A way of measuring social mobility by comparing an adult's present occupation or income with that of the family she or he was born into. It therefore shows how much social class mobility there has been between two generations.

**Intragenerational social mobility** A way of measuring social mobility by comparing a person's present occupation or income with her or his first occupation. It therefore shows how much mobility an individual has achieved within her or his lifetime.

there are declining numbers of working-class jobs, and growing numbers of middle-class jobs – there is 'more room at the top', enabling middle-class children to stay middle-class, while also enabling some working-class children to become middle-class.

- Nearly 80 per cent of working-class adults, and about three-quarters of those in the middle class, were born to parents of the same class.

- There is a close link between the social class of origin (the class people are born into) and the social class of destination (the one they end up in as adults) – at least 40–50 per cent of children today can expect to find themselves in the same class position as their parents, whether measured by income or by occupational group.

- Not everyone has the same chance of achieving upward social mobility. A child from a working-class background has only about half the chance of entering the upper middle class as an adult, compared to one from the lower middle class. A child born into the upper middle class has about four times the chance of being in that class as an adult compared to one from a working-class background. For example, the typical doctor or lawyer today grew up in a family with an income two-thirds higher than that of the average family. This shows a clear lack of equal opportunity for all to have the same chance of getting the top jobs (see cartoon).

The 1:2:4 pattern of unequal opportunity
Whatever the chance a boy from a working-class background has of reaching the upper middle class as an adult, a boy from a lower-middle-class family has about twice that chance, and a boy born into the upper middle class has about four times the chance of being in that class as an adult. This clearly shows an inequality of opportunity in the chances of upward mobility in Britain.

- Social-class background is still the major factor influencing success in the education system, which is crucial for upward social mobility. Those from middle- and upper-middle-class backgrounds and those privately educated dominate the universities. Those 7 per cent of the population who can afford to attend fee-paying private schools dominate the top institutions of power in the UK, with three out of four judges, one in two senior civil servants, about half of top professionals, and a third of MPs and Cabinet ministers privately educated.
- The land-owning upper class still remains largely closed, as much wealth is inherited rather than achieved through work or talent. The best way to get rich in modern Britain is still to be born to rich parents.

*Intragenerational social mobility*  The chances of upward mobility during a person's career, such as moving from a manual job to a higher-status professional and managerial or technical job, have declined. Higher-status positions are increasingly filled directly by graduates from the education system, and most of these graduates themselves come from higher social-class backgrounds.

---

### Activity

Go through the following list, writing down for each one 'upward mobility', 'downward mobility' or 'no change', *and* 'intergenerational mobility' or 'intragenerational mobility'. Refer to the occupational scales earlier in the chapter (see pages 387–8) if you find any difficulty.

1 A nurse who decides to become a labourer on a building site.
2 The daughter of a miner who becomes a bank manager.
3 A teacher who decides to retrain as a social worker.
4 A doctor's son who becomes a taxi driver.
5 An immigrant from a poor farming background in Africa who gets a job in Britain as a farm labourer.
6 The daughter of a skilled manual worker who becomes a routine clerical worker.
7 A postal worker who becomes a traffic warden.
8 A pilot whose son becomes a police constable.
9 The owner of a small shop whose daughter becomes the manager of a large supermarket.
10 A sales assistant in a shop who becomes a priest.

---

## Obstacles to social mobility

While levels of social mobility have grown since the 1970s – though not by very much – there remain very large inequalities of opportunity, and a number of obstacles to social mobility and the development of a truly 'open' society.

- Education is a key factor in enabling social mobility. Despite free and compulsory state education, there remains widespread inequality of educational opportunity, as seen in chapter 4. Many working-class children face a number of obstacles and disadvantages in the way of success in education, which mean they do not do as well as their ability should allow them to, and this restricts their chances of upward mobility.

- There remain biases in recruitment to the upper-middle-class elite jobs. For example, judges and top civil servants are recruited almost exclusively from people who have attended very expensive (largely boys') public schools and then gone to Oxford or Cambridge Universities. This is a major obstacle for children from working-class backgrounds, who can't afford these schools and are therefore often denied the chance of getting into these top jobs.

- Women face a range of obstacles in achieving upward mobility, because of a number of factors which hinder their ability to compete in the labour market on equal terms with men (see later in this chapter).

- Disadvantages in education, and **racism** in education, training and employment, often present obstacles to the upward social mobility of some minority ethnic groups. Consequently, a high percentage of people of African-Caribbean and Pakistani/Bangladeshi origin are represented in the working class.

> **Racism** Treating people as inferior, and encouraging hostility towards them, on the grounds of racial or ethnic origins – usually based on skin colour or other physical or cultural characteristics.

---

**Activity**

1 Look at the box below, and explain how each of the factors might encourage or limit the possibilities of upward social mobility.
2 Suggest what steps you might take to ensure that the most well-paid and responsible positions in society are filled by the most able and committed people, regardless of their social class, gender or ethnic origins.

---

| Factors encouraging social mobility | Factors limiting social mobility |
|---|---|
| • Family support for children, in the form of money, support in education, values and networks of contacts | • Inequality of educational opportunity and lack of success in education |
| • Raising educational standards and ensuring access to further and higher education for all | • Lack of family support |
| • Equality of opportunity for all, based on meritocracy, with fairer recruitment policies by employers | • Poor attitudes, expectations and lack of ambition |
| • Drive, ambition and a willingness to seize opportunities and take risks | • Barriers to some occupations, such as the legal profession, for those from the 'wrong' social class or educational background |
| | • Racial and sexual discrimination |
| | • Childhood poverty |

## Conclusion on social mobility

Britain has one of the lowest social-mobility rates in Europe. The chances of social mobility (compared to family occupation or income) have changed little since the early 1980s. Britain remains highly unequal, and the life chances of children remain closely tied to the social class of the families into which they were born. Children born to poorer families continue to have fewer chances of success in education, poorer employment opportunities and poorer health than those from more affluent backgrounds, creating barriers to upward mobility. Social-class inequalities in social mobility (and also inequalities due to gender and ethnicity, which are discussed later in this chapter) persist as major features of life in contemporary Britain, and most people do not achieve much upward social mobility from the family into which they are born.

## Social-class inequality and life chances

Social classes do not exist merely in the mind of the sociologist: there are wide, measurable differences in life chances between social classes. The higher the social class of an individual, the more access she or he will have to society's resources, such as better housing, food, holidays, income and job security. She or he will live a longer and healthier life, and will have more influence in society. The following section examines some examples of these class differences, and further examples are discussed in other parts of this book (see particularly chapter 4 on inequalities in education, and online chapter 8 on inequalities in health at www.politybooks.com/introsoc).

### Social-class inequalities in wealth and income

- Wealth refers to property which can be sold and turned into cash for the benefit of the owner. The main forms of wealth are property such as housing and land, bank deposits, shares in companies, and personal possessions.
- Income refers to the flow of money which people obtain from work, from their investments, or from the state in the form of welfare benefits. Earned income is income received from paid employment (wages and salaries). Unearned income is that received from investments, such as rent on property, interest on savings, and dividends on shares.

**The distribution of wealth and income**   Figure 6.8 shows that, in 2014–16, the poorest 50 per cent of the population owned only 9 per cent of the wealth, while the richest 50 per cent owned 91 per cent; 30 per cent of the population possessed over three-quarters (76 per cent) of the nation's household wealth.

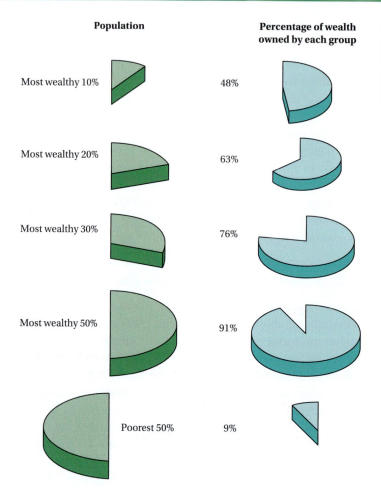

**Figure 6.8** Distribution of household wealth: Great Britain, 2014–2016

*Source: Wealth in Great Britain, Wave 5: 2014–16*, Office for National Statistics, 2018

Population | Percentage of wealth owned by each group

Most wealthy 10% — 48%

Most wealthy 20% — 63%

Most wealthy 30% — 76%

Most wealthy 50% — 91%

Poorest 50% — 9%

As figure 6.9 shows, income is also unequally distributed, with the richest fifth (20 per cent) of the population getting 44 per cent of total income in 2017–18 – more than twice their fair share if income were equally distributed, and more than the bottom three-fifths got between them. The poorest fifth got only about 5 per cent, only a quarter of their fair share if income was equally distributed.

### Who are the rich?

- *The traditional aristocracy.* They are major landowners, such as the Duke of Westminster, who owns sizeable chunks of London, Cheshire, North Wales and Ireland, forests and shooting estates in Lancashire and Scotland, and properties in North America and the Far East. According to the 2018 Rich List published by the *Sunday Times,* the Duke of Westminster is Britain's tenth-richest person, with an estimated wealth of £9.96 billion (£9,960,000,000).

**Figure 6.9** Changes in the distribution of income, by fifths of the population: United Kingdom, 1979–2017/18

*Source: Households Below Average Income, Department of Social Security, 1997, and Department for Work and Pensions, 2019*

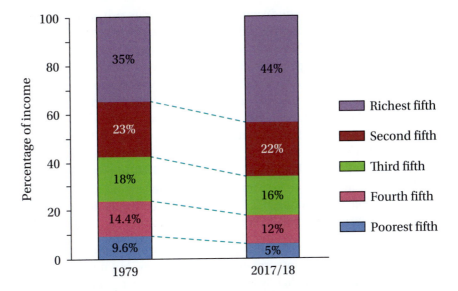

**The UK income procession**

Imagine that everyone's height was based on their income, so the more you earned, the taller you were. Suppose the entire population of the UK marched past you in one hour, ranked in order of their income. This is what you might see. For the first half an hour, you would be greeted by a parade of very small people, and you wouldn't see a person of average height (income) go by until around 37 minutes had passed. After that, a fair few people of average stature would pass by. After 57 minutes, mini-giants of 3.45m appear. In the last few minutes, great giants would emerge, and during the last few seconds their heights would be measured in kilometres.

**Activity**

Study figure 6.9 and answer the following questions:
1 Which group increased its share of income between 1979 and 2017–18?
2 Which group suffered the largest cut in its income share between 1979 and 2017–18?
3 By how much did the percentage share of the poorest fifth of the population fall between 1979 and 2017–18?
4 How might the evidence in figure 6.8 be used to show that the rich were getting richer between 1979 and 2017–18 while the poor, in comparison, were getting poorer?
5 Draw a pie chart to illustrate the distribution of income in 2017–18.

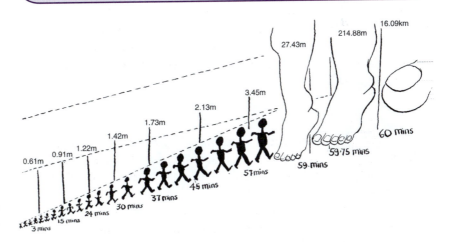

- *The owners of industry and commerce* – the corporate rich of the business world. This includes chemical billionaire Jim Ratcliffe, the richest person in the UK, worth £21.05 billion; Sir Richard Branson of Virgin, Britain's twenty-ninth richest person in 2018, with estimated assets of £4.53 billion; and the Perkins family, owners of Specsavers, worth £1.7 billion.
- *Stars of entertainment and the media.* These include J. K. Rowling, author of the Harry Potter books, on £700 million; former Beatle Sir Paul McCartney, and his wife Nancy Shevell (£820 million); David and Victoria Beckham (£340 million); Sir Elton John (£300 million); Sir Mick Jagger (£260 million); and, among the relatively impoverished, Adele struggles along on £140 million; Daniel Craig (James Bond) on £125 million; Harry Potter stars Daniel Radcliffe (£87 million) and Emma Watson (£50 million); and Ed Sheeran (£80 million).

Around 94 per cent of the 1,000 richest people in the UK built their own fortunes, some through the internet or other technology, but much wealth is still inherited among the slightly less rich – giving them a good opportunity to become super-rich – with those inheriting doing nothing to earn their riches. Many of the rich live on unearned income from investments rather than from employment. The starkness of these inequalities is made clear by the Queen, one of Britain's richest women, with personal assets estimated at £370 million in 2018. If she were to pop this into her local high street bank in 2018 (assuming a mere 1 per cent rate of interest), she would receive at least £4.11 in unearned income each minute all day, of every day, every year (after paying higher-rate tax). This is an hourly rate of about 33 times greater than someone on the National Living Wage in 2018 (who might earn only for 8

The Queen is one of Britain's richest women, though there are other women and men who are *much* richer. Her wealth could produce an hourly unearned income, 24 hours a day, about 33 times as much as someone on the National Living Wage, and her unearned income every year, after tax, would take an employee on average wages about 100 years to earn. Do you think such inequalities can be justified? Explain why or why not.

hours a day, rather than the Queen's 24-hour income). Her unearned income each year after tax would take a full-time employee on average wages (after paying tax and who was never ill) about 100 years to earn, and the Queen would still have her original £370 million.

High earners and the self-made rich do not necessarily put in more work than those who receive low pay; it is simply that society places different values on people in different positions, and rewards them more or less highly. Senior executives in large companies, bankers, and music and film stars and other celebrities will probably not have to work as hard for their high incomes as an unskilled manual labourer working long hours in a low-paid job.

## Attempts to redistribute wealth and income

The massive inequalities in wealth and income which have existed this century, and the inequalities in life chances these have caused, have provoked various measures by governments to redistribute wealth and income more equally. Some of these measures are:

- *inheritance tax*, which is a tax payable when people give gifts of wealth either before or after death, and is intended to limit the inheritance of vast quantities of wealth from one generation to the next.
- *capital gains tax*, which is intended to reduce profits from dealing in property or shares, and is payable whenever these are sold.
- *income tax*, which is payable on unearned and earned income, and it rises as earnings increase.
- *social welfare benefits* from the state, like Universal Credit, which are attempts to divert the resources obtained through taxation to the needy sections of society.

### Why have attempts to redistribute wealth and income failed?  Despite these measures, attempts to redistribute wealth and income have been largely unsuccessful. Little real redistribution has occurred, and what redistribution has taken place has mainly been between the very rich and the lesser rich, and the gap between the richest and the poorest sections of society has actually grown wider in recent years. Most people wrongly believe the richest face the biggest tax burden, but research by the Equality Trust in 2016 found the poorest 10 per cent of households paid 12 per cent more of their income in taxes than the richest 10 per cent. There are five main reasons for this:

- Their investments often mean the wealthy can make their wealth grow at a faster rate than that at which it is taxed.
- *Tax relief.* The state allows tax relief, a reduction in the amount paid in tax, on a wide variety of things such as business expenses and private

pensions. These are expenses which only the better-off are likely to have. This means that they pay a smaller proportion of their income in tax than a person who is poorer but who does not have these expenses.

- *Tax avoidance schemes* are perfectly legal, and are often thought up by financial advisers and accountants to find loopholes in the tax laws and beat the tax system, thereby saving the rich from paying some tax. Such schemes involve things like living outside Britain for most of the year, investing in pension schemes to avoid income tax, investing in tax-free or low-tax areas such as the Channel Islands and the Cayman Islands, giving wealth away to kin well before death to avoid inheritance tax, or putting companies or savings in other people's names, such as those of husband/wife, children or other kin.

- *Tax evasion* is illegal, and involves people not declaring wealth and income to HM Revenue and Customs. This is suspected to be a common practice among the rich.

- *A failure to claim benefits.* Many people fail to claim the welfare benefits to which they are entitled. Some reasons for this are discussed later in this chapter.

## Social-class inequalities in health

Despite the welfare state and the National Health Service, major differences in health chances (the life chances relating to health) continue to exist between social classes. There is a social gradient in health (see figure 6.10) that runs, like a ladder, from social class 7 at the bottom to social class 1 at the top. With every step up the ladder, there is an improvement in health and how long people are expected to live. There is a mass of evidence which shows that lower-working-class people live shorter, unhealthier lives and suffer more from almost all diseases than those in the upper middle class.

- People in social class 7 (lower working class), compared to those in social class 1 (upper middle class), have, on average:
  - twice the **death rate** – the number of people dying per thousand of the population each year
  - about 7 years' less **life expectancy** – how many years they live
  - twice the chance of dying before the age of 5, and of dying before reaching state pension age
  - between two and five times greater risk of dying from accidents of all types
  - a 50 per cent higher risk of long-standing illness
  - around three times the risk of developing heart disease.
- Four times as many women die of cervical cancer in the lower working class as in social class 1.

> **Death rate** The number of deaths per 1,000 of the population per year.

> **Life expectancy** An estimate of how long people can be expected to live from a certain age. It is commonly estimated from birth, but it can be given from any age.

- Lung cancer and stomach cancer occur twice as often among men in manual jobs as among men in professional jobs.
- For the majority of cancers, there is a five-year gap in the survival rates between the best- and worst-off.

***Explaining class differences in health and life expectancy***   These differences are often explained by the following features of working-class life, which are less likely to be experienced by those in middle-class occupations:

- longer working hours, with shiftwork and overtime
- poorer conditions at work, with more risks to health and safety through accidents and industrial diseases
- less time off work with pay to visit the doctor
- lower income, leading to poorer diets and housing
- more likelihood of working-class areas being at risk through industrial and traffic pollution
- poorer medical care in working-class areas, with longer hospital waiting lists and overworked GPs, and lack of sufficient income to make use of private medicine or purchase non-prescription drugs
- lower levels of education, which often mean less awareness of health and the services which are available, and less self-confidence in questioning the judgements of health professionals

**Figure 6.10** The social gradient in health

- poverty in old age, due to the lack of an occupational pension and inadequate earnings while working to save for retirement
- smoking and obesity, both of which lie behind many diseases, tend to be more common in the working class
- higher levels of unemployment and poverty, and therefore more stress-related illnesses.

## Class inequalities in employment

The different status of occupations is backed up by different terms and conditions of employment under which people work. These improve with movement upwards through the social-class hierarchy.

In general, those lower down in the social-class hierarchy, compared to those higher up:

- get lower pay, despite working longer hours with shiftwork and overtime
- have shorter paid holiday leave
- work in more dangerous and less hygienic conditions, with greater risks of accident and disease
- are more supervised at work, having to clock in, getting pay 'docked' for lateness, and not being allowed time off with pay for personal reasons
- receive less training in their work
- are less likely to receive full pay during sickness, or to belong to an employer's pension scheme
- have much less job security: the risk of unemployment is much greater for an unskilled manual worker than for someone in social class 1.

### Explaining class differences in employment

- *Functionalists* suggest class differences in employment are often explained or justified by the higher education, training and increased management responsibility of many non-manual workers.

Those in lower social classes often work in more dangerous jobs or unhealthy working conditions

- *Weberians* explain them by differences in market situation (see pages 383–4).
- *Marxists* explain them by the need to retain non-manual workers' commitment and loyalty to the firm to protect the firm's interests, investments and secrets. The tighter control and poorer working conditions of manual workers suggest they are not trusted by management, are considered more dispensable, and can be more easily replaced.

---

**SOCIAL-CLASS INEQUALITIES IN EDUCATION AND CRIME**

Don't forget there is also evidence of social-class inequalities:

*in education* (see pages 246–64 and 240–3) – working-class underachievement and the 'old boys network' based on private education and elite universities;

*in crime* (see pages 332–9) – selective law-enforcement and the leniency shown to white-collar and corporate criminals compared to those from the working class.

---

## Does social class still matter?

Many people today suggest that social class is no longer very important, often blaming sociologists for highlighting class inequalities which don't really have much impact on people's lives. Social class is thought to have little influence on people's lifestyles, and to be of declining importance today as a source of identity – how people see themselves and how others see them. Some commentators suggest that people today identify themselves not as being working-class or middle-class, but in terms of their gender identity or ethnic identity. Postmodernists (see page 49) suggest people now create their own identities through the goods they choose to consume and the choices they make in how they live their lives. People are less influenced by their social class, close communities and work situations, and they can now choose, 'pick and mix', chop and change any identities they want from a range of different lifestyles presented to them through the media, and by the choices they make in their leisure activities and the lifestyles they express through their consumer spending.

In fact, British Social Attitudes surveys have shown that most people still identify with social class, with six in ten seeing themselves as working class, and around a third as middle class – only about one in twenty didn't identify with any class. However, even if people today didn't identify themselves with their social class as much as they once did, this wouldn't undermine the significance of social class. There are greater similarities between black and white children from working-class families than between working-class and middle-class children from the same ethnic group; there are greater similarities between women from the same social class than there are between

Social class is like living in a goldfish bowl: you can't see the sides, but you'll soon realize they exist when you bump into them

women of different social classes, and working-class women are likely to identify themselves more with other women of their own social class than they are with middle- and upper-class women.

Pretending that social classes don't exist will not make them go away, any more than not being able to see a plate-glass door will stop you from hurting yourself when you walk into it.

Ask yourself why you don't buy expensive clothes, houses and cars, or travel first-class by train. Why don't you go to exotic foreign countries for long holidays several times a year? Why don't you eat out at restaurants all the time instead of cooking? Why don't you try to skip National Health Service waiting lists by paying for private medicine? What stops you from forging out your own identity by going on expensive shopping trips to buy goods to reinvent yourself?

Much of this chapter – and the chapters on education and crime – shows how, whatever anyone might think, social class and social class inequalities are significant features of contemporary Britain, and remain the key influences on people's life chances.

## GENDER STRATIFICATION AND INEQUALITY

Stratification by gender is a feature found in most societies, with men generally being in a more dominant position in society than women. Our gender has major influences on how we think about ourselves, how others think about us, and the opportunities and life chances open to us. Men have traditionally been seen in a wide range of active and creative roles – as warriors, hunters and workers, as political leaders or successful business executives, as scientists, engineers, inventors or great artists.

And what roles have women been traditionally seen in? As homemakers and mothers confined to the home and caring for their husbands and children. Even when working outside the home, women's jobs often seem to be an extension of their caring roles in the home, looking after others as receptionists, secretaries, personal assistants, nurses, teachers, social workers, shop and kitchen assistants, or cleaners. We might almost be forgiven for thinking that men and women exist in two different worlds, united only by belonging to the same species. Chapter 1 discussed the way these differences between males and females in modern Britain are constructed through socialization (see pages 25–38), and the sections below will examine some of the continuing inequalities between women and men which are, in part, a product of this socialization.

## Theories of gender stratification

### Functionalist theories

Functionalist writers, such as Parsons, argue that the differences between the sexes are inborn and biologically based:

- Men are biologically more suited to performing the instrumental role of provider/breadwinner.
- Women are more naturally suited to remaining in the private/domestic sphere of the home, performing the expressive role of nurturing, caring and providing emotional support.

These biologically based differences are reinforced by the socialization process, which creates gender differences – the culturally created differences between men and women.

Most sociologists reject the view that the biological differences between men and women are the main reason for the inequalities between them in contemporary societies. They emphasize the role of socialization from an early age, which encourages men and women to adopt different roles. Evidence for the cultural, rather than biological, creation of inequalities between men and women is also shown by the different and changing roles adopted by men and women in different societies.

### Marxist theories

**Patriarchy** Power, status and authority held by men.

Marxists, like feminists, see the subordination of women arising from **patriarchy** (see below). They also emphasize the role women perform as a

**reserve army of labour** – a group of people who can be called on as workers when the economy is doing well and needs them, and can be pushed back into the home as mothers and homemakers when the economy has vacancies mainly for men.

> **Reserve army of labour** A section of the labour force which is held in reserve, to be called into the workforce when the need arises.

## Weberian theories

Weberians would argue that, because of patriarchy, women have lower status and less power than men. They have a weaker market situation due to the demands of housework and childcare. This means they lack the same flexibility as male employees. They also have interrupted careers, due to time off for childbearing, which limits their promotion opportunities.

## Feminist theories

Feminists argue gender inequalities are a result of patriarchy, which keeps women in a subordinate position. Walby (1990) described six patriarchal structures (see pages 57–9 in chapter 2) which segregate women mainly into low-paid, low-status positions where they are collectively exploited, thereby maintaining patriarchal domination of society.

## The changing status of women in Britain

During the twentieth century, there was a gradual improvement in the status of women in Britain, the outlines of which it is useful to list here. However, as will be seen later, women still face major inequalities compared to men, particularly the conflicting demands of family life and career success.

- Women have achieved more political equality with men, beginning with the powerful and often violent campaign waged by the Suffragette Movement at the beginning of the last century, and, by 1928, women in the UK had for the first time the same voting rights as men.
- Women today have equal rights with men in education. It is now illegal to discriminate against women or men by denying them access to certain subjects and courses at school, or in further and higher education, because of their gender.
- More types of job are seen as suitable for women today, and many more women are going out to work in paid employment. Women now make up about half of the workforce in Britain, which gives them more financial independence.
- Equal-opportunity laws have helped women to get a better deal and overcome prejudice and discrimination. For example, laws like the Equal Pay Act (1970), the Sex Discrimination Act (1975) and the Equality Act (2010) have made it illegal for employers to offer different rates of pay to men and women doing the same or similar work, and to distinguish between men and women in work, leisure and educational

opportunities. The Equality and Human Rights Commission (www.equalityhumanrights.com/en) helps to enforce these laws and to promote equality of opportunity between men and women.

- Women now have won equal rights with men in property ownership, and, in the event of a divorce, all property now has to be divided between husband and wife.
- Women have had equal rights with men in divorce since 1923.
- The welfare state has provided more support for lone-parent families – the majority of which are headed by women – and for women caring for dependent husbands and the elderly in the home.
- Girls have exceeded boys in educational success, and women are increasingly well qualified, and better qualified than men in the younger age groups.

### Activity

Go to www.equalityhumanrights.com and investigate the kinds of things done by the Equality and Human Rights Commission in relation to gender inequalities. In the light of your findings, suggest three ways the Commission is fighting to improve the position of women, and to prevent discrimination against anyone because of their sex.

## Why has the status of women changed?

The changing status of women in Britain over the last century can be explained by a number of factors, which are summarized in figure 6.12 on page 416.

*The Suffragette Movement*   The Suffragette Movement, which started at the turn of the twentieth century and lasted until 1918, aimed to achieve voting rights for women that were equal with men's in parliamentary elections. This involved a long and often violent struggle against men's ideas about a woman's role. It was the first major struggle by women for equality with men – hence it is often referred to as 'first-wave feminism' – and began to change the ideas held by both men and women about a woman's role. The success of this campaign gave women political power in elections for the first time, and MPs (Members of Parliament) had to begin to take women's interests into account if they were to be elected.

*Two world wars*   During the First (1914–18) and Second (1939–45) World Wars, women (as the reserve army of labour) took over many jobs in factories and farms which were formerly done by men, as the men went off to be soldiers. Women showed during these war years that they were quite capable of doing what had previously been seen as men's jobs, and this began to change people's ideas about a woman's role.

***Compulsory education of children*** Compulsory schooling since 1880, and particularly since 1944, has reduced the time necessary for the care and supervision of children in the family. Recent improved childcare provision, and access to preschool for all 3- and 4-year-olds, have reduced this time further. This has given women with children greater opportunities to go out to paid work, with more authority derived from having their own income.

***The women's movement*** The women's movement – 'second-wave feminism' – first emerged in the 1960s (as the women's liberation movement), and was concerned with the fight to achieve equality with men in a wide range of areas. This movement was not a single group, but consisted of a large number of different women's groups with various aims, both in Britain and abroad. These groups were united by the need to improve the status and rights of women, and to end patriarchy.

The women's movement challenged many ideas about the traditional role of women, particularly the stereotype that 'a woman's place is in the home'. It campaigned for:

- better nursery facilities
- free contraception and free abortion on demand, and 'a woman's right to choose' whether to have an abortion or not
- equal pay and job opportunities

The suffragettes at the beginning of the twentieth century (around 1897–1918) were an important landmark in the long and continuing struggle for women's equality in the UK. The picture on the right shows Emmeline Pankhurst, a prominent suffragette who was arrested several times for her activism

- the removal of tax and financial discrimination against women
- freedom from violence against women
- the right of women to define their own sexuality.

*Third-wave feminism*   There is in contemporary Britain a new 'third wave' of feminism, following on from the women's movement that began in the 1960s. This recognizes that the fight for equality for women is far from over. It focuses more on issues such as violence against women, sexual harassment, women's individual identity, and the differences between women. It has a new focus on intersectionality (see the box below) and the way

## WHAT IS INTERSECTIONALITY?

Intersectionality refers to the idea that different forms of discrimination (and privilege) can become intensified when they combine, overlap or intersect (or interconnect). Intersectional feminists point out, for example, that there are substantial differences in the experience of women from different social classes, from different ethnic groups, and for those who are non-disabled compared to those who are disabled. A woman might experience gender discrimination because of her sex; she might face additional discrimination if she is also black, more if she is working class, and still more if she is disabled too. Religion –e.g. Islamophobia (see page 451) – and sexuality – e.g. homophobia (see page 451) – can also combine with and shape these. This intersectionality is shown in figure 6.11, and there's a short video explaining it here: https://youtu.be/PjpS9CftpVo.

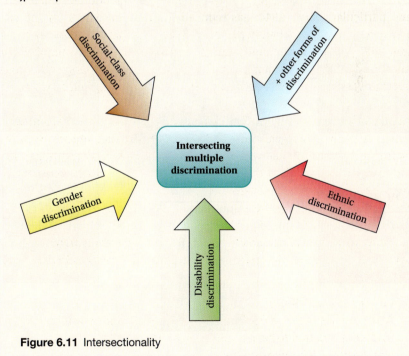

**Figure 6.11** Intersectionality

different women experience multiple layers of oppression, caused, for example, by the interlinking or overlapping of gender, ethnicity, social-class, disability and other inequalities – in each of which women come off worst.

The women's movement challenged many people's ideas about women, and has created a climate of expectation in which women now expect to be treated equally and not simply as lovers, homemakers and mothers. It is mainly because of pressures from the women's movement that

**Figure 6.12** Why has the status of women changed over the last century?

## Activity

1 *Either:* use the internet and find out what you can about the kinds of actions carried out by women in their campaigns to achieve equality with men. You will find www.historylearningsite.co.uk/suffragettes.htm useful to investigate the suffragettes and the campaign for 'Votes for Women', and www.redstockings.org gives information on the women's liberation movement in the USA (where it started). The Fawcett Society (www.fawcettsociety.org.uk) has a useful website for investigating current issues.
   *Or:* interview some older female relatives about women's fight for equality in the women's liberation movement of the 1960s and 1970s.
2 How do you think these activities might have changed both men's and women's views on women's traditional roles?

**Sexism** Prejudice or discrimination against people (especially women) because of their sex.

equal-opportunity laws have been passed, and that **sexism**, or prejudice and discrimination against people because of their sex, is increasingly seen as unacceptable behaviour.

***Reliable contraception*** Modern contraception has become a much more reliable means of preventing unwanted pregnancies. Since the 1960s, the contraceptive pill has proven very effective, despite some health risks to women, and has enabled women to take control of their fertility, giving them more control over their lives.

***Smaller family size*** The declining size of families is both a cause and a consequence of the improving status of women. This has reduced the time spent in child rearing and given women greater opportunities to enter paid employment. Increasingly, women are having fewer children, or none at all, and they are having them at an older age after they have established their careers.

***More jobs for women*** There are more types of job seen as suitable for women today, and legal obstacles to the employment of women have been removed in most cases. Although there still remains a lot of prejudice and discrimination by employers about the suitability of some jobs for women, the way women took over men's jobs during the world wars, and the pressures of the Suffragette Movement and, more recently, the women's movement and third-wave feminism have helped to erode hostility to female workers among many male bosses and workers. This increase in employment opportunities for women has come about because of:

- *the expansion of light industry, manufacturing and the tertiary sector of the economy* – concerned with services, finance, administration, distribution, transport and government agencies, such as the NHS, the social services and education. The expansion of this sector has increased the number of routine clerical and administrative jobs, which are over-whelmingly done by women.

- *an increase in the number of jobs in the lower professions*, such as teaching, social work and nursing, which employ many women.
- *the provision of maternity benefits and maternity and paternity leave*, which provide additional encouragement and opportunity for women to return to work after childbirth, as their jobs are kept open for them while they are absent having children.

The fact that more women are working gives them greater financial independence, and therefore more authority, in both the family and society.

*Technology in the home* Advances in technology have brought many improvements to the home environment, including better housing standards – e.g. central heating; labour-saving devices like washing machines, microwave cookers, food processors and vacuum cleaners; and manufactured foodstuffs such as canned and frozen foods, ready meals and fast food. It has been suggested that these improvements have reduced the time spent on housework. However, others argue that these developments have simply meant higher standards are expected. For example, automatic washing machines mean that washing is done several times a week instead of just once on 'washing day', and people change their clothes more often. This also creates, of course, more ironing. Similarly, vacuum cleaners mean that houses are expected to be kept cleaner than they used to be.

---

**Activity**

1  Despite the improvements in the position of women outlined above, suggest two ways that women may still face obstacles or problems in their careers today that men don't.
2  Suggest how you might remove or overcome each of the obstacles or problems you have identified.

---

## Gender inequality and life chances

### Gender inequalities in paid employment

Many of the factors discussed above explaining the changing status of women have brought about a large increase in their employment in the last forty years. In 2019, women made up nearly half of the workforce (47 per cent), compared with less than 30 per cent at the beginning of the twentieth

century. About 72 per cent of women aged 16–64 were in employment in 2019 (81 per cent for men) compared to 53 per cent (91 per cent for men) in 1971. Much of this increase has been among women with dependent children: less than 10 per cent of women with dependent children were working in the early twentieth century, but this has now increased to about 74 per cent.

Although women have obtained job opportunities and rights previously denied to them, women's position at work is still unequal to men's. The following section summarizes the key features of women's employment situation, and describes and explains the main inequalities women face in the labour market.

***The sexual division of labour*** The processes of gender role socialization outlined in chapter 1 still have the general effect of emphasizing girls' domestic responsibilities of housework and childcare. As seen in chapter 3, women continue to take on the major responsibilities for housework and childcare, often alongside paid employment. The different socialization of males and females continues to show itself in the **sexual (or gendered) division of labour** in the job market, with jobs being divided into 'men's jobs' and 'women's jobs', with women generally working in different types of jobs from men. This sexual division of labour involves:

**Sexual (or gendered) division of labour** The division of work into men's jobs and women's jobs.

- *vertical segregation* – this means that in general the jobs women do tend to be concentrated at the lower end of the salary and occupational-status scale, with lower pay, poorer promotion prospects and lower status than men's. Women are more likely than men to be in non-manual work, though this is usually in the more 'menial' non-manual occupations, such as routine clerical/administrative work and as sales assistants. Even those women in the professions are most commonly found in the lower ones such as teaching, nursing and social work. Men are more likely to be employed in higher-skilled jobs than women, which generally have higher pay.

● *horizontal segregation* – this means that women's jobs are spread over a far narrower range of jobs, which are also of a different type from men's.

### EVIDENCE FOR VERTICAL SEGREGATION

As shown in figure 6.13, men are much more likely to be employed in the top higher managerial and professional group, and table 6.3 shows that few women in this group are in the highest-status and most well-paid and powerful professional jobs. Figure 6.13 also shows that women are mainly employed in jobs which are concentrated at the lower end of the occupational scale: in intermediate and semi-routine occupations, such as administrative and secretarial, personal service and sales and customer service jobs, many of which require little or no training.

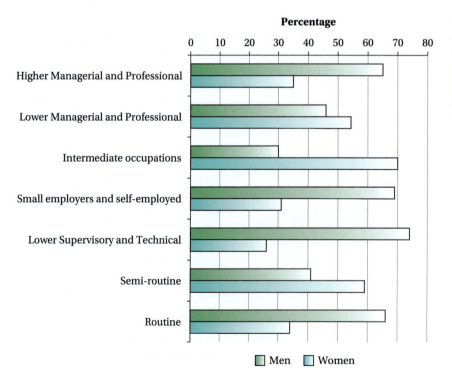

**Figure 6.13** The occupations of men and women: UK, 2019

*Source:* dataset: *EMP11: Employment by Socio-economic Classification, Labour Force Survey,* Office for National Statistics

## Table 6.3 Women and men in some top professional jobs: UK 2017–2018

| Job | Women (%) | Men (%) |
| --- | --- | --- |
| Senior civil servant | 40 | 60 |
| Senior police officer (Chief Inspector and above) England and Wales | 25 | 75 |
| MP (June 2017) | 32 | 68 |
| Cabinet minister (2018) | 22 | 78 |
| UK Member of the European Parliament | 41 | 59 |
| Local government chief executive | 33 | 67 |
| Armed forces senior officer (Lieutenant-Colonel and above) | 9 | 91 |
| Court of Appeal judge | 24 | 76 |
| High Court judge | 24 | 76 |
| Circuit judge | 29 | 71 |
| Queen's Counsel (QC) | 16 | 84 |
| Barrister | 37 | 63 |
| Partner in top 100 UK law firms | 21 | 79 |
| Trade union general secretary | 36 | 64 |
| Employer Association leader | 26 | 74 |
| Secondary-school headteacher (England) | 38 | 62 |
| General medical practitioner (GP) | 55 | 45 |
| Directors in top FTSE 100 UK companies | 29 | 71 |
| University professors | 25 | 75 |
| All managers, directors and senior officials | 35 | 65 |

*Sources:* Institute for Government; Home Office; BBC; House of Commons Library; European Parliament; Fawcett Society; Ministry of Defence; Courts and Tribunals Judiciary; Bar Standards Board; PwC UK; Certification Officer; Department for Education; General Medical Council; Cranfield University; Advance HE; Office for National Statistics.

### Activity

Refer to figure 6.13 and table 6.3, and answer the following questions:

1 In which three occupational groups in figure 6.13 were there more women employed than men?
2 What evidence is there in figure 6.13 of vertical segregation in the labour market?
3 What is the source of the data in figure 6.13?
4 Which three top professional groups in table 6.3 show the greatest inequality in the representation of women?
5 In which two professional groups in table 6.3 was the representation of men and women the most equal?
   (a) Suggest three explanations for the under-representation of, or obstacles facing, women in top professional jobs.
   (b) Suggest two actions that might be taken to overcome the obstacles facing women that you have identified in (a) above.

### EVIDENCE FOR HORIZONTAL SEGREGATION

Figure 6.14 shows that about three-quarters of women are employed in four main occupational groups: Professional, Associate Professional and Technical occupations (especially in education, welfare and health); Administrative and Secretarial; Sales and Customer Service (where around 63 per cent are cashiers or sales assistants); and Caring, Leisure and Other Services (where around 88 per cent are involved as care workers, in childcare, and hairdressing and beauty). Figure 6.15 shows the occupations in which women dominate, and, as will be considered below, those occupations which are female-dominated are also often the lowest-paid.

Women are mainly employed in low-grade and low-paid jobs which are seen as 'female occupations'. These are often extensions of the traditional domestic roles of homemakers and mothers into which many women continue to be socialized. These involve serving and waiting on people, caring for them, cleaning and clearing up after others – all jobs that women have traditionally done in the home. Such jobs include nursing, primary-school teaching, secretarial and routine clerical work, low-grade catering work such as that of waitresses and canteen assistants, and working as shop assistants, supermarket 'shelf-fillers' and check-out operators. For example, secretaries serve their (still usually male) bosses, organizing the office to make things easier for them, making them coffee, and providing papers for and clearing up after their meetings; primary-school teaching involves childcare; nursing is caring for the sick; catering involves cooking, serving and clearing up meals.

***Part-time work*** As shown in figure 6.16, in 2019 around three out of four part-time workers were women, and about 42 per cent of women

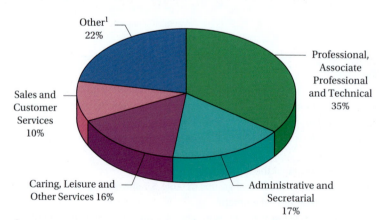

Figure 6.14 Occupational distribution of working women: UK, 2018

*Source: All in employment by status, occupation and sex, Labour Force Survey, Office for National Statistics*

[1] includes Managers and Senior Officials, Process, Plant & Machine Operators, Skilled Trades, and Elementary Occupations

**Figure 6.15** The percentage of workers in each occupation group that are women, 2018, UK

*Source*: *Labour Force Survey*, Office for National Statistics

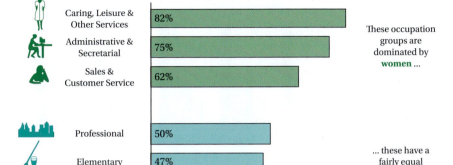

The percentage of workers in each occupation group that are women, 2018, UK

These occupation groups are dominated by **women** ...

... these have a fairly equal gender split ...

... and these are dominated by **men**.

in paid employment worked only part-time, compared with 13 per cent of men.

Surveys suggest this is closely related to women's responsibilities for children and other domestic tasks. Many working women are limited in the jobs they can do and the hours they can work because they are still expected to carry the *dual burden* of housework and childcare on top of paid work, and to be at home for the children leaving for and returning from school. There

**Figure 6.16** All those in employment, by full-time and part-time work, and gender

*Source*: *Labour Force Survey*, Office for National Statistics

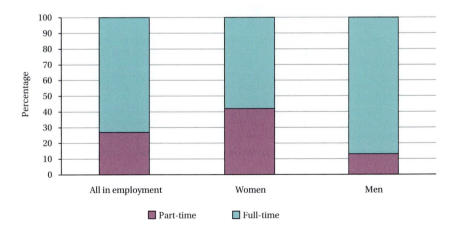

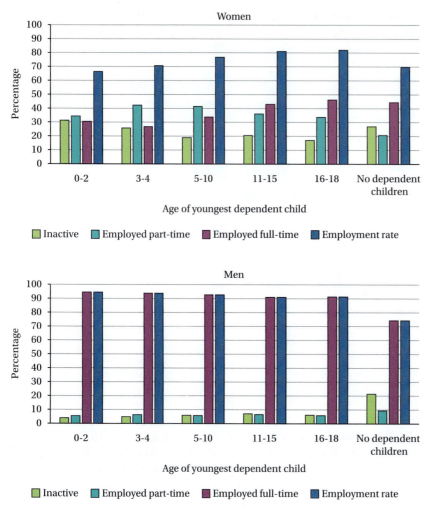

**Figure 6.17** Economic activity[1] and employment rates[2] of women and men (aged 16 to 64) with dependent children,[3] by age of youngest dependent child, including the percentage who work full- or part-time: UK, 2019

[1] People are 'active' when they are employed, or unemployed and seeking work. 'Inactive' refers to those who are not seeking work, as they are looking after the family and/or home, or for other reasons (e.g. disability or long-standing illness).

[2] The employment rate refers to the proportion of those who are in employment and unemployed but actively seeking work. It includes here women and men with dependent and non-dependent children, or no children.

[3] Dependent children are those living with their parents and either aged under 16, or aged 16–18 in full-time education. Children aged 16–18 who have a spouse, partner or child living in the household are not classified as dependent children.

*Source*: adapted from *Working and Workless Households in the UK: January to March 2019*, Office for National Statistics

are still few workplaces today with childcare facilities, which would allow working mothers to take full-time jobs. The presence of dependent children (under the age of 16, or 18 if in full-time education) and the age of the youngest child are the most important factors related to whether or not women are in paid employment, and whether they work full- or part-time. Figure 6.17 illustrates the importance of this link between dependent children and women's patterns of working in paid employment, and how, by contrast, the employment rates of men, and whether they work full- or part-time, are unaffected by the age of their youngest dependent child.

### Activity

Study figure 6.17 and answer the following questions:
1 What is meant by a 'dependent child'?
2 What percentage of women with children between the ages of 3 and 4 were in full-time employment in 2019?
3 Using the data in figure 6.17, write a short paragraph explaining how the age of the youngest dependent child affects the employment rates of women and men.
4 Approximately what percentage of women, compared to men, with children between the ages of 5 and 10, were in full-time employment?
5 What evidence is there in figure 6.17 that having dependent children seems to have a far greater impact on the working lives of women than of men?
6 Suggest a suitable research method to investigate a sample of women in paid employment who have small children, with the aim of discovering any problems or role conflict they experience at work and in the home arising from motherhood. Give two reasons why you chose that research method, and explain why you think it would be the best method for investigating this topic.

*Limited career opportunities*   Women have more limited career opportunities than men for a number of reasons:

- *Gender stereotyping*, at school and in the wider gender-role socialization process, means women, even when they have the necessary educational qualifications for the top jobs, often lack the self-confidence and assertiveness to apply for them.
- *Male prejudice* about women in career jobs and senior positions. There is evidence that some men are reluctant to be supervised by female managers.
- *Women with children are often seen by employers as unreliable.* It is often assumed by employers that any woman of childbearing age will eventually have children. Surveys suggest some employers try to avoid hiring or

Many employers still ask women discriminatory questions

promoting women who are likely to become pregnant, and many continue to ask potential women employees about their family plans, even though such questions are illegal under discrimination laws.

There is a common assumption that mothers will be unable to cope with the demands of the job, or to balance work and family life, and will try to avoid work during school holidays, or be absent to look after sick children. Research by the Equality and Human Rights Commission in 2015 estimated that as many as 54,000 women a year were forced out of their jobs as a result of becoming pregnant, and around 1 in 5 new mothers experienced harassment or negative comments from their colleagues, employer or manager when pregnant or returning from maternity leave.

- *The glass ceiling.* Even successful women in career jobs often find they come up against what has been called the **glass ceiling** – an invisible barrier of discrimination which makes it difficult for women to reach the same top levels in their chosen careers as similarly qualified men. These factors mean women are often overlooked for training and promotion to senior positions by male employers.

- *Career breaks or interrupted careers.* Women with promising careers may have to leave jobs temporarily to have children, and therefore miss out on relevant experience, training and promotion opportunities. Top jobs require a continuous career pattern in the 20–35 age period – yet these are the usual childbearing years for women, so while men continue to work and get promoted, women miss their opportunities.

- *Married or cohabiting women are still more likely to move house and area for their male partner's job promotion than for their own.* This means women interrupt their careers and have to start again, often at a lower

> **Glass ceiling**
> An invisible barrier of discrimination which makes it difficult for women to reach the same top levels in their chosen careers as similarly qualified men.

level, in a new job, which means the men are getting promotion at the expense of lost opportunities for their partners.

*Limited access to training*    Women are less likely than men to enter training for better-paid and more secure skilled work. Often women are denied training, and therefore promotion opportunities, because employers, parents, teachers and sometimes the women themselves see training as 'wasted' on women. Employers, as a result of gender socialization, may assume women will leave work to produce and raise children. They may therefore be unwilling to invest in expensive training programmes for women. Rather, they prefer to employ women in low-skilled jobs where they can be easily and quickly trained and replaced. Of the small number of women who do obtain training, the vast majority are employed in 'feminine occupations' such as hairdressing, beauty and clerical work, which are generally low-paid with limited career prospects.

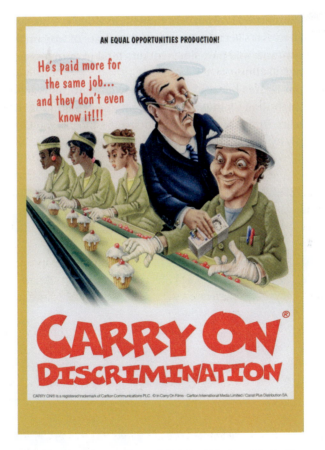

Reproduced with permission of the Equal Opportunities Commission (now incorporated into the Equality and Human Rights Commission)

*Lower pay – the gender pay gap* The **gender pay gap** refers to the difference between women's hourly earnings and those of men. While the Equal Pay Act (1970), now part of the Equality Act (2010), gives equal pay to women if they do the same (or similar) work as men, it has been shown above that women often do not do the same work as men, and consequently have no one to claim equal pay with. For example, many more women work in the low-paid 'caring' occupations than men, and there may often be no males to compare their wages with. In 2018, women made up six in ten of all low-paid workers, and around 27 per cent of women in employment were on low pay, compared to about 11 per cent of men. Women have fewer opportunities than men to increase their pay through overtime, shift payments or bonuses.

According to the Office for National Statistics, in 2018 the average hourly pay of full-time women workers was only 91.4 per cent of that of men – a gender pay gap of 8.6 per cent. This gender pay gap for full-time workers was entirely in favour of men for all occupations. For all workers (both full- and part-time), men earned 17.9 per cent more than women. The gender pay gap is larger for all workers because a much higher share of women than men are employed part-time, and part-time workers tend to earn less per hour than those working full-time.

Government figures released in 2018 showed that there are almost four times more men than women in Britain's highest-paid jobs (earning over £100,000 a year). In contrast, the ten worst-paid jobs in the UK are all performed mainly by women (see box opposite).

> **Gender pay gap**
> The difference between the hourly earnings of women and men.

A 2017 report by the British Medical Association found that women doctors working full-time were paid thousands of pounds less (34 per cent) each year than their similarly qualified male colleagues

The reasons for the gender pay gap include:

- *Women being concentrated in low-skilled and part-time work*, which lacks promotion prospects and trade union protection, and often sick pay, holiday pay and redundancy payments – a situation which does not apply to the majority of men.
- *Sex discrimination* – it's illegal, but still happens.
- *Women's greater caring responsibilities* – e.g. for children, the sick or the elderly. This leads them into more part-time jobs, which generally pay less and have fewer promotion opportunities.
- *Career breaks for childbirth and child rearing*, interrupting promotion opportunities.
- *Women's primary responsibility for unpaid work in the home* (domestic labour). Women's dual burden and their triple shift (see page 134 in chapter 3) limit their access to and advancement in paid work.

## Gender inequalities in unpaid work: domestic labour

When talking about women at work, many people assume this refers to paid employment. However, it is important to remember there is one job which is still seen as primarily the responsibility of women – unpaid house-work or domestic labour, including cooking, cleaning, doing the washing, childcare and looking after the sick and elderly. This is true in the major-ity of cases even when both partners are working full-time outside the home in paid employment. The inequalities in domestic labour are dis-cussed in more detail in chapter 3, pages 181–3, and you should refer to these now.

---

**THE TEN LOWEST-PAID JOBS IN THE UNITED KINGDOM …**

1 School midday and crossing patrol
2 Leisure and theme park attendant
3 Playworker
4 Waiter, waitress
5 Bar staff
6 Cleaner and domestic
7 Care escort
8 Sports and leisure assistant
9 Retail cashier / check-out operator
10 Kitchen and catering assistant

*… and they're nearly all done by women!*

*Source: Annual Survey of Hours and Earnings:2018*, Office for National Statistics

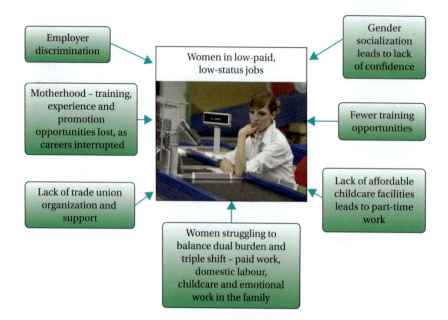

**Figure 6.18** Why are women concentrated in lower-paid and lower-status jobs than men?

## Women and social mobility

Women have traditionally had poorer chances of mobility than men. However, the better performance of women in education, their growing participation in the labour force, and equal opportunities policies at work are now giving women more favourable opportunities for upward mobility. Nevertheless, for the reasons considered above, women still face major difficulties in entering skilled manual and higher managerial, technical and top professional occupations. They have less chance of promotion than men, and many women experience downward mobility as they abandon careers with bright futures to take care of children, only to return to work at a lower status, and with less pay, than when they left. There are still very few women compared with men in the top elite positions in society – those in the small

---

**GENDER INEQUALITIES IN THE FAMILY, EDUCATION AND CRIME**

Don't forget there is also evidence of gender inequalities:

- *in the family* (see pages 134 and 181–4) – women's dual burden, their triple shift and inequalities in power and authority.
- *in education* (see pages 219–20 and 278–80) – the underachievement of working-class girls (and boys). Even girls who beat boys in education still don't do as well as they might because of patriarchy in the classroom.
- *in crime* (see pages 194–6, 317 and 357) – the double jeopardy faced by women who both commit serious crimes and violate the norms of traditional gender roles. Women are the main victims of domestic violence and sexual offences.

**Activity**

This section has mainly focused on the inequalities facing women in paid and unpaid work.

1   What other inequalities do women face in their daily lives compared with men? Think about things like going into pubs alone, fear of attack and sexual assault, politics and so on. List all those you can think of.

2   In the light of the issues raised in this chapter and your responses to the activity above, consider what steps might be taken to break down these inequalities. To help you do this, draw three columns. In the first column, list all the inequalities you can think of that women still face today compared with men; in the second column, list the causes of these inequalities; in the third column, list the changes that would need to be made in society to remove these inequalities.

3   Describe and explain two reasons why, despite the inequalities they continue to face, there are more women in top jobs in the UK today than there were in the 1950s.

**Race** The division of humans into different groups according to physical characteristics, such as skin colour.

groups of occupations which hold a great deal of power, such as judges, leaders of industry, top civil servants, and MPs and government ministers.

# ETHNIC STRATIFICATION AND INEQUALITY

## Race, ethnicity and minority ethnic groups

**Ethnicity** The shared culture, including language, religion, cultural traditions and characteristics, of a social group, which gives its members an identity in some ways different from other groups – e.g. Black, Asian and Minority Ethnic (BAME) groups.

The idea of **race** refers to the attempt to divide humans according to physical characteristics (like skin colour) into different racial groups, such as white or black. Such classifications have little scientific basis, and sociologists generally regard this as a rather pointless exercise, as it has no value in explaining human culture, such as social inequality. This is because human behaviour is largely a result of socialization, and cannot be explained by purely biological characteristics.

**Ethnicity** is a more valuable idea. This refers to the common culture shared by a social group, such as language, religion, styles of dress, food, shared history and experiences, and so on. An **ethnic group** is any group which shares a common culture, and a **minority ethnic group** is a group which shares a cultural identity that is different from that of the majority population of a society. This means that groups such as Travellers, the Polish and the Irish are all minority ethnic groups in Britain, as well as ethnic groups of a different skin colour, such as Asian, Chinese and Black communities.

**Ethnic group** A group of people who share a common culture.

**Minority ethnic group** A social group which shares a cultural identity that is different from that of the majority population of a society.

There is a wide range of ethnic groups who have emigrated to Britain over the years, such as Irish, Chinese, Jews, Poles, Indian, Pakistani and Bangladeshi Asians, and Black Africans, Black Caribbeans (together termed 'Black' or 'African-Caribbeans') and, more recently, people from Eastern

Europe, such as the Czech Republic, Romania, Bulgaria, Estonia, Hungary, Latvia and Lithuania. Traditionally, White British people saw 'minority ethnic groups' as people of a different racial origin – typically those of Black or Asian origin – but recent White immigrants and migrant workers from Eastern Europe are also becoming commonly seen as minority ethnic groups. It is important to recognize that not all Black, Asian and Minority Ethnic (BAME) groups share the same cultural features. For example, Asians and African-Caribbeans show especially strong cultural differences, and Indian Asians may be Sikhs (the largest group in Britain) or Hindus, while Pakistanis and Bangladeshis are more likely to be Muslims. Recent migrants from Eastern Europe come from a range of different cultural backgrounds.

At the 2011 census, about 13 per cent of the population of the UK were non-white, and these make up a small minority of all immigrants. British Asians and African-Caribbeans together form about 10 per cent of the UK population; 94 per cent of British Black Caribbeans and over half of people from Pakistani and Bangladeshi backgrounds were actually born in the UK, so it is misleading to regard them as immigrants.

## Ethnic inequality and life chances

While some BAME groups are doing very well in Britain, they often face a series of disadvantages and poorer life chances than their White British counterparts. Pakistanis, Bangladeshis and African-Caribbeans in particular face a series of disadvantages in Britain compared with the white majority, although there are differences within each group. Particular groups seem to suffer an 'ethnic penalty' in some situations – a range of inequalities which

She has good reasons to look worried – although some of those from minority ethnic groups are doing very well in Britain, BAME groups still face a series of disadvantages and poorer life chances than their White British counterparts. Why might that be?

cannot be explained by any other factors apart from ethnicity, suggesting that the causes lie in direct and indirect discrimination. For example, in education, black pupils face higher risks of being excluded from school than white pupils committing similar offences, and have lower levels of achievement than those from similar social-class backgrounds. If you are black, you are up to forty times more likely to be stopped and searched by the police, three times more likely to be arrested, and four times more likely to be in prison than someone who is white.

Some of these inequalities and disadvantages are discussed in chapter 4 on education (see pages 264–9), chapter 5 on crime and deviance (see pages 340–4 and 358), and chapter 7 on the media (see pages 551–3). You should refer to these sections. This section will examine additional inequalities in employment, pay, poverty and housing.

## *Employment and unemployment*

Nearly all BAME groups are less likely to be in paid employment than similarly qualified White British men and women. During the economic recession of 2008–10, black and Asian unemployment grew at a faster rate than that for white people, and in 2009, nearly half (48 per cent) of 16- to 24-year-old black people were unemployed, compared to 20 per cent of white people of the same age. Other findings show:

- African-Caribbeans, Pakistanis and Bangladeshis are less likely than White British people to secure the best jobs. These groups are under-represented in non-manual occupations, particularly in managerial and professional work. They are hugely under-represented in Parliament and the top elite occupations. In 2017, barely 3 per cent of Britain's most powerful and influential people, such as business leaders, top civil servants, newspaper editors, Supreme Court judges and top police and military officers, were from BAME groups (see https://goo.gl/RzuoYU for more detail).

- BAME groups are over-represented (that is, there is more of them than there should be, given their proportion in the population) in low-paid, semi-skilled and unskilled manual occupations, and they are more likely to work in particular low-paid sectors such as sales, catering, hairdressing, textiles and clothing – occupations with limited opportunities for promotion and pay increases. They often work longer and more unsociable hours (shiftwork and night work) than white people. Black and Asian people are less likely to get employed when competing with White British people with the same qualifications for the same job.

- People from BAME groups are more likely to face unemployment, as shown in figure 6.19. Those with university degrees are around two and half times more likely to be unemployed than their white peers.

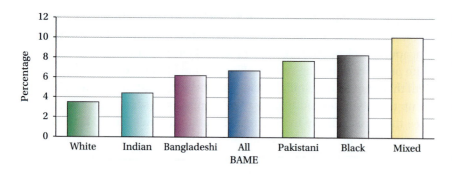

**Figure 6.19** Unemployment rates,[1] by ethnic group: United Kingdom, October–December 2018

[1] The unemployment rate is the number unemployed as a percentage of all those active in the labour market.

*Source: Labour Force Survey,* Office for National Statistics, February 2019

## Lower pay – the ethnicity pay gap

Black and Asian people have lower average earnings than white people, even when they have the same job level. On average, Pakistani and Bangladeshi employees earn about 17 per cent less, while African-Caribbeans earn about 14 per cent less.

According to the Equality and Human Rights Commission (*The Ethnicity Pay Gap,* 2017), despite some specific ethnic minority groups, such as the Chinese, receiving higher earnings than white workers on average, ethnic minority groups:

- are more likely to work in low-paying industries, with security, hospitality and textiles employing the highest proportions
- are over 50 per cent more likely to be paid at the national minimum wage, compared to all those employed.

## Poverty

The Department for Work and Pensions showed that in 2017–18:

- BAME groups were far more likely than white people to be in the poorest fifth of the population, as figure 6.20 shows
- Over a third (36 per cent) of people from BAME groups lived in low-income households, compared to a fifth (20 per cent) of white households.
- Nearly half of people from Bangladeshi and Pakistani ethnic backgrounds lived in low-income households;
- Around 45 per cent of all BAME children lived in low-income households compared to 26 per cent of white children.

## Housing

BAME groups overall face the following housing inequalities.

- They tend to live in inferior housing to white people and in poorer and 'less desirable' areas of towns and cities.

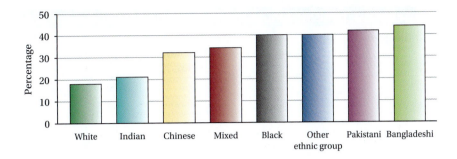

**Figure 6.20** Percentage of each ethnic group in the poorest fifth of the population: United Kingdom, 2017–18

*Source: Households Below Average Income: 1994/95 to 2017/18*, Department for Work and Pensions, 2019

- They tend to live in older properties than whites, and are more likely to live in a terraced house or flat.
- BAME groups generally face higher levels of overcrowding than white households. For example, around 30 per cent of Bangladeshi households are overcrowded, and they are fifteen times more likely to live in over-crowded accommodation than White British people.
- They are more likely to live in rented accommodation, as table 6.4 shows. Indian Asians, however, are more likely to be owner occupiers than white people, although the quality of the Indian Asians' housing is often poor, and tends to be in the least desirable and cheaper areas.
- They are more likely than white people to be homeless. Around a third of those accepted as homeless by local authorities in England are from BAME groups – nearly three times as many as there should be given their proportion of the population.

## Theories and explanations for ethnic stratification and inequality

The following explanations for ethnic disadvantage should be considered together, as they are cumulative, in that one aspect of discrimination or disadvantage can lead to further disadvantage in other areas. It is also important to remember that the social-class and gender inequalities discussed earlier in this chapter also combine with, or intersect with (see the box on page 415 on intersectionality), ethnic disadvantages to make ethnic inequality worse. An example is Bangladeshi working-class women, who are probably the most deprived group in Britain. It is also important not to develop crude stereotypes like 'ethnicity equals poverty'. This overlooks the great successes of some people from all ethnic backgrounds, particularly those of Indian and Chinese ethnicity. It also disguises the fact that there are widespread disadvantages facing the White British lower working class as well.

### Table 6.4 Housing tenure by ethnic group, England, 2017–18

| Ethnic group | Owner occupier % | Rented from social sector (council or housing associations) % | Rented privately % | All households (thousands) |
|---|---|---|---|---|
| White | 66 | 16 | 18 | 20,487 |
| Black | 31 | 40 | 29 | 787 |
| Indian | 72 | 7 | 21 | 558 |
| Pakistani or Bangladeshi | 59 | 18 | 23 | 502 |
| Other | 36 | 24 | 40 | 937 |
| All BAME groups | 46 | 24 | 30 | 2,785 |
| All ethnic groups | 63 | 17 | 20 | 23,272 |

*Source*: adapted from *English Housing Survey headline report 2017 to 2018: section 1 household tables*, Ministry of Housing, Communities and Local Government, 2019

### Activity

1  Refer to table 6.4.
   (a) Which ethnic group is most likely to occupy homes they own?
   (b) Which ethnic group is least likely to rent their home privately?
   (c) What is the difference in the percentage of white people who own their own home compared to all BAME groups?
2  Look back over the section so far on ethnicity and inequality, and answer the following questions:
   (a) Which BAME group is most likely to be unemployed?
   (b) Which BAME group is most likely to be living in the poorest fifth of the population?
   (c) Which BAME group appears to face the greatest overall disadvantages? Give reasons for your answer, and refer to some evidence.
   (d) Suggest two forms of inequality facing BAME groups *other than* those in employment, pay, poverty and housing.
   (e) BAME working-class women are frequently the most disadvantaged social group of all. Drawing on your knowledge of gender, ethnic and class divisions, suggest possible explanations for this.

## Functionalist theories

- *Underachievement in education* (see pages 264–9 in chapter 4). Functionalists argue that society is meritocratic, and those with the drive and ability will make it to the top. The reasons some BAME groups experience poor life chances is because they lack the qualifications to reach the top in a meritocratic society.

- *Failure to assimilate.* Some BAME groups are socialized into ethnic subcultures, which marks them out as having some different norms and values from the White British majority. The disadvantages of some BAME groups will gradually disappear as their socialization patterns change to enable them to absorb and become assimilated into the dominant culture, and to become accepted by the White British ethnic majority.
- *The underclass.* The functionalist-related New Right (see pages 52–4 and 486–8) views some BAME groups as having cultural features which make them part of the underclass, right at the bottom of the social hierarchy. These cultural features mean they have only themselves to blame for their disadvantage.

## Marxist theories

- *Many of those in BAME groups are working-class.* They therefore face the same problems encountered by all working-class people, regardless of their ethnic origin. This would explain their disadvantage compared with the population as a whole.
- *Divide and rule* – discrimination against BAME groups acts to divide the working class along ethnic lines. BAME groups are used as scapegoats to blame for problems that are not their fault. This disguises that the real source of problems lies in the structure of inequality in capitalist societies, and hinders the development of class consciousness (see page 380) in a united working class, which might threaten the wealth and power of the dominant social class.
- *Cheap labour* – BAME groups provide a source of cheap labour for the capitalist class, and a reserve army of labour that can be drawn on in times of economic boom, and easily discarded in times of economic recession.

## Weberian theories

Weberians argue that BAME groups:

- *have lower status* than white people in a predominantly white society due to racism and discrimination (see below).
- *have a weaker market situation.* This is due to poorer educational qualifications or other skills, which, combined with racism, means they face poorer rewards or unemployment when they try to sell their labour in the labour market.
- *have less power than white people.* This is partly because of their lower status and weaker market situation, which means they have less access

to positions of influence in society. A related explanation is that some BAME groups lack **social capital**.

This refers to the social networks of influence and support that people have, such as links of friends and family connections, and knowing the 'right people' – who to talk to, who to get advice from, and who is in a position to help them (or their children) in times of difficulty or need, and to influence others in their favour. Possession of social capital is highest in the white middle and upper classes, and can provide a network of skills and support to help their children's education and find the best schools, and connections to help them get jobs and take advantage of opportunities. BAME groups may either have weaker social capital, or less influential networks to help them take up opportunities.

## Racial prejudice and discrimination

**Racial prejudice** and **racial discrimination** are key explanations for the social position of BAME groups, and underlie the functionalist, Marxist and Weberian explanations above.

The 1965 Race Relations Act was the first of a series of pieces of legislation in the UK to make it illegal to discriminate against people on the 'grounds of colour, race, or ethnic or national origins'. Much of this anti-discrimination legislation has since been rolled up into the 2010 Equality Act. In the UK, it is now illegal to discriminate against people on ethnic grounds.

However, there is widespread evidence that racial discrimination in employment, housing and other areas continues, particularly against those with a skin colour other than white. Part of the problem is that it is difficult to prove racial discrimination. For example, a BAME person who is turned down for promotion at work in favour of a white person may be told the white person was simply more suited to the job in some way.

Discrimination might well mean that BAME people are more likely to be singled out for redundancy when the axe falls, or overlooked for promotion, and there is evidence of discrimination among private landlords, letting agencies and council officials in allocating housing to black and Asian people.

The most straightforward explanation for disadvantages in employment and pay is that they result from racism and prejudice by employers, who either refuse to employ some BAME groups, or employ them only in low-status and low-paid jobs, or refuse to promote them. This view has been confirmed by a number of surveys in which it was found that white workers received more positive responses in job applications than similarly qualified and experienced applicants from BAME groups. For example, a 2017 survey by the BBC (see https://goo.gl/gpEsye) found that a job-seeker with an English-sounding name ('Adam') was offered three times the number of

**Social capital**
The social networks of influence and support that people have.

**Racial prejudice**
A set of assumptions about an ethnic group, which people are reluctant to change even when they receive information which undermines those assumptions.

**Racial discrimination** When people's racial prejudice causes them to act unfairly against an ethnic group. For example, a racially prejudiced police officer might use his or her power to pick on BAME people more than white people, perhaps by stopping and searching them in the street and asking what they're up to.

interviews that an applicant with a Muslim name ('Mohamed') with identical skills and experience was offered.

The fear of racism affects where BAME groups choose to live, as they seek to reduce the risks of racial abuse and attack by avoiding neighbourhoods they know to be racist and therefore unsafe for them. This restricts their choices in housing and the areas they can live in, even without the direct discrimination of racist landlords.

## The news is not all bad …

Being black or Asian in Britain is often portrayed as a story of racial inequality, prejudice and discrimination. Yet the news is not all bad. The existence of institutional racism (see pages 343–4 in chapter 5) has now been officially recognized, and action taken to tackle racism in a wide range of public services and private organizations. A series of Race Relations Acts and the 2010 Equality Act have sought to tackle racism in all areas of social life, and every single public service in Britain, including schools, now has a legal obligation to positively promote race equality and better race relations. National and local government and some large companies and organizations in Britain are trying to improve the under-representation of BAME groups in important areas of social life, using measures such as:

- advertising jobs in minority ethnic newspapers
- race awareness courses for staff handling recruitment
- monitoring of job applications for ethnic bias

**Activity**

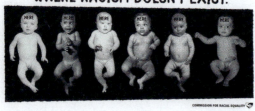

1 Refer to the 'Babies' poster from the Commission for Racial Equality (now incorporated into the Equality and Human Rights Commission). What point is the poster making?

2 Below are four possible explanations for racism. Study them carefully, discuss them in your group, and think of any other reasons why BAME groups face racial prejudice and discrimination. Then, for each explanation, suggest a means of overcoming it.

   (a) *History*. Our society has a long history of white domination of African and Asian countries. Slavery and colonization were often justified on the basis of ideas about the supposed superiority of white people to those of other ethnic origins. These ideas still tend to linger on.

   (b) *Stereotyping*. A stereotype is a generalized, over-simplified view of the features of a social group, allowing for few individual differences between its members. Often the media portray degrading and insulting stereotypes of minority ethnic groups which fuel racism.

   (c) *Scapegoating*. Scapegoats are individuals or groups blamed for something which is not their fault. When unemployment, poverty and crime rates rise, it becomes easy to find simple explanations by scapegoating easily identifiable minorities, such as BAME groups or asylum-seekers.

   (d) *Cultural differences*. In any society where there are cultural differences between groups, such as in religious beliefs, values, customs, food, dress and so on, there are bound to be conflicts from time to time between the minority cultures and the majority culture.

3 In three columns, as suggested below, make a list of all the inequalities facing BAME groups, including those from the other chapters referred to at the beginning of this section. In the second column, put down some of the causes for the inequality you've identified, and in the third column suggest policies or steps that could be taken to overcome these inequalities.

INEQUALITY FACED        POSSIBLE CAUSES        POSSIBLE SOLUTIONS

4 Identify and explain one advantage and one disadvantage of using unstructured interviews to investigate the extent of racism experienced by BAME groups.

- equal opportunities policies to combat discrimination in schools, colleges and private- and public-sector employers
- multicultural education in the school curriculum.

In some areas, such as education, some minority ethnic groups are doing better and are much more likely to continue their education beyond the age of 16 than their white counterparts, and there is a growing black and Asian middle class.

# AGE STRATIFICATION AND INEQUALITY

Age is not in itself a significant feature of inequality in contemporary Britain, and the age group to which you belong does not in itself have a major impact on your life chances, in the way that social class, gender or ethnicity does. Nonetheless, for the two extremes of the age range – children and young people (roughly 0–18) and older people (state pension age 65/6 and older) – there are some significant differences from people of other ages.

## The social construction of age

When something is a social construction, it means it is created through the individual, social and cultural interpretations, perceptions and actions of people. Age and age groups are social constructions, as how old you are is not simply, or most importantly, a matter of biological development. The status allocated to people of different biological ages is created by society and social attitudes.

Attitudes to age vary between cultures. In some societies, old people have high status as the 'elders' of a community, while in modern Britain older people generally tend to lack status and authority, though this can vary between ethnic groups. In the Asian and Chinese communities, for example, elderly people are still often held in high esteem.

Social attitudes to people of different ages can change over time. In medieval times, childhood did not exist as a separate status. Children often moved straight from infancy, when they required constant care, to working roles in the community. Children were seen as 'little adults'. They did not lead separate lives, and dressed like, and mixed with, adults. Childhood was certainly not the specially protected and privileged time of life we associate with children today, with their legal protection, extended education and freedom from work.

The social construction of age means that we tend to think of people in terms of age groups in contemporary British culture, such as 'infants',

These women are all of a very similar age. However, their levels of physical activity, independence and knowledge of the latest technology are very likely to determine which one you consider to be the 'oldest'

'children', 'teenagers', 'youth', 'young' and 'mature' adults, the 'middle-aged', 'pensioners' or the 'old'. The age group to which we belong can have important consequences for status in society, particularly for the young and the old.

## Is age a significant source of social inequality?

It sometimes seems there are large inequalities separating today's younger **generation** of 'millennials', born between roughly 1980 and 2000, and the older 'baby-boomer' generation born between about 1945 and 1965, who are or soon will be state pensioners.

**Generation** Those born in the same 15- to 30-year period.

The baby-boomer generation as a whole have done much better financially than previous generations. They have benefitted, for example, from huge gains in the value of their homes, free higher education, relatively secure lifetime jobs, earlier state pension ages and more generous work-related pensions, which means they are able to enjoy a more comfortable retirement than any generation before or after them. The typical pensioner household income is now, for the first time, higher than that of the average working-age household.

By contrast, today's younger generation of millennials finds itself struggling to even buy a home, faces huge costs and years of debt for higher education, often insecure and poor conditions of employment, reduced promotion opportunities, poorer work-based pensions, and ever-extending years before they can draw their state pensions. They are financially propping up by their taxes the costs of the welfare state created by the expanding older generation, such as their demands on the NHS and the rising cost of state pensions as older people live longer and longer.

However, this view of generational inequality ignores the huge inequality that exists between different groups within the *same* generation of people, such as similarly aged middle-class and working-class people, and this inequality is greater than inequality between generations. These inequalities reflect the social class, gender and ethnic inequalities discussed earlier, and have nothing to do with age.

## Inequalities among older people

There are huge social-class inequalities among older people, such as those in wealth, income, poverty, health, housing, access to and use of public services – particularly health services – and life expectancy (how long people live). These include factors like the social class in which they grew up in childhood, their own educational achievements and occupations as adults, and periods of unemployment. For example, people from low-paid occupational backgrounds are more likely to be in poor health and living in poverty when they are older, even if they have been employed for all of their working lives. Official statistics published in 2018 showed that the average pensioner living in the affluent City of London enjoyed a pension income that was three times higher – £25,600 more – than the average pensioner living in poorer Stoke-on-Trent.

Gender differences also create inequalities among older people. Women in lower-classed occupations are less likely to be working in later life, and though women live longer than men, they spend more years in poor health, and are more likely than men to be in poverty when they are older.

People of all ages from ethnic minority groups in the UK are more likely to have poor physical and mental health, and to have lower pensions in later life, compared with White British groups.

## Inequalities among younger people

White British young people from higher social-class backgrounds continue to enjoy the same advantages as ever. Grandparents and parents will probably help with buying their first home, help get them jobs, and provide financial support in higher education and help them to avoid or pay off student loans, with a generous inheritance when their grandparents and parents die. Those from the most disadvantaged backgrounds will have none of these benefits.

The following sections examine some inequalities linked only to age, rather than social class, gender and ethnicity. However, it is likely that these inequalities are experienced in different ways by those from different social-class, gender and ethnic backgrounds.

## Young people and inequality

### Legal inequality

Inequalities among young people, say from ages 0 to 21, primarily arise from a desire to protect their overall health and safety, security and well-being, to protect them from exploitation and harm, and to prevent them from engaging in activities which they are thought not yet to be sufficiently mature or responsible to participate in, such as marriage (minimum age 16 with parent/guardian's consent, otherwise age 18), driving a car (minimum age 17), voting and becoming a Member of Parliament or a local councillor (minimum age 18). There are, therefore, a mass of laws that, in effect, give them fewer legal rights than those of other ages, and stop them from doing and buying things until they reach certain ages. There are also laws that try to protect them against exploitation – such as restrictions on working hours and minimum wage regulations – and against child abuse and paedophilia. Some examples of these are shown below.

- Those under 14 (13 in some areas) aren't allowed to undertake paid work, except for odd jobs for a parent, relative or neighbour, babysitting, light work like a paper round, and some specially licensed sport, advertising, modelling or appearing in plays, films, television shows or other entertainment.
- Young workers (over school leaving age and under 18) are not allowed to be employed in factory, construction or transport work.
- Those under school leaving age are not allowed to work during school hours or for more than two hours on any school day or 12 hours in any week, or before 7 a.m. or after 7 p.m.
- Those under the age of 16 (the age of consent) cannot legally engage in sexual acts.
- Shopkeepers cannot legally sell lottery tickets, aerosol paints and petrol to under-16s, or cigarettes, tobacco, solvents, lighter fuel, knives and alcohol to under-18s.
- Cinema films, DVDs, video and computer games have '12', '15' and '18' age restrictions.

## Pay inequality

Young people are often at risk of exploitation when they are employed, and, like adults, are protected by a legally set national minimum wage. No employer can pay less than this legal rate without breaking the law. However, the law allows age discrimination in minimum wages, and there are separate rates for those under age 18, those aged 18–20, and those aged 21–4, which are all less than the minimum adult rate – the 'national living wage', which starts for those over age 25. This means more than a million young people are being paid up to £3.45 an hour less for doing the same jobs as older workers. While this is a clear inequality, the reason given by government is to discourage young people from going into employment before they have finished the preferred options of education and training, which bring long-term benefits.

However, a 2017 survey by the Young Women's Trust found that this leads to a quarter of young people in the UK being constantly in debt. Nearly half of young people borrow money, work extra hours or skip meals to make their cash last to the end of the month.

## Unemployment

Young people are particularly vulnerable to unemployment, especially during periods of economic recession, as firms stop hiring and usually make their least-skilled workers redundant first. The unemployment rate at the begining of 2019 for 18- to 24-year-olds was 9.8 per cent, about two-and-a-half times higher than that for the population as a whole (3.9 per cent).

## Older people and inequality

One in three children born today can expect to live to the age of 100, and the average person can expect to live a quarter of their lives in retirement. In mid-2015, more than one in three people (36 per cent) in the UK were aged 50 or over, and by 2041, nearly a quarter of all adults will be over state pension age, and the number of people over 85 will have doubled. Greater life expectancy means people may be in the 'older' age group for perhaps longer than in any other age group. This means that more people than ever before face an extended period of living with the social-class, gender and ethnic inequalities discussed in this chapter, and that have blighted their lives, with these worsening as their health and income decline as they leave paid work and grow older.

People aged between 50 and 64 have the highest disposable income (uncommitted spending money) of any age group, and the 'grey pound' (older people's spending) is very important to businesses, and, increasingly, new businesses are opening up that market to older people and are dedicated to their needs, such as SAGA.

## Age discrimination: ageism

Despite being a significant proportion of the population and a major market for business, older people are likely to encounter age discrimination or **ageism**. This means they face prejudice and discrimination, with negative stereotyped assumptions that they are less intelligent, forgetful, 'grumpy' and 'moaning', in poor health, incapable and dependent on others, unable to learn new skills and so on – simply because they are old.

Ageism can have detrimental effects on older people, and they may face being called derogatory (offensive and belittling) names and having negative media images ('dirty old man', 'boring old fart', 'grumpy old woman'), being infantilized (treated like infants/children), being denied a sexual identity, encountering barriers to proper medical treatment (such as not

**Ageism**
Stereotyping of, or prejudice and discrimination against, individuals or groups on the grounds of their age.

Discrimination on age grounds is a major inequality facing older people. Ask a few of your older relatives whether they have experienced any form of age discrimination

being referred to a consultant due to being too old) and losing jobs or facing obstacles to getting jobs on the grounds of age.

Age UK (www.ageuk.org.uk) suggests other examples of ageism include:

- being refused interest-free credit, a new credit card, car insurance or travel insurance because of your age
- receiving a lower quality of service in a shop or restaurant because of the organization's attitude to older people
- being refused membership of a club or trade association because of your age.

Age discrimination was outlawed by the Equality Act of 2010, but, as with racial discrimination discussed earlier, age discrimination may turn out to be difficult to prove in some circumstances.

Many elderly people are discouraged by employers from continuing in work beyond state pension age, even if they are still perfectly capable of doing their jobs. The employment rate of those over state pension age was around 11 per cent (2019), despite the fact that a majority of people say they would like to do some kind of work for longer than this.

One more positive aspect of inequality in relation to older people that gives them advantages over all other age groups is the extra benefits that come from the state, such as free prescriptions, free eyesight tests and free off-peak bus travel for the over-60s, and free TV licences for those over 75. However, it might well be argued these benefits have been earned through a lifetime of working and paying taxes, and in all too many cases they do not do much to overcome the lifetime effects of the social-class, gender and ethnic inequalities discussed in this chapter.

## Theories explaining age inequalities

### *Functionalist theories*

Functionalist theories suggest age inequalities arise at the two extremes of childhood / young adulthood and old age. The different roles associated with age are vital for the smooth running of society.

- *Children and young adults* are still undergoing the process of socialization to fit them into society. Their lack of status arises as they are still making the transition from the ascribed status of the family to the achieved status of full independent adults and involvement in the adult labour market.
- *Older people* lack status as they are disengaging (or actively removing themselves) from their previous roles. Many older people's willingness and ability to work will diminish with age, and retirement makes way for the new, younger workforce to the advantage of the whole society. A criticism of this is that the skills and expertise of the older worker are lost to the economy.

### *Marxist theories*

These emphasize that:

- both young and older people provide a source of cheap labour for capitalism
- media stereotypes and negative labelling of both groups, and moral panics over the behaviour of the young (see pages 300 and 548–9), help to justify their exploitation
- the elderly, in capitalist societies, are regarded as of less use as labour power and as a source of profit by employers, as they are more expensive to employ than younger people
- the elderly become an increasing drain on resources – for example, through their growing use of the NHS and the high cost of providing their state pensions – and become less productive and useful as they grow older
- the elderly retired working class are of less use as a source of profit through their diminishing consumption of consumer goods as their spending power reduces as they leave paid employment
- it is the young and the elderly working class who suffer the greatest exploitation.

## Weberian theories

Weberian theories suggest that young people lack status as they have a weak market situation because they lack skills, knowledge, training and experience, and lack power to bargain for a better position. Older people who have retired lose the status and power derived from being part of the paid labour force.

## Feminist theories

Feminist theories emphasize the role patriarchy plays in the different experiences of both younger and older women, who are frequently less valued than their male counterparts. Older women, regardless of wealth and background, have a lower status than men. Ageing women often find they face additional pressures that ageing men do not – for example, they often have additional caring responsibilities for older and younger relatives, and they are less likely to have high-profile/visible roles in the media. Elderly women become 'invisible' in a variety of social situations, and particularly the media, in a way older men do not.

# STRATIFICATION, INEQUALITY AND DISABILITY

An **impairment** is some loss, limitation or difference of functioning of the mind or body, on a long-term or permanent basis, either that one is born with or that arises from injury or disease. **Disability** occurs when this physical or mental impairment has a substantial and long-term unfavourable effect on a person's ability to carry out normal day-to-day activities. An impairment only results in disability when it prevents people from taking part in the usual everyday activities that others can.

- The *biomedical model of disability* regards disability as a form of abnormality. Those with impairments are seen as needing treatment and rehabilitation to help 'normalize' them – make them as like those without impairments as possible.
- The *social model of disability* suggests that disability is socially constructed. This means that it is not the result of the state of people's minds or bodies, but socially created by the actions and attitudes of those in society who don't consider the needs of those who do not conform to a society's ideas of what is 'normal'. It is discrimination and prejudice in social attitudes and policies which turns people with impairments into disabled people. For example, the design of buildings may create obstacles for those who use wheelchairs so they can't carry out the same activities as others. In this way, the way society is set up *disables* the person using a wheelchair.

**Impairment** Some loss, limitation or difference of functioning of the mind or body, on a long-term or permanent basis, either that one is born with or that arises from injury or disease.

**Disability** A physical or mental impairment which has a substantial and long-term unfavourable effect on a person's ability to carry out normal day-to-day activities.

## Inequalities in life chances

Disabled people share with others the same advantages or disadvantages in life chances arising from their social-class, gender and ethnic backgrounds discussed earlier. But they face additional prejudice and discrimination because of their impairments, compared to those who are not disabled. The disabled are over-represented among women, those from lower social classes and from BAME groups.

Disabled people overall have the following disadvantages compared to the non-disabled. In 2018, they were:

- less qualified, nearly three times as likely to have no formal qualifications at 19 years of age, and twice as likely to be NEET (not in any form of education, employment or training)
- over twice as likely to be unemployed
- more likely to be working part-time than full-time
- more likely to be found in manual than in non-manual jobs
- less likely to get jobs or promotions they are qualified for
- around three times more likely to be economically inactive (not looking for work)
- earning significantly less than those with similar qualifications
- more likely to be dependent on state benefits
- more likely to be living in poverty
- more likely to encounter obstacles in leisure opportunities – e.g. finding it hard to get into clubs, pubs, sports facilities, cinemas, etc.
- more likely to have inadequate medical care – e.g. not having their conditions properly diagnosed and treated or not being referred to specialists for treatment
- more likely to face negative media portrayals – e.g. presented as violent, scary, threatening, evil, incapable, etc.
- more likely to face mocking, patronizing, abusive or dismissive attitudes from others – e.g. people may talk directly to a disabled person's carer and ignore the person with an impairment; being seen as a nuisance, etc.

### *Reasons for these inequalities*

- Overt and direct discrimination – e.g. employers refusing to give them jobs (which is illegal).
- Inaccessible workplaces and reluctance by employers to make workplace adaptations to make them disabled-friendly.
- GPs and other healthcare professionals often do not have much training in understanding, diagnosing and treating patients with some impairments.

- Covert or hidden discrimination – e.g. establishing rules or physical barriers which make it difficult for disabled people to apply for jobs or access workplaces; inaccessible public transport making it hard to get to work.
- Difficulties arising from their impairment in accessing public, commercial and leisure goods and services.
- Lack of understanding by the non-disabled of what disabled people can do – particularly by employers.
- Inadequate welfare benefits, which don't recognize the extra costs that disability brings – e.g. the need to pay for carers, taxis and various aids and medications.
- Prejudiced and stereotyped social attitudes.

---

### Activity

1 Describe one explanation for the inequalities disabled people face that might be offered by:
   (a) Functionalists
   (b) Marxists
   (c) Weberians
   (d) Feminists

2 Imagine you want to investigate disabled people's experiences of prejudice and discrimination in everyday life using postal questionnaires. Identify and explain one advantage and one disadvantage or weakness of using this method.

---

## RELIGION AND SEXUALITY AS DIMENSIONS OF INEQUALITY

Religion and sexuality can also have an impact on life chances. While these do not necessarily take the form of generalized inequalities in many spheres of life in the same way social class, gender, ethnicity, age and disability do, they are significant in that they can provide a basis for prejudice and discrimination against, and bullying of, the groups concerned. Individuals may become victims of **hate crime** – any crime that is perceived by the victim, or any other person, to be motivated by hostility or prejudice towards someone based on a personal characteristic, such as their ethnicity, disability, religion, beliefs or **sexual orientation**. Much of this hate crime is directed against BAME groups in the UK, in the form of racial abuse and racial attacks, but disability, religion and sexuality can also provide a basis for hate crimes.

**Hate crime** Any crime that is perceived by the victim, or any other person, to be motivated by hostility or prejudice towards someone based on a personal characteristic, such as their ethnicity or race, disability, religion, beliefs or sexual orientation.

**Sexual orientation** The type of people that individuals are either physically or romantically attracted to, such as those of the same or opposite sex.

## Religion

**Islamophobia**
An irrational fear and/ or hatred of, or aversion to, Islam, Muslims or Islamic culture.

In contemporary Britain, Muslims are exposed to **Islamophobia** – an irrational fear and/or hatred of or aversion to Islam, Muslims or Islamic culture. Some sections of the mainstream media regularly scaremonger about Muslims, and make anti-Muslim hatred become more socially acceptable. There has been in recent years a rise in attacks against mosques, physical and verbal abuse of Muslims in schools and the wider society, hate mail, and online abuse against Muslims through social media. In 2017–18, the police recorded 8,336 religious hate crimes – 9 per cent of all hate crimes – and many of these were directed against Muslims. Islamophobia not only affects the immediate victims, but can also contribute to a general climate of anxiety and fear among all Muslims, which has a negative effect on the quality of their lives and their health. It can also contribute to wider discrimination, as shown in the earlier example of the BBC research on job applications using the 'Adam v. Mohamed' names (see pages 438–9).

## Sexuality

**Homophobia**
The irrational hatred, intolerance and fear of lesbian, gay, bisexual and transsexual (LGBT) people.

Lesbian, gay, bisexual and transsexual (LGBT) people often face shocking levels of crime and discrimination motivated by **homophobia** – the irrational hatred, intolerance and fear of LGBT people. Stonewall, the LGBT charity, released research in 2017 that showed the proportion of LGBT in Britain who had experienced hate crime had increased by 78 per cent in five years, from 9 per cent in 2013 to 16 per cent in 2017. One in five LGBT people had experienced a hate crime or incident due to their sexual orientation and/or gender identity in the previous twelve months. Among school students, 45 per cent of gay pupils faced bullying because of their sexuality – most typically in the form of insults or gossip. But for some there were physical attacks and death threats. In 2017–18, 14 per cent of hate crimes recorded by the police were against LGBT people. The Stonewall research found four out of five LGBT people who experienced a hate crime or incident didn't report it to the police, so the real number of crimes is likely to be much higher. Like Islamophobia, homophobia not only affects the immediate victims, but can also contribute to a general climate of anxiety and fear among all LGBT people, who are at constant risk of encountering abuse and discrimination in many areas of life.

> **Activity**
>
> Write a short essay (around 15 minutes) answering the following question: 'How far do sociologists agree that social class, rather than age, gender or ethnicity, is the most important division in society today?'

# STRATIFICATION AND INEQUALITIES IN POWER AND AUTHORITY

Power is the ability of people or groups to exert their will over others and get their own way, even if sometimes others resist this.

A distinction is often made between two types of power:

- **Authority** is power which is accepted and obeyed because it is seen as legitimate (fair and right) by those without power. We obey those with authority because we accept they have the right to tell us what to do.
- **Coercion** is that type of power which is not accepted as legitimate by those without power, as the powerholders rule without the consent of those they govern. People only obey because they are forced to by violence or the threat of violence.

> **Authority** Power which is accepted and obeyed because it is seen as legitimate (fair and right) by those without power.

> **Coercion** Power that is only obeyed because of violence or the threat of violence.

## Formal and informal sources of power

- *Formal power* relates to the organized power structure in a group or organization. For example, an employer will have formal power through owning or managing a company, and teachers will have power over students because of their position in the school's hierarchy and the authority which is linked to that position to enable them to do their job, such as controlling classroom behaviour.
- *Informal power* arises from things like a person's superior knowledge and experience, or their ability to persuade others to do as they wish because people respect and admire them, even if they have no formal power. In peer groups, for example, some individuals may have informal power because they are trusted and have personalities and leadership qualities that others respect, which encourages others to follow their lead.

Weber (1947) saw three different sources of power based on three main types of authority, which explain why people accept this use of power as legitimate:

- **Traditional authority** is accepted and obeyed because power is based on established traditions, customs or inherited status, such as that of the British monarchy.
- **Charismatic authority** is accepted and obeyed because of the powerholder's charismatic personality – exceptional personal charm and magnetism – which encourages devotion and obedience among others, e.g. German Nazi dictator Adolf Hitler, or religious leaders like Jesus Christ.
- **Rational-legal authority** is power accepted and obeyed because it is based on shared and impersonal formal rules and laws, and people have

> **Traditional authority** Power which is seen as fair and just as it is based on established traditions and customs.

> **Charismatic authority** Power which is seen as fair and just as it is based on a powerholder's exceptional personal charm and magnetism.

> **Rational-legal authority** Power which is seen as fair and just as it is based on shared and impersonal formal rules and laws.

In what circumstances might the rational-legal authority of police officers become coercion instead?

power because it is an accepted part of their job, such as that of a police officer, a teacher or the prime minister.

## Power in everyday life

Power relations are found in all aspects of everyday life. The basis of this power is usually because one person or group is dependent on another in some way – what they can do is limited by what the powerholder allows, though there may often be a power struggle between them. For example, employers have power over employees, as employees need work and wages to live. However, this doesn't mean employers can treat their staff in any way they wish: workers have legal employment rights and may have **trade unions** to prevent unfair treatment. The same applies with the power of parents over children, teachers over students, and men over women. In all these cases, power is limited by the law, which makes it illegal to smack children, beat pupils, and use domestic violence as forms of control.

**Trade unions**
Organizations of workers whose aim is to protect the interests of their members and improve their life chances.

## The distribution of power in society

- *Functionalists* suggest that power in society is held by those who are the best qualified, the most talented and who have the greatest leadership skills, and who use their power for the benefit of society as a whole.
- *Marxists* argue that political power in society is held by the bourgeoisie – those who own and control the means of production. The owning class is also a ruling class (see pages 55 and 379). The dominant elites in society

## Activity

1   Look at the following examples of where power is used in everyday life. In each case:
    (a)  Describe with an example what the basis of the power relationship might be.
    (b)  Explain whether the power used in your example is coercion or authority; and if it is authority, which of the three kinds of authority it is (traditional, charismatic or rational-legal).
    (c)  Describe with an example what form a power struggle might take.

Here are two examples of the power of children over other children to help you get started.

(i)   A child might have power over other children because they are physically stronger, and use *coercion* through unwanted physical bullying to dominate and control them – the resulting fight is a form of power struggle.

(ii)  A child might have power over others because they are an elected representative on a school council, and so have *rational-legal authority* to set the rules for other children. Children in the minority who didn't like the rules being set might struggle against the representative by organizing to get a replacement elected, while the present representative might try to whip up enough support to keep their position.

   Now do the same in the following relationships:
   (i)     Parents and children
   (ii)    Teachers and students
   (iii)   Police and the public
   (iv)    Prison warders (guards) and prisoners
   (v)     Landlords and tenants
   (vi)    Husbands and wives or cohabiting couples
   (vii)   Doctors and patients
   (viii)  MPs or councillors and the public

2   Look at the following situations in which people are using their power in modern Britain. In each case, briefly explain whether they are using authority or coercion; and if authority, which type. Give reasons for your answer. Be warned – some may involve bits of both authority and coercion, and so it may be worth discussing your answers with someone else.
    (a)  A white police officer who stops and searches people simply because they're black, and then arrests them for objecting.
    (b)  A traffic warden who gives someone a parking ticket for illegal parking.
    (c)  A school pupil who beats up other pupils if they won't give him or her money.
    (d)  A teacher in a school who puts a student in detention for not doing his or her homework.
    (e)  A couple who beat their children because they won't do as they're told.
    (f)  A prime minister who orders his or her detectives to clear a restaurant of other customers so he or she can eat in peace.
    (g)  A manager who tells workers to stop chatting and get on with their work.

> (h) A man who beats his female partner because she displays too much independence.
> (i) A prison officer who puts a prisoner in solitary confinement for refusing to follow orders.
> 3  What do you think are the circumstances which influence whether the use of power is seen as fair or not?

who control society's institutions – such as the police, the army, the legal system, the civil service and the media – mainly come from privileged backgrounds. Those who have attended fee-paying public schools and elite universities form the 'old boys' network' (see pages 242–3), giving them power and influence in society far greater than their numbers deserve, and regardless of whatever political party forms the elected government. Its control of the media means it also controls the dominant ideas in society. The ruling class uses its power not for the benefit of everyone, but to protect its own interests.

- *Weberians* argue, like Marxists, that power is linked to high socio-economic classes (with strong market situations), and to high-status groups, such as upper-middle-class white males. Those with weak market situations or low status, such as the poor and unemployed, also lack power and influence in society, particularly as they often lack the resources to make their voices heard and get them listened to by powerholders.
- *Feminists*, such as Walby (see pages 57–9) emphasize that society is patriarchal. Power in society is held predominantly by men, who use their power to protect their interests. Feminists point to the under-representation of women in elite positions in society as evidence of this.

**Dictatorship**
A form of government in which power is concentrated in the hands of one person or a small powerful ruling elite.

**Democracy**
A form of government in which people enjoy many individual rights and freedoms, and the people participate in political decision-making, usually by electing individuals to represent their views.

## How ordinary people can exercise power

There are differences between societies in the amounts of power ordinary people have to influence government decisions, and these differences are shown in two opposing political systems: **dictatorship** and **democracy**.

### Dictatorship

In a dictatorship, society is controlled by an individual or a small powerful group – an elite – and ordinary people lack any control over the state or government decision-making. There are no free elections and no civil liberties, and most of the features found in a democracy (see figure 6.21) do not exist. The government rules by coercion rather than consent. People are forced to obey the government because of its control of the police, the courts and the army. All the major social institutions – such as the economy, the education system, religion, the legal system, the police and the media – are strictly controlled by the government. Ideas opposed to those of the government are censored, and any opposition organizations crushed by force. Examples of dictatorships include Hitler's Germany in the 1930s and 1940s, the contemporary People's Republic of China ('Communist' China), North Korea and Syria.

## Democracy

Democracy is a system of government which basically involves 'government of the people, by the people, for the people', in which ordinary people have some control over government decision-making. It is impractical for everyone in society to be permanently and directly involved in political

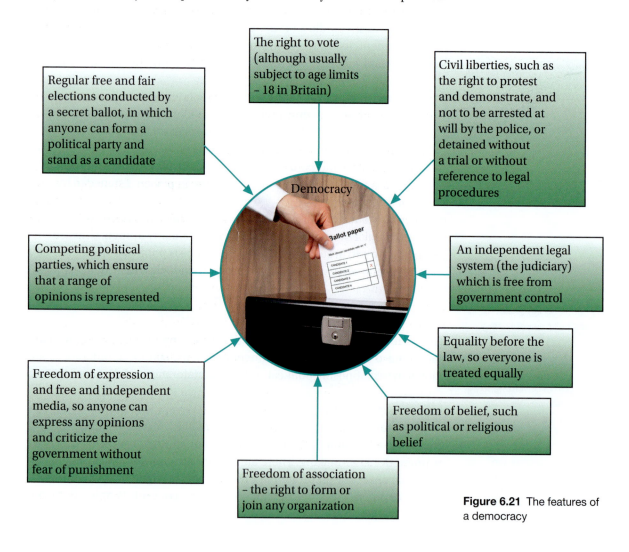

The right to vote (although usually subject to age limits – 18 in Britain)

Civil liberties, such as the right to protest and demonstrate, and not to be arrested at will by the police, or detained without a trial or without reference to legal procedures

Regular free and fair elections conducted by a secret ballot, in which anyone can form a political party and stand as a candidate

Democracy

Competing political parties, which ensure that a range of opinions is represented

An independent legal system (the judiciary) which is free from government control

Equality before the law, so everyone is treated equally

Freedom of expression and free and independent media, so anyone can express any opinions and criticize the government without fear of punishment

Freedom of belief, such as political or religious belief

Freedom of association – the right to form or join any organization

**Figure 6.21** The features of a democracy

decision-making, so often representatives are elected to represent people's opinions – such as MPs (Members of Parliament) and local councillors in Britain. This is known as representative or parliamentary democracy, and is found, for example, in Britain, France, Germany, the other countries of the European Union, India and the USA. In such democracies, people use a whole range of means to put pressure on those they elect to represent them, to ensure they do what they want them to do. While electing representatives is an important part of a democracy, a democratic society usually includes many other features to ensure that representatives can be replaced if they follow unpopular policies, and that people can freely express their opinions. Figure 6.21 illustrates the main features of a democracy.

## Influencing decision-making in a democracy

There are a number of ways individuals can have some power and influence the decision-making process in a democracy, or protest against policies adopted or proposed for implementation. Joining a **political party** – a group of people organized with the aim of forming the government in a society, such as the Labour or Conservative parties – is an obvious way, which enables people to take part in formulating the policies of that party, which may eventually become government policy if the party wins a general election.

The existence of competing political parties, combined with free elections and freedom of speech, means that parties must represent a range of interests if they are to be elected or to stay in power: the need to attract voters means parties have to respond to the wishes of the electorate – those eligible to vote. Voting is the most obvious way ordinary people can influence political decisions, and is an important part of their responsibilities, as well as their rights, as citizens. A further method is by writing to or emailing their local MP or councillor to try to have their concerns taken up, or by contacting the media and using public opinion to put pressure on elected politicians. However, individuals on their own have limited power, and the most effective way of influencing decision-making is to join together with others concerned about the same issue, by forming or joining a protest group of some kind, such as pressure groups and social movements.

*Pressure groups*   Pressure groups are organizations which try to put pressure on those with power in society to implement policies which the groups favour, or to prevent unpopular policies which may harm them from being implemented. They usually focus only on one issue or a group of issues relating to their members. Pressure groups are important in a democracy as they help to keep political parties and governments in touch with the opinions of the citizens who elected them, and are an important means for ordinary

**Political party**
A group of people organized with the aim of forming the government in a society.

people to use their 'people power' to influence powerholders in society. Examples of pressure groups include:

- the AA – the Automobile Association, representing the interests of motorists (www.theaa.com/about-us)
- Age UK – representing the interests of the elderly (www.ageuk.org.uk)
- the NSPCC – the National Society for the Prevention of Cruelty to Children (www.nspcc.org.uk/what-we-do)
- trade unions, like the National Education Union, protecting and promoting the interests of teachers and children in schools (https://neu.org.uk/working-neu)
- professional associations, like the British Medical Association, representing doctors (www.bma.org.uk/about-us)
- employers' organizations, like the CBI (the Confederation of British Industry) representing business (www.cbi.org.uk/about/about-us)
- the Child Poverty Action Group, concerned with eliminating child poverty (www.cpag.org.uk/about-cpag)
- environmental action groups, like Greenpeace (www.greenpeace.org.uk/about) and Friends of the Earth (https://friendsoftheearth.uk/who-we-are).

*Social movements*   Another way individuals can influence powerholders in a democracy is through identifying and involving themselves with a social movement. Social movements are a form of pressure group involving a broad movement of people who are united around the desire to promote, or block, a wide set of social changes in society, and often focus on global issues, not just national ones. They differ from political parties and more conventional pressure groups in the following ways:

- They are more likely to operate outside the existing political framework.
- They use more unconventional and sometimes illegal tactics, such as civil disobedience, demonstrations (sometimes violent) and direct action, like protesters blocking roads, breaking up meetings and destroying animal-testing laboratories.
- They are less likely to have full-time staff and a formal national organization.
- They are more likely to work informally through the active involvement, commitment and participation of supporters via a network of small, independent locally based groups. These groups are linked to one another informally – and to similar groups internationally – and rally their support through the internet and social media.
- They are more likely to gain support from men and women of all social classes and ethnic groups, with a wide range of different beliefs and values.

**STOP THE WAR (WWW.STOPWAR.ORG.UK )**

The 'Stop the War' coalition in 2003, against the invasion of Iraq by Britain and the USA, was the largest coordinated political protest ever seen, with over 2 million people protesting on the streets of London, and many millions more across the world. These people were drawn from all sections of society, and the internet enabled tiny groups with virtually no resources to mobilize millions of people, through websites, smartphones, and emails to press and supporters, leading to protest spreading across the globe like a Mexican wave. The internet and other new media like Facebook, Twitter and Instagram have enabled such social movements to engage with people in a way the conventional political parties have failed to do, and have proven to be a key means of mobilizing support for a social protest movement.

It has been suggested that social movements represent attempts by the non-powerful, the non-wealthy and the non-famous to make their voices heard by the powerful.

Social movements have emerged over issues like opposition to war, damage to the environment, climate change, human rights and civil liberties denied through institutional discrimination and marginalization –as in anti-racism, women's and LGBT rights and equality – and concerns over animal welfare, the world refugee crisis and more specific issues such as Brexit. Examples of social movements include the feminist movement, Black Lives Matter (https://blacklivesmatter.com/about), the Stop the War coalition (https://goo.gl/1F2vi6) and the anti-globalization movement.

Figure 6.22 illustrates a range of methods used by pressure groups and social movements to influence public opinion, political parties and governments.

## How much power in society do ordinary people really have?

### *Unequal protest groups*

Not all pressure groups and social movements are equally effective in achieving change in society, and this can often leave individuals feeling powerless.

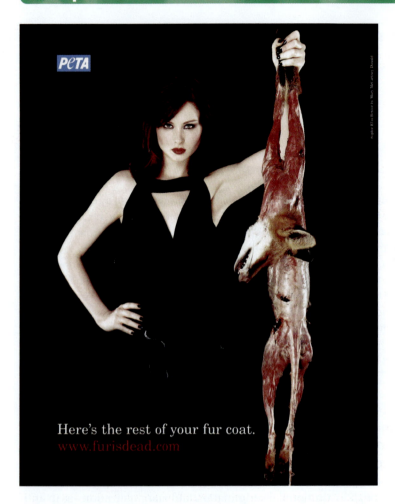

PeTA

Here's the rest of your fur coat.
www.furisdead.com

Shocking images are sometimes used by pressure groups and social movements to attract attention, like this one by PETA (People for the Ethical Treatment of Animals)

The effectiveness of protest groups on powerholders will depend on factors like:

- their size – how many people they represent, how influential those people are and their level of public support
- their money (to organize campaigns, advertise, employ staff, etc.)
- their economic power – how significant they are in the economy, e.g. university lecturers going on strike has little effect on the wider economy, but train drivers doing so can wreak economic chaos as people are unable to get to work
- their access to and influence on those with power – particularly government policy makers
- the government's view of the importance of the group
- the strength of their organization and leadership.

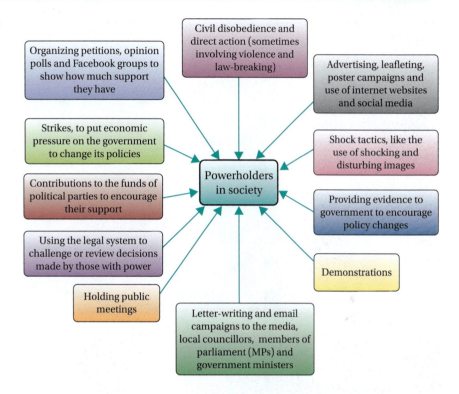

**Figure 6.22** Some methods used by pressure groups and social movements

Organizing petitions, opinion polls and Facebook groups to show how much support they have

Civil disobedience and direct action (sometimes involving violence and law-breaking)

Advertising, leafleting, poster campaigns and use of internet websites and social media

Strikes, to put economic pressure on the government to change its policies

Shock tactics, like the use of shocking and disturbing images

Contributions to the funds of political parties to encourage their support

Powerholders in society

Providing evidence to government to encourage policy changes

Using the legal system to challenge or review decisions made by those with power

Demonstrations

Holding public meetings

Letter-writing and email campaigns to the media, local councillors, members of parliament (MPs) and government ministers

Not all interests are represented through pressure groups and social movements, and not all groups in the population are equally capable of forming them. Disadvantaged groups such as the poor, the unemployed, the homeless, some BAME groups, the disabled and the mentally ill often lack the resources, education or other ability to make their voices heard. Substantial wealth and education mean some groups can run more effective campaigns to bring their concerns to the attention of powerholders, such as employers' organizations like the CBI.

Not everyone has the same chance of meeting or influencing top decision-makers: those most likely to succeed are those who come from the same social-class background as those with power. 'Friends in high places' and the 'old boys' network' mean that the interests of the upper and middle classes are generally more effectively represented than those of the working class or marginalized groups.

## Non-elected rulers

Democracy is meant to involve governments reflecting the interests of the people through elected representatives. However, the House of Lords is not elected, but has considerable power in controlling which laws are passed.

Protest groups in action, top left to bottom right: a publicity stunt against Sizewell B nuclear reactor; collecting signatures for a petition to save a fire station from closure; and a demonstration in London in 2016 to show solidarity with refugees

## Elite rule

As Marxists and feminists point out, wealth remains highly concentrated in the hands of a small upper class, mainly comprised of men, which therefore has major influence on economic decision-making. For example, this class can decide where businesses should be located and whether they should be opened or closed down, and it can control the workforce through hiring and firing. Democratically elected governments cannot afford to ignore this power, as they might face rising unemployment and other social problems if the upper class decided not to invest its money.

Most of those in the top elite jobs who run the various institutions controlling society – like Parliament, central and local government, the civil

Anglican archbishops and bishops have seats in the House of Lords, which plays an important role in making laws. But they are unelected, and unaccountable to voters

service, the legal institutions (courts), the police and the army – are white men who come from public schools and upper- and upper-middle-class backgrounds. They wield enormous power and influence in this country. Even among Labour MPs, few come from working-class backgrounds. This raises questions about the extent to which the voices of women, BAME groups and the working class are even heard – let alone listened to – by those in power.

## Deciding the issues

The political parties – not the population as a whole – often decide what the important issues are and which ones they are going to fight elections around. The media are mainly privately owned and controlled by a rich and powerful minority and have a conservative bias. They have an important role in forming public opinion and, like political leaders, can decide the issues around which elections are fought.

The sections above suggest that ordinary people have little chance of expressing their opinions and influencing decision-making. This is likely to be true particularly of those holding radical opinions who want to change the way society is presently organized.

## Activity

1 Imagine that you wanted to campaign against something, such as the proposed closure of a local school, plans to build a new airport or road, or to build a waste incinerator in your area. Choose any issue you like, and plan out how you might organize a campaign to achieve your aims. Think carefully of how you might get people together and all the activities you might engage in to influence those with power. What obstacles, including the need to raise money, might you find in organizing a successful campaign?

2 You want to carry out a survey about the extent to which people have power in everyday life over the decisions that affect them.
   (a) Give one reason why you should try to obtain a representative sample.
   (b) Describe one source you might use to obtain such a representative sample.
   (c) Describe one research method you might use to collect information from people about their attitudes to the power they have in everyday life, and explain two reasons why you chose this method.

## POVERTY

Earlier it was shown that large differences in wealth and income remain in Britain, combined with a range of other social class inequalities. Nothing highlights more the extent of inequality in Britain than the continued existence of widespread poverty. A walk through the streets of any large city will reveal stark contrasts between the mansions, the luxury cars and the expensive lifestyles of the rich, and the poverty and hardship of many of those

who are unemployed, sick or old, who are lone parents, who are homeless or living in decaying housing, and who are faced with a future of hopelessness and despair. Poverty is essentially an aspect of social-class inequality, affecting above all those from the working class, because other classes have savings, occupational pensions and sick pay schemes to protect them when adversity strikes or old age arrives.

One of the key issues in discussing poverty, and certainly the most controversial, is the problem of defining what poverty is.

## Absolute poverty

**Absolute poverty**
Poverty defined as lacking the minimum requirements necessary to maintain human health and life.

**Absolute poverty** or subsistence poverty refers to a person's biological needs for food, water, clothing and shelter – the minimum requirements necessary to subsist and maintain life, health and physical efficiency.

A person in absolute poverty lacks the minimum necessary for healthy survival. While the minimum needed to maintain a healthy life might vary – for example, between hot and cold climates and between people in occupations with different physical demands – absolute or subsistence poverty is roughly the same in every society. People in absolute poverty would be poor anywhere at any time – the standard does not change much over time. The solution to absolute poverty is to raise the living standards of the poor above subsistence level. Absolute poverty is most associated with the countries of the less-developed world, such as those in Africa, where it remains a widespread problem. It is unlikely many people live in absolute poverty in Britain today, where poverty is basically relative poverty (see below).

Absolute poverty, shown here in Somalia, is generally associated with the less-developed countries like those in Africa, where famines and starvation occur, and people lack on a daily basis the minimum subsistence needs for biological survival.

# THE GLOBAL EXTENT OF ABSOLUTE POVERTY

- Around 769 million people in the world are living in extreme poverty – on US$1.90 (about £1.45 in 2019) a day or less.
- 815 million people are undernourished – 11 per cent of the world's population.
- The world's richest 1 per cent of people receive over twice (20 per cent) as much income as the poorest 50 per cent (9 per cent).
- 82 per cent of all wealth created in the world in 2017 went to the richest 1 per cent of the world population.
- 750 million adults are illiterate.
- Easily preventable diseases, such as pneumonia, diarrhoea, malaria and measles, kill nearly 3 million children under the age of 5 each year – over 8,000 every day.
- About 2.1 billion people lack access to safe drinking water at home, and 4.5 billion people lack safely managed sanitation.
- 303,000 women die each year from preventable causes related to pregnancy and childbirth – over one every 2 minutes.

**Distribution of people living on less than US $1.90 (around £1.45 in 2019) a day**
**Global estimate: 769 million people (2016)**

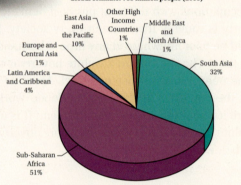

**Distribution of undernourished people Global total: 815 million people (2016)**

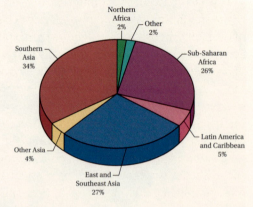

**Figure 6.23** Social inequalities, income poverty and hunger

*Sources*: World Inequality Lab (2017), *World Inequality Report 2018*; United Nations (2017) *The Sustainable Development Goals Report 2017*; UNESCO Institute for Statistics (2017), *Fact Sheet No. 45, September 2017, FS/2017/LIT/45*; Oxfam International (2018), *Reward Work, not Wealth*; World Health Organization / UNICEF (2017) *Progress on Drinking Water, Sanitation and Hygiene: 2017 Update and Sustainable Development Goal Baselines*; International Bank for Reconstruction and Development / The World Bank (2016) *Taking on Inequality*; FAO, IFAD, UNICEF, WFP and WHO (2017), *The State of Food Insecurity and Nutrition in the World, 2017*

## Relative poverty: poverty as social exclusion

**Relative poverty** involves defining poverty in relation to a generally accepted standard of living in a specific society at a particular time. This takes into account social and cultural needs as well as biological needs.

Relative poverty is a condition in which individuals or families are deprived of the opportunities, comforts and self-respect which the majority of people in their society enjoy. Minimum needs are then related to the standard of living in any society at any one time, and will therefore vary over time and between societies, as standards of living change. For example, those living in slum housing in Britain would be regarded as poor here, but their housing would appear as relative luxury to poor rural labourers in developing countries. Similarly, running hot water and an inside bathroom and toilet would have been seen as luxuries 100 years ago in Britain, but today are seen as basic necessities, and those without them would be regarded as poor by most people.

Townsend (1979) was a key pioneering poverty researcher, and provided the classic definition of relative poverty:

> Individuals ... can be said to be in poverty when they lack the resources to obtain the types of diets, participate in the activities and have the living conditions and amenities which are customary, or at least widely encouraged or approved, in the societies to which they belong. Their resources are so seriously below those commanded by the average individual or family that they are, in effect, excluded from ordinary living patterns, customs or activities.
>
> (P. Townsend, *Poverty in the United Kingdom*, Penguin, 1979)

Townsend used this definition to measure the extent of poverty in the UK. His research was based on questionnaires issued to a representative sample of over 2,000 households and more than 6,000 individuals located in various geographical areas in the UK. He devised a deprivation index (an example of a similar index appears on page 469) covering a large number of factors, including diet, fuel, clothing, housing conditions, working conditions, health, education and social activities. Each household was given a score on this deprivation index, and Townsend then calculated the extent of relative poverty in the UK at around 22 per cent of the population. Townsend's methods and conclusions were criticized at the time by those who argued that his index was inadequate and produced potentially misleading results – for example, the absence of fresh meat and cooked meals might not be an indicator of poverty but of individual choice.

Townsend's research laid the basis for future and contemporary poverty research, with the use of more sophisticated deprivation indices (plural

---

**Relative poverty**
Poverty defined in relation to a generally accepted standard of living in a specific society at a particular time.

of 'index') to take into account individual choice, and what the general population – rather than just poverty researchers like Townsend – regard as necessary for an acceptable standard of living in contemporary Britain (see 'the consensual idea of poverty' below).

## Social exclusion

The relative definition of poverty is closely linked with the idea of social exclusion. Social exclusion is where people are marginalized or excluded from participation in education, work, community life and access to services and other aspects of life seen as part of being a full and participating member of mainstream society. Those who live in relative poverty lack the resources and are denied the opportunities to live the normal life enjoyed by the majority of people. They lack power and control over their lives, are given low status, lack access to decision-makers, and lack the resources to change opinions of them as being other than lazy and inadequate. They are excluded from full participation in society.

## The consensual idea of poverty

A third idea of poverty – overcoming the problem of researchers defining what counts as poverty – is to ask the public what they regard as being poor, and what items they (and not just researchers) think are necessary for a

### Activity

1 Either alone, or through majority agreement in a group, go through the Poverty and Social Exclusion deprivation index in table 6.5 opposite, and decide which items or activities you think all adults should have in Britain today to have a reasonable standard of living. Make two lists:

2 (a) necessities, which all adults should be able to have if they want or choose them, and which they should not be forced to go without because they can't afford them

  (b) desirable, but not necessary.

3 Compare your lists with that of another person or group. How do your decisions compare with others'? Were some items clear-cut and others borderline? Discuss the reasons for any differences of opinion about what count as necessities.

4 Now go to the Poverty and Social Exclusion in the UK national survey at https://goo.gl/6QUA9H and compare your findings with those of the national survey conducted in 2012. How far do your lists agree or disagree with these national findings?

5 Do you think if you were in a very poor country you would have the same list of necessities? Give reasons for your answer.

## Table 6.5 The Poverty and Social Exclusion Necessities of Life Survey list

1. Enough money to keep your home in a decent state of decoration
2. Enough money to replace any worn-out furniture
3. Enough money to replace or repair broken electrical goods such as refrigerator or washing machine
4. A small amount of money to spend each week on yourself, not on your family
5. Two pairs of all-weather shoes
6. Regular savings (of at least £20 a month) for rainy days
7. Car
8. Washing machine
9. A warm waterproof coat
10. Replace worn-out clothes with new (not second-hand) ones
11. A roast joint (or vegetarian equivalent) once a week
12. Presents for friends or family once a year
13. Damp-free home
14. Mobile phone
15. Television
16. Telephone at home (landline or mobile)
17. Home computer
18. Internet connection at home
19. Meat, fish or vegetarian equivalent every other day
20. Household contents insurance
21. Heating to keep home adequately warm
22. Two meals a day
23. To be able to pay an unexpected expense of £500
24. Hair done or cut regularly
25. A dishwasher
26. Fresh fruit and vegetables every day
27. An outfit to wear for social or family occasions such as parties and weddings
28. Appropriate clothes to wear for job interviews
29. All recommended dental work/treatment
30. Curtains or window blinds
31. A table, with chairs, at which all the family can eat
32. Regular payments into an occupational or private pension
33. A hobby or leisure activity
34. A holiday away from home for one week a year, not staying with relatives
35. Friends or family round for a meal or drink at least once a month
36. Going out socially once a fortnight
37. Celebrations on special occasions such as Christmas
38. A meal out once a month
39. Holidays abroad once a year
40. Visits to friends or family in other parts of the country 4 times a year
41. Going out for a drink once a fortnight
42. Attending weddings, funerals and other such occasions
43. Visiting friends or family in hospital or other such institutions
44. Attending church, mosque, temple, synagogue, or other places of worship
45. Going to the cinema, theatre, or music event once a month
46. Taking part in sport/exercise activities or classes

*Source*: adapted from *Omnibus Survey 2012: PSE UK Necessities of Life Module*. Reproduced by permission of www.poverty.ac.uk, part of the ESRC PSE: UK research programme

minimum standard of living in Britain. This approach aims to establish a widespread agreement (a consensus) on what ordinary people think makes up the minimum standards required for life in Britain in the first two decades of the twenty-first century. The *Poverty and Social Exclusion Necessities of Life Survey* list in table 6.5 on the previous page – a form of deprivation index similar to that used by Townsend – of some popular items, and the activity following it, explore this idea of a consensual notion of poverty based on contemporary standards of living.

## The controversy over poverty

The idea of relative poverty and its measurement have been particularly controversial. Many Conservative politicians and the New Right (see pages 52–4) attack the idea of relative poverty and the suggestion that many people in Britain are poor. Item A below presents this view. Item B presents an alternative view put forward by the Child Poverty Action Group, with which many sociologists would agree.

### Activity

Read items A and B, and then answer the questions which follow.

**Item A**

Some Conservatives attack the idea of relative poverty and the view that many people in Britain are poor. They argue that poverty in the old absolute sense of hunger and want has been wiped out, and it is simply that some people today are 'less equal' than others. They claim that the lifestyle of the poorest 20 per cent of families today represents affluence beyond the wildest dreams of the Victorians. Starving children and squalid slums have disappeared, and they point out that half of today's so-called 'poor' have a telephone, car and central heating, and virtually all have a refrigerator and television set. They argue that it is therefore absurd to suggest that more than a fifth of the population is today living in poverty. They claim the idea of relative poverty amounts to no more than simple inequality, and that the use of the concept of relative poverty means that, however rich a society becomes, the relatively poor will never disappear as long as there is social inequality. As one former Conservative minister commented, 'The poverty lobby would, on their definition, find poverty in Paradise.'

**Item B**

The Child Poverty Action Group (CPAG) supports the view that poverty should be seen in relation to minimum needs established by the standard of living in a particular society, and all members of the population should have the right to an income which allows them to participate fully in society rather than merely exist.

Such participation involves having the means to fulfil responsibilities to others – as parents, sons and daughters, neighbours, friends, workers and citizens. Poverty filters into every aspect of life. It is about not having access to material goods and services such as decent housing, adequate heating, nutritious food, public transport, credit and consumer goods.

But living on the breadline is not simply about doing without things; it is also about experiencing poor health, isolation, stress, stigma and exclusion.

Poverty curtails freedom of choice. The freedom to eat as you wish, to go where and when you like, to seek the leisure pursuits or political activities which others accept; all are denied to those without the resources … poverty is most comprehensively understood as a state of partial citizenship.

The gradual raising of the poverty line simply reflects the fact that society generally has become more prosperous and therefore has a more generous definition of a minimum income. The poor should not be excluded as the general level of prosperity rises.

*Source*: adapted from Carey Oppenheim, *Poverty: The Facts*, CPAG

1   With reference to item A, explain briefly in your own words Conservative objections to the idea of relative poverty.
2   Explain in your own words what the former Conservative minister meant when he said 'The poverty lobby would, on their definition, find poverty in Paradise' (highlighted at the end of item A).
3   On the basis of what you have studied so far in this chapter, what definition of poverty do you think the Conservatives in item A support? Give reasons for your answer.
4   With reference to item B, identify three factors apart from material goods and services which the CPAG thinks should be taken into account when defining poverty.
5   Explain what is meant by 'exclusion' and 'poverty is most comprehensively understood as a state of partial citizenship' in item B (highlighted).
6   What definition of poverty do you think the CPAG supports? Give reasons for your answer.
7   Go to https://goo.gl/y6qH2J. Explain how this comedy sketch illustrates, in a very amusing way, why poverty is best understood as a relative concept and can only be judged in relation to the lifestyles of others in the society to which a person belongs.
8   Discuss in your group whether or not you think poverty really exists in modern Britain, given the starving populations in developing countries elsewhere in the world.

## The measurement of poverty in Britain: the poverty line

The **poverty line** is the dividing point between those who are poor and those who are not. The official poverty line used in Britain today, and by the European Union, is 60 per cent or below of **median income** (see glossary box).

Sociologists often also take into account those who are living on the margins of this poverty line, as those whose incomes are low often slip between being just above the poverty line and on or below it.

## The extent of poverty in the UK

In 2017–18 in the UK:

● 14,000,000 people were living in poverty (below 60 per cent of median income) – 22 per cent of the population
● Nearly a third (30 per cent) of all children were living in poverty

The numbers of the poor, and the changes between 2002–3 and 2017–18 are shown in figure 6.24.

## Who are the poor?

The identity of the major groups in poverty suggests that poverty is caused not by idleness, but by social circumstances beyond the control of the poor themselves. The unemployed, the low-paid, lone parents, pensioners and the sick and disabled account for most of the poor. Those living in poverty

> **Poverty line** The dividing point between those who are poor and those who are not. The official poverty line used in Britain today, and by the European Union, is *60 per cent of median income.*

> **Median income** The middle income point where half of the population have income above that amount, and half have income below that amount.

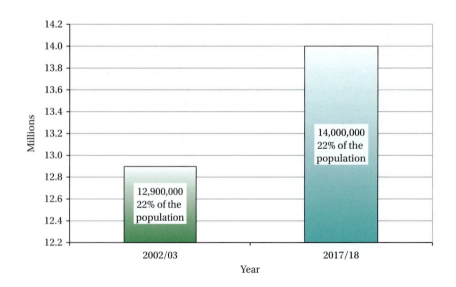

**Figure 6.24** Numbers of people living in poverty (below 60 per cent of median income after housing costs): UK, 2002–3 and 2017–18

*Source*: *Households Below Average Income*, Department for Work and Pensions, 2019

**Activity**

Study figure 6.24 and answer the following questions:
1  By how much did the percentage of the population living on below 60 per cent of median income change between 2002–3 and 2017–18?
2  What percentage of the population had below 60 per cent of median income in 2002–3?
3  How many more people had below 60 per cent of median income in 2017–18 than in 2002–3?
4  What percentage of the population were living on below 60 per cent of median income in 2017–18?
5  Suggest possible reasons for the change in the numbers of those living in poverty between 2002–3 and 2017–18.

(low-income households on or below 60 per cent of median income) in 2017–18 are shown below

● *Those without work* – 45 per cent were workless.
● *The low-paid* – 57 per cent were in full-time or part-time work. Many of the poor work long hours in low-paid jobs.
● *Pensioners* – 15 per cent were pensioners. Many elderly retired people depend on state pensions for support, and these are inadequate for maintaining other than a very basic standard of living.
● *Lone parents* – 16 per cent were lone parents. Lone parents are often prevented from getting a full-time job by the lack of affordable childcare facilities, or only take part-time jobs, which generally get lower rates of pay. The costs of childcare often mean lone parents cannot afford to work. The majority of lone parents are women, who in any case get lower pay than men.
● *The sick and disabled* – around a quarter of all disabled people were in poverty. Disability brings with it poorer employment opportunities, lower pay, and dependence on state benefits.
● *Children* – about 4.1 million children were living in poverty – nearly 1 in 3 (30 per cent) of all children.
● *Minority ethnic groups* – just over a third (36 per cent) of people from ethnic minorities were living in poverty – nearly twice the rate for white people (20 per cent). Nearly half of people from Bangladeshi and Pakistani ethnic backgrounds were living in low-income households, and more than one out of two Bangladeshi and Pakistani children.

Figure 6.25 illustrates which groups made up most of those living in poverty in 2017–18, by family type and by economic status, and figure 6.26 shows the risk of being in poverty by various groupings.

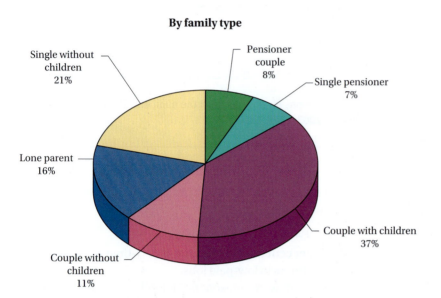

**By family type**

Single without children 21%

Pensioner couple 8%

Single pensioner 7%

Lone parent 16%

Couple with children 37%

Couple without children 11%

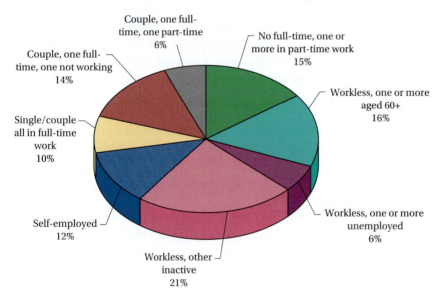

**By economic status of adults in the family**

Couple, one full-time, one part-time 6%

Couple, one full-time, one not working 14%

No full-time, one or more in part-time work 15%

Single/couple all in full-time work 10%

Workless, one or more aged 60+ 16%

Self-employed 12%

Workless, one or more unemployed 6%

Workless, other inactive 21%

**Figure 6.25** Who are the poor? There were 14,000,000 people living in low-income households (60 per cent or less of median income after housing costs) in the United Kingdom in 2017–18. This figure shows the family and economic features of those making up the total living on low incomes

*Source: Households Below Average Income*, Department for Work and Pensions, 2019

**By family type**

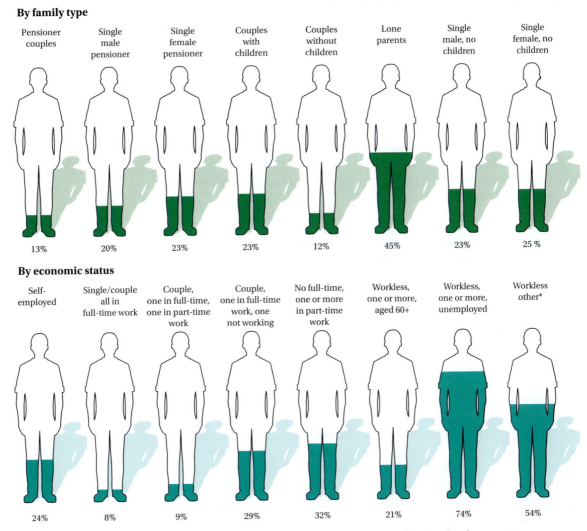

| Pensioner couples | Single male pensioner | Single female pensioner | Couples with children | Couples without children | Lone parents | Single male, no children | Single female, no children |
|---|---|---|---|---|---|---|---|
| 13% | 20% | 23% | 23% | 12% | 45% | 23% | 25 % |

**By economic status**

| Self-employed | Single/couple all in full-time work | Couple, one in full-time, one in part-time work | Couple, one in full-time work, one not working | No full-time, one or more in part-time work | Workless, one or more, aged 60+ | Workless, one or more, unemployed | Workless other* |
|---|---|---|---|---|---|---|---|
| 24% | 8% | 9% | 29% | 32% | 21% | 74% | 54% |

\* Other = all those not included in previous groups, eg. long-term sick, disabled people, and non-working lone parent

**Figure 6.26** The risk of poverty: percentage of individuals in particular groups living in poverty (below 60 per cent of median income after housing costs): United Kingdom, 2017–18

*Source*: *Households Below Average Income*, Department for Work and Pensions, 2019

**Activity**

Refer to figure 6.25.

1 What percentage of those living on a low income in 2017–18 were single pensioners?
2 Which family type made up the greatest proportion of those in poverty in 2017–18?
3 What percentage of the poor were made up of those who were workless? Refer to figure 6.26.
4 What percentage of self-employed people were living in poverty in 2017–18?
5 What percentage of couples with children were living in poverty?
6 What evidence is there in figure 6.26 that might be used to show that low pay is a cause of poverty?
7 What difference is there between the proportion of couples with children and that of couples without children living in poverty?
8 Which two groups overall have the highest risk of poverty?
9 Which group overall has the least risk of being in poverty?
10 Suggest how the evidence in figure 6.26 might be used to show that the poor are victims of unfortunate circumstances rather than being themselves to blame for their poverty. Could any of the evidence in the figure be used to support the opposite view?

## Criticisms of the poverty line

Many people are critical of the definition of poverty simply in terms of income, because it takes no account of all the extras most of the population take for granted, such as coping with household emergencies, going on holiday, going out for a drink with friends, and taking part in other leisure activities. Poverty is not simply a matter of how much income someone has, but can also involve other aspects of life such as the quality of housing and the quality and availability of public services like transport, hospitals, schools and play areas for children.

Some aspects and consequences of poverty apart from shortage of income are shown below. While not all of those in poverty will experience all of these multiple deprivations, the list below shows how poverty can be like a spider's web, trapping the poor in a deprived lifestyle in many aspects of their lives.

- *Homelessness.* In 2017–18, around 57,000 households were officially accepted as unintentionally homeless and in priority need by local authorities in England. There were more homeless than this, such as those regarded as intentionally homeless, or not in priority need, or who simply don't come to the attention of local councils or other authorities. There were an estimated 4,677 rough sleepers, living in the streets.
- *Environmental poverty.* Environmental poverty refers to features of the environment in which people live. The poor often live in areas that lack

**Figure 6.27** Reasons for homelessness: households officially accepted as homeless by local authorities, by reason for loss of last settled home, England 2018

*Source*: Ministry of Housing, Communities and Local Government, 2018

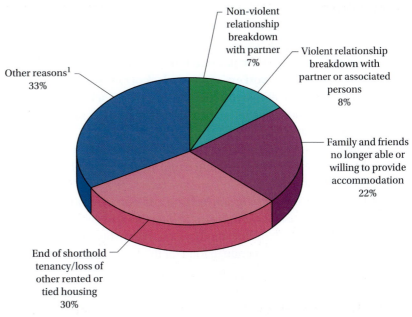

Non-violent relationship breakdown with partner 7%

Violent relationship breakdown with partner or associated persons 8%

Other reasons[1] 33%

Family and friends no longer able or willing to provide accommodation 22%

End of shorthold tenancy/loss of other rented or tied housing 30%

[1] Other reasons include: racially and non-racially motivated violence or harassment, leaving local authority care, mortgage and rent arrears, fire or flood / other emergency

access to essential services such as GP surgeries, shops, schools, post offices and public transport, and close to polluting industries and busy roads where air quality is poor, leading to health problems like breathing difficulties and asthma.

- *Poverty in healthcare*
  - There are fewer doctors practising in inner-city areas (where many of the poor live), and those who do are often overworked, because the poor have more health problems.
  - The poor are less likely to get time off work with pay to visit the doctor.
  - They face longer hospital waiting lists.
  - Many are not fully aware of what health services are available to them, and the poor tend to be less vocal in demanding proper standards of care from doctors.
- *Poverty at school*
  - Inner-city schools often have a concentration of social problems, such as social deprivation, drugs, discipline problems and vandalism, and consequently a higher turnover of teachers.
  - Parents are less able to help their children with their education, and have less money than non-poor parents to enable the school to buy extra resources.

- *Poverty at work*
  - *Poor working conditions.* These include: a neglect of health and safety standards and a high accident rate; working at night and long periods of overtime because the pay is so low; lack of trade union organization to protect the workers' interests; lack of entitlement to paid holidays; and no employers' sick pay or pension schemes.
  - *Insecure employment,* often with high risks of job loss with very short notice of dismissal.
- *Poor health,* such as respiratory problems like asthma and infectious diseases, as a result of poor diet and damp, environmental pollution and overcrowded housing.
- *Going short of food, clothing and heating,* and not being able to replace household goods or carry out household repairs and decoration. Poor parents, and particularly lone mothers, on welfare benefits are much more likely to go without enough food for themselves, in order to feed their children, than mothers not receiving benefits. Many poor families have an unhealthy diet, not because they don't know or care about nutritionally healthy food, but because they can't afford it.
- *Isolation and boredom.* Making friends may be hard because there is no money to get involved in social activities.
- *Stress and depression,* in the face of mounting bills and debts, perhaps leading to domestic violence, family breakdown and mental illness.
- *Low self-esteem,* brought on by dependence on others, the lack of access to the activities and facilities others have, and difficulties in coping with day-to-day life.

Why do you think some people become homeless? How might being homeless affect other aspects of people's lives?

Poverty means going short materially, socially and emotionally. It means spending less on food, on heating and on clothing than someone on an average income. But it is not what is spent that matters, but what isn't. Poverty means staying at home, often being bored, not seeing friends, not going out for a drink and not being able to take the children out for a trip or treat or a holiday. It means coping with the stresses of managing on very little money, often for months or even years. It means having to withstand the onslaught of society's pressure to consume. It impinges on relationships with others and with yourself. Above all, poverty takes away the tools to build the blocks for the future – your 'life chances'. It steals away the opportunity to have a life unmarked by sickness, a decent education, a secure home and a long retirement. It stops people being able to take control of their lives.

(Carey Oppenheim, *Poverty: The Facts*, CPAG)

## The effects of globalization on poverty

**Globalization** refers to the growing interconnectedness of societies across the world. Businesses now have to compete with other companies in a global economy, and they can move jobs, money, technology and raw materials across national borders quickly and easily. Competition from countries with lower-paid workers has led companies to keep down wages, and to increase the speed of work to reduce costs and maximize profits. Some work and production that used to be performed in the UK has been moved to other countries where wages are lower – such as call centres, which are often relocated to India. Globalization has increased inequality both nationally and internationally, and the gap between the rich and the poor is now greater than it has ever been.

Globalization has had the following effects on the poor:

- *more insecure jobs*, as employers require greater flexibility in the number of workers they employ in the face of global competition. These jobs are often temporary, part-time, on short-term contracts or on zero-hours contracts (whereby employees are 'on call' by employers, with no guarantee of work, to be employed and paid only if and when needed).
- *lower pay* – many of those who are poor are now in employment, and work for many now no longer provides a route out of poverty. More people are now experiencing uncertainty about their earnings, and in 2015–16, six in ten of those in the poorest fifth of households had no savings at all to fall back on if they found themselves workless. Growing numbers of people in low-paid work are now having to use food banks, which give out emergency food parcels on a weekly basis to people in hardship.

**Globalization**
The growing interconnectedness of societies across the world, with the spread of the same culture, consumer goods and economic interests across the globe.

- *increased risks of unemployment* – many people now live in constant dread of losing their jobs to competition from other countries, and it is typically those already in low-paid work who are most at risk.

## Sociological perspectives on poverty

### Functionalism

Functionalists, such as Davis and Moore (see pages 376–7), examine the ways in which poverty can be seen as necessary and as performing useful functions for the maintenance and stability of society in the following ways:

- It ensures some people have no other choice but to undertake the most undesirable, dirty, dangerous or menial low-paid jobs that most people don't want, but which are important to the smooth running of society.
- It provides necessary incentives and motivation for people to work.
- It creates jobs for those who deal with the effects of poverty, e.g. social workers, social security staff, debt advisers and the police.
- It reinforces conformity by demonizing the poor as lazy misfits and scroungers, and thereby provides a living example to the non-poor of what they should avoid. This reinforces the mainstream values of hard work, seizing opportunities and planning for the future.

Functionalist explanations have been criticized on the grounds that the poor may well feel resentment and bitterness at their low income and poor life chances, which may create conflict and divisions that actually threaten the stability of society rather than support it.

### Marxism

Marxists argue that the problem of poverty is really the problem of the unequal distribution of wealth, and the exploitation of the poor by the rich in unequal class-divided capitalist societies.

- Poverty is the inevitable result of capitalism, and low-paid workers provide the source of profits which enables the rich to achieve high incomes.
- The threat of poverty and unemployment motivates workers for the capitalist class.
- The existence of the poor helps to keep wages down, boosting the profits of the owners of private businesses, and provides a pool of cheap labour – a reserve army of labour – which threatens the jobs of the non-poor should their wage demands become excessively high.
- Poverty divides the working class, by separating off the poor from the non-poor working class, and prevents the development of working-class unity and a class consciousness that might threaten the stability of the capitalist system.

## Weberians

The Weberian perspective suggests poverty arises from the different market situations of individuals – the different skills that people have and the different rewards attached to them when they sell (or can't sell) their labour in the job market.

- The poor have a weak market situation: they often have few skills, and the demand for unskilled and unqualified labour is declining, so pay is low.
- Many in poverty live in circumstances that exclude them from competing in the labour market at all – e.g. the long-term sick, lone parents and the disabled.
- The poor lack power to change their position, because they do not have the financial resources to form powerful groups to change public opinion, and they are often badly organized. Combined with their low status and lack of access to powerful decision-makers, this makes it difficult for them to change their situation.

## Feminism

Feminists emphasize that women face a greater risk of poverty than men – what is called the feminization of poverty – particularly lone parents who are mainly women, and single female pensioners. The box below outlines this feminization of poverty, and the effects of poverty on women in low-income households.

---

**THE FEMINIZATION OF POVERTY**

Women are more likely than men to experience poverty. In 2017–18, 20 per cent of all women (and 23 per cent of single female pensioners) lived in low-income households compared to 18 per cent of men (and 20 per cent of single male pensioners)

- Women are more likely to be in low-paid and part-time work. In 2018, around three-fifths of low-paid workers were women.
- They are more likely than men to be lone parents with sole responsibility for children, leading to reduced possibilities for employment and dependence on inadequate state benefits.
- Women live longer than men, and therefore spend a greater proportion of their lives beyond state pension age. However, because of low pay throughout their lives, they are less likely than men to have savings, and are less likely than men to be entitled to employers' pensions.
- In many low-income households, it is often mothers rather than fathers who bear the burden of trying to make ends meet, and in the face of poverty sacrifice their own standard of living to shield the rest of the family from poverty, and provide food, clothing and extras for the children.

## Tackling poverty

### *The welfare state*

The main measures taken to help the poor have largely developed with the welfare state. In the UK, the Beveridge Report in 1942 recommended the development of welfare services run by the state, aimed at the destruction of the 'five giants' of Want (poverty), Disease (ill health and lack of healthcare), Squalor (poor housing), Ignorance (lack of educational opportunity) and Idleness (unemployment), and the creation of a society in which each individual would have the right to be cared for by the state from womb to tomb.

The welfare state provides a wide range of benefits and services including:

- a variety of welfare benefits through the social security system for many groups such as the unemployed, those injured at work, the sick and disabled, widows, the retired, expectant mothers, lone parents, and children – for example, state pensions, Job Seeker's Allowance, Employment and Support Allowance, and Income Support (all – except state pensions – now included in a single benefit called Universal Credit).
- a comprehensive and largely free National Health Service, including ante- and post-natal care, hospitals, GPs, dentists and opticians (although some charges are payable – for example, to dentists and opticians).
- free and compulsory state education and training for all, to the age of 18.
- social services provided by local councils, such as social workers, and special facilities for the disabled, the elderly and children. Local councils are also responsible for housing the homeless, and for the adoption and fostering of children.

The Beveridge Report of 1942 recommended tackling the 'five giants' of Want (poverty), Disease (ill health and lack of healthcare), Squalor (poor housing), Ignorance (lack of educational opportunity) and Idleness (unemployment). These principles laid the basis for the state's role in tackling social problems we see in today's welfare state

- a national minimum wage and national living wage to help the poorest-paid and to prevent their exploitation.

The welfare state, run by national and local government, is not the only provider of welfare and means of tackling poverty. The informal and voluntary sectors also play important roles, often working alongside state provision.

## Informal welfare provision

This is provided informally by family, friends and neighbours, such as offering the homeless temporary accommodation or meals, or providing financial help in times of distress. Informal help for the poor often means care by women, as it is women who take on the main caring responsibilities, and who are often the main helpers in food banks and charity shops, and help family members going through periods of crisis. Women, generally, take on more volunteering work than men.

## Voluntary organizations

These are non-official, non-profit-making organizations, often charities, which are 'voluntary' in the sense that they are neither created by, nor controlled by, the state. They employ both salaried staff and voluntary helpers, and are funded by donations from the public and grants from, or sale of services to, central and local government. They try to fill some of the gaps left by the safety net provided by the state, by providing help and information in areas where this is missing. Voluntary organizations have high levels of expert knowledge, and work in specialized areas – such as domestic violence, homelessness, debt, mental illness, disability, rape and sexual abuse – where state provision may be under pressure, inadequate or non-existent. However, they often lack adequate funds to be as effective as they might otherwise be, and they do not exist in all areas where they are needed. Examples of such groups that tackle poverty include: the Salvation Army, which provides hostel accommodation and soup kitchens for the homeless; the Trussell Trust, which runs a network of over 400 food banks, giving emergency food and support to people in crisis across the UK; and the Child Poverty Action Group, which promotes action for the relief of poverty among children, and families with children.

## The persistence of poverty: why the poor remain poor

The welfare state in Britain was originally seen as a way of providing 'womb-to-tomb' care, and of eradicating poverty. However, while it may have removed the worst excesses of absolute poverty, widespread deprivation remains in modern Britain, and the welfare state has yet to solve the real problems of relative poverty. Why is this?

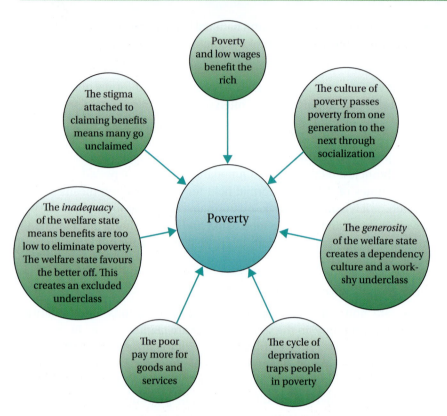

**Figure 6.28** Why the poor remain poor

A good way to remember the various explanations of poverty is to think of them as 'blaming theories' – where is the blame placed for poverty?
The explanations below variously:
- blame the *generosity* of the welfare state (the 'nanny state')
- blame the *inadequacy* of the welfare state
- blame the culture of the poor
- blame the cycle of deprivation
- blame the unequal structure of power and wealth in society.

## Blaming the generosity of the welfare state: the dependency culture and the underclass (version 1)

The New Right (see pages 52–4) argues that poverty continues because the welfare state has created a **dependency culture** (sometimes called a *culture of dependency*). This is where people develop a set of values and beliefs and a way of life centred on dependence on others. The New Right believes the generosity of 'handouts' from the 'nanny' welfare state undermines personal responsibility and self-help. This encourages the poor to abandon reliance on work to support themselves. They become content to live on welfare-state

> **Dependency culture** A set of values and beliefs, and a way of life, centred on dependence on others. Normally used in the context of those who depend on welfare-state benefits. Sometimes called a 'culture of dependency'.

benefits, rather than taking responsibility themselves for improving their situation. The more the welfare state provides benefits for people, the less they will do for themselves, leading to a situation where people learn to become dependent on others.

*Universal versus selective, means-tested benefits* The New Right believes that universal welfare benefits (which are available to everyone regardless of income, such as the basic state pension, and free healthcare and education) should be withdrawn from all those who are capable of supporting themselves. These benefits should instead be targeted only at those who genuinely need them, such as the disabled and the long-term sick. Universal benefits should therefore be replaced by selective benefits, targeted by means-testing. Means-testing involves people having to pass a test of their income and savings (their 'means') before receiving any benefits, and only if these are low enough would they receive any benefits. The arguments over means-testing are presented in the box below.

---

### ARE MEANS-TESTED BENEFITS A GOOD IDEA?

| Yes | No |
|---|---|
| • Benefits are targeted only at those who really need them. People who are able to work should support themselves. More money would then be available to invest in the economy, create jobs and cut taxes. | • Means-tested benefits may lead to some people being worse-off if they take a low-paid job. They may lose means-tested benefits like housing or council tax benefits, and the extra they earn by working is not enough to compensate for the lost income. This 'poverty trap' discourages people from taking work. |
| • Means-testing stops unemployment being an option for some people, and fights the welfare dependency culture. | • Because of the poverty trap, means-testing might drive people into a dependency culture and a reluctance to get a job. |
| • Families, communities and voluntary organizations are strengthened as alternative sources of support. | • Families and communities caught in the poverty trap are likely to be weakened by poverty and stress. |
| • Selective means-tested benefits will enable more benefits for the most disadvantaged, by no longer wasting money on those who can afford to support themselves. | • Often the most deprived do not take up or make full use of universal benefits, as they're unsure of how to do so. Means-tested benefits attach a stigma to those who claim them, and make it even more unlikely they will claim benefits to which they are entitled. |

## UNCLAIMED BENEFITS

Many poor people do not claim the welfare benefits to which they are entitled, particularly those which are means-tested. According to the Department for Work and Pensions' own estimates, released in 2018, between about 10 per cent and 40 per cent of those entitled to some income-related benefit were not claiming it, representing overall up to about £10.1 billion left unclaimed in 2016–17. This is around 24 per cent of the money that was paid out. The failure to claim benefits is often because of:

- the complexity of the benefits and tax system
- inadequate publicity or lack of awareness about the availability of the benefits
- the sometimes difficult language of leaflets and complex means-testing forms, which mean people often do not know what their rights are or the procedures for claiming benefits. This is particularly important as the poor are among the least-educated sections of the population.
- people's lack of confidence about whether or not they are entitled, or because they regard the effort involved in claiming as too great for the amounts involved
- government policies which discourage claiming by some groups
- the stigma attached by the media to benefit claimants, such as campaigns and headlines about 'scroungers' and benefit fraudsters.

### Activity

Refer to the 'Unclaimed benefits' box and the image of newspaper headlines above, and answer the following questions or discuss them in your group.

1 Do you agree or disagree with the view that the media give the impression that people receiving benefits are 'scroungers'? Give reasons for your answer.
2 Do you think most people receiving welfare benefits are deserving? How would you go about finding out?
3 Do you think benefits discourage people from taking more responsibility for their own lives? Give reasons for your answer.
4 Do you think it is reasonable that people should be expected to take a job even if they will be worse-off than if they received benefits?

*The underclass – version 1: the poor as welfare scroungers and social misfits* Murray (1984), writing from a New Right perspective, argues that the generosity of the welfare state, and the dependency culture, have created a poor, antisocial, deviant underclass – right at the bottom of the social hierarchy – who have developed a lifestyle and set of values and attitudes which make them reluctant to take jobs. Murray argues that welfare benefits discourage self-help and self-sufficiency, and undermine mainstream values such as honesty, family life and hard work. Growing numbers of lone parents and young people lose interest in getting jobs, and develop

Do you think newspaper reports like this might attach a stigma to welfare claimants and deter some people from claiming benefits to which they are entitled?

alternative values that tolerate crime, cheating the benefit system and various forms of antisocial behaviour. They are scroungers willing simply to live off the welfare state. Murray's view of the underclass also regards some of the poor as social misfits, who share the following features which makes them different from the rest of society:

- high levels of illegitimacy, lone parenthood, cohabitation (rather than marriage) and family instability
- lack of morality and commitment to mainstream values
- drunkenness and 'yob culture'
- crime, drug abuse and benefit fraud (note: benefit fraud made up just 1.2 per cent of the total benefits bill in 2018–19)
- exclusion from school, and educational failure.

Murray's solution to poverty is to cut welfare benefits to encourage self-reliance through marriage or work. This approach has become increasingly common over the last twenty years, in part based on a series of myths about the generosity of the welfare state spread by government and the media.

Consequently, in Britain's towns and cities, poor people from vulnerable groups who have slipped through the protection of the safety net of the welfare state – or been forced out of it by harsh government policies – are increasingly visible. Many of the poorest in our society have been abandoned, to turn to a poorly funded voluntary sector or food banks to survive, or just cope – or not cope – alone.

These ideas of the dependency culture and the underclass are also implied in the later 'culture of poverty' explanation (see pages 489–91).

Many sociologists reject Murray's view of the underclass. This alternative view of the underclass is explored below in version 2.

## Blaming the inadequacy of the welfare state: the underclass (version 2)

An alternative explanation for the persistence of poverty is offered by those who argue that benefit levels are too low to lift people out of poverty. From this viewpoint, the welfare state is not generous enough. Middle-class people also gain more from the welfare state than do the poor. For example, the middle class gain more from state spending on education, because they keep their children in education longer (in further and higher education). The middle class also gain more from the health service, partly because they are more demanding and assertive in their dealings with doctors, and partly because the middle class are generally healthier. This means that doctors in middle class areas are less overworked, and so are able to spend more time dealing with patients and their problems. Poor people, by contrast, get less time with their doctors and face longer hospital waiting lists. Tax relief on private pensions also benefits the middle-class more, as they are more likely to have private pension schemes. This bias towards the middle class has been called the **inverse care law** – that those whose need is greatest get the least resources, and those whose need is least get the greatest resources.

*The underclass – version 2: poverty and social exclusion*   This failure of the welfare state to provide sufficient help to the poor has led to an alternative view of the underclass to that of Murray and the New Right discussed above. This alternative view suggests the underclass consists of disadvantaged groups whose poverty means they are excluded from taking part in society to the same extent as the non-poor. This excluded underclass consists of groups such as the disadvantaged elderly retired, lone-parent families, the homeless and the long-term unemployed. These groups are forced to rely upon inadequate state benefits which are too low to give them an acceptable standard of living. This prevents them from participating fully in society, and gives them little opportunity to escape the poverty trap.

Sociologists who take this view argue that the evidence shows that the attitudes and values of the poor are no different from those of the non-poor: they have conventional attitudes and morality, and want the same stable relationships and paid employment as the rest of society, but just lack the means to achieve them. It is not the attitudes of poor people which are to blame for their poverty, but the difficulties and misfortune they face, which are beyond their control – such as unemployment, mental illness, disability or sickness. In this view, it is government policies that have neglected to tackle low pay, allowed the living standards of those on some benefits to stagnate or decline,

**Inverse care law** In relation to the welfare state, including the National Health Service, the suggestion that those whose need is least get the most resources, while those in the greatest need get the fewest resources.

and failed to give the poor the opportunities and incentives needed to get off benefits. The members of the underclass are victims of social inequality rather than the cause of social problems. This view suggests government policies should do more to improve the living standards of those on benefits (e.g. through higher pensions and benefit levels), and give incentives to the poor to get off benefits by ensuring there are enough decently paid and secure jobs available.

---

### Activity

**Two views of the underclass**

**Version 1**
A group who have developed a lifestyle and set of attitudes which mean they are no longer willing to take jobs. They have evolved a dependency culture, which means they are not prepared to help themselves but are prepared to live off the welfare state. They lack morality, and have high levels of crime, cohabitation and lone parenthood. Their workshy 'sponging' attitudes and lack of social responsibility are the causes for their poverty. Most of the poor have only themselves to blame.

**Version 2**
A group whose poverty means they are excluded from taking part in society to the same extent as the non-poor, even though they want to. They consist of groups like the disadvantaged elderly retired, lone parents, the disabled, the homeless, the low-paid and the long-term unemployed. Their attitudes are the same as those of the rest of society, but they are forced to rely upon low pay, zero-hours contracts or inadequate state benefits – or no benefits – which are not high enough to give them an acceptable standard of living. This prevents them from participating fully in society, and gives them little opportunity to fulfil their ambitions and escape the poverty trap.

Compare the two models of the underclass above:
1  Which view do you think provides the most accurate picture of poor people? Give reasons for your answer.
2  Suggest two solutions to the problem of the underclass for each version.

---

## Blaming the culture of the poor: the culture of poverty

Another explanation for the persistence of poverty is the theory of the **culture of poverty**.

This suggests it is features of the poor themselves – their values, culture and way of life – that cause poverty and social exclusion. These features include:

**Culture of poverty**
A set of beliefs and values thought to exist among the poor, which prevents them escaping from poverty.

- *resignation* – they are resigned to their fate, and make little effort to change their situation, and seldom take opportunities to escape poverty when they arise
- *fatalism* – a view that nothing can be done to change their situation
- *lack of future planning*
- *marginalization* – not identifying themselves as part of mainstream society.

In this view, the poor make little effort to change their situation, or to help themselves overcome their social exclusion. They won't use their initiative and involve themselves in mainstream society or try to break free of their poverty, even when opportunities to do so arise. Children grow up in this culture, and learn these values from their parents, and so poverty and social exclusion continue from one generation to the next.

The weakness of this type of explanation is that there is little clear-cut evidence that children inherit their parents' attitudes, and it tends to blame the poor for their own poverty. However, if the poor do develop a culture of poverty – and this is hotly disputed – it may well be a *result* of poverty, and not a *cause* of it. For example, the poor cannot afford to save for a 'rainy day', planning for the future is difficult when the future is so uncertain, and it is hard not to give up and become resigned to being workless when any jobs

---

**TRAPPED IN POVERTY: THE POOR PAY MORE**

One of the great ironies of poverty is that poor people have little choice but to spend money in less economical ways, and the cost of living is higher for the poor than the non-poor. This hinders them in their attempts to escape poverty. The poor pay more because:

- They often live in poor-quality housing, which is expensive to heat and maintain.
- They have to buy cheap clothing, which wears out quickly and is therefore more expensive in the long run.
- They have to pay more for food as they can only afford to buy it in small quantities (which is more expensive than buying in bulk), and from small, expensive corner shops as they haven't cars to travel to supermarkets. They also lack storage facilities such as freezers for buying in bulk.
- The cost of house and car insurance is higher as a result of more theft and vandalism in poor areas.
- They pay more for credit; banks and building societies won't lend them money as they consider them a high risk. Loans are therefore often obtained from 'loan sharks' at exorbitant rates of interest.
- They suffer more ill health, and so have to spend more on non-prescription medicines, such as cold cures and pain-killers.

on offer are so poorly paid, insecure and menial, or after endless searching for jobs that don't exist.

The culture-of-poverty explanation, and the earlier 'dependency culture' one, are convenient ones for those in positions of power, as they put the blame for poverty on the poor themselves. If these explanations are adopted, then the problem of poverty will be solved by policies such as cutting welfare benefits to the poor, to make them stand on their own two feet, and job training programmes to move them from welfare to work.

## Blaming the cycle of deprivation

A further explanation for poverty is what has been called the cycle of deprivation. This suggests that:

- *the poor are trapped in a web or vicious circle* by material circumstances which, regardless of attitudes or ability, offer little chance of escape (see, for example, the box 'Trapped in poverty: the poor pay more').
- *poverty is cumulative*, in the sense that one aspect of poverty can lead to further poverty. For example, a child born in a poor family may have poor-quality housing and diet. This may cause ill health, absence from school, educational underachievement and consequently a low-paid job or unemployment, and therefore poverty in adult life.

Figure 6.29 illustrates examples of possible cycles of deprivation. The problem with this explanation is that, while it explains why poverty continues, it does not explain how poverty begins in the first place. The final type of explanation does try to do this.

## Blaming the unequal structure of power and wealth in society

These are structural explanations, which explain poverty in terms of the structure of society, with its unequal distribution of wealth and income, and the inadequate assistance given to the poor. Poverty is seen as an aspect of social inequality and not merely an individual problem of poor people. These are mainly the Marxist and Weberian arguments outlined on pages 480–1 and the feminist views on pages 57–9, 412 and 481, which suggest that the reason the poor remain poor is because they are exploited by the rich in an unequal, patriarchal capitalist society, and low-paid workers, especially women, provide the source of profits which enables the rich to achieve high incomes.

In this view, it is not being unemployed, mentally ill, homeless, a lone parent, long-term sick, disabled or old that causes poverty. Rather, it is government policy and the structure of society which mean some people face misfortune through no fault of their own, and are penalized for it by low pay, inadequate benefits, a deprived lifestyle and poor life chances.

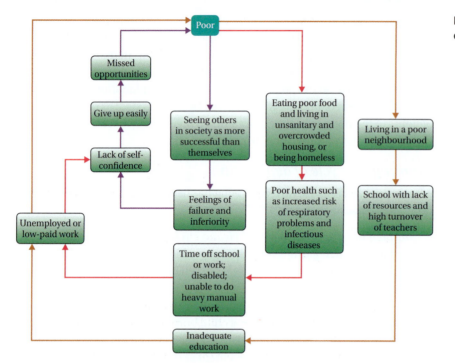

**Figure 6.29** Cycles of deprivation

What factors push people into a cycle of deprivation and prevent them escaping from poverty?

Structural explanations suggest that any serious attempt to abolish poverty would involve a widespread redistribution of wealth and income. This would mean the creation of improved social services, higher welfare benefits, and more secure and better-paid jobs, with the introduction of higher taxes on the rich to pay for these reforms.

## Activity

1   Describe and explain two differences between absolute and relative poverty.
2   Describe and explain two reasons why lone parents may be living in poverty.
3   Identify and explain two reasons why poverty continues despite the welfare state.
4   Imagine you wanted to carry out a small survey asking people their views about poverty. Identify the research method you would use, and explain why you think the method you chose would be better than other methods you could have used.
5   Imagine you have become the prime minister, with a huge majority in Parliament enabling you to carry through a successful campaign against poverty. Think carefully about all the explanations for poverty you have read of in this chapter, and the groups in poverty. Devise a series of policies which would help to reduce poverty. Explain in each case why you think your proposed policy would help to reduce poverty.
6   Write a short essay (10–15 minutes) answering the following question: 'How far do sociologists agree with the view that the culture of the poor is the main reason for their poverty?'

## CHAPTER SUMMARY AND REVISION CHECKLIST

After studying this chapter, you should be able to:

- explain why social inequality is an important social issue

- explain what is meant by social stratification

- describe the main features of slavery; the caste, estate and class systems; and the differences between them

- describe the main features of consensus and conflict theories of social class, including those of the functionalists, Marxists and Weberians, and some problems with them

- outline Davis and Moore's contribution to the functionalist theory of stratification, and make some criticisms of it

- explain why sociologists often use occupation as an indicator of social class, and explain the problems in the use of occupation and occupational scales

- outline the main social classes in Britain today

- describe some of the main changes in the class structure in the past 100 years, including changes in the working class and the middle class, and the discussions over embourgeoisement and proletarianization

- outline Levine's research on the embourgeoisement thesis

- describe some of the features of, and obstacles to, social mobility in contemporary Britain

- describe and explain a range of social-class inequalities in life chances, including inequalities in wealth and income, health, employment, education and crime, and why attempts to redistribute wealth and income have failed

- explain why social class continues to be of importance in contemporary Britain

- outline functionalist, Marxist, Weberian and feminist theories of gender stratification, including Walby's theory of patriarchy

- explain what is meant by the 'sexual (or gendered) division of labour'

- describe how, and explain why, the position of women has changed in Britain over the past century

- describe and explain a range of gender inequalities in life chances, including inequalities in paid and unpaid work, the gender pay gap and social mobility, and in the family, education and crime

- explain why women overall get only around 82 per cent of the average male wage and are poorly represented in top jobs

- explain what is meant by the terms 'ethnicity', 'ethnic group' and 'minority ethnic group'

- describe and explain a range of inequalities in life chances faced by ethnic minorities in contemporary Britain, including in relation to employment, low pay, poverty, housing, education and crime

- outline functionalist, Marxist and Weberian theories of ethnic inequality

- explain what is meant by racial prejudice and racial discrimination, and suggest some explanations for them

- describe how age is a social construction, some age-related inequalities, and assess how important age inequalities are in affecting life chances compared to inequalities arising from social class, gender and ethnicity

- outline functionalist, Marxist, Weberian and feminist theories of age stratification

- explain the difference between an impairment and a disability, and the biomedical and social models of disability

- outline a number of ways in which disability can affect life chances

- outline how religion (Islamophobia) and sexuality (homophobia) can be a basis for inequality

- outline how stratification is linked to inequalities in power and authority, including: the distinctions between authority and coercion; formal and informal sources of power; Weber's theories of traditional, charismatic and rational-legal authority; and how power is exercised in everyday life

- outline functionalist, Marxist, Weberian and feminist views on the distribution of power in society

- explain the difference between a dictatorship and a democracy, and outline a range of ways in which ordinary people can influence powerholders in a democracy, including pressure groups and social movements, the methods they use and the factors affecting their ability to influence powerholders

- explain the difference between absolute, relative and consensual definitions of poverty, and how the poverty line is measured in contemporary Britain

- outline the work of Townsend on poverty, and his view of relative poverty

- identify the main groups in poverty in modern Britain, and briefly explain why each of them is poor

- describe aspects of poverty apart from lack of income

- identify some ways globalization has affected poverty

- outline functionalist, Marxist, Weberian and feminist views and explanations of poverty
- examine some ways the state and voluntary organizations have attempted to tackle the problem of poverty (mainly the welfare state)
- give a number of explanations why the poor remain poor despite the welfare state, including the generosity of the welfare state and the dependency culture, the inadequacy
- of the welfare state, the culture of poverty, the cycle of deprivation, and functionalist, Marxist, Weberian and feminist structural explanations
- discuss the different versions of the view that the poor are an underclass, including Murray's New Right theory and features of the underclass

## KEY TERMS

Definitions can be found in the glossary at the end of this book, as well as these terms usually being defined in the margin where they first appear in the chapter. You can also find the glossary online by following the link at www.politybooks.com/browne. Put it in your phone for ready reference.

| | | | |
|---|---|---|---|
| absolute poverty | embourgeoisement | life expectancy | relative poverty |
| affluent workers | endogamy | market situation | reserve army of labour |
| ageism | ethnic group | means of production | ruling-class ideology |
| authority | ethnicity | median income | sexism |
| bourgeoisie | false class consciousness | minority ethnic group | sexual (or gendered) |
| caste system | feudalism | occupational status |     division of labour |
| charismatic authority | gender pay gap | open society | sexual orientation |
| class consciousness | generation | party | slavery |
| class struggle | glass ceiling | patriarchy | social capital |
| closed society | globalization | petty bourgeoisie | social class |
| coercion | hate crime | political party | social mobility |
| Communism | homophobia | poverty line | social movement |
| culture of poverty | impairment | pressure groups | social stratification |
| death rate | income | proletarianization | status group |
| democracy | intergenerational social | proletariat | trade unions |
| dependency culture | mobility | race | traditional authority |
| deskilling | intragenerational social | racial discrimination | underclass |
| dictatorship | mobility | racial prejudice | wealth |
| disability | inverse care law | racism | white-collar workers |
| economic inequality | Islamophobia | rational-legal authority | |

There are a variety of free tests and other activities that can be used to assess your learning – mainly aimed at AS- and A-level sociology students, but you might find them useful – as well as an online searchable glossary, at

www.politybooks.com/browne
You can also find new contemporary resources by following Ken Browne on Twitter

@BrowneKen

# Contents

**KEY ISSUES**

- What are the media?
- Traditional and new media
- Patterns of media use – who uses the media, and what for?
- The significance of the new media in contemporary society
- The role of advertising in the media
- Ownership and control of the media
- The content of the media: media bias, public opinion and social control
- Censorship, freedom of the media and democracy
- The media and socialization
- Media representations and stereotyping
- The influence of the media – the effects of the media on audiences
- Violence and the media
- Into the future

# WHAT ARE THE MEDIA?

The term 'media' refers to the technology, organizations and products involved with communication with large mass audiences without any face-to-face personal contact. The main media of mass communication include terrestrial (earth-based) and satellite television, radio, newspapers and magazines (print or online), books, films, advertising, the internet, computer games and social media (websites and apps and other online means of communication that are used for social interaction among large groups of people, whereby they create, share and exchange information and develop social and friendship networks).

# TRADITIONAL AND NEW MEDIA

The media are now often divided into the traditional and the new media.

## The traditional media

The traditional or 'old' media refers to those media that communicate in a one-way process to very large mass audiences. This is the type of media

The traditional media include separate devices such as printed books, television and newspapers, and are a one-way 'take it or leave it' process of mass communication

associated with traditional broadcasting, like the terrestrial television channels (BBC 1 and 2, ITV 1, and Channels 4 and 5) and BBC radios 1 and 2, and mass-circulation national and Sunday newspapers. There is little consumer choice, beyond a few TV channels, radio stations or newspapers and magazines.

## The new media

The 'new media' refers to those media using new technology which first emerged in the late twentieth and early twenty-first centuries, which distribute their content using screen-based, digital (computer) technology. These include computers and the internet; electronic e-books; digital cable and satellite TV; and set-top boxes like Sky Q and Virgin TV's V6, enabling customized, individualized television viewing with a choice of hundreds of television channels; digital media like mp3; internet downloads and streaming of films, videos and music onto smartphones and tablets; user-generated media content via apps and websites like Snapchat, Facebook, YouTube and Instagram; and interactive video/computer games through PlayStations and Xboxes.

While the traditional media involve different devices for different media content – such as printed format for books, newspapers and magazines, radios and mp3 players to listen to music and radio programmes, televisions to watch shows, and phones to make calls – new media technology often involves using a single device doing several things. For example, the latest media technology, like Apple's iPhones and iPads, enable users, on a single device, to make phone calls, read books, send text messages and emails, take photos and record videos and send them to friends and upload them to internet sites, browse the internet, play music, watch films and TV,

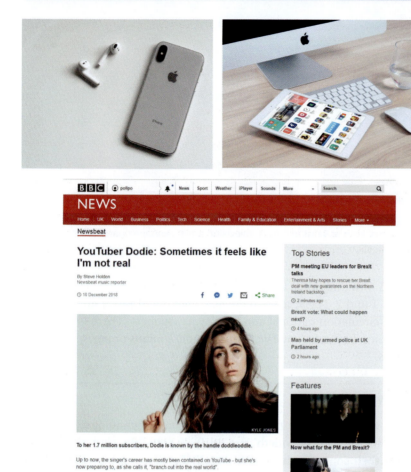

New media involve digital (computer) screen-based technology, often integrating many uses into a single device, as in Apple's iPhone and iPad shown here. Traditional print and TV are also now competing with the internet, as shown by the BBC website pictured here

consult maps, and hundreds of other applications. Likewise, businesses and advertisers are able to communicate with millions of people at the same time through a single device.

## Differences between the traditional and new media

The new media differ from traditional forms of the media in several ways:

### *They are digital (digitality)*

Essentially, this means 'using computers', whereby all data (text, sound and pictures) are converted into computer code which can then be stored, distributed and picked up via screen-based devices, such as smartphones, digital TVs and computers.

## *They are interactive (interactivity)*

This means consumers have an opportunity to participate in, engage with and interact with the media, creating their own material, and customizing the media to their own wishes, with much greater choice compared with the passive consumption and 'take it or leave it' features of the traditional media. For example, people don't just have to watch the news or other content that media professionals provide: they can actually create it themselves, by uploading videos to YouTube, posting items on the internet, blogging and vlogging for all to see, and spreading their ideas on Facebook and Twitter; they can vote people on or off reality TV shows, like *I'm Celebrity, Get Me Out of Here* or *Strictly Come Dancing*, buy things from advertising programmes and rent films to view, and they can set their own TV schedules, using DVD recorders, set-top boxes and BBC's iPlayer.

## *They are hypertextual (hypertextuality)*

Much of the internet is linked together through hypertext. These are embedded links to other items that make it easy to search for and interact with information.

## *They are dispersed (dispersal)*

This means it is less centralized and controlled than traditional media, and more adapted to individual choices. There is a massive growth in media products of all kinds, and there is huge scope for people to create and spread their own information which is more outside the control of large media companies and the agencies of social control.

For example, people are now making their own videos and posting them on the internet. In 2018, there were around 300–400 hours of consumer-generated video uploaded to YouTube every minute. Blogs are beginning to rival traditional journalism as sources of information and news. Estimates of the number of blogs vary wildly, but all agree there are now hundreds of millions of blogs in the online world.

## The effects of new media on traditional media

All the traditional media companies are massively involved in the new media. For example, all the major newspapers and TV channels now have their own websites and apps, and their online readerships far exceed the circulation of their printed formats or live broadcast programmes. Some of the changes arising from the development and growth of new media and

**Activity**

1  Go to www.en.wikipedia.org  and look up 'digital media', 'interactivity', 'hypertext' and 'virtual reality'. Follow the hypertext links given in Wikipedia, and give two examples of contemporary media that use each of these.

2  Go to www.youtube.com, do a search on sociology, and report your findings on any two sociology videos.

3  Go to www.bbc.co.uk/news/uk and watch the UK news, making a note of the latest headline stories. Now do the same with https://news.sky.com.  Compare the two sets of news stories, and whether they seem to be covering the same material. What might this suggest to you about how the media influence our views of the world?

4  Discuss with others in your group, or do a small survey, and find out what people use the new media for, and whether they use them more or less than the traditional media like newspapers, books and television.

new media technologies which have had an impact on the traditional media include:

- *a decline in advertising in traditional media* – internet advertising is now the largest category of advertising spending in the UK. Traditional news outlets, such as printed newspapers and TV, face an increasingly uphill struggle to make money, since a large part of their income came from advertisers placing adverts in their newspapers or between their programmes.

- *a huge decline in printed newspaper and magazine sales*, and a general downward trend in live broadcast TV viewers, as stories are easily and more rapidly accessible via social media on smartphones and tablets

- *the use of new media to gather news* and other stories for traditional media

- *shifts in traditional news flow cycles* – online, news events are reported far faster and more frequently than traditional media can report them. Journalists working in traditional media have far less time to process and check stories

- *traditional media and media owners have less power t*o dictate what the public gets to know about – anything they don't report is likely to be covered elsewhere online

- *more control by media audiences*, such as the use of smartphones to obtain and report news, rather than TV or newspapers. News stories, for example, often appear first on social media like Twitter, and traditional media often spend their time playing catch-up.

# PATTERNS OF MEDIA USE – WHO USES THE MEDIA, AND WHAT FOR?

The new media are rapidly threatening, and taking over from, the traditional media as a means of mass communication.

People are spending more time watching, streaming and consuming media than ever. On-demand and streamed content delivered over the internet is an important part of the way in which people watch television: 67 per cent of adults now use online services to watch TV, like BBC iPlayer, and 45 per cent pay to subscribe to streaming services such as Netflix and Amazon Prime.

While traditional broadcast TV is still the main way people consume media, the gap with new media is closing fast. In 2016, people worldwide spent an average of around 43 minutes more each day viewing TV (174 minutes) than using the internet (131 minutes). By 2018, the gap had reduced to around 7 minutes more time watching TV, and forecasts suggested that by 2020 this would reverse, and daily time spent using the internet (180 minutes) would overtake television (168 minutes) by 12 minutes a day.

In the UK, around 90 per cent of households had internet access at home in 2018, and 98 per cent of these had a fixed broadband connection. The smartphone is the device that adults are most likely to own (76 per cent) – more than laptops (64 per cent) or tablets (58 per cent); 73 per cent of adults used the internet 'on the go' using a smartphone. An estimated three out of four internet users have a social media profile or account, most of them on Facebook, which is the largest social-network service in the UK, and the third most frequently used website after Google and Microsoft sites.

## Users of the media

There is an element of stratification within both the traditional and new media, with differences between users based on gender, age, social class and ethnicity.

### *Gender differences*

- Males overall spend more time than women online on a laptop or desktop, but young women (aged 18–34) spend more time than young men online using their smartphones.
- Males spend more time than females playing computer games and using fixed game consoles, watching videos online and using email and chatrooms.
- Females are slightly more likely to use social-networking sites.

- E-readers are more popular among females (probably because they generally read more than males).
- Females are more likely to send and receive texts, and make more phone calls, and to use the internet for studying and research, whereas men use it more for personal pleasure and fun.
- Research shows that males prefer sport, action movies and documentaries on TV; women prefer soaps and costume dramas.
- Men are more likely to be in control of media technology in the home.

## Age differences

### Traditional media

- Watching live broadcast TV is declining overall, but it is going down fastest among young people, and is actually rising among over-64s.
- Younger households are more likely to have satellite or cable television services than older households.
- Young people visit the cinema more – Hollywood movies are mainly aimed at young people more than older people.
- Young people are less likely than older people to consume media in traditional formats, such as print newspapers, and TV on TV sets.
- Younger people are less likely to access news from TV, radio or print newspapers.
- Print newspaper readership is declining among younger audiences, who prefer digital media. The average age of the *youngest* print newspaper reader in the UK in 2017 was 43. Print newspapers are increasingly becoming the preserve of older people.

### New media

There is a substantial generation gap in access to and in the use of new media – this difference is hardly surprising given that young people have grown up with the latest technological developments; they have learnt to use the internet at school, at home and from their peers; and they are consequently more media-savvy than older generations. But this generation gap is diminishing, as use of the internet and apps has become crucial for people in the UK to communicate, shop, and find information and entertainment, and they increasingly underpin people's ability to participate fully in society. The age differences in 2017–18 showed that:

- while use of social and communications apps was high among all age groups, older people were less likely to use new media and the internet, and use of social media apps declines with age. Nonetheless, in 2018 nearly half (45 per cent) of over-75s were internet users, though they use it less often than younger people, and four in ten internet users over 75 had a social media profile or account.

- viewers aged 18–24 spent more time watching YouTube videos than any other age group.
- smartphone ownership is highest among younger adults, and use of smartphones by people aged 65 and over was lower than for other age groups. But in 2017 it was increasing sharply, and the over-65s were the only age group for which smartphone use was increasing.
- adults are now less likely to go online via computers and more likely to use their smartphones. A quarter of young adults (aged 16–34) *only* used a device other than a computer to go online
- The age group 16–24 is more likely to consume media in a variety of formats – e.g. watching TV on their mobile, laptop or tablets rather than a TV set – and is more likely to go online using their mobile.

### Social-class differences

Apart from printed newspapers (see below), there are diminishing social-class differences in media use. Households that only have access to Freeview TV, as opposed to satellite or cable TV and paid-for subscription services like Netflix or Amazon Prime, are more commonly found in the lower social classes.

In general, the more educated a person is (typically linked to their social class), the more they will use the internet. The middle classes are more likely than average to own smartphones, laptops and desktops, and have traditionally been the biggest users of the new media. This is because they have the economic means to do so – e.g. purchasing a computer, hardware and a monthly broadband subscription.

The box on the next page shows the major UK print newspapers, which can be separated into three main groups – 'quality', 'mid-market' and 'red tops' – which mainly reflect social-class differences in their readership.

### Ethnic differences

There are relatively few Black, Asian and Minority Ethnic (BAME) journalists in mainstream media, and BAME media consumers often call out mainstream media for racist stereotyping and under-representing BAME groups. Surveys suggest four out of five people believe that media coverage of BAME groups promotes racism.

- **Television:** Satellite and cable TV and the internet mean BAME groups whose first language is not English have access to programmes in their own language, and BAME groups spend up to 50 per cent of their TV-viewing time watching ethnic channels, such as the Hindi-language ZEE TV, ZEE Cinema (the home of Bollywood blockbusters), B4U Movies and Star Plus for Asian audiences. Asian channels make up the second-largest collection of channels on Sky after general entertainment.

## BRITAIN'S NATIONAL DAILY AND SUNDAY NEWSPAPERS

### The 'quality' newspapers

These include *The Times*, *The Guardian*, *The Telegraph* and *The Financial Times*, and, on Sunday, *The Sunday Times*, *The Observer* and *The Sunday Telegraph*. These are fairly serious in tone and content, use a lot of text, and are concerned with news and features about politics, economic and financial problems, sport, literature and the arts, and give in-depth, analytical coverage in longer articles and news stories. These are more likely to have a middle-class readership.

### The 'middle-brow' or mid-market newspapers

These are the *Daily Express* and *Daily Mail*, and the *Sunday Express* and the *Mail on Sunday*. These are in-between the qualities and the red tops, and include features of each. While they tend to have a slightly more serious tone and content than the red tops, they also cover a range of the more colourful issues found in them. They are aimed primarily at the middle-brow middle/lower-middle class, but have readers drawn from the whole social spectrum.

### The popular or red-top tabloid press

These are the mass-circulation, daily and Sunday newspapers aimed at mass audiences – commonly called the tabloid press. They are *The Sun*, *Daily Mirror* and *Daily Star*, and the *Sunday Mirror*, *Sunday People* and *Daily Star Sunday*, and are generally referred to as 'red tops' because of the colour of their masthead logos. These aim to entertain as much as providing news, and are dominated by images/photos. They concentrate on the sensational aspects of the news, like political scandals and crime, and human interest stories, such as sex scandals and celebrity gossip, plus entertainment, loads of sport and other light topics, written in very simple language combined with large headlines and many colour photographs. They are primarily aimed at a working-class readership.

- **Print media:** Most BAME groups in the UK have their own publications, which are either printed in ethnic minority languages, and/or provide coverage of their countries of birth or topics of interest to their community in the UK. An estimated 67 per cent of Asian TV viewers read Asian newspapers or magazines. There are around seventy print publications produced for BAME communities in the UK, many of which have linked websites. Examples include:
  - *African Voice* (http://africanvoiceonline.co.uk) – a Black African newspaper with the latest news from Africa, including African entertainment, politics and culture
  - *The Voice* (www.voice-online.co.uk) – a national black weekly newspaper aimed at the British African-Caribbean community

> **Activity**
>
> Look at the box on Britain's national daily and Sunday newspapers.
>
> 1 Compare one quality and one red-top newspaper for the same day, by either getting hold of a copy of each or viewing them online on their related websites. Study the kinds of stories, advertisements, photographs and cartoons, and the language they use. List all the differences between them. In the light of your findings, suggest and explain carefully three reasons why these two types of newspapers are, in general, read by members of different social classes.
>
> 2 Carry out a small survey asking people:
>
>    (a) What their main source of news is, such as radio, television, newspapers, internet, social media and so on.
>
>    (b) Which medium they think is the most believable or reliable source of news, giving the most truthful accounts, and why.
>
>    (c) Which medium they think is the most unbelievable source of news, least likely to give a truthful account of events, and why.
>
>    (d) Draw up conclusions about which source of news people generally seem to use the most and which they find the most reliable/truthful, and summarize their reasons for this. Compare your results with others in your group, and try to reach an overall conclusion about what people find to be the most believable/reliable news source, and why people seem to find some news sources more reliable than others.

    ○ *Eastern Eye* (www.easterneye.biz) – Britain's best-known and most respected Asian weekly newspaper with national coverage

    ○ *Polish Express* (www.polishexpress.co.uk) – delivers news, entertainment and advice for the Polish community living in the UK and is the largest Polish-language newspaper published outside of Poland, and the second-largest BAME newspaper in the UK.

● **New media:** BAME groups are more likely to have a broadband connection compared to the UK average, and they are more likely than the white population to use the internet for social networking and video calling, as well as accessing websites relating to their ethnic identity.

## Uses of the new media

The box below represents some of the uses of the new media. It is important to remember that, in most cases, the individual consumer is only one of millions, and those providing the service, albeit customized to individual use, are communicating with millions of people, with funding and profits provided, in most cases, by advertisers.

---

**USES OF THE NEW MEDIA (INCLUDING THE INTERNET)**

- Buying and selling products
- Education
- All kinds of research
- Finding information of all kinds, such as on health or religion
- Contacting support groups
- Finding and making friends, and building social networks, including online dating and chat rooms
- Entertainment
- Communicating with friends and family
- Banking, paying bills and other financial transactions
- Political campaigning (especially on social media)
- Downloading, uploading, filesharing and listening to music
- Sharing and viewing photos and videos
- Reading or watching the news, including online newspapers, and sports results
- Creating and uploading text and photo/video content
- Blogging
- Viewing pornography
- Playing games, like Candy Crush Saga on Facebook (which had 50 million monthly users in 2018)
- Accessing information about government, local council or health services
- Buying travel services, like train and flight tickets, and booking hotels
- Watching television, including catch-up TV through applications like the BBC iPlayer, watching films and video clips and listening to the radio

---

# THE SIGNIFICANCE OF THE NEW MEDIA IN CONTEMPORARY SOCIETY

There is little doubt that new media technology has had a massive impact on contemporary society. For example, around two-thirds of the world's population had a mobile phone in 2018, and for a variety of uses, like those discussed above, other than making phone calls; and over half of the world's 7.6 billion people were using the internet.

There are very wide debates about the new media and their significance in contemporary society. Some have an optimistic view, seeing the new media as playing a positive role in society, while others are more pessimistic. The following sections summarize these two sides of the discussion.

## Optimistic views of the new media

### Widening consumer choice

There are now hundreds of digital cable and satellite TV channels, websites and online newspapers and magazines for people to choose from. People can now make their own TV schedules, for example.

## More media-user participation

Interactive digital TV, online news sites, blogging, tweeting and **citizen journalism** (where the public, rather than professional journalists, collect and report news), video- and photo-sharing websites like YouTube and Instagram, and social-networking sites like Facebook (1.59 billion monthly active users) and WhatsApp (1 billion monthly users) are all giving consumers more opportunities to participate in using and producing media content.

## More access to information

Everyone now has access to huge amounts of information from all over the world. This potentially gives people more power in society, as they can now access information for themselves, and on practically any topic, rather than relying on others for it. An everyday example might be people being able to check symptoms of illness online, through websites such as NHS Choices (www.nhs.uk/pages/home.aspx) and Netdoctor (www.netdoctor.co.uk), and also to check any risks associated with prescribed medicines they have been given. This gives patients more power through information, rather than leaving them solely dependent on doctors. Other examples might be using Trip Advisor (www.tripadvisor.co.uk) to check out holiday and hotel locations, and to post your own reviews of places you've stayed at.

## More democracy

(See pages 456–9 if you're not sure what a democracy is.) Some suggest that new media technology can give more power to ordinary people. There is now a far wider range of news sources, and a vast ocean of information available to all. More people, not just large media corporations, have the opportunity to communicate with vast numbers of other people.

This can empower people, by enabling them to learn about, and providing information about, things they didn't know before. For example, ordinary

The internet gives individuals more access to information than ever before, giving them more power and control over their lives rather than being dependent on others. Websites, like NHS Choices and Netdoctor shown here, enable individuals to check their symptoms online and receive health advice, without being obliged to visit GPs' surgeries

people can now publish their thoughts on Twitter (www.twitter.com), attack those in power on Blogger (www.blogger.com) or Wordpress (https://wordpress.com), and report on events excluded from other mainstream media by sending their own news stories and photos to citizen journalism sites like Demotico (www.demotico.com). Protest groups of all kinds have built websites to spread their messages across the world, including terrorist websites seeking to recruit and promote their views. Protesters can now reach, in ways never before possible, a worldwide audience very rapidly. Public outrage can bring websites to their knees, by overwhelming them with emails and hits, and targeting advertisers to get them to withdraw advertising from the sites.

This electronic technology of the new media can make it increasingly difficult for the mainstream-media newspapers and news channels to ignore stories they might have dropped in the past, and gives more power to the once powerless. For example, video shot on a mobile phone by a protester at a London demonstration in April 2009 provided evidence that it was police brutality that caused the death of a man there, which the police had tried to cover up before the video emerged. This forced the mainstream media to accept the protesters' version of events, rather than that of the police.

## Social life and social interaction are enhanced

The new media have opened up new channels for communication and interaction, enhancing or supplementing existing face-to-face interactions. People can stay in touch via email when they are away from home, or meet anonymously in chat rooms or social-networking sites, which may lead to face-to-face meetings. Social-networking and sharing sites can enhance

How might mobile phone technology be used to give more power to ordinary people, and expose wrongdoing by the already powerful?

social networks, re-establish lost contacts between old friends, create online communities and bring people together. It is also possible for alternative identities to be constructed in cyberspace or virtual worlds, and the media may become part of the means by which people express themselves.

## Pessimistic views of the new media

### Problems of the validity of information – the problem of fake news

It is often difficult to know the source and truth (validity) of messages in the new media – who they come from, who is sending them and whether or not they are true or false. It is therefore often hard to validate information, and to know what to believe. There may be no journalists, TV crews or independent witnesses on the ground to verify whether stories, videos and photos are true, doctored, fake or exaggerated. Similarly, much so-called 'factual' public information on the internet, such as health information, is often little more than disguised advertising for health-related products. Such material is often shared and recycled without anyone checking the information or sources. New technology, for example, allows sound and video to create realistic-looking news footage of public figures appearing to say whatever you want them to say. It is now more necessary than ever to question everything we read, see and hear to avoid the trap of believing fake news.

> You can find out more about fake news, its creation and how to spot it at https://goo.gl/BWAUnA

### A threat to democracy

While there is evidence that the new media can give more power to ordinary people, the new media are not public property open to all. Transnational corporations like Microsoft, Apple, Google, Yahoo!, Vodaphone and News Corporation control the internet technology, the satellite channels and mobile networks. This poses a threat to democracy and enhances the power of the already powerful, as more and more of what we know is dominated and controlled by global corporations. Google holds massive amounts of information about people's web browsing, monitors billions of webpages, and in a sense is watching everything we do on the internet. If anyone can be said to control the internet, it is Google.

New technology is providing governments with tools for increased social control over their citizens, through surveillance of emails, tweets and Facebook posts, and monitoring of websites, intercepts of mobile calls, tracking mobiles, etc. Google, for example, withdrew from China in 2010 because the Chinese government was hacking into Google to track human rights activists. Facebook has been blocked from time to time in several countries. Wealthy and powerful people, corporations and governments can still control the new media, and the same media that can give power to ordinary people can simultaneously give more power to the already powerful.

## The lack of regulation

The global nature of the new media, such as the internet and satellite broadcasting, means there is a lack of regulation or control, by national bodies like Ofcom (see later). This means undesirable things like bias, fake news, internet crime, terrorism, human trafficking, paedophilia, pornography, drug smuggling, violence and racism can thrive virtually unchecked. Other undesirable effects include internet trolling and cyberbullying, in which individuals are bullied online and from which it is difficult for victims to escape, unlike other forms of bullying. Twitter, particularly, has come in for a lot of criticism as individuals and their families have faced malicious and savage abuse, and rape and death threats from those disagreeing with their views.

## There is no real increase in consumer choice

There is poorer-quality media content, with dumbing-down to attract large audiences, much of the same content on different TV channels, and endless repeats. Celebrity culture replaces serious programming, and national newspaper websites chase after large audiences by replacing serious news reporting with 'infotainment' (information wrapped up as entertainment).

## The undermining of human relationships and communities

A 2017 study suggested that heavy use of media such as Facebook, Twitter, Snapchat and Instagram is associated with feelings of social isolation. People lose the ability to communicate in the real world as they spend less quality time with family and friends, and more time wrapped up in solitary electronic media. There will consequently be a loss of **social capital** or the useful social networks which people have, as they spend less time engaging with the communities and neighbourhoods in which they live.

> **Social capital**
> The social networks of influence and support that people have.

## The digital divide

Not everyone has access to the new media, and there is inequality, or a **digital divide**, between those who can and those who can't afford access to the digital and information technology underpinning the new media, such as pay-to-view satellite channels, computers, smartphones and broadband internet access. This creates national and global inequalities, and a new digital underclass, who are excluded from the alleged benefits of the new media. For example, in 2018, 10 per cent of UK households did not have an internet connection at home, and 10 per cent of adults said they did not

> **Digital divide**
> The gap between those people with effective access to the digital and information technology making up the new media and those who lack such access.

Will new media technology lead to an increase in social isolation? What do you think?

intend to get internet access in the next twelve months. The new media, and particularly the internet, are used most heavily, and by the largest proportion of people, in the Western world. Europe and North America make up around 24 per cent of the world's internet users, even though these areas comprise just 15 per cent of the world's population. This contrasts with 11 per cent of the world's internet users in Africa, which makes up about 17 per cent of the world's population. Around 43 per cent of the world's population are not internet users. Many of those living in the world's poorest countries do not have internet access due to the lack of resources to build the digital networks required, and private businesses won't provide them as there aren't sufficient numbers of customers willing or able to pay enough for them to make a profit. Language and cultural barriers can also be a problem, as about 55 per cent of websites are in English, and most web content is generated in the USA and Western Europe. The internet and other new media are now such a part of the social fabric that many of those who lack access to information and communication technology, and the skills and confidence to use them, face social exclusion. Figure 7.1 illustrates this digital divide.

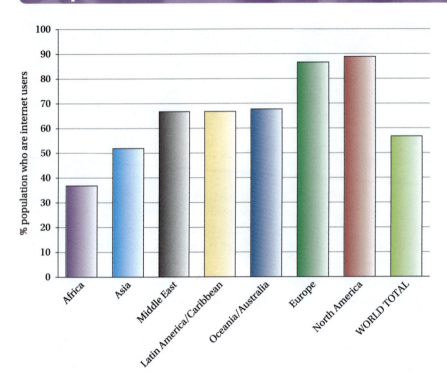

**Figure 7.1** The digital divide: percentage of population using the internet, March 2019

*Source*: www.internetworldstats.com

## Activity

1  Describe and explain how use of the internet, including social media, is changing the way people interact with each other.
2  Explain what is meant by 'the new media is more interactive'.
3  Examine the arguments and evidence in the previous section and, drawing on your own experiences, try to reach a conclusion about whether the new media are, overall, having a good or bad effect on society. If you are in a group, you might divide yourselves up into two groups for and against, and debate the issue.
4  Refer to figure 7.1 and answer the following questions:
   (a) What percentage of the population in which area of the world had the highest level of internet users in 2019?
   (b) In what region did approximately 52 per cent of the population use the internet?
   (c) Approximately what percentage of the world population were internet users in 2019?
   (d) Describe two ways that not having access to the internet, via a computer, tablet and/or a smartphone, might disadvantage households in contemporary Britain.
5  Write a short essay (about 15 minutes) answering the following question: 'How far is it true to say that there is a digital divide in the new media?'.

# THE ROLE OF ADVERTISING IN THE MEDIA

The media, both traditional and new, are predominantly run by large business corporations with the aim of making money, and the source of much of this profit is advertising. Advertising helps to offset media production costs, and allows all kinds of media to be sold cheaply, or provided free – that is why, for example, there are free newspapers, free news websites, and why you don't have to pay to use Facebook, Instagram and Twitter. It is this dependence on advertising which explains why so much concern is expressed about ratings for television programmes, the circulation figures of newspapers and the social class of their readers, the number of 'hits' a website gets, or the number of users of social-media apps. Advertisers will usually advertise only if they know that there is a large audience for their advertisements, or, if the audience is small, that it is well-off and likely to buy their products or services.

The importance of advertising income means that, increasingly, websites have to appeal to mass audiences if advertisers are to be persuaded to advertise. Spam (unasked-for electronic bulk messages via texting or email) is becoming a cheap means for advertisers to reach masses of people. Over 60 per cent of all media advertising in the UK in 2018 was digital (internet-based) advertising. This is causing growing financial difficulties for traditional media companies. Many national and local newspapers and TV stations now have their own websites, reaching millions more people and making more money from advertisers than their own printed papers or TV channels do.

## Advertising and media content

The importance of advertising affects the content of the media in the following ways:

- *Audiences or readers must be attracted.* If they are not, then circulation or viewing figures will fall, advertisers will not advertise, and the particular channel, website or newspaper may go out of business. This means that what becomes 'news' is partly a result of commercial pressures to attract audiences by selecting and presenting the more colourful and interesting events in society. It also gives private businesses some control over media content, as they will not advertise in media with which they strongly disagree.
- *In order to attract the widest possible audience or readership, it becomes important to appeal to everyone and offend no one.* This leads to a conservatism in the media, which tries to avoid too much criticism of the

way society is organized in case it offends the readers or advertisers. This may mean that minority or unpopular points of view go unrepresented in the mainstream media.

- *It may lead to a distortion of the news* by concentrating on sensational stories, conflict, celebrity gossip and scandal, which are more likely to attract a mass audience than more serious issues are. Alternatively, for those media which aim at a 'select' audience from the upper and upper-middle classes, it is important that the news stories chosen should generally be treated in a conservative way, so as not to offend an audience which has little to gain (and everything to lose) by changes in the existing arrangements in society.

- *Advertising becomes embedded in content without audiences realizing it.* Watching TV sport often involves constant exposure to advertising, such as adverts around the football pitch and on players' shirts, or alongside the track in motor racing. In many Hollywood films, advertisers will pay for product placement – where their products are actually used and shown in the films, such as Audi in the *Iron Man* trilogy, Heineken and Aston Martin in the James Bond films, and Pepsi in *World War Z*.

- *Media content becomes infiltrated by advertisers,* as advertising follows new-media consumers by cookie tracking of searches. For example, you might be viewing news or celebrity stories, but adverts pop up relating to consumer products you were searching earlier, or sites you had earlier logged onto. Google searches over time build up a profile of a person's identity, and this can then result in advertisements appearing that appeal to that person's identity, even when they're viewing totally unrelated content. This is why an increasing number of new-media users are turning to ad-blocking software, which hides or stops the loading of irritating and intrusive advertisements which interrupts the enjoyment of their web browsing.

---

### Activity

The popular media often seem obsessed with the activities and lives of royalty, celebrities, and health issues such as obesity, anorexia, size-zero fashion models and offering health advice of doubtful quality.

1  Study two of the red-top newspapers or popular magazines, either in print or online. Make a list of the types of stories and pictures they include.
2  As a sociologist and probable consumer of such material, suggest reasons why these media cover these issues, and why people buy or view these media in such large numbers.

# OWNERSHIP AND CONTROL OF THE MEDIA

## Ownership of the media

The media are very big business. The ownership of the main media in modern Britain is concentrated in the hands of a few large companies, which are interested in making profits. The details of who owns what are continually changing, as take-overs and mergers regularly occur, but in 2018 in the UK, for example:

- Three companies (News UK, Daily Mail and General Trust, and Reach (formerly Trinity Mirror)) dominated around 90 per cent of the national daily and Sunday newspaper market. One individual, Rupert Murdoch of News UK, owned the *Sun, Sunday Sun, The Times* and the *Sunday Times* – newspapers which made up about 39 per cent of all national daily and Sunday newspaper sales in Britain in 2018.
- Six companies owned around 80 per cent of local newspaper titles.
- Sky, effectively controlled by Rupert Murdoch's 21st Century Fox empire, is by far the UK's biggest private broadcaster and dominates pay TV.
- Channel 5 was owned by the US giant, Viacom International.
- Two companies controlled around half of all local radio stations, and most radio news is provided either by the BBC or by Sky.
- Two companies – Openreach (a subsidiary of BT) and Virgin Media – owned the cable networks for delivering phone, TV and internet, and in 2018 just four companies (BT, Sky Broadband, Virgin Media and TalkTalk) provided 96 per cent of internet services, as well as phone and TV. Four companies (EE/BT, O2, Vodaphone and Three) controlled 90 per cent of mobile networks.
- Google accounted for 85 per cent of UK internet web searches, and it also owned YouTube, and the Android operating system used on smartphones.

Rupert Murdoch of News Corporation was in 2018 one of the world's most powerful media owners, with substantial interests in TV satellite broadcasting, websites, films, and newspaper, magazine and book publishing across the world

- Facebook was by far the most popular social-media site, and it also owned the most popular apps, Instagram and WhatsApp.

As well as this concentration of ownership, the features of media ownership include:

- *Vertical integration* – there is concentration of ownership of all aspects of a single medium. For example, Rupert Murdoch owned (until March 2019) 21st Century Fox, which owns TV and film studios, and a large chunk of Sky, so he owned both the programme- and film-making facilities, and the means of transmitting them to consumers through Sky TV. Netflix is now not only streaming TV programmes and films made by others, but is increasingly creating its own original content, and will likely be acquiring its own film production facilities.
- *Horizontal integration and diversification* – media organizations now often have interests in a range of different types of media, such as films, TV, newspapers and magazines, book publishing, music and websites. Rupert Murdoch, for example, also owns HarperCollins, one of the world's largest English-language book publishers.
- *Global ownership* – media ownership is international, and the owners have global media empires stretching across the world. The world's largest media companies are now based in the United States, and US transnational media and communications corporations, such as Alphabet (which owns Google), the Walt Disney Company, Comcast, Facebook, Bertelsmann and Viacom dominate global communications.
- *Conglomeration* – media companies are often part of huge global conglomerates. These are large companies or corporations that own a series of different businesses around the world that have a wide range of interests in products besides the media. The Walt Disney Company, for example, owns retail stores and theme parks, as well as its extensive media interests.
- **Synergy** – this means a media product is produced in different forms which are promoted together to consumers, by one or several companies, to enable greater sales than would be possible through the sale of a single form of that product. For example, 'Harry Potter' was originally a series of books, and 'Star Wars' a series of films, but the 'brands' were licensed to several companies which produced a vast range of related media and consumer merchandise, such as spin-off films, books, DVDs, clothing, bags, toys, computer games, visitor attractions, etc. (see, for example, https://goo.gl/UxDB8q and https://goo.gl/2C8vGg). This synergy turned Harry Potter and Star Wars into household names and money-spinning global phenomena, which would have been much less likely to have happened if Harry Potter and Star Wars had only existed in their original single book and film forms.

**Synergy** Where a media product is produced in different forms which are promoted together to enable greater sales than would be possible through the sale of a single form of that product or by the efforts of one company.

This concentration of ownership in the hands of a few companies gives a lot of power to business people who are neither elected nor accountable to the public.

This poses a threat to democracy and enhances the power of the already powerful, as more and more of what we know is dominated and controlled by global corporations.

> **Activity**
>
> Explain why the concentration of ownership of the media might be of some concern in a democracy (refer to pages 456–9 if you're not really sure what a democracy is).

## Control of the media and media content

There is a debate over the extent to which the concentration of private ownership of the media means that the owners actually control the content of the media. There are three main views on this.

### The Marxist approach

Marxists suggest the content of the media reflects the wishes of the media owners. The views of the most powerful and influential members of society are given greater weight than those of less powerful groups. It is the rich, powerful and influential who are more likely to be interviewed on TV, to appear on chat shows, to be quoted in newspapers, and so on. Not all groups in society have equal influence on editors and journalists to get their views across, and only very rich groups will have the resources required to launch major media companies or websites to get their views across independently.

Marxists argue that:

- Media owners are part of a wealthy ruling elite. They directly influence and manipulate media content to protect their interests and spread the dominant ideology – the beliefs and values which justify and defend the interests of the dominant social class.
- The media promote incomplete and distorted news stories which the ruling class would like audiences to believe, and which influence the way people think and act.
- Editors, managers and journalists may have some professional independence from owners, but still generally choose to support the dominant ideology. This is because they are predominantly white, middle-class and male, and thus act in keeping with the dominant ideology, from which they benefit.
- Journalists' careers are dependent on gaining approval of their stories from editors. Owners appoint editors, and dismiss those who step too

far out of line, so editors are unlikely to challenge the ideas of their owners.

- The media present the values and beliefs of the dominant ideology as reasonable and normal, and form a consensus – widespread agreement – around them. This means the ideas of the dominant class in society become part of everyday common sense. Ideas, groups and behaviour outside this established consensus and everyday common sense created by the media – especially those which threaten the status quo (the existing arrangements in society) – are seen as unreasonable nonsense, and attacked, ridiculed or ignored.
- Media audiences – the public – are fed on a dumbed-down mass diet of undemanding, trivial and uncritical content, such as stories about royalty and celebrities, and exaggerated or made-up stories about crime, welfare 'scroungers' and such like, which stops people focusing on and challenging serious issues and problems in society.
- Much media news is little more than a **propaganda** system for the elite interests which shape and control it.

> **Propaganda**
> One-sided, misleading or untrue information used to promote a particular cause or point of view.

## *The pluralist approach*

**Pluralism** is a view that suggests that power in society is spread among a wide variety of groups and individuals, with no single one – such as a dominant class – having a monopoly on power and influence. Pluralists disagree with the Marxist view that media content is simply that which is decided by owners and defends their interests. They argue it is consumers who influence media content through their market power – audiences will simply not watch TV programmes, view webpages or buy newspapers and magazines and so on which do not reflect their views. If media companies do not satisfy their audiences, they'll go out of business.

> **Pluralism** A view that sees power in society spread among a wide variety of groups and individuals, with no single one having a monopoly on power and influence.

Pluralists argue:

- The media's owners are primarily concerned with making profits. Media managers and journalists need to attract large audiences and to gain advertisers if they are to produce profits for the owners. The only means of doing this is to provide what the audiences – not the owners – want. Media competition and the need to attract audiences means that sometimes journalists do occasionally develop critical, anti-establishment views, expose injustice, or corruption in government and business, and therefore are not always or simply in the pockets of the powerful.
- The internet, cable, satellite and digital television, and the global reach of modern media technology, offer such a huge range and choice of media products and access to knowledge from across the world that no single group or class can impose its views on others. The media now cover all kinds of interests and all points of view.

- Ordinary people now have the opportunity to create their own media products, which enables them to present alternative views to those of the media establishment and its owners. People can set up their own websites and blogs, online magazines or newspapers, and use apps like Facebook, Facebook Messenger, WhatsApp, Instagram and Twitter to get their views across and distribute them to millions of people around the world. There is therefore no link between ownership of the media and media content.
- The state regulates media ownership, so no one person or company has too much influence.

Marxists criticize the pluralist view as they argue that people have been socialized by the media into the belief that they are being provided with what they want. The media may have actually already created their tastes, so that what audiences want is really what the media owners want.

## *The postmodernist approach*

> ### POSTMODERNISM – A NOTE TO STUDENTS
> Postmodernism is mainly considered in this book in relation to this media chapter. It is not normally required for GCSE and similar-level introductory courses, but if you are doing the Cambridge IGCSE you will need some awareness of it. More general introductory courses to sociology may wish you to have at least some familiarity with postmodernist ideas. Having said this, if you do mention postmodernism (correctly) in GCSE answers, the examiners are likely to be extremely impressed.

Postmodernism (see page 49 in chapter 2) stresses that society is changing rapidly, and there has been a loss of trust in the superiority of rational thought and science as a means of understanding and improving the world. We are now moving into a 'post truth society', based on feeling, emotion and instinct, and detached from hard reality. For example, whether media news is regarded as 'the truth' or 'fake news' is simply a matter of someone's own interpretation.

Postmodernists view the media in the following ways:

- The wide range of globalized media offers the world's population more choices in terms of their consumption patterns and lifestyles. The media open up access to a wide range of cultures, bringing people unlimited opportunities to form their identities unconstrained by the limited horizons of local norms and traditions. This wide choice means media owners have little opportunity to influence content, because – as the pluralists suggest – audiences will just go elsewhere.
- Society is media-saturated – media images and messages are everywhere and constantly bombard us. These dominate and distort the

way we see the world. This distorted view of the world is called **hyper-reality**, in which appearances are everything, with the media presenting **simulacra** – artificial make-believe images or reproductions/copies of real events which bear little or no relationship to the real world. For example, media images replace reality to such an extent that laser technology and video reportage have eliminated the blood, the suffering and the corpses from war. The media news presents a sanitized or cleaned-up version of war, with wars as media-constructed spectacles, which have such an air of unreality about them that it is hard to distinguish between image and reality, as they appear like Hollywood movies or computer games.

- People increasingly live through media-led virtual lives rather than their real ones – e.g. the new media provide opportunities to create 'virtual identities' which may bear no resemblance to what a person is really like, for instance fake profiles on Facebook.

- The media no longer reflect reality but actively create it – e.g. reality TV shows like *The Only Way is Essex*, *Made in Chelsea* and *Love Island*, and social-networking and video-sharing sites such as Facebook and YouTube, are blurring the distinction between 'reality' and 'hyper-reality', leaving audiences confused about what is real and what is media-created.

- Media-saturated society creates desires and pressures to consume, and many of us actually mould our identities – how we see and define ourselves and how we want others to see us – in terms of media imagery. It is not the quality of the clothes or mobile phones we buy that matters, but whether they conform to media-induced images, styles, brand names and trends. The media-promoted designer labels of popular culture become more important than the quality of the products; in films, it is not the story that matters so much as how good the special visual and sound effects are – not the script or the writing, more the icon and the big-name stars.

*Criticisms of postmodernist views of the media*   Postmodernist views have been criticized because they assume that, in a media-saturated society, people are passively submerged in media hyperreality; they do not allow for the fact that people have experiences of their own to draw on, and they can discuss, interpret, ignore or reject media imagery and messages. Marxists emphasize that the media choice alleged by postmodernists (as well as pluralists) is a myth, as transnational media conglomerates control the major media and forms of communication and influence. Many poor people cannot afford to adopt media-based identities as they don't have the money to buy the consumer goods – like trainers or the latest smartphone – necessary to support such identities.

---

**Hyperreality** A view of the world which is created and defined by the media, with the image of an event seen as more real than the actual event it is meant to be depicting.

**Simulacra** Media images or reproductions and copies which appear to reflect things in the real world but have no basis in reality.

## THE CONTENT OF THE MEDIA: MEDIA BIAS, PUBLIC OPINION AND SOCIAL CONTROL

The media play a key role in providing the ideas and images that people use to interpret and understand much of their everyday experience, and they colour, shape and even construct our view of the world, and people's ideas, attitudes and actions.

Most people use and believe the media, particularly television, as their main source of news. The media therefore have an important role in forming public opinion: most people will base their opinions and attitudes not on personal experience, but on evidence and knowledge provided by newspapers, television, the internet and other media.

The media obviously cannot report all events and issues happening in the world every day. Of all those happenings, those owning and working in the media make decisions about which events they decide are newsworthy and worth reporting, and how these reports are presented to media audiences. The news, like any other product for sale, is a manufactured item. The media don't simply report the facts, on which people can then form opinions. They select facts and put an interpretation on them, frequently stressing the more conservative values of society. The media can then be said to act as an agency of social control.

These points raise the general questions of what factors influence the content of the media, and of whether the media give false impressions of what is happening in society. Do the media show **bias** – do they present subjects in a one-sided way, which favours one point of view over other

**Bias** A subject being presented in a one-sided way, favouring one point of view over others, or deliberately ignoring, distorting or misrepresenting issues.

alternative views, and do they deliberately ignore, distort or misrepresent issues? What are the implications of this in a democracy?

The sections below discuss some of the factors that influence the content of the media, and may cause bias in them, and how the media consequently act as an agency of social control. Figure 7.2 on page 529 summarizes these factors.

## Agenda-setting and gatekeeping

**Agenda-setting** is the idea that, even if you don't believe the media tell us *what* to think, it does tell us what to think *about*. This is because the agenda, or list of subjects, for public discussion is laid down by the media.

Obviously, people can only discuss and form opinions about things they have been informed about, and it is the media which provide this information in most cases. This gives those who own, control and work in the media a great deal of power in society, for what they choose to include in or leave out of their newspapers, programmes and websites will influence the main topics of public discussion and public concern. This may mean that some subjects are never discussed by the public because they are not informed about them.

The media's deliberate and routine refusal to include reports on some issues is called **gatekeeping**.

Such issues are frequently those potentially most damaging to the values and interests of the dominant class in society. For example, strikes are widely reported (nearly always unfavourably), while industrial injuries and diseases, which lead to a much greater loss of working hours (and life), hardly ever get reported. This means that there is more public concern with tightening up trade union laws to stop strikes than there is with improving health and safety laws. Similarly, crime committed by BAME people, migrant workers and asylum-seekers gets widely covered in the media, but little attention is paid to attacks on these people by white racists. This tends to reinforce people's racial prejudices. A final example is the way welfare-benefit fraud by poor people is widely reported, but much less so tax evasion by the rich. This means there are calls for tightening up benefit claim procedures and cracking down on fraud, rather than strengthening agencies concerned with chasing tax evaders, who cost taxpayers in the UK at least three times more than benefit fraud.

## Norm-setting

**Norm-setting** means the process whereby the media emphasize and reinforce conformity to social norms, and seek to isolate those who do not

**Agenda-setting**
The process whereby the media select the list of subjects to report and bring to public attention.

**Gatekeeping** The media's refusal to cover some issues.

**Norm-setting**
The process whereby the media emphasize and reinforce conformity to social norms, and seek to isolate those who don't conform by making them the victims of unfavourable public opinion.

## Activity

1 Study the main newspaper, radio, television or internet and social media news stories for three days. Draw up a list of the top five trending headline stories, perhaps under headings such as 'quality newspapers', 'red tops', 'BBC TV news', 'ITN news', 'BBC news website', 'Sky News', 'Radio 1 news' and so on. This is easiest to do if a group of people divide up the work. The following websites may help in this:

www.bbc.co.uk/news
www.itv.com/news
www.theguardian.com/uk
www.thetimes.co.uk
www.thesun.co.uk
www.mirror.co.uk
www.sky.com/skynews

2 Compare your lists, and see whether there is any evidence of agreement on the 'agenda' of news items for that week. If there are differences between the lists (check particularly the newspapers), suggest explanations for them.

conform by making them the victims of unfavourable public opinion. This is achieved in two main ways:

- *Encouraging conformist behaviour*, such as not going on strike, obeying the law, being brave, helping people, and so on. Advertising, for example, often reinforces the gender role stereotypes of men and women.
- *Discouraging non-conformist behaviour*. The media often give extensive and sensational treatment to stories about murder and other crimes of violence, riots, welfare-benefit fraud, football hooliganism, animal rights and environmental protesters, and so on. Such stories, by either emphasizing the serious or undesirable consequences which follow for those who break social norms, or presenting them in negative ways, are giving lessons on how people are expected *not* to behave. For example, the early treatment of AIDS in the media nearly always suggested it was a disease that only gay men could catch. This was presented as a warning to those who strayed from the paths of monogamy and heterosexuality – both core values of British society.

Stan Cohen illustrates this idea of norm-setting very well in the following passage:

A large amount of space in newspapers, magazines and television and a large amount of time in daily conversation are devoted to reporting and discussing behaviour which sociologists call deviant: behaviour which somehow departs from what a group expects to be done or what it considers the desirable way of doing things. We read of murders and drug-taking, vicars eloping with members

The media often give very negative or hostile treatment to groups and issues of all kinds that they regard as holding values and beliefs that are outside the boundaries of sensible society, such as stories about animal rights activists

of their congregation and film stars announcing the birth of their illegitimate children, football trains being wrecked and children being stolen from their prams, drunken drivers being breathalysed and accountants fiddling the books. Sometimes the stories are tragic and arouse anger, disgust or horror; sometimes they are merely absurd. Whatever the emotions, the stories are always to be found, and, indeed, so much space in the mass media is given to deviance that some sociologists have argued that this interest functions to reassure society that the ==boundary lines between conformist and deviant==, good and bad, healthy and sick, are still valid ones. The value of the boundary line must continually be reasserted: we can only know what it is to be saintly by being told just what the shape of the devil is. The rogues, feckless fools and villains are presented to us as if they were playing parts in some gigantic morality play.

(From introduction to Stanley Cohen, ed., *Images of Deviance*, Penguin, 1982)

---

**Activity**

1 How is deviance defined in the passage above by Stanley Cohen?
2 What does the passage suggest is one of the functions of the media's interest in deviance? Give examples from the passage of: (a) two types of deviant behaviour which are not regarded as criminal in contemporary Britain; and (b) two types of deviant behaviour which are regarded as criminal in contemporary Britain.
3 Think of one example of deviance which is currently receiving a lot of attention in the media and is of major public concern. Explain how this might be reasserting the value of the 'boundary lines between conformist and deviant' behaviour (highlighted in the text).
4 Look at a range of newspapers and news websites and try to find examples of norm-setting headlines and stories. Explain in each case what types of behaviour are being encouraged or discouraged.

## The owners

As seen on pages 519–22, there are differing views among Marxists, pluralists and postmodernists about the extent to which the private owners of the media are able to impose their own views on their editors. However, even when the owners don't directly impose their own views, it is unlikely that those who work for them will produce stories which actively oppose their owners' prejudices and interests, if they want to keep their jobs. The political leanings of the owners and editors are overwhelmingly conservative.

## Making a profit

The media are predominantly run by large business corporations with the aim of making money, and the source of much of this profit is advertising. As seen earlier (see pages 515–16), advertising can have a direct effect on media content, as the media can't afford to offend audiences or advertisers if they want to stay in business.

## News values and newsworthiness

Journalists obviously play an important role in deciding the content of the media, as it is journalists who basically select what the news is and decide on its style of presentation. News doesn't just happen, but is made by journalists. Research has shown that journalists operate with values and assumptions about which events are 'newsworthy' – these assumptions are called **news values**. These guide journalists in deciding what to report and what to leave out, and how what they choose to report should be presented.

The following features are required for an issue or event to be considered newsworthy:

**News values** The values and assumptions held by journalists which guide them in choosing what to report and what to leave out, and how what they choose to report should be presented.

- *Clarity* – issues that are easily understood.
- *Unexpectedness* – events that are in some way out of the ordinary, such as disasters or terrorist attacks, are more likely to make it into the news.
- *Drama* – events that have some human drama or interest to them and that involve conflict, excitement and action.
- *Personalization* – events that can be personalized and linked to individuals in some way, such as scandals or other activities of celebrities and famous personalities.
- *Proximity* – events that are considered close to (have proximity to) and relevant to the media audience. Events in the home country are generally considered more important than those happening in the rest of the world, and national events are generally considered more important than local ones.

- *Meaningfulness* – stories which it is assumed will be of interest to the media audiences – giving the readers and viewers what they want. This is of great importance if the audience or readership is to continue to be attracted, and viewing figures kept up or papers sold.

The idea of news values means that journalists tend to play up those elements of a story that make it more newsworthy, and the stories that are most likely to be reported are those which include many newsworthy aspects. These features affecting the content of the media suggest that the media present, at best, only a partial, and therefore biased, view of the world.

## Selection

The processes of agenda-setting, gatekeeping and norm-setting mean some events are simply not reported and brought to public attention. Some of those that are reported may be singled out for particularly unfavourable treatment. In these ways, the media can decide what the important issues are, what news is, what the public should and should not be concerned about, and what should or should not be regarded as normal behaviour in society.

## The presentation of news

The way items are presented may be important in influencing how people are encouraged to view stories. For example, the physical position of a news story in a newspaper or webpage (front page / lead story, or small inside column or hyperlink), the order of importance given to stories in TV or internet news bulletins, the choice of headlines, and whether there is accompanying film or photographs will all influence the attention given to particular items. A story may be treated sensationally, and it may even be considered of such importance that it justifies a 'breaking news' newsflash. Where film is used, the pictures shown are always selected from the total footage shot, and may not accurately reflect the event or may have a hidden bias. For example,

**Figure 7.2** Sources of bias and social control in the media

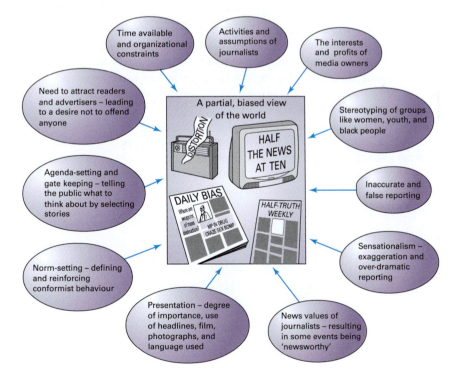

Time available and organizational constraints

Activities and assumptions of journalists

The interests and profits of media owners

Need to attract readers and advertisers – leading to a desire not to offend anyone

A partial, biased view of the world

Stereotyping of groups like women, youth, and black people

Agenda-setting and gate keeping – telling the public what to think about by selecting stories

DISTORTION

HALF THE NEWS AT TEN

DAILY BIAS

Where are weapons of mass destruction!

MP IN DRUG CRAZE SEX ROMP

HALF-TRUTH WEEKLY

Inaccurate and false reporting

Norm-setting – defining and reinforcing conformist behaviour

Presentation – degree of importance, use of headlines, film, photographs, and language used

News values of journalists – resulting in some events being 'newsworthy'

Sensationalism – exaggeration and over-dramatic reporting

in the reporting of industrial disputes, employers are often filmed in the peace and quiet of their offices, while workers are seen shouting on the picket lines or trying to be interviewed against a background of traffic noise. This gives the impression that employers are more calm and reasonable people and have a better case than the workers.

The media can also create false or biased impressions by the sort of language used in news reporting, such as the use of words like *handout*, *scrounger*, *fraudster*, *workshy*, *lazy* and *scum*, sometimes associated with those claiming welfare benefits.

## Activity

1. Refer to the three news stories below, or any major news stories which are currently receiving wide coverage in the media. List the features of these stories that you think make them newsworthy. To find more details on any story, try a Google search on the internet.

2. Take one contemporary big news story. Study one quality and one red-top newspaper, or their related website, of the same day and compare their coverage of this story. For example, do they sensationalize it and present new or different angles? What evidence is there, if any, that the news values of red tops differ from those of the quality press? Give examples to back up your answer.

3. Imagine you wanted to run a campaign to prevent a local school or hospital closing (or choose any topic of interest to you). In the light of your expert knowledge about news values, suggest ways you might get the attention of journalists, and activities you might undertake to achieve media coverage of your campaign. Explain why you think the activities you identify might be considered newsworthy.

**The terrorist attack** on the 'Twin Towers' of the World Trade Center in New York on 11 September 2001 was a massive international news story. Two passenger aircraft were hijacked, and deliberately crashed into the twin towers, causing both towers to collapse, and killing around 3,000 people. This dominated world news for weeks and months afterwards, and provoked a range of conspiracy theories on the internet.

The 'Twin Towers' of New York's World Trade Center before their destruction

**The Grenfell Tower fire** broke out on 14 June 2017 at the 24-storey Grenfell Tower block of public-housing flats in North Kensington in London. It caused at least seventy-two deaths and over seventy injuries. The fire started accidentally in a fridge-freezer, but spread rapidly due to the building's exterior cladding. The fire led to major concerns about the neglect and safety of public-housing blocks, and resulted in a public inquiry. The fire received huge national and international coverage in the media.

Royal weddings are always big news stories. **The wedding of Prince Harry and Meghan Markle** was held on 19 May 2018. A total of 18 million people were reported to have watched the wedding in the UK, and the global audience was estimated to be in the hundreds of millions, and it was front-page news in every newspaper.

### Activity

Study the language of newspaper reporting – the red-top tabloids are probably the easiest – and find some examples of language which might give a distorted or biased impression of particular individuals or groups, such as animal rights activists being described as 'nutters'.

## Inaccurate and false reporting and the creation of moral panics

Other influences on media content, and possible sources of bias, lie in inaccurate reporting, because important details of a story may be incorrect. Politicians are always complaining that they have been inaccurately quoted in the press. False reporting, through either completely making up stories or inventing a few details, and the media's tendency to dramatize and sensationalize events out of all proportion to their actual significance in society – typical of much reporting of the royal family and of crime – are devices used to make a story more interesting and attract audiences. This is particularly common in the mass-circulation red-top press and their related websites.

Such false, inaccurate or exaggerated and sensationalized reporting in the media can sometimes generate a moral panic. This is a wave of public concern about some exaggerated or imaginary threat to society. Moral panics are generated around activities or social groups that are defined as threatening to society or dominant social values. Media-generated moral panics often arise from many of the pressures discussed so far in this chapter, such as the ever-growing need in the competitive world of the media to attract audiences through sensationalized, interesting and exciting dumbed-down news stories and infotainment (information wrapped up to entertain), and thereby make money from advertisers. Such methods mean the media can be accused of socially constructing the news and manufacturing unwarranted anxiety in their audiences. There is a fuller discussion of moral panics and the role of the media in the social construction of crime and deviance on pages 299–303 in chapter 5, and you should refer to this now.

Moral panics show the media's power to define what is normal and what is deviant, unacceptable behaviour, and to reinforce a consensus around the core values of the dominant ideology, while at the same time making money through attracting audiences. Such methods mean the media can be accused of manipulating their audiences.

## Organizational constraints

People's habits in the way they keep up with the news have changed, with less use of newspapers (where sales are falling) and TV, and growing use of social media to access and spread news. People now expect to be able to access up-to-date news at all times and wherever they happen to be, through their mobile phones, tablets and laptops, or computers at home or work. These changes place growing organizational pressures on media organizations, which have little alternative but to respond to this changed situation. Digital media technologies and networks mean that news reporting is now almost instantaneous, with news reporting becoming rolling 'breaking news', with TV news programmes like the BBC News Channel, and websites like the BBC (www.bbc.co.uk/news), The Guardian (www.theguardian.com) or Daily Mail Online (www.dailymail.co.uk) delivering breaking analysis all day long, with constant updating of reports.

Competition means media organizations have to work within very tight time schedules to meet ever-shortening deadlines. This means that shortcuts to news gathering may need to be taken. There may be a greater emphasis on getting a news story first rather than getting it right, with inadequate evidence collected to justify any conclusions drawn. Stories aren't checked as carefully as they should be, to verify facts and to ensure it is real information rather than speculation or 'fake news'. For example, the media may rely on police or government press releases for stories, but this means reporters only report what they have been told, and they often haven't done the legwork to check stories for themselves. (See also 'churnalism' below.)

## The assumptions and activities of journalists

The views and assumptions of journalists can have an important influence on media content – after all, they are the ones who actually report and write stories.

Journalists tend to be mainly white, male and middle-class, and this influences whose opinions they seek for comment, what issues they see as important, and how they think issues should be presented and explained to audiences. Journalists are likely to give greater importance to the views of powerful people, as their views appear more 'reasonable' to reporters, and they tend to ignore or treat less favourably what they regard as extremist or radical views.

Journalists are busy, and they like to keep their work as simple as possible. This means they often obtain information from news agencies, government

News reporting is highly competitive, with companies around the world all competing to get the best coverage of the very latest up-to-the-minute events. How do you think this might cause bias in news reporting?

press releases, public relations consultants and so on. This means powerful and influential groups such as businesses, the government, political parties, and those with power and wealth are more likely to be able to influence journalists.

## The rise of churnalism

The term '**churnalism**' refers to the process of journalists *churning* out articles based on second-hand reports, rather than digging out the news for themselves. There is a growing trend in the media to churnalism, with media content wholly, mainly or partially constructed from recycled second-hand material, from social-media sources such as Twitter, or from pre-packaged material from press releases provided by news agencies, governments, advertisers and by the public relations industry. This is often reproduced without journalists doing further research or checking whether the 'facts' are true or false. Sometimes media content is little less than 'advertorials' – branded content paid for by advertisers and promoting their products but masquerading as journalists' news articles, e.g. 'Is this the end of overeating? New scientific breakthrough helps you lose weight without hunger or cravings.' The result of churnalism is a blurring of advertising, information, news and entertainment and a reduction of quality and accuracy, as what is presented as news is wide open to manipulation and distortion.

> **Churnalism**
> A form of journalism in which journalists produce media content based on pre-packaged material, such as press releases and social-media reports, without doing further research or checking facts.

The rise of churnalism is linked to many of the issues discussed so far in this topic: the desire of media owners to cut costs, and attract audiences and advertisers in a hugely competitive global media market, coupled with the time pressures on journalists arising from the intensity of 24/7 rolling news in the context of ever-expanding new media.

All these features discussed above, and the later sections on media stereo-typing (see pages 545–58), suggest that the media generally present, at best, only a partial and biased view of the world.

## CENSORSHIP, FREEDOM OF THE MEDIA AND DEMOCRACY

**Censorship** The restriction of freedom of speech through the control or suppression of media content by a government or other official body.

**Censorship** refers to a government or other official body controlling or suppressing media content, and thereby restricting freedom of speech. Some undemocratic, repressive regimes, like those in China, North Korea and Iran, monitor and control what appears in both traditional and new media. The internet, and particularly social-networking sites and email, face government censorship and surveillance using web filtering/blocking and surveillance technology which can monitor email and web traffic and block access to websites. For example, the majority of China's social networks employ content management teams to censor messages which might cause political problems with the government. In such societies, media content may be little more than one-sided, misleading or untrue propaganda used to promote or protect government interests.

Although the media in Britain are generally free to report whatever they like, and the state and government have no power in normal times to stop the spreading of any opinions through censorship, there are some formal limits to this freedom. The government and the state have a number of direct and indirect controls over the media, and operate a system of media regulation – control or guidance on how the media should operate. It should be remembered that the following media regulators operate mainly with British-based media and media-providers, and there are some forms of media, such as satellite broadcasts and the internet, that can be extremely difficult for the regulators in any single country to control.

### Activity

1. Describe two examples of media censorship.
2. Describe and explain two reasons why the internet, social media and other new media technology might have made it more difficult for governments to censor news and ideas.

## Media regulation: formal controls on the media

### The law

The law restricts the media's freedom to report just anything they choose in any way they like.

- *The laws of libel* forbid the publication of an untrue statement about a person which might cause him or her to suffer contempt, ridicule, dislike or hostility in society.
- *The Official Secrets Acts* make it a criminal offence to report without authorization any official government activity which the government defines as an 'official secret'.
- *Defence and Security Media Advisory Notices*, or 'DSMA-Notices', are issued by the government as requests to journalists not to report defence and counter-terrorist information which the government believes might be damaging to national security.
- *The Racial and Religious Hatred Act of 2006 and the Equality Act (2010)* forbid the expression of opinions which will encourage hatred or discrimination against people because of their ethnic group or religious beliefs.
- *The Obscene Publications Act* forbids the publication of anything that the High Court considers to be obscene and indecent, and likely to 'deprave and corrupt' anyone who sees, reads or hears it.
- *Contempt of Court* provisions forbid the reporting and expression of opinions about cases which are in the process of being dealt with in a court of law, or that are likely to prejudice a fair trial.

### Ofcom

Ofcom (Office of Communications) is the main regulator of broadcast and new media in the UK, with responsibilities across television, radio, telecommunications and wireless communications services.

This has responsibility for:

- ensuring that a wide range of television, radio, electronic media and communications services with broad appeal are available in the UK, with high-speed, high-quality services
- protecting the public from any offensive or potentially harmful effects of broadcast media, and to safeguard people from being unfairly treated in television and radio programmes, or having their privacy invaded
- ensuring, through its broadcasting code, that reporting is accurate and impartial
- monitoring the performance of Public Service Broadcasting (see box below).

## PUBLIC SERVICE BROADCASTING

Public Service Broadcasting (PSB) is an attempt by the state to regulate the quality and content of some of the media. PSB includes all the BBC and the main ITV channels: Channel 4 and Channel 5. The BBC and Channel 4 are publicly owned (by the state), while the others are private companies. PSB channels have a legal obligation – unlike other media channels – to provide TV content that:

- informs our understanding of the world – e.g. through providing news, information and analysis of current events and ideas
- stimulates knowledge and learning – e.g. providing coverage of arts, science and history
- reflects UK cultural identity – e.g. coverage of shared national events
- represents diversity and alternative viewpoints – e.g. coverage of different cultures and alternative viewpoints;

and to provide TV programmes that are:

- high quality
- well funded and well produced
- original and new UK content (not repeats or purchased elsewhere)
- innovative, with new ideas and approaches
- challenging – to make viewers think
- widely available – free to view.

## The BBC

The BBC is a largely state-funded body, established by Royal Charter, and is governed by the BBC Board, some of whose members are appointed by the Queen on advice from government ministers. The Board aims to represent the interests of licence-fee payers (TV viewers and radio listeners) and to ensure the BBC remains independent and impartial and resists pressure and influence from any source. The BBC is a Public Service Broadcaster (see box above), and is regulated by Ofcom. It is financed by the state through the television licence fee, plus income from a series of private spin-off companies, which top up the licence-fee income with substantial profits. The state can therefore have some control over the BBC by refusing to raise the licence fee. Although the BBC is not a private business run solely to make a profit like the independent commercial broadcasting services (see below), and is not dependent on advertising for its income, it still has to compete with commercial broadcasting by attracting audiences large enough to justify the licence fee.

## Independent broadcasting

Independent broadcasting includes all the non-BBC television and radio stations. These are regulated by Ofcom, which licenses the companies which can operate in the private sector, and is responsible for the amount, quality and standard of advertising and programmes on independent television and radio, and deals with any complaints.

### The Independent Press Standards Organisation (IPSO)

The Independent Press Standards Organisation (IPSO) is a voluntary regulator for the newspaper and magazine industry. It was established by the newspaper industry itself. IPSO seeks to monitor and maintain the standards of journalism set out in what is known as the Editors' Code, which deals with issues such as accuracy, invasion of privacy, intrusion into grief or shock, and harassment. IPSO considers and investigates complaints against the content of newspapers that breaches acceptable standards of newspaper journalism. As a voluntary body, it has no real power to enforce effective sanctions as a result of these complaints.

## The media, power and democracy

Much of this chapter so far has suggested that the media act as an agency of social control, are a conservative influence in society, giving only a biased view of the world, and are tightly controlled. However, some argue that the wealth of information provided by the media encourages and promotes a variety of opinions, and this enables the population to be informed on a wide range of issues, which is essential in a democratic society. These viewpoints are discussed above in the section 'More democracy' (pages 509–10) and 'A threat to democracy' (pages 511–12). The box below summarizes briefly some of the competing views on this aspect of the role of the media in modern Britain.

**THE MEDIA PROMOTE DEMOCRACY**

- Because the media in Britain are not controlled by the state, the risk of censorship by governments is reduced, and free speech is protected. Journalists are free to report and comment – within legal limits.

- The wide variety of privately owned media means a range of opinions are considered and public debates take place. By criticizing the actions of governments, the media can play an important watchdog role, and keep governments in touch with public opinion.

**THE MEDIA RESTRICT DEMOCRACY**

- The media (particularly newspapers) reflect the conservative views of their wealthy owners. While journalists are often critical and expose wrongdoing, they will frequently avoid issues which might cost them their jobs by upsetting newspaper owners or TV-station bosses.

- The variety of opinions presented is limited. The ideas and actions of the least powerful groups are the most likely to be excluded. Those who in some way present a challenge or threat to the status quo – the existing way society is organized – are presented as irresponsible or unreasonable extremists.

- The media give an unbiased account of news. TV news has to be impartial.

- News values, agenda-setting, norm-setting and other sources of bias mean only some issues are covered, and these are not presented in neutral ways. The media choose what to report and how to report it, and therefore provide a biased view of the world.

- The media accurately reflect public opinions that already exist in society rather than creating new ones. People wouldn't read newspapers or view TV and websites unless they were providing what their audiences wanted.

- The media do not simply reflect public opinion, but actively form and manipulate it. People can only form opinions on the basis of the knowledge they have, and the media are primarily responsible for providing this knowledge. The owners of the media hold overwhelmingly conservative views, and their ownership gives them the power to defend their position by forming favourable public opinion.

- Anyone can put his or her views across, by setting up a website, a blog, citizen journalism or a newspaper, distributing leaflets, putting up posters, and other means of communicating ideas.

- Only the rich have the resources necessary to publish and distribute a newspaper on a large scale, or to set up a television or radio station, and it is the wealthy who own and control the main means of electronic communication through social media. A small powerful group of media owners can control access to ideas, information and knowledge.

## Activity

That the media in Britain are owned by a small group of individuals and companies which control the spread of ideas and information, and who are not elected or answerable to the public, means people's opinions are manipulated by a small minority. Far from promoting democracy, the media in Britain are a major threat to it.

Identify and explain three arguments for this view, and three against, and then discuss this statement with others if you are in a group. Make sure you consider the effects the internet and social media might have on the spread of alternative ideas and opinions.

# THE MEDIA AND SOCIALIZATION

## The significance of the media as an agency of socialization

As considered in chapter 1, there is a wide range of agencies involved in people's socialization, and the media are only one influence on the way people might think and behave. Nonetheless, the media are now major influences in socialization, not least because they play such a central part in many people's lives. For example, there are 28 million televisions in British homes, with the typical viewer watching broadcast television for about 25 hours a week in 2017 – around 3½ hours a day, with many more viewing media on smartphones and tablets. In 2019, around 4½ million national newspapers were sold every day, with nearly 29 million people viewing online news sites. This is on top of people viewing social media, billboards and advertising on a daily basis, and time spent online at work, or school and university.

The media have therefore become a key agency of secondary socialization and informal education, as they become ever more important sources of information, entertainment and leisure activity for large numbers of people. Our view of the world, our political and social attitudes, our view of others – such as political leaders – are more and more formed through our impressions gained from the media, rather than through personal experience. These impressions can influence how we think we should live our lives and how we should act, how we might vote in elections, and our own personal senses of identity.

Use of the new media is now a feature of everyday life, and they play an important role in secondary socialization

## The media, consumption and identity

The explosion of the new media in recent years has meant that, as postmodernists emphasize, society is becoming media-saturated, and the media are present in very many aspects of our lives and play a growing part in shaping the world we live in.

Postmodernists argue that what we see, hear or read in the media often has important influences on our identity – how we see ourselves, how others see us and how we want other people to see us. The media are used:

- by individuals to confirm or explore their identities, values and interests
- to help people make choices about their lifestyles, such as finding out and keeping up with the latest social attitudes, or trends in fashion, music, cooking or home decorating
- to create desires and pressures to buy things, and shape our ideas about the things we should buy – our consumer choices.

Many people often come to see and define their self-image, and the image they want to present to other people, in terms of media imagery, whether this be a gender identity, an ethnic identity, a national identity, a social-class identity, a hybrid identity (mixing different identities) or any other identity they might wish to adopt. For example, people may adopt media-induced images, styles, brand names and trends, with celebrities, fashion models, musicians, soap stars or other media figures as role models in their own lives; they may find out from the media about the latest lifestyle trends, such as in dress, music and clubbing, and incorporate them into their chosen identities.

## The media and political socialization

The media play an important role in political socialization. This is concerned with informing the public on important local, national and international political issues and government policies that affect them, and forming people's political beliefs and the political party for which they vote in elections.

The mainstream media generally present a very conservative view of society – supporting the establishment and the existing arrangements in society. This helps to create a long-term climate of opinion that encourages people to support the way things are currently organized, and favours the mainstream political parties at the expense of smaller parties which might want to make radical changes.

### *Print and online newspapers*

These each tend to put forward a particular political opinion, and therefore take a one-sided approach to news reporting. Through their choice of stories, pictures and headlines, they try to influence their readers to vote for one

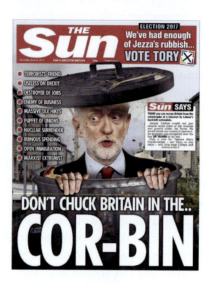

The influence of the media on voting is most likely to take place over the longer term, by endlessly praising parties and leaders it wishes to see win elections, and relentlessly attacking those it wishes to see lose, as shown in these two front pages from the Labour-supporting *Daily Mirror* and the Conservative-supporting *Sun*

political party (see, for example, the two newspaper front pages from the 2017 General Election in the UK). However, this does not mean that all voters are persuaded by the newspaper they read. Many people buy a newspaper for various reasons, such as sport or celebrity pictures or gossip, and may not be influenced by what they read about politics. Because newspapers tend to put forward a particular political opinion, many people see them as unreliable sources of evidence, and turn to the television instead.

## TV and radio

Media regulation means that TV and radio have, by law, to avoid political bias and be fair and balanced in their news reporting and analysis, and are expected to report the facts. This is especially true of the Public Service Broadcasters (see page 537). The exceptions to this are formal party political broadcasts, in which parties are given TV time to address voters.

There is little evidence to suggest that party political broadcasts or party leaders' live debates on television have much influence in changing people's voting habits, except in the case of **floating voters**. These are undecided voters who find it difficult to make up their minds which way to vote, and who therefore might regularly switch votes between parties from one election to the next. It is these voters who are most likely to be influenced by the media, and it is at these floating voters that many TV party election broadcasts are aimed.

**Floating voters**
Undecided voters who have no fixed political opinion or commitment to any political party.

## New media

People now have a much wider range of media to draw on, such as social media, citizen journalism and the global internet. This enables people to have almost unlimited access to information outside of the traditional media, which means they can be better informed than ever before, and gives political parties the opportunity to connect directly with voters and to get their opinions across.

Social media played a larger role than ever in the 2017 General Election in the UK, but YouGov research found that traditional news sources such as newspapers, and particularly television, still remained more influential among voters than social media for accessing political news and how they chose to vote. This included 18- to 24-year-olds, who are the biggest users of social media. For them, social media were the second-greatest influence on their voting, with TV still having the most influence.

## The influence of opinion polls

The media can also affect voting by their reporting of opinion polls (see page 90 in chapter 2). Opinion polls provide the basis for reports about the 'state of the parties', which are regularly published in both traditional and new media, often in the form shown in figure 7.3 below, and in election periods polls are conducted daily.

There is some evidence that opinion polls published in the media might not simply reflect voters' opinions, but actually help to form and change them, and therefore affect the eventual election results. For example, the polls may predict a voter's preferred party will lose, and therefore that voter switches to another party they think is more likely to win.

Because published opinion polls can affect the results of elections, some suggest they should be banned immediately before elections, and this has occurred in several European countries where polls are not allowed to be published in the media shortly before elections.

**Figure 7.3** Opinion polls on how people intend to vote are frequently published in the media. They are usually presented in a format like that shown here, showing the parties' share of the vote and how this has changed since the last poll. There is some evidence that polls published in the media may sometimes affect how people vote.

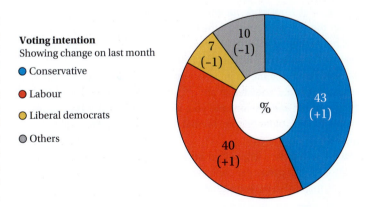

**Voting intention**
Showing change on last month

- Conservative
- Labour
- Liberal democrats
- Others

## THE MEDIA AND VOTING: KEY FINDINGS

- Where people already have established political views, the media are more likely to reinforce those views than to change them.
- People tend to be selective in their choice of viewing and reading, and they only see and hear what they want to. They will either select information which confirms their existing opinions and avoid anything that conflicts with them, or reject those aspects which do not conform with their existing ideas (see the audience selection model of media effects on pages 561–2).
- The media are unlikely to change people's voting behaviour in the short term (such as in the run-up to a general election), but they might be effective in changing attitudes over a longer period of time. For example, they might gradually change people's perception of a particular party or political leader, by constantly rubbishing, day in, day out, over a long period, those it wants to see lose, and similarly endlessly praising those it wants to see win (see the cultural effects model of media effects on pages 562–3) .
- The media are most likely to be influential on issues, parties and leaders that are new to people, and about which people have little knowledge or experience.
- Most of the media have, in the long run, supported the Conservative (or Tory) Party. This can create a long-term climate of opinion in which more people favour the Conservatives, and in which opposition parties stand at a disadvantage.

### Activity

1 Work out approximately how many hours in a typical week you spend engaging with media – e.g. watching television, videos or DVDs; playing computer games; using the internet and social media; listening to the radio or music; reading print or online newspapers and magazines; or at the cinema, and so on.
2 Work out approximately how many hours a week you spend sleeping.
3 There are 168 hours in a week. Take away the number of hours you spend sleeping from this total. Now work out what percentage of your waking life you spend under the direct influence of the media (you can do this by dividing the number of hours spent watching TV, browsing social media, etc., by the number of waking hours and multiplying by 100).
4 List all the ways you think the media influence you in your life – e.g. in relation to your lifestyle and identity, knowledge about current affairs, attitudes and opinions, tastes in music and fashion, and your views of different social groups, such as women and men, older people, minority ethnic groups, the disabled and the elderly.
5 Do you think the media have a large effect on your beliefs and values, your sense of identity and your consumer choices? What other influences on your beliefs and values might also be important?

# MEDIA REPRESENTATIONS AND STEREOTYPING

One of the issues that has interested sociologists has been the ways in which the media can contribute to the formation of impressions about social groups, such as those based on ethnicity, gender, age, social class and disability. The media do this through the reports and images they use to portray groups when they present them to media audiences. These portrayals are known as **media representations**.

Media representations very often conform to and create stereotypes. Stereotypes are generalized, oversimplified views of the features of a social group, allowing for few individual differences between members of the group. Stereotyping often distorts and exaggerates some characteristics of some individuals in a group, and assumes they apply to everyone in that group. These media representations and stereotypes, whether true or distorted, may influence the way people think about these groups, particularly when they have no personal experiences with which to form their own impressions.

As well as stereotypes, media representations are also linked to two further ideas: the **media gaze** and **symbolic annihilation**.

- *The media gaze* – the term 'gaze' was first used in a media context to describe the '**male gaze**' – the way media content produced by men looked at women as sexual objects. It can equally well be applied in a wider sense to describe a general media gaze. This refers to the way the media establishment views society and social groups. This 'gaze' of the media establishment means that media content does not reflect the social diversity that characterizes our society, but the point of view of the predominantly male, able-bodied white upper and middle class who own, control and work in the media.

- *Invisibility and symbolic annihilation* – this refers to the way some groups are excluded altogether from the media and become invisible, or are under-represented (not appearing as much as they should, given their proportion in the population), condemned or trivialized, or only appear in a limited number of stereotyped roles. This process is called 'symbolic annihilation' and gives a distorted impression of some social groups, or erases them from public consciousness altogether.

The following sections will review some examples of media representations and stereotypes. As you read them, you should remember that media representations and stereotypes do not necessarily mean that people will accept or believe these representations. The various theories of media effects discussed later on pages 559–64 suggest that media audiences do not

**Media representations** The way the media present groups to media audiences, which may influence how people think about these groups.

**Media gaze** The way the media view society and represent it in media content.

**Symbolic annihilation** The lack of visibility, under-representation and limited roles of certain groups in media representations, as they are, in many cases, omitted, condemned or trivialized.

**Male gaze** Where men look (gaze) at women as sexual objects.

necessarily react to or interpret the same media representations in the same way. For example, media representations of ethnic minorities or of disabled people may not have the same meaning to those who are from a minority ethnic group or who live in multicultural communities, or to those who are disabled or know disabled people, as to those who lack such experiences. People may therefore accept, ignore or reject media representations.

## Media representations of gender – gender stereotyping

Marxists and feminists argue that representations of gender are filtered through the media gaze of a predominantly male-dominated media establishment. This gives rise to media representations and stereotypes of women and girls which reflect the male gaze, whereby they are very often portrayed as sexual objects for men's satisfaction – e.g. models used in advertising. Feminists emphasize that media representations of women often spread a patriarchal ideology – a set of ideas that supports and justifies the power of men over women.

> There is an extensive discussion of media stereotyping of gender, and representations of men and women, and how and why they're changing, in chapter 1 (see pages 33–8). It is very important for you to refer to this section now.

### *Harmful consequences of media stereotyping of gender*

The media frequently expose people to images of 'perfection' in print and online newspapers and magazines, on TV, in films, on websites, in music videos and advertisements, which in most cases do not conform to the reality of their everyday lives. This may have harmful effects on their mental health, by inducing feelings of guilt, inadequacy and lack of self-confidence among the majority of women and men who don't measure up to the media stereotypes. This may partly explain why so many more women than men are concerned with slimming and dieting, and why anorexia and other eating disorders are illnesses affecting mainly teenage girls.

Many surveys have found teenage girls to be obsessed with body image and the desire to acquire a 'perfect' celebrity body, expressing unhappiness and seeking continual reassurance about their own physical appearance. Even girls under the age of 10 link happiness and self-esteem with being slim and pretty. These harmful consequences of media stereotyping are also beginning to affect men more, with evidence of them having mounting concerns over their appearance and sexual attractiveness, their body size and shape, their diet, health and dress sense. The growing use by men of cosmetics and cosmetic surgery – as well as the increase in eating disorders among men – all suggest that the factors that have traditionally affected women are now also beginning to have an effect on men.

## Media representations of age – age stereotyping

Representations of different age groups – children, young people / teenagers / youth, and older people – tend to be filtered through the media gaze of young to middle-aged male adults who dominate the media establishment. Overall, older people are under-represented in the media, and children and youth are over-represented.

### Representations of children

Children (roughly the pre-teens) are generally represented in a positive way: as innocent, in need of protection and sources of fun and pleasure. They often figure as consumers of toys and games in advertising, or as comedy sources in sitcoms.

Headliners (www.headliners.org), a journalism site run by young people, monitored national newspaper output for one week, and found seven stereotypes of children, in the following order of frequency.

1 *Kids as victims* – children portrayed as good children led astray by bad influences, or as victims of crimes committed against them by others.
2 *Cute kids* – providing the feel-good factor in advertising and other stories.
3 *Little devils* – stories of evil children and young hooligans, often in comedies and drama.
4 *Kids are brilliant* – exceptional children who excel in some way.
5 *Kids as accessories* – used to somehow enhance their parents' image, like those of celebrities.
6 *Kids these days!* – showing lost childhood and adults' nostalgia for their own childhoods, with young people now knowing so much more than their parents used to at their age, being corrupted by social media and other things that (allegedly) didn't happen when their parents were children.
7 *Little angels* – children who can do no wrong.

### Representations of teenagers/youth

The media often create a negative stereotype of young people (from roughly the teens to the early twenties) as a problem group in society – as troublemakers, druggies, layabouts, yobs and vandals. They are frequently depicted in the context of crime, gang, knife and gun culture, and antisocial behaviour. These representations are driven by media news values, as exaggerating the occasional deviant behaviour of a few young people out of proportion to

The media frequently present young people as a trouble-making problem group, rather than as the fairly conformist future adults most are, like the students shown here

its real significance in society can generate exciting stories and sensational headlines that help to boost media audiences.

The media provide for many people the only source of information about events, and therefore distort people's attitudes and give a misleading impression of young people as a whole. Older people, who tend to be more home-based, are particularly vulnerable to such stereotypes, as their impressions are likely to be formed strongly by the media.

*Folk devils and moral panics*   In his book on the Mods and Rockers of the 1960s, *Folk Devils and Moral Panics*, Stan Cohen suggested that media stereotypes of young people, particularly where unusual or exceptional behaviour is involved, provide exciting stories and sensational headlines, and help to attract media audiences. He argues that young people have been used as scapegoats – blamed for things that are not their fault – to create a sense of unity in society, by uniting the public against a common enemy.

Young people are relatively powerless, and an easily identifiable group to blame for all of society's ills. Some young people who get involved in relatively trivial deviant or delinquent actions or groups, such as antisocial behaviour or vandalism, face labelling in the media as folk devils, or groups posing an imaginary or exaggerated threat to society. This may cause a moral panic in society – an overreaction of public concern stirred up by overblown and sensationalized reporting in the media, suggesting that society itself is under threat. Editors, politicians, church people, police, magistrates and social workers then pull together to overcome this imagined threat to society.

The folk devils become visible reminders of what we should *not* be. In this view, young people play much the same role as witches in the past – an easy scapegoat to blame for all of society's problems. As a result of these moral panics, all young people may then get labelled and stereotyped as a potentially troublesome problem group.

It should be remembered, though, that it is these same young people who are the major users of the new media. This means that stereotyping in the media can be combated by young people themselves through texting, tweeting, YouTube and the other devices of citizen journalism. This means that mainstream media organizations may over time be forced to change their traditional media stereotypes of young people.

There is more discussion of media labelling, scapegoating, folk devils, moral panics and how the media can amplify deviance (deviancy amplification) – or make it worse – on pages 299–303 and you should refer to this section now.

**Activity**

Go to http://en.wikipedia.org/wiki/Mods_and_Rockers. Read what it says about the Mods and Rockers in the 1960s, and suggest reasons, with evidence, why they might have been seen as folk devils causing a moral panic in society. Is there any evidence they posed any real threat to society?

## Representations of older people

Older people – say, in their late fifties onwards – are often largely invisible or under-represented in the media, or presented in quite negative ways. Elderly people suffer from negative stereotyping in the media perhaps more than any other identifiable social group apart from youth. Old age is generally represented as an undesirable state. Typical stereotypes include being:

- poor
- in ill health
- a burden
- forgetful
- antisocial
- interfering
- incapable of work
- not interested in sex
- personally difficult, stubborn, moaning and grumpy.

There are sometimes different stereotypes for men and women. It is not uncommon to see older men presented in a positive light, for example as sexual partners of younger women in Hollywood movies, or as distinguished, experienced and informed 'wise old men', such as Dumbledore in the Harry Potter book and films, political and religious leaders, successful business-people, experts of various kinds, and as established and authoritative media journalists and commentators. By contrast, there are few positive images of older women, who are often rendered invisible – symbolically annihilated – because women are, in media imagery, expected to be forever young and youthful, and there are not many positive roles for them as they grow older.

Negative representations of older people are beginning to change, as most Western countries have an ageing population (see pages 151–5) – a growing proportion of older people compared to younger people – and around one in five people in the UK are now over the age of 65. The growing numbers of older people in the population with money to spend – the 'grey pound' – mean we might expect more positive images of ageing to emerge, and more positive roles for older women, as media companies pursue the growing older people's market, as shown in the Dove Pro·Age campaign marketing beauty products to older people.

### Activity

The Dove Pro-Age campaign shown above sought to market a range of beauty products avoiding traditional media stereotypes of gender and age. Study the four images, and suggest ways they may, or may not, challenge media stereotypes of gender and/or age.

## Media representations of ethnicity – ethnic stereotyping

There's a general under-representation of BAME groups in media ownership and management, in TV and film roles, and in advertising.

Representations and stereotypes of non-white BAME groups are often filtered through a White British media gaze – the 'white eye' – of a predominantly White British middle-class-dominated media establishment. BAME groups make up only about 13 per cent of the population of Britain, yet frequently this minority are presented in quite negative ways in the media, and as if they were major causes of conflict and social problems that otherwise wouldn't exist. Black and Asian people – particularly black people – and more recently white migrants from Eastern Europe (e.g. from Romania and Bulgaria) are often only represented in the media in a limited range of degrading, negative and unsympathetic stereotypes, in the context of trouble of various kinds, and as scapegoats on which to blame a range of social problems.

### *Media stereotypes of BAME groups*

1   *As deviants and law breakers* – e.g. drug dealers, terrorists, welfare cheats, 'muggers' (who commit street robbery with violence), and involved in gang, gun and knife criminal subcultures.
2   *As posing a threat* – possessing a culture that is seen as alien and a threat to British culture. BAME cultures are a kind of 'enemy within', with immigration seen as a threat to the British way of life and the jobs of White British workers. Media reports of rare events such as sexual grooming of young white women, forced marriages (in which one or both of the parties is forced into marriage against his or her will) and honour killings (the murder of a family member, usually of women, by other members, due to a belief that the victim has brought dishonour on the family), give a misleading impression of all BAME groups.

    Muslims and Muslim culture are frequently presented as a threat to British values (see Islamophobia, below), and recently migrants from Eastern European countries such as Romania and Bulgaria have suffered negative media stereotyping for the same reasons.
3   *As people causing social problems, conflict and trouble* – as in stories about terrorism, racial problems, ethnicity-related riots, disruption caused by underachieving black students in schools, immigration (whether legal or undocumented ['illegal']), welfare fraud, lone parents and so on. These are often presented in the context of people with individual inadequacies or 'badness', rather than people with social problems generated by things like poverty, racial discrimination, poor housing, and racist intimidation and attacks by white people.

Asylum-seekers are often represented as bogus, as really economic migrants seeking to work illegally, rather than as people escaping from persecution, including possible torture or death, in the countries from which they have fled.

4 *As having limited talents and skills* – they are often portrayed as low-paid workers, in jobs like cleaning, in nail bars or car washes, as educational failures, or as people who often do well in sport and music, but are rarely portrayed as academic or professional successes.

5 *As people who have problems internationally* – for example, who originate from countries with corrupt leaders; where people live in poverty,

---

**ISLAMOPHOBIA AND THE MEDIA**

Islamophobia (see page 451 in chapter 6) is an irrational fear and/or hatred of or aversion to Islam, Muslims or Islamic culture. Some sections of the mainstream media regularly focus on the activities of a tiny minority of Muslims in Britain, linking them to terrorism, suicide bombings, extremist preachers, forced marriages and the oppression of women. This has led to the stereotyping in the popular imagination of all Muslims, and a moral panic around Muslims as a threat to British social values and public safety. Such scaremongering by the media has increased Islamophobia in British society, and made anti-Muslim prejudice and hatred more widespread and more socially acceptable.

Such media representations and moral panics bring with them harassment and fear for many British Muslims, who have little sympathy with the tiny minority of Muslim extremists or terrorism of any kind, and whom surveys repeatedly show are moderates who accept the norms and values of British life and Western democracy.

famine and drought conditions (images of starving babies); where there are always tribal conflicts, civil wars, military coups and so on, and who need the white Western countries to provide aid and to help solve their problems for them.

Many media stories that focus on BAME groups are often either completely absurd, untrue or massively exaggerated. The media rarely report on the successes and achievements of BAME groups, their history and culture, or about the discrimination and deprivation they often face in employment, pay, poverty and housing (see pages 432–5), education (see pages 264–70) and criminal justice (see pages 340–4). Attacks on BAME groups by White British racists rarely receive media coverage.

## Changing stereotypes of BAME groups

There is a slowly growing acceptance in the media of BAME groups as a mainstream part of British society.

- There are more black and Asian figures appearing in music, arts, TV dramas and soaps, and as TV presenters.
- BAME groups have more access via new media, and satellite and cable TV, to programmes relevant to them. This puts pressure on mainstream media organizations to be more responsive to their needs in order to retain media audiences and advertising revenue.
- Young people from BAME groups are greater users of social media than the average in the UK, and this gives them more power to counter negative ethnic stereotypes and reports in mainstream media.

## Media representations of disability – stereotyping of the disabled

> There is a section on pages 448–50 in chapter 6 on disability, to which you might wish to refer to help you understand what sociologists mean by disability, and some of the inequalities faced by disabled people.

The media gaze which forms representations and stereotypes of disabled people is mainly filtered through the eyes of the predominantly able-bodied who control the media industry.

Disabled people are so seriously under-represented among those who work in the media industry and in the whole range of media content, and are so often portrayed in negative ways, that they effectively face symbolic annihilation.

Disabled people are rarely portrayed as a normal part of everyday life, as workers, parents, etc., who happen to have an impairment as well. In most cases, disabled people only appear where their disability is a central feature of their role – they appear because they are either disabled or playing a disabled character, rather than as other characters who also have an impairment.

Most of us learn about disability as part of the socialization process, and media stereotyping plays a major role in this process, and forms people's views about disability. The vast majority of representations and information about disability in books and films, on television and in print and online media is extremely negative, consisting of stereotypes which medicalize, patronize, criminalize and dehumanize disabled people. Disabled people are often represented as an abnormal group that is not part of, and unable to participate in, daily life in mainstream society, and as lacking commitment to mainstream norms. For example, the media frequently suggest that disabled people in receipt of welfare benefits are 'scroungers', 'cheats' and 'skivers', and disability, particularly mental health-related disability, is often linked with threats posed by madness, badness and violent 'psycho' stereotypes.

### Media stereotypes of disability

Barnes in *Disabling Imagery and the Media* suggests the media often show the following stereotypes of disabled people:

- *as pitiable or pathetic* – e.g. in TV charity appeals such as *Children in Need*
- *as sinister or evil* – e.g. Frankenstein, wicked witches in fairy tales, or exaggerated headline stories in the tabloid press about the dangers allegedly posed by people with mental illness
- *as super cripples*, assigned superhuman, almost magical, abilities – e.g. in media coverage of the Paralympics
- *as laughable or an object of ridicule* – e.g. the fool or 'village idiot'

How might enthusiastic coverage of Paralympic Games and the Invictus Games give an inaccurate representation of life with a disability? What might the positive and negative effects of such coverage be?

- *as a burden* – the view of disabled people as helpless and having to be cared for by others
- *as sexually abnormal* – as 'perverts', or non-sexual and lacking sexual feelings.

These negative media stereotypes do not provide accurate or fair reflections of the actual experience of disabled people, and reinforce negative attitudes towards them, and ignorance about the nature of disability. Disabled people, and those who have some personal experience of disability, may well ignore, resist, reject or reinterpret such general stereotypes. However, for the many who lack such experience to draw on, the media may have a role in forming distorted and negative impressions of all disabled people.

---

### Activity

This activity could be divided up if working in a group, with people taking different media.

1 Drawing on media you use, such as websites, internet advertising, video games, films, TV programmes, newspapers and magazines, and so on, list the types of disability/impairments you come across in a one-week period.

2 Identify the response you think each example is designed to evoke in the audience, such as horror, outrage, pity or fear.

3 Identify from your survey a range of examples to illustrate the stereotypes mentioned above.

4 Present your findings to the rest of the group, and discuss what conclusions might be drawn about the representation of disability in the contemporary media.

## Media representations of social class – stereotyping of social classes

The mainstream media gaze means representations of social class are filtered through the eyes of the rich and powerful upper-class media owners and the middle-class media professionals who produce media content. In general, this has three consequences:

1 *More favourable stereotypes of the upper and middle classes than the working class or the poor.* The media give the impression that the values and lifestyles of the middle class are the norm, to which everyone should aspire. The working class and the poor/underclass are presented as in some ways abnormal/deviant and/or as figures of fun.
2 *An over-representation of the upper and middle classes and an under-representation of the working class and the poor.* When the working class and the poor are represented, they are typically stereotyped in negative ways, with their failings seen as arising from their lack of conformity to middle-class values, norms and lifestyles.
3 *The portrayal of the working class in a more restricted range of roles* than the middle class.

Media news values mean the rich and famous are more newsworthy than similar stories about working-class people. There is little media content that explicitly discusses class privilege, class inequality and the differences in power and life chances with which Marxist and Weberian sociologists are concerned (see chapter 6, pages 401–10, 453 and 455 for more on this).

### WHAT IS THE CHAV STEREOTYPE?

The chav underclass stereotype has a huge range of 'failings': ignorance, immorality, vulgarity, bad taste (bling jewellery, fake designer gear), lack of education, drug abuse, alcoholism, crime, sexual promiscuity, lone parenthood, waste, obesity and a tendency for violence. Chavs are thugs who own dangerous dogs, irresponsible parents with out-of-control children, aggressive men and excessively fertile women, who are workshy, welfare dependents, committing benefit fraud, who subsist on junk food and live in filthy council houses on run-down estates, with unwashed dishes and clothes everywhere, and where dogs crap on threadbare and filthy carpets.

A still from the Channel 4 documentary *Benefits Street*, criticized for perpetuating a negative chav stereotype attached to those in deprived areas

## Representations of the working class

The working class and the poor are typically stereotyped in negative ways, such as the hostile 'chav' stereotype (see box) which merges the working class with the poor. The poorest sections of the working class are frequently stereotyped as benefit 'scroungers' or as criminals, and they only become newsworthy when they reinforce the popular impression that the poor are poor because of their own failings – the 'undeserving poor' – and this under-mines any public sympathy for their plight.

### Stereotypes of the working class include:

- *As dumb and stupid buffoons:* figures of fun who may be well intentioned, but are immature, irresponsible, inarticulate, incompetent, lacking in common sense, and who are coping only ineptly with life.
- *As a source of trouble and conflict:* particularly working-class youth, in the context of trouble, such as crime and antisocial behaviour, e.g. as undesirable welfare 'scroungers', as lone parents, and as inadequate parents who are unable to cope with their uncontrollable delinquent children and other difficulties.
- *As living in idealized/romanticized working-class communities:* the working class is presented most positively as living in traditional working-class communities, where people are seen as respectable and hard-working. Life rotates around pubs, shops and close and supportive networks of family and friends, where people struggle to overcome adversity in their lives. These are the stereotypes portrayed in TV programmes like *EastEnders, Coronation Street* and *Call the Midwife.* The values of those living in these communities are often praised, but they have little relation to reality, as such working-class communities have largely disappeared with the decline of traditional industries.
- *As an underclass of white trash and scum – 'chavs'* (see box)*:* this is the most negative, hostile and offensive stereotype of the working class, which first emerged in the late 1990s / early 2000s. It is now probably the most dominant one in the media, which seems to have replaced the media stereotype of the hard-working and respectable traditional working class. The confrontational ITV daytime chat show *The Jeremy Kyle Show* frequently featured for the entertainment of viewers 'chav-like' dysfunctional working-class people whose lives were in turmoil.

## Representations of the middle class

The middle class and its lifestyles receive the greatest exposure in the media – in drama, sitcoms, advertising, magazines and newspapers. Middle-class tastes and lifestyles are regarded positively, and are presented as the norm to which everyone should aspire. Middle-class people are generally presented in a positive light – as mature, sensible, educated and successful, and coping with problems, in sharp contrast to the portrayals of the working class. This reflects the media gaze of a middle-class-dominated media establishment. This helps to justify the existing class structure and class inequalities, by suggesting that people who are higher up the class structure are more competent and successful, and therefore more worthy of respect than those below them.

## Representations of the upper class

The upper class – rich and powerful aristocrats, businesspeople and celebrities – is generally portrayed very positively, as 'well bred', cultured and superior. The lavish lifestyles of the upper class are celebrated, particularly in the form of luxury homes, cars, exotic holiday locations and expensive fashion accessories. These often provide media content for mass audiences, in TV, the mass-circulation and online tabloid press, and magazines, especially in celebrity magazines such as *OK!* (www.ok.co.uk) and *Hello!* (www.hellomagazine.com), and their related websites.

The upper class is often portrayed in a romanticized, nostalgic way in the context of costume/period dramas like *Downton Abbey*, which suggest that somehow life was once better, even for the poor who worked for the upper class.

Marxists see media representations of the upper class as a celebration of hierarchy and wealth, which encourage admiration and envy by other social classes, and acceptance of the existing social hierarchy as natural, normal and desirable. Pluralists, on the other hand, see such content as simply providing what media audiences want.

### Activity

1 Based on your own media use, try to identify a contemporary example of each of the stereotypes of the different social classes described above. If you're in a group, collect your answers and explain how each of the examples demonstrates a stereotype. Discuss whether the various examples you've found provide an accurate or fair view of the social classes concerned.
2 Choose one media social-class stereotype, and give two reasons why the stereotype you have selected might be regarded as newsworthy and worth covering by most of the media.
3 Describe two ways in each case that the media might provide for individuals
   (a) a source of identity
   (b) role models for their own behaviour.
4 Outline any two contemporary media representations with which you are familiar, and explain in each case why they might be harmful to the groups concerned – e.g. Muslims linked to terrorism and brutal punishments; disabled people defined only by their disability.

**THE MEDIA, CRIME AND DEVIANCE**
The media provide knowledge about crime and deviance for most people in society, but media reports tend to be very selective. Reports often dramatize, exaggerate and sensationalize crime and deviance, thereby giving a false and misleading impression of their real pattern and extent in society. **There is extensive coverage of the media and crime and deviance on pages 299–303 in chapter 5, and you should refer to these pages to find out more about this topic.**

## THE INFLUENCE OF THE MEDIA – THE EFFECTS OF THE MEDIA ON AUDIENCES

Much of this chapter suggests that the content of the media may have some effect on the audience. However, this cannot be taken for granted. People are conscious, thinking human beings, not mindless robots. They might not swallow everything they come across in the media, and they might respond in a variety of ways to what they read, hear or see. For example, they might dismiss, reject, ignore, criticize, forget or give a different meaning to a media message, and this is likely to be influenced by factors such as their own social experiences, their ethnic origin, social class, gender and so on. For example, a black person is likely to reject a racist message in a TV broadcast or newspaper report. It therefore becomes very difficult to generalize about the effects of the media.

We also need to be aware that the media is only one influence on the way people might think and behave, and there is a wide range of other agencies involved in people's socialization. People can form their own judgements on media content, and it would be somewhat foolhardy to suggest all behaviour can be explained by exposure to the media. Families, friends, schools, workplaces and workmates, churches and religious groups may all influence individual and group behaviour and attitudes.

There are a number of different approaches that sociologists have adopted to the question of whether media content does actually have an influence or effect on audiences, mainly centred around the issue of whether audiences are:

- **passive** – mindless dopes who passively consume, accept, believe and react to media content
- **active** – people who actively and critically interpret media content, giving it their own meanings and interpretations rather than just passively accepting everything the media tells them.

Four of these different approaches or models are summarized below.

## 1 The hypodermic syringe model: a passive audience approach

This approach, sometimes called the 'magic bullet' theory, suggests the media act like a hypodermic syringe (or a bullet), injecting powerful and influential content (norms, values, lifestyles, opinions, news, etc.) into the 'veins' of media audiences, with immediate effects – for example, seeing violence on television, and then going out and attacking someone. Media audiences are seen as entirely passive – unthinking, gullible and easily manipulated robots, who are unable to resist the 'drug' injected by the media.

Three main criticisms of this model are:

- It is outdated, oversimplified and overexaggerates the power and influence of the media on audiences. It assumes people are completely passive – like blank sheets of paper waiting to be written on. There are many influences on people's behaviour apart from the media.

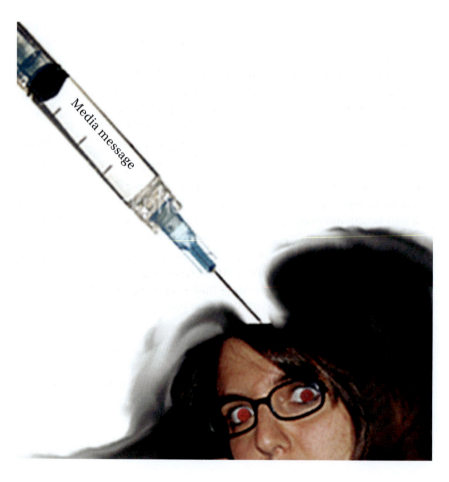

Media message

The hypodermic syringe model suggests that the media inject messages into the 'veins' of media audiences, with an immediate effect on their behaviour

- Audiences don't all react the same way – this will depend on their socialization, their own ideas and how they interpret what they see or hear.
- There is little research evidence to support this view of media effects, but there is much research suggesting the media doesn't have such an effect.

## 2 The audience selection model – selective filtering or decoding: an active audience approach

This model suggests that those who produce media content intend it to contain – or encode it with – a particular message that audiences are encouraged to believe. For example, it might be encoded with messages that all women should be slim and attractive, that many Muslims are terrorists or that people on welfare benefits are lazy and undeserving.

These media messages could be decoded or interpreted by audiences in one of three ways:

(a) *acceptance of the message as intended* – e.g. people on welfare benefits are lazy and undeserving.

(b) *acceptance of the message, but amended to fit the audiences' own beliefs and experiences* – e.g. some of those on welfare benefits might be lazy and undeserving, but it's not true of the people I know.

(c) *outright rejection of the media message* – e.g. it's not true that most people on benefits are lazy and undeserving, and most are the victims of unfortunate circumstances beyond their control.

The particular interpretation of the message adopted by audiences will be influenced by their own knowledge and life experiences, and the social groups to which they belong, such as their social class, gender, age, ethnicity and disability.

This suggests that people are not blank pieces of paper waiting to be written on by the media, but have choices and experiences of their own, and interpret – or decode – and filter what they read, see or hear in the media. They do this by **selective exposure**, **selective perception** and **selective retention**.

- *Selective exposure* means people may only watch or read media output that fits in with their existing views and interests.
- *Selective perception* means people will filter and interpret media output, so they only see or hear that which fits in with their own views and interests.
- *Selective retention* means people will ignore or forget media output that is not in line with their own views and interests.

**Selective exposure** Individuals exposing themselves only to media output that fits in with their existing views and interests.

**Selective perception** Individuals filtering and interpreting media output so they only see or hear that which fits in with their own views and interests.

**Selective retention** Individuals ignoring or forgetting media output that is not in line with their own views and interests.

This approach means that it is impossible to know what the effects of the media on audiences will be, as this will depend on the values, attitudes, beliefs and life experiences of those audiences. This means, using the examples given above, that obese women, Muslims and those receiving welfare benefits – or those who know and have experience and knowledge of such people – are likely to react quite differently to the same media message from those who have no such experience of their own to draw on. Similarly, feminists are likely to reject what they see as patriarchal media messages, and Marxists will reject what they see as media content protecting the interests of the dominant class. An example of the application of these filters might be the way people respond to party political election broadcasts, depending on which political party they personally support, as suggested in the cartoon below.

## Activity

Selective exposure, selective perception and selective retention

Explain how the cartoon above illustrates the idea that people filter what they view in the media.

## 3 The cultural effects model – the 'drip drip' effect: an active audience approach

This model is a Marxist view. This suggests that media content is heavily influenced by the interests of the dominant and most powerful groups in society. The media have an effect on audiences, but the model does not see media audiences as simply passive consumers of media.

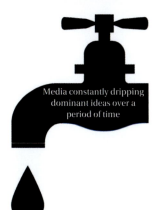

Media constantly dripping dominant ideas over a period of time

The cultural effects model agrees to some extent with the audience selection approach, and it accepts audiences will interpret the media they consume differently and will respond to it in different ways. The majority are likely to support and agree with the content and 'slant' of media messages, as they have no experiences of their own to judge media content by. Some may be critical of or even reject that content, depending on their social characteristics, such as their social class, gender or ethnicity, and their own life experiences.

The cultural effects model disagrees with the audience selection / selective filtering approach because it argues that the audience selection model exaggerates the extent to which audiences can give whatever interpretations they choose to media content. This is because, over a period of time, the media will sooner or later undermine people's capacity to overcome media bias. Through a slow, steady, drip-drip effect, media content acts like a subtle, ever-present process of brainwashing. This will eventually fill people's minds – just as a dripping tap will eventually fill a bath – with the dominant ideas in society, and shape people's everyday taken-for-granted common-sense ideas and their view of the world. For example, if we see minority ethnic groups nearly always portrayed in the context of trouble and crime, or Muslims nearly always linked to terrorism or women portrayed only as mothers, lovers and sex objects, over time this will come to form the stereotypes we hold of these groups, to the exclusion of other aspects of their lives. Through this process, media audiences eventually come to accept that the dominant ideas put out by the media are just common-sense, and the only sensible way of seeing the world.

There are two main difficulties with the cultural effects model:

1 It doesn't recognize that the media don't always spread the dominant ideas in society. Journalists and film- and programme-makers have some independence in their work, and can sometimes be very critical of the dominant ideas and existing arrangements in society. This can provide 'hooks' for audiences to themselves become more critical of media content.

2 It doesn't allow for the influence of social media and the huge sharing of ideas by citizen journalists (see pages 509–10) and others that are very critical of society. This means audiences have more access to alternative ideas to challenge those put out by mainstream media.

## 4 The uses and gratifications model: an active audience approach

This model suggests the effects of the media will depend on what the audiences use the media for, and their own various pleasures and interests (*gratifications*). The question then becomes not what the media do to people, but what people do with the media.

People use the media in different ways, such as for pleasure, information, relaxation, company, keeping up with trends, and as background 'wallpaper' while doing other things. This approach makes it difficult to generalize about the effects of the media, as these are likely to vary depending on what people use the media for.

## Activity

1  Explain how the cartoon above illustrates the ways people use the media for different purposes and gratifications.
2  On which individuals in the cartoon do you think the media are having the most effect and the least effect? Give reasons for your answer.
3  Refer to the section above on the effects of the media on audiences. Which approach best fits your own media habits? Which do you find the most persuasive? Give reasons for your answer.
4  Suppose you wanted to study the effects of a TV programme on an audience. Suggest how you might go about researching this.
5  Carry out a short survey finding out what use people make of the media in their daily lives – for example, for leisure, relaxation, information, background 'wallpaper' while doing other things, exploring and confirming their identities, and so on.
6  Identify four ways in which you think you are influenced by the content of what you see or read in the media.
7  Explain briefly *in your own words* what is meant by each of the hypodermic syringe, audience selection, cultural effects, and uses and gratifications models of the effects of the media on audiences.
8  Write a short essay (around 15 minutes) answering the following question: 'How far do sociologists agree with the view that the media are mainly concerned with helping the ruling class maintain its powerful position in society?'

## VIOLENCE AND THE MEDIA

Violence – including pornography – on the internet, in computer games, in TV news reports and dramas, and in films and videos is now part of popular culture, and more people are exposed to such violence than ever before.

Such media violence is often blamed for increasing crime and violence in society. An example of this view occurred after the murder in 1993 of 2-year-old James Bulger by two 10-year-old boys. The judge in the case commented: 'I suspect that exposure to violent video films may in part be an explanation.'

Assertions, like that in the Bulger murder, that media violence generates real-life violence are commonplace, and masses of research have been done to investigate whether such a link really exists, particularly in relation to children. However, despite all the research, there is little reliable and undisputed evidence about whether violence in the media leads to an increase in aggressive behaviour, though the weight of evidence suggests there is no such link. For example, a 2003 report by the Broadcasting Standards Commission found that children are fully aware that television production is a process and that they are not watching reality, with the report concluding: 'They are able to make judgements … they are not blank sheets of paper on whom messages can be imprinted'. Children displaying tendencies to violence may have had such tendencies regardless of television viewing.

Much media violence is fictional, and there is a problem in defining what counts as 'violence'. Boxing and wrestling, fights in TV dramas, parents hitting children, police attacking protesters, shooting, news film of warfare and many children's cartoons all depict violent scenes, but they are unlikely to have the same effects on every individual. Researchers and audiences may

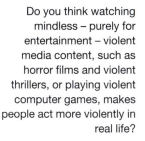

Do you think watching mindless – purely for entertainment – violent media content, such as horror films and violent thrillers, or playing violent computer games, makes people act more violently in real life?

not all view scenes showing real-life violence, fictional violence and cartoon violence in the same way.

The box below shows some competing claims about the effects of media violence. Even if there were evidence it did have some effects, the earlier section on media effects on audiences suggests media violence is unlikely to have the same effects on everyone, and it may actually reduce, rather than increase, real-life violence.

---

**SOME COMPETING CLAIMS ABOUT THE EFFECTS OF VIOLENCE IN THE MEDIA**

- *Copycatting:* like a hypodermic syringe injecting a drug, exposure to media violence causes children to copy what they see and behave more aggressively in the real world.
- *Catharsis:* media violence does not make viewers more aggressive but reduces violence, as it allows people to live out their violent tendencies in the fantasy world of the media, rather than in the real world.
- *Desensitization:* repeated exposure of children to media violence has gradual 'drip-drip' long-term effects, with increased risk of aggressive behaviour as adults, as people tend to become less sensitive and disturbed when they witness real-world violence, have less sympathy for its victims, and become socialized into accepting violence as a normal part of life.
- *Sensitization:* exposure to violence in the media can make people more sensitive to and less tolerant of real-life violence.
- *Media violence causes psychological disturbance in some children:* watching media violence frightens young children, causing nightmares, sleeplessness, anxiety and depression, and these effects may be long-lasting.
- *Media violence causes some people to have exaggerated fears*, such as about crime, and their personal safety and that of their family and their communities.

---

The problems of researching whether violence in the media causes real-life violence include:

- It is difficult to decide whether it is the media or other agencies (such as the peer group or an abusive family) that affect a person's behaviour.
- The spread of new media means there is such a wide choice of media that it is almost impossible to know in the real world which media are watched, what violence people are exposed to, the context in which it occurs, and what meanings people give to what they see. It is therefore very difficult to know which, if any, will have an impact on behaviour.
- In a media-saturated society, where everyone is constantly bombarded by media imagery from across the globe, it is almost impossible to find

anyone who has not been exposed to violent media images of some kind. This makes it hard to find out what people would be like without any influence from the media, and, in any case, real-world violence existed long before the media became a general feature of society.

The simplest answer to the question 'Does media violence cause violent behaviour?' is 'We don't really know.' But detailed analysis of hundreds of research studies suggests the reason for this is because the link is either very weak or does not exist at all.

---

### Activity

1  Refer to the earlier sections on the effects of the media on audiences, and suggest two possible effects on audiences of violent media content for *each* of the hypodermic syringe, audience selection, cultural effects, and uses and gratifications models.

2  Refer to the box above headed 'Some competing claims about the effects of violence in the media'.

   (a)  Suggest three different ways people might react to watching a violent movie.

   (b)  Look at each of the possible effects, and try to make at least one criticism of each one, as in the following example:

| **Effect of violent media content** | **Criticism** |
|---|---|
| *Desensitization:* repeated exposure to media violence increases the risk of aggressive behaviour, as people become less sensitive and disturbed when they witness real-world violence, have less sympathy for its victims, and become socialized into accepting violence as a normal part of life. | Violent media content might so horrify and sensitize people to it that they become opposed to violence in real life. |

3  Suggest reasons why children might be more vulnerable to media violence than adults.

---

## INTO THE FUTURE

We are living in the middle of the most dramatic communications explosion of all time. New technology is changing the media so rapidly that new developments are occurring almost daily. Digital broadcasting enables us to receive hundreds of cable and satellite television channels; interactive television enables audiences to participate in what they are watching; there are millions of webpages to view; and there is the possibility of doing a range of electronic-based communication tasks on single devices which slip inside a jacket pocket or a bag. The huge growth in social media means we can all now develop social networks, post news stories and interact with very many people across the globe.

The media have become a gigantic international business, with instant news from every part of the globe. International marketing of TV programmes and films to international audiences is backed by huge investments. The internet has millions more people going online every year. All-dancing, all-singing computers and smartphones are replacing televisions, stereos and landline phones in our homes, with instant access to colossal amounts of information and entertainment from the entire globe. Printed newspaper sales have been steadily declining, and may well continue to do so, as more and more news services and newspapers appear online. Printed books are facing growing competition from e-readers, such as Amazon's Kindle which can hold upwards of 1,500 books, or devices like Apple's iPad.

The speed of technological change is now so great that the world is said to be rapidly becoming a 'global village'. This means that the whole world has become like one small village, with everyone (at least those who are affluent enough) exposed to the same information and messages through media which cut across all national frontiers. It remains to be seen how the media will develop during the twenty-first century, but it seems likely there will be an enormous increase in the power of the already powerful media companies.

## CHAPTER SUMMARY AND REVISION CHECKLIST

After studying this chapter, you should be able to:

- explain what is meant by the term 'media'

- describe what is meant by the 'traditional' and the 'new' media, and some of the differences between them

- describe how the development of new media has affected traditional media

- describe differences between social groups (gender, age, social class and ethnicity) in media use, and a variety of purposes for which people use new media

- describe different views on the significance of the new media in contemporary society

- describe and explain the significance of advertising in the media

- describe the main features of media ownership and control, and explain how these might influence media content, including Marxist, pluralist and postmodernist approaches to the media

- describe and explain how and why the media might be biased, including in reporting the news, and explain a variety of ways they might act as agents of social control and influence public opinion, including the concepts of agenda-setting, gatekeeping, norm-setting, news values, moral panics and churnalism

- describe what is meant by censorship, and briefly identify a number of formal controls on the media, including the law and bodies set up to regulate them

- examine competing views of the role of the media in democratic societies
- outline a variety of ways in which the media contribute to socialization, including consumption patterns and identity, and political socialization and voting
- outline and explain, with examples, some of the ways the media represent and form stereotypes in relation to gender, different age groups, ethnicity, disability and different social classes

- outline and explain how the media might give false impressions of crime, amplify deviance and create moral panics
- discuss different views of the effects of the media on audiences, including the hypodermic syringe, and the audience selection, cultural effects, and uses and gratifications models
- describe different arguments about the effects of media violence, and some difficulties of researching these effects.

## KEY TERMS

Definitions can be found in the glossary at the end of this book, as well as these terms usually being defined in the margin where they first appear in the chapter. You can also find the glossary online by following the link at www.politybooks.com/browne. Put it in your phone for ready reference.

| | | |
|---|---|---|
| agenda-setting | hyperreality | selective exposure |
| bias | male gaze | selective perception |
| censorship | media gaze | selective retention |
| churnalism | media representations | simulacra |
| citizen journalism | news values | social capital |
| digital divide | norm-setting | symbolic annihilation |
| floating voters | pluralism | synergy |
| gatekeeping | propaganda | |

There are a variety of free tests and other activities that can be used to assess your learning – mainly aimed at AS- and A-level sociology students, but you might find them useful – as well as an online searchable glossary, at

www.politybooks.com/browne
You can also find new contemporary resources by following Ken Browne on Twitter

@BrowneKen

# CHAPTER 8 Health and Illness

## Contents

### KEY ISSUES

- The social construction of the body, health and illness
- Defining health, illness and disease
- The biomedical and social models of health and illness
- Becoming a health statistic
- How society influences health
- The food industry
- Sociological theories of health and illness
- Inequalities in health

Chapter 8 is available as a download at www.politybooks.com/introsoc.

# AQA and WJEC-Eduqas 'classic text' references

These are the 'classic texts' which the AQA and WJEC-Eduqas require students to be aware of. These are identified in the text by the author name(s) and date, and they are also included in the index so they can easily be found in the book.

Ball, S. J. (1981) *Beachside Comprehensive: A Case Study of Secondary Schooling*. Cambridge University Press.

Ball, S. J., Bowe, R. and Gerwitz, S. (1994) 'Market Forces and Parental Choice' in S. Tomlinson (ed.), *Educational Reform and its Consequences*. London: IPPR / Rivers Oram Press.

Becker, H. S. (1963) *Outsiders: Studies in the Sociology of Deviance*. New York: Free Press.

Bowles, S. and Gintis, H. (2011 [1976]) *Schooling in Capitalist America*. Chicago: Haymarket Books.

Carlen, P. (1988) *Women, Crime and Poverty*. Milton Keynes: Open University Press.

Cohen, A. K. (1971 [1955]) *Delinquent Boys: The Culture of the Gang*. New York: Free Press.

Davis, K. and Moore, W. E. (1967 [1945]) 'Some Principles of Stratification' in R. Bendix and S. M. Lipset (eds.), *Class, Status and Power*. London: Routledge & Kegan Paul.

Delphy, C. and Leonard, D. (1992) *Familiar Exploitation: A New Analysis of Marriage in Contemporary Western Societies*. Cambridge: Polity.

Devine, F. (1992) *Affluent Workers Revisited*. Edinburgh University Press.

Durkheim, E. (1973 [1925]) *Moral Education*. Glencoe: Free Press.

Francis, B. (2005) 'Not/Knowing their Place: Girls' Classroom Behaviours', in G. Lloyd (ed.), *Problem Girls*. Abingdon: RoutledgeFalmer.

Halsey, A. H., Heath, A. F. and Ridge, J. M. (1980) *Origins and Destinations: Family, Class and Education in Modern Britain*. Oxford: Clarendon Press.

Heidensohn, F. (1985) *Women and Crime*. London: Macmillan.

Marx, K. (2000) *Selected Writings*, 2nd edition, ed. D. McLellan. Oxford University Press.

Merton, R. K. (1968 [1949]) *Social Theory and Social Structure*. New York: Free Press.

Murray, C. (1984) *Losing Ground: American Social Policy, 1950–1980*. New York: Basic Books.

Oakley, A. (1982) 'Conventional Families' in R. N. Rapoport, M. P. Fogarty and R. Rapoport (eds.), *Families in Britain*. London: Routledge & Kegan Paul.

Parsons, T. (1959) 'The Social Structure of the Family', in R. N. Anshen (ed.), *The Family: Its Functions and Destiny*. New York: Harper and Row.

Parsons, T. (1964) 'The School Class as a Social System' in T. Parsons, *Social Structure and Personality*. New York: The Free Press.

Rapoport, R. N. and Rapoport, R. (1982) 'British Families in Transition' in R. N. Rapoport, M. P. Fogarty and R. Rapoport (eds.), *Families in Britain*. London: Routledge & Kegan Paul.

Townsend, P. (1979) *Poverty in the United Kingdom*. Harmondsworth: Penguin.

Walby, S. (1990) *Theorizing Patriarchy*. Oxford: Blackwell.
Weber, M. (1947) *The Theory of Social and Economic Organization*. New York: Free Press.
Willis, P. (1977) *Learning to Labour: How Working Class Kids Get Working Class Jobs*. Farnborough: Saxon House.

Young, M. and Willmott, P. (1973) *The Symmetrical Family*. Harmondsworth: Penguin.

Zaretsky, E. (1976) *Capitalism, the Family and Personal Life*. London: Pluto Press.

# Glossary

Words in coloured type within entries refer to terms found elsewhere in the glossary.

**absolute poverty**   Poverty defined as lacking the minimum requirements necessary to maintain human health and life. *See also* relative poverty.

**accordion family**   A multigenerational family which constantly changes in size as people move into or out of the family home. Fully adult children either don't leave and continue to live with their parents, or keep leaving and returning, and grandparents leave their own homes and come to live with their adult children either temporarily or permanently.

**achieved status**   Status which is achieved through an individual's own efforts. *See also* ascribed status.

**affluent workers**   Highly paid manual workers.

**ageing population**   A population in which the average age is getting higher, with a growing proportion of elderly people, and a declining proportion of younger people.

**ageism**   Stereotyping (*see* stereotype) of, or prejudice and discrimination against, individuals or groups on the grounds of their age.

**agencies of social control**   State organizations – e.g. the criminal justice system (police, courts, probation service, prisons, etc.) – or other groups and institutions – e.g. the family, religion, the education system, the peer group and the media – that control people's behaviour to compel conformity to social norms and values.

**agencies of socialization**   Groups and social institutions that are responsible for, or involved in, the socialization process – e.g. the family, the education system, religion, the media, the workplace and the peer group.

**agenda-setting**   The process whereby the media select the list of subjects to report and bring to public attention.

**agents of social control**   The actual people who carry out social control in the agencies of social control. For example, in the criminal justice system, the agents of social control are people such as police officers, judges and magistrates.

**agents of socialization**   The actual people who carry out socialization in the agencies of socialization. For example, in the family and education system, parents and teachers may be regarded as agents of socialization.

**alienation**   The feeling of a lack of power and control over their lives that many people experience. Marxists link this to oppression and exploitation in capitalist societies, and the unfulfilling work that people have to perform.

**anomie**   Confusion and uncertainty over social norms.

**anti-school (or counter-school) subculture**   A group within a school organized around a set of norms, values, attitudes and behaviour in opposition to the main values, norms and aims of a school. Sometimes called a counter-school subculture.

**arranged marriage**   A marriage which is arranged by the parents of the marriage partners, with a view to compatibility of family background and status. More a union between two families than two people, and romantic love between the marriage partners is not necessarily present.

**ascribed status**   Status which is given to an individual at birth and usually can't be changed. *See also* achieved status.

**authority**   Power which is accepted and obeyed because it is seen as legitimate (fair and right) by those without power.

**beanpole family**   A multi-generation extended family, which is long (multi-generational) and thin, with few people in each generation. This is because fewer children are being born in each generation, but people are living longer.

**bias**   A subject being presented in a one-sided way, favouring one point of view over others, or deliberately ignoring, distorting or misrepresenting issues.

**bigamy**   Where monogamy is the only legal form of marriage / civil partnership, the offence of marrying/civil-partnering another person while still legally married/civil-partnered to someone else who is still living.

**birth rate**   The number of live births per 1,000 of the population per year.

**boomerang family**   A family in which adult children who had left home return to live with their parent(s).

**boomerang generation**   A generation of young adults who return – or keep leaving and returning – to live with their parent(s).

**bourgeoisie**   Class of owners of the means of production.

**capitalism**   A form of society or economic system in which the means of production are privately owned; goods are produced for sale in the free market (rather than for personal use) to make profits for their owners; and the majority of people only make the money needed to survive by selling their labour to the owners in exchange for wages.

**case study** Research that focuses on the intensive study of a single example of a place, person, group, institution or event.

**caste system** A stratification system (*see* social stratification) based on Hindu religious beliefs, in which an individual's position is fixed at birth and cannot be changed.

**censorship** The restriction of freedom of speech through the control or suppression of media content by a government or other official body.

**cereal-packet family** The stereotype of the best and most desirable family found in the media and advertising. It is generally seen as involving first-time married opposite-sex parents and their own natural children, living together, with the father as the primary breadwinner and the mother as primarily concerned with the home and children.

**charismatic authority** Power which is seen as fair and just as it is based on a power-holder's exceptional personal charm and magnetism.

**chivalry thesis** The suggestion that the male-dominated criminal justice system, such as the police and the courts, takes a more benevolent, protective and patriarchal view of female offending, and treats women more leniently than men.

**churnalism** A form of journalism in which journalists produce media content based on pre-packaged material, such as press releases and social-media reports, without doing further research or checking facts.

**citizen journalism** Where members of the public, rather than professional journalists and media companies, collect, report and spread news stories and information.

**citizenship** The legal, social and political rights and responsibilities of individuals (citizens) living in a society.

**class consciousness** An awareness in members of a social class of their real interests.

**class deal** The material rewards – money – that women gain from working in paid employment.

**class struggle** Conflict and struggle between the two major social classes in capitalist society – the bourgeoisie (capitalist class) and the proletariat (the working class).

**classic extended family** A family in which several related nuclear families (see nuclear family) or family members live in the same house, street or area. It may be horizontally extended, where it contains aunts, uncles, cousins, etc., or vertically extended, where it contains more than two generations.

**closed society** A stratification system (*see* social stratification) where social mobility is not possible.

**coercion** Power that is only obeyed because of violence or the threat of violence.

**cohort** A group of people with a shared characteristic.

**communes** Self-contained and self-supporting communities, where all members of the community share property, childcare, household tasks and living accommodation.

**communism** An equal society, without social classes or conflict, in which the means of production are the common property of all.

**compensatory education** Extra educational support for those coming from disadvantaged groups to help them overcome the obstacles they face in the education system and the wider society.

**comprehensive school** One which accepts children of all abilities, without any selection by examination.

**conflict theory** A sociological approach that emphasizes social differences and conflicts, with inequalities in wealth, power and status all creating conflicts between individuals and groups. *See also* consensus theory.

**conjugal roles** The roles played by partners in couples who live together. *See also* joint (or integrated) conjugal roles; segregated conjugal roles.

**consensus theory** A sociological approach that emphasizes the shared norms and shared values that exist between people, and sees society made up of individuals and social institutions working together in harmony, without much conflict between people and groups.

**consumer (or consumption) goods** Products and services that people buy to satisfy their needs and desires, such as food, clothes, furniture, TVs, tablets, smartphones and leisure activities, like paying to go to cinemas, clubs and concerts.

**content analysis** A way of analysing documents and other qualitative material by quantifying them – e.g. counting the number of times a particular item appears in the media.

**conventional family** A nuclear family composed of a legally married couple living with their children.

**corporate crime** Crimes committed by large companies, or by individuals on behalf of large companies, which directly profit the company rather than individuals.

**correspondence principle** (or theory) The way the hidden curriculum in schools corresponds closely to, or mirrors, many features which are expected in the workplace.

**counter-school (or anti-school) subculture** A group organized around a set of norms, values, attitudes and behaviour in opposition to the main values, norms and aims of a school. Sometimes called an anti-school subculture.

**covert role** A hidden role, where the researcher in participant observation conceals from the group being studied his or her true identity as a researcher, to gain access to the group and avoid disrupting its normal behaviour.

**crime** Behaviour which is against the law – law-breaking.

**criminal justice system** (CJS)   All the different agencies and organizations that are involved in law, order and the control and punishment of crime and other offending, such as motoring offences. It includes the police, Crown Prosecution Service (CPS), courts, prisons and the probation service.

**cultural capital**   The educational level of parents, their knowledge, attitudes and values, language use and other educational resources that exist in the home that enable parents to support their children in education, and the children themselves to make good progress at school.

**cultural deprivation**   The idea that some young people fail in education because of supposed cultural deficiencies in their home and family background, such as inadequate socialization, failings in pre-school learning, inadequate language skills and inappropriate attitudes and values.

**cultural diversity**   Cultural differences between social groups and different societies, based on factors such as history, religious beliefs, ethnic group, social class and age.

**culture**   The language, beliefs, values and norms, customs, roles, knowledge and skills which combine to make up the way of life of any society.

**culture clash**   A clash or conflict between the cultural values of different individuals, groups and institutions – e.g. between the cultural values of the home and those of the school.

**culture of poverty**   A set of beliefs and values thought to exist among the poor, which prevents them escaping from poverty.

**customs**   Norms which have existed for a long time.

**dark figure of crime**   Crimes that are undiscovered, unreported and unrecorded by the police.

**death rate**   The number of deaths per 1,000 of the population per year.

**deferred gratification**   Putting off immediate rewards and pleasures in order to achieve higher rewards in the future.

**democracy**   A form of government in which people enjoy many individual rights and freedoms, and the people participate in political decision-making, usually by electing individuals to represent their views.

**demography**   The term used for the study of the characteristics of human populations, such as their size and structure and how these change over time.

**dependency culture**   A set of values and beliefs, and a way of life, centred on dependence on others. Normally used in the context of those who depend on welfare-state benefits. Sometimes called a 'culture of dependency'.

**dependent**   Someone who is maintained by another person, e.g. a dependent child is supported by his or her parent(s).

**deschooling**   A term used in two ways: one view is that schools should be abolished in society as they promote conformity, repress children, and stifle creativity and independent critical thinking. Alternatively, the term is used to describe the process whereby parents decide to remove their children from formal schooling (to deschool them) and teach them at home.

deskilling  The removal of skills from work by the application of new machinery which simplifies tasks.

deviance  Failure to conform to social norms and values – rule-breaking behaviour.

deviancy amplification  The process by which the media, through exaggeration and distortion, actually create more crime and deviance.

deviant career  Where people who have been labelled (see labelling) as deviant (see deviance) find conventional opportunities blocked to them, come to accept a deviant self-identity and so are pushed towards deviant subcultures and into committing further deviant acts.

dictatorship  A form of government in which power is concentrated in the hands of one person or a small powerful ruling elite.

digital divide  The gap between those people with effective access to the digital and information technology making up the new media and those who lack such access.

disability  A physical or mental impairment which has a substantial and long-term unfavourable effect on a person's ability to carry out normal day-to-day activities.

discrimination  The unfair or unfavourable treatment of people because of the group with which they are identified, e.g. by gender, ethnicity, religion, social class or age.

division of labour  The division of work or occupations into a large number of specialized tasks, each of which is carried out by one worker or group of workers.

divorce rate  The number of divorces per 1,000 married people per year.

domestic division of labour  The division of roles, responsibilities and work tasks within a family or household.

domestic labour  Unpaid housework, including cooking, cleaning, child-care and looking after the sick and elderly.

dominant ideology  The ideas and beliefs of the most powerful and wealthy groups in society, which influence the ideas and beliefs of the rest of society.

dual burden  The two jobs of paid employment and unpaid domestic labour taken on, nearly always, by women.

dual-career families  Those in which both partners have their own careers, with the hope and expectation of future promotions.

dual-earner families  Those in which both partners earn money from paid employment.

dysfunctional family    A family which doesn't work as it should, causing physical and psychological harm affecting the safety and development of children and other family members.

economic inequality    Refers to differences in all those material things that affect the lives of individuals, such as their wealth, their income and the hours they work.

edgework    Voluntary risk-taking behaviour of any kind that explores and challenges the edges or boundaries of what is normally allowed or accepted.

elaborated code    A form of language use involving careful explanation and detail. The language used by strangers and individuals in some formal context, such as a job interview, writing a business letter, or in a school lesson or textbook, and which uses a much wider vocabulary than the restricted code.

elite    A small group holding great power and privilege in society.

embourgeoisement    The idea that the differences between the middle class and working class are disappearing, with well-paid manual workers merging into the middle class. The opposite of proletarianization.

emigration    The flow of people leaving their usual country of residence and entering another country for at least a year, which then becomes their new country of residence.

emotional work    Tasks concerned with maintaining the bonds of affection, moral support, friendship and love.

empty-shell marriage    A marriage in which the marital relationship has broken down, but the couple continue living together and no divorce or separation has taken place.

endogamy    Where marriage must be to a partner of the same kinship or social group.

equality of educational opportunity    The idea that every child, regardless of his or her social class background, ability to pay school fees, ethnic origin, gender or disability, should have an equal chance of doing as well in education as his or her ability will allow.

equality of opportunity    The opportunity to compete on the same terms as everyone else.

ethics    Ideas about what is morally right and wrong.

ethnic group    A group of people who share a common cultural identity.

ethnicity    The shared culture, including language, religion, cultural traditions and characteristics, of a social group, which gives its members an identity in some ways different from other groups – e.g. Black, Asian and Minority Ethnic (BAME) groups.

ethnocentric curriculum    The curriculum of a school which gives priority to the culture of a particular ethnic group, whilst disregarding or downplaying other cultures.

ethnocentrism  A view of the world in which other cultures are seen through the eyes of one's own culture, with a devaluing of the others. For example, school subjects may concentrate on White British society and culture, rather than recognizing and taking into account the cultures of different ethnic communities (*see* ethnic group).

expressive role  The nurturing, caring and emotional role, often seen by functionalists as the natural role for women in the family, linked to women's biology.

extended family  A family grouping including all those linked by kinship ties. There are two main types of extended family: the classic extended family and the modified extended family.

false class consciousness  A failure by members of a social class to recognize their real interests.

family diversity  The wide range of different family types and family lifestyles.

feminism  A view, and a movement, which believes that women are disadvantaged in society, and aims to achieve gender equality so women have rights, power and status equal to those of men. Anyone supporting this view is known as a feminist.

feminist  Someone who believes that women are disadvantaged in society, and should have rights, power and status equal to those of men.

feral children  Children who display wild, undomesticated, animal-like behaviour, as a result of missing out on some important stages of human learning, as they have been removed from human contact and the normal processes of human socialization.

fertility rate  The number of live births per 1,000 women of childbearing age (15–44) per year. *See also* total fertility rate.

feudalism  A closed (*see* closed society) system of stratification (*see* social stratification) based on land ownership and legal inequalities.

floating voters  Undecided voters who have no fixed political opinion or commitment to any political party.

focus group  A form of group interview in which the group focuses on a particular topic to explore in depth, and people are encouraged to talk to one another as well as the interviewer.

folk devils  Individuals or groups posing an imagined or exaggerated threat to society.

forced marriage  One in which someone is compelled, often by violence or the threat of violence, to marry without their consent.

formal rules  Written rules and laws, which can bring about formal negative sanctions (punishments) if broken.

formal social control  Control of people's behaviour by agencies of social control and agents of social control that have the specific purpose of ensuring social conformity and the maintenance of social order – e.g. the criminal justice system, police officers and judges.

functional prerequisites   Basic needs that must be met if societies are to survive.

functionalism   A sociological perspective which sees society made up of parts – such as the family, education system and religion – which work together to maintain society. Society is seen as basically harmonious and stable, because of agreement on basic values (value consensus) and on the everyday rules of social life established through socialization.

gatekeeping   The media's refusal to cover some issues.

gender   The culturally created differences between men and women which are learnt through socialization.

gender deal   The material and emotional rewards and status that women gain from fulfilling their traditional roles in the family and home, with material and emotional support from a male breadwinner.

gender pay gap   The difference between the hourly earnings of women and men.

gender role   The pattern of behaviour which society expects from a man or woman.

generation   Those born in the same 15- to 30-year period.

geographically mobile   Able and willing to move home from one area to live in another area, region or country.

glass ceiling   An invisible barrier of discrimination which makes it difficult for women to reach the same top levels in their chosen careers as similarly qualified men.

global culture   The way cultures in different countries of the world have become more alike, sharing increasingly similar consumer products and ways of life. This has arisen as globalization has undermined national and local cultures.

globalization   The growing interconnectedness of societies across the world, with the spread of the same culture, consumer goods and economic interests across the globe.

group interview   Where the researcher interviews several people at the same time, with the researcher controlling the direction of the interview, with responses directed to him or her.

halo effect   When pupils become stereotyped (see stereotype), either favourably or unfavourably, on the basis of earlier impressions.

hate crime   Any crime that is perceived by the victim, or any other person, to be motivated by hostility or prejudice towards someone based on a personal characteristic, such as their ethnicity or race, disability, religion, beliefs or sexual orientation.

**Hawthorne effect** (or observer effect)   When the presence of a researcher, or an individual's or group's knowledge that it has been specially chosen for research, changes the usual behaviour of the individual or group, raising problems for the validity of research.

**hidden curriculum**   The learning of values, attitudes and behaviour through the school's organization and teachers' attitudes, but which is not part of the formal timetable – e.g. obedience, punctuality and conformity to school rules.

**homophobia**   The irrational hatred, intolerance and fear of lesbian, gay, bisexual and transsexual (LGBT) people.

**household**   An individual living alone, or a group of people (not necessarily related) who live at the same address and who share cooking facilities and a living room, sitting room or dining area.

**hybrid families**   Those where the couple come from two different cultural or ethnic backgrounds, creating new family relationships and values arising from the merging of the two cultures.

**hyperreality**   A view of the world which is created and defined by the media, with the image of an event seen as more real than the actual event it is meant to be depicting.

**hypothesis**   An idea that a researcher guesses might be true, but which has not yet been tested against the evidence.

**identity**   How individuals see and define themselves, and how other people see and define them.

**immediate gratification**   Taking opportunities and enjoying yourself now, rather than waiting for higher rewards in the future.

**immigration**   The flow of people entering another country, and making it their place of residence for at least a year.

**impairment**   Some loss, limitation or difference of functioning of the mind or body, on a long-term or permanent basis, either that one is born with or that arises from injury or disease.

**imposition problem**   The risk that, when asking questions in interviews or self-completion questionnaires, the researcher might be imposing their own views or framework on the people being researched, rather than getting at what they really think.

**income**   The flow of money which people obtain from work, from their investments or from the state in the form of welfare benefits.

**indictable offences**   More serious criminal offences that are tried at crown court before a judge and jury. Lesser offences are tried at a magistrates' court.

**infant mortality rate**   The number of deaths of babies in the first year of life per 1,000 live births per year.

**informal rules**   Unwritten rules or social norms which aim to control behaviour and ensure conformity in particular situations in everyday life.

**informal social control**   Control of people's behaviour by agencies and agents whose primary purpose is not social control, but that act in various ways to ensure social conformity through approval and disapproval of behaviour in everyday life – e.g. social pressure from agencies such as the family and peer groups, and from agents such as parents and neighbours, friends and workmates.

**informed consent**   The ethical (*see* ethics) requirement that those taking part in research should, whenever possible, have agreed to do so and have given this consent based on a full understanding of the nature, aims and purposes of the research, any implications or risks taking part might have, and the uses of any findings of the research.

**institutional racism**   'The collective failure of an organization to provide an appropriate and professional service to people because of their culture, colour or ethnic origin. It can be seen or detected in processes, attitudes and behaviour which amount to discrimination through unwitting preju-dice, ignorance, thoughtless and racist stereotyping which disadvantages minority ethnic people' (Macpherson Report, 1999).

**instrumental role**   The provider/breadwinner role, often seen by function-alists as the natural role for men in the family.

**interactionism**   A social-action perspective that is concerned with under-standing human behaviour in face-to-face and small group situations, and how individuals, groups and situations come to be defined in particular ways through their everyday encounters with other people.

**intergenerational social mobility**   A way of measuring social mobility by comparing an adult's present occupation or income with that of the family she or he was born into. It therefore shows how much social-class mobility there has been between two generations.

**interpretivism**   An approach that believes it is only possible to understand society by using methods that provide an understanding of the interpreta-tions and meanings people give to social situations, and of how they see and understand the world around them.

**intersectionality**   The way different forms of discrimination can become intensified when they combine, overlap or intersect (or interconnect).

**interviewer bias / interviewer effect**   The answers given in an interview being influenced or distorted in some way by the presence or behaviour of the interviewer.

**intragenerational social mobility**   A way of measuring social mobility by comparing a person's present occupation or income with her or his first occupation. It therefore shows how much mobility an individual has achieved within her or his lifetime.

inverse care law   In relation to the welfare state, including the National Health Service, the suggestion that those whose need is least get the most resources, while those in the greatest need get the fewest resources.

Islamophobia   An irrational fear and/or hatred of, or aversion to, Islam, Muslims or Islamic culture.

joint (or integrated) conjugal roles   Where there are few divisions in household and other tasks and the roles performed by partners in couples who live together.

juvenile delinquency   Crime committed by those between the ages of 10 and 17, though the term 'delinquency' is often used to describe any antisocial or deviant behaviour by young people, even if it isn't criminal.

kibbutz   A community established in Israel, with the emphasis on equality, collective ownership of property, and collective child rearing.

kinship   Relations of blood, marriage/civil partnership or adoption.

labelling   Defining a person or group in a certain way and as having particular characteristics – as a particular 'type' of person or group.

labour power   People's capacity to work. According to Marxism, labour power is sold to the owners of the means of production in exchange for wages.

law   An official legal rule, formally enforced by the police, courts and prison, involving legal punishments if it is broken.

leading questions   Questions which are worded in such a way as to encourage people (lead them) into giving a particular answer.

life chances   The chances of obtaining those things defined as desirable, and of avoiding those things defined as undesirable, in a society.

life course   The various significant events individuals experience during the course of their lives – e.g. marriage or cohabitation, becoming a parent, divorce and retirement.

life expectancy   An estimate of how long people can be expected to live from a particular age. It is commonly estimated from birth, but it can be given from any age.

longitudinal study   A study based on a sample of people from whom data are collected at regular intervals over a period of years.

macro approach   An approach to studying society that focuses on the large-scale structure of society as a whole, rather than on individuals and small groups.

male gaze   Where men look (gaze) at women as sexual objects.

malestream   Sociology that concentrates on men, is mostly carried out by men, and then assumes that the findings can be applied to women as well.

**marginalization**   The process whereby some groups or individuals are pushed by poverty, ill health, lack of education, racism, sexism and so on to the margins of society, and are unable to take part in the life enjoyed by the majority of people. *See also* social exclusion.

**market situation**   The rewards that people are able to obtain when they compete to sell their skills in the labour market, depending on the scarcity of their skills, the demand for them, and the power they have to obtain high rewards.

**marketization**   Where something is left to free market competition and the forces of supply and demand. In education, this refers to the process whereby schools and colleges become more independent, and compete with one another for students, and become subject to the free-market forces of supply and demand, based on competition and parental choice.

**marriage rate**   The number of marriages per 1,000 unmarried people aged 16 and over per year.

**Marxism**   A sociological theory which sees society divided by conflict between two main opposing social classes (*see* social class): a small richer class which owns the majority of society's wealth, which exploits a much larger class of non-owners.

**master status**   The dominant status of an individual – such as that of an 'ex-con' or thief – which overrides all other characteristics of that person.

**matriarchy**   Power and authority held by women.

**matrifocal family**   Where mothers head families and fathers play a less prominent role in the home and in bringing up children.

**means of production**   The key resources like land, labour, raw materials, property, factories, businesses and machinery which are necessary for producing society's goods.

**media gaze**   The way the media view society and represent it in media content.

**media representations**   The way the media present groups to media audiences, which may influence how people think about these groups.

**median income**   The middle income point where half of the population have income above that amount, and half have income below that amount.

**meritocracy (or meritocratic society)**   A society in which social and occupational positions (jobs) and pay are allocated purely on the basis of people's merits, such as their individual experience, talents, abilities, qualifications and skills.

**micro approach**   An approach to studying society that focuses on small groups or individuals, rather than on the structure of society as a whole.

**migration**   The movement of people between one country or area and another, who remain for at least a year.

minority ethnic group    A social group which shares a cultural identity (*see* culture) which is different from that of the majority population of a society.

mixed methods    The use of both quantitative and qualitative methods within a single study (also referred to as methodological pluralism).

modified extended family    A family type in which related nuclear families (see nuclear family), although living apart geographically, nevertheless maintain regular contact and mutual support through visiting, phone calls, Skype, letters, email and social media.

monogamy    A form of marriage / civil partnership in which a person can only be legally married/civil-partnered to one partner at a time.

moral panic    A wave of public concern about some exaggerated or imaginary threat to society, stirred up by overblown and sensationalized reporting in the media.

multicultural society    A society in which there are a range of different cultures (ways of life) which exist alongside the shared overall culture of society.

NEET    A young person (aged 16–24) who is **N**ot in **E**ducation, **E**mployment or **T**raining.

net migration    The *difference* between immigration and emigration, and therefore whether the population of a country has gone up or down when both immigration and emigration are taken into account.

New Right    An approach to social and political policies that stresses individual freedom; self-help and self-reliance; reduction of the power and spending of the state; the free market and free competition between private companies, schools and other institutions; and the importance of traditional institutions and values.

news values    The values and assumptions held by journalists, which guide them in choosing what to report and what to leave out, and how what they choose to report should be presented.

non-conformity    Acting in a way that goes against a society's or group's norms and values.

norm-setting    The process whereby the media emphasize and reinforce conformity to social norms, and seek to isolate those who don't conform by making them the victims of unfavourable public opinion.

norms    Social rules which define correct or appropriate behaviour in a society or group.

nuclear family    A family with two generations, of parents and children, living together in one household. *See also* privatized (or isolated) nuclear family.

objectivity   Approaching topics with an open mind, avoiding bias and being prepared to submit research evidence to scrutiny by other researchers.

occupational status   The ranking of occupations based on the amount of status or social standing (admiration and respect) in society attached to a job, usually based on factors such as its power, income and the training and educational qualifications required. Sometimes referred to as socio-economic status.

open society   A stratification system (*see* social stratification) in which social mobility is possible.

over-representation   When too many from a particular group are represented, compared to that group's proportion of the total population.

overt role   A non-hidden or revealed role, where the researcher in participant observation reveals to the group being studied his or her true identity and purpose.


particularistic values   Standards and rules that give priority to personal relationships.

party   Any group which is concerned with holding power, making decisions and influencing policies in the interests of its membership

patriarchal ideology   A set of ideas that supports and justifies the power of men over women.

patriarchy   Power, status and authority held by men.

peer group   A group of people of similar age and status, with whom a person mixes socially.

peer pressure   Pressure from those in a group to which one belongs to encourage conformity to group norms.

personal documents   Those produced for a person's own use, which are usually private, and record part of a person's life – e.g. diaries and letters.

perspective   A way of looking at something.

petty bourgeoisie   A social class of small-business owners, squeezed between the bourgeoisie and the proletariat.

pilot survey   A small-scale practice survey carried out before the final survey to check for any possible problems in the way it is designed.

pluralism   A view that sees power in society spread among a wide variety of groups and individuals, with no single one having a monopoly on power and influence.

police caution   A formal warning given by the police to anyone aged 10 or over for minor crimes, such as graffiti.

political party   A group of people organized with the aim of forming the government in a society.

polyandry A form of marriage in which a woman may have two or more husbands at the same time.

polygamy A form of marriage in which a member of one sex can be married to two or more members of the opposite sex at the same time.

polygyny A form of marriage in which a man may have two or more wives at the same time.

positive discrimination Giving disadvantaged groups more favourable treatment than others to make up for the disadvantages they face.

positivism An approach that believes society can be studied using similar methods to those used in the natural sciences, such as physics, chemistry and biology.

postmodernism An approach that stresses that society is changing so rapidly and constantly that it is marked by chaos, uncertainty and risk, and is fragmented into many different groups, interests and lifestyles.

poverty line The dividing point between those who are poor and those who are not. The official poverty line used in the UK today is *60 per cent of median income* – the definition of poverty used by the European Union.

power The ability of people or groups to exert their will over others and get their own way, even if sometimes others resist this.

pressure groups Organizations that try to put pressure on those with power in society to implement policies which the groups favour, or to prevent unpopular policies from being implemented.

primary data Information that sociologists have collected themselves. *See also* secondary data.

primary socialization Socialization during the early years of childhood, carried out by the family or close community. *See also* secondary socialization.

privatized (or isolated) nuclear family A self-contained, self-reliant and home-centred nuclear family unit that is largely separated and isolated from its extended kin (see kinship), neighbours and local community life.

proletarianization The process of decline in the pay and conditions of sections of the middle class (*see* social class), so they become more like the working class. The opposite of embourgeoisement.

proletariat The class (*see* social class) of workers, who have to work for wages to survive as they do not own the means of production.

propaganda One-sided, misleading or untrue information used to promote a particular cause or point of view.

public documents Those produced for public knowledge and available to all.

qualitative data    Information about people's feelings and the meanings and interpretations they give to some issue or event, expressed in their own words rather than in statistical form.

qualitative methods    Research methods used to collect information about people's feelings and the meanings and interpretations they give to some issue or event, usually in their own words.

quantitative data    Information that can be expressed in statistical or number form.

quantitative methods    Research methods used to collect quantitative/statistical information.

race    The division of humans into different groups according to physical characteristics, such as skin colour.

racial discrimination    When people's racial prejudice causes them to act unfairly against an ethnic group.

racial prejudice    A set of assumptions about an ethnic group, which people are reluctant to change even when they receive information which undermines those assumptions.

racism    Treating people as inferior, and encouraging hostility towards them, on the grounds of racial or ethnic origins – usually based on skin colour or other physical or cultural characteristics.

rational-legal authority    Power which is seen as fair and just as it is based on shared and impersonal formal rules and laws. *See also* authority, charismatic authority, power, traditional authority.

reconstituted or blended or stepfamily    A family in which one or both partners have children from a previous relationship, combining to form a new family.

relative deprivation    A sense of lacking things (deprivation) compared to the group with which people identify and compare themselves.

relative poverty    Poverty defined in relation to a generally accepted standard of living in a specific society at a particular time. *See also* absolute poverty.

reliability    Whether another researcher, if repeating research using the same method for the same topic on the same group, would achieve the same results.

representative sample    A smaller group selected from the survey population for study, containing a good cross-section of the characteristics of the survey population as a whole.

representativeness/generalizability    Whether a group being studied contains similar characteristics to those of a wider group, enabling the results of research to be applied more generally (generalized) to a wider population beyond just the one studied.

reserve army of labour    A section of the labour force which is held in reserve, to be called into the workforce when the need arises.

respondent    The person answering – responding to – questions in questionnaires and interviews.

response rate    The number of people who respond to questionnaires compared to the total number of questionnaires distributed.

restricted code    A form of language use which takes for granted shared understandings between people. The informal, simple, everyday language, sometimes ungrammatical and with limited explanations and vocabulary, which is used between friends or family members. *See also* elaborated code.

role conflict    The conflict that arises between the successful performances of two or more roles at the same time, such as those of worker and mother.

role model    A pattern of behaviour which others copy and model their own behaviour on.

roles    The patterns of behaviour which are expected from individuals in society.

ruling-class ideology    The ideas and beliefs of the dominant class which controls society.

sample    A small representative group drawn from the survey population for questioning or interviewing.

sampling frame    A list of names of all those in the survey population, from which a representative sample is selected.

sanction    A reward (positive sanction) or punishment (negative sanction) to encourage social conformity.

sandwich generation    A generation of people (typically aged anywhere between their 30s and 60s) who are sandwiched between having to care for their ageing parents and, at the same time, supporting their own children.

scapegoats    Individuals or groups blamed for something which is not their fault.

school ethos    The character and atmosphere of a school.

secondary data    Information that already exists and which the researcher hasn't collected herself or himself. *See also* primary data.

secondary socialization    Socialization which takes place beyond the family and close community. It is carried out through agencies of secondary socialization such as the education system, the peer group, the workplace, the media and religious institutions. *See also* primary socialization.

secularization    The process whereby religious thinking, practice and institutions decline and lose influence in society.

segregated conjugal roles    A clear division and separation in household and other tasks and the roles performed between the partners in couples who live together.

**selective exposure**   Individuals exposing themselves only to media output that fits in with their existing views and interests. *See also* selective perception, selective retention.

**selective law enforcement**   When the police and courts use their discretion to decide whether someone has broken the law, whether to arrest them, to charge them, and whether or how to punish them.

**selective perception**   Individuals filtering and interpreting media output so they only see or hear that which fits in with their own views and interests. *See also* selective exposure, selective retention.

**selective retention**   Individuals ignoring or forgetting media output that is not in line with their own views and interests. *See also* selective exposure, selective perception.

**self-fulfilling prophecy**   The process in which people act in response to a prediction of their behaviour, thereby making the prediction come true. Often applied to the effects of streaming in schools.

**self-report studies** (or surveys)   Studies or surveys where people are asked to own up to committing crimes, whether or not they have been discovered.

**serial monogamy**   A form of relationship in which a person keeps marrying/civil-partnering/cohabiting with and divorcing or separating from a series of different partners, but only forms a relationship with one person at a time.

**setting**   Putting school students into different groups – sets – for a particular subject, according to their ability in that subject.

**sex**   The biological differences between men and women.

**sexism**   Prejudice or discrimination against people (especially women) because of their sex.

**sexual (or gendered) division of labour**   The division of tasks into 'men's jobs' and 'women's jobs'.

**sexual orientation**   The type of people that individuals are either physically or romantically attracted to, such as those of the same or opposite sex.

**simulacra**   Media images or reproductions and copies which appear to reflect things in the real world but have no basis in reality.

**slavery**   A stratification system (*see* social stratification) in which some people are regarded as the property of others.

**social capital**   The social networks of influence and support that people have.

**social class**   An open (*see* open society) system of stratification (*see* social stratification) consisting of broad groups of people (classes) who share a similar economic situation, such as occupation, income and ownership of wealth.

**social cohesion**   The bonds or 'glue' that bring people together and integrate them into a united society.

**social conformity**  Acting in a way that follows a society's or group's norms and values.

**social construction** (or social construct)  Something that is created by people's actions, beliefs and interpretations in a society or culture, rather than something that exists in biology or nature. It only exists because people have constructed it by choosing to give it a particular meaning, interpretation and label – e.g. the definitions of crime, deviance, health, gender or race.

**social control**  The process of persuading or forcing individuals to conform to values and norms.

**social exclusion**  The situation where people are marginalized (*see* marginalization) or excluded from full participation in mainstream society, as they lack the resources and opportunities most people take for granted.

**social facts**  Social phenomena which exist outside individuals but act upon them in ways which mould their behaviour – e.g. social institutions such as the family, the criminal justice system and the education system.

**social inequality**  The unequal access people have to resources such as wealth, income, power and status, and the unequal distribution of opportunities linked to these, such as in education, health, housing and employment.

**social institutions**  The various organized social arrangements that are found in all societies.

**social interaction**  The relationship between two or more individuals, and how those individuals act and react to those around them.

**social issues**  Issues that affect people and the way they live their lives.

**social media**  Websites, apps and other online means of communication that are used to create, share and exchange information and connect people together – e.g. Facebook, Instagram, YouTube and Twitter.

**social mobility**  The movement of groups or individuals up or down the social hierarchy.

**social movement**  A broad movement of people who are united around the desire to promote, or block, a broad set of social changes in society. Unlike a political party or pressure groups, they are often only informally organized through a network of small, independent, locally based groups.

**social order**  A relatively stable state of society, with some shared norms and values which establish orderly patterns that enable people to live together and relate to one another in everyday life.

**social policy**  The packages of plans and actions adopted by national and local government or various voluntary agencies to solve social problems (see social problem) or achieve other goals that are seen as important.

**social problem**  Something that is seen as harmful to society in some way, and that calls for something to be done to sort it out. *See also* social policy.

**social processes**   The various influences that control and regulate human culture and behaviour, and help to keep societies running more or less smoothly and with some day-to-day stability.

**social solidarity**   The integration of people into society through shared values, a common culture, shared understandings, and social ties that bind them together.

**social stratification**   The division of society into a hierarchy of unequal social groups.

**social structure**   The social institutions and social relationships that form the 'building blocks' of society.

**socialization**   The process of learning the culture of any society. *See also* primary socialization, secondary socialization.

**society**   A large group of people who are involved with one another and generally share the same geographical territory or country and a similar way of life, language and beliefs.

**sociological perspective**   An approach adopted by a sociologist when studying society.

**sociology**   The systematic (or planned and organized) study of human groups and social life in modern societies.

**status**   The amount of prestige, importance or respect attached to individuals, social groups or positions in any society by other members of a group or society. Status involves people's social standing in the eyes of others. *See also* achieved status, ascribed status.

**status frustration**   A sense of frustration arising in individuals or groups because they are denied status in society.

**status group**   A group of people who share a similar social standing (status) and lifestyle in any society.

**stereotype**   A generalized, over-simplified view of the features of a social group, allowing for few individual differences among its members. The assumption is made that all members of the group share the same features. An example might be 'all those on welfare benefits are on the fiddle'.

**stigma**   A label or mark of shame or disgrace showing strong disapproval of behaviour that is seen as wrong, abnormal or immoral – e.g. the shame (stigma) attached to having a criminal record.

**streaming**   Putting school students into the same group for all subjects according to their ability.

**structural differentiation**   The process of more specialized institutions emerging to take over functions that were once performed by a single institution. For example, some once-traditional functions of the family have been transferred to the education system and the welfare state.

**structuralism**   (or structural theory/structural approaches)   A sociological perspective that bases its explanations on the study of the overall social structure and culture of society, rather than by focusing on individuals or small groups.

subculture   A smaller culture shared by a group of people within the main culture of a society, in some ways different from the main culture, but with many aspects in common.

survey   A means of collecting primary data, often from large numbers of people, in a standardized statistical form, by questioning them using interviews and questionnaires.

survey population   The section of the population which is of interest in a survey.

symbolic annihilation   The lack of visibility, under-representation and limited roles of certain groups in media representations, as they are, in many cases, omitted, condemned or trivialized.

symmetrical family   A family in which the roles of partners who live together in couple relationships have become more alike (symmetrical) and equal.

synergy   Where a media product is produced in different forms which are promoted together to enable greater sales than would be possible through the sale of a single form of that product or by the efforts of one company.

total fertility rate   The average number of live children born to women of childbearing age. *See also* fertility rate.

trade unions   Organizations of workers whose aim is to protect the interests of their members and improve their life chances.

traditional authority   Power which is seen as fair and just as it is based on established traditions and customs. *See also* authority, charismatic authority, power, rational-legal authority.

trend   How the pattern shown in statistics changes over time, such as an increase or decrease.

triangulation   The use of a variety of methods, and different types of data, to cross-check that the results obtained by another method are valid (*see* validity) and reliable (*see* reliability).

tripartite system   The system of secondary education established in 1944 in which pupils were selected for one of three types of secondary school according to their performance in the 11+ exam.

triple shift   The three periods of working time spent, nearly always by women, on paid employment, unpaid domestic labour and emotional work.

underachievement   The failure of people to achieve as much as they are capable of, and to fulfil their full potential.

underclass   A social group who are right at the bottom of the social-class hierarchy, who are in some ways cut off or excluded from the rest of society.

**universalistic values**   Standards and rules that apply equally to everyone, regardless of who they are.

**validity**   Whether statistics or the findings of research actually provide a true, genuine and authentic picture of what is being studied.

**value consensus**   A general agreement around the main norms and values of society.

**value freedom**   The idea that the beliefs and prejudices of the sociologist should not be allowed to influence the way research is carried out and evidence interpreted.

**values**   General beliefs about what is right or wrong, and the important standards and goals which are worth maintaining and achieving in any society.

*verstehen*   The idea of understanding human behaviour by putting yourself in the position of those being studied, and trying to see things from their point of view.

**victim surveys**   Surveys that question people on whether or not they have been a victim of a crime, whether or not they reported it to the police. This tries to discover how much crime goes unreported by victims and unrecorded by the police.

**wealth**   Property which can be sold and turned into cash for the benefit of the owner.

**white-collar crime**   Offences committed by individuals who abuse their positions in middle-class jobs for personal gain, at the expense of the organization or clients of the organization.

**white-collar workers**   Non-manual clerical workers, sales personnel and other office workers, whose work is non-professional and non-managerial.

# Answers to questions in chapter 2

p. 63    (Table 2.1 activity) (1) 44,000. (2) 11,000. (3) 51,000. (4) 99,000. (5) 11.9. (6) 29.3 per cent. (7) 158,000.

p. 63    (Describing a trend activity) (1) Upward trend, increasing by 4.2, from 5.9 in 1971 to 10.1 in 2011. (2) Upward trend from 74,000 in 1971 to 158,000 in 1991, then it declines after 1991 to 118,000 in 2011. (3) Upward trends for both husbands and wives to 1991, but then declines between 1991 and 2011, especially for wives. Increasing by 10,000 for husbands, compared to 33,000 for wives. Those granted to wives have increased more than those granted to husbands between 1971 and 1991, though the gap between them narrowed after 1991.

p. 64    (Graphs Figure 2.5 activity) (1) About 79,000. (2) About 172,000. (3) Upward trend, rising from about 80,000 in 1971 to about 173,000 in 1991, then decreasing to 130,000 by 2011.

p. 65    (Graphs Figure 2.6 Activity) (1) About 44,000. (2) There are four trends you could mention: total divorces increasing up to 1991, then a decline; divorces granted to husbands increasing up to 1991, then stable before a slight decline; divorces granted to wives increasing up to 1991, then a decline; the divorces granted to wives increased far more than those granted to men up to 1991, but the gap between them narrowed after 1991.

p. 66    (Bar chart Figure 2.7 Activity) (1) About 30 per cent (2) An increasing/upward trend, from about 9 per cent in 1971 to about 29 or 30 per cent in 2011.

# Illustration credits

# Index